POLITICS OF CONFRONTATION

POLITICS OF CONFRONTATION

The Foreign Policy of the
USA and Revolutionary Iran

BABAK GANJI

Revised paperback edition published in 2011 by I.B.Tauris & Co Ltd
6 Salem Road, London W2 4BU
175 Fifth Avenue, New York NY 10010
www.ibtauris.com

Copyright © 2011, 2006 Babak Ganji
First published in hardback by Tauris Academic Studies, an imprint of I.B.Tauris & Co Ltd, 2006

The right of Babak Ganji to be identified as the author of this work has been asserted by the author in accordance with the Copyright, Designs and Patent Act 1988.

All rights reserved. Except for brief quotations in a review, this book, or any part thereof, may not be reproduced, stored in or introduced into a retrieval system, or transmitted, in any form or by any means, electronic, mechanical, photocopying, recording or otherwise, without the prior written permission of the publisher.

ISBN: 978 1 84885 964 7

A full CIP record for this book is available from the British Library
A full CIP record for this book is available from the Library of Congress

Library of Congress Catalog Card Number: available

CONTENTS

	Acknowledgements	vii
1	US Policy towards Iran	1
2	The Carter Administration's Regional Strategy and Policy towards Iran	11
3	The development of religious opposition to the Shah	29
4	The formation of the Tripoli Bloc and the radical challenge to the regional order	40
5	Revolutionary crisis in Iran	49
6	Policy currents and the Iranian revolution	62
7	The intensification of the revolutionary crisis	86
8	US policy during the collapse of the ancien regime and the victory of the revolution	100
9	The regional impact of the Iranian revolution	118
10	The Carter administration's modus vivendi with the revolutionary regime	131
11	US strategies and the Iranian hostage crisis	147
12	The Soviet invasion of Afghanistan and the hostage crisis	169
13	The Failure of the hostage rescue mission and the continuation of the negotiations	187
14	Iran-Iraq war and developments in the hostage crisis	206
15	Post-election shift of US strategy in Iran and the region	225
16	Conclusion	237
	Notes	241
	Bibliography	301
	Index	315

ACKNOWLEDGMENTS

This study is partly based on my doctoral thesis at the University of Newcastle-Upon-Tyne. I am deeply grateful to my supervisor Rod Hague for encouraging me and sharing his insights into US foreign policy with me throughout this project. I would also like to thank my examiners Professor John Dumbrell and Professor David Campbell, as well as the Department of Politics and the Robinson Library. A number of people helped me complete this project. Dr Rob Morrison encouraged me to finish this study after a long illness. I would also like to thank former US officials, Gary Sick and William Quandt, for discussing various aspects of the period under study with me. I am grateful to Patrick Seale, Mostafa Alamuti and Colonel Isa Pejman for sharing their insights into Middle Eastern and Iranian politics with me. Professor Richard Thornton was very helpful with regard to US strategy during the Nixon-Kissinger and Carter periods. I would like to thank him for reading parts of this study and making helpful suggestions. I would like to thank Dr Lester Crook and Kate Sheratt at I.B. Tauris, my copy-editor, Audrey Daly and Carol Anne Martin who formatted the manuscript.

A number of my good friends and colleagues also gave me tremendous moral support during this project. I would like to thank Lesley Simm, Nazenin Ansari, Izabella Aladysheva, Nel Hodge, Elena Best-Shaw, Farzad Besharat, Farhang Jahanpour and Indrek Utsal. Above all, I would like to thank my mother for all the support she gave me while I was working on this project. Without her support, this project would never have been completed. Needless to say, I alone am responsible for any errors.

1

US POLICY TOWARDS IRAN

This study primarily focuses on US policy towards Iran during the Carter administration. However, any such study will also have to grapple with the history of that policy. The nature of the America-Iranian relationship changed in 1969 with the advent of the Nixon administration. The Shah had already begun to pursue a more independent foreign policy in the 1960s and British withdrawal from the East of Suez enabled him to improve his bargaining position vis-à-vis the US, which was deeply involved in Vietnam. Thus what the Carter administration inherited was a relationship that had been dramatically transformed as a result of the policies pursued by Richard Nixon and Henry Kissinger.

Perhaps the most valuable source for studying US policy during this period has been US documents seized by the Iranian students after the occupation of the US embassy. Those documents reveal that, contrary to the prevailing view, US officials were well aware of the discontent in Iran and the nature of the opposition to the Shah. Moreover, they were also worried about the consequences of the Shah's increasing independence in the international arena.

Accounts of US policy towards Iran written by former officials, such as President Jimmy Carter, Zbigniew Brzezinski, Cyrus Vance, Gary Sick, John Stempel, and William Sullivan all provide a wealth of information.[1] However, like most memoirs, they are self-serving and reflect these former officials' biases. For example, Carter, Brzezinski, and Sick blamed the State Department and Ambassador Sullivan for the intelligence failure in Iran. Sick contended that Sullivan had his own plan for managing the transition to a post-Shah regime. Brzezinski also argued that some State Department officials welcomed the Shah's overthrow.[2] Cyrus Vance and William Sullivan blamed Brzezinski for hampering their efforts to effect a smooth transition. On the whole, John Stempel has presented a less biased view of the Iranian revolution.

Studies of US policy towards Iran

Generally speaking, as far as US policy towards Iran is concerned, nearly all the students of the Iranian revolution have focused on two issues: inadequate US contacts with opposition groups in Iran, and lack of good intelligence on Iran.[3] Ofira Seliktar has argued that the failure of US policy in Iran falls into the category of "a fundamental failure that occurred at the *paradigmatic, policy* and *intelligence dimensions* of the predictive process".[4] According to Seliktar, such a "fundamental failure triggers a revision of the epistemic level of knowledge, often referred to as a paradigm".[5] A prominent historian of Iran, Nikkie Keddie has observed that academics, including those engaged in research in Iran, nearly all failed to predict the downfall of the Shah.[6] Therefore, one important area US policy towards Iran is the role of experts in influencing US policy. The author has decided to deal with two such cases: Richard Cottam and James Bill both of whom have been highly critical of the Carter administration's policy towards Iran. Bill has also been chosen because he has criticized American academics for their failure to predict and explain Middle Eastern events.[7]

Richard Cottam and James Bill

Richard Cottam was a former CIA and Foreign Service Officer with extensive experience of Iran. Cottam was convinced that the US had damaged its long-term interests by supporting the Shah. During the Iranian revolution, he reported to the State Department on his meetings with opposition figures. In his account of Iranian-American relations, Cottam has blamed Brzezinski for preventing the State Department from establishing contact with the Khomeini camp. His account is biased in that he has sought to exonerate both himself and those State Department officials who called for siding with Khomeini.

Iranian clerics told Cottam that Khomeini was among the most obscurantist clerics in Iran. Yet he reported to the State Department that Khomeini and his entourage were among the most enlightened Iranian groups.[8] However, in his study of US policy towards Iran, Cottam said nothing about the substance of his discussions with Khomeini's clerical opponents.[9] Nor did he make any reference to official contacts between the Carter administration and the Khomeini camp. All these omissions sharply reduce the value of his study. Even after the Iranian revolution and a time when executions were occurring and radical clerics were consolidating their hold on power, Cottam continued to argue that Khomeinism was an ideology which wanted to give Iran "genuine independence, free institutions, and a revival of Islamic and Iranian cultural values". He believed that Khomeini would play only "a boundary-setting role".[10]

Like Richard Cottam, James Bill also had extensive experience of Iran and even after the revolution, he continued to argue that the clergy did not want to play a leading role in Iranian politics.[11] However, Bill's involvement in US policy-making was only peripheral. Nevertheless, his study of US policy towards Iran, *The Eagle and the Lion*, has been widely recognized. Bill's study suffers from several shortcomings. Firstly, he fails to inter-relate important regional events such as the Soviet invasion of Afghanistan and the Iran-Iraq war to the formulation of US policy towards Iran. Secondly, he went so far as to argue that the US completely failed to predict the revolution owing to the influence of the pro-Shah constituency in the US and blamed Zbigniew Brzezinski for the US 'failure' to establish contact with the Khomeini camp. Bill has also ignored US contacts with the Khomeini camp.[12]

In fact the Carter administration did very little to save the Shah, and it *did* establish contact with the Khomeini camp. Moreover, US intelligence was well aware of the importance of religion in Iranian and Middle Eastern politics, and indeed encouraged Islamists at certain junctures.[13] Bill has also sharply criticized Brzezinski for focusing on the Soviet threat. In fact, a report submitted by CIA analyst Ernest Oney in 1976, had warned that the Soviets had had contacts with the Iranian clerical establishment, which it identified as the

Shah's most dangerous opponent, to turn the opposition in an anti-American direction. Events proved Brzezinski right. The Soviet Union supported the non-aligned orientation of revolutionary Iran.[14]

Policy currents and the study of US policy

This study relies on the concept of policy currents as a tool for explaining US foreign policy behaviour during the Iranian crises examined. The concept of policy currents was, arguably originally formulated by Franz Schurmann in his book, *The Logic of World Power*. For Schurmann policy currents reflect the perceptions, as well as the organizational and ideological affiliations, of policy-makers.[15]

The most important difference between this study and that of Schurmann concerns the sources of policy currents. In this study, policy currents refer to the various long-term tendencies or mind sets that have influenced US foreign policy over the years. Another writer who has made use of the notion of policy currents is Walter Russel Mead.[16] Mead's greatest achievement is his ability to combine the interplay of American foreign policy traditions and the bureaucratic, institutional and policy rivalries in the US.[17]

Contending strategic visions in the post-1969 period

In the post-1969 period, the foreign policy context in the US became a far more complex process. Vietnam had such a huge impact on US foreign policy that a new current of opinion emerged in the Democratic Party which sought to distance the US from right-wing dictatorships in the Third World. It saw regimes such as the Shah's or Somoza's as long-term liabilities for the US. Indeed, such a trend had briefly emerged during the Kennedy presidency.

Vietnam led US foreign policy-makers to seek to harness the strength of potential regional powers for the purpose of maintaining US preponderance. The Nixon doctrine was based on the assumption that such US allies could defend themselves if the US sold them arms, thereby obviating the necessity of US intervention.[18] However, in the 1960s there emerged another influential liberal current in US foreign policy whose proponents were primarily associated with the journal, *Foreign Policy*. Such luminaries as Anthony Lake, Leslie Gelb, Patricia Derian and Morton Halperin argued that the US had to be prepared to accommodate change in the Third World.[19]

The strength of this liberal current in the State Department was one reason why US relations with Iran were strained during the Carter period. When the Carter administration came to office the US foreign policy-making elite was at a crossroads. The US foreign policy establishment increasingly ascribed the failure of US global strategy to Soviet misbehaviour and bad faith.[20] However, the liberals remained strong in the Democratic Party and they greatly influenced US foreign policy in the first two years of the Carter administration. In her study of the Carter administration's policy towards Iran, Ofira Seliktar has also offered a variant of the policy current explanation. However, she has divided US policy-makers into the categories of realpolitikers, such as Brzezinski, and moralpolitikers, such as some of Vance's subordinates in the State Department. The moralpolitikers were associated with supporters of George McGovern and Walter Mondale in the Democratic Party. They also included officials such as chief of the State Department's Policy Planning Staff Anthony Lake, the head of the Bureau of Political and Military Affairs at the State Department, Leslie Gelb, and the head of the Office of Human Rights at the State Department Patricia Derian. These officials were profoundly influenced by America's experience in Vietnam and tried to disassociate their country from Third World dictatorships. Moreover, they did not believe that the primary cause of unrest in the Third World was Soviet activism. They placed far greater emphasis on domestic political and economic factors.[21]

However, Seliktar's explanations are, in some cases, factually incorrect. For example, she contends that the realpolitikers were "all but silenced by the defeat of the shah" and supported the view that "moderates" would prevail in the power struggle following the fall of the Shah.[22] However, as we shall see in the relevant chapters, all US officials were realpolitikers and the realpolitikers to whom Seliktar refers in her study were not silenced by the fall of the Shah and they certainly did not believe that the so-called "moderates" would prevail in the power struggle. Indeed, even the so-called moralpolitikers did not consistently count on the "moderates" to prevail in the power struggle. Paradoxically, in some parts of her study, Seliktar comes close to accepting this interpretation, but she seems to have entrapped herself in the categories she initially created, thereby obfuscating her own analysis.[23]

The main flaw in Seliktar's study, however, is the absence of any reference to the energy crisis and Iran's role as an oil producer. Nor does she analyse US policy towards Iran within the framework of US regional and global strategies. In that context, US policy towards Saudi Arabia was particularly important during the Carter period because the Carter administration sought to strengthen Saudi Arabia to force the Shah to change his oil-price policy and to lessen US dependence upon Iran. The Shah's oil-price policy was the main cause of some prominent US officials' dissatisfaction with him and in the 1960s and 1970s the price of oil was the most important issue over which the Shah disagreed with the US. As we shall see in this study, it is noteworthy that the Carter administration significantly toned down its criticisms of the Shah and began to listen to his demands for more weapons systems after he agreed to refrain from pressing for further price increases.

As we shall see in this study, bureaucratic rivalries, institutional conflicts and power struggles served as transmission belts for the expression of different foreign policy currents. From the very beginning, the Carter administration was divided over the question of America's world role. The main protagonists in the debate were Secretary of State Cyrus Vance and National Security Adviser Zbigniew Brzezinski. Both Brzezinski and Vance firmly believed that the US should preserve its global primacy. Vance believed that the emergence of global interdependence had ushered in a new era of international relations, which required the US to move towards creating a new multipolar international order.

Zbigniew Brzezinski was an advocate of the strategy referred to in this study as neo-containment. Neo-containment advocates argued that the Soviet Union had become much more assertive globally, particularly in the Third World. They called for ensuring US global primacy by matching the Soviet military build-up.

The emergence of the Committee of the Present Danger symbolised this trend. Members of the committee, such as Richard Pipes and Paul Nitze, raised profound questions about détente and contended that the Soviet Union's increasingly assertive international behaviour necessitated a major change in US global strategy.[24] Brzezinski's views were somewhat different from those of the Committee on the Present Danger. However, Brzezinski supported détente only as long as it imposed a self-denying ordinance on the Soviet Union and led to irreversible changes in the Soviet bloc.

Foreign policy currents and Iranian crises: The case of Richard C. Thornton

One historian who has recognized the significance of contending foreign policy visions is Richard C. Thornton. Thornton's studies of the Nixon-Kissinger, Carter and Reagan periods show the importance of contending foreign policy visions in US administrations.

According to Thornton, the Vietnam War and the relative decline of US led to sharply divergent US responses to the problems caused by the relative decline of the US. The two approaches, which Thornton has characterized as containment and détente, were brought into sharp focus in a number of different foreign policy crises which beset Nixon-Ford, Carter and Reagan administrations. In each administration advocates of containment sought to strengthen US positions around the Soviet periphery before embarking upon negotiations with the Kremlin, whereas advocates of détente placed greater emphasis on the importance of relaxation of tensions and engaging the Soviet Union in arms control negotiations.

As far as the Iran crisis is concerned, Thornton has argued that there were vast differences between National Security Adviser Zbigniew Brzezinski and Secretary of State Cyrus Vance over US global strategy.[25] Brzezinski sought to consolidate the US position around the Soviet periphery prior to negotiating détente with Moscow, whereas Vance wanted to reduce US geopolitical pressure on the Soviet periphery while negotiating with the Soviet Union.[26] Iran played an important role in Brzezinski's scheme of things, but for Vance it was important to reduce the geopolitical pressure on the Soviet Union. The Carter administration, according to Thornton, sought to broaden the base of the Shah's regime to stabilise it. In the event, the policy backfired and culminated in the Iranian revolution.[27]

Vance, however, believed that a regime led by Khomeini would not necessarily harm long-term US interests, and opposed the use of force to crush the revolution. After the revolution, the US sought to befriend revolutionary Iran. However, Khomeini's visceral hatred of the US led to the Iranian hostage crisis and the rupture of ties.

There are several major differences between this study and that of Thornton. Firstly, the author disagrees with Thornton's premise that advocates of détente sought to reduce the geopolitical pressure on the Soviet periphery.[28] During the Nixon-Ford administrations, Kissinger, who was an advocate of détente, played a key role in facilitating the sale of vast quantities of arms to Iran and he closely collaborated with the Shah to expel the Soviet Union from the Middle East.

Secondly, although Thornton devotes a considerable part of his volumes on the Nixon-Ford and Carter administration to the question of oil, there are absolutely no references to the disagreements between the US and the Shah over the issue of oil and US support for Saudi Arabia. The main dispute in the

Carter administration was over the issues of political and military containment. It is to this issue that we must now turn.

The State Department and the Shah

Vance and his advisers strongly opposed some of the Shah's key policies such as pursuit of a high oil-price policy, expanding Iran's nuclear programme, a huge military build-up aimed at dominating the Persian Gulf and the Indian Ocean and the suppression of dissent in Iran. Vance did not have a background in Iranian affairs and he was assisted by a number of advisers. These were: director of the Iran desk at the State Department, Henry Precht; US ambassador to Iran, William Sullivan; and Assistant Secretary of State for Near Eastern and South Asian Affairs, Harold Saunders. In late 1978, Richard Cottam who had served in the CIA and maintained extremely close ties with Khomeini's advisers also emerged as an unofficial adviser to the State Department.

Vance and his advisers did not have exactly the same views on how the US should deal with the Shah. However, they agreed on a number of important points. They believed that by equating Iran with the Shah and refusing to listen to the opposition groups' demands, the US had removed itself from playing a role in political developments in Iran. They also agreed that the US should establish contact with leaders of Iranian opposition groups, particularly the National Front and the Iran Liberation Movement.

Vance believed that Iran would not substantively change its foreign policy because of the Soviet threat to Iran's national security. Precht and Sullivan even believed that by helping the opposition come to power, the US would protect its interests in the post-Shah Iran.

Vance, however, had to be politically sensitive because the fall of the Shah could alienate powerful American political figures and have a deleterious impact on the strategy of détente. Coming in the wake of the fall of Saigon and a number of Soviet interventions in the Third World, opponents of Carter's policies, such as Henry Kissinger, argued that the Carter administration's abandonment of the Shah had contributed to the victory of the Iranian revolution. Thus it is not surprising that Vance was reluctant to make a deal with the Iranian opposition as early as some of his advisers.

The National Security Council

The National Security Council's (NSC's) perspective on the Iranian crisis was shaped primarily by National Security Adviser Zbigniew Brzezinski. The Polish-born Brzezinski, who was one of the West's leading Sovietologists, took a dim view of the Soviet Union's commitment to détente. He saw Third World conflicts through an East-West prism and argued that détente had imposed a self-denying ordinance on the US. Brzezinski believed that the Soviet Union's attainment of strategic parity would enable it to change the global balance of power to the detriment of the US.[29]

Former CIA Director Robert Gates, who at the time served as one of Brzezinski's assistants on the NSC, has also argued that US policy-makers mainly worried about the psychological balance and the geopolitical implications of the changing strategic balance.[30] Secretary of State Cyrus Vance was convinced by the arguments put forward by his Soviet affairs adviser Marshall Shulman that the US should try to coexist with the Soviet Union because of its nuclear capability.[31] However, the debate over strategy towards Iran can best be summed up in terms of political versus military containment of the Soviet Union and New World Order versus global primacy. Vance saw the Soviet challenge as a political challenge. Moreover, his belief in multi-polarity meant that countries such as France, West Germany and Japan would have greater roles to play in Iran and the Middle East.

Brzezinski, however, saw the Soviet challenge as both political and military and he consistently favoured the build-up of US forces in Southwest Asia. He believed in re-establishing US global primacy and ensuring that the US maintained its predominance in Iran. Brzezinski shared Kissinger's geopolitical view of international relations and saw Iran as the key state in the containment of the Soviet Union in the Middle East.

Unlike Kissinger, who emphasized the importance of Egypt, Brzezinski believed that Saudi Arabia had a key role to play in the region.[32] Brzezinski wanted to increase direct US presence in the Persian Gulf and the Indian Ocean. It is noteworthy that Brzezinski tasked his friend Samuel Huntington who served on the NSC staff between 1977 and 1978 to prepare a study of the global balance of power between the US and the Soviet Union. As a result of Huntington's study, the NSC contributed to the formulation of Presidential Review Memorandum Number 10 which called for strengthening US military presence in Southwest Asia.

Huntington had long been interested in the study of political change in the developing world and his study, *Political Order in Changing Societies*, had delineated some of the dilemmas that modernising traditional monarchs such as the Shah faced. Huntington's prognostications about the future of traditional monarchies were bleak.[33] Huntington was also acutely aware of the difficulty of persuading the Shah to establish a constitutional monarchy.[34] Huntington's analysis of the Shah's fate was unlikely to have comforted US officials and Brzezinski and Huntington opposed the decision to compel the Shah to open up the Iranian political system.[35]

Moreover, it is also important to note that Brzezinski's deputy, David Aaron, as well as other NSC officials Jessica Tuchman and Robert Hunter did not particularly like the Shah's style of governance. Vice-President Mondale, David Aaron and the director of the State Department's Policy Planning Staff, Anthony Lake, employed a number of officials, who served in the second and third tiers of government, and whose ideas were consistent with the so-called new internationalists' conception of international relations. For example, both the Assistant Secretary of State For Human Rights Patricia Derian and Stephen Cohen, who was in charge Iran's human rights affairs, were supporters of George McGovern who had been highly critical of American support for right-wing dictatorships.[36] Both Mondale and Aaron had contacts with the Iranian opposition in the US and considered the Shah to be "a highly illegitimate ruler, whose behaviour should be modified".[37]

Some observers have speculated that Mondale imposed Aaron on Brzezinski. However, Brzezinski has denied rumours that he did not want Aaron on the NSC. He has said that he was impressed by Aaron and, in fact, recommended him to Mondale as a foreign policy adviser in the early 1970s when Mondale was thinking about his presidential campaign.[38] Despite Aaron's views, during the revolutionary turmoil he was not a strong supporter of the Iranian revolutionaries.[39] Moreover, Brzezinski and Aaron had similar views on the Soviet Union and Aaron "provided strong support to Brzezinski at critical times".[40] The reason Brzezinski became concerned about developments in Iran was his fear of instability and revolutionary upheaval in a country of major strategic importance. Brzezinski advised Carter to support a military crackdown with or without the Shah. Paradoxically, the NSC's Iranian affairs specialist, Gary Sick, believed that only a genuine constitutional monarchy could prevent a total collapse of the Iranian regime.[41]

Brzezinski, who believed that the Iranian revolution would destabilise the entire region, called for strengthening US military presence in the Persian Gulf and Southwest Asia. However, only after the Iranian revolution did Brzezinski manage to influence US regional strategy.[42] On the whole, Carter tended to side with Vance, but Brzezinski's sheer determination influenced the course of US global and regional strategies at key junctures.[43]

Human Rights Policy

The Carter administration human rights policy has been the subject of many controversial debates. It is important to note that the Vietnam war and Congressional hearings into CIA covert operations during the Ford administration provided the background against which US diplomacy was conducted during the Carter administration. President Carter vociferously expressed support for the human rights policy, emphasising that the US would reformulate its policies towards its authoritarian Third World allies.[44]

For Carter, Vietnam had been a turning point in US foreign policy. He argued that democratization was the only long-term solution to US foreign policy problems.[45] Carter said that human rights must be 'a fundamental tenet of our foreign policy'. Like President Kennedy, Carter believed that evolutionary change introduced from above would prevent revolutionary change or leftist take-overs.[46]

In fact, as early as 1971, Anthony Lake, who served as the State Department's director of the Policy Planning Staff during the Carter administration, had articulated the essential tenets of the human rights policy.[47] Some critics of the administration's human rights policy, such as Ofira Seliktar, have interpreted the policy in terms of the rise of a new internationalism in the US in the aftermath of the Vietnam war. Seliktar has argued that some officials, such as the director of the Iran desk at the State Department, whom she describes as moralpolitikers, wanted the Shah out of power for doctrinal reasons.[48] Indeed, David Newsom, who served as Under-Secretary of State for Political Affairs at the State Department later observed that supporters of the human rights policy ion the administration "came into the Department dedicated to the idea of seeing the overthrow of rightist regimes".[49] The Shah himself later held McGovernites responsible for his downfall, contending that "McGovernites in the second echelon of the State Department were anxious to see me go".[50]

Secretary of State Cyrus Vance sympathized with the McGovernites. When he was the president of the New York Bar Association, Vance encouraged William Butler of the International Commission of Jurists who was pressuring the Shah to liberalize.⁵¹ However, it is important to note that human rights diplomacy was particularly important in the cases of Iran, Nicaragua and South Korea where the US sought to re-define its strategic relationships with the Shah and Anastazio Somoza and Park Chun Hee. No such concerns were expressed with regard to countries with much worse human rights records such as Saudi Arabia and Indonesia. Indeed, conservative authors such as Jeane Kirkpatrick and Joshua Muravchik would later sharply criticize the Carter administration for its double standards.

Kirkpatrick argued that regimes, such as that of the Shah, were traditional dictatorships, which did not seek to dominate all aspects of their people's lives. Kirkpatrick argued that totalitarian regimes could not be democratized, whereas traditional polities could be democratized over time. She blamed the Carter administration for the collapse of the Shah and Somoza.⁵²

Kirkpatrick was right in that the Carter administration's approach to the issue of human rights was selective at best. According to a member of the International Commission of Jurists, in 1976, the Shah was 'way down the list of tyrants. He would not even make the A-list.'⁵³ During the period, 1977–79, Khmer Rouge was by far the worst human rights violator in the world. It took Carter 16 months to speak out against 'the genocidal policies' of the Khmer Rouge.⁵⁴ Moreover, when Vietnam defeated Cambodia, the Carter administration began to support the Khmer Rouge indirectly.⁵⁵

US policy towards Iran was, in a sense, a microcosm, which reflected the dispute over strategy in the Carter administration. Iran had been a key component of the strategy of containment for most of the post-war period. It is not surprising that the dispute between Brzezinski and Vance should have become so serious over the issue of Iran.

US policy towards resurgent political Islam

The Carter administration was the first US administration to encounter the problem of Islamic resurgence. Recently, scholars of US policy towards radical Islam, such as Maria Do Ceu Pinto and Fawaz Gerges, have divided US policy-makers into confrontationalists and accommodationists.⁵⁶ However, during the period under study, US policy-makers were primarily concerned about the Soviet threat.

During the revolution, Brzezinski feared that the Soviet Union supported the Iranian revolution, and that the Shah's overthrow would lead to the establishment of a radical regime which would threaten US strategic interests throughout the region. Brzezinski, therefore, strongly advised Carter to support a crackdown with or without the Shah.

Vance, however, believed that despite leftist support for the revolution, Khomeini and his supporters would be able to withstand the pressure from the left and that they would establish a regime which would maintain Iran's security relationship with the US. Vance's views were influenced to a large extent by the views of Ambassador Sullivan and the director of the Iran desk at the State Department, Henry Precht.

As far as Brzezinski was concerned, the only good thing about the Iranian revolution was that Khomeini, who was strongly anti-Communist, led it. However, Brzezinski was well aware of the fact that the vast majority of Soviet

Muslims were Sunnis and were unlikely to be influenced by the Iranian revolution. The occupation of the US embassy in Tehran changed Brzezinski's mind and he called for Khomeini's removal. Brzezinski saw the crisis as a threat, as well as an opportunity to build up US military power in the Middle East.

Vance remained steadfast in his opposition to confrontation with the revolutionary regime even after the occupation of US embassy in Tehran. Vance's resignation over Carter's decision to launch a hostage rescue mission was motivated by his fear of a wider regional conflagration and a possible Soviet intervention in the crisis.

Regional policy currents

President Carter and his principal advisers, particularly Vance, believed that the US had to strengthen its ties with Saudi Arabia and broaden the base of the Shah's regime. US regional strategy was based on strengthening the position of Crown Prince Fahd in the royal family. The fall of the Shah and US failure to broker a comprehensive regional settlement were major setbacks for Fahd who lost the policy war to his half-brother Prince Abdullah. Abdullah wanted to reach a modus vivendi with revolutionary Iran and he was extremely reluctant to support an Arab-Israeli peace agreement.

The Saudis' failure to improve relations with revolutionary Iran led them to provide assistance to Sunni fundamentalist groups to contain revolutionary Iran. Moreover, Saudi Arabia sought to broaden its international ties to reduce its dependence on the US security guarantee. The advent of the Reagan administration led to a major improvement of US-Saudi ties.

Importance of policy currents

The concept of foreign policy currents provides a useful tool for analysing US policy towards Iran because it explains why US policy-makers proved to be remarkably intractable even during periods of acute crisis. The study attempts to reopen the debate about such subjects as intelligence failures and US policy towards radical Islam to contribute to the further study of this important period in US and Iranian history.

2

THE CARTER ADMINISTRATION'S REGIONAL STRATEGY AND POLICY TOWARDS IRAN

US relations with Iran in the post-war period were influenced by the Cold War and control over Middle East oil resources. Until 1945, Great Britain and Russia and then the Soviet Union had been the major external actors on the Iranian scene. The 1907 Anglo-Russian agreement dividing Iran into spheres of influence was symptomatic of the country's vulnerability to external pressure. The advent of the Soviet Union sharply increased the importance of Iran to Great Britain and then to the US because the country's geography, as well as the strength of its communist party, the Tudeh, made it a bastion of the containment of the Soviet Union.

The nationalization of the Iranian oil industry in 1951 was a major turning point in Iran's relations with great powers. An examination of the oil nationalization crisis and the 1953 coup d'etat is beyond the scope of this study. Suffice it to say that Great Britain and the US overthrew the government of Mohammad Mossadeq, the leading Iranian nationalist of the early post-war period. However, Great Britain's influence in Iran, which was already declining prior to the coup, declined even further as a result of the formation of the oil Consortium. Henceforward American oil companies would have a substantial share of Iranian oil resources. US relations with Iran expanded dramatically following the coup.

However, it would be wrong to argue that US policy in Iran proceeded smoothly in the period 1953–1979. The arrest of members of the Tudeh's military network in 1955 demonstrated the strength of communism in Iran. In fact, almost immediately after the 1953 coup d'etat the Eisenhower administration became concerned about the corruption and lack of accountability of the Iranian regime. In 1957, the Eisenhower administration tacitly supported a coup attempt by the head of Iranian military intelligence, General Valiollah Qarani, which was aimed at compelling the Shah to dismiss Prime Minister Manuchehr Eqbal, who was seen as subservient to the Shah, and replace him with Ali Amini. The Qarani coup attempt was foiled. However, in 1961 the Kennedy administration, which feared that corruption and despotism would only encourage the communists compelled the Shah to appoint Amini. The Shah could only dismiss Amini after agreeing to implement a far-reaching economic and social reform programme, later known as the White Revolution. However, as we shall see in a later chapter, the White Revolution alienated the clergy who vehemently opposed the Shah.

One of the main reasons the Shah agreed to the implementation of a reform programme was his desire to establish Iran as a regional power. As early as the mid-50s, the Shah had come to the conclusion that it would be only a matter of time before Great Britain withdrew its forces from the Persian Gulf. To the chagrin of US officials, the Shah had always placed greater emphasis on military modernization programmes than on social reform. As British influence in the Persian Gulf and the Middle East declined, the Shah changed his focus. He saw Arab radicalism, rather than Soviet communism, as a greater threat to Iranian security interests. Indeed, in the 1950s, Iranian regional strategy resembled British and Israeli regional strategies far more closely if only because of the three countries' opposition to Egyptian President Gamal Abd al-Nasser.[1]

Then in 1959, the Shah embarked upon a policy of détente with the Soviet Union and, to the consternation of the Eisenhower administration, even toyed with the idea of neutralism as a means of pressuring the Eisenhower administration to increase the export of US military equipment to Iran. During the Kennedy administration some US officials, most notably chief of the Iran desk, John Bowling, argued that the Shah had no choice but to distance himself from the US in order to maintain political control. In the 1960s perceptive US officials recognized that the Shah was becoming increasingly independent. However, both the Kennedy and Johnson administrations were deeply concerned about the stability of Iran and the Shah's ability to respond effectively to the challenges posed by nationalism and Islamism.[2]

The Vietnam War and Britain's economic difficulties, which led to the Wilson government's decision to withdraw British forces from the East of Suez, enabled the Shah to establish Iran as the regional hegemon. However, the Johnson administration was extremely reluctant to endorse Iranian hegemony over the Persian Gulf. Johnson's failure to persuade Wilson to maintain UK military presence East of Suez led US officials, particularly National Security Adviser Walt Rostow, to call for the build-up of Iran as the preponderant regional power.[3]

In the Nixon administration, Henry Kissinger was the principal advocate of supporting the Shah's regional ambitions. During his May 1972 visit to Iran President Richard Nixon approved of selling all kinds of US weaponry to Iran except nuclear weapons. Nixon and Kissinger also approved of the Shah's plan to covertly assist Iraqi Kurds to put pressure on the Iraqi regime which was involved in a territorial dispute with Iran over the Shatt al-Arab.[4] Nixon and Kissinger also tacitly supported the Shah's high oil-price policy, which was designed to finance Iran's military build-up and economic modernization programmes. Advocates of high oil price policy believed that higher prices would damage America's economic rivals, West Germany and Japan. However, by 1975, if not earlier, it was clear that the policy had been a major failure since West German and Japanese economies recovered from the impact of higher prices more quickly than the US economy. Moreover, by 1975 higher prices threatened the very fabric of the world economy.[5]

Unlike Kissinger and Nixon, State Department officials also saw Iran as a major source of instability in the area:

> Iran's military superiority in the Persian Gulf, its concern about radical Arab forces, and the political fragility of some Arabian peninsula states has created an Iranian propensity to intervene which could result in a

confrontation damaging to our relations with the Arabs. The arms race in the Gulf, sparked as much by Iranian acquisitions as by any other factor, could lead to the rapid escalation of local conflicts, increased great power involvement in the Gulf, and new generations of weaponry in the Arab-Israeli complex. Iran's military power - and its superior attitudes - may cause growing Saudi resentment, and Saudi pressure on us to restrain Iran.[6]

Moreover, there was a dispute in the administration between Kissinger, who sought to maintain close relations with Iran for geopolitical reasons and Treasury Secretary William Simon, who called for exerting political pressure on the Shah to force him to change his policy. Kissinger argued that pressuring the Shah might lead to his overthrow and that the Soviet Union and radicals would be the main beneficiaries of the fall of the Shah.[7] In 1975, the Shah ended Iran's dispute with Iraq and the two countries signed a peace agreement in Algiers. As a result of the agreement, the Shah ended Iran's assistance to the Iraqi Kurds. Kissinger was sharply criticized for the curtailment of the assistance to the Kurds, but he has argued that the US had no choice but to do so given the reality of the situation in Iraqi Kurdistan.[8]

He pressed forward with his policy of broadening the ties between the two countries. Two weeks after meeting the Shah in Zurich, Kissinger and the Iranian Minister of Economy and Finance Hushang Ansary signed a 15 billion-dollar economic agreement. According to Amir Asadollah Alam's diaries, Iran signed the bilateral agreement 'in the mistaken belief that it might placate' the US over oil prices.[9] The agreement was 'the largest agreement of its kind ever signed by two countries'. It required Iran to spend 15 billion dollars on American goods and services over the next five years. The US would assist Iran in the construction of eight nuclear power plants, which were estimated to provide Iran with eight thousand megawatts of electricity. By April 1975, US officials were privately saying that the two countries non-military and non-oil trade could reach 23 to 26 billion dollars over the next six years.[10]

However, in 1975-1976, some US officials began to seriously question the value of a strategic relationship with Iran. In 1976, a CIA analyst of Iranian affairs, Ernest Oney, reported that the Iranian elite was sclerotic and that the Soviet embassy had established close relations with a number of clerics in the expectation that it would be able to guide any upheaval in a radical anti-American direction.[11] Oney tried to get the agency to commission a study of Iranian religious leaders. However, his superiors were not receptive to the idea. Some officials also dismissed him as 'Mullah Ernie'.[12] Nevertheless, as we shall see in the following chapters, US officials in the field did provide enough intelligence to their superiors in Washington to enable them to understand the nature of the opposition to the Shah. By the mid 1970s, some US officials were also pointing out that the Shah was becoming increasingly independent and that he would harness US strategy for his own purposes.[13]

The CIA was also becoming increasingly concerned about the Shah's policies. According to 1975 press reports, a CIA psychological profile of the Shah described him as a 'a dangerous megalomaniac, who is likely to pursue his own aims in disregard of U.S. interests'.[14] There has also been much debate about the CIA's intelligence on the Shah's health. Sir Shapoor Reporter, a

British intelligence agent stationed in Iran, has said that in 1974 he informed former British Prime Minister Lord Home that the Shah had cancer.[15] Two reports prepared by the State Department's INR before the onset of the revolutionary crisis indicate that the State Department did not know of the Shah's illness. In May 1976 the INR reported: 'Only 55 years old, in good health, and increasingly careful about security, he [the shah] has a good chance to be able to lead Iran for many more years.' Then in January 1977: 'At age 57, in fine health, and protected by an elaborate security apparatus, the Shah has an excellent chance to rule for a dozen or more years.'[16] According to one account, the French did not discover the Shah's illness until June 1978.[17]

However, according to the former head of the CIA's Near East Division, Charles Cogan, the French knew that the Shah had cancer as early as 1972 'because one of the doctors that was treating the shah was in some way affiliated with the French intelligence service'.[18] According to Cogan, US officials became aware of the 'gravity' of the Shah's illness in 1976. According to another CIA official: 'We knew the shah was ill. We had reports from-well, from a very good source.'[19] David Long, who served at the State Department's Bureau of Intelligence and Research (INR) has also said that US officials knew that the Shah had cancer.[20]

In 1975, the State Department's Bureau of Intelligence and Research (INR) took the initiative in formulating an important National Intelligence Estimate (NIE) on Iran.[21] This study contained a large section on opposition forces in Iran and warned of the importance of religion in Iranian politics. It bluntly said: 'Prominent in the opposition are religious leaders.' It particularly emphasized the increasing ties between secular opposition elements and religious leaders. The sections on the vulnerability of the Shah's regime remained intact and the sceptics provided extensive evidence of the increasing opposition to the Shah's regime. US embassy officials in Tehran and US Air Force analysts sharply disagreed with the negative attitude of the NIE towards Iran. Nevertheless, the Pentagon reluctantly accepted it, but Kissinger's State Department ignored it.[22] Despite the embassy's disagreement with the NIE, it informed the State Department that the monarch had become more dictatorial. The Shah's decision to abolish Iran's two-party system was interpreted as a move to reduce the power of Prime Minister Hoveyda.[23]

By the mid 1970s, Iran's relations with the Consortium had also deteriorated and the Shah's oil price policy had alienated the Ford administration. The Ford administration decided to change US policy and exert political pressure on the Shah to change his oil-price policy. In fact, the Ford administration started to put pressure on the Shah regarding the price of oil in 1975, and Ford even threatened to change US policy towards Iran.[24] This was part of a broader effort to co-ordinate US economic policies with those of West Germany and Japan. Such co-ordination was also reflected in the formation of an elite institution, the Trilateral Commission, which was a symbol of US efforts to share the burdens of maintaining global primacy with Western Europe and Japan.[25]

Ford even threatened to reappraise US policy towards Iran. Indeed, in 1975, the Shah believed that General Khatami was involved in an US-backed coup d'etat against him. Khatami was killed when his hang-glider crashed.[26] However, US arms sales to Iran continued unabated despite the Pentagon's objections and thanks largely to Kissinger's influence. The US also approved of the sale of nuclear reactors to Iran despite concerns about the impact of such sales on US non-proliferation policy. The Ford administration supported the Shah's plans to build large nuclear energy industry, while negotiating a multibillion dollar deal that would have enabled Iran to acquire large quantities of enriched uranium and plutonium. After hesitating initially, President Ford signed a directive in 1976 offering Iran a US-built reprocessing facility for extracting plutonium from nuclear reactor fuel. The agreement gave Iran the complete 'nuclear fuel cycle'. According to Kissinger: 'I don't think the issue of proliferation came up'.[27]

However, the Shah also embarked upon a covert nuclear programme with the assistance of South Africa.[28] Moreover, despite the Ford administration's generosity regarding the supply of nuclear energy, the Shah remained defiant on the oil-price issue and continued to pursue a high-price policy. British and Israeli officials became seriously concerned about the stability of the Shah's regime in the mid-1970s. For some US officials, the British and the Israelis were the best sources of intelligence on Iran. Henry Precht, who served as the director of the Iran desk at the State Department during the Iranian revolution has said that his 'best sources' on Iran were the British. According to Precht, the British 'were much more informed, much more insightful. And their reporting, their assessments were not upbeat'. The Israelis had excellent sources in the Iranian bazaar. Moreover, according to Precht, the Israeli representative to Iran, Uri Lubrani, warned him as early as 1976 that the Shah was facing a serious crisis.[29] One reason why the British and the Israelis were better informed about Iranian affairs might have been their close relations with the Special Intelligence Bureau headed by General Hossein Fardust. We shall address this issue in chapter 5. Suffice it to say that the Special Intelligence Bureau liaised closely with the SIS and the Mossad because the Shah did not trust the CIA. By the mid-1970s, Fardust, who had excellent contacts among the clergy had come to the conclusion that the Shah was in deep trouble.

By the time the Carter administration entered office, Kissinger's regional strategy had failed and there was a debate about the course of US policy towards Iran. For the Carter administration, as for all other post-war US administrations, US control over Middle East oil was one of the most important objectives of US regional strategy. The main US objectives were to maintain its primacy in the Persian Gulf in order to reduce Soviet influence in the region and compete favourably with West Germany and Japan.

The Shah increasingly sought to exclude the US and the Soviet Union from the Persian Gulf/Indian Ocean/Red Sea region. He believed that greater US involvement in the aforementioned region would provoke a Soviet response, which Iran must prevent. Saudi Arabia, on the other hand, saw the US as a counterweight to Iran and Iraq.

By 1977 the Shah had purchased over 6 billion dollars' worth of arms from the US and had more than 12 billion dollars' worth on order.[30] However, the Shah's military build-up and his profligacy had driven Iran to the brink of bankruptcy. By 1977 Iran's budget deficit had risen to nearly 6 billion dollars.[31] In 1975 the US was Iran's first trading partner with nearly 20 percent share of Iran's non-military imports. By 1977 the US had slipped into third place with 15 percent of the share. West Germany was in the first place and Japan in the second. Thus not only had West Germany and Japan succeeded in recovering from the 1973 oil shock, but they had also increased their economic influence in Iran.

It is not clear to what extent foreknowledge of the Shah's illness led US officials to advise American companies not to take risks in Iran. According to one former CIA official: 'I left Iran in 1976, and I told four close friends to get their money out of the country, that Iran was going down the tubes.'[32] By 1977 such famous companies as IBM, B.F. Goodrich, Dow Chemical and Union Carbide were leaving Iran.[33] So gloomy were the prospects for the Iranian economy that in 1977 the US embassy informed Americans that 'it appears fairly certain that few if any new major projects will be identified in the next three or four years'.[34] As early as 1976 the US embassy estimated that 1 billion dollars had left the country. Other estimates indicated that twice that amount had left the country. A State Department official observed that Iranians 'voted with their money long before they voted with their feet'.[35] According to one estimate as much as 15 billion dollars left the country during the revolutionary crisis.[36]

By now Iran's rival, Saudi Arabia, had emerged as a global economic power and as America's most important trading partner in the region. At the end of 1976 Saudi reserves constituted over one-fourth of the world's total.[37] Unlike Iran, Saudi Arabia provided a favourable environment for foreign investors.[38]

As early as 1972 Saudi Oil Minister Zaki Yamani had proposed a long-term special relationship with Washington in return for a change in US policy towards Israel. The Nixon administration rejected Yamani's proposal.[39] Moreover, the Saudis failed to persuade Washington compel the Shah to change his oil policy.[40] Initially, Kissinger refused to pressure the Shah for fear of destabilising Iran. However, the Ford administration began to shift the fulcrum of US strategy to Saudi Arabia in 1976. After the 1973 oil price increases, the US had become increasingly dependent on Saudi oil. Western Europe and Japan were far more dependent on Iranian oil and they imported 16 percent - over two million barrels per day and 20 percent - almost one million barrels per day - of their oil from Iran.[41] Moreover, economic and military and agreements ensured that US had preferential access to Saudi oil.[42]

Relations between the US and Saudi Arabia expanded considerably during the Ford administration. US intelligence cooperation with Saudi Arabia also expanded and the two countries co-operated on a range of regional issues to prevent Soviet expansionism in the Persian Gulf, Southwest Asia and the Red Sea. The Safari club symbolized this co-operation. The club was a private intelligence network, which brought together the US, Iran, Saudi Arabia, France and Egypt for the purpose of opposing Soviet global activities, particularly in Africa. Despite the fact that Saudi Arabia had been financing Islamist organizations across the world it was still wary of supporting Islamist take-overs in the region. Thus the Saudis were frightened of the possibility of the Shah's replacement by his Islamist opponents.[43] However, as we shall see, the policy of weakening the Shah was very much part of US regional strategy after the Carter administration came into office and this fitted in perfectly with the administration's policy of building up Saudi Arabia as a regional power.

Cyrus Vance later unfairly criticized the Ford administration for not changing US policy towards Iran despite US congressional criticisms of the Shah's military build-up and the fact that he appeared to be extending his ambitions beyond the Persian Gulf.[44] The Carter administration's policy towards Saudi Arabia and the Arab-Israeli conflict was based on the Trilateral Commission's premise that the supply of oil was linked to the settlement of the Arab-Israeli conflict.[45]

The Carter administration and policy currents in Saudi Arabia

It is important to note that the Saudi leadership was not unified on the question of the Arab-Israeli conflict and Saudi oil-price policy. Crown Prince Fahd was the only Saudi leader who wanted to use the kingdom's spare oil-production capacity to prevent price increases.[46] Fahd's rivals, most notably King Khalid, and the commander of the National Guard, Prince Abdullah, did not want to antagonize radical Arab states, and opposed high levels of oil production.[47] Saudi Arabia had huge financial surpluses, which had been recycled by US and other Western banks or invested in the US, UK and other Western countries.[48]

US strategy was based on the premise that Washington's support for a comprehensive Middle Eastern settlement would reduce radical Arab pressure on Saudi Arabia and enable Riyadh to prevent dramatic increases in the price of oil.[49] The US security relationship with Saudi Arabia was a symbol of US commitment to the survival of the House of Saud.[50] However, the Iranian-Saudi rivalry further complicated US policy towards the Middle East because both countries made efforts to influence Washington and purchase US weapons.[51]

The Carter Administration distances the US from the Shah

As soon as the Carter administration entered office, it downplayed the importance of US relations with Iran. Before the 1976 election, the Shah had made clear his pro-Republican sympathies.[52] Indeed, according to one account, the Shah had contributed several million dollars to the Ford campaign.[53] Nevertheless, during the US presidential elections, he said that the election result 'would not have the slightest effect on Iran-American relations. Iran controlled a good part of the free world's energy resources and the free world could not tolerate the loss of Iran, and any threat to Iran's vital interests would lead to war'.[54] Despite such bravado, privately the Shah was deeply concerned about Carter's victory and he was reported to have observed that 'it looks like we are not going to be around much longer'.[55]

After the Iranian revolution, former CIA director and ambassador to Iran, Richard Helms, argued that there was no effective opposition to the Shah when President Carter came to office.[56] However, the US was well aware of the strong religious opposition to the Shah's rule.[57] A State Department transition paper observed that the clergy 'do not accept the present monarchy or its reform policies'.[58] Many Carter administration officials believed that there was a 'need for fundamental change in Iran'.[59] According to Vance, despite continuities in several policy areas, there were 'marked differences in the way in which we conducted our bilateral relation, particularly as regards arms sales and human rights'.[60] During the transition period the Carter administration requested a paper on the Shah as an ally of the US. The report was prepared by the State Department's Bureau of Intelligence and Research (INR) and it raised serious questions about the Shah's style and the stability of his regime. Academic Iran experts supported the INR's analysis. However, the NSC and the White House had no intention of dramatically changing US policy.[61]

Moreover, even the INR observed that despite terrorism Iran would be stable over the next several years.[62] The INR described the opposition to the Shah as 'more a state of mind than readiness to act'.[63] However, the report only led the Shah's opponents in the administration to compare the Shah to the former South Vietnamese dictator, Ngo Din Diem, arguing that the Shah had lost his legitimacy and that he had to liberalize or be replaced. Opponents of the policy of weakening the Shah, led by National Security Adviser Zbigniew Brzezinski, contended that sudden liberalization would destabilize Iran. Brzezinski asked his friend, Samuel Huntington, who specialized in the process of change in Third World countries, and his assistant William Odom to study the issue. Brzezinski and Huntington were both worried about liberalization in dictatorial regimes which they called 'dismantling the tiger'. Brzezinski opposed the policy of liberalization on the grounds that local customs would prevent that process.[64]

As we saw in the first chapter of this study, the dispute over Iran policy was part of a broader conflict within the administration over the choice of global strategy. One of the administration's first decisions was to commission a study of the US-Soviet strategic balance. Samuel Huntington was tasked with conducting the review, which led to the formulation of Presidential Review Memorandum (PRM) 10. The main conclusion of the memorandum was that the Soviet Union had primarily made progress in the military field and that the US had to build up its military capability, particularly in the Persian Gulf to protect its vital interests.[65] Huntington and Odom both believed that Iran was the country in which a US-Soviet confrontation was most likely. According to Odom, Huntington 'really provided a first-class conceptualization of the problem' and 'had five or six criteria that drove you right to Iran as the most probable location'.[66] PRM-10 led to the drafting of Presidential Directive-18 which was signed on 24 August 1977. The directive recommended that the US maintain a 'deployment force of light divisions with strategic mobility' for 'global contingencies', particularly in the Persian Gulf region.[67]

The debate over the drafting of PD-18 sharply polarized the administration. Advocates of détente sought to guide US policy in the direction of reducing US forces in Europe and South Korea. They also favoured arms control negotiations with the Soviets to resolve the security issues of the Persian Gulf-Indian Ocean region. Brzezinski, however, warned of the increasing vulnerability of the Persian Gulf region and Soviet power projection capabilities in Southeast Asia, Africa and even the Caribbean. The final version broadly reflected the NSC's views on NATO, the rapid deployment force and Korea.[68] Brzezinski also influenced the administration's policy towards the Soviet Union by convincing President Carter to take measures to 'attack the internal legitimacy of the Soviet government'. Thus as early as March 1977 President Carter approved 'covert propaganda' against the Soviet Union proper and not just the Eastern European satellite states.[69] However, the evidence suggests that the issue of Iran was addressed through measures to force the Shah to change his oil price and arms procurement policies. At the same time, US policy sought to broaden the base of the Iranian regime and make America less dependent on the Shah for the protection of its interests in the Persian Gulf.

The debate over PRM-10 and PD-18 masked a fundamental strategic choice made by President Carter almost immediately after he took office. Carter sided with officials who wanted to weaken the Shah. The president set his policy in motion by distancing the US from the Shah. After Carter was elected the Shah sent him a cable of congratulation to which he never formally replied. Carter's rudeness did not go unnoticed in Iran. Moreover, for several months, the administration issued no statements about who was going to succeed Ambassador Richard Helms. In fact, Kissinger had already selected William Sullivan, a career diplomat, for the post.[70]

Sullivan had previously served as ambassador to the Philippines and as Kissinger's aide in Vietnam peace negotiations held in Paris. Henry Paolucci has argued that Kissinger's decision to recommend Sullivan for the Iran post was an indication of his decision to reformulate US policy towards Iran because Sullivan was extremely adept at easing out US clients, such as South Vietnamese leader Ngo Din Diem, who had outlived their usefulness. Sullivan had also co-operated with Kissinger to facilitate US withdrawal from South Vietnam.[71]

According to the former head of the CIA's Near East Division, Charles Cogan:

> Vance, and shall we say, the State Department in general looked forward towards the possibility of a smooth transition whereby the monarchy would cede some power to the dissidents who were considered to be not just Khomeini but moderates around him, and there were some, and this could be a successful transition to the parliamentary constitutional monarchy.[72]

It is noteworthy that National Security Adviser Zbigniew Brzezinski also initially approved of the policy of encouraging the establishment of a constitutional monarchy in Iran because Americans believed that the Shah was 'flagrantly violating human rights', but also because constitutionalism would ensure Iran's internal stability.[73]

The Carter administration combined its decision to downplay the importance of military containment of the Soviet Union with an effort to moderate Iran's military build-up. However, the State Department recognized that the administration's decision to limit arms transfers to the region and US human rights policy would cause problems with Iran and the region.[74]

The State Department argued that US geopolitical interests were to strengthen Iran to prevent 'Soviet aggressiveness' and to stabilize the Middle East and South Asia. The US also had an interest in maintaining its intelligence facilities.[75] Moreover, it had to safeguard 'a reliable source of petroleum to the West, Japan, and Israel at as low a price as possible ... bearing in mind the limited leverage we possess on Iranian price positions'.[76]

Iran's increasing independence meant that the US had to reappraise its security relationship with it. Although the country had emerged as a significant regional power, it still relied on the US to deter direct Soviet aggression.[77] The State Department warned that the US would find it difficult to 'moderate Iran's military build-up' because the Shah had already proved that he was quite prepared to purchase arms even from the Soviets. Thus the only way to persuade the Shah to do so was to impose 'a general moratorium of arms transfers to the area by all arms suppliers'.[78] As we will see, the Carter administration failed to persuade the Shah to reduce his arms purchases.

The Carter administration and the energy crisis

By the summer of 1977 it had become clear that the Saudis did not have the 11.8 million barrels per day production capacity they claimed they had. Nevertheless, such claims enabled the incoming Carter administration to justify establishing closer relations with Riyadh.[79] During this period, a CIA report warning that the Soviet Union was running out of oil generated a great deal of controversy. The Agency predicted that the Soviet Union would resort to the use of force against Middle Eastern oil producers to obtain energy.[80]

The discovery of huge natural gas reserves would almost certainly have refuted the administration's claim about an impending energy crisis in the US. An Energy Research and Development Agency (ERDA) study completed in early April 1977 concluded that natural gas reserves in the US alone were likely to exceed America's total energy requirements well in to the twenty-first century. The report was censored and the official responsible for undertaking the study was dismissed.

Nevertheless, the director of the US geological survey, Dr Vincent McKelvey announced publicly that America's natural gas reserves were 'about ten times the energy value of all previously discovered oil, gas, and coal reserves in the US combined'. He said that the geopressured zones in Texas and Louisiana contained the equivalent in gas of 'about 4 trillion barrels of oil, roughly twice the conventional estimate of ultimate world petroleum resources'. Dr McKelvey was immediately fired.[81]

Not only was there no energy crisis, but the likelihood of an oil glut would imminently become apparent. However, a low-cost energy situation would prevent the US from improving its economic position vis-à-vis West Germany and Japan. Despite the favourable energy situation, on 18 April 1977, Carter declared that the US was facing an energy crisis, describing the situation as the 'moral equivalent of war'.[82]

The administration's policy was reflected in its amalgamation of energy-related bureaucracies in the Energy Department. On the legislative front, the Carter administration adopted policies aimed at enhancing energy conservation measures. It sent the energy bill to Congress in April 1977, but this bill was not approved until 15 October 1978. However, Carter did not enunciate the second part of his programme until the spring of 1979, i.e. after the fall of the Shah.[83]

The Shah's reaction to Saudi oil diplomacy

The Shah saw Saudi Arabia's new oil policy as a major threat to the stability of his rule. He believed that the US had encouraged the Saudis to use its oil power to bankrupt his country.[84] The monarch believed that Iran was 'broke' and that oil production was likely to fall by 30 percent. He even contemplated the possibility of blacklisting regular customers if they tried to 'take advantage' of Iran's predicament.[85] The Shah and his Court Minister Amir Asadollah Alam agreed that it was time to launch a reform programme to ensure the stability of the regime. Moreover, Alam was determined to get rid of his rival, Prime Minister Amir Abbas Hoveyda, whom he described as a CIA agent.[86] Initially the Shah disagreed with Alam.[87] However, later he made Hoveyda a scapegoat.

The Shah also turned to Israel for help to stop US media attacks on the Iranian government,[88] but the Carter administration was not responsive to Israel's advice on Iran-related issues and repeatedly ignored it.[89] The Shah also sought to improve relations with Riyadh. In early April, he announced that he supported a Saudi proposal for a conference to promote internal security co-operation among Persian Gulf countries, and on 15 April he sent a delegation to meet King Khalid in Riyadh to negotiate a compromise agreement on oil prices. In return, the Saudis agreed to loan Iran 3 billion dollars.

The Shah and president Carlos Andres Perez of Venezuela sent conciliatory messages to the Saudi leadership in early May apprising Riyadh of their decision to moderate their price policy. The Saudis appreciated the amicable tone of the Shah's message.[90] The Shah also expanded Iran's economic ties with its archrival, Iraq.[91]

The Shah made another important concession to the Carter administration. In April 1977 Iran and the US agreed to cooperate and exchange technical information on nuclear safety matters.[92] However, Iran still continued its covert nuclear cooperation with Israel and South Africa.[93] Indeed, Iran and Israel concluded a secret agreement on technological cooperation. Iran agreed to fund a number of sensitive projects in Israel, one of which was the development of a surface-to-surface missile which was capable of carrying a nuclear warhead.[94] According to the deputy Iranian Minister of Defence for procurement, General Hasan Tufanian, Iran decided to embark upon the project after Iraq's decision to acquire Soviet Scud missiles and the Carter administration's refusal to supply Lance missiles to Iran. Israel had failed to persuade the US to fund nuclear-related projects. As a result, Iran and Israel concluded a secret agreement to pursue nuclear-related research without informing the Carter administration.[95]

Until the revolution, Iran continued to pay Israel regularly for these projects by delivering oil secretly to a Swiss broker who sold it and transferred the funds to Israel. The transactions were conducted under the supervision of an Iranian-born-Israeli official Meir Ezri who served as Israel's representative to Iran for 12 years. The last such payment, 260 million dollars' worth of oil, was made by Tufanian shortly before the victory of the Iranian revolution. However, Iran 'never received a single screw'. Tufanian was so concerned about maintaining the secrecy of the project that he sent all the relevant documents on one of the last El Al flights out of Iran. Officials of the new Iranian regime, however, learned 'the general outline' of the programme, but they did not have a detailed knowledge of the transactions.[96]

Failure of US regional strategy and elite rivalry in Saudi Arabia

By May 1977 the Carter administration had failed in its attempt to use Saudi Arabia's spare capacity to undermine the Shah's position in OPEC. Moreover, King Khalid's illness widened the rift in the Royal Family over the issue of succession.[97] There were serious concerns about the vulnerability of Saudi oil installations to sabotage following a fire at Ras Tanura which reduced Saudi production to 8.462 million barrels per day.[98] Soon afterwards it was reported that Iraq and Libya had financed a coup against the Saudi regime.[99] In October and November 1977, 17 officers and a large number of civilians were tried for hatching plot against the regime.[100]

Given the pressure on the kingdom from the radical Arab states and the rifts in the Royal Family, it is not at all surprising that even Crown Prince Fahd had to link Saudi production policy to a comprehensive settlement of the Arab-Israeli conflict.[101]

US-Saudi co-operation suffered another setback in early June when the North-South negotiations collapsed.[102] Soon afterwards, Saudi Arabia announced that it would increase its oil prices at mid-year by an additional 2% above what had been previously planned.[103] After July 1977, Saudi Arabia substantially lowered its production forecasts.[104]

The Carter administration increases the pressure on the Shah

After Saudi Arabia's failure to raise its oil production, the Carter administration began to directly put pressure on the Shah on the issue of oil prices. Initially, the Shah resisted US attempts to coerce him into changing his oil-price policy.[105] The Shah had sought to shift to the use of nuclear energy in order to preserve Iran's oil resources. He told Ambassador Sullivan 'that Iran, Saudi Arabia, and other oil-producing countries had been defrauded of their just economic benefits by the international oil companies over the years and that their return on a barrel of oil had been far less than they deserved'.[106]

Different offices within the State Department held different views of the stability of the Shah's regime. For example, in a 4 May report from Iran, US charge d'affaires in Iran, Jack Miklos opposed the policy of putting pressure on the Shah on the grounds that there was a 'wide gap between some Western images of current day Iran' and Iranian political culture. He and other opponents of the liberalization policy would later argue that proponents of the human rights policy had prevented a meaningful discussion from taking place within the administration.[107] However, others were not too worried about the stability of the Shah's regime. On 13 May Alfred Atherton of the Near Eastern Bureau who briefed Secretary Vance for his first meeting with the Shah told him: 'The shah is in a stronger position internally than any previous time in his long rule.'[108] However, the State Department's Bureau of Intelligence and Research (INR) had a completely different view. In May 1977 INR's office of External Research hired outside experts to assess the situation in Iran. The decision to ask outside experts to comment on Iran policy was the result of a tug of war among State Department officials over Iran policy. The Human Rights Bureau wanted to replace Ambassador Richard Helms with a person who would represent the new internationalist current in US policy. However, acting on the advice of former Secretary of State Dean Rusk, Carter chose William Sullivan, who had previously served in Laos and the Philippines. Sullivan's opponents accused him of 'bombing Laotian peasants' and denigrated him by describing him as 'security-minded'.[109] The experts recommended by INR, however, told Ambassador Sullivan that the Shah should start a dialogue with opposition figures and share power in order to prevent a revolution.[110]

The Carter administration acted on the INR's advice and increased the human rights pressure on the Shah. Vance's trip to Iran in May 1977 set the stage for increasing that pressure. Before he went to Iran, the US embassy had sent the State Department a translated copy of a letter from Ali-Asghar Haj Seyyed Javadi, one of the Shah's leading intellectual opponents, sharply criticizing the regime for its violation of human rights. Vance told the Shah that respect for human rights was 'a key element of our foreign policy'. Moreover, Vance 'repeated more or less verbatim the points made by Haj Seyyed Javadi'.[111]

However, he noted that the US welcomed the improvement in the treatment of prisoners. The Shah told Vance that because his regime was under attack from communists and their allies, he could not do much to restrain his security forces. He contended 'that if Iran were to slip into civil strife, only the Soviet Union would stand to gain'. The Shah 'had no objection' to US human rights policy, 'as long as it was a question of general principle and not directed at him or did not threaten his country's security'.[112]

The Shah warned that the Soviet Union, facing the prospect of long-term energy shortages, sought to control the oil resources of the Middle East.[113] After his meeting with Vance, the Shah was 'more insecure in his relations with the Americans than ever'.[114] During the trip Vance apparently leaked word to the National Front that the Shah was told to 'liberalize or be removed'.[115] The new US ambassador to Iran, William Sullivan, encouraged contacts with dissidents. According to Charles Naas, a senior political officer at the US embassy in Tehran, Sullivan encouraged the embassy's political section to contact dissidents 'including a few people who had a good feel for the religious leaders'. According to Naas, the Shah 'was aware that we had changed our m.o. and had started encouraging the opposition' In fact, the Shah was deeply concerned about US policy towards his country.[116] Iranian opposition leaders, who were encouraged by the Carter administration's critical attitude towards the Shah, stepped up their activities during the summer of 1977.

AWACS sale and the removal of Prime Minister Hoveyda

The most significant decision taken during this period was the administration's attempt to tacitly link the sale of AWACS planes to the introduction of political reforms in Iran. The White House's policy on arms sales was delineated in Presidential Directive-13 which limited US arms sales 'except to countries of strategic importance'. Since Iran was not mentioned in the directive, observers began to speculate about the Shah's status.[117] The available evidence suggests that Vance used the AWACS sale as a means of persuading the Shah to make concessions. During his visit to Iran in May, Vance told the Shah that the Carter administration intended to sell AWACS planes to Iran, but he did not inform his State Department colleagues that he had made such a promise.[118]

However, it is highly unlikely that Vance's colleagues did not know about the proposed sale. As early as January 1977, Vance had told the House International Relations Committee that AWACS would enable Iran to defend itself against the Soviet Union and Iraq.[119] Moreover, the US Air Force, which sponsored the programme, wanted to sell the plane to other countries 'to spread its research and development costs'.[120]

It appears that the Carter administration did decide to sell the AWACS to Iran, but not before the Shah had been seriously weakened. State Department officials were the leading opponents of the sale of AWACS planes to Iran. Within the State Department, the most prominent opponents of the sale were; Leslie Gelb, Anthony Lake and Patricia Derian.[121] Moreover, deputy National Security Adviser David Aaron declared that the 'shah has to learn that is not the Nixon-Kissinger administration anymore'. By withholding information on this matter, Vance allowed opposition to the sale to develop in the State Department. In the meantime Ambassador Sullivan who had not yet arrived in Iran, had issued a statement to Congress alluding to the existence of religious opposition to the Shah. The Shah was furious. He believed that Sullivan and the Carter administration did not know that the Soviets were manipulating his opponents.[122]

The Carter administration submitted the proposed sale to Congress on July 7, 1977.[123] During the Congressional hearings on the sale of AWACS planes to Iran, the participants openly discussed the possibility of instability in Iran.[124] As a result, the House International Relations Committee rejected the proposal. Carter then withdrew it to prevent the Congress from rejecting it altogether.[125] Indeed, the debate about the sale of AWACS turned into one about the legitimacy of his rule.[126]

The Shah was furious with Carter and sent an angry message to him threatening to purchase similar equipment elsewhere. Carter held firm. He did not 'care whether he buys them from us or not'.[127] At a meeting with US Ambassador William Sullivan, the Shah declared that Iran had reached a 'turning point' and that the issue of Iran's relations with the US would have to be studied.[128] However, the State Department considered the threat serious enough and Sullivan assured the Shah that 'the AWACS sale would be approved with only very minor modifications'.[129] The Shah changed his mind and the proposal was resubmitted to Congress in September.

During the row over the sale of AWACS to Iran, the US also began to pressure the Shah to dismiss Prime Minister Hoveyda. From early 1977 onwards, Hoveyda began to worry that the Shah might sacrifice him to disassociate himself from allegations of corruption.[130] According to a SAVAK report dated 18 July 1977, an American diplomat had said that the Carter administration had seriously asked the Shah to replace the Hoveyda government. According to the report, Carter and other US officials were furious about the Iranian government's contribution to the Ford campaign.[131]

Hoveyda had served as Prime Minister for 13 years and many Iranians believed that he was responsible for the spread of corruption in the country. The Shah replaced him with Jamshid Amuzegar whom he regarded as pro-American. Hoveyda became Court Minister, replacing the Shah's close friend Amir Asadollah Alam who was dying of cancer.[132]

The Shah launched his liberalization programme in August 1977. It included revitalizing three institutions, which scrutinized the government's execution of policy decisions, greater tolerance of criticism and a cabinet reshuffle.[133] Moreover, in May and June the Iranian government invited the International Red Cross to inspect Iranian prisons. The Shah pledged to improve prison conditions, ban the use of torture by SAVAK, strengthen the judicial rights of defendants and relax the laws on the freedom of the press and assembly.[134]

The Shah's conviction that the US had abandoned him was reinforced by French intelligence reports that persuaded him that Carter intended to overthrow him out of sheer ignorance and naive hatred of dictatorship.[135] Indeed, the then head of French intelligence Count Alexandre De Merenches told the Shah that Carter had decided to replace him and he even gave the monarch the names of officials who had been put in charge of the operation. The Shah said that he did not believe him, but De Marenches merely said: 'And what if the Americans make a mistake?'[136]

However, the Shah came to believe in a gigantic Anglo-American plot to overthrow him.[137] Although ex post facto accounts of the Iranian revolution tend to portray religious fundamentalism as its main driving force,[138] nationalist and radical Marxist groups also played an important role in the Iranian revolution.[139] Initially, it was the intelligentsia that began to express open and concerted opposition to the regime.[140] The then British ambassador to Iran Sir Anthony Parsons has argued that the Carter administration's policy of distancing the US from the Shah encouraged his opponents to redouble their activities.[141]

Indeed, according to Mehdi Bazargan, who was to serve as the first prime minister of revolutionary Iran: 'Carter's election made it possible for Iran to breathe again.'[142] In June 1977 National Front leaders wrote an open letter to the Shah, accusing him of; practising 'despotism in the guise of monarchy'; wasting Iran's oil resources; violating human rights; and tolerating corruption and flattery. The letter asked him to respect the constitution and the Universal Declaration of Human Rights, abandon one-party rule, allow exiles to return and permit the establishment of a government based on majority representation.[143]

However, the nationalists were split between secular nationalists and the Liberation Movement,[144] whose leader, Mehdi Bazargan, favoured an alliance with Khomeini.[145] However, secularist politicians such as Bakhtiar were contemptuous of Khomeini and his followers who they considered to be obscurantist, foreign agents and terrorists.[146] Moreover, any hint of an alliance amongst the National Front, religious groups, and the leftists could lead the Shah to crack down.[147] In an effort to co-opt his opponents, the Shah proposed that the National Front be given a few seats in the next parliament, which was due to be elected in June 1979. However, the National Front could not even submit the names of 25 candidates.[148]

Gary Sick and the then British Ambassador to Iran Anthony Parsons have claimed that the Shah decided to embark upon his liberalisation programme in order to prepare the ground for his son's succession. Sick has, rather astonishingly, contended that the Shah's Swiss education made him a liberal.[149] However, the Shah and members of the Iranian Royal Family made it abundantly clear that he had no intention of introducing Western-style democracy.[150] The Shah only agreed to introduce reforms under pressure from the US and as we will see, once that pressure subsided he backtracked.

Oil price issue resolved?

The Carter administration continued to press the Shah on the oil price issue. Sullivan repeatedly reminded the Shah that there was a direct relationship between the price of oil and inflation in the West. Sullivan himself favoured a quiet approach on the question of oil prices, but Deputy Treasury Secretary Anthony Solomon sharply criticized the Shah for pursuing a high-price policy. Treasury Secretary Michael Blumenthal was also inclined to confront him directly on the issue of oil prices. Sullivan disagreed with that approach. The Shah had a meeting with Blumenthal, Solomon and Sullivan in late 1977 during which the price of oil and the OPEC summit were discussed.[151]

The Shah told Blumenthal that he did 'not want to be known as a price hawk'.[152] Moreover, he had already decided to accept an invitation from President Carter to visit Washington, and wanted to avoid turning that meeting into a confrontation over the price of oil. Despite the diplomatic tone of US communications with the Shah, the Carter administration made it abundantly clear to the monarch that it would not be responsive to his concerns on the arms supply and geopolitical issues unless he agreed to a price freeze.[153]

The Shah's visit to Washington in November 1977 set the stage for a rapprochement between the two countries. However, the visit was marred by clashes between pro and anti-Shah demonstrators. The American police had to fire tear gas to disperse the crowd, and the gas drifted over the White House's south lawn, causing the Shah to clean his face with a handkerchief.[154] The incident deeply influenced the perceptions of both the Shah's supporters and opponents. There were student demonstrations in Tehran, and fifty-six lawyers, judges and professors, who were mostly associated with the National Front, signed an open letter calling for free elections and the abolition of SAVAK.[155] The Shah's supporters saw the demonstration as a deliberate American attempt to weaken the Shah.[156]

At his private meeting with the Shah, Carter was effusive in his praise for the monarch, declaring that Iran had 'blossomed forth under enlightened leadership', and that it had become 'a very stabilizing force in the world at large'. However, Carter raised the oil price and human rights issues and emphasised 'the punishing impact of increased oil prices on the industrial economies'. He 'pressed' the Shah to support a price freeze at the next OPEC meeting. Then he assured the monarch that the military alliance between the US and Iran was 'unshakeable' and that the two countries had 'unbreakable ties'.[157] However, referring to the congressional dispute over the sale of AWACS to Iran, Carter 'explained that managing the U.S.-Iranian arms supply relationship would be easier if Iran would reduce its arms requests'.[158]

The Shah agreed that 'Western economies were hurting and that in the long run this was bad for Iran'.[159] He agreed to 'give Western nations a break.' However, he said that this was merely a 'palliative' and called for the formulation of long-term policies.[160]

He, however, 'insisted' that his country needed 140 F-16s and 70 F-14s. Carter was not at all enthusiastic about this request and he merely agreed to consult with Congress. However, he 'warned' the Shah not to expect Congress to agree to 'another large aircraft sale so soon after the narrow AWACS victory'.[161]

The Shah was encouraged by his talks with Carter.[162] Carter was right about congressional opposition. In November, Senate majority leader, Robert Byrd called for a moratorium on arms sales.[163] However, the Shah's supporters in Congress were vociferously supporting him. In 1977, the US Senate released a study sponsored by Senator Henry 'Scoop' Jackson, chairman of the Committee on Energy and Natural Resources. The study argued that the US might have to support Iranian military intervention in the Arabian peninsula should changes of policy or regime disrupt the flow of oil to the US or its allies.[164]

Carter ignores warnings of Shah's predicament

Barely six weeks after his visit to Washington, the Shah met Carter again, this time in Tehran. By now, it was becoming increasingly clear that the Shah was in deep trouble. As early as September 1977, the CIA had argued that Iranians saw his 'reforms' as 'a long series of artificial creations to give the appearance but not the reality of political freedom'.[165] Moreover, Carter's briefing materials for his visit to Iran included reports on clashes between human rights activists and Iranian authorities. One NSC paper argued that 'the shah undoubtedly sees this as a potential threat to his rule'.[166]

After the monarch's visit to the US, NSC official Gary Sick prepared a memorandum on the demonstrations in Iran. According to Sick, several American experts on Iran had argued that the monarch faced strong opposition and he 'wondered perhaps if the shah was truly running scared'. However, despite these observations no one in the US government argued that the Shah was likely to be overthrown.[167]

At the end of 1977, Israel's Minister to Washington and deputy to the ambassador, Hanan Bar-On, presented the State Department with his government's 'detailed assessment of the situation in Iran'. The report contained a 'sombre warning' and it was taken so seriously that the State Department 'red-flagged' it and gave it 'wide priority dissemination, including President Carter'.[168] According to former director-general of the Israeli Foreign Ministry, David Kimche: 'The report was read, filed and forgotten.'[169]

In fact, in a toast to the Shah, Carter described Iran 'as an island of stability in a turbulent corner of the world'.[170] Moreover, during the visit, the Shah presented Carter with list of more than 10 billion dollars worth of military equipment.[171] By January 1978, the Shah had accepted US demands for a moderate oil price policy. In return, he expected the US to continue to sell vast quantities of sophisticated weaponry to Iran. Moreover, he tried to justify Iran's military purchases by drawing attention to Iraq's arms procurement programmes.[172]

The State Department's Bureau of Political and Military Affairs under Leslie Gelb completed a study of Iran's military requirements. Most US officials believed that Iran should not be exempted from the policy on limiting arms sales. However, they thought that 'it would be very difficult' for the Carter administration 'to tell the shah what his own military needs were'.[173]

Sullivan believed that if they could demonstrate that the US had a programme for reducing its oil imports and utilizing alternative sources of energy, the Carter administration would be able to persuade Iran to continue to pursue a moderate oil-price policy. His advice was to ask the World Bank to carry out a study of Iran's future without oil, despite the resistance of his Iranian counterparts.[174]

Sullivan had established good relations with the Shah. He advised Carter to contact the monarch from time to time to reassure him.[175] Sullivan believed that Iran's policies towards such issues as the Arab-Israeli conflict and nuclear non-proliferation were in harmony with US policies. He had also expanded the embassy's contacts with opposition groups. The embassy would continue to pressure the Iranian government to increase the US share of the Iranian market. The US had one major deal, which involved the sale of nuclear reactors to Iran estimated at 10 billion dollars.[176] As we will see in the next two chapters, the Shah's domestic and regional policies would generate a backlash.

3

THE DEVELOPMENT OF RELIGIOUS OPPOSITION TO THE SHAH

Analysts of US policy towards Iran, such as James Bill, Richard Cottam and Amir Taheri, have blamed the CIA for the US failure to understand the roots of the religious opposition to the Shah. Analysts of Iranian politics such as Ervand Abrahamian, Shaul Bakhash, Baqer Mo'in and Vanessa Martin have dealt with the development of the Khomeini movement in depth.[1] However, these authors have not addressed the issue of the relationship between the Iranian state apparatus and religious organizations.

Early observers of Middle Eastern politics sought to explain the Islamist resurgence in terms of the uneducated masses' inability to cope with the dilemmas of modernization.[2] However, they failed to explain the popularity of Islamism among educated classes in the Middle East. As scholars such as Daniel Pipes, Martin Kramer and Bassam Tibi have observed, Islamism is a product of modernity and it has served as a vehicle for furthering the interests of a counter-elite which sees itself as disenfranchised.[3] In the Arab world of the 1960s and 1970s, Islamists were influenced by the Muslim Brotherhood and the ideas of the Pakistani theoretician, Abolala al-Mawdudi and Egyptian Islamists Hasan al-Banna and Muhammad Sayyid Qutb.[4]

The Brotherhood's success in Arab countries depended to a very large extent on its ability to develop clandestine cells which infiltrated the military, the police and the judiciary, not to mention a host of social institutions. Iran's distinct Shi'a identity meant that the influence of any Sunni Muslim organization would be limited in religious terms. In Iran, the Muslim Brotherhood's structure influenced the thinking of Fada'iyan-e Islam (the self-sacrificers of Islam), an extremist Islamist group that vehemently opposed the secularization of Iranian society in the 1940s and 1950s and which was responsible for the assassination of Iranian Prime Minister Haji Ali Razmara in 1951 and the attempted assassination of Prime Minister Hossein Ala in 1955. The leader of Fada'iyan- Islam, Navvab Safavi, was executed. During his formative period, Khomeini had close ties to Ayatollah Abolqasem Kashani (1882–1962) who was a founder of Fada'iyan-e Islam. During the oil nationalization crisis, Kashani abandoned Prime Minister Mohammad Mossadeq and sided with the Shah. Kashani played a major role in the CIA-organized campaign against Mossadeq. Khomeini opposed Mossadeq during the oil nationalization crisis. However, as we shall see, he became anti-American in the 1960s. Fada'iyan-e Islam also contributed to the radicalization of Egyptian politics. According to Bernard Lewis, Fada'iyan-e Eslam was partly responsible for the Muslim Brotherhood's decision to stage an uprising against Egyptian President Gamal Abd al-Nasser in 1954.[5] The Muslim Brotherhood tried to assassinate Nasser in October 1954.[6] As we shall see, the Khomeini camp had ties to the Muslim Brotherhood in the 1970s.

National-Religious Opposition to the Shah

After the 1953 coup d'etat, the Shah increasingly dominated Iranian politics and crushed the opposition to his rule forcefully. The creation of a centralized secret police, SAVAK, in 1957 was a major step towards the creation of a strong dictatorial regime. The SAVAK was formed with the assistance of the CIA. However, after chief of military intelligence General Valiollah Qarani tried to overthrow the Shah in 1957, the Shah became increasingly suspicious of the CIA and tried to replace CIA advisers with Mossad officials.[7] The advent of the Kennedy administration in 1961 put the Shah on the defensive because of the administration's call for major reforms. Indeed, in the early 1960s, the National Front began to organize themselves and US diplomats and CIA officials also maintained contact with opposition figures.[8]

The Kennedy administration also put pressure on the Shah to appoint a reformist aristocrat, Ali Amini, as Prime Minister in 1961. Amini was expected to introduce wide-ranging socio-economic reform programmes. He managed to gain considerable influence among middle and upper classes. Indeed, his popularity alarmed the Shah who dismissed Amini after he persuaded the Kennedy administration that he would introduce the required reforms himself.

However, the Shah's reform programme alienated members of the landed aristocracy and the clergy who were his main supporters.[9] The Shah sought to broaden the base of his regime through selective co-optation of his opponents in the nationalist National Front and the communist Tudeh parties, but he failed to gain sufficient long-term support among the middle classes and students.

After the crushing of the Second National Front in the early 1960s, the Liberation Movement of Iran led by Mehdi Bazargan emerged as the main nationalist opposition group to the Shah.[10] However, it would be extremely misleading to describe Bazargan as a secularist.[11] Bazargan wholeheartedly accepted the oversight of government by a committee of Islamic jurists as set out in the 1906 constitution.

It is astonishing that even those who have recognised Bazargan's religiosity should describe his devotion to the 1906 constitution as being reflective of his liberalism.[12] The Iran of 1979 was vastly different from the Iran of 1906 and its is difficult to see how a committee of Islamic jurists could respond to the needs of a modernising country. Bazargan, who believed that the most important cause of Mossadeq's downfall was the lack of religious support for the National Front, called for extensive clerical participation in governmental affairs including such fields as security, administration, and finance. One cleric who welcomed Bazargan's activities was Ayatollah Khomeini.[13]

The main difference between Bazargan and Khomeini was that Bazargan sought to further what he perceived to be Iran's national interests, whereas Khomeini rejected nationalism as an un-Islamic concept. However, the differences between Bazargan and Khomeini did not become public until after the revolution. Bazargan's closest ally among the clerics was Ayatollah Taleghani and together they formed the Iran Liberation Movement to establish a link between universities and theological seminaries.[14] Bazargan also co-operated with Ayatollah Morteza Mottahari.[15]

Bazargan broke away from the National Front in 1962 because he believed that its leadership was too conciliatory. The leaders of the Liberation Movement remained in prison until 1966. Between 1966 and 1977 they continued their activities underground and abroad. A number of Liberation Movement members broke away and formed the Mojahedin Organization, which began to wage guerrilla warfare against the Shah.[16]

The Mojahedin Organization's (later Mojahedin-e Khalq) ideology was syncretist in that it combined Islamist and Marxist ideologies. The most influential exponent of syncretism was the French-educated Dr Ali Shari'ati (1933–1977) who argued that a true Islamic society was a classless one.[17] Shari'ati drew on the works of Fanon, Weber, Sartre, and Durkheim to condemn 'Westoxification' which he blamed for the backwardness and subjugation of Iran and other Third World countries.[18] Shari'ati also contended that the clergy had allowed Islam to be co-opted by corrupt rulers.[19]

Despite his commitment to anti-imperialism, Shari'ati was an elitist who vehemently opposed democracy.[20] He believed that a revolutionary vanguard party had to be formed to wage armed struggle against the Shah. As early as 1964, Shari'ati, Ebrahim Yazdi and Mostafa Chamran formed the Liberation Movement Abroad. Shari'ati returned to Iran and took up a post as a university lecturer. Yazdi and Chamran went to Egypt in 1964 for guerrilla training.[21] Shari'ati's mingling of Islam and Marxism influenced one of Iran's most violent guerrilla organizations, the Mojahedin-e Khalq, whose members the Shah denounced as 'Islamic Marxists'.[22]

The Mojahedin-e Khalq carried out a number of terrorist attacks, including the attempted kidnapping of the son of Shah's twin sister, Princess Ashraf the son of the Shah's twin sister, Princess Ashraf, in October 1971 and the attempted bombing of a Tehran power station during the Shah's celebration of 2,500 years of Iranian monarchy at Persepolis in 1971.[23] Hundreds of members of Mojahedin-e Khalq, as well as of the Marxist Fada'iyan-e Khalq and the Revolutionary Organization of the Tudeh were arrested. As a result those groups escalated their terrorist attacks. However, at least another 28 guerrillas were killed by the end of 1972.[24] The Mojahedin's terrorist attacks declined after 1972. In 1975, there was a major split in the organization when the paths of the Muslim and Marxist factions diverged.[25]

The Marxist Mojahedin then carried out a series of terrorist attacks including the assassinations of two American military officers, three American employees of Rockwell International and an Iranian employee of the US embassy. The Muslim factions also carried out terrorist attacks, including the bombing of a Jewish emigration office in Tehran.[26]

The overseas branch of the Liberation Movement, the Liberation Movement of Iran Abroad, established close ties with all the major opposition groups.[27]

Ebrahim Yazdi, in particular, played a key role in establishing a link between Khomeini and guerrilla organizations opposing the Shah. Yazdi was an US-trained pathologist who met Khomeini in 1964 and became his chief representative in the United States in the early 1970s.[28]

In the 1970s Khomeini gave Yazdi the responsibility for co-ordinating the armed opposition to the Shah. Yazdi established a close relationship with the Mojahedin Organization. However, when the Mojahedin Organization fell under the influence of Marxists, Yazdi distanced himself from it.[29]

However, Khomeini refused to intervene in the dispute between Ali Shari'ati and his conservative religious opponents.[30] In the 1970s Khomeini moved closer to radical and leftist Islamic groups in order to broaden his support base among the intelligentsia.[31]

The emergence of conservative religious opposition: Khomeini's doctrine

Iran's clerical establishment had played an important role in other tumultuous periods of Iranian history, most notably, the Tobacco Movement (1891–92) which forced the Shah to revoke the tobacco concession; the Constitutional Revolution (1905–1911) and the oil nationalization crisis.[32]

Khomeini's views on Islam and the role of religion in politics were outlandish.[33] In fact, even during the revolution, the clerics who supported Khomeini were in a minority. Khomeini was born in 1902. He was an ally of Grand Ayatollah Borujerdi who was the supreme religious leader in Iran. Borujerdi, however, was opposed to clerical interference in politics and formed a de facto alliance with the Shah. Khomeini did not express his opposition to the Shah explicitly until the advent of the Shah's White Revolution.[34]

Two of the most important planks of the White Revolution were land reform and voting rights for women. The traditional aristocracy strongly opposed the Shah's limited reform programmes. The traditionalists had supporters in the Royal Court, the government, the Majlis, and the intelligence services. They organized opposition to the Shah across the country and sought to bring down the government of Amir Asadollah Alam.[35]

Even the quietist Ayatollah Borujerdi strongly opposed the Shah's policy.[36] It was during this period that Ayatollah Khomeini opposed voting rights for women and organized opposition to the Shah across the country, particularly in the religious city of Qom. The Shah viewed Khomeini as a British agent whose mission was to keep Iran backward.[37] The Shah and Alam suppressed the Khomeini-led uprising in Qom brutally and jailed Khomeini. However, Khomeini was released a few months later after the then SAVAK Director General Hasan Pakravan asked the Shah not to execute him.[38]

In 1963 Khomeini created an underground religious network whose task was to recruit sympathizers and wage war against the Shah. The group was called the Islamic Coalition Society because it was a coalition of six Islamic groups. However, initially, Khomeini strongly opposed the pursuit of armed struggle against the Shah because he believed that it would be ineffective.[39]

The Shah's decision to grant immunity from prosecution to American military personnel stationed in Iran in 1964 led Khomeini to reorganize religious opposition to the government. This time the regime arrested Khomeini and exiled him to Turkey. Khomeini moved to Iraq a year later.[40] The

Islamic Coalition Society subsequently set up an armed wing, which was supported by clerics including Ayatollah Morteza Mottahari and Mohammad Hoseini-Beheshti. The group drew up a list of people whom it wanted to assassinate; the Shah, his influential physician Dr Abdolkarim Ayadi, thirteen members of the government, director of SAVAK, General Ne'matollah Nasiri, former Prime Minister Manuchehr Eqbal, eleven civil servants and newspaper editors who had criticized Khomeini and the clergy.[41]

The Islamic Coalition Society assassinated the then Prime Minister Hasan Ali Mansur. Those involved in the attack were arrested and jailed in 1965. However, soon afterwards another Islamist party, the Islamic Nations Party, was formed.[42] The ideology of the Islamic Nations Party was different from that of the Islamic Coalition Society in that it believed in socialism.

The Islamic Nations Party sought to emulate the organizational structure of Arab socialist and Nasserist organizations, but it attached greater importance to Islam. The leader of the group was Kazem Bojnurdi who was the son of a grand ayatollah who had lived in Iraq and had been influenced by pan-Islamic ideas.[43] The Islamic Nations Party sought to wage armed struggle against the Shah. Bojnurdi managed to recruit dozens of people through the Khomeini movement.[44]

It is important to note that Islamist opponents of the Shah did not form an ideologically monolithic organization.[45] Islamist groups realized that they had to praise the virtues of democracy and nationalism in order to legitimise their opposition to the Shah.[46] Khomeini's supporters included highly educated people who considered the Shah to be an American puppet who had allowed Western imperialists to plunder his country's resources. They embraced Islamism as a means of eliminating the influence of foreign powers in Iran.[47] Islamism served as an ideology that could rally the religious masses against the Shah and as a vehicle for mobilizing potential members of the Iranian counter-elite whom the Shah had failed to co-opt.[48]

The basis of Khomeini' view of government was the doctrine of the guardianship of the supreme jurisconsult (*Velayat-e Faghih*). Significantly, Khomeini did not fully develop his views until 1970, when he was nearly 70.[49] Khomeini argued that the people were 'minors' who should be guided by the jurisconsult.[50] Moreover, Khomeini vehemently opposed nationalism and embraced pan-Islamism.[51]

Some authors such as Gary Sick and Ervand Abrahamian have gone so far as to argue that even some of Khomeini's closest advisers were unaware of the Ayatollah's views.[52] A far more plausible interpretation is that they understood Khomeini's reactionary views only too well, but decided to support him in order to defeat the Shah.[53]

Khomeini and his advisers concentrated on criticizing the greatest weaknesses of the Shah as perceived by a large majority of the people, namely, dictatorship, dependence on the US, and widespread corruption.[54] Khomeini would repeatedly declare: 'The source of all our troubles is America. The source of all our troubles is Israel. And Israel also belongs to America.'[55] Khomeini believed that the Jews wanted nothing less than world domination.[56] Moreover, contrary to the Shah's view of him as a British agent, Khomeini criticized Britain just as harshly as he criticized Israel and the US.[57]

After the defeat of leftist guerrilla organizations, religious networks were the only well-organized sources of opposition to the Shah's regime.[58] John Stempel, the US embassy's political officer, estimated that there were approximately 180,000 to 200,000 clerics and 80,000 to 90,000 mosques.[59]

Khomeini relied on hundreds of theologians whom he had trained to propagate his ideas.[60] He and his supporters had spent millions of dollars among their followers and constituents.[61] After the arrest of its members for the assassination of Mansur in 1964, the Islamic Coalition Society concentrated on disseminating its message through propaganda while building up its urban guerrilla capability.[62]

Moreover, it also set up schools and charity organizations to spread its influence. Thus, in the event of a crackdown, it could claim that it was involved in cultural activities.[63] Moreover, by now the leaders of the organization in Iran, Morteza Mottahari, Mohammad Hoseini Beheshti, Mohammad-Javad Bahonar and Mohammad Mofatteh were discussing the issue of uniting all the militant clerics in a nation-wide organization.[64] In 1976, Mottahari who served as the leader and chief ideologue of the society visited Khomeini in Najaf and the two of them discussed the resumption of the struggle against the Shah.[65]

As a result of the discussion between Mottahari and Khomeini, the Militant Clergy Society was formed in 1977. Moreover, by 1977 the Islamic Coalition Society had set up eight branches in Tehran which were involved in recruiting youth, organizing strikes, distributing Khomeini's leaflets and tapes and providing food and fuel to the people. Indeed these groups were later instrumental in forming local revolutionary committees.[66] By 1977, Mottahari, controlled as many as six hundred highly trained guerrillas who formed the hard core of the Tehran crowds opposing the Shah.[67]

Khomeini also drew on the support of numerous traditional organizations, which felt they had been abandoned and replaced by regime-sponsored organizations. Moreover, there were 'interest-free loan' funds, which benefited from Iran's economic boom and offered many banking services.[68] However, it is important to note that most clerics were either non-political or favoured the implementation of the constitution. The most senior cleric in the country, Ayatollah Shari'atmadari, did not call for the Shah's overthrow and strongly opposed Khomeini's doctrine of the guardianship of the supreme jurisconsult. Khomeini and his entourage considered Shari'atmadari to be a 'puppet' of the regime if only because the Shah supported him as the source of religious emulation in 1970. Indeed Shari'atmadari's views were closer to those of nationalists and liberals than to those of Khomeini.[69]

The security services and religious networks

It would be extremely naive to suggest that Khomeini could defeat the regime's ruthless and efficient security apparatus by relying on contributions from the bazaar and sending tapes of his sermons to his followers in Iran.[70] Some students of the Iranian revolution, such as Jahangir Amuzegar, believe that SAVAK failed to understand the depth of dissatisfaction in the country.[71] The consensus of opinion is that Iranian intelligence services were so concerned about the activities of leftist guerrilla groups and the Tudeh Party that they failed to penetrate Islamic fundamentalist groups and their secret networks.[72] However, few academics have studied the behaviour of the Iranian intelligence establishment prior to the revolution.

In fact, the Shah was so concerned about Khomeini's activities that the SAVAK's internal security division, Department Three, was instructed to infiltrate Khomeini's entourage in Najaf.[73] However, the Shah also considered Islamists as a useful counterweight to his nationalist and leftist opponents. Thus he sought to isolate Khomeini, while permitting Islamist groups to pursue their activities. According to SAVAK records confiscated in February 1979, 'the secret police had at least slight contact with over 1,200 religious leaders. Very few were full-time collaborators, but they had compromised themselves at one time or other'.[74]

The Shah was convinced of the efficacy of religious propaganda to prevent the spread of leftist ideas, particularly in the universities, but he also believed that the clergy were his most implacable enemies.[75] Indeed, Seyyed Hoseyn Nasr, who served as the head of the Empress's bureau in 1978, had extensive contacts with Islamists. Long after the revolution, Nasr described himself as follows: 'Perhaps I was the first Islamic thinker who, having studied extensively in the West and having become deeply immersed and formally educated in different facets of Western thought, rejected the very foundation of modern thought and returned to the bosom of traditional Islam.'[76]

Nasr saw Islamists as a useful counterweight to secularists and leftists whom he believed were undermining traditional Iranian values. An advocate of traditionalist philosophy, Nasr maintained contact with the head of Khomeini's secret organization in Iran, Ayatollah Mottahari.[77] It is not known whether Nasr knew about Mottahari's activities, but Islamist groups saw Nasr as a figure who could establish a balance of power between themselves and the royal court and prevent 'chaos'.[78]

During the revolution, Nasr told the US embassy that younger clerics had been educated 'by men who are fully capable of combining mystic Shi'ite doctrine with Marxist politics'. Nasr warned the US embassy that Khomeini's advocacy of violence could cause a rift within Shi'a Islam and the break-up of Iran along ethnic lines.[79]

The Shah also funded Shi'a groups such as *al D'awa al-Islamiya* (Islamic Call) in Iraq and the Imam Musa Sadr's network in Lebanon.[80] These groups later emerged as networks of pro-Khomeini activity. Moreover, there were sharp differences of opinion in the highest echelons of SAVAK on the issue of religious opposition. For example, there were differences between General Ne'matollah Nasiri and General Fardust, the director of the Special Intelligence Bureau. There were also differences between General Naser Moghaddam, who served as director of SAVAK's internal security department and later as the director of Military Intelligence before being appointed as SAVAK director in April 1978, and General Nasiri.[81]

In the early 1970s, the disagreements within SAVAK caused major problems in its confrontation with urban guerrilla groups.[82] There are indications that by the early 1970s some officials in SAVAK's internal security department, Department Three, had come to see Shari'ati as a useful de facto ally against the leftists.[83] However, by the late 1970s Shari'ati had become a threat to the regime and SAVAK may have even played a role in his death in 1977.

The most prominent intelligence official who advocated forming an alliance with the clergy against the leftists was the chief of the Special Intelligence Bureau General Hossein Fardust. Fardust maintained contact with the clergy through his close friend Hedayatollah Eslaminia who was a senior SAVAK agent in charge of religious affairs.[84] Eslaminia also served as Amir Abbas Hoveyda's channel to the clergy while the latter served as Prime Minister and Court Minister.[85]

Hojjatieh, the Islamic Coalition Society and the Khomeini organization

It is important to note that Khomeini did not have the largest religious network or the largest number of followers among Shi'i Muslims. However, by 1977 Khomeini had succeeded in forming alliances with both the conservative clergy and radical Islamists and leftists. The largest religious organization in the country was a semi-secret society known as the Hojjatieh which was formed to oppose the influence of Baha'i religion in Iran. Baha'is were viewed as apostates because they believed that the Koran was not the final revelation and that the writings of a nineteenth writer, Baha'ollah, provided further revelation. The Shah considered Hojjatieh to be a useful anti-Communist force.[86] The Hojjatieh was covertly supported by SAVAK, as well as several prominent grand Ayatollahs such as Golpayegani, Mar'ashi and Kho'i. Others who also lent their support included Grand Ayatollah Borujerdi and Sheikh Mohammad Taghi Falsafi.[87]

Another prominent member of Hojjatieh was Ayatollah Mohammad Hoseini-Beheshti. According to a former diplomat of the Islamic Republic of Iran, Mir Ali Akbar Montazam, General Hossein Fardust established close relations with Ayatollah Beheshti. According to Montazam, Beheshti initially worked for SAVAK's internal security department, but he was later transferred to Department Seven.[88]

By 1977, the Hojjatieh was said to have 12,000 members throughout the country.[89] Ayatollah Kho'i, a supporter of Hojjatieh, had the most extensive religious network of followers and former students. Kho'i's influence stretched from Lebanon to Afghanistan and the former Soviet Azarbaijan. However, Ayatollah Kho'i always rejected the concept of the guardianship of the supreme jurisconsult.[90] Thus, the majority of Shi'a Muslims did not believe in Khomeini's conception of an Islamic state.

The Islamic Coalition Society served as the main vehicle for propagating Khomeini's message in Iran.[91] The leaders of the Islamic Coalition Society in Iran were Ayatollah Beheshti and Ayatollah Mottahari, both of whom were employees of the Iranian Ministry of Education. Their tasks included writing religious textbooks for the government.[92] They took advantage of the government's tacit support for Islamism to set up schools, charities and religious education classes. The key to Khomeini's success was the formation of an alliance between the Islamic Coalition Society and elements of Hojjatieh. Ayatollah Beheshti played a key role in this context. He was a member of the Hojjatieh and also co-ordinated the activities of the Islamic Coalition Society.[93]

As late as 1977 prominent Hojjatieh members such as Ayatollah Beheshti and Ayatollah Mahdavi-Kani were still trying to work within the system while planning the Shah's removal.[94] By the early 1970s Hojjatieh had become radicalized and some of its youth organizations, such as Askariyun and Mahdiyun, worked with other clerically led religious societies against the Shah.[95] One of the main reasons for the radicalization of the Hojjatieh and its cooperation with the Khomeini camp was the growth of Baha'i influence in Iran. The Shah's physician Dr Abdolkarim Ayadi and Prime Minister Amir-Abbas Hoveyda, SAVAK Director General Ne'matollah Nasiri and chief of SAVAK's Department Three, Parviz Sabeti, were among the most influential officials who were rumoured to be Baha'is. Increasingly, SAVAK resorted to repression in order to quell religious opposition to the regime. In the 1970s the regime took over the distribution of religious endowments organization so as to control the distribution of religious funds.[96]

SAVAK kept clerics who supported Khomeini under close surveillance.[97] In 1975, Khomeini strongly opposed the formation of the one-party-system and the establishment of the Resurgence Party from his exile in Iraq. Shortly afterwards, SAVAK arrested a number of Khomeini's followers, including Ayatollah Beheshti, Ayatollah Montazeri, Ayatollah Hossein Qomi, Hojjat ol-eslam Khamene'i and Hojjat ol-Eslam Kani.[98] According to Mehdi Bazargan, sometime in 1974 to 1975, Ayatollah Mottahari, Ayatollah Taleghani, and Seyyed Ali Khamene'i (Iran's current supreme leader) established a secret group whose objective was the development of 'an Islamic world outlook'. SAVAK, however, found their index cards in a house in Mashhad.[99]

SAVAK did not succeed in eliminating religious opposition to the regime, but it partially co-opted two of the founders of the Islamic Coalition Society, Ayatollah Beheshti and Mottahari and it allowed the Islamic Coalition Society to pursue its activities. Moreover, SAVAK's success in crushing armed opposition groups led Khomeini and his followers to concentrate on organizing a mass uprising against the Shah.[100]

Despite vast differences between the Hojjatieh and Khomeini over doctrinal issues such the role of the jurisconsult, cooperation between the Hojjatieh and the Khomeini camp increased after 1977. The most important religious organization dominated by the Hojjatieh was the Association of the Combatant Clergy, which was founded by a Hojjatieh member Ayatollah Mahdavi-Kani in 1976.[101] The Association of the Combatant Clergy was an underground revolutionary religious organization involved in mobilizing support for Khomeini during the Iranian revolution.[102]

Khomeini also appealed to Ali Shari'ati's supporters even though he did not approve of Shari'ati's attitude towards Islam.[103] Shari'ati's message found audiences in places as far apart as Cairo and Jakarta. In Iran Shari'ati influenced Iranian radicals who proceeded to form Islamic Marxist organizations such as the Mojahedin-e Khalq and Habibollah Peyman's Movement of Combatant Muslims.[104] After 1970 Khomeini placed much greater emphasis on liberating the 'downtrodden' masses.[105] This enabled Khomeini to co-opt leftist and even communist groups in 1978.[106]

The external connections of Khomeini's organization

Khomeini also relied on a network of external support to foment revolution against the Shah. Much has been made of the Khomeini camp's ties to Sa'id Ramadan who has been described as the CEO of the Muslim Brotherhood.[107] Ramadan was married to the daughter of the founder of the Egyptian Muslim Brotherhood, Hasan al-Banna. He travelled across the Middle East and built Muslim Brotherhood cells all over the region. He also co-operated with

Pakistani Islamists, particularly Abul-Ala al-Mawdudi, who established the Muslim Brotherhood-style Islamic Group. In the 1950s, some American officials, such as US ambassador to Egypt, Jefferson Caffery, considered Ramadan to be a potential ally against communist and radical leftist groups. Ramadan also lived in Switzerland and the Swiss authorities suspected him of being a British and American agent. There is no evidence that the British or the Americans recruited Ramadan. Ramadan established the Islamic Centre of Geneva, which became a major centre of Islamist activity and a forum for Islamist activists from across the Islamic world. He also teamed up with a Brotherhood financier, Youssef Nada who helped him establish the group's bank, Al-Taqwa.[108] However, Ramadan considered US intelligence to be incompetent and the evidence suggests that he was only interested in furthering his own group's political interests, namely the export of Islamism.[109] By 1978 the Muslim Brotherhood had established cells in many Middle Eastern countries and it even had cells in the US.[110] Ramadan also had extensive contacts with the Saudi regime and he helped the Saudis establish the Muslim World League in 1962. Throughout the 1960s and 1970s, the Saudis were strongly encouraging the spread of radical Islam as a bulwark against communism and radical nationalism.[111] In Iraq, the Sunni Egyptian Muslim Brotherhood had ties to the Iraqi Da'wah (Call) Party which was founded by Khomeini's close allies Ayatollah Muhammad Baqer al-Sadr and Ayatollah Muhsin al-Hakim. Sadr and Hakim had been concerned about the spread of communism in Iraq and Hakim issued a fatwa attacking communism in 1960.[112] Ramadan also encouraged Khomeini to think in terms of exporting the Islamic revolution, arguing that African-Americans were likely to be influenced by Khomeini's message and that they could be recruited as secret agents for staging Islamic revolutions in other countries.[113] However, the Muslim Brotherhood was not the Khomeini camp's main ally in the Middle East. The Ba'thist Syrian regime of Hafiz Asad was Khomeini's main source of external support.[114]

Hafiz Asad started supporting Khomeini in 1973.[115] Syria and the PLO were also involved in training leftist Iranian guerrilla groups such as Mojahedin-e Khalq and Cherikha-ye Fada'i-ye Khalq. Those groups' ideologies were primarily influenced by Arab radicals. Khomeini's organization was provided with money and training and Khomeini's close aides such as Sadegh Ghotbzadeh were given Syrian passports.[116]

In the late 1960s, Khomeini's ally Musa Sadr had agreed to provide Lebanese training camps and sanctuaries to Khomeini's followers.[117] Sadr had previously worked for SAVAK. However, he later turned against the Shah and joined Khomeini.[118] Sadr and Khomeini played important roles in shoring up the regime of Hafiz Asad in the early 1970s. Asad's regime was accused by the Sunni majority of being heathen because Asad was an Alawi who had embraced secularism.[119]

Asad was desperate to find an ally to quell the religious opposition to his regime. At Khomeini's suggestion, Sadr declared that the Alawis were faithful Muslims and continued to legitimize the Alawi faith in his sermons. As a result, it became increasingly difficult for Asad's opponents to question his religious credentials. It would not be an exaggeration to argue that Asad owed Khomeini a debt of gratitude.[120] In return for Sadr's assistance to his regime, Asad agreed to help Khomeini overthrow the Shah.[121]

Despite the improvement in Asad's religious standing, the Syrian Muslim Brotherhood started its campaign of violence against Asad in 1976.[122] However, Asad was not loyal to Khomeini, and as we shall see in a later chapter he was prepared to shut down pro-Khomeini camps in Syria in return for the resumption of Iranian hostility to Iraq.[123]

Moreover, the Syrian-Libyan axis, which was supported by Moscow, provided funds and training to Khomeini's supporters. It is important to note that by now Syria was virtually a Soviet client state. The role of the Ba'thist regime in Iraq is particularly complex. Iraq also had close ties with the Soviet Union. Iraq's peace treaty with Iran expressly prohibited the signatories from allowing subversive groups to use their territory. However, despite the fact that Khomeini was under close surveillance, much of the funding for Iranian guerrilla groups was sent by religious sources through Khomeini's headquarters in Iraq.[124]

It was not until the summer of 1978 that Saddam Hussein began to indicate that he was willing to move against Khomeini. Syria was supporting Khomeini and Iraq's decision to allow Khomeini to continue his activities may well have been because of the influence of President Ahmad Hasan al-Bakr and opponents of Saddam Hussein in the Iraqi leadership who had close ties with Syria.

The Iraqi leadership may also have been concerned about the outbreak of domestic unrest if it restrained Khomeini.[125] Moreover, the Shah's secret alliance with Israel and his support for Sadat's peace-making efforts alarmed Iraq, Syria and Libya. The Shah was fully aware of the strong clerical opposition to his alliance with Israel. Indeed, one reason that he refused to publicize Iran's secret cooperation with Israel was his fear of a domestic backlash. Despite the fact that the Shah saw Khomeini as a British agent, he also believed that conservative clerics were useful allies in his fight against communism and Khomeini. Perhaps the Shah's contradictory perceptions of the role of the clergy best explain his failure to either crack down on or accommodate the clerical establishment during the Iranian revolutionary crisis.

4

THE FORMATION OF THE TRIPOLI BLOC AND THE RADICAL CHALLENGE TO THE REGIONAL ORDER

US regional strategy was aimed at stabilizing the price of oil and US policies towards Iran, Israel and Saudi Arabia were influenced by the pursuit of that goal. The Carter administration saw Saudi Arabia as the key to its energy and Middle East policies. Secretary of State Cyrus Vance continued to dominate US foreign policy until May 1978 when the Afghan coup led to a massive dispute in the administration.

The ultimate objective of Vance's global strategy was the gradual reduction of US military power in the Eurasian landmass and its gradual replacement by stable collective security structures.[1] In the Middle East, the most important such structures would be an Iran-Iraq-Saudi Arabia security pact in the Persian Gulf and a comprehensive Arab-Israeli settlement.

The opposition of the Jewish lobby to Carter's policies led him to support a bilateral Israeli-Egyptian peace, which could serve as a vehicle for reaching a broader settlement later on.[2] Moreover, the effort to support Egyptian President Anwar Sadat's peace-making efforts led radical Arab states, Syria, Libya and South Yemen, as well as a faction of the Iraqi regime around President Ahmad Hasan Al-Bakr, to form an alliance against Sadat. Syria was, undoubtedly, the key member of this alliance.

In an effort to counter the expected defection of Egypt from the radical camp, the alliance, which was backed by the Soviet Union and the PLO, provided strong support to Khomeini to overthrow the Shah. At the same time, the KGB began to consider plans to assassinate Sadat and the Soviet Union also played a more active role in Afghanistan, the Horn of Africa and South Yemen.[3]

The Shah and regional détente

After the Shah's reversal of Iran's oil policy in late 1977, the price of oil was no longer a matter of dispute between Iran and Saudi Arabia. Iran continued to improve its relations with Iraq. There were several high-level visits during this period and a number of bilateral agreements on trade, economic relations and cultural cooperation were concluded, and technical committees met for detailed negotiations on specific issues.[4]

Despite the differences between Iran and Iraq over oil price policy and Iraq's military build-up and nuclear programme, Iran began to cooperate with Iraq and Saudi Arabia on a Persian Gulf security pact.[5] In the aftermath of Sadat's visit to Jerusalem, however, the Saudis were anxious to placate Iraq.[6] The Shah sent the

Iranian foreign minister to Baghdad for consultations and the Iraqis were more receptive to the idea of discussing a regional security arrangement. In April 1978, Saudi Defence Minister Prince Sultan visited Iran and Iraq to discuss security cooperation among the three countries.[7]

However, nothing came of Sultan's visit to Iraq, probably because the US Congress was debating a major arms deal package for Israel, Egypt and Saudi Arabia. The two countries did not resume their talks on security issues until May, after the coup d'etat in Afghanistan which heightened concern in the region.[8]

Soviet response to the Shah's regional strategy

Despite the worsening economic crisis and the growing opposition to the regime the Soviets did not believe that a revolution was imminent in Iran. The KGB was pessimistic about the prospects of Iranian leftist groups. It believed that the most likely alternative to the Shah would be a regime dominated by the military.[9] The KGB suffered a major set-back in Iran when its main agent, General Ahmad Mogharebi, code-named MAN, was arrested by SAVAK in September 1977. He had been recruited in the early years of the Cold War and in the final years of the monarchy he was involved in Iranian arms purchases from the US and other Western countries. According to Soviet defector Vladimir Kuzikchin, Mogharebi was 'regarded as the Residency's best agent' and had 'innumerable connections in various spheres of Iranian life, including the court of the Shah, the government and SAVAK'.[10] Despite the fact that he had originally been recruited apparently as an ideological agent, Mogharebi was increasingly motivated by financial considerations. In 1972 his salary was increased from 150–200 to 330 convertible rubles a month. In 1976 his salary was raised to 500 rubles. However, his increasing contacts with the KGB made SAVAK suspicious of him and he was arrested in September 1977.[11]

The Soviet Union had another important agent in Iran, code-named ZHAMAN, who was also recruited in the early years of the Cold War. He was a relative of Amir Abbas Hoveyda who served as the Shah's Prime Minister and Court Minister. ZHAMAN was particularly useful to the Soviets because he passed Soviet disinformation to the Shah, as well as to his American, Egyptian, Somali and Pakistani contacts. In 1977, the KGB gave ZHAMAN a thousand-dollar pair of cufflinks for his efforts to promote Soviet active measures.[12] Soviet ambassador Vladimir Vinogradov also tried to cultivate Hoveyda himself. Hoveyda told Vinogradov that he had seen a SAVAK report to the Shah complaining that they had been having 'long political discussions'.[13]

By 1977, the Shah's policies towards Iraq, Egypt and Afghanistan had significantly undermined Moscow's regional strategy. Soviet officials believed that dissidence in Iran was encouraged by Washington to punish the Shah for pursuing independent foreign and oil policies. However, they believed that the Shah and his American supporters would not permit a revolution to occur.[14] Nevertheless, in response to the Shah's regional activism, Moscow activated the Baku-based National Voice of Iran (NVOI) and the Soviet embassy in Tehran printed Navid, the organ of the Iranian communist party, Tudeh. Indeed, US officials had been aware for some time that the Kremlin had been interested in the removal of the Pahlavi dynasty.[15] Nevertheless, in his memoirs, Vance, who was the leading advocate of détente in the administration, argued that Moscow did not want to destabilize Iran because it 'feared Islamic revival'.[16] Vance, therefore, completely ignored Moscow's contacts with radical Iranian clerics and its support for leftist guerrilla organizations. Moreover, as we will see, Moscow's allies among radical Arab states also provided a great deal of assistance to the Khomeini camp.

Moscow also sought to halt the move towards a separate Egyptian-Israeli settlement by constructing a coalition of radical Arab states to confront US allies. The Kremlin also increased its involvement in Syria, even though KGB officials considered Asad to be a 'petit-bourgeois ego maniac'.[17] Asad feared that Syria would be isolated and Israeli hegemony in the Levant consolidated as a result of Sadat's policies. Other Arab leaders shared Asad's fears of a separate Egyptian-Israeli peace.[18]

Hafiz Asad's regional strategy

By 1977 Syria had emerged as the Soviet Union main ally in the Middle East. Despite the deterioration of relations in 1976 because of Syrian intervention in the Lebanese civil war, the two countries improved their relations in 1977 partly because of Sadat's attempts to make peace with Israel. Indeed, in 1976, Brezhnev indicated that Syria was the Soviet Union's main ally in the Middle East. Soviet arms exports to Syria in 1977 were worth 825 million dollars. In 1978, they were worth more than one billion dollars.[19] According to KGB files, in December 1977, Syrian President Hafiz Asad approved of a secret meeting in Damascus between his intelligence chiefs and the Popular Front for the Liberation of Palestine to discuss Sadat's assassination.[20]

In late 1977 Syrian President Hafiz Asad revealed that the purpose of his regional strategy was the creation of a greater Syria federation composed of Syria, Lebanon, Jordan, and the West Bank.[21] He also strengthened his country's ties with the PLO to undermine Sadat's efforts to make peace with Israel and to counter the Israeli-Maronite alliance in Lebanon.[22] However, neither Syria nor the PLO was strong enough to compensate for the loss of Egypt. Asad's long-term goal was to create a Greater Syria. The centrepiece of the new Syrian-Soviet regional strategy was the formation of a bloc of radical states to counter US allies, Iran, Egypt and Saudi Arabia. This strategy was set in motion in December 1977, when Asad tried to form a new alliance of radical Arab states, the 'Tripoli Bloc', with Libya and Iraq.[23]

The main obstacle to the formation of this alliance was the long-standing enmity between Syria and Iraq.[24] President Bakr and his proteges were more inclined than Saddam Hussein to compromise with Syria.[25] Iraq's refusal to attend the Tripoli conference was undoubtedly a blow to Soviet regional strategy. Nevertheless, Moscow warmly endorsed the 'Tripoli Declaration', which called on Arabs to assist Syria and the PLO and condemned Sadat's visit to Jerusalem. It was later reported that Libya had pledged to finance a billion dollars' worth of Syrian arms purchases from the Soviet Union.[26]

Asad's failure to draw the Shah into an anti-Iraq alliance and support for Khomeini

In an important message to the Shah at the end of 1977, Asad asked the Shah to resume his military assistance to the Iraqi Kurds. In return, Asad promised to curtail the activities of Khomeini's followers and to ensure that the Shi'i cleric

Musa Sadr 'will no longer play a role in Lebanon'.[27] The Shah's refusal to go along with Asad led the latter to resume his assistance to the Khomeini camp.[28]

Asad believed that he could attain his regional objectives by severing Iran's ties with Israel and persuading Iran to abrogate the Algiers peace treaty with Iraq.[29] He believed that Iran was sufficiently large and powerful to replace Egypt in his regional strategy. Providing assistance to Khomeini and his followers was an important part of Asad's alliance with Arafat.[30]

Soviet and PLO involvement in the Iranian revolution

In late 1977 the PLO leader, Yaser Arafat, who was involved in training thousands of Iranian leftist guerrillas, approached the Shah to persuade him to change his policy towards Israel. Saudi Arabia and Jordan supported Arafat's efforts and urged the Shah to meet Arafat and agree to the establishment of a PLO office in Iran. PLO 'Foreign Minister' Faruq Qoddumi met the SAVAK representative in Cairo and travelled to Iran twice to meet Iranian officials. The Shah continued to procrastinate, but he had indicated that he might accept the establishment of a Palestinian state.[31]

As the situation in Iran deteriorated, the Shah received reports on the PLO's involvement in destabilizing Iran. When Israeli Prime Minister Menachem Begin visited Iran on 22–24 February, the Shah expressed his deep frustration with the US. He warned Begin that the clergy had formed an alliance with the communists in order to overthrow him, and asserted that the US did not understand the situation in the Persian Gulf. The Shah was also concerned about the situation in Afghanistan and predicted that a communist coup would occur in the near future. Begin shared the Shah's concerns about Soviet expansionism in the region. He assured the monarch that Israel was prepared to resume talks with Egypt without any preconditions.[32]

Israeli intelligence indicated that the Shah's opponents were being trained in PLO camps in various Arab countries. Moreover, other Iranians were being trained for infiltration into the Iraqi Shi'a community to destabilize the Iraqi regime.[33] After March 1978 Israel stepped up its assistance to the Maronites in the Lebanese civil war to destroy the PLO's infrastructure in Lebanon and dismantle Khomeini's organization in that country.[34]

SAVAK was also receiving intelligence on Libyan support for Iranian revolutionaries from a rogue CIA agent, Edwin Wilson. Wilson had close relations with SAVAK in the mid 1970s, but in late 1975 he began to work with Libyan intelligence for money. However, Wilson still believed that he was also working for the CIA. Wilson gathered intelligence indicating that the KGB was assisting the Libyans and funding, through East German intelligence, assassination and guerrilla training programmes for opponents of the Shah, as well as such groups as the Nicaraguan Sandinistas.[35] He also gathered intelligence indicating that hundreds of the Shah's opponents had received paramilitary and assassination training by Libyan intelligence. Wilson has said that between 1976 and 1979, he provided SAVAK, either directly or through his CIA associates, the names of the Iranian 'students' being trained by the Libyans and that SAVAK launched a massive campaign of assassination against them throughout the world.[36] However, Wilson also gave the Libyans SAVAK intelligence. He has said that had SAVAK discovered his treachery, he would have been almost certainly assassinated.[37]

Iran had long been one of the main targets of the KGB's subversive operations. According to Soviet defector, Vladimir Kuzikchin, Soviet leader Nikita Khruschev personally approved of an assassination attempt against the Shah in 1962.[38] Between 1967 and 1973, a number of landing sites, arms dumps and bases in Iran had been selected and photographed. Moreover, the Azerbaijani, Kazakh and Kyrgyz KGBs were instructed to recruit illegal agents (agents not under official cover) who could pass as members of Iranian ethnic groups. In Tehran, the KGB had drawn up detailed plans for the bombing of 23 buildings, including royal palaces, SAVAK and police headquarters, ministries, the main railway station and TV and radio stations. The defection of Oleg Lyalin, a KGB officer at the London residency, in 1971 led to the recall of many KGB officers involved in sabotage operations and the KGB scaled back some of its plans. However, in 1977 KGB illegals hid a secret weapons cache of 27 Walther pistols and 2,500 rounds of ammunition in a dead letter box. Apparently the cache was to be used in the event of an uprising against the Shah.[39] In early 1978, SAVAK was informed that a large number of PLO and Muslim Brotherhood terrorists had illegally arrived in Iran and had established contact with Iranian mullahs and religious leaders.[40] SAVAK also discovered a large PLO weapons cache in Tehran. SAVAK informed the Shah of the PLO's plan to destabilize Iran, but he instructed the organization not to arrest the saboteurs for fear of intensifying the human rights pressure on the regime. He wanted SAVAK to keep the saboteurs under surveillance and arrest them if they resorted to violence.[41]

Some Iranians incorrectly believe that Israel played an important role in overthrowing the Shah.[42] Their suspicions were fuelled by the behaviour of SAVAK's internal security department, Department Three, which closely liaised with the Israeli Foreign intelligence service, the Mossad. The head of Department Three, Parviz Sabeti, was reportedly trained in Israel, and some observers of Iranian politics believe that Sabeti was a Mossad agent of influence.[43]

As we will see in later chapters, during the Iranian revolution, Sabeti conducted agent provocateur operations in an effort to persuade the Shah to institute a crackdown. However, the operations had calamitous consequences for the Shah because they intensified opposition to the regime.

The Brzezinski-Vance dispute over US response to Soviet strategy

The Carter administration was not particularly concerned about the impact of the formation of the Tripoli bloc on internal developments in Iran. One of the administration's biggest mistakes during this period, which undoubtedly contributed to the failure of its policy towards Iran, was its refusal to support a Congressional bill on the imposition of sanctions on state sponsors of terrorism. Following a hostage incident in Somalia during which West Germans rescued their hostages, the Carter administration undertook a review of its counter-terrorism policy. The review was completed by Brzezinski's assistant William Odom and resulted in Presidential Security memorandum 30 (PSM30) signed by President Carter on 16 September 1977.[44] Brzezinski and his assistant William Odom strongly supported the Special Forces Operational Detachment-DELTA, or Delta Force, set up to carry out hostage rescue operations.[45] However, Odom merely reinforced his boss's view of terrorism, namely that 'as a phenomenon terrorism did not exist'. He contended: 'When it happens here, it is a crime'. 'When it happens abroad, it is war.'[46] Nevertheless, PSM-30 gave the NSC an important role in formulating the country's counter-terrorism policy. It also set up a new Working Group on terrorism. However, these measures did not satisfy some prominent law-makers such as Senator Abraham Ribicoff, and Senator Jacob Javits. Senator Ribicoff introduced a new bill on 24 October 1977 calling on the executive branch to create new institutions to combat terrorism and impose sanctions on countries that 'aid and abet terrorism'.[47]

Despite the fact that the bill was supported by many senators, the administration encouraged a debate about the definition of terrorism to kill the bill. The NSC disliked the bill's proposal to re-organize the executive branch in pursuit of counter-terrorism . Moreover, US officials were also concerned that the bill would undermine US efforts to negotiate an Arab-Israeli peace settlement especially because Ribicoff and Javits had indicated that they wanted sanctions to be imposed on four Arab countries that supported Palestinian terrorism.[48]

In fact, at the time, the prevailing view seemed to be that the PLO had accepted a two-state solution to the Arab-Israeli conflict, as outlined in UN Resolution 242, and that it was ready to renounce terrorism. The NSC believed that terrorists were intent upon drawing attention to themselves and that the more attention they got the more they would try to repeat their actions.[49] Like the rest of the administration, the NSC did not link developments in Iran to those in the rest of the Middle East. The NSC, led by Brzezinski, was fixated on the Soviet threat and ignored the activities of radical Arab states, which in some cases were acting as Soviet clients. In fact, even after the Carter administration left office, Brzezinski's hawkish assistant, William Odom, refused to cooperate with the Reagan administration which had a Soviet-centric view of international terrorism.[50] The Soviets were not directing all international terrorist activities. However, they did have very close relations with some of the worst state sponsors such as Syria and Libya.

Initially, the Soviets were suspicious of Arafat because of his close relations with Romanian dictator Nicolae Ceausescu. However, a Politburo resolution of 7 September 1973 instructed the KGB residency in Beirut to maintain contact with Arafat's intelligence service.[51] More importantly, the KGB had extremely close relations with Wadi Haddad, the head of the foreign operations of the Popular Front for the Liberation of Palestine (PFLP). Haddad was the controller of the notorious terrorist Carlos 'the Jackal'. In 1972, Haddad formed a breakaway faction of the PFLP, the Special Operations Group, after PFLP leader George Habbash condemned terrorism. The new group's headquarters was in Baghdad and Haddad continued to maintain extremely close relations with the KGB. KGB chief Yuri Andropov was hopeful that the KGB could to some extent control Haddad's activities. The most spectacular terrorist attack Haddad planned was probably the kidnapping of OPEC oil ministers in 1975. Haddad's death in 1978 of cancer did not put a stop to the KGB's attempts to cultivate Palestinian terrorists. The KGB also tried to expand its intelligence liaison with Arafat's Fatah faction. Arafat had visited Moscow on a number of occasions. During Arafat's visit to Moscow in 1974, an official communiqué recognized the PLO as 'the sole legitimate representative of the Arab people of Palestine'. In June 1978, a member of the Fatah Central

Committee and the head of Arafat's intelligence service visited Moscow for talks with the KGB and the International Department.[52]

The State Department was primarily interested in reducing the Shah to a figurehead monarch and cultivating his opponents. As far as the issue of regional radicalism was concerned, the Carter administration was far more concerned at this stage about the increasing Soviet influence in the Horn of Africa. Soviet activity there prompted the Carter administration to order an extensive review of US strategy.[53] Vance argued that Moscow was merely taking advantage of opportunities to increase its influence in the Third World. Brzezinski, however, contended that the purpose of Soviet intervention in the Horn of Africa was to gain control over Saudi Arabia, the oil pipelines, and the Suez Canal.[54]

Carter did accept one of Brzezinski's main policy recommendations, namely the creation of a rapid deployment force. Soviet commentators argued that the US sought to turn the Persian Gulf into an 'area of strategic influence of the United States'.[55] The Carter administration also pressed forward with its policy of strengthening Saudi Arabia.

Matters were further complicated by a dispute between the Carter administration and Israel regarding the sale of F-15, F-16 and other equipment to Saudi Arabia.[56] The Saudis warned that they would reverse their oil policy and stop supporting the dollar if the Carter administration succumbed to pro-Israeli pressure.[57] Despite vigorous lobbying by Prime Minister Begin and pro-Israeli groups, the Carter administration proceeded with the sale and the Senate approved it after a divisive debate.[58]

The Coup d'etat in Afghanistan and Regional Security

By early 1977, the Shah's policy of drawing Afghanistan into Iran's orbit had been so successful that it was leading to an Iranian-Soviet confrontation.[59] Daoud Khan's decision to improve his country's ties with the US, Iran, Egypt, Saudi Arabia and Turkey infuriated Soviet leaders.[60] Daoud believed that the unrest in Iran would probably lead the Kremlin to take pre-emptive action in Afghanistan to prevent US military intervention in Iran.[61] Soviet ambassador to Afghanistan Alexander Puzanov expressed his country's serious concern about the events in Iran, hinting that should the unrest in Iran 'acquire an international dimension' his country would not 'remain indifferent'.[62]

The Afghan coup, which led to the establishment of a communist regime, reinforced the Shah's belief that an alliance of 'the red and the black' had been created to overthrow him.[63] During his visit to Washington in November 1977, the Shah had given Carter a lengthy presentation on Afghanistan.[64] The Shah was convinced that as a result of US-Soviet détente, the Soviet Union was altering the strategic balance in the Middle East, Southwest Asia and the Indian Ocean and that the Afghan coup was a portent of things to come in his own country.

The KGB was involved in the Afghan coup which led to the murder of Daoud Khan and his entire family, as well as those of 7,000 officers and officials. Subsequently, the KGB assisted the new regime to suppress Afghan Islamists.[65] Communist Afghanistan also became an important base for KGB and GRU activities against the Shah.[66] 'Afghanistan as Finland is probably inevitable', observed NSC official Gary Sick, 'but an Afghan Hungary is a positive danger to the long-term stability of the entire region.' Sick advised Brzezinski that the US should cooperate with Iran and other US allies in the region to overthrow the Afghan regime. Brzezinski agreed with Sick and recommended 'an active political response to the coup'.[67] However, the evidence indicates that Brzezinski failed to convince Carter.[68] Carter, Vance and CIA Director Stansfield Turner downplayed Moscow's role in the Afghan coup so as not to jeopardize détente.[69]

In early May, the Shah sent a letter to Carter about developments in Afghanistan. He said that he had predicted the coup against Daoud but it had occurred earlier than he had expected. He indicated that he would build up Iran's military power and rely on the US to supply some of its military requirements. He also expressed his dissatisfaction with the Oil Consortium. He informed Carter that the Consortium had sharply reduced its off-take of Iranian oil, thereby jeopardizing Iranian military programmes.[70]

Carter's response to the Shah's letter has not been documented by any of his advisers. However, events after the Afghan coup and embassy reports indicate that the president sided with the State Department. Cyrus Vance has falsely claimed that there were doubts about Soviet involvement and that US allies were urging the Carter administration to adopt a restrained policy towards the new Afghan regime.[71]

In fact, it was the State Department that prevailed upon Carter to persuade the Shah to adopt a 'wait and see attitude' and continue to assist Afghanistan financially.[72] However, Iran began to cooperate with Israel and China to organise an anti-Soviet alliance in Afghanistan. Israel's foreign intelligence service, the Mossad, brought SAVAK and the Chinese intelligence service together for that purpose.[73] The evidence suggests that Iran and China did not involve the CIA in their plans.[74]

On 9 June, in a small meeting with his senior advisers, Carter made it clear that Vance was his 'chief foreign policy spokesman'.[75] Brzezinski would be Carter's 'inside adviser and not a spokesman for foreign policy'.[76] As a result, Vance dramatically reversed US foreign policy in virtually all areas.[77]

Iraq's Changing Regional Strategy

One of the most important side effects of the pro-Soviet coup in Afghanistan was Iraq's decision to distance itself from the Soviet Union. After the Afghan coup, Saddam Hussein immediately cracked down on the Iraqi Communist Party (ICP).[78]

Moreover, from the autumn of 1977 onwards, Hussein began to prepare the ground for a coup against President Ahmad Hasan al-Bakr. Several reshuffles in the Iraqi leadership strengthened Saddam Hussein's position.[79] The executions of Iraqi communists reflected the Iraqi regime's fear that Moscow might use the communists to overthrow it.[80] Hussein was also concerned that Khomeini might succeed in establishing a Shi'a fundamentalist regime in Iran which would be hostile to Iraq. Thus he stepped up cooperation on internal security matters with Iran.

Despite Bakr's earlier protests about the Carter administration's decision to form a Rapid Deployment Force,[81] Iraq was so concerned about the Soviet threat to the region that it did not protest when Bahrain renewed the lease of its naval facilities to the US. It also agreed to discuss Oman's proposal for Persian Gulf security in May 1978.[82] Moreover, Iran, Iraq and Saudi Arabia were close to concluding a pact that could lead to 'a major shift in the strategic balance of the oil producing area'.[83] However, Iraq was suspicious of Iran and Saudi Arabia because of their close associations with the US. And, both Iraq and Saudi Arabia were suspicious of the Shah's regional ambitions. Iran blamed Iraq and Saudi Arabia for the collapse of the talks.[84]

In August, Crown Prince Fahd of Saudi Arabia tried to revive the talks on a Persian Gulf security pact. By the end of the summer both Iraq and Saudi Arabia had become concerned about the turmoil in Iran. Both countries repeatedly expressed their support for the Shah and Iraq received Empress Farah as late as 11 November 1978.[85]

Ayatollah Khomeini's presence in Iraq was a serious obstacle to the improvement of Iranian-Iraqi relations. The Shah asked Saddam Hussein to expel Khomeini from Iraq. Hussein sent his half-brother, Barzan al-Takriti to Iran for talks with the Shah. Al-Takriti informed the Shah that Iraq was quite prepared to arrange a 'suitable accident' for Khomeini to silence him for ever. Hussein believed that the Shah had to get tough with the clergy and was prepared to offer assistance.[86] The fact that Khomeini was not expelled from Iraq until October 1978 strongly suggests that Bakr and his supporters protected him. However, the power struggle in Iraq, which was also inextricably intertwined with the country's geopolitical orientation, prevented Iran and Iraq from concluding an anti-Soviet security pact.

5

REVOLUTIONARY CRISIS IN IRAN

The onset of revolutionary crisis in Iran was an indirect result of the Carter administration's policy. However, until late 1977, two of the leading figures in Khomeini's secret organization in Iran, Ayatollah Mohammad Hosseini Beheshti and Ayatollah Mohammad Raza Mahdavi-Kani, were still prepared to work within the system to change the regime from within.[1] The change in the Shah's oil-price policy led the Carter administration to reduce the human rights pressure on the Shah. However, by now, the Shah's opponents, most prominently Ayatollah Khomeini and his supporters, had come to the conclusion that the time was ripe for challenging the monarch. The Shah's problems were compounded by the rivalry between the Royal Court and the government, and policy differences and rivalries within SAVAK.

Intra-elite discord and agent provocateur operations

The Shah's appointment of Jamshid Amuzegar as Prime Minister turned SAVAK and the Royal Court against the government. SAVAK Director General Nasiri believed that the Carter administration wanted to overthrow the Shah. He had observed that if Carter were elected, the Shah would 'collapse'.[2] Director of SAVAK's internal security division, Department Three, Parviz Sabeti, believed that the Shah's liberalization programme would result in 'a popular revolt'.[3] Sabeti had prime ministerial ambitions even when the crisis was virtually out of control.[4] He regularly received reports from his contacts in the clerical establishment and was well aware of the intensifying revolutionary crisis.[5] Sabeti believed that all the opponents of the regime had to be eliminated but he also called for launching an anti-corruption campaign. Sabeti's office closely monitored the economic activities of Iranian officials and elite, including members of the Royal Family. Sabeti regularly briefed his close friend, Amir Abbas Hoveyda, when the latter served as prime minister, on the economic activities of the Iranian elite. Some of Sabeti's reports on the illegal activities of members of the Royal Family infuriated the Shah who threatened Sabeti for filing 'one particularly damaging' report.[6]

As far as the issue of opposition to the regime was concerned, the Shah believed that if the situation in the country worsened perceptibly, he could justify a crackdown.[7] According to former SAVAK official, Mansur Rafizadeh, SAVAK agent provocateurs set fire to banks and indirectly manipulated armed opposition groups to rob banks to provide the Shah with a pretext to crack down. After Carter was elected president, the Shah ordered General Nasiri to intensify SAVAK's agent provocateur operations to make the Carter administration understand that its human rights policy would only result in a communist take-over of Iran.[8]

Court Minister Amir Abbas Hoveyda was concerned by reports he received from his close friend Hedayatollah Eslaminia who was one of SAVAK's, as well as the US embassy's, contacts with senior clerics. Eslaminia warned Hoveyda that US officials were intent upon forming an alliance between Amuzegar and the military in order to ease the Shah out of power.[9] Hoveyda suffered a setback in January 1978 when Amuzegar persuaded the Shah to allow him to combine the premiership and the secretary generalship of the Rastakhiz Party.[10]

Stories were leaked to the press comparing Carter to Kennedy. According to Iranian press reports, Kennedy had used economic pressure to compel the Shah to introduce reforms and appoint Ali Amini as Prime Minister. In October the Iranian press castigated Amini as an American agent. Several US officials believed that the Shah wanted to warn Carter that similar pressure tactics would not work.[11]

Intensification of religious opposition to the Shah

By late 1977 the religious opposition had concluded that the Carter administration had decided to overthrow the Shah. Richard Cottam, who served as an adviser to the State Department on Iranian affairs and was in contact with the Khomeini camp, observed in early 1978: 'There is not the slightest question that the timing of opposition activity is directly related to Carter's pronouncements on human rights.'[12] In November 1977, after the Shah's visit to the US, Khomeini's adviser, Dr Ebrahim Yazdi, contacted him, saying that the Carter administration had abandoned the Shah.[13]

In the same month Khomeini issued a *Fatwa* against the Shah. Khomeini declared that he was 'exercising' his 'religious authority' and that he had 'deposed the Shah and abrogated the Constitution'. He called for a campaign of total disobedience. The letter was sent to thousands of addresses in Iran, especially to clerics throughout the country. The SAVAK learned 'almost immediately' of the *Fatwa* but it chose not to inform the Shah.[14]

The Shah was not informed until more than a week after the event.[15] By late 1977 SAVAK reports indicated that there was growing cooperation between Khomeini's religious followers, nationalist groups and Islamists. Sabeti reported that Khomeini was highly popular among lower classes and that his supporters were taking advantage of adverse social conditions. According to Sabeti, different groups that were seeking to overthrow the regime had started co-ordinating their activities and bazaaris and businessmen had contributed substantial sums to radical religious groups.[16]

In December 1977, Khomeini gave an interview to *Le Monde* in which he called for the overthrow of the Shah.[17] The Shah, who was angered by the *Le Monde* interview, agreed to act on Hoveyda's proposal to respond to Khomeini's attacks.[18]

The Shah and Hoveyda provoke religious opposition

Towards the end of December 1977, the Shah set up an ad hoc committee under the chairmanship of Court Minister Hoveyda for responding to Khomeini's propaganda. The committee persuaded the Shah to build up Khomeini as the main threat to the regime and a mad man who wanted to return Iran to the dark ages.[19] The Shah, who thought that Carter's visit to Iran was a sign of strong US support for him, decided to challenge Khomeini head-on.

At the same time, the Shah limited Prime Minister Amuzegar's contacts with US officials. For example, he even refused to brief Amuzegar on his discussions with President Carter, saying that he had discussed foreign affairs and oil with the US president.[20] Hoveyda sought to destabilize the Amuzegar government by embroiling it in a conflict with the religious opposition.[21] He wanted to demonstrate that Amuzegar was incapable of governing the country and persuade the Shah to re-appoint him as Prime Minister.[22]

Unrest in the country would also show the Carter administration that liberalization would only encourage instability.[23] The committee sent two letters, which were supposedly written by two individuals to the editors of *Kayhan*, and *Etelaat*, Iran's two main dailies. The Shah himself read and edited the letters, which were sent by Information Minister Dariush Homayun.[24] The letters described Khomeini as a British agent and a mad homosexual Indian poet. In one of the letters the clergy were described as 'a race of parasites, engaged in sodomy, usury, and drunk most of the time'.[25]

The following day Khomeini's secret committee in Iran, Ayatollahs Beheshti, Mottahari, and Mofatteh, held a meeting. They thought that the Shah had decided to crack down.[26] According to one account, Hoveyda's contact with the religious establishment, Hedayatollah Eslaminia, began to stir up the situation in Qom as well. Homayun also provoked the opposition.[27]

Shortly afterwards the religious city of Qom exploded. Five thousand militant religious students, clerics and bazaaris led by Hojjat-al Islam Sadegh Khalkhali went on the rampage, attacking banks, government offices and other public places. The police withdrew from the scene. Finally the army arrived on the scene and dispersed the crowd. Over a hundred people were arrested and released after Ayatollah Kazem Shari'atmadari intervened on their behalf. Some school children, seven demonstrators and two policemen were killed in the clashes.[28]

SAVAK described the Qom incident to the Shah as a 'minor incident'.[29] Sabeti explicitly instructed all SAVAK offices and branches and security agencies of the regime to refrain from disclosing the real reason for the detention of pro-Khomeini activists and to say that they had been arrested on charges of affray and sedition.[30] The militant group of theology students called themselves Hezbollah (Party of God). Their leader was Sheikh Hadi Ghaffari, whose father had been jailed by SAVAK for five years and had died under torture in 1975.[31]

On 11 January, another major demonstration occurred in Qom. The security forces attacked Shari'atmadari's house and they killed a *talabeh* there.[32] After the Qom incident Sabeti asked Prime Minister Amuzegar to order a crackdown. He wanted to arrest 3,500 people in two separate operations. When Amuzegar refused to do so, Sabeti asked Court Minister Hoveyda to convince the Shah.[33] The evidence suggests that Sabeti resorted to agent provocateur activities to inflame the situation to persuade the Shah to order a crackdown.

As we saw earlier, the Shah had been thinking along the same lines. Apparently fear of US reaction, as well as his distrust of Sabeti, prevented the monarch from taking action. However, SAVAK action squads had already started a campaign of intimidation against secular opposition groups. Some opposition leaders were told: 'You are agents of the US, prepare for death.'[34] On 8 April, 1978, bombs exploded at the homes of five founders of Iran' Committee for the Defence of Human Rights, including leader of the Liberation Movement Mehdi Bazargan and leader of the National Front Karim Sanjabi.[35] US officials were well aware of the security services' harassment of opposition leaders and dissidents.[36]

Sabeti repeatedly called for a crackdown to put an end to demonstrations against the regime. He believed that after suppressing the opposition, the regime should allow a loyal opposition to emerge which should also be given free reign to criticize the system and members of the Royal Family.[37] In April, Sabeti approached his close friend Court Minister Hoveyda to call on the Shah to ask him to suppress the opposition to the regime. Hoveyda was also concerned about the growing opposition to the regime and was concerned about the regime's lack of a 'strategic' crisis management plan. The Shah asked for a plan and Sabeti sent him a list of 1,500 people whose arrest he believed would put an end to the unrest in the country.[38] The Shah agreed to the arrest of 300 people only.[39] Moreover, the Shah repeatedly refused to grant Sabeti an audience during the revolutionary crisis even though the director of SAVAK's Department Three probably knew more than any other official in the country about the weaknesses of the regime and its vulnerability to revolutionary activities.[40]

It is important to note that the disintegration of Iran's security apparatus was partly caused by the dispute over strategy between the US and Israel. Sabeti and Nasiri, who were closer to Israel, called for a crack down, whereas Generals Fardust and Moghaddam who were closer to British and US intelligence services advocated co-opting the religious opposition and the National Front. However, both the Sabeti and Fardust-Moghaddam factions wanted to reduce the involvement of members of the Royal Family in politics. Sabeti, who was vehemently opposed to the Khomeini movement, seems to have been thinking in terms of allowing the re-emergence of political parties in Iran to stabilize the regime. Fardust and Moghaddam, however, were thinking along the lines of forming a de facto alliance with the Islamists whom they saw as a counterweight to leftist and communist groups. Not surprisingly, as former senior SAVAK officers, Fardust and Moghaddam had allies in SAVAK. Indeed, Moghaddam would return to SAVAK in June as director. A SAVAK intelligence report written as late as February 1978 named several of the prominent figures in Khomeini's group as 'our potential allies' in the war with 'Communist and terrorist groups'.[41]

The Qom incident provided the Shah's Islamist opponents with a pretext to hold a series of memorial services which turned into demonstrations against the Shah. Henceforward Khomeini and his followers would portray the Shah as a godless dictator who was willing to massacre Muslims to remain in power.[42] Once the security forces began to kill the demonstrators, the bazaaris offered financial support to the victims' families and, from September onwards, to the striking workforce. What had begun as an internal power struggle prepared the ground for the Iranian revolution. During this period, the Khomeini camp also began a massive smear campaign against the Shah alleging that he had converted to Zoroastrianism, Judaism or Mithraism. The Shah was also portrayed 'traitor', a 'dog' and an Israeli and American agent.[43] At the same time, leaders of Khomeini's organization in Iran, Ayatollahs Beheshti and Mottahari, organized 'spontaneous' demonstrations in front of the houses of National Front leaders, who had little following in the country to assure Western media and middle-class Iranians that a democratic revolution was under way against the tyrannical Shah.[44]

The available evidence suggests that despite the growing religious opposition to the Shah, Fardust and Moghaddam, who were rivals of SAVAK Director General Nasiri, took advantage of Hedayatollah Eslaminia's contacts with Ayatollah Shari'atmadari to prepare the ground for Nasiri's dismissal. Eslaminia met several times with Ayatollah Shari'atmadari and accused Nasiri of wrongdoing and Baha'ism. Shari'atmadari, who knew nothing about Nasiri's activities, began to criticize the SAVAK director and repeatedly called for the establishment of a constitutional monarchy in Iran.[45]

US assessments of the situation in Iran

John Stempel, who served as the US embassy's political officer during the revolution, has claimed that the US relied on SAVAK and because SAVAK underestimated the depth of religious opposition to the regime the US failed to recognize Khomeini's mass appeal.[46] In his book on intelligence, which was highly praised by two Carter administration officials, National Security Adviser Zbigniew Brzezinski and Energy Secretary James Schlesinger, Walter Laqueur argued that the CIA had relied heavily upon SAVAK and failed to study the Shah.[47] Laqueur's argument is also factually incorrect. Firstly, SAVAK had excellent intelligence on the activities of Islamists. However, as we have seen SAVAK and Iranian intelligence were divided and as we will see, a cross-section of Iranian intelligence was undermining the Shah during the revolutionary turmoil in an attempt to reduce him to a figurehead. More importantly, as we have seen in this study, some US officials believed in weakening the Shah or removing him altogether. While it is true that the decimation of the CIA's clandestine service under President Carter had significantly weakened the agency and made it more dependent upon foreign intelligence services, such as SAVAK, the agency did have enough intelligence on the Islamist opposition to the Shah to persuade the administration to pursue a different policy. Indeed Brzezinski did recommend an alternative policy, but by the time Carter began to listen to Brzezinski it was too late to save the Shah or the Iranian monarchy.

However, there is no doubt that President Carter and Vice-President Mondale were hostile to the CIA. Mondale had served on the Church Committee, which had investigated the CIA's covert operations and sharply criticized the agency for gross misconduct.[48] During the presidential campaign, Carter had described the CIA as a 'disgrace'.[49] His first nominee for the post of CIA director, Theodore C. Sorenson, had been 'a conscientious objector and a harsh critic of intelligence', but he was rejected by the US Senate.[50] Carter's second nominee, Admiral Stansfield Turner, was not any better as far as the CIA's clandestine activities were concerned. Carter put Vice-President Mondale in charge of reforming the agency. Mondale was assisted by his protégé, deputy

National Security Adviser David Aaron. Turner placed far greater emphasis than his predecessors on technical intelligence and demonstrated his lack of respect for the clandestine service by dismissing more than 800 of its members, thereby severely weakening the agency.[51]

As far as Iran was concerned, the departure of two of the CIA's experienced Iran watchers Charles C. Rudolph and Ernest R. Oney was particularly damaging to US policy.[52] However, as we will see in this study, US failures in Iran were caused by wrong-headed policy decisions and by sheer incompetence not by intelligence failures. In fact, the CIA had been funding the Iranian clergy. The payments began in 1953 and continued regularly until 1977 when President Carter abruptly stopped them. One 'informed intelligence source' estimated that the CIA paid the clergy as much as 400 million dollars a year. Other sources believe that this amount is far too high. Nevertheless, the cut-off of subsidies to the clergy was one of the factors, which accelerated the fall of the Shah.[53] American investigative journalist Joseph Trento has claimed that the CIA had actually facilitated Khomeini's move from Turkey to Iraq in 1964 and that after the Ba'thists came to power in 1968, Saddam Hussein permitted the CIA to plant a number of 'Iranian-born' agents in Khomeini's entourage.[54] According to Trento: 'Right up until Khomeini returned to Teheran from France, Richard Helms was convinced that the men around Khomeini were loyal United States intelligence agents.'[55]

Ambassador Helms, according to Trento, was so concerned about maintaining close relations with the Shah that he failed to warn Washington of the consequences of its policy. In any case, by the summer of 1977 John Stempel had even informed his academic colleagues of the increasing influence of religious opposition groups in Iran.[56] A ten-page analysis of the Iranian opposition written by the US embassy in July 1977 concluded that Bakhtiar, Khomeini, Beheshti, and Bazargan would play important roles in Iranian politics.[57] Helms' successor Ambassador William Sullivan was shrewd enough to recognize that Islamic fundamentalism had emerged as a regional phenomenon and was a force in Pakistan, Turkey and Saudi Arabia.[58]

Indeed Sullivan realised that religious opponents of the Shah had formed a tactical alliance with the leftists and that they were both taking advantage of the administration's human rights policy.[59] Sullivan expected the regime to co-opt the opposition. He predicted that anti-regime dissidents would be harshly dealt with if they threatened the Shah's position. Sullivan advocated a policy of privately encouraging the Shah's opponents, while keeping a low profile in public given 'the long history in Iran of connection between foreign intrigue and dissidence'.[60]

As early as October 1977 students demonstrating in Tehran had called for Khomeini's return to Iran.[61] US officials understood that the Qom incident in January 1978 was a watershed in the Iranian monarchy's relations with the religious opposition. On 24 January, the US embassy reported:

> As a result of the Qom incident organized Moslem establishment is potentially in strongest position since 1963 vis-à-vis GOI [Government of Iran] Moslems far from wholly unified, but GOI demonstrating considerable uncertainty in facing up to the challenge ...[62]

Sullivan had expanded the embassy's contacts with opposition groups.[63] The embassy reported that the key figure behind the Qom disturbances was Ayatollah Shari'atmadari. This report demonstrated considerable knowledge of Shari'atmadari. However, the US embassy had no contacts with Ayatollah Shari'atmadari before Sullivan's arrival in Iran.[64] Sullivan recognized this deficiency. He also observed that the embassy had limited contacts with bazaar merchants.[65]

Just before the Qom incident Sullivan reported to Washington that he wanted to expand the embassy's contacts with emerging groups in Iran.[66] The State Department's Bureau of Intelligence and Research, INR, warned that the Shah's Islamist opponents had never been so strong since 1963.[67]

A 29 January 'Morning Summary', which was authored by the State Department and served as briefing from Vance to Carter, put forward a similar argument.[68] As early as 2 February 1978, Sullivan began to define the situation in Iran as revolutionary. He argued that 'a post revolutionary Shi'a movement would have broad popular support' and that it would be strongly anti-Communist and anti-Western.[69]

Ayatollah Shari'atmadari's call for a strike and his subsequent order to stop the unrest in Tabriz indicated that Khomeini was not the only leader calling for respect for Islam.[70] The American consul in Tabriz Mike Metrinko reported after the Tabriz riots of 18 February that the riots demonstrated that the regime's control over the provinces 'can be seriously threatened'.[71]

Vance does not seem to have conveyed the recommendations of such reports to Carter. At this stage he did not even forcefully advocate maintaining contact with opposition leaders.[72] In a memorandum to Brzezinski, NSC official Gary Sick said that despite the Iranian regime's characterization of the opposition as Communist-inspired, 'the reactionary Muslim right wing' posed the 'true threat' to the Shah's rule.[73]

At a March 1978 meeting of the State Department's Bureau of Intelligence and Research, INR, a paper was presented entitled 'Monarchy in Crisis' which was very sombre about the future of the Pahlavi dynasty: 'Time is not on the side of the Shah'.[74] In the same month, Iran expert James Bill presented a paper at a State Department seminar, entitled 'Monarchy in Collapse'. Bill predicted that the escalation of violence would mean that the Shah would lose his 'capacity' to maintain political control. He predicted that 'the American future in Iran can in no way be considered bright'.[75]

By April it was clear that there was concerted religious opposition to the Shah. Gary Sick warned that the Shah had unleashed a wave of repression in response to the demonstrations in the country, adding: 'Most observers believe the danger is still latent, but cracks in the facade of Iranian social stability are becoming difficult to ignore.'[76]

Sullivan, however, recognized that the opposition to the Shah was primarily political and in late April he reported that the 'breakdown of communication' between the Shah and the religious conservatives could lead to 'serious internal instability', which leftists and the National Front would probably seek to exploit. Sullivan observed that dissidence in Iran was deeply rooted and that 'economic improvement' would not eliminate it.[77]

US contacts with the opposition

In May, US embassy political officer John Stempel established contact with

Mohammad Tavakkoli of the Liberation Movement. At first, senior officials of the Liberation Movement were cautious because they suspected Stempel of being a CIA agent and were unsure of US motives.[78] Stempel held several meetings with Mehdi Bazargan, Mohammad Tavakkoli and Ezatollah Sahabi in May and June 1978. Bazargan blamed the US for putting the Shah back on the throne in 1953. Moreover, according to one of Stempel's reports: 'All three Liberation Front leaders insisted that the Shah must have been forced to liberalize and they attributed this wholly to President Carter's human rights policy.'[79]

Tavakkoli warned Stempel that unless the Liberation Movement was given the opportunity to participate in politics, terrorist groups would step up their activity. Stempel claimed that the CIA was not responsible for overthrowing Mossadeq, that US influence was less than it appeared, that SAVAK was confused about the situation and that the Carter administration's human rights policy was only one of the factors that had led the Shah to liberalise.[80]

Stempel warned his interlocutors that the clerics could use their alliance with the Liberation Movement to take power. Tavakkoli vehemently rejected Stempel's argument, arguing that the choice for Iran was between Islam and Marxism and that the clergy 'merely wished to measure conformity of religious law with civil law.' Stempel was sceptical and they 'agreed to disagree'.[81] When Stempel argued that some clerics such as Ayatollah Shari'atmadari wanted to preserve the Shah, Tavakkoli said that if Shari'atmadari said so, the people would desert him.[82]

Nevertheless, the US embassy concluded that the Liberation Movement was eager to maintain contact with the embassy and was fascinated to learn that former CIA and State Department official, Richard Cottam, was still in close contact with it.[83] The US embassy continued its contacts with the Liberation Movement, even though it knew full well that its interlocutors were taking advantage of US human rights policy to overthrow the Shah.

The Shah's change of internal security policy

Some observers believe that the head of the Special Intelligence Bureau, Major-General Hossein Fardust, played a key role in bringing about the downfall of the Shah. Both the Shah and his twin sister, Princess Ashraf, as well as some senior officials of the monarchical regime, believed that Fardust had supported Khomeini. Princess Ashraf went so far as to write that Fardust had been plotting with Khomeini to overthrow the Shah.[84]

The Special Intelligence Bureau was responsible for overseeing SAVAK and Military Intelligence. It was set up under the supervision of the British Secret Intelligence Service, SIS (MI6). Indeed, Fardust's SIS connection was perhaps the most important reason why the Shah was initially wary of cultivating Ayatollah Shari'atmadari. At the time, Iran was involved in a massive dispute with the BP-led Consortium over the renewal of the Consortium agreement. The Shah was convinced that London was responsible for generating the religious opposition to his rule to force him to make concessions or overthrow him.[85]

It would be wrong to argue, as Amir Taheri has done, that the clergy deceived SAVAK into thinking that leftists and terrorists caused all the instability.[86] Fardust was in contact with senior clerics through his close friend

Hedayatollah Eslaminia who reported to him every week.[87] By early 1978, some military officers had come to the conclusion that the US had abandoned the Shah and began to explore the possibility of staging a coup to save the regime without the Shah. However, they then decided to support a constitutional monarchy.[88]

Fardust's protege Naser General Moghaddam seems to have been one of the ring-leaders. When he was the director of Military Intelligence, G-2, General Moghaddam sought to instigate an uprising against the Shah. Moghaddam began his campaign in 1977 when during a trip to the US he contacted Mansur Rafizadeh, deputy SAVAK station chief in the US, who regularly reported to the CIA. According to Rafizadeh, Moghaddam said that he wanted to overthrow the Shah and execute the then SAVAK Director General Nasiri.[89] Moghaddam probably wanted to test Washington's reaction to his overture.

In April, Moghaddam sent a thirty-page report to the Shah through his personal channels to the Royal Family. Moghaddam warned that the US would abandon the Shah if he failed to end the unrest and that a revolution would overthrow the Shah unless real reforms were introduced. Even the US would desert the Shah if he failed to stop the disorder in Iran.[90] The most cursory glance at General Moghaddam's proposals indicates that he could not have possibly forwarded them to the Shah without strong US support. This was essentially a repeat performance of the 1957 Qarani coup attempt. Qarani and his followers had also contemplated the possibility of staging an uprising to overthrow the Shah if he did not introduce reforms. In 1978, Qarani was closely co-operating with the revolutionaries and he would serve as the revolutionary regime's first chief of staff in 1979.

Moghaddam's proposal included; the arrest of all corrupt government ministers, the dissolution of Majlis and the Senate, and the arrest and trial of all corrupt members of the Royal Family, members of parliament and senators and the return of all the assets of the Royal Family to the Iranian people.

General Moghaddam expected the Shah to reject his proposals and force him to retire. The Shah did indeed reject these proposals. He asserted that he would not act against the constitution![91] What he meant was that he would not stage a coup against himself. Not only did the Shah not dismiss Moghaddam, he actually appointed him as the new chief of SAVAK in June 1978.

By now Ayatollah Shari'atmadari had split from Khomeini because of the latter's opposition to the monarchy.[92] US officials were hopeful about exploiting such divisions. On 11 April US political officer, George Lambrakis, reported that a National Front leader, Hedayatollah Matin-Daftari, had told him that Khomeini was more influential than Shari'atmadari and that the latter's followers 'do not dare to stand up to the edicts from Khomeini'.[93] Fardust and Moghaddam's protégé, Hedayatollah Eslaminia, informed US embassy officials George Lambrakis and John Stempel that on 13 May 1978, all chiefs of security and police services in Iran had held a meeting to discuss the unrest in the country.

SAVAK chief General Nasiri advocated crushing the opposition, but head of the Special Intelligence Bureau, General Fardust, opposed the use of force because he thought it would further exacerbate the situation in the country. The participants accepted Fardust's approach and Fardust then persuaded the Shah to pursue this policy.[94]

Eslaminia also reported that Ayatollah Shari'atmadari had told Hoveyda's deputy, Behbahanian, that he did not agree with Khomeini's views, but he wanted the government and Princess Ashraf to refrain from interfering in religious affairs.[95] Eslaminia encouraged the US embassy to persuade the Shah to dismiss Prime Minister Amuzegar, the head of the National Iranian Oil Company, Hushang Ansari, and SAVAK Director General Nasiri.[96] Eslaminia declared that henceforward the Shah should only attack the communists and avoid 'lumping together the religious opposition with the communists'.[97]

The Shah would not introduce major reforms until the summer. In the meantime, Iranian ambassador to the US, Ardeshir Zahedi, who was rather unfamiliar with the internal situation of his own country, turned to old CIA hands to save the Shah's throne. It is to this issue that we should now turn.

Kermit Roosevelt and Miles Copeland conclude the Shah is finished

Immediately after the Afghan coup in April 1978, Brzezinski began to urge the Shah to crack down on the opposition. Iran's ambassador to the US, Ardeshir Zahedi, sent Brzezinski's message to the monarch.[98] Moreover, Zahedi repeatedly complained to one of the architects of the 1953 coup d'etat, Kermit Roosevelt 'that the US Government was bombarding the Shah with conflicting advice'.[99]

In May 1978, Zahedi asked Roosevelt if he was prepared to travel to Tehran 'to discuss with the Shah a repeat performance of 1953'.[100] Roosevelt was convinced that the Shah could not be saved. Indeed he had just published a book about his role in the 1953 coup d'etat. Some prominent Iranians believed that Roosevelt had deliberately sought to accelerate the Shah's downfall by tarnishing his image.[101]

Roosevelt told Zahedi that former CIA official Miles Copeland was the most qualified person to assess the situation in the country. If Copeland decided that nothing could be done, then there would no point in attempting a coup. Zahedi said that he accepted Roosevelt's advice. Roosevelt was convinced that the Shah could not be saved and he informed Copeland of his views. However, Roosevelt did not tell Zahedi what he had told Copeland in his absence.[102]

Roosevelt told Zahedi that Copeland would only try to assess the chances of implementing a successful covert operation. However, even before his arrival in Iran, Copeland blew the cover of his operation. In an extensive discussion with an official of the State Department's Human Rights Bureau during his flight to Tehran, Copeland boasted that he was a CIA agent who was travelling to Iran 'as a special emissary of President Carter' to cooperate with SAVAK to stage a military take-over which would be followed by 'a pogrom in which all Communists and religious leaders of any importance would be publicly executed'.[103] To make matters worse for the Shah and Carter, this State Department official was a liberal with a background in the student protest movement.[104]

Copeland did not inform CIA Director Admiral Stansfield Turner of his visit to Iran. He met General Nasiri, and General Moghaddam, the new director of SAVAK. Nasiri, whom Copeland thought was stupid, made it clear that unless the Shah cracked down before the religious month of Muharram (in December), he would be overthrown.[105]

Copeland also met a Mossad agent who was collaborating with Nasiri. A contingency plan drawn up by Iranian officials concentrated on preventing the arrest and assassination of the Shah and prominent government officials. Copeland even met his contacts from 1953, but he had concluded that a limited covert operation could not save the regime. After his discussions with Moghaddam and Nasiri, Copeland was convinced that nothing could be done and he 'decided not even to seek an appointment' with the Shah.[106]

Copeland believed that even a massive US military intervention would guarantee no more than a 'breathing space' for the Pahlavi dynasty. Roosevelt agreed with Copeland. Zahedi also appeared to agree.[107] But as we shall see, Brzezinski and Zahedi would press forward with their plans for a coup.

The State Department sought to compel the Shah to embark on a wide-ranging reform programme, which would reduce him to a figurehead. In keeping with this policy, the State Department's Human Rights Bureau even refused to approve the sale of tear gas to Iran.[108] As late as October 1978, the State Department and Ambassador Sullivan were still seeking to deny Iran the crowd control equipment needed to quell the unrest in the country.[109]

It is clear that Copeland and Roosevelt wanted to turn off the Brzezinski-Zahedi initiative even before it had started. That is probably why Copland informed the State Department official of his mission. Copeland and Roosevelt served the interests of oil companies who were then locked into a conflict with the Shah. At the time, negotiations were proceeding on the renewal of the Consortium agreement in Tehran. By May 1978, the Shah was complaining bitterly to President Carter about the companies' decision to reduce their production level. US oil companies, which were also members of ARAMCO, were particularly blameworthy. They were more concerned about their position in Saudi Arabia than the Shah's regional ambitions. In 1978 US oil companies regarded the Shah as a threat to their international position and welcomed his downfall.[110] The Shah wrote in 1980:

> I suspected that Big Oil financed the demonstrations and that the CIA helped organize them. I know this sounds contradictory since both of these powerful interests had also supported my rule. But I do believe now that the West created an organized front against me to use whenever my policies diverged from theirs.[111]

Most Western observers have simply dismissed these observations as the conspiratorial musings of a fallen monarch.[112] However, we should not assume, as the Shah did, that the companies' intention was to replace the Shah with a government led by Khomeini. The companies' cut-back of their production and the Carter administration's human rights pressure were designed to compel the Shah to change his policies.

US officials' assessment of the unrest in Iran

Throughout the spring of 1978, the State Department's *Morning Summary* warned the Carter administration that 'continued unrest would precipitate a crackdown, that confrontations would become more violent, and that SAVAK officials feared these would present a growing threat to the government'.

Nevertheless, in May and June both the CIA and State Department publications expressed 'modest optimism' about the regime's prospects.[113]

Sullivan continued to downplay the gravity of the situation in Iran. For example, as late as 21 May he reported that the Shah had all the 'necessary instruments of power' and that he could 'shift tactics' whenever necessary.[114]

The consensus among US intelligence officials was that the Shah's religious opponents were not prepared to compromise. For example, on May 11, the National Intelligence Daily which was prepared mainly by the CIA, reported:

> There appeared to be little room for compromise between the Shah and conservative Muslim opponents, who believe that reforms instituted by the Shah and his father threaten the future of Islam in Iran. The Shah is gambling that his program of modernization has enough popular support to allow him to take measures against conservative Muslims – a community that, in his opinion, wants to turn the clock back to the Middle Ages.[115]

By the spring of 1978, American and British publications noted the emergence of an alliance between Islamic traditionalists and other opposition groups. Yet, during this period the National Intelligence Daily, 'which had quite early noted the potential of any such alliance, did not report on its actual existence until June 17, and even then with some uncertainty'.[116]

One reason that the State Department took a benign view of the activities of the pro-Khomeini opposition was its Arab rather than Soviet connections.[117] During this period, the Israeli Mossad and the French intelligence service, SDECE, also warned of the threat to the Shah's rule.[118] In early June, the Israeli representative in Tehran, Uri Lubrani wrote a report predicting that 'the shah may not survive for more than two or three years'.[119] In June, Lubrani sent a long cable to Tel Aviv and the Israeli authorities became so alarmed that they encouraged Iranian Jews to leave the country.[120] There were reports that Lubrani's warning was passed on to Washington, but that US officials had not taken it seriously.[121]

According to a former head of Israeli military intelligence Shlomo Gazit, Lubrani's report was passed to the CIA, but the agency did not believe such Israeli or French reports. The CIA did not have much faith in French intelligence and the Carter administration believed that the Lubrani report was aimed at scaring it because of the political pressure on Israeli Prime Minister Menachem Begin to negotiate with Arab countries.[122] CIA Director Stansfield Turner had also sharply reduced the CIA's reliance upon Israeli intelligence as part of the administration's even-handed approach to the Arab-Israeli conflict.[123]

Gary Sick has said that Lubrani's report was never given to the White House. Lubrani later said publicly that he had discussed his concerns with Sullivan. However, Sullivan did not mention Lubrani's warning in his reports or during the discussions he held in Washington during the summer of 1978.[124]

Sick has argued that Sullivan and other US officials were reluctant to raise the issue of instability in Iran because the entire US regional strategy depended on the survival of the Shah.[125] However, Sick's account does not stand up to scrutiny when one examines the documentary evidence. However, the situation was so serious by the spring of 1978 that even Secretary Vance had to share his concerns with President Carter. The unrest in Iran, called the 'Tehran spring' could no longer be ignored. On 10 May, Vance informed Carter that the unrest was 'the most serious anti-shah activity since 1963'.[126]

The available evidence strongly suggests that Ambassador Sullivan, Secretary Vance and other State Department officials sought to keep the NSC in the dark as long as possible in order to gain time to implement their own strategy. The State Department strategy, political containment, was based on the premise that Iran was a country which would be beholden to the US because of its geopolitical circumstances.

Sullivan, and apparently also Vance, were not at all perturbed by the possibility that a successor Iranian government might pursue anti-Zionist policies. Indeed, as we will see in a later chapter, Sullivan would argue that an anti-Zionist policy would not damage US regional interests.

The Shah's policy decisions indicate that he was not completely aware of the conflict over the choice of strategy in Washington. Washington's inability to speak with one voice only confused the Shah and led him to conclude that US officials were trying to overthrow him.

6

POLICY CURRENTS AND THE IRANIAN REVOLUTION

Although the Shah had agreed to change his oil price policy, he had refused to make any concessions regarding the Consortium agreement or Iran's military build-up. The dispute with the Consortium was long-standing and the evidence suggests that the Carter administration was unable or unwilling to compel the Consortium to reach an agreement with Iran. The Consortium was only taking three million barrels of oil from Iran despite the fact that the agreement with Iran obliged it to take a minimum of five million barrels. The collapse of the Consortium negotiations and the unrest in the country brought the Iranian economy to a standstill in October 1978.[1]

William Engdahl has argued that the BP-led Consortium organized the opposition to the Shah and that the fall of the Shah was a plot hatched in London and Washington. Firstly, Engdahl has not provided any evidence to prove his case. Secondly, Engdahl does not seem to be aware of the fact that Iran cancelled the Consortium agreement shortly after the revolution, thereby dealing a severe blow to British and US interests in the Middle East. Thirdly, by the time US officials concluded that the situation in the country was revolutionary, they knew full well that Iran under any successor government would not be as close to the US as it had been under the Shah.

The available evidence tells a completely different story, namely that advocates of the New World Order strategy led by Cyrus Vance sought to pressure the Shah into changing his policies and establishing a constitutional monarchy in Iran. The implementation of the New World Order strategy in Iran was predicated upon the activities of the director of the Special Intelligence Bureau, Major-General Hossein Fardust, and the director of SAVAK, General Naser Moghaddam, who was Fardust's protégé.

The assumption behind the strategy seems to have been that a constitutional monarchy or the Shah's replacement by his son would broaden the base of the regime, reduce corruption, ensure the renewal of the Consortium agreement and moderate Iran's military build-up. One can hardly describe the failure of US policy during this period as a failure of intelligence. The failure was primarily a failure of judgement on the part of the proponents of the New World Order strategy.

The Shah equated détente with appeasement of the Soviet Union. At a meeting with former US Secretary of State Henry Kissinger in early June, the

Shah said that the Carter administration might have reached a secret agreement with Moscow to divide Southwest Asia into spheres of influence and even partition Iran. Kissinger assured the Shah 'that the United State-especially under Jimmy Carter-was psychologically incapable of such a spheres-of influence policy'.[2]

As early as the spring of 1978, Viktor Kazakov, a KGB officer under diplomatic cover at the KGB's Tehran residency, told an American contact that the Shah would be removed by 'oppressed masses rising to overthrow their shackles'.[3] In the summer of 1978 most of the KGB's Middle East experts still believed that the Shah's regime was stable. KGB chief Yuri Andropov was more concerned about the Shah's alliance with the US and its threat to the Soviet Union than with the consequences of a revolution in Iran. At a meeting in Moscow with the KGB's Tehran resident, Ivan Anisimovich Fadeykin, in July 1978, Andropov ordered Fadeykin to increase the active measures against the Shah to destabilize his regime and damage Iran's relations with the US and its allies.[4] The KGB fed the Shah disinformation that the CIA was intent upon causing unrest in Iran and that the US was looking for a successor who could stabilize the country with the assistance of SAVAK and the military. KGB active measures probably influenced the Shah and made him more suspicious of the US. However, the Shah also suspected the superpowers of trying to divide his country between themselves.[5] There can be little doubt that the Shah and his family did not trust the Americans. The Shah's son and his heir, Reza Pahlavi, for example, believed that the Americans bombarded his father with radiation which caused the malignant lymphoma which later killed him.[6]

However, the Shah was far too psychologically dependent on the US to directly confront Carter.[7] He compared his predicament to that of his father in 1941 who was removed by the British. He thought that only a spontaneous show of public support for him or an intervention by the military after he left the country might maintain him in power. He came to the conclusion that he could save the throne for his son only by continuing his liberalization programme.[8]

The Shah's decision to press forward with his liberalization policy was made at the worst possible time. The oil boom was receding and the regime was less capable of satisfying popular demands. The 'open political climate' permitted the Shah's traditional enemies – the fundamentalist clergy, the radical left, the nationalists, and the liberals to mobilise, and eventually unite in opposition to the monarchy.[9]

Reform of SAVAK and attempts to co-opt the opposition

Between May and September 1978 the State Department dominated Iran policy and US policy. This was despite the fact that the Carter administration was becoming increasingly concerned about Soviet foreign policy in the Middle East and the Horn of Africa. On 1 June 1978, the intelligence community presented a new estimate to President Carter. According to the new estimate, the Soviet Union was deeply involved in a number of Third World trouble spots. Former CIA Director Robert Gates, who served under Brzezinski on the NSC, has described the new estimate as a 'cold shower' for the advocates of détente.[10] On 15 August, a policy review committee chaired by Secretary of State Cyrus Vance noted the growing Soviet influence in the 'arc of crisis' in Asia and Africa. On 24 August,

President Carter signed a Presidential Review Memorandum calling for the containment of the Soviet Union along the 'arc'. This was a success for National Security Adviser Zbigniew Brzezinski and the Pentagon because they had been calling for the formulation of just such a strategy. However, the policy disputes in the administration between Brzezinski, who favoured containment, and Vance, who advocated the continuation of SALT II negotiations with the Soviet Union, prevented it from responding to the Soviet challenge in a coordinated fashion.[11]

As far as Iran was concerned, the State Department continued to dominate US policy-making in the summer of 1978. The director of the Iran desk at the State Department, Henry Precht, was the most influential US official during this period. Precht who had been one of Leslie Gelb's senior assistants in the State Department's Bureau of Political and Military Affairs, had replaced Charles Naas as the head of Iran desk. Precht, who also served a tour of duty in Iran, believed that the Pahlavi dynasty was in serious trouble. Regardless of whether Precht reached this conclusion as a result of 'an honest analysis of day-to-day events' or his moral convictions or his policy preferences,[12] or a combination of the aforementioned factors, he dramatically influenced the course of US policy during this period. This was partly because President Carter's principal foreign policy advisers, Zbigniew Brzezinski and Cyrus Vance, were preoccupied with other important foreign policy issues such as SALT and the Arab-Israeli peace process.[13]

Precht contended that without wide-ranging reforms the Shah and the Pahlavi dynasty would be overthrown.[14] At the same time, Precht was convinced that the National Front would come to power in the event of the Shah's downfall. Without naming Precht as the leader of the anti-Shah group in the State Department, Ambassador Sullivan argued that the group was so vehemently opposed to the monarch that 'they wished to see him collapse' regardless of 'the consequences' for the US or its allies.[15] According to Brzezinski, Precht 'was motivated by doctrinal dislike of the shah and simply wanted him out of power altogether'.[16]

Throughout the crisis the Shah was operating on the assumption that London and Washington were destabilizing Iran. He sought to accommodate conservative clerics such as Ayatollah Shari'atmadari, while excluding the National Front, the Liberation Movement, Khomeini's supporters and leftists from the political process. The Shah believed that accommodating conservative clerics, whom he saw as British agents, would placate London and secure the throne for his son. The Shah's new policy was reflected in the organizational changes made in SAVAK during this period.

The Shah agreed to Prime Minister Amuzegar's request to dismiss SAVAK Director General Nasiri, whom Amuzegar believed was destabilizing the country to discredit his government.[17] Amuzegar recommended General Moghaddam as Nasiri's successor and the Shah appointed him on 6 June.[18] Moghaddam was appointed despite the Shah's preference for Nasiri's deputy General Mo'tazed.[19] Indeed Moghaddam had even alienated Empress Farah because he named some of her relatives in his report to the Shah in April, saying that they were corrupt.[20] Later, Henry Precht 'was credited with pressuring' the Shah to dismiss Nasiri.[21]

Undoubtedly one of the main reasons that the Shah appointed Moghaddam was that Moghaddam was expected to follow Fardust's policy of cultivating conservative clerics.[22] Court Minister Hoveyda and General Nosratollah

Mo'inian, Director of the Special Bureau agreed with Fardust.[23] Moreover, the evidence suggests that the CIA may well have recommended Moghaddam to the Shah.[24] He was trusted both by the National Front and the Liberation Movement. In fact, Moghaddam wanted to give the National Front a role in government.[25] However, as we saw earlier, the Shah's intention was not to placate the National Front. As late as July 1978, the Shah described his nationalist opponents as 'even more traitorous than the Tudeh Party'.[26]

General Moghaddam's machinations and the issue of the Shah's abdication

By appointing Moghaddam as chief of SAVAK the Shah thought he could mollify the Carter administration and the opposition.[26] Given the Shah's psychological dependence on the US, it is highly unlikely that he would have allowed Moghaddam to remain in his post, had the US not strongly supported Moghaddam's policy position. Immediately after taking over, Moghaddam purged a number of senior SAVAK officers. The Shah also released several hundred political prisoners in the spring and autumn of 1978. The hard-liners in SAVAK led by Parviz Sabeti were infuriated by these actions. The Shah's decision demoralized these officials and might have even led them to change their loyalties.[28] In July word leaked that the Shah had introduced a code of conduct for his family. In July and August 1978, most members of the Shah's family left the country.[29] Moreover, the Shah himself repeatedly said privately that he intended to travel abroad.[30]

Moghaddam instructed all directors of SAVAK throughout Iran to accommodate the prevailing anti-regime current by siding with 'the people'.[31] Moreover, according to one account, Moghaddam, who was in possession of intelligence indicating that the opponents of the regime were smuggling guns into the country, did nothing to stop such smuggling.[32] Moghaddam did not inform the head of SAVAK's Department Three, Parviz Sabeti, of his talks with the opposition either.[33]

The most important move that Moghaddam made after taking over as SAVAK Director was relaxing the pressure on the Khomeini organization. In the summer of 1978, the leader of the Lebanese Maronites, Bashir Gemayel, apparently acting on an Israeli request, arrested several leaders of the Khomeini organization. They were, Ebrahim Yazdi, one of Khomeini's chief aides and the head of the Khomeini organization in the US, Mostafa Chamran, who was instrumental in training hundreds of Khomeini's disciples in PLO terrorist camps, Mohammad Montazeri, the son of Ayatollah Montazeri who was co-operating closely with Muammar Qadhafi to overthrow the Shah, and Sadegh Ghotbzadeh, another one of Khomeini's chief aides who was close to Syria.

These men were to be flown to Oman and handed over to the Iranian government. At the last minute, Moghaddam ordered the plane back to Lebanon.[34] Moreover, Moghaddam began to search for allies among SAVAK officials to assist him in removing the Shah.[35] He tried to prepare the ground for the Shah's abdication in favour of his son. He even managed to persuade Empress Farah, who knew that the Shah had cancer, to cooperate with him. Throughout the summer of 1978, Moghaddam, the Empress, and former Prime Minister Ja'far Sharif-Emami were trying to find a way to persuade the

Shah to abdicate. Sharif-Emami would become the power behind the throne. The Empress feared that the Shah would reject the proposal and did not put the proposal to him.[36]

Fardust and Moghaddam, who knew that the Shah was gravely ill, informed the US embassy, through their protégé Hedayatollah Eslaminia, of the Shah's illness in an effort to persuade US officials to put pressure on him to abdicate. Eslaminia informed the US embassy that Fardust and Moghaddam had told him that the Shah appeared to be ill and that blood tests had been ordered. He said that the US and other countries should monitor the Shah's health and, if necessary, 'they should urge him to convene the Regency Council and prepare Iran for change'. The US embassy contended that this might be premature, but noted that rumours were circulating in official circles that the Shah was gravely ill.[37]

Senior Iranian officials almost certainly guessed that the Shah was a dying man.[38] In early July, as John Stempel has written, rumours began circulating 'that the Shah was terminally ill with (take your choice): leukaemia, lung cancer, or irreversible pneumonia. 'Medical reports' were for sale to diplomats and newsmen to document different allegations'.[39]

Meanwhile, unrest continued in the country. The Shah was convinced that the security forces could deal with the guerrilla threat. What alarmed him was the participation of ordinary people in anti-Shah demonstrations. Moreover, the Shah believed that 'Western public opinion has been misled by crypto-Communists in the media'.[40]

However, he told Ambassador Sullivan that the unrest in the country was far too systematic and well planned to be spontaneous, adding that he did not believe that the KGB was capable of orchestrating such a sophisticated campaign. Sullivan assured the Shah that the US supported him and was not plotting against him.[41]

The issue of US intelligence failure

As we saw in chapter 1, much has been of the US 'intelligence failure' in Iran. Some authors, such as James Bill and Ofira Seliktar, have gone so far as to argue that the failure was so fundamental that the whole basis of US knowledge of Iran had to be called into question.[42] US officials' comments have lent credence to such explanations. For example, Brzezinski later observed that the 'failure is not so much a matter of particular intelligence reports or even specific policies . . . [b]ut a deeper intellectual misjudgment of a central historical reality'.[43] Vance has claimed that State Department experts, the CIA and foreign governments assured the US that although the Shah might have to compromise with his opponents, his rule was not jeopardized.[44] Despite all the reports warning of the deterioration of the situation in Iran, the CIA reported that no revolutionary upheaval was likely in the near future.[45]

According to one report, 'the military was loyal to the monarchy and that those who were in opposition, both the violent and the nonviolent, did not have the capacity to be more than troublesome in any transition to a new regime'.[46] Carter has quoted this CIA report to justify his decision not to respond to the crisis in the summer of 1978.[47] However, it is important to note several factors. Firstly, the reference to 'in any transition to a new regime' suggests that the CIA was already thinking in terms of regime change in Iran. Secondly, at the time, the majority of opposition leaders were demanding a return to the 1906 constitution.

Much has also been made of reporting restrictions imposed on mid-level officials because of America's close relations with Iran. Former NSC official, Gary Sick: 'The Shah basically made it very clear that he didn't like us messing around in his domestic politics, but at his request the United States basically backed off.'[48] According to the then CIA Director Admiral Stansfield Turner: 'There was this sense that if you criticized the Shah very vigorously, there was a very real chance that this would come back to haunt you and that you would end up working in some other part of the government rather than working on Iran policy.'[49] After the Iran debacle, Kissinger and Brzezinski were sharply criticized for their hostility to those who reported on the Shah's failures as a statesman. One critic, James Bill, contended that pro-Pahlavi bias was such a serious problem in various US institutions that it blinded many American diplomats and other officials to the realities of the Shah's rule.[50]

Long after the revolution, Brzezinski still defended himself, arguing that he had never imposed any restrictions on reporting from Iran and that neither he nor President Carter 'had a special stake in favorable reporting from Iran'. However, he also conceded that it was 'conceivable that in a setting in which Iran seemed to be a favored ally of the United States insofar as the region is concerned that perhaps some mid-level bureaucrats, analysts, felt it would be not good for them. That they would not feel secure in rocking the boat so to speak'.[51] However, as we will see in a later chapter, Brzezinski would even undermine a former senior official, George Ball, whom he himself recruited to report on Iran.

Another issue often raised in discussions of US intelligence 'failure' in Iran is US officials' close association with the Shah's supporters. Turner later observed that US officials' association with Westernized Iranians had blinded them to the reality of the situation in Iran. At the same time, according to Turner: 'We didn't have enough people who truly understood Iran, spoke the language. The people we sent out to the field were too wont to get their information at cocktail parties.'[52] Turner's statement is correct and it has been verified by none other than James Bill who has written extensively on US officials' 'ignorance' of Iranian political realities.[53] For example, he has observed: 'While fewer than 10 per cent of American diplomatic personnel in Iran spoke and read Persian fluently in 1970, the comparable figures for the British and Soviet embassies were 45 and 70 percent.'[54]

Turner himself has been sharply criticized for dismissing more than 800 members of the CIA's clandestine division, including an experienced Iran analyst, Ernest Oney. Moreover, veteran chiefs of station were replaced with officials who had no knowledge of the culture or language of the country.[55] Gary Sick later observed that US officials were ignorant of the reality of the situation in Iran.[56] Ofira Seliktar has argued that US officials' secular outlook and their linear definition of progress prevented them from understanding the religious nature of the unrest in Iran. Moreover, according to Seliktar, US officials focused on formal and official centres of power, thereby ignoring the important role of Islamism in Iranian politics.[57]

However, the documentary evidence indicates that enough information was provided by US officials in the field on Islamist and other types of opposition to the Shah to enable policy-makers to understand that the Shah was in serious trouble. Indeed, by the summer of 1978 much of this information was not even secret. Turner himself observed later that in the case of Iran 'there was relatively little secret information that was pertinent'.[58] However, as we shall see, US failure in Iran was primarily caused by sharp differences between US officials, most notably Brzezinski and Vance, over strategy, and by incompetence. President Carter was responsible for such institutional failures because he failed to restrain his officials and, more importantly, he failed to define a coherent presidential strategy. Leslie Gelb later observed that Carter could not choose between or combine the two approaches. Carter also refused to fire both or one of his principal foreign policy advisers. He was ultimately responsible for the 'disarray' in his administration.[59]

US officials were well aware of the growing religious opposition to the Shah and the de facto alliance between religious extremists and leftists. The Defence Intelligence Agency (DIA) reported that Khomeini had emerged as a very influential leader of the opposition and the Tudeh party had reportedly sided with Khomeini's extremist followers. The DIA had found no evidence that various groups opposing the Shah had begun to co-ordinate their strategies.

The DIA reported that the security services wanted a crackdown.[60] However, it predicted that the Shah would hold a dialogue with the religious opposition, but that he would react firmly to violent opposition to his rule. The DIA, on the other hand, only expected 'continuing tests between the government and the opposition'.[61]

The State Department was more pessimistic about the future of the Shah's regime. In August Assistant Secretary of State for Near Eastern and South Asian Affairs, Harold Saunders, informed Vance:

> The Shah's strongest opponents come from the Shia religious leadership, split in two apparently co-operating factions, one an ultra-conservative group headed by Khomeini (exiled in Iraq) and the other by the more moderate Shari'atmadari of Qom, Iran. Drawing their support from the poorer classes, the traditional bazaar merchants, single men who have been uprooted from their villages for work in the cities, and unemployed youths, the mullahs probably are also helped by covert left-wing groups.[62]

Saunders concluded that 'an early end to the disorders is not a prospect'.[63] On 5 August, the Shah promised free parliamentary elections in 1979 and the participation of opposition elements in government, but warned that he would deal harshly with those who instigated violence.[64] The embassy warned that the Shah was 'on a tight rope' and that he had to meet the opposition's demands and prevent the security forces and the military from cracking down.[65]

US embassy reported that in conversations with Sullivan, US charge d'affaires, Charles Naas, and most foreign visitors, the Shah had emphasized that he wanted to prepare the ground for his son's accession to the throne. US embassy observed correctly that despite their rhetoric, most of the Shah's opponents were authoritarian.[66] It argued that the main reason the Shah had not resorted to crushing the opposition was his fear of Western opposition to such a policy.[67]

Nevertheless, US embassy had 'no doubt' that the Shah would crack down if only to save his throne.[68] In August, US embassy reported that the Shah and his entourage had underestimated the Islamist challenge. It observed that the government had no choice but to deal with Islamists.[69]

As far as the religious opposition was concerned, there were those who were calling for reforms, as well as figures such as Khomeini and his followers who called for the removal, and even the assassination, of the Shah.[70] US embassy noted that the Shah would not accept religious control of the government and would only accept a constitutional monarchy if his son were to take over.[71]

Embassy officials wanted to turn the Iranians' intense suspicions of US influence to their advantage.[72] They argued that if the Shah could bring the 'moderates' into the political process by making token concessions, then the security forces could deal with the 'extremists who are undoubtedly receiving help from ex-Tudeh party elements, and other outside forces'. However, embassy officials cautioned that even concessions might not enable the Shah to split the opposition.[73] In late August, Sullivan reported that the Shah was now firmly convinced that Iran had become far too unstable to be ruled through 'benevolent authoritarianism'.[74]

The Shah's failure to split the clerical establishment

In his reports to the US embassy, General Fardust's and General Moghaddam's protégé, Hedayatollah Eslaminia, consistently argued that Shari'atmadari supported the Shah on condition that the monarch reduced his involvement in politics.[75]

In a 21 June report, US political officer, George Lambrakis, reported that Shari'atmadari had distanced himself from Khomeini because of the latter's radicalism and vehement opposition to the Shah. At the same time, the embassy advised against pushing the human rights issue.[76] However, in July 1978, Eslaminia informed the embassy that the Shah had told generals Fardust and Moghaddam that he was 'most distressed that Shari'atmadari had not disassociated himself from Khomeini'. According to Eslaminia, the respect for Khomeini 'among the mass of illiterate population' meant that Shari'atmadari could not publicly disassociate himself from him.

Eslaminia believed that the power struggle among 'all senior ayatollahs' would prevent the emergence of a 'centrist' position.[77] He argued that it was imperative to split the communists from Khomeini and contain corruption.[78] Despite this grave warning, the embassy downplayed the gravity of the situation in Iran.[79]

General Moghaddam's contacts in the religious establishment, including Shari'atmadari's son-in-law, indicated that Shari'atmadari wanted the Shah to replace Amuzegar and hold some corrupt officials accountable for their activities.[80] He also wanted the Shah to stop his family's political and financial activities.[81] Shari'atmadari's declared that if the Shah dared to imprison him, 'the whole country will blow up'.[82] The embassy's religious source believed that Ja'far Sharif-Emami was 'the best candidate' as Amuzegar's replacement 'because he is a very religious man himself and has solid political backing'.[83]

On 18 August, the Shah declared his commitment to Islamic principles and preserving the Shi'a faith.[84] During this period, the conflict between

Shari'atmadari and Khomeini over the issue of constitutionalism escalated and Shari'atmadari challenged Khomeini to go to Iran to demonstrate his strength.[85] Khomeini called on Iranian army and police officers not to fire on crowds and oppose the government, but they did not heed Khomeini's message.[86]

The Khomeini camp responded by intensifying its terrorist activities. On 19 August, the Rex Cinema in Abadan was set on fire, killing 477 people.[87] Another estimate has put the minimum number of people killed at 600, including many children. A further 300 people were injured.[88] The Rex Cinema fire 'was by all accounts the single most horrific event in Iran's contemporary history'.[89]

At the time the opposition's claim that SAVAK was responsible for the atrocity was taken at face value. Criticisms of the regime also spread to the Majlis and the Senate.[90] After the revolution, it became increasingly clear that Islamist radicals had set the cinema on fire.[91]

After the Rex cinema fire, instability and revolutionary turmoil spread to Iran's oil-rich province of Khuzestan.[92] In late August, General Moghaddam, who had reduced the pressure on religious opposition groups, asked Iraqi intelligence chief Sa'dun Shaker to silence Khomeini in accordance with the 1975 Algiers accord. Khomeini told Shaker that if the Iraqis attempted to silence him, he would leave Iraq.[93]

SAVAK advised Iraqi officials to isolate Khomeini. It believed that keeping Khomeini in Iraq would benefit both regimes. Shaker told SAVAK that Khomeini was stubborn.[94] Shaker also warned Alexander Count de Marenches, the then director-general of French intelligence, of the dangerous repercussions of Khomeini's activities.[95] De Marenches sent Saddam Hussein a message warning him that Khomeini could destabilize the whole region.[96] Nevertheless, Khomeini stayed in Iraq until October 1978 and continued his militancy.

The Shah appoints Sharif-Emami Prime Minister

At a meeting with Sullivan in late August, the Shah said that he was convinced that the CIA was plotting against him. Sullivan reported that the Shah wanted to broaden the base of his regime, but the military opposed concessions. Sullivan wanted President Carter to send a letter to the monarch to demonstrate US support for him. According to Gary Sick, the letter drafted by Sullivan was extremely flattering.[97]

At the end of August, the Shah appointed Ja'far Sharif-Emami as Prime Minister. He was one of the most corrupt Iranian politicians and was regarded as a British agent. He was Grand Master of the Grand Lodge of Iran and the most senior Freemason in the country. The main reason the Shah decided to appoint Sharif-Emami as Prime Minister was his belief that Britain was destabilizing Iran and that the appointment would placate London.[98] Indeed, Sharif-Emami himself argued that the British had been destabilizing Iran to undermine Amuzegar who was pro-American.[99]

The director of the Special Intelligence Bureau, General Fardust, believed that Sharif-Emami was a capable man.[100] Fardust's protégé, Moghaddam, however, wanted one of the National Front leaders to be appointed as Prime Minister.[101] He asked the Empress to beg the Shah to change his mind and warned her that the regime would be overthrown by a revolution.[102] The Empress conveyed Moghaddam's message to the Shah, but she could not change her husband's mind.[103]

Many members of the new government were old-style politicians and the government also included several former members of the Tudeh party.[104] The Sharif-Emami government simply contained too many corrupt individuals.[105] A group of radicals led by Manuchehr Azmun, Hushang Nahavandi, Mohammad Baheri and Kazem Vadi'i wanted to carry out a widespread purge. Another group wanted to deal with the crisis in a measured way.[106]

Sharif-Emami abolished one-party rule and took cosmetic measures such as restoring the Islamic calendar which had been abolished two years earlier, closing casinos and so forth.[107] However, he stopped short of bribing the clergy to stop their opposition.[108] At the same time, Sharif-Emami capitalized on the unrest in the country, using it to curtail the Shah's powers.[109]

Both Sharif-Emami and Deputy Prime Minister Azmun were in contact with clerics and some ministers were in contact with opposition figures.[110] On 29 August, it was reported that Sharif-Emami had sent a delegation to Najaf to persuade Khomeini to return to Iran.[111] However, religious leaders complained about Sharif-Emami and Azmun's corruption.[112] Nevertheless, the government freed almost all the jailed clerics. It was during this period that two clerics called publicly for the first time for the overthrow of the Shah and the establishment of an Islamic government.[113]

By September, US intelligence analysts had become extremely pessimistic about the Shah's long-term chances of survival. However, this pessimism was not reflected in policy.[114] After a meeting with the representative of the Liberation Movement of Iran, Mahmud Tavakkoli, in late August, the US embassy's political officer, John Stempel, concluded that the gulf between the Shah and the Liberation Movement was so wide that there was no chance of compromise between them.[115] Indeed in his correspondence with Khomeini, Bazargan argued that creating an 'Islamic government had to be the only and ultimate aim of every Muslim'. But Bazargan proposed to create an Islamic Republic in stages.[116]

The State Department's failure to change the Shah's military policy

By September 1978, it was clear that the State Department had not achieved its aim of moderating Iran's military build-up.[117] Arms sales, nuclear non-proliferation and human rights were the issues which divided the two countries.[118] On 6 September, the US received Iran's five-year plan for military purchases from the US. The total package would have been worth at least twelve billion dollars over the next four years.[119] In fact, during this period SAVAK was conducting a covert operation to smuggle nuclear material from the US to Iran.[120] It is not clear to what extent US officials were aware of SAVAK's activities.

The role of intelligence in policy conflicts in Washington

On 1 September, the State Department's Bureau of Intelligence and Research (INR) warned that the Shah could only continue to govern through 'substantial use of force'. However, the INR speculated that this might actually aggravate opposition to the Shah's rule and call into question the loyalty of the army and security forces.[121] INR analysts warned that 'the shah will lose the support of the army and be forced to step down by 1985'.[122]

In September, CIA Director Admiral Turner abandoned the attempt to formulate a National Intelligence Estimate (NIE) on Iran. There was serious disagreement among government analysts. The draft NIE was not particularly insightful about Iran and was cautiously optimistic about the situation. It was presented to the National Foreign Intelligence Board in early September 1978. Turner criticized and abandoned the NIE in September 1978 on the advice of the director of the INR.[123] In fact, Turner was in an excellent position to know about the Shah's opponents. According to Turner, the British ambassador to Iran, Anthony Parsons, was one of the agency's main sources of intelligence on that country.[124] According to Parsons, by early September 'the whole Pahlavi apparatus was in danger'.[125]

Turner's action suggests that he had tacitly sided with the State Department, which opposed a crackdown. Although Brzezinski and his assistant Gary Sick have complained about an intelligence failure, sufficient intelligence was available to convince them that the Shah was in trouble.[126]

Talk of military crackdown

At a meeting with the Iranian ambassador to the US, Ardeshir Zahedi, in late August, Brzezinski said that the Shah had to construct a political framework to accommodate the forces that his 'modernization' programme had unleashed. Zahedi agreed with Brzezinski and said that the Shah needed to 'clean house' and engage in a 'dialogue' with the people.[127]

Zahedi, whose father had led the coup against Mossadeq in 1953, believed that the Shah could save his throne by ordering a crackdown. He returned to Iran on 5 September to organize an effort to maintain the Shah in power. The White House had received reports that Zahedi saw the crisis as an opportunity for himself to become Prime Minister or Court Minister.[128]

Zahedi was one of the most corrupt and incompetent Iranian officials and his role as ambassador was to cultivate American politicians.[129] Nevertheless, Brzezinski remained in contact with Zahedi throughout the crisis. Zahedi wanted a Chilean-style crackdown along the lines of the 1973 coup. He held extensive talks with the Chilean ambassador to Washington on the Pinochet coup. Some of Zahedi's associates had even drawn up plans for detaining up to 100,000 troublemakers in various sports stadia in Iran.[130]

Zahedi led the military to believe that Washington supported a crackdown. Zahedi and his associates wanted the Shah to order the arrest and public trial of a large number of former officials, most notably former Prime Minister Amir-Abbas Hoveyda, and to impose martial law and arrest tens of thousands of troublemakers throughout the country.[131] Zahedi also sought to construct a coalition of military hard-liners and conservative clerics, most probably with himself as Prime Minister.[132] However, he failed to do so.[133] So serious was the situation that finally on 8 September, the State Department authorized the export of riot control equipment to Iran.[134]

The Continuing unrest in Iran and the failure of the Sharif-Emami government

According to Brzezinski, the reports of his assistant Gary Sick 'though isolated and in conflict with both Embassy reporting and CIA analysis, reinforced my growing uneasiness about Iran'.[135] On 7 September, Sick sent a memorandum to Carter, warning him that both government and academic Iran specialists were 'universally pessimistic' about the situation in Iran, adding that 'Iran may be ripe for full-scale revolution'.[136] Sick could not have possibly reached this conclusion without relying on the intelligence provided by the State Department and the CIA because the NSC did not possess an independent intelligence-gathering capability.

By early September, it was clear that the Sharif-Emami government had failed to stabilize the country.[137] Moreover, leftist guerrilla groups, operating independently of the Khomeini camp, had been involved in a series of clashes with the police.[138] General Moghaddam, who had been trying to co-opt the opposition, informed the National Security Council that communists and Islamic Marxists were responsible for the unrest and persuaded the National Security Council to impose martial law on the country.[139]

On 8 September, there were clashes between the army and demonstrators at Zhaleh Square in eastern Tehran in which scores of demonstrators were killed. That day became known as Black Friday. The order to fire on the crowd was given by the Tehran Martial Law Administrator General Gholamali Oveisi.[140] The military expected terrorist attacks and strikes to continue. The Shah was now convinced that the Soviet Union was destabilizing Iran. He told Sullivan that he would submit the legislation on freedoms of assembly and the press to the Majlis and hold free elections in June 1979.

The Shah made it clear that he had no intention of abdicating or leaving Iran, although he realized that martial law might drive his opponents underground and force them to resort to terrorism. Sullivan reported that the Shah had sided with advocates of reform.[141]

Carter called the Shah on 10 September to express his support for him. The Shah said that his opponents had taken advantage of his liberalization programme to plot his removal. However, he made it clear that there was no alternative to liberalization.[142] The Shah was not reassured by Carter's call and he wrote in his memoirs that Carter never called him during the crisis. There could be no doubt that the Zhaleh Square massacre was a setback for the regime. Khomeini declared that Israeli soldiers had been deployed to kill Iranians.[143]

Assessments of the situation in Iran

From September onwards US embassy officials began to warn of the dire consequences of military rule. In an internal embassy memorandum, John Washburn argued that the unrest in Iran made it:

> quite possible that the Shah would be removed in the next decade by assassination, coup, or irresistible population pressure. The best possible future government would be one dominated by an alliance between civilians and younger military officers. The worst would be a regime dominated by senior military officers.

Washburn contended that because most Iranians disapproved of military rule, the US had to discourage military rule 'no matter in what straits the Shah finds himself, or what chaos initially succeeds him'.[144] Washburn argued that the US should distance itself from the Shah while pressuring him to liberalize.[145]

In September, former State Department and CIA Iran specialist, Richard Cottam, who had maintained contact with the Khomeini camp, approached Gary Sick to argue that the US should support the opposition. Cottam claimed that 'moderates' and 'secularists' would succeed the Shah. Sick vehemently disagreed with this optimistic analysis.[146]

Cottam believed that the Shah deliberately inflated the Soviet threat to justify his hegemonic policies in the Persian Gulf. Moreover, according to Cottam, the Shah had used Iran's good ties with the Soviet Union to exert diplomatic leverage on the West.[147] By September Sullivan was convinced that the Shah and 'moderate' clerics had failed to reduce the level of support for Khomeini because they had nothing to offer the most disadvantaged people.[148] Sullivan argued that the Shah had to deal with the root causes of discontent because otherwise he would be overthrown.[149]

According to Sullivan, the Khomeini organization had 'reportedly been penetrated and is assisted by a variety of terrorist, crypto-communist, and other far left elements'. However, moderate politicians lacked the organizational base to challenge Khomeini and Islamists.[150]

French intelligence analyst Alain De Beaupuy told his American colleagues in September 1978 that 'if the Shah does not undertake extensive activity in the next two weeks' he would have to leave Iran 'by the end of October'.[151] De Beaupuy believed that the Shah had to permit the establishment of a constitutional monarchy.[152]

Vance was still reporting that the US had not yet received any evidence of external involvement in the unrest.[153] In fact, the embassy had already reported on de facto ties between the Khomeini camp and the Tudeh which was an instrument of Soviet policy.[154] Indeed in September Soviet MIGs violated the Iranian air space in an apparent attempt to intimidate the Shah.[155] By now even General Fardust was advising the Shah that Khomeini should be arrested immediately if he decided to go back to Iran. The Special Intelligence Bureau recommended that Iran should threaten to reappraise its relations with whichever country decided to give Khomeini permission to stay.[156]

At the same time, the Special Intelligence Bureau and SAVAK sought to accommodate the Liberation Movement of Iran despite SAVAK reports saying that the US embassy was encouraging Bazargan's Liberation Movement.[157] Moreover, General Moghaddam tacitly continued to support the activities of Ayatollah Shari'atmadari and former Prime Minister Ali Amini whose bid for premiership Khomeini also supported in the hopes of undermining the Shah.[158]

The Shah makes another effort at splitting the clerical establishment

In September, the Shah asked British ambassador, Anthony Parsons, if Britain could use its influence with moderate clerics to persuade them to back down. Parsons turned the Shah down flat, declaring that Britain had severed its ties with clerics in order to preserve its relationship with him.[159] Parsons said that unfulfilled expectations had led the people to turn to the clergy, that 'Khomeini was implacable and that nothing but the removal of the Shah would satisfy him'.

Parsons argued that the National Front would not be easily mollified because the Shah had maltreated its members.[160] The monarch warned Parsons that any alternative regime would be far worse for the West. Parsons reassured him that Britain fully supported him.[161]

On 17 September, Shari'atmadari declared that there should be no negotiations with the Shah and a week later he stated that it would be unacceptable to co-operate with the Sharif-Emami government and martial law administrators.[162] In late September, Parsons told the Shah that Britain and the US were not plotting against him and that he had to call free elections because the only alternatives would be his overthrow or 'savage military repression'. Parsons warned him that 'Khomeini was determined to overthrow the monarchy and his following in the country was strong'. He advised the Shah to instruct Sharif-Emami to negotiate with 'moderate' clerics to split them from the Khomeini camp.[163]

The Shah told Parsons that he was no longer sure of the survival of the monarchy. However, he wanted to prepare the ground for his son's succession.[164] The Shah was operating on the assumption that Khomeini would be isolated because of his extremism and that his own control over the military would enable him to ensure his predominance.

On 23 September, Khomeini issued a statement, saying: 'U.S. and Soviet agents should be killed if they try to intervene.'[165] On the same day, the Iraqi government put Khomeini under house arrest. Representatives of the Liberation Movement complained to John Stempel that either the US or the Soviet Union was responsible for Khomeini's arrest. They sought to persuade the embassy to abandon the Shah and support the transition to a new regime. They said that Shari'atmadari supported Khomeini and would not negotiate with the Shah, adding that several clerics had intended to call on the people to kill American citizens in Iran. Stempel said that the Iraqis had taken action for various reasons and also because they feared the Soviets. Stempel argued that the US considered the Shah to be the best agent for effecting the transition to constitutionalism.[166]

The US embassy supported Sharif-Emami's initiative to split conservative clerics and the Liberation Movement from Khomeini.[167] The Sharif-Emami government and conservative clerics reached an accommodation because they both feared that leftist groups were hiding behind Khomeini. Indeed, by now even the Liberation Movement and the National Front held Tudeh agitators responsible for much of the unrest in the country.[168]

Agent provocateur operations to destabilize the Sharif-Emami government

Khomeini's departure from Iraq and arrival in Paris on 6 October dramatically changed the situation in Iran. The Shah believed that if Khomeini went to a radical Arab state, such as Syria or Libya, he would be able to intensify his opposition to the regime. He did not expect Khomeini and his followers to use modern means of communications effectively to destabilize Iran.[169] Moreover, by now SAVAK hard-liners led by Parviz Sabeti were seeking to bring about the downfall of Moghaddam and Sharif-Emami by encouraging agent provocateurs. Moghaddam failed to curb the activities of Sabeti and his supporters.[170]

SAVAK cells operating under such names as the 'Underground Committee for Vengeance' and the 'Resistance Corps' attacked opposition figures.[171] Deputy Prime Minister Manuchehr Azmun played an important role in other agent provocateur operations aimed at inflaming the situation to prepare the ground for a crackdown. Azmun was a SAVAK official who had also been briefly a member of the Tudeh Party when he was a student in West Germany. His acerbic exchanges with other cabinet officials led to the resignations of three ministers. Azmun was Sabeti's close friend and he regularly reported to him on religious developments. He believed that the regime could end the crisis by executing scores of prominent people.

Moghaddam vehemently opposed Azmun's recommendations and even threatened to ensure his execution.[172] Before the Sharif-Emami government collapsed, Azmun resigned from his post in the cabinet and with Sabeti's assistance he set up a new party called the Union of Iran's Proletariat.[173] Sharif-Emami believed that SAVAK was destabilizing the country to demonstrate that the Shah's liberalization policy was flawed.[174]

According to Sullivan's report to Washington, Sabeti's agent provocateur operations had led to clashes and caused destruction in Kerman, Ravar, Kermanshah, Hamedan, Gorgan, Rezayieh, Amol, Baneh, Maragheh, Sanandaj and other cities. Sabeti had bragged about two of these incidents shortly after his trip to Kurdistan. Sullivan believed that the Shah had authorized Sabeti's agent provocateur operations.[175]

Sharif-Emami informed the Shah of Sabeti's activities, but the Shah rejected his reports. However, he gave him carte blanche when Sharif-Emami showed him a report on Sabeti's involvement in provoking unrest in the Shahr-e Rey oil refinery. Sharif-Emami ordered Sabeti's dismissal. In October, Sabeti and 33 members of SAVAK's Department Three were dismissed. Sabeti continued to provoke unrest in the country, but Sharif-Emami chose not to arrest him and allowed him to leave the country quietly.[176]

Sharif-Emami's continuing efforts to conciliate religious opposition

By early October, Sharif-Emami had made a deal with Ayatollah Shari'atmadari who had 'admitted some Marxist infiltration of religious groups'. In the Majlis the Sharif-Emami government presented evidence of leftist involvement in the unrest.[177] Shari'atmadari sent a message through SAVAK channels to the Shah saying that many people wanted Khomeini to return to Iran. He proposed that Khomeini be given the opportunity to return on condition that he respected the constitution. Shari'atmadari argued that Khomeini would not accept the offer and the Shah's position would be strengthened among the Shi'a throughout the world.[178]

On 10 October the Shah told Sullivan that he was thinking about inviting Khomeini to Iran. Sullivan told the Shah that he 'would be out of his mind to issue an unconditional invitation'.[179] During this period, the Shah ordered an investigation into the Royal Family's endowments. Moreover, two ministers were arrested, the head of the Atomic Energy Department was dismissed and former SAVAK chief General Nasiri, who had been appointed Iranian ambassador to Pakistan, was recalled to Iran to be interrogated by a military tribunal.[180] On 17 October, the Sharif-Emami government formally promulgated the end of press censorship.[181]

Above all, Sharif-Emami tried to use the negotiations with the opposition to increase his own powers.[182] However, he told Parsons, that the government could not compete with Khomeini's huge expenditures on theology students and bazaaris.[183] Sharif-Emami and Shari'atmadari brokered an agreement as part of which religious leaders had agreed to form a coalition with National Front politicians.[184]

Shari'atmadari's friend, Naser Minachi, told John Stempel that religious leaders believed that the Shah would protect the country against 'anarchy and communism'. However, Sharif-Emami failed to persuade Khomeini to mute his opposition despite his tacit cooperation with Bazargan and the most senior clerics in Iran, Grand Ayatollahs Shari'atmadari, Golpayegani, and Mar'ashi.[185]

In the first half of October Sharif-Emami sent envoys to Paris to warn Khomeini that he could never overthrow the Shah and that his opposition had only cost Muslim lives.[186] However, Khomeini threatened to call on his supporters to abandon 'peaceful resistance'.[187] Throughout October the government failed to control the unrest and an oil workers' strike paralysed the economy. Strikers demanded the return of Khomeini and the lifting of martial law. The chairman of the National Iranian Oil Company Hushang Ansari failed to persuade the strikers to go back to work and fled the country.[188]

Leftist groups were deeply involved in organizing the strikes. By the end of October, 37,000 oil workers were on strike. They demanded higher wages, expulsion of all foreign workers, and an end to the martial law.[189] Military commanders advised the Shah to order a crackdown.[190]

By mid-October Sullivan felt that even religious leaders could not bring the situation under control.[191] Sharif-Emami, Ayatollah Shari'atmadari and the Liberation Movement had reached an agreement stipulating that the Shah must 'reign, not rule'. However, Sharif-Emami failed to persuade the Shah to surrender control over the military.[192] The monarch was unwilling to order his troops to fire indiscriminately.

The military was becoming increasingly uneasy about the Shah's attitude.[193] Generals Fardust and Moghaddam had already established contact with the leaders of the Khomeini camp in Iran. They did not inform the Shah of these negotiations.[194] They had written off the monarch and were trying to form an alliance with religious groups.[195]

Sullivan and Parsons discourage supporters of military government

By mid-October rumours that the Tehran Martial Law Administrator Oveisi would lead a military coup were gaining currency in Iranian political circles. Oveisi wanted to detain 20,000 opponents of the regime.[196] Some hard-liners even suggested that Iran should invade Afghanistan to divert attention from the revolution.[197]

By mid-October ambassadors Sullivan and Parsons were so worried about a crackdown that they warned Oveisi: 'The effect of a military coup on Iran's Western friends and allies would be disastrous.'[198] At a meeting with the Shah on 24 October, Parsons and Sullivan said 'that in their view a military solution was a non-starter'. Sullivan did not consult the White House on this matter.[199]

The Shah proposed two options: a military government, or a coalition, which would include members of the opposition. Sullivan and Parsons urged the Shah to bring members of the opposition into the government.[200] The Shah agreed with his interlocutors. Indeed Parsons thought that the Shah was 'implacably opposed to a military take-over'.[201]

In Washington, Gary Sick recommended that the Carter administration make a statement or issue a joint statement with its allies or even send Brzezinski to Iran to demonstrate US support for the Shah.[202] However, the State Department made it clear that the US should strongly oppose military rule.[203] Moreover, Sullivan argued that the US should not send crowd-control equipment to Iran or issue any more statements of support for the Shah or plan visits by high-level emissaries. Sullivan wanted the US to avoid contact with Khomeini and work with the Shah whom he believed was trying to establish a broad-based government.[204]

Failure of efforts to the split clerical establishment

Sharif-Emami's agreement with Ayatollah Shari'atmadari and the Liberation Movement was only in force until the end of October.[205] Khomeini refused to meet the Shah's envoys Ali Amini or Ardeshir Zahedi. He also warned other political figures not to negotiate with the Shah.[206] At the end of October, Shari'atmadari declared his support for Khomeini and even threatened to start an armed uprising.[207]

In October, the Liberation Movement presented a transition plan to the US embassy, arguing that the US could secure its long-term strategic and economic objectives in Iran and the Persian Gulf by abandoning the Shah. The embassy concluded that it was 'an appeal deliberately designed for Western ears', arguing: 'Khomeini's anti-American statements contradicted Liberation Movement arguments'. Washington did not reply to Sullivan's proposal that it acknowledge 'the suggestion'.[208]

Bazargan met Khomeini and Ebrahim Yazdi in Paris on 30 October – their first meeting since 1962. Bazargan called for free elections to change the regime from within. Khomeini rejected Bazargan's proposal, adding that the US would not try to prevent the revolution because 'its cause was just'. Bazargan concluded that Khomeini was a 'turbaned' Shah. However, it later emerged that Khomeini had asked Bazargan to draw up a list of trustworthy people who could advise him after his return on whom he should support as candidates in parliamentary elections or appoint to the cabinet.[209] Two days later Bazargan gave Khomeini a list of names. The list included the names of Ayatollah Beheshti, Ayatollah Mottahari, Ayatollah Zanjani, Hojattoleslam Rafsanjani, and Hojjatoleslam Mahdavi-Kani from the clergy, all of whom were members of Khomeini's organization.[210]

In the last week of October National Front leader Karim Sanjabi went to Paris and made a deal with Khomeini.[211] Upon his arrival in Iran, Sanjabi was arrested by martial law administrators for opposing the Shah.[212] Bazargan and Sanjabi's tacit alliance with Khomeini demonstrated that the crisis could not be settled by peaceful means.

The Oil Factor

The Shah believed that the BP-led Consortium was destabilizing Iran to force him to change his oil policy and maintain its predominant position in Iran. The Shah stalled the companies, issuing no instructions to the NIOC chairman Hushang Ansari who was negotiating with the companies. The negotiations were deadlocked.[213]

By now the failure of US oil policy had become clear. The depreciation of the dollar and heavy oil imports had failed to suppress polycentric tendencies in the Western alliance.[214] West Germany's and Japan's reserve holdings reached a historic high vis-à-vis US holdings.[215] Moreover, the European Monetary System (EMS) could become a rival bloc to the dollar.[216]

The Congressional approval of F-15 sale to Saudi Arabia to a large extent contributed to the Saudi decision to support the dollar.[217] However, OPEC remained acutely concerned about the depreciating value of the dollar.[218] Saudi Arabia called for a price freeze until the end of 1978. In late November, the Shah told visiting US Treasury Secretary Michael Blumenthal that he would continue his low oil-price policy. Blumenthal appreciated the Shah's concession. The Shah told Blumenthal that he wanted to form a civilian government. Carter informed the Shah that he supported his efforts.[219]

However, Algeria, Iraq, and Kuwait demanded a price rise.[220] In 1977 the net inflow of OPEC capital into the US was 7.3 billion dollars. This was more than a six-fold increase during the post-1973 period.[221] The net inflow of capital since the oil embargo was 38 billion dollars. This had been sufficient to counterbalance the entire trade deficit and could have caused several stock market crashes had the investors decided to withdraw their money. However, OPEC capital had not moved into a control position in US businesses. Nevertheless, it was extremely difficult to estimate the amount of OPEC's investments in the US because OPEC members often used intermediaries.[222]

As we saw earlier, one reason for US pressure on the Shah was alleviating Saudi concerns about Iran's military build-up. However, Saudi leaders did not support a revolution in Iran. Zbigniew Brzezinski argued that it was important to show the Saudis that the US stood by its friends.[223] Saudi Arabia was an important country. As the *Petroleum Economist* observed, 'with its official reserves alone of more than 50 billion dollars, any decision by Saudi Arabia to throw its weight about in the market could terrify other investors'.[224]

From October 1978, the Carter administration shifted from a depreciating to an appreciating dollar policy and to a reduction of oil imports. Indeed this strategy laid the foundations of the Reagan administration's high-dollar policy.[225] In effect, the Carter administration undertook a 30 billion-dollar intervention in financial markets to buttress the dollar-the largest intervention in American history.[226]

The crisis of US strategy and the formation of military government in Iran

As late as 28 October, Sullivan reported that the Shah could 'on the one hand, restrain the military and, on the other hand, lead a controlled transition... I would strongly oppose any overture to Khomeini'.[227] However, in an Inter-agency Intelligence Memorandum (IIM) on 29 October, the INR said that the Shah might not survive for more than eighteen to twenty four months.[228]

At a meeting with Sullivan on 31 October, the Shah said that Sharif-Emami was totally ineffective. Although the Shah said that military dictatorship 'would at best be a quick fix and in the long run no solution at all', he also indicated that he was unenthusiastic about a coalition government.[229]

On the same day, Sullivan cabled that one had to seriously examine the assumption that there was 'no viable alternative' to the Shah.[230] Sullivan reported that the Shah could not simply continue his liberalization programme because of Shari'atmadari and Khomeini's refusal to compromise.[231]

Sullivan opposes military crackdown

By now the Sharif-Emami government had virtually no support in the Majlis.[232] At a meeting with ambassadors Parsons and Sullivan on 1 November, the Shah declared that he would 'rather leave the country than submit' to the National Front's call for a referendum on the monarchy. The Shah told Sullivan and Parsons that the hard-liners were pressuring him to establish a military government. Indeed, during the meeting, Ambassador Zahedi called the Shah and recommended organizing pro-regime mobs to attack the Shah's opponents, even if that meant starting a civil war. But the Shah rebuffed Zahedi, saying that 'this is not 1953 and is not even the same situation that existed two weeks ago'.[233]

The three men concluded that another attempt should be made to form a coalition government, possibly by threatening the formation of a military government. If that initiative failed, the Shah would attempt to 'form a neutral government for the sole purpose of holding elections'.[234]

Sullivan reported that if the Shah remained in the country he could only rule by forming a military government. Should he decide to leave Iran, 'the military would be expected to take over in a coup without the Shah'.[235] Sullivan argued that a military take-over would damage long-term US interests, but it would be inevitable in the event of continuing chaos. General Oveisi had already approached a number of people to serve in his government of 'national salvation'. The embassy believed that the military would not officially stage a take-over without the Shah's permission, but expected the military to tell the Shah to order a crack down or leave the country.[236]

In 1978 Zahedi and his associates organized attacks on mosques and crowds. The attacks angered the demonstrators and resulted in clashes between the military and the crowds. Zahedi tried to persuade the Shah to execute a few prominent politicians, including former Prime Minister Hoveyda, to mollify the opposition.[237]

The Shah did not have much respect for Zahedi as a political operator.[238] Despite the Shah's apparent reluctance, coup planning continued. The embassy reported that the monarch had set up two committees of five members to organize support for him throughout the country.[239]

Sullivan reported that it was 'quite likely' that Zahedi had advised the Shah to form the two committees. He now believed that the Shah's telephone conversation with Zahedi in the presence of himself and Parsons was 'stage-managed to impress them with [the] Shah's innocence as pro-Shah incidents backfire'.[240] Sullivan's Iranian sources with access to the Shah interpreted these moves in terms of the Shah's inability to understand 'the gravity' of the monarchy's 'predicament'.[241]

On 2 November, Sullivan again reported that Zahedi had failed to form a coalition, which included the clergy. Sullivan had received intelligence indicating that Zahedi had masterminded agent provocateur attacks in Kerman in late October where a mosque had been attacked. A Kurdish tribal leader (Salar Jaaf) had also been accused of ordering his henchmen to attack demonstrators in Paveh. Other such demonstrations and agent provocateur operations had been carried out in Zahedan and Birjand (by supporters of the Alam family).[242] Sullivan did not believe that Zahedi could succeed. He reasoned:

> In 1953, the bazaaris and mullahs led mobs in support of the monarchy. In 1978, they are leading mobs against the monarchy. Zahedi cannot switch the bazaaris and mullahs of today. Recourse to mob violence under present conditions would assist the polarization between [the] Shah and Khomeini supporters which we all hope to avert.

Sullivan wanted a negotiated solution which relied on 'moderates of the centre'.[243] The embassy believed that any military take-over would involve arresting thousands of people. Sullivan predicted that the situation in the country would resemble those in Greece under the Colonels or in Latin American countries under juntas. Moreover, a military take-over would increase left-wing terrorist attacks on Americans in Iran. The Shah would lose his credibility, the moderates would be swept aside by the radicals and there would be an international outcry against the use of force.

Moreover, the military did not have the expertise to run the oil fields. However, if the Shah waited long enough for the situation to deteriorate further and then imposed military rule and combined his actions with a sophisticated public relations ploy, he might succeed in convincing anti-communist conservatives to support him. However, so far the government had proven to be incapable of mounting an intelligent public relations campaign.[244]

On 2 November, in an important memorandum to Vance, the INR argued that the Shah's meetings with ambassadors Sullivan and Parsons showed that he lacked confidence as in 1953. The INR warned that 'only drastic measures by the Shah hold any promise for staving off a descent into chaos'. Intelligence reports indicated that moderate opposition figures and religious leaders were trying to form a government with the Shah as a figurehead. Khomeini, however, was an obstacle in their path.[245]

Ayatollah Shari'atmadari had threatened armed struggle unless the Shah met religious leaders' demands.[246] According to the INR, the Shah would have to offer 'the moderates' a deal that would isolate Khomeini, adding that the Shah might succeed only if he relinquished power.[247] If the Shah chose to do nothing he would be overthrown or replaced by the military. However, the INR did not expect a military government to last more than six months.[248]

On the same day, the strategic debate between advocates of New World Order and neo-containment in Washington came to a head.[249] Brzezinski wanted to encourage the Shah to crush the opposition, whereas Vance and his State Department advisers wanted to urge him to restrain the Iranian military. Brzezinski criticized ambassadors Sullivan and Parsons, thinking that the Shah's overthrow was a real possibility. He had received a call from former Vice-President Nelson Rockefeller who had criticized the Carter administration for 'doing nothing'.[250]

Vance and the State Department were operating on the assumption that any future Iranian government would co-operate with the US if only to maintain stability and contain communism. However, US-Iranian relations would be 'far less intimate'.[251] Admiral Turner also supported the State Department position. Secretary of Defence Harold Brown generally supported Brzezinski. He argued that 'a military government with the shah was better than one without the shah'.[252]

At a meeting of the NSC's Special Co-ordinating Committee on 2 November, it was decided, after Carter's intervention, to inform the Shah that the US supported him 'without reservation'. The message asked the Shah to take 'decisive action' and demonstrate 'leadership'. However, once the Shah had restored 'order and authority', the administration hoped that he would 'resume prudent efforts to promote liberalization and to eradicate corruption'.[253]

Brzezinski later claimed that the Shah's opponents in the US government, including Iran desk director Henry Precht, never explicitly called for his removal and couched their arguments in terms of democratization and formulating transition plans.[254]

On 3 November, Sharif-Emami warned Sullivan that 'the shah was incapable of making any decision'.[255] On the same day, Brzezinski telephoned the Shah and expressed 'the unshakeable support of the U.S. government' regardless of Iran's type of government. Brzezinski emphasized that the US 'did not encourage any particular solution', but argued that 'concessions alone would only make the situation more explosive'.[256] The Shah asked pointedly, 'Is your ambassador briefed?', implying that Sullivan was recommending a different policy.[257] The Shah thought the messages were 'confusing and contradictory'.[258]

The difficulty of forming a military government was compounded by the Shah's fear of being overthrown by such a government. In fact, after 1953, coup planning had proceeded under the pretext of contingency planning for staging a military take-over in the event of the Shah's assassination. The favourite candidate for leading a military take-over was General Oveisi who was also responsible for contingency planning. The Shah knew full well that in the past, some US administrations had shown an inclination for replacing him with a strong military leader. In the 1940s and 1950s General Razmara was grooming himself for such a role.[259] In the late 1950s and early 1960s the US chose General Valiollah Qarani and then General Teimur Bakhtiar the then Director of SAVAK for such a role.[260] In the 1970s the Shah discovered that General Khatami might have been involved in an US-backed coup. Khatami was killed shortly afterwards in a mysterious accident.[261]

After Khatami's death, General Oveisi was responsible for staging a take-over in the event of the Shah's assassination. In early November, Zahedi, who had been in contact with Brzezinski, urged a group of generals to approach Oveisi to discuss coup planning without the Shah. Oveisi, who thought this was a plot by the Shah to test his loyalty, made it clear that he would not act against the Shah's will.[262]

The CIA also approached deputy SAVAK station chief in the US, Mansur Rafizadeh, to discuss another coup plan with Oveisi. The CIA officials who talked with Rafizadeh claimed that they were unaware of the first approach to Oveisi. They told Rafizadeh that the Carter administration was behind the coup plan and asked him to warn Oveisi not to inform Sullivan. Oveisi turned Rafizadeh down flat, observing that the US government was divided and there was no one in charge. When Rafizadeh told Oveisi that Sullivan was not informed of the plan, Oveisi mocked the scheme.[263]

The Shah confronts Sullivan and Parsons

At a meeting with ambassadors Sullivan and Parsons on 4 November, the Shah said that he had received a telephone call from Brzezinski, saying that Washington either supported the formation of a military or a coalition government.[264] Sullivan said that the Brzezinski phone call did not mean that Washington supported a military government, but that it would support the Shah's decision 'if he had absolutely no other choice'. Parsons said that he had no instructions, but repeated that London wanted a political solution and that he personally strongly opposed a military government.[265]

The Shah told Sullivan and Parsons that he was still trying to form a coalition government with the National Front. However, he had no intention at all of considering the National Front's proposal of a referendum on the monarchy.[266] The Shah argued that Iranian generals were 'pressing him harder than ever' to form a military government and indicated that the Iranian military leaders had been aware of the Brzezinski call. The Shah said that 'it was all very well for Brzezinski to talk, but he still believed that unleashing the military would solve nothing.'[267]

The Shah wanted a constitutional government which was supported by 'moderate' clerics. If the government or the military, he argued, faced a coalition of the National Front, the moderate clergy and Khomeini, Khomeini would declare a holy war and cause 'a bloodbath'.[268]

Parsons argued that the situation was completely different from the one in 1953 and that the military could not subdue the people.[269] Parsons left the meeting, fearing that the Shah could no longer resist the pressure from the military particularly because the generals believed that Washington supported them.[270]

The Shah was also discouraged by Sullivan's reply on 4 November. Sullivan had received instructions to tell the Shah that the US government supported him, but he said that he had received no instructions.[271] The fact that Sullivan did not so much as mention this meeting in his memoirs suggests that he did not support the Shah.[272]

By now Generals Tufanian, Rabi'i, Oveisi, Admiral Habibollahi and the director of SAVAK General Moghaddam were meeting frequently to chart an independent course of action. Indeed, they even visited the US embassy individually.[273] Perhaps one reason they did not succeed was Moghaddam's contacts with the opposition.[274]

On November 4 and for the next two days SAVAK carried out acts of sabotage and violence in Tehran. The targets were selected carefully to draw attention to the fact that the regime's opponents were anti-Western. SAVAK set fire to the British embassy, Western business establishments, tourist hotels, banks, cinemas, and liquor stores. The agitators also evicted American advisers at the Ministry of Labour from their offices. Genuine revolutionaries who thought Khomeini had ordered these actions immediately entered the fray and caused even more destruction.[275]

There are two interpretations of the events of November 4–5. Ambassadors Parsons and Sullivan have argued that SAVAK and the hard-liners in the military decided to carry out agent provocateur operations to force the Shah to crack down.[276] However, former SAVAK official, Mansur Rafizadeh, later wrote that the Shah had planned the operations to persuade Washington to agree to a crackdown.[277] The available evidence does not support Rafizadeh's claim.

Indeed, the CIA later reported that the Shah had rejected the hard-liners' advice because Khomeini might call for 'a holy war' and conscripts' loyalties would be 'severely tested'.[278] After the events of 4 November, the Shah decided to appoint General Oveisi as Prime Minister. However, Sullivan and Parson's opposition to Oveisi's appointment led him to change his mind and appoint General Azhari instead.[279]

The Shah told Sullivan and Parsons that he had reluctantly decided to form a military government. The Shah assured Sullivan that he would not order the arrest of National Front leaders because he wanted to bring them in to a coalition government later. However, there were rumours that some National Front leaders would be arrested. Sullivan reported that the military might have sought to derail the Shah's programme for forming a coalition government.[280]

In Washington, Brzezinski saw the Shah's decision to form a military government as a sign of his determination to stamp his authority on the situation.[281] According to Iranian government documents, Brzezinski advised Zahedi to ask the Shah not to tie his hands by declaring a timetable for lifting the martial law and holding elections.[282]

The Shah was apologetic when he announced the formation of the military government. He said: 'I once again repeat my oath to the Iranian nation and undertake not to allow the past mistakes, unlawful acts, oppression and corruption to recur but to make up for them ... I heard the revolutionary message of you people, the Iranian nation. I am the guardian of the constitutional monarchy, which is a God-given gift, a gift entrusted to the shah by the people.'[283]

To prove that the government was military in name only, the Shah appointed one of the most incompetent and ineffectual generals, Gholamreza Azhari, as Prime Minister. Indeed, the Shah told ambassadors Sullivan and Parsons that he had deliberately chosen Azhari because he was ineffectual.[284] The Shah's formation of a military government alienated moderate opposition groups. At the same time, his conciliatory speech alienated his hard-line supporters. Commander of the Navy Admiral Habibollahi later observed that the Shah's speech 'was a blow to the officer corps, a sign of the approval of the revolution, and was actually the beginning of the transfer of power'.[285]

The Shah also met Ambassador Parsons who persuaded him to look in to the affairs of the Royal Family and the Pahlavi foundation. The Shah assured Parsons that his friend, former Prime Minister and Court Minister Hoveyda, would not be arrested. However, Hoveyda was arrested on 8 November. Sullivan reported that the Shah displayed 'a sensitivity bordering on panic in his efforts to placate critics'.[286] Had the Shah been somewhat more imaginative in his approach, he might have been able to wean some of Khomeini's key supporters, such as bazaar merchants, away from him.[287] However, his assumption that London and Washington were responsible for his predicament sealed his fate.

'An Intelligence Disaster of the First Order'

On 6 November, NSC official Gary Sick complained to Brzezinski that 'this has been an intelligence disaster of the first order' because of the paucity of intelligence on the opposition, infiltration of opposition groups and strikers' demands.[288] Brzezinski distrusted the State Department and sent Gary Sick to review the cables from the US embassy in Tehran.[289] Sick concluded that the embassy 'had done a good job of reporting on the basic facts'. However, he also contended that 'there was very little digging below the surface'.[290] When it was finally ready, the National Intelligence Estimate (NIE) on Iran was not exactly full of insights. For example, it reported that the Soviet Union was reluctant to directly intervene in Iran lest such intervention damage bilateral relations. The NIE expected Soviet interests to be jeopardized by a military or religious government, but it expected the Soviets to take advantage of the instability in the country.[291]

The most important part of the CIA's analysis was its prediction that in the long run, even a government led by the Shah was expected to dramatically reduce Iran's dependence on the US. Iran's most immediate foreign policy objective was to maintain Iranian preponderance in the Persian Gulf region, but Iran and its Arab neighbours were unlikely to agree on collective security arrangements.[292]

Given the internal unrest, Iran was expected to shift resources from military and nuclear programmes to transport and agriculture.[293] According to the estimate, the country was likely to decline as a regional power. Its oil production capacity was approaching its peak and would begin to fall probably in the early 1980s and natural gas could not replace oil as a source of revenue. Foreign investment would decline unless the Shah stabilized the domestic situation.[294]

The intelligence estimate on Iran had been completely overtaken by the course of events. By now, Ambassador Sullivan and some of his State Department colleagues were coming to the conclusion that the US had no choice but to change its Iran policy.

7

THE INTENSIFICATION OF THE REVOLUTIONARY CRISIS

The crisis in Iran brought the strategic debate in the Carter administration to the fore. Secretary of State Cyrus Vance and his supporters believed that the US should limit its goals in Iran to the preservation of Iran's territorial integrity, continued access to oil and denial of political power to leftists. National Security Adviser Zbigniew Brzezinski, on the other hand, saw the Iranian revolution as increasingly Soviet inspired and a threat to US regional and global positions. CIA Director Admiral Turner sided with Vance most of the time, whereas Secretary of Defence Harold Brown and Secretary of the Energy James Schlesinger sided with Brzezinski.

The military government, religious and leftist opposition and the oil strike

Despite its name, the Iranian military government believed that the solution to the crisis was political.[1] It continued the Shah's anti-corruption campaign by arresting officials such as former Prime Minister Hoveyda and former SAVAK Director General Nasiri who were symbols of corruption in the country. The Shah was worried about arresting Hoveyda who had served as Prime Minister for thirteen years.[2] Indeed, the Shah had said that arresting Hoveyda would be tantamount to putting the system on trial.[3] However, Hoveyda's opponents, most notably, Ardeshir Zahedi, persuaded the Shah that it was a good idea to make Hoveyda a scapegoat to mollify the opposition.[4]

Such palliatives were ineffective. By now, leftist guerrilla groups had entered the fray.[5] The National Voice of Iran (NVOI), the Soviet Union's clandestine radio station, increased its broadcasts and supported those in 'the battle to oust imperialism, particularly U.S. imperialism'.[6]

Oil workers and public utility employees went on strike. Few of the people involved in such strikes had even heard the names of Khomeini's closest advisers, Beheshti, Mottahari and Rafsanjani.[7] Iran's economic woes continued because of the government's failure to end the oil strike.[8] At the same time, the regime's supporters were alienated by Azhari's efforts to accommodate the religious opposition.[9] SAVAK showed documents from the Tudeh Party's secret branch, the Navid organization, to Brian Crozier, who was associated with the Institute for the Study of Conflict in London. According to Crozier, copies of the newsletter, *Navid*, were produced in the Soviet embassy. The documents were translated and the institute published a study, entitled, 'The Campaign to Destabilize Iran' by Robert Moss.[10]

A *New Republic* article by Robert Moss, entitled 'Who's Meddling in Iran?', influenced Brzezinski's thinking. According NSC official Gary Sick, 'at a critical moment the article attained the status of a key policy document.'[11] Almost immediately after the formation of the military government, US ambassador William Sullivan and British ambassador Anthony Parsons began to explore ways of facilitating the transition to a post-Shah regime. Parsons was still thinking in terms of preserving a constitutional monarchy.[12]

Sullivan was thinking much further ahead than Parsons. Judging from John Stempel's account, the embassy learned some time in October that the Shah was suffering from cancer.[13] By early November Carter, who had become increasingly concerned about the State Department's attitude towards the Shah, instructed Vance to ensure that State Department officials supported the monarch.[14] Carter was also concerned about Soviet military intervention in Iran.[15]

On 9 November, Sullivan sent a cable to the White House, entitled 'Thinking the Unthinkable: Iran without the Shah'. Sullivan believed that Khomeini and younger military officers were strongly anti-Communist so Khomeini could return to Iran as part of an accommodation between the military and the religious opposition. According to Sullivan, Khomeini would play a 'Gandhi-like' role and elections would be held to establish an Islamic Republic, which would be strongly pro-Western.[16]

Sullivan wanted to compel Khomeini to 'eschew the 'Nasser-Qadhafi' types, whom I assumed he would prefer' and appoint figures such as Bazargan to key positions. Sullivan believed that his proposal would serve US interests because,

> it would avoid chaos, ensure the continued integrity of the country, preclude a radical leadership, and effectively block Soviet domination of the Persian Gulf. In these circumstances, the major losses, as I saw them would be a reduction in the intimacy of our military and security relations, a shift on Iran's part from a pro-Israeli to an anti-Zionist position, and a certain aloofness in our overall dealings. While this situation would certainly be less appealing than the arrangements we had enjoyed under the shah, it would obviously be better than one in which an inchoate revolution would succeed and the integrity of the armed forces be destroyed.[17]

Sullivan however, noted that a single mistake 'could produce unforeseeable consequences'.[18] According to Brzezinski, Sullivan's cable encouraged those State Department officials 'who were generally inclined to argue that the fall of the Shah would have benign consequences for American interests'.[19] Sullivan later blamed Brzezinski for killing off his plan. He said that the failure to implement it permitted leftist influence to grow in Iran after the revolution.[20]

Soviet intervention and the crisis of US Strategy

Until September 1978 Soviet officials believed that the Carter administration supported Khomeini in order to compel the Shah to make more concessions or to replace him with a more compliant regime.[21] The Soviets believed that the US wanted to punish the Shah for his independent oil policy. However, they also believed that the US policy had backfired.[22] The unrest in Iran and the Shah's failure to clamp down persuaded the Soviets that Iran was ripe for a full-scale revolution.[23]

The KGB residency in Tehran was hostile to Khomeini. It reported that he had described Iranian communists as 'unpatriotic puppets of Moscow' and was infuriated by the communist coup in Afghanistan in April 1978 which he believed had prevented that country from establishing an Islamic regime. The KGB residency reported on Khomeini's increasing popularity in the country, but it did not expect the ayatollah to seek to replace the Shah.[24] By November, Soviet leaders had decided to actively support the revolution. On 18 November, Brezhnev sent a letter to Carter warning the US against intervening in Iran.[25] He implicitly invoked the 1921 Iranian-Soviet treaty, saying 'that any interference, especially military interference in the affairs of Iran' would affect Soviet security interests. In effect, Brezhnev threatened to respond militarily to US military moves to save the Shah.[26]

Only five days before Carter had announced in a news conference that there was no evidence of Soviet attempts to destabilize the Iranian regime.[27] Brezhnev's message was considered as extremely important 'since it marked a clear shift in Soviet policy'.[28] Brzezinski believed that Brezhnev's letter indicated that a 'more ominous international dimension' had emerged.[29] He became increasingly convinced that the revolution was Soviet inspired.[30]

Carter, who sought to avoid a confrontation with the Soviet Union, sent a message to Brezhnev saying that the US would not intervene but would 'honour' its 'commitments to Iran' and that the US supported the Shah whole-heartedly.[31] Vance also declared that the US had no intention of interfering in Iran and it expected the Soviet Union to refrain from doing so as well.[32] The Shah concluded that the US had decided not to honour its security commitment to Iran.[33] He later claimed that he had decided to allow Prime Minister Azhari to continue the liberalization programme because of US and British pressure.[34]

Changes in the Tudeh Party's leadership

During this period, Moscow moved to change the leadership of the Tudeh Party. The General-Secretary of the Party, Iraj Eskandari, who favoured an alliance with Iran's Liberation Movement and Ayatollah Shari'atmadari, in pursuit of a constitutional monarchy, was replaced by Nureddin Kianuri who called for supporting Khomeini to overthrow the Shah.[35]

According to Eskandari, there were two tendencies in Soviet strategy at the time. One led by the chief of the International Department, Boris Ponomarev, favoured Eskandari's approach, whereas another group of officials, particularly chief of Azerbaijan KGB Heidar Aliev, supported Kianuri.[36]

According to Eskandari, Aliev believed that US military intervention to support a client regime would lead to a Soviet counter-invasion and he wanted the Tudeh's military branch to prepare for leading a coup. Aliev, who believed that Kianuri would be the most suitable candidate to establish a pro-Soviet government in Iran, engineered Eskandari's removal.[37]

Eskandari had already been weakened and he had made token concessions to Kianuri. For example, Eskandari praised Khomeini, the clergy and the National Front and called for a united front strategy to oust the Shah.[38] The US embassy in Tehran feared that Eskandari's statement indicated a change in Soviet policy 'to more active meddling in current Iranian troubles'.[39] The Shah told Sullivan that Eskandari's statement was 'a signal that the Soviets were preparing to back Khomeini by sending weapons into Iran and promoting civil war'.[40]

The Shah's reluctance to use force and disagreements in Washington

The Shah told Sullivan that he had received many messages from Zahedi, saying that the Americans were urging him to get tough. He told Sullivan that he would not kill young people to rule Iran.[41] However, efforts to form a coalition government failed because of the National Front's alliance with Khomeini. The Shah would not abandon his role as commander-in-chief and Zahedi also undermined former Prime Minister Ali Amini's efforts to form a coalition government.[42]

On 20 November, the CIA reported that it did not believe that any compromise solution could include a role for the Shah, adding that Khomeini was prepared to throw Iran into chaos to overthrow the monarch.[43] During this period, there were also a sharp disagreements among US officials over the Shah's state of mind. Even before the formation of the military government, the State Department's Bureau of Intelligence and Research (INR) had been concerned about the monarch's behaviour. On 2 November, INR reported that the Shah had 'reversed to the moods of depression and vacillation'.[44] On 21 November, Treasury Secretary Michael Blumenthal, who had visited Iran, also reported that the Shah was suffering from serious depression. During his meeting with Blumenthal the Shah had repeatedly said that he did not know what to do. Blumenthal told Brzezinski: 'You've got a zombie out there'. He also advised the national security adviser to develop a 'fallback position', adding: 'You've got to understand that we can't count on the Shah any more.'[45]

However, only one day later, the CIA's assessment of the Shah's psychology stated that 'his mood is not inappropriate to this situation, that he is not paralyzed by indecision'.[46] Brzezinski's main contact in Iran, Ambassador Zahedi, repeatedly claimed that the Shah wanted him to be Court Minister or Prime Minister. Carter was reluctant to support Zahedi because the intelligence he had received indicated that Zahedi was wrong.[47] He sided with Vance who instructed Sullivan to advise the Shah to form another civilian government.[48]

Vance emphasized that the US had no contingency plans for saving the Shah and that the US would only evacuate US citizens if there were further unrest in Iran.[49] Vance and the State Department instructed Sullivan to advise the Shah to form a coalition government. However, Brzezinski intervened and cancelled Sullivan's instructions.[50] Brzezinski was trying to galvanize support for a crackdown and he tried to compel the State Department to encourage the Shah to use the iron fist.[51] Brzezinski also tried to include the military option in a letter to Tehran. However, when a draft was sent to the State Department, Vance warned President Carter that the use of force would lead to a large number of casualties and possibly even the outbreak of civil war and Soviet intervention in Iran.[52]

As late as 30 November, the official US position was that the Shah genuinely wished to 'reign but not rule'.[53] US officials did not believe that Khomeini would accept a negotiated solution to the conflict because of his thirst for revenge. Nevertheless, the embassy believed that a negotiated solution was the only way to preserve Iran, if only because many groups saw Khomeini as only a symbolic figure.[54]

However, the embassy's contacts amongst the opposition were now calling for the Shah's immediate departure.[55] The religious month of Muharram was thought to be of critical importance. On 23 November, Khomeini had called on Iranians 'to go into the streets' and described Muharram as 'a month of blood and vengeance'.[56]

Escalating violence and intensification of opposition to the Shah

By now State Department reports indicated that Khomeini's popularity had been waning even among the clergy who complained of his single-minded opposition to the Shah and leftist influence on his organization. Khomeini remained the most powerful religious leader in the country primarily because his potential opponents, such as Ayatollah Shari'atmadari and Ayatollah Kho'i who was in Iraq, were unwilling to challenge him head-on.[57] Moreover, by now, armed leftist groups such as Mojahedin-e Khalq and Cherikha-ye Fada'i-ye Khalq were playing an important role in attacking military bases.[58]

The CIA warned that in the past religious ceremonies had been used to express opposition to the regime.[59] CIA Director Admiral Turner warned that the Shah might not survive Muharram.[60] CIA officials saw 'almost no chance' of a political compromise between the Shah and 'moderate' leaders of the opposition. Indeed they warned that religious leaders could no longer control their followers. However, the Shah could not rely on a policy of repression either.[61]

As far as CIA officials were concerned the Shah was no longer a viable political force. However, the CIA had an extremely optimistic view of the ability of National Front leaders:[62] The Defence Intelligence Agency (DIA) was more optimistic about the Shah, arguing that if the Shah managed to survive Muharram, he might still make a deal with 'moderate' opposition figures.[63]

The debate about Soviet policy in Iran, Vance calls for US acceptance of the revolution

As we saw earlier, Brzezinski believed that the Soviets were involved in orchestrating the opposition to the Shah. Vance recognized that the Soviet Union might have decided to even 'go so far as to encourage the Party to co-operate with Khomeini and other opposition leaders to avoid raising the spectre of a red menace in Iran'.

Vance argued that continued unrest would present the Soviet Union with an opportunity to increase its influence in the Persian Gulf. However, the Soviets did not want a military or an Islamist government on their southern borders. Vance concluded that the Soviets wanted a weak constitutional monarchy which curtailed the Shah's military programmes, while permitting the Soviet Union to wield influence 'perhaps through a legalized Tudeh Party'.[64] He was concerned about the impact of the Iranian upheaval on the Persian Gulf and

Southwest Asia.⁶⁵ However, he believed that détente would prevent Soviet expansionism.⁶⁶ After visiting Iran, deputy CIA director, Robert Bowie, however, concluded that leftists played an important role 'behind the scenes'.⁶⁷

US intelligence was guilty of another kind of omission. In the months before Khomeini seized power, Michael Ledeen from the *New Republic*, Stephen Rosenfeld from the *Washington Post* and Judith Miller from *The New York Times* obtained copies of Khomeini's writings and speeches. They were 'alarmed to discover' that Khomeini held reactionary, anti-Semitic and anti-American views.⁶⁸ They shared their concerns with Senator Henry 'Scoop' Jackson who discussed the issue with Iran specialists at the CIA. However, CIA officials told Jackson that the documents in question 'were forgeries put out by the Israeli Mossad'.⁶⁹ According to Ledeen, CIA officials almost certainly knew the truth, but they either preferred to please the State Department and the White House or they had their own 'agenda'.⁷⁰

By then Vance was predicting 'some combination of military rule with the support of top religious leaders and National Front politicians'. Vance argued that such a regime would be nationalistic, but only the tone, rather than the substance, of its policies would differ from those of the Shah.⁷¹

The opposition had voiced strong criticism of Israel, but it was prepared to maintain Iran's close ties with the US, if it abandoned the Shah.⁷² The new regime would also pursue a high-oil price policy. Iran would sever its ties with Israel and South Africa, prefer to trade and purchase armaments from France or Britain and sharply reduce intelligence co-operation with the US. It would also support Islamic fundamentalist opposition groups in Afghanistan.⁷³ Nevertheless, Vance believed that Iran's economic development needs would ensure its pro-Western foreign policy orientation.⁷⁴

Meanwhile the Shah was trying to form the Regency Council. The State Department never really considered this as anything more than a stopgap measure.⁷⁵ Brzezinski compared all such transition proposals to the formation of the Kerensky government in Tsarist Russia, and the Shah finally rejected the plan on Zahedi's advice.⁷⁶

By early December, Brzezinski had concluded 'that a military government without the Shah was our only viable option'.⁷⁷ Zahedi was consulting closely with General Gholam-Ali Oveisi and Lieutenant-General Manuchehr Khosrowdad about staging a coup. Apparently, they sought to remove the Shah, execute former Prime Minister Amir-Abbas Hoveyda to prove their even-handedness, and then crush the clergy and leftist groups.⁷⁸

Brzezinski sought to remove the opponents of the coup option from the US decision-making process. Brzezinski believed that 'lower echelons at State, notably the head of the Iran Desk, Henry Precht, were motivated by doctrinal dislike of the Shah and simply wanted him [out] of power altogether'.⁷⁹ Brzezinski sought to exclude Precht from the SCC meetings on Iran.⁸⁰ Moreover, Brzezinski requested the Department of Defence to draw up contingency plans for US occupation of southern Iran so as to control the oil fields.⁸¹

The proposal was put to Carter on 5 December. Carter instructed Secretary of Defence, Harold Brown, to 'move expeditiously on this matter'. However, Carter refused to send Brzezinski, or Secretary of Energy Schlesinger, to Iran to signal US support.⁸² At the same time, Brzezinski accepted a proposal from Treasury Secretary Michael Blumenthal that former Under-Secretary of State George Ball should prepare a report on the situation in Iran.⁸³

George Ball's proposal for transition to a post-Shah regime

George Ball, who had long experience of Iranian affairs, had a very low opinion of the Shah and was well aware of the discontent in Iran.[84] Brzezinski 'came to regret' his decision to call on Ball when he discovered that Ball was Vance's 'good friend'.[85] The Shah considered Ball as one of 'those Americans who wanted to abandon me and ultimately my country'.[86]

In the meantime, Vance tried, but failed, to close the Brzezinski-Zahedi channel.[87] At a mini SCC meeting on 5 December to consider Ball's proposals, deputy CIA director Robert Bowie reported that leftists were playing an increasingly important role. However, Henry Precht argued that Khomeini and his religious supporters were the main force in the country.

Ball called for the establishment of a 'Council of Notables' to find a political solution. He said that any government formed by the Shah would not be acceptable to the opposition. Ball's proposals had already been incorporated into a draft State Department policy paper written by Assistant Secretary of State for Near East and South Asian Affairs, Harold Saunders. Ball's recommendations were sent to Sullivan for comment and apparently even co-ordination.[88]

Ball's involvement enabled mid-level State Department officials who opposed the Shah to influence US policy.[89] Sullivan informed Saunders that even Khomeini favoured US involvement but only if it forced the Shah to abdicate. He wanted to ensure that the military would participate in future discussions with 'moderate' opposition figures and senior clerics.

Nevertheless, Sullivan did not believe that Khomeini would make concessions. He warned that the Shah had until the beginning of January to find a solution. Otherwise, 'some more dramatic move would be necessary to prevent the country from chaotic collapse'.[90]

Carter abandons the Shah

It was against the background of growing turmoil in Iran that Carter told a group of reporters on 7 December, that it was up to the Iranians to decide whether they wanted the Shah.[91] His remarks were construed as a vote of no confidence in the monarch. Sullivan reported that Carter's remarks had 'plunged' the Shah 'into a deep depression'.[92] The State Department's 'clarification' and Brzezinski's assurances to Zahedi did not have much effect.[93]

General Oveisi had warned the Shah that unless demonstrators were fired upon, they would march on the palace.[94] The army did open fire on the demonstrators and about 1,500 people were killed between 20 November and 10 December.[95] The Shah decided not to give Oveisi carte blanche after he was informed that SAVAK Director Moghaddam opposed a crackdown.[96] By 8 December, the military government decided to lift the ban on demonstrations in return for a promise that the rallies would be 'orderly and non-violent'.[97]

Nevertheless, there were massive demonstrations on 10 and 11 December. The defection rate from the military was one thousand a day and rising.[98] Even uniformed military officers were taking part in demonstrations against the Shah. More importantly senior military officers, particularly in SAVAK, the police and the office of Martial Law Administration, had begun collaborating with the Khomeini camp.[99]

Opposition groups' infiltration of the military

SAVAK Director General Naser Moghaddam did not inform the Shah or the Iranian high command of the extent of disaffection in the military. Moreover, military intelligence (G-2) reports focused primarily on communist, but not religious, infiltration of the military.[100] Above all, Moghaddam had not given the relevant reports to the counter-intelligence unit of the General Staff and had merely told the Shah that the infiltrators were under surveillance. When General Gharabaghi later asked him why he had not arrested the infiltrators, Moghaddam said that the time was not right.[101]

After the revolution many officers declared that they had started supporting opposition groups several months before the revolution.[102] On 11 December, a small group of non-commissioned officers and enlisted men opened fire on the officer's mess of the elite Imperial Guard at a military base in Lavizan, killing dozens of officers.[103] According to General Fardust's' purported memoirs, shortly after the incident SAVAK supplied the names and addresses of the members of the Revolutionary Council to the Shah, but the monarch instructed SAVAK not to make a move.[104] The Shah felt depressed, but he apparently continued to believe that the armed forces would remain intact.[105] However, in the second half of December, desertions among the conscripts continued to increase and there were acts of sabotage at a number of bases.[106]

The Shah opts for coalition government, the State Department opts for Khomeini

On 5 December, a CIA update had stated that the unrest might 'threaten the survival of the monarchy'. The report concluded that the Shah could not reach an accommodation with the opposition.[107] In December, former CIA station chief in Iran, Arthur Callahan, visited Iran and concluded that the fall of the Shah was imminent.[108] Moreover, on 5 December, the State Department's Bureau of Intelligence and Research (INR) reported that the Shah 'is a spent force [who] sooner or later will be replaced by others no matter what we do'.[109]

At a meeting with Sullivan on 12 December, the Shah said that he was convinced that 'Khomeini commanded enormous power.'[110] He said that surrender would result in the disintegration of the country and that the only option was a coalition government.[111] He said that he had been in contact with National Front figures Shapur Bakhtiar, Karim Sanjabi, and Gholam-Hossein Sadighi.[112]

At this point, the State Department decided to establish direct contact with the Khomeini camp. On 12 December, the head of the State Department's Iran desk, Henry Precht, an American academic Marvin Zonis, who was an adviser on Iranian affairs to the State Department, and Robert Hirschman met one of Khomeini's chief advisers, Ebrahim Yazdi. Yazdi said that Khomeini would establish a transition government in Iran until 'free elections' decided the nature of the future government. He even claimed that people hostile to Islam would not be persecuted.

According to Yazdi, the future regime would not sell oil to Israel and South Africa and would cancel the Shah's arms contracts. Yazdi dismissed the possibility of Soviet intervention and averred that the communists lacked support in Iran. His only concern was that Iraq would seek to take advantage of the unrest in Iran.

Yazdi accused President Carter of supporting the Shah and humiliating the opposition, particularly Khomeini. He claimed that Khomeini was not in favour of violence, but he declared that in the event of a military crackdown, Khomeini would call upon his followers to arm themselves. He said that continued US support for the Shah would lead Khomeini to probably call for attacking Americans in Iran and 'the U.S. would suffer the same fate as the Shah in Iran'. Both sides agreed that neither of them 'would acknowledge that there had been any official contact between Khomeini and the U.S. Government'. Precht's report took many of Yazdi's claims at face value and described Yazdi as an idealist.[113]

The Special Co-ordinating Committee considers George Ball's proposal

The next day, 13 December, the Special Co-ordinating Committee was convened to consider George Ball's report. On the same day, Sullivan reported that the Shah had said that he had three options: (i) a national coalition with himself as a figurehead monarch; (ii) his departure and the establishment of a Regency Council which would relinquish political power to the opposition; (iii) a military junta led by the Shah.[114]

The Shah favoured the first option. Sullivan and Ball proposed that the Shah might form a Council of Notables that would act as a guarantor for any kind of agreement with the opposition.[115] Ball's report said the US 'bore much of the responsibility for the shah's megalomania' and that a crackdown would turn Iran 'into another Lebanon'. Ball urged Carter to establish a 'disavowable channel of communication' with the Khomeini camp.[116] Brzezinski argued that Ball was transferring power to the opposition and called for a military government 'which in time can become increasingly civilianized, as in Turkey or Brazil'.[117]

Carter sided with Vance who 'strongly advocated a political solution with the shah remaining as constitutional monarch, if possible, but without him if necessary, coupled with efforts to preserve the Iranian military as an institution'.[118] Harold Brown feared that too rapid a move towards a civilian government would destabilize the country further and divide the military.[119] Ball, however, managed to torpedo the proposal to send Brzezinski to Iran.[120]

Carter told Ball, in Brzezinski's presence, that he would not follow his policy prescriptions.[121] Vance wanted to ask the Shah to make clear his view of the future of his regime and devise a 'solution short of a military government'. Carter agreed to Vance's proposal. Brzezinski was unenthusiastic, but he felt that if all the other alternatives to a strong military government were exhausted, then Carter would have no choice but to adopt his policy.[122]

The Shah tries to form a coalition government again

The Shah could not make a deal with any of his prime ministerial candidates; Karim Sanjabi, Ali Amini or Gholam Hossein Sadighi.[123] He indicated that he accepted the role of the constitutional monarch but he would remain the commander of the armed forces. Vance correctly concluded that the Shah was 'still unwilling to share enough power with a coalition government to split the moderate nationalists off from the Khomeini followers'.

Vance believed that the Shah was manoeuvring to get the US to support the formation of a firm military government.[124] State Department officials, particularly Henry Precht, believed that Brzezinski's contacts with Zahedi were undermining their efforts. The State Department tried to close the Zahedi channel.[125] Precht argued that the US should try to find 'a graceful exit for the Shah while gaining a fair amount of credit in doing so for the U.S.'.[126]

Sullivan reported to Washington that he intended to immediately implement the contingency plan described in his cable of 9 November which proposed to arrange for the departure of the Shah and senior officers and bring about an accommodation between the military and the national-religious opposition. Sullivan received no reply to his cable, but he heard from Washington that the administration continued to support the Shah and expected him to survive.[127]

On 21 December, NSC official Gary Sick sent a memorandum to Brzezinski, arguing that the US could not possibly support repression in the long run, adding that the Shah had to immediately accept the role of a constitutional monarch and form a government of national salvation.[128] However, even relatively moderate Iranian politicians no longer wanted a constitutional monarchy.

The State Department's refusal to support the 'iron fist' option

The Shah asked Sullivan point-blank on 26 December whether the US would 'support a policy of brutal repression'.[129] Vance instructed Sullivan to inform the Shah that the US would not support repression and that he should quickly form a civilian government. Vance urged Carter to instruct Sullivan to prepare the ground for the formation of a coalition government with strong military support.[130]

On 26 December, the INR warned that the US should seek to establish channels of communication among major opposition groups 'to stave off complete collapse'.[131] By now Shapur Bakhtiar had emerged as the main candidate for the post of Prime Minister. General Moghaddam recommended Bakhtiar to the Shah.[132] The Shah later wrote that he had appointed Bakhtiar 'with reluctance and under foreign pressure'. He described Bakhtiar as 'an Anglophile and an agent of British Petroleum'.[133] According to the Shah, his final decision was made after he met former British Foreign Secretary Lord George Brown who endorsed Bakhtiar and asked him to leave the country. On 29 December, Bakhtiar was asked to form a civilian government.[134]

Bakhtiar was anything but Anglophile. A thoroughly Francophile individual, he likened himself to General de Gaulle and indicated that he might become the head of state.[135] As early as October 1978, Bakhtiar had told Congressman Stephen Solarz and US embassy counsellor George Lambrakis that the US should support the National Front since it 'offered the only alternative to today's corrupt regime or to a Soviet take-over'. Bakhtiar had said that he would not cut off the supply of oil to Israel.[136] He was prepared to work within the parliamentary system, but he did not want to preserve the Shah.[137]

Bakhtiar and National Front leader Karim Sanjabi believed that Khomeini's advisers Yazdi and Ghotbzadeh, whom they considered to be foreign agents, had encouraged him to reject the National Front's overtures.[138] However,

National Front leaders believed that the only way to further their objectives was to form an alliance with Khomeini and gradually undermine his position.[139]

Richard Cottam's contacts with the Iranian opposition

Richard Cottam continued to report to the State Department on his contacts with the Khomeini camp. At a meeting with Khomeini on 28 December, he declared that Mossadeq had failed because he overestimated the power of the US. He advised Khomeini not to make the same mistake.[140]

Cottam warned the US embassy that all opposition groups feared that the unrest would serve communist interests.[141] He advised the embassy to support nationalist and religious opposition forces.[142] He described Khomeini as a 'boundary-setting charismatic leader', who had told him that he did not want a theocracy. Cottam correctly identified Beheshti as one of the main leaders of the movement in Iran.[143]

However, Cottam's knowledge of the leaders of the opposition was very shallow and his reporting was internally inconsistent. For example, according to Cottam, the 'overwhelming majority' of his Iranian contacts had said that Khomeini was a reactionary cleric. Nevertheless, Cottam argued that Khomeini was misperceived because of his movement's decisions to accept Ali Shari'ati's concept of Islamic socialism and downplay Mossadeq's influence on it.[144]

Cottam even believed that Khomeini supported 'an improved role for women'. He was convinced that Khomeini's view of religion was 'centrist and reformist'.[145] Apparently, he was also unaware of the fact that Khomeini had opposed the Shah's reform programme in 1963.

In early January Ambassador Sullivan began to implement the State Department's unofficial policy of effecting the transition to a successor regime led by nationalists and the religious opposition. He did not inform the White House of the substance of his negotiations with the Khomeini camp and he contacted the State Department by telephone or teletype.[146]

The Bakhtiar solution

By now Sullivan was trying to persuade Washington that Shapur Bakhtiar would not be able to govern Iran. He also argued that transferring control over the armed forces to Bakhtiar would cause a major confrontation, which would result in 'the disintegration of the armed forces and eventually in the disintegration of Iran'. The White House's response to Sullivan called into question his 'loyalty' and 'instructed' him to support Bakhtiar. Sullivan decided to resign, but he delayed his resignation until he had safely evacuated the Americans living in Iran.[147]

Carter has misrepresented Sullivan's position to indicate that Sullivan supported Khomeini,[148] and Gary Sick has criticized Sullivan for his failure to understand the weakness of Iranian nationalists.[149] In fact, Sullivan's plans distinguished between a government led by Khomeini and one led by Bazargan and Beheshti. He was trying to stop Khomeini from establishing a radical regime.[150]

Ebrahim Yazdi has indicated that the Khomeini organization was deeply worried that Sullivan would succeed in co-opting younger military officers. If the US influence in Iran declined precipitously then a coup led by younger officers, similar to Sudanese and Libyan coups, might be executed after the revolution.[151]

On 2 January, the Shah told Sullivan that he had decided to appoint Bakhtiar as Prime Minister. Bakhtiar would not control the military and the Shah was sceptical about Bakhtiar's chances of success. However, the Shah made it clear that repression would not work. He also indicated that he would not leave the country if this led to increasing unrest.[152] Sullivan knew full well that the Shah distrusted Bakhtiar.[153]

Sullivan later argued that the Shah considered Bakhtiar to be only a 'figleaf' that would enable him to leave Iran 'in good constitutional form'.[154] However, as we shall see, at the time Sullivan was worried that the Shah would not leave Iran. He warned that the Regency Council was the only other option. By then neither Bakhtiar nor any other politician could prevent a full-scale revolution.[155]

Sullivan's coup warning and the Huyser mission

By now Sullivan had negotiated a transition plan with the Khomeini camp. In return for a hundred senior generals leaving the country with the Shah, the Iranian opposition would select their replacement. In return, the leaders of the 'moderate opposition' would pledge to refrain from arresting or taking revenge against military officers.[156] Sullivan informed the State Department that Khomeini had to approve of this 'tentative agreement'. He proposed a direct approach to Khomeini.[157] Sullivan and the State Department decided that the inspector-general of the Foreign Service, Theodore L. Eliot, Jr., who spoke Persian, would meet Khomeini in Paris to negotiate a transition 'with a minimum of bloodshed'.[158]

On 3 January, Sullivan sent an eyes only message to Vance, saying that 'the moment of truth' had arrived and that all the moderates believed that the Shah had to leave immediately. However, a group of military officers were urging the Shah to abandon Bakhtiar and crack down. Other Iranian generals had threatened to stage a coup to overthrow the Shah if he did not make up his mind.[159] Sullivan warned that the monarch would not leave Iran unless President Carter told him to do so. If Carter did not do so within the next few days, Sullivan warned, the military would stage a coup.[160]

In his memoirs, Vance has said that Carter and his advisers met to discuss Sullivan's assessment of the situation on 4 January. However, according to Carter's memoirs, Vance called him in Guadeloupe on 4 January to inform him of Sullivan's warning. According to Carter's diary entry, on 4 January 'top military leaders' had informed Sullivan that they would prevent the Shah from leaving Iran. They would then a stage a coup and would only give Bakhtiar 'token' support.[161] Sullivan, however, had reported that the Shah was involved in the plan.[162]

Had Vance informed the group of coup planning on 3 January, the day the coup option was discussed, he would have strengthened the supporters of such a coup. Brzezinski was not at all keen on establishing contact with Khomeini and said that the Shah had to be informed first. Sullivan immediately contacted the Shah who, according to Sullivan, listened 'gravely and without enthusiasm'. However, he did not oppose the idea.[163]

Those present at the 3 January NSC meeting were divided over the question of whether they should tell the Shah to 'step aside'. Vance and CIA Director Admiral Turner argued that the US should tell the Shah to leave Iran. Brzezinski contended that the US should not do this because it would alarm US allies in the region and trigger a civil war in Iran.[164]

Nevertheless, two important decisions were made. Firstly, a message to the Shah said that the US supported the Bakhtiar government and that he would be welcome in the US. It concluded by emphasizing the importance of preserving the military.[165]

Secondly, the US would also send the deputy-allied commander in Europe, General Robert Huyser, to Iran. Brzezinski was disappointed with the message, arguing that the US 'should have encouraged the military to stage a coup'.[166] Carter disagreed with Brzezinski who contended that all the US had to do was to 'give a clearer signal and a leader will emerge'. Brzezinski was hoping that the Iranian military would interpret Huyser's orders as encouragement to crush the revolution.[167]

On 5 January, Vance sent Sullivan a cable saying that the Carter administration wanted a civilian government under a Regency Council. The US wanted the military to support Bakhtiar, but if Bakhtiar proved to be unsuccessful, then the military had to have contingency plans to 'restore order'.[168]

The Purpose of the Huyser Mission

The Huyser mission has generated a great deal of controversy. Carter has said that one of Huyser's tasks was to preserve the military in the Shah's absence.[169] He has acknowledged that there were discrepancies between Sullivan's and Huyser's evaluations of the situation and that he 'came to trust Huyser's judgement'.[170]

According to Brzezinski, US officials thought 'the formation of the Bakhtiar government meant that the Shah's regime was finished'. The point at issue was whether the new regime could withstand strong religious opposition. Moreover, US officials differed over the purpose of preserving the military.[171] Brzezinski argued that the military and the security services would survive in the Shah's absence. The CIA totally disagreed with his analysis.[172]

Vance and his advisers, however, were highly sceptical about Bakhtiar whom they thought lacked support among the masses.[173] Nevertheless, Carter believed that Bakhtiar could reach an accommodation with Khomeini.[174] Vance, Christopher, and Mondale wanted Huyser to persuade the military to support a post-Shah civilian government.

Brzezinski stressed the need for publicly supporting Bakhtiar, but he also supported a coup in the event of Bakhtiar's failure. Secretary of Defence Brown, Deputy Secretary of Defence Charles Duncan and Secretary of Energy James Schlesinger supported Brzezinski. Therefore, Huyser's instructions contained a provision for a coup.[175]

According to Sullivan, one of Huyser's tasks was to persuade the Iranian high command to disregard their oath of allegiance to the Shah and support Bakhtiar.[176] This was, of course, tantamount to a coup against the Shah.[177] British Ambassador Sir Anthony Parsons has said that the purpose of Huyser's mission was to prevent a pro-Shah military coup.[178] His mission was to ask the military to abandon the Shah and if the monarch refused to transfer power to Bakhtiar, he would 'explore the possibility' of a coup.[179]

Huyser has claimed that he felt the Shah should stay in Iran since the generals had threatened to leave with the Shah or execute a coup.[180] He has made so many contradictory statements that one wonders if those statements were not made to mollify his critics.[181] In any case, what Huyser felt is not particularly important because he followed Washington's instructions.

The Iranian high command's opposition to Shah's removal was the main obstacle to the implementation of any policy. In fact, the Bakhtiar government was not approved by the Majlis until two days *after* Huyser's arrival in Iran.[182] The Shah had indicated that he had been forced to appoint Bakhtiar by the US and Britain.[183] Iranian generals believed that Washington had imposed the Bakhtiar government on the Shah.[184]

Iran's then Chief of Staff, Major-General Abbas Gharabaghi, has contended that Huyser's mission was to prepare the ground for a Khomeini take-over.[185] Bakhtiar's objective, however, only tactically coincided with that of Huyser. He wanted to establish a republic.[186] According to General Gharabaghi, one of Huyser's main tasks was to ensure the Shah's immediate departure.[187]

The military, Gharabaghi has contended, never had a coup plan and had specifically been instructed by the Shah not to stage a coup. The most obvious sign that the Carter administration had abandoned the Shah was that Huyser did not even inform him that he was in Iran until six days after his arrival in the country.[188] As far as the Iranian high command was concerned, the formation of the Bakhtiar cabinet meant that the opposition had won.[189]

8

US POLICY DURING THE COLLAPSE OF THE ANCIEN REGIME AND THE VICTORY OF THE REVOLUTION

US policy during the final days of the Iranian revolution was characterized by bickering and conflicts over strategy. Moreover, by now, two high-ranking Iranian officers, director of the Special Intelligence Bureau, General Hoseyn Fardust, and the chief of staff, General Abbas Gharabaghi, had begun to collaborate with the Khomeini camp.[1]

Brzezinski and General Huyser who had been sent to Iran to study the military situation, continued to argue, however, that the military would be able to maintain its cohesion despite the defections and that, if necessary, it would be able to execute a coup d'etat.[2] However, the political culture of the Iranian officer corps was an obstacle to executing a coup d'etat. Unlike their counterparts in Turkey or Latin American countries, Iranian officers were not politicized. Iranian leaders' perception of one another was often coloured by conspiratorial notions and this made it very difficult for them to work together. However, the debates within the Carter administration no longer affected the pace of developments in Iran.

The Guadeloupe Summit

The summit of Western leaders in Guadeloupe sealed the Shah's fate. President Carter, British Prime Minister James Callaghan, French President Valery Giscard D'Estaing and West German Chancellor Helmut Schmidt attended the summit. Giscard D'Estaing had already abandoned the Shah after a visit to Iran by his adviser Michel Poniatowski in late December. The Shah had bluntly told Poniatowski that any attempt to crush the revolution would only lead to civil war, Soviet intervention, and the disintegration of Iran. He asked Poniatowski to advise D'Estaing to persuade other Western countries to adopt a common position on Soviet policy towards Iran at the Guadeloupe summit.[3]

Poniatowski argued that the West had to form a coalition between the military and the clergy to prevent Iran's drift into the Soviet orbit. He also warned that such a regime might be destabilized as a result of future elections.[4] According to one account, at Guadeloupe, Giscard D'Estaing argued that if the Shah remained in Iran, the US would be embroiled in a civil war and the Soviet Union would intervene in Iran.

D'Estaing said that what Europe needed was Iran's oil and stability in the Middle East. He strongly advised Carter to make a deal with Khomeini.[5] Moreover, the French president informed Carter that the Shah had asked him not to expel Khomeini because he might go to Iraq or Libya and increase his activities.[6]

The unanimity at the Guadeloupe summit did not prevent the participants from blaming one another for the fall of the Shah.[7] According to Giscard D'Estaing, Carter declared that the Shah's position had become untenable and he had to leave Iran immediately.[8] However, according to Carter, the three other leaders told him that the Shah had to leave, but they did not support Khomeini. They agreed that the military had to be preserved.[9]

Coup threats and the Shah's departure

By early January, the military was convinced that Bakhtiar's goal was to establish a republican regime.[10] High-ranking military officers feared that if Bakhtiar succeeded in establishing a republic, he would purge the military High Command in retaliation for the anti-Mossadeq coup of 1953.[11]

On the day Huyser arrived in Iran, Ambassador Sullivan sent an 'eyes only' message to Vance and 'angrily demanded that Huyser be instructed to co-ordinate with him'.[12] Sullivan told Huyser that the US should abandon Bakhtiar and recognize a new regime. He said, however, that a group of military officers were urging the Shah to abandon Bakhtiar and order a crackdown. Vance agreed with Sullivan's assessment that the Shah must leave immediately.[13]

Vance immediately informed Huyser that his instructions had been changed and that he should not contact the Iranian High Command until he received further instructions.[14] He then called Carter, who was in Guadeloupe, and warned him of the military's plan to crack down. Vance advised Carter to revise Huyser's instructions to inform the 'the Iranian military that we will not support this'.[15] He recommended that the US should 'stay away from both the military and the Shah'.[16]

Clearly, Vance was circumventing the president to smooth the transition to a regime led by Khomeini. Carter, however, said that he would not change Huyser's instructions. He wanted Sullivan to ascertain the Shah's position on the military take-over and instructed Vance to tell Huyser not to 'deliver the last message to the Shah, which was urging him to leave the country'.[17]

Carter's instructions to Vance were diametrically opposed to the decision of the day before.[18] He was uncertain about the future orientation of a successor regime and he now believed that the Shah, the military and Bakhtiar would 'prevail'.[19] Thus the US would support a military take-over.[20] Sullivan was instructed to see the Shah to find out whether he supported the military.[21] However, US officials have said that no coup planning had taken place and Brzezinski noted that the Shah had told Sullivan that he had merely been trying 'to put pressure on Bakhtiar'.[22]

Huyser has claimed that no planning had been done.[23] However, he has also written that the Iranian military had begun planning for a take-over in November 1978. In fact, Huyser was anxious to discover if the military had a secret plan.[24] The available evidence suggests, rather strongly, that Sullivan foiled the coup.

The Shah refuses to support a military take-over

The Iranian military had begun planning for a take-over during the Sharif-Emami government.[25] In fact, in December 1978, copies of a highly detailed coup plan were circulating in Tehran.[26] According to former Israeli intelligence official Ari Ben-Menashe, in December, some elements in the CIA sought to enlist SAVAK and the Israeli intelligence in a scheme to assassinate Khomeini and stage a coup d'etat. The Israelis, however, did not think that the Shah could govern Iran. According to Ben-Menashe, former Israeli representative to Iran, Uri Lubrani, presented the plan, which was drafted by Prime Minister Begin's counter-terrorism adviser Rafi Eitan, to the Shah, but the monarch rejected the proposal, arguing that he did not want any bloodshed. Lubrani concluded that neither the Shah nor the military were capable of suppressing the revolution.[27]

In fact, the Shah had rejected a SAVAK proposal to order Khomeini's assassination, arguing that Khomeini was a British agent and that he had to be left alone.[28] The Israeli government sent Uri Lubrani to Iran after appeals from Iranian Air Force General Rabi'i and deputy Defence Minister General Tufanian.[29] Lubrani arrived on 5 January and he had meetings with General Tufanian and 'several people with access to Khomeini's circle'.[30]

Lubrani reported that the Shah would be overthrown and that the revolutionaries would not resume Iran's oil supplies to Israel. In addition, he reported that they would also cancel joint defence projects.[31] Nevertheless, the Israeli government was still hoping that there would be a military take-over in Iran.[32] Moreover, there have been reports that Ariel Sharon had called for Israeli military intervention to prevent the fall of the Shah.[33] However, there is absolutely no evidence that any Israeli official thought of such a risky intervention.

Sullivan seems to have exploited the threat of a coup and the military's call for US assistance to pressure the Shah into leaving the country.[34] The Shah indicated that he would leave Iran soon to strengthen Bakhtiar and that the military would stage a take-over in the event of Bakhtiar's failure.[35] On 6 January, he announced that he would be leaving Iran. However, a group of hard-liners led by General Khosrowdad declared that the military would prevent his departure.[36]

The Shah was worried that the generals could stage a take-over with Israeli or American assistance and refuse to restore him to power.[37] He removed General Oveisi who later left Iran for 'medical treatment'.[38] Moreover, the Shah sharply curtailed the powers of hard-liners such as the commander of the airborne division, General Manuchehr Khosrowdad, commander of the Air Force, General Amir-Hossein Rabi'i, and General Hasan Tufanian who was responsible for arms procurement.[39]

The coup plan was foiled not least because some members of the military High Command were actively collaborating with the opposition. The Khomeini camp even had access to the intelligence on coup planning and it informed Richard Cottam of this.[40] Bakhtiar was also anxious to prevent a coup in order to accelerate the Shah's departure.[41] The Iranian High Command was divided between those who wanted to stage a take-over, such as Generals Rabi'i and Badre'i, and those such as Gharabaghi who sought to form a coalition with the religious opposition to crush the leftists.[42]

Iranian military intelligence reports, which were compiled with the cooperation of US military advisers, made clear that the revolution was instigated by leftist and Islamic Marxist groups and that Islam was only a veneer. The Iranian High Command made it clear to Huyser that the US was obliged to come to their assistance in accordance with the 1959 treaty between Iran and the US.[43] They held Sullivan responsible for the Shah's departure.[44] Huyser, somewhat disingenuously, argued that Shah was leaving of his own free will.[45]

Bakhtiar's efforts to negotiate with opposition

Bakhtiar was prepared to allow Khomeini to return to Iran as a religious leader, but he wanted to 'steal the revolution' from Khomeini.[46] Indeed this was also the policy pursued by some of Iran's veteran politicians such as former Prime Minister Ali Amini.[47] However, the Iranian High Command expected Huyser to do everything for them, deal with ambassadors Sullivan and Parsons, silence the BBC and retrieve the situation.[48]

Bakhtiar began to negotiate with Khomeini even before the Shah's departure from Iran.[49] He sent a message to the Khomeini camp, saying that he was prepared to set up a republic, but not an Islamic republic.[50] Moreover, Bakhtiar indicated that he could not prevent a military crackdown and that he was particularly worried about Israeli activities.[51]

The boldest transition plan was put forward by former Prime Minister Ali Amini who sought to combine the Regency Council and Khomeini's Islamic Council. The Shah even agreed to Ayatollah Beheshti's membership of the Regency Council.[52] Ali Amini would take over the premiership and would welcome Khomeini, but he would not allow the clergy to run the country.[53]

Khomeini rejected Amini's proposal. At the same time, the Khomeini camp was becoming increasingly fearful of the Soviet Union's response to the establishment of an Islamic republic and US support for a crackdown.[54]

Vance's call for negotiations with Khomeini and transition proposals

Despite Khomeini's intransigence, Vance was determined to negotiate with the Khomeini camp. On 7 January, Vance called Carter in Guadeloupe, urging that he 'be authorized to open a direct channel to Khomeini in Paris'.[55] He told Carter that he wanted to tell Khomeini that if Bakhtiar failed, the communists would lead the radical left. Vance had already instructed retired ambassador Theodore Eliot to go to Paris to meet Khomeini.[56] Carter believed that approaching Khomeini would fragment the military and undermine Bakhtiar. He was surprised to learn that the Shah had himself approved of the proposal.[57] Brzezinski managed to persuade Carter to cancel the Eliot-Khomeini meeting.

On 8 January, Carter sent a message to Khomeini through the office of the French President, asking him to stop opposing Bakhtiar. He said that the Shah was leaving and warned that the military might intervene if the situation deteriorated.[58] Ambassador Sullivan, James Bill and Richard Cottam have argued that the cancellation of the Eliot mission radicalized the opposition and prevented a peaceful transfer of power.[59] That is simply not true. The Carter administration continued to negotiate with the Khomeini camp.

According to Ebrahim Yazdi, the Khomeini camp held talks with the US during this period. Yazdi spoke to NSC official Gary Sick, who told him the US wanted direct contact with Khomeini, and held several meetings with US representative Warren Zimmerman.[60] One reason that Khomeini agreed to hold indirect talks with the US was that even his clerical supporters inside Iran had become wary of his radical pronouncements.[61]

Ambassador Sullivan's transition plan

Ambassador Sullivan thought that Bakhtiar was unrealistic and cabled his views to Washington. His cable caused some consternation in the White House because the administration's official policy was to support Bakhtiar. Sullivan simply ignored the White House's instructions and pressed forward with his own plans.

He contacted Ayatollah Beheshti and apparently persuaded General Huyser to advise senior Iranian generals to do so as well. Then he met Bazargan and Ayatollah Musavi Ardebili. Bazargan wanted the military to cooperate with his government. He and his associates had a list of military officers who would be required to leave Iran but who could take their possessions with them and escape any punishment. Both Bazargan and Musavi-Ardebili wanted to preserve Iran's ties with the US.[62]

US embassy political officer, John Stempel, also held meetings with Abbas Amir-Entezam of the Liberation Movement and the head of the Committee for the Defence of Human Rights, Naser Minachi. They agreed to refrain from attacking Bakhtiar in return for US restraint regarding a coup.[63] Meanwhile, the US signed a memorandum of understanding (MOU) with Iran regarding the termination or restructuring of a number of military contracts. By the time of the Iranian revolution, the Iranian government had twelve billion dollars' worth of military equipment on order.[64] The memorandum of understanding was concluded by a Pentagon official, Eric Von Marbod.[65] Gharabaghi has accused Bakhtiar of colluding with Huyser to conclude the MOU. He has argued that that is one of the main reasons that Bakhtiar was reluctant to talk about the Huyser mission.[66]

On 9 January, Huyser reported that the military was concerned that senior officers might leave with the Shah and that the military would then disintegrate.[67] On the same day, Secretary of Defence Harold Brown reported to Carter that the military was still not ready to stage a coup and that Huyser had advocated forming a coalition between the military and the religious opposition. Brown thought that Huyser's advice was 'unrealistic'.[68]

Vance's renewed call for negotiations with Khomeini and the Shah's departure

At a meeting of senior US officials on 9 January, Vance called for a coalition government and a 'direct channel to Khomeini'. Brzezinski, however, was worried that negotiating with Khomeini 'would demoralize the top military leaders and accelerate their exodus'.[69] It was decided that the US should approach Khomeini through the French and warn him to give Bakhtiar a chance to stabilize the situation.

Moreover, Sullivan's plan, which called for an alliance between the military and Khomeini, was rejected. Carter and Brzezinski, in particular, were concerned about the impact of abandoning the Shah on US allies in the region.[70] The most important results of the meeting were, Carter's approval of the Shah's immediate departure, and the preservation of the Iranian military. Brzezinski agreed to the Shah's departure because he thought that the Shah was an obstacle to the resolution of the crisis.[71]

The tenuous alliance between Bakhtiar and the military

The 10 January decision regarding the alliance between the military and Bakhtiar implied transfer of control over the military to Bakhtiar. The administration's decision was immediately relayed to General Huyser. Huyser's task would be to tell the Shah that his rule was over and that he must leave Iran immediately. He was also instructed to stop any pro-Shah military coup by warning the Iranian High Command that if they moved to seize power the United States would cut off all their supplies.[72]

Carter's decision was also relayed to Sullivan. Sullivan, who totally disagreed with the decision to rely on Bakhtiar, fired off an angry cable to Washington describing Carter's decision as 'insane'. Carter instructed Vance to 'get Sullivan out of Iran', but Vance refused to do so. Carter 'reluctantly' agreed to allow Sullivan to remain in Iran, but he increasingly relied on Huyser to provide him with information on developments there.[73]

At his second meeting with the Iranian High Command on 10 January, Huyser made a U-turn and argued that the Shah's immediate departure was essential.[74] Huyser urged Gharabaghi to meet Ayatollah Beheshti and Mehdi Bazargan.[75] General Rabi'i later told the revolutionary tribunal that Huyser threw the Shah out like a dead mouse.[76]

The Iranian military's Crisis Committee decided that they had to prevent the Shah's departure and Khomeini's return. The Shah agreed with this decision and Gharabaghi made it clear to Huyser that if Khomeini returned, there would be a bloodbath.[77]

Huyser continued to ask Gharabaghi to negotiate with Bazargan and Beheshti, but Gharabaghi said that such a meeting would be useless. The Iranian High Command concluded that the US had thrown its weight behind Khomeini.[78] General Gharabaghi reported Huyser's recommendation to the Shah, who merely said that he knew Beheshti.[79] The issue was brought to a head the next day when Huyser and Sullivan met the Shah. According to the monarch, the only thing that interested Huyser and Sullivan was the date and hour of his departure.[80]

Huyser raised the issue of transferring control of the military to Bakhtiar, but the Shah did not give a clear reply.[81] After the meeting, the Shah was convinced that he had lost US support.[82] In his report to Washington, Sullivan pointed out that the US must abandon the Shah and advised Carter to make the Shah aware of the US assessment that the military and religious forces had to form an alliance to preserve Iran's territorial integrity and contain communism.[83] Sullivan also warned Carter not to support or meet the Shah when the latter reached his exile.[84] The Carter administration did not even reply to Sullivan's cable. Brzezinski and the Pentagon instructed Huyser to prepare the military for a crackdown.[85]

The Carter administration's contacts with the Khomeini camp

By 11 January, all senior US officials except Brzezinski advocated reaching an accommodation with Khomeini whom they believed would not pose a threat to US interests because he did not know how to govern. The majority of US officials believed that the new regime would be a coalition of the military and National Front elements, with Khomeini as a figurehead. Thus, they argued that it was imperative for the US to help the opposition oust the Shah and Bakhtiar as quickly as possible.

The NSC, however, vehemently disagreed with this optimistic analysis.[86] On 12 January, Brzezinski sought to convince Carter to support a coup, arguing that he disagreed with 'some Iran experts' who believed that Khomeini would play the role of a 'venerable sage'.[87] Carter disagreed with Brzezinski.[88] The Shah, in any case, feared that a military crackdown would lead to Soviet intervention and the intensification of secessionist tendencies. He told Gharabaghi to formally deny the veracity of the rumours of a coup and prevent a coup.[89]

The Shah left Iran on 16 January amid scenes of jubilation staged by the Iranian people. On the same day, Zimmerman met Yazdi in Paris and told him that Sullivan had reported that Huyser had prevented a coup. Zimmerman invoked the military's fear of the Tudeh to persuade Yazdi to delay Khomeini's return to Iran. The military was concerned that the Tudeh had a masterplan for provoking a confrontation between the military and Khomeini's supporters. Zimmerman made it clear that Khomeini must delay his return to Iran and authorize Beheshti to meet the military commanders. Moreover, the US warned that if Khomeini tried to overthrow Bakhtiar, the military would stage a coup.[90]

Yazdi's notes show that Beheshti had started negotiating with the military without Khomeini's authorization.[91] Khomeini wanted the US to prevent a coup, but he did not want to negotiate with the military. However, Beheshti persuaded Khomeini to authorize him to do this.[92]

Khomeini replied, through Yazdi, to the US message. He said, rather absurdly, that the military and the communists were in tacit collusion to destroy the Islamic movement. He wished to know if the US wished to preserve the monarchy or the military. He also asked if the US was destroying or removing all the military equipment from Iran.[93] Yazdi believed that the US was using the threat of a coup and Tudeh activities to delay Khomeini's return, thereby enabling Bakhtiar to change the constitution and steal the revolution from Khomeini. Moreover, he feared that the US proposal of an alliance between the military and Khomeini might later enable the military to stage a coup against Khomeini.[94] Nevertheless, after the Shah's departure the Liberation Movement thanked the US embassy for preventing a coup.[95] However, they were only interested in a deal that would abolish the monarchy.[96]

By now the US and the Iranian military had intelligence indicating that the PLO was smuggling arms into Iran.[97] Moreover, the Soviets, who were supporting the opposition, were warning that the US would stage a coup if Bakhtiar collapsed.[98] However, it was difficult for the Iranian military to stage a coup. Moreover, Bakhtiar opposed a crackdown.[99] Bakhtiar was trying to modify the constitution and make a deal with Khomeini.[100] However, he feared that hard-line generals would remove him if he made a deal with Khomeini.[101]

Negotiations between the military and religious opposition

The day after the Shah's departure, General Huyser again advised the Iranian

High Command to establish contact with religious leaders.[102] Huyser informed Secretary of Defence Harold Brown that the military could hold together, while coup planning continued. However, Brown was worried that it might collapse.[103] Huyser said that the military and religious leaders would hold talks on the 18th and that, if necessary, in about a week, the military would be ready to stage a takeover.[104] When Brown enquired about estimated casualties in the event of a coup, Huyser responded that, 'Some 10,000 deaths now could save a million lives later'.[105] Huyser, however, reported that Sullivan and other embassy officials still believed that the Iranian military was 'a paper tiger'.[106]

Failure of Efforts to Construct a Religious Counterweight to Khomeini

Bakhtiar had concluded that Ayatollah Shari'atmadari and other conservative clerics would consider his government as more acceptable than Khomeini's brand of Islam.[107] Shari'atmadari and other conservative clerics opposed Khomeini because they believed that the Ayatollah was surrounded by radicals and communists who would take advantage of his call for violence to establish a leftist government in Iran.[108] Shari'atmadari challenged Khomeini's use of the title of Imam and his comparison of the Iranian revolution with the advent of Islam.[109] Khomeini's followers described Shari'atmadari as a puppet of the Shah and the US.[110]

Acting through generals Fardust and Moghaddam's protégé, Hedayatollah Eslaminia, Shari'atmadari tried to persuade the US embassy to prevent Khomeini from coming to power.[111] US embassy officials believed that Shari'atmadari and other religious leaders regarded the Shah as a 'bulwark against Bolshevism.' The embassy, however, had concluded that it was too late to construct a 'moderate' alternative to Khomeini.[112]

Moreover, Sullivan did not inform Huyser that Shari'atmadari had requested extensive US support and argued that the establishment of an Islamic Republic would be inevitable.[113] On 20 January, Sullivan's British counterpart, Anthony Parsons, sent his last analysis to London, arguing that the generals had to 'transfer their allegiance' to Khomeini and that the only man who could effect the transition was Mehdi Bazargan.[114]

Bakhtiar's efforts to negotiate with Khomeini and the issue of coalition

The greatest threat to Khomeini's position came from the Mojahedin-e Khalq and the Cherikha-ye Fada'i-ye Khalq. These groups began to operate independently in mid-January.[115] Some clerics appealed to the left not to act independently until after the change of government.[116] Khomeini knew full well that democracy would not reduce the appeal of the left.[117] His religious supporters, the Hezbollahis, attacked leftist gatherings and universities shouting 'Death to Communism'.[118] The conflict between the Hezbollah and the Mojahedin-e Khalq also surfaced during this period.[119]

Generals Fardust and Moghaddam believed that a coup would only exacerbate the situation and prepare the ground for Soviet intervention. Some former Iranian officials believe that the Shah instructed Fardust to co-operate with the Khomeini camp in order to prevent Iran's slide into the Soviet camp.[120] According to Fardust's purported memoirs, he paid no attention to Bakhtiar's instructions and acted independently. Fardust has claimed that he sent a message to Bakhtiar asking him to resign.[121]

According to Iranian counter-intelligence and military sources, Fardust was the link between the military and the leaders of the opposition, at least since the Shah's departure.[122] Mehdi Bazargan consulted Fardust before making appointments in the Iranian military and promised Moghaddam to retain him as the SAVAK director or the director of military intelligence after the revolution.[123] Fardust also played an important role in foiling coup attempts.[124]

From 17 January onwards, Bakhtiar, supported by Moghaddam, began to hold talks with the opposition in an effort to find a way of bringing Khomeini into a coalition government. The main point at issue was the terms of Bakhtiar's resignation.[125] Sullivan was optimistic that Khomeini's decision to delay his return to Iran would enable the US to prepare the ground for negotiations between Bakhtiar and the opposition.[126] Indeed, John Stempel concluded that Bakhtiar had already made a deal with the opposition.[127]

Bakhtiar's negotiations with the opposition and Brzezinski's support for a coup d'etat

On 18 January, the Iranian High Command bluntly told Huyser that Bakhtiar would collapse the following day and that they had to stage a coup. The commanders were also concerned about 'an increased level of alert in Iraq, Turkey, Afghanistan, and the Soviet Union'.[128] Huyser said that 'the US would take care of all external threats'. He dissuaded the military from staging a coup.[129]

Bakhtiar exploited the coup threat to gain leverage in his negotiations with Khomeini.[130] He warned Khomeini that a lot of his supporters were in fact communists and that the clergy strongly opposed him.[131] He said that he would not allow the Revolutionary Council to run alongside his own government,[132] but he indicated that he was prepared to accept the abolition of the monarchy.[133] He dispatched Seyyed Jalaleddin Tehrani, who had saved Khomeini's life, to negotiate with Khomeini.[134]

On 18 January, Carter indicated at a news conference that he was preparing his country for a change of regime in Iran.[135] Once again, Brzezinski tried to persuade Carter to support a military coup. On 18 January, he warned Carter that,

> Iran was likely to shift piecemeal to an orientation similar to that of Libya or in to anarchy, with the result that our position in the Gulf would be undermined, that our standing throughout the Arab world would decline, that the Israelis would become more security-oriented and hence less willing to compromise, that the Soviet influence in south-western Asia would grow, that our allies would see us as impotent, that the price of oil would increase, that we were likely to lose some sensitive equipment and intelligence capabilities germane to SALT, and that there would be severe domestic political repercussions.[136]

Brzezinski argued that over the next two weeks the US might have to support a military coup. Harold Brown agreed with Brzezinski. Brzezinski urged

Carter to discuss the matter with such figures as former Secretary of State Henry Kissinger, former President Gerald Ford, and Senator Robert Byrd to maximize domestic support for a coup d'etat. He warned that the US was perceived as being supportive of 'a post-Bakhtiar coalition government, including perhaps Khomeini, and that this was devastating to our credibility'.[137]

Carter's support for Brzezinski and collapse of coalition negotiations

Brzezinski's memorandum influenced Carter who told his advisers that the US should tell Bakhtiar that it would oppose a coalition that included Khomeini.[138] Carter had concluded that the US could only rely on the military and officials of the Shah's regime. Vice-president Mondale and Vance, on the other hand, supported a coalition with Khomeini.[139] However, Carter strongly supported Brzezinski, declaring: 'The threat of a military coup is the best way to prevent Khomeini from sliding in to power.'[140]

Huyser's new instructions said that Bakhtiar had to broaden his base of support by gaining the support of non-communist forces, particularly religious groups. However, 'There was no question of transforming the government into a coalition with Khomeini'.[141]

Huyser concluded that the reason Brown had given him new instructions was that Sullivan had been pressing for a coalition with Khomeini.[142] Negotiations between Bakhtiar and the Khomeini camp collapsed on 20 January because Khomeini was not prepared to negotiate with Bakhtiar's envoy Seyyed Jalaleddin Tehrani.[143] According to Abolhasan Bani-Sadr, the negotiations collapsed due to US threats to support a coup.[144]

On 20 January, the US embassy sent a report to the State Department on the state of the Iranian military, describing it as 'a paper tiger'. It warned that desertions were increasing, adding: 'If Khomeini came back, practically the whole lot would defect.'[145] Chief of Staff General Gharabaghi proved Sullivan right when he declared on 21 January that the military would not stage a coup or back any particular group and that it would only intervene to preserve the territorial integrity of Iran. Moreover, Gharabaghi tendered his resignation to Bakhtiar.[146]

Bakhtiar persuaded Sullivan, through Huyser, to ask Gharabaghi to withdraw his resignation. Sullivan agreed to his request, against his better judgement.[147] Huyser has said that he did not trust Gharabaghi because the general was in contact with the opposition and was not decisive.[148] Indeed, on the same day that Gharabaghi tendered his resignation, Khomeini told the British media that he had made a deal with the military.[149]

Bakhtiar failed to persuade senior religious figures such as Ayatollah Shari'atmadari to side with him. Khomeini's followers called Shari'atmadari a SAVAK agent, and it was reported that Khomeini's and Shari'atmadari's followers had clashed in Tabriz.[150]

At the same time, Ayatollah Shari'atmadari and other prominent clerics were concerned that Khomeini's rejection of constitutional processes would trigger a coup d'etat in Iran.[151] Shari'atmadari and the internal opposition were trying to combine the Regency Council and Khomeini's Islamic Council.[152]

Bakhtiar's manoeuvres

US embassy continued its efforts to bring Bakhtiar and the opposition groups together.[153] Mehdi Bazargan and the Revolutionary Council in Tehran tried to persuade Khomeini to hold direct negotiations with Bakhtiar in Paris.[154] A dispute followed in the Khomeini camp about whether Khomeini should meet Bakhtiar. According to Ebrahim Yazdi, Khomeini did not really want Bakhtiar to resign because he believed that Bakhtiar's resignation would trigger a military coup and that even a failed coup would culminate in a bloodbath.[155]

Moreover, Ayatollah Beheshti had also contacted Khomeini and advised him to establish contact with the military. Khomeini wanted to ensure that the army would not stage a coup and he asked Beheshti to assure military officers that a revolutionary government would treat them better.[156] The main preoccupation of US officials remained the containment of leftist groups. The US embassy reported: 'Marxist-Islamic issue, long denied by many oppositionists, is now too obvious to be ignored.'[157]

Ayatollah Shari'atmadari's confidant Naser Minachi told the US embassy that he was concerned that hard-liners in the military might attempt to assassinate Khomeini. Shari'atmadari and other conservative religious leaders wanted to prevent a coup d'etat or the disintegration of the military and civil war. The embassy strongly advised the opposition and the military to unite.[158]

Carter refuses to support efforts to bring about the fall of Bakhtiar

Ambassador Sullivan sought to bring down Bakhtiar as quickly as possible. In a personal message to Vance, Sullivan said that Bakhtiar was determined to succeed, but he 'was not amenable to American advice'. The military commanders, Sullivan reported, were negotiating with Beheshti and would not support Bakhtiar. They would only act as a 'neutral guarantor of the constitution and public order'.

Sullivan and Huyser's main concern was that clashes between the clergy and the military would prepare the ground for a leftist take-over. According to Vance, Huyser requested that if Bakhtiar failed, the military should 'attempt to negotiate an understanding with Khomeini'.[159] On 23 January, the State Department reported that both Sullivan and Huyser had requested Washington to allow them to proceed with their plan to form a coalition government between the military and the religious elements.[160] In fact, the record suggests that Huyser was thinking of staging a coup to prevent Khomeini's return.

In his account, Vance has cleverly linked Huyser with the proposal to form a coalition between the military and religious elements and downplayed the significance of his own and Sullivan's actions.[161] However, Huyser drew a sharp distinction between Beheshti and Khomeini. Huyser welcomed the appearance of Marxists because this proved that they 'were not a figment of the military imagination'. Moreover, according to Huyser, this meant that the US 'should be able to make some form of common cause with the religious leaders against this menace'.[162]

Harold Brown feared that Khomeini's return would result in a premature coup or the disintegration of the military.[163] Huyser discussed with Moghaddam the idea of informing Khomeini that he would be assassinated upon his arrival in Iran. Moghaddam said that he was negotiating with the religious opposition

and warned Huyser that the military would prevent Khomeini from staging a take-over.[164] Washington, however, instructed Huyser that 'Khomeini's return was not in itself a cause for implementing the contingency plans.'[165]

Bakhtiar wanted to delay Khomeini's return to gain time to abolish the monarchy. The main point at issue in the negotiations between Bakhtiar and the Khomeini camp was Bakhtiar's own resignation. However, when Bakhtiar failed to persuade the military and Khomeini to accept the modification of the constitution, he decided to threaten Khomeini. Harold Brown reported that Bakhtiar had told General Huyser that he would divert Khomeini's plane and arrest him.[166]

Brzezinski advised Carter to give Bakhtiar the green light to arrest Khomeini. Vance, however, argued that any attempt to block Khomeini's return or to arrest him on arrival would result in the fall of Bakhtiar and the disintegration of the military.[167] Carter initially agreed to give Bakhtiar the go-ahead to arrest Khomeini. However, Vance contended that 'Khomeini might even get killed in the process, setting in motion altogether unforeseeable consequences.'[168] The administration continued to hold meetings on the subject on 23 and 24 January. Brzezinski and Brown argued that the US should support Bakhtiar's initiative, but Vance continued to oppose it. Carter eventually approved Bakhtiar's decision.[169]

On 23 January Bakhtiar asked French officials to send a message to Khomeini, warning him that his return to Iran would result in a bloodbath. The French reluctantly agreed to carry the message. However, they made it clear to Bakhtiar and the Khomeini camp that they did not want to interfere in Iran's internal affairs.[170]

The French decision was tantamount to supporting Khomeini because Bakhtiar was negotiating from a position of weakness. On 24 January, he sent a personal messenger to Paris with a letter proposing a constitutional assembly on condition that Khomeini delayed his return to Iran for three weeks.[171] According to Gharabaghi, Bakhtiar wanted to change the constitution and steal the revolution from Khomeini.[172]

On 24 January, Warren Zimmerman met Ebrahim Yazdi to deliver a message partially written and approved by Bakhtiar. The message warned Khomeini that unless appropriate constitutional procedures were followed, there would be 'a direct, extraconstitutional confrontation' which would hurt everyone including 'religious elements and their followers'. The message also drew the Khomeini camp's attention to the Tudeh Party's statement supporting the Revolutionary Council and the provisional government. It warned Khomeini that it would be 'premature' for him to return to Iran.[173]

The failure of the coup option

Meanwhile the Shah's supporters were planning to stage a coup d'etat. Until now the Shah had refused to listen to Ambassador Zahedi, but it seems that in late January when he was in Morocco he briefly contemplated the possibility of staging a military take-over similar to the one which returned him to power in August 1953.[174]

Zahedi and Colonel Jahanbani, however, formulated a hare-brained scheme to hijack Khomeini's plane and force him to negotiate a deal at gunpoint. If

Khomeini refused to make a deal they would kill him.[175] The conspirators would carry out these actions as 'renegades'. The Shah could then condemn their actions or order their arrest and execution.[176] According to the conspirators the Shah rejected this scheme, saying, 'You must be mad. If you carry on like this I will ask [King] Hassan to put you behind bars.'[177]

Despite the Shah's expressed opposition to a coup, the Iranian military had done extensive contingency planning and the hard-liners intended to implement their plans on 11 February.[178] Indeed, some of the generals had developed plans for assassinating Khomeini and crushing the revolution.[179]

The available evidence suggests that General Moghaddam and General Fardust informed the opposition. Moghaddam was killed a few months after the revolution under suspicious circumstances. Indeed, some believe that he was the victim of revenge killing and that he was not executed.[180] Moghaddam believed that the communists were taking advantage of Khomeini's opposition to the regime to achieve their own objectives.[181] However, he told other generals that killing Khomeini would exacerbate the situation and result in more bloodshed.[182]

Moghaddam informed deputy SAVAK station chief in the US, Mansur Rafizadeh, that General Khosrowdad and his supporters had decided to shoot down Khomeini's plane, adding that he had placed Khosrowdad under surveillance. He asked Rafizadeh to inform the CIA. According to Rafizadeh, the CIA asked him to send Moghaddam a message, saying that Khosrowdad should be prevented from issuing orders to shoot down the plane. The CIA believed that such an act would only cause unnecessary bloodshed.[183] Rafizadeh passed the CIA's message to Moghaddam who agreed to prevent Khosrowdad from acting.

Moghaddam believed that he could secure his position in a post-Shah government because he had prevented more bloodshed.[184] He did not believe that Khomeini would be the future leader of Iran. He thought that Bazargan would succeed Bakhtiar and that Ebrahim Yazdi would resolve the crisis with US assistance.[185]

Moghaddam was simultaneously negotiating with Bazargan to prepare the ground for the transition to a post-Shah regime. Moghaddam indicated that Khomeini's life was in danger and that the military was anxious to prevent bloodshed. Bazargan gave him Beheshti's telephone number so that the two of them could arrange a meeting.[186]

The Khomeini camp believed that Bakhtiar's and Moghaddam's overtures were made on Washington's instructions and that Washington was exaggerating the influence of leftist groups and the threat of a coup to force them to surrender.[187] According to Ebrahim Yazdi, the French informed the Khomeini camp that there was a plot to assassinate their leader. Khomeini's entourage believed that the CIA was plotting against him.[188]

The French informed Khomeini's entourage that Bakhtiar would either order an attack against Khomeini's plane or seek to divert it and have Khomeini arrested.[189] The Khomeini camp also received warnings from other sources.[190] Khomeini himself was also concerned about being poisoned and a special food taster was soon appointed to ensure that he would not be poisoned.[191]

Nevertheless, Khomeini decided to delay his return to Iran. Khomeini and his advisers thought that if Bakhtiar resigned the hard-liners would stage a coup. The leader of the Liberation Movement, Mehdi Bazargan, however, continued his efforts to form a coalition with Bakhtiar.[192]

The question of Bakhtiar's resignation

By the night of 24 January Bakhtiar had personally agreed to Khomeini's return to Iran. More importantly, Bakhtiar 'approved of Khomeini's initial programme'.[193] After the Iranian revolution, Bakhtiar said that he had decided not have Khomeini's plane shot down because he believed that Khomeini would become a martyr.[194] Khomeini's advisers Ayatollahs Mottahari and Zanjani asked Bakhtiar to resign. He said that he would not oppose the establishment of a republic, but he believed that making an announcement on the issue would be tantamount to declaring war on the military.[195]

Indeed Bakhtiar and Mottahari agreed to draft a letter in which Bakhtiar would accept to serve as Khomeini's Prime Minister.[196] Bakhtiar was also negotiating with Ayatollah Beheshti. Beheshti, however, did not fear military intervention.[197] According to another version of events, Bakhtiar wrote his resignation letter but he refused to sign it.[198] Nevertheless, by January 27, Beheshti had persuaded Bakhtiar to go to Paris to negotiate with Khomeini.[199] According to Bani-Sadr, Beheshti and Rafsanjani agreed with Bakhtiar's decision not to resign.[200] However, Beheshti's agreement with Bakhtiar intensified Khomeini's distrust of Beheshti.[201]

Bakhtiar's negotiations with the Khomeini camp broke down because of differences within the Khomeini camp.[202] Later hard-liners would accuse Yazdi and Beheshti of colluding with Bakhtiar and the Pahlavi regime to strike a bargain, which would prevent a complete collapse of the regime.[203]

In an effort to appeal to the US, Khomeini nominated Mehdi Bazargan as provisional Prime Minister. Khomeini's nomination of Bazargan and the latter's declaration that the clergy would remain 'in the background as the guiding political and spiritual force of the revolution' satisfied Secretary Vance, who wanted a smooth transition.[204] As a result, Vance abandoned Bakhtiar immediately.[205]

After holding talks with ambassadors Sullivan and Parsons, Bakhtiar decided to open the airports and allow Khomeini to return to Iran. He took his decision without consulting the Iranian National Security Council.[206] Bakhtiar dismissed objections to his decision, arguing that people would realize that Khomeini was incompetent and he would lose support in the country. Moreover, he told General Gharabaghi that he had negotiated the terms of Khomeini's return to Iran. General Moghaddam supported Bakhtiar in the Iranian National Security Council's discussions.[207]

At the meeting of the Iranian National Security Council on 29 January, the Iranian High Command discussed the possibility of staging a coup to prevent Khomeini from coming to power. Those in favour of staging a coup were Tehran martial law administrator, General Rahimi and the commander of the Gendarmerie, General Mohagheghi. General Moghaddam argued that the opposition was trying to destroy the basis of Iran's national power, which he believed was the military. However, he argued that the use of force would result in the disintegration of the military itself.[208] At the end of the 29 January meeting, the Iranian High Command decided to find a political solution to the crisis.[209]

Indeed, on the same day, Generals Gharabaghi and Moghaddam met opposition leaders Mehdi Bazargan and Ezatollah Sahabi. Gharabaghi made a deal with Bazargan and Sahabi.[210] The military agreed to Khomeini's return to Iran. However, the two sides could not agree whether the Regency Council should continue or whether it should be modified.[211]

Bakhtiar's resignation letter was delivered to Bazargan and Beheshti on 29 January,[212] but Bakhtiar and Khomeini still did not agree on the terms of the resignation.[213] However, the government made no further attempts to prevent Khomeini from returning to Iran.

General Gharabaghi informed General Huyser that the military would support Bakhtiar if he reached an agreement with Khomeini. However, if Khomeini formed a rival government, the military would move only protect key installations and buildings.[214]

Khomeini arrived in Iran on 1 February. Before leaving Paris, he indicated that the opposition had been in contact with the military and said that contacts would be resumed if necessary.[215] As soon as he arrived in Iran, Khomeini made a speech, saying that he accepted neither the government nor the Majlis. Khomeini made it clear that the next government, which would be a caretaker one, had to be appointed by the Revolutionary Council. The caretaker government would then supervise the holding of a referendum and if the people voted for the establishment of a republic, then a republican government would be formed.[216]

Despite Khomeini's intransigence, talks between Bakhtiar and the Liberation Movement resumed immediately after Khomeini's arrival in Iran, but the terms of Bakhtiar's resignation and the issue of the referendum, positing a choice between a monarchy and an Islamic Republic, remained unresolved.[217] Unlike his entourage, Khomeini refused to compromise. The Liberation Movement informed John Stempel of what had transpired.[218] Khomeini made it clear that the only acceptable solution was a temporary Islamic government to supervise the referendum; he was convinced that the military could not withstand a showdown.[219]

By now, even Huyser was convinced that staying in Iran was futile, and the Pentagon approved his departure. Brzezinski, however, feared that the military would see Huyser's departure as a US disengagement from Iran. Vance agreed with Brzezinski's assessment and Huyser was instructed to stay in Iran.[220]

Huyser informed JCS chairman General Jones that the military were ready to stage a coup without him, but he added that he had reservations about General Gharabaghi's ability to lead a coup. He repeated that Sullivan 'who had far wider sources of information' believed that the military was incapable of staging a coup. Huyser made it clear that Sullivan wanted to accommodate Khomeini.[221] President Carter later agreed to Huyser's departure, but he decided to instruct Huyser's deputy General Philip C. Gast to continue Huyser's preparations.[222]

Despite its initial opposition to the formation of a coalition between Bakhtiar and Khomeini, the White House continued to support Bakhtiar long after it had become clear that he was trying to form such a government. For example, Sullivan was instructed to meet Khomeini if Bakhtiar asked him to do so, but if Khomeini asked to meet Sullivan, Sullivan had to consult Bakhtiar first.[223]

Huyser left Iran on 3 February. On 4 February Khomeini appointed Bazargan as Prime Minister and declared that opposition to Bazargan would be 'tantamount to opposing Islamic principles'.[224] On 5 February, General Huyser reported personally to President Carter. He made it clear that he and Sullivan disagreed regarding the Iranian military's ability to crush the revolution. Moreover, 'Sullivan believed that if Khomeini established an Islamic republic, the drift would be eventually toward democracy.' Huyser, however, contended that 'the drift would be toward communism'.[225]

Despite Carter's expression of support for Bakhtiar, State Department officials predicted that Bakhtiar would last only another two or three days. Carter was enraged and convened a meeting with State Department officials, threatening to summarily dismiss them for disloyalty.[226] In spite of this, disagreements persisted over Iran policy between the White House and the State Department.

As Brzezinski had predicted, what ultimately determined the outcome of the power struggle in Iran was the Iranian military's position. Bakhtiar sought to convey the impression that he could not prevent the military from staging a coup if the Khomeini camp did not make concessions.[227] General Fardust and General Moghaddam undermined him, seeking to form a coalition with Khomeini.

General Fardust, the failure of the coup option and a declaration of neutrality

The military split during the final days of the regime. Generals Fardust and Moghaddam played important roles in ensuring that the military would declare itself neutral.[228] Fardust was probably instrumental in foiling the coup scenario favoured by Brzezinski. According to the then CIA Director Stansfield Turner, Brzezinski called for a covert operation to strengthen Khomeini's opponents and politicians who were prepared to cooperate with the Pahlavi dynasty. In early December, Brzezinski wrote to Vance and asked him to persuade US allies to support this effort. Turner claimed that he was 'dumbfounded' that such a proposal could be put forward to support the 'so-called moderate political elements'. Turner claimed that the CIA lacked a covert operation capability in Iran.[229] The evidence suggests that Turner failed to restrain Brzezinski. In early February, George Nathanson, whom the US embassy described as an 'American businessman and self-styled intriguer', arrived in Iran to discuss plans for a coup with Iranian military commanders. Nathanson was assisted by Frank Burroughs, the executive director of Iran-America Chamber of Commerce. There is no evidence that Brzezinski had sent Nathanson to Iran. However, according to his own memoirs, Brzezinski continued to press for the implementation of the coup option until the day the revolution triumphed.

The US embassy bluntly told Nathanson that the US 'will not intervene to save the regime'. Nathanson also approached Fardust. It is highly unlikely that Fardust would have met Nathanson had a high-ranking US government official not sent him to Iran. Fardust rejected Nathanson's proposal for staging a coup and advised him to help Khomeini. He argued that '[the] British and [the] Russians are co-operating in fomenting this crisis'. Fardust said that he wanted the US to work with pro-Western figures like himself and to concentrate on 'moderating Khomeini', arguing that if Khomeini failed, 'the communists are sure to seize power'. Fardust even speculated that Khomeini might accept the constitution and that the Shah might be able to return, 'provided he agrees to reign, not rule'.[230]

Fardust also recommended that the US must ensure that 'the army should support neither Bakhtiar nor Khomeini.'[231] The embassy was astonished at Fardust's contention that the British and the Soviets were co-operating to destabilize the regime and his claim that the existence of a pro-Western government and even the Shah's return would depend upon Khomeini's success. However, the embassy could not 'overlook the strong possibility that this is a provocation'.[232]

General Huyser has written that he suspected Fardust of acting as a Soviet agent because the Soviets were receiving intelligence on his discussions with the Iranian military.[233] General Gharabaghi has disputed his claim, arguing that several high-ranking officers had been in contact with the opposition and that the opposition was responsible for such leaks.[234]

According to some accounts, after the Iranian revolution Fardust was appointed as the chief of the new regime's security service, the SAVAMA. In 1983 he was arrested and charged with spying for the Soviet Union. According to General Fardust's biographer Colonel Isa Pejman, the Shah instructed Fardust to co-operate with Khomeini to prevent the country from going communist.[235]

The evidence strongly suggests that the main reason the Iranian High Command decided to surrender to the Khomeini camp was its fear of a communist take-over.[236] By now opposition groups were openly arming themselves and the mosques were arming Khomeini's supporters. Meanwhile, Bakhtiar continued his efforts to change the constitution.[237]

At a meeting of the National Security Council on the same day, Bakhtiar instructed General Moghaddam to set in motion SAVAK's emergency plan for arresting opposition figures. Gharabaghi has argued that Bakhtiar was only seeking to demonstrate his toughness to retain the military's support for his government.[238]

The evidence suggests that at this point, faced with a choice between a republic led by Bakhtiar and one led by Khomeini, the officers who were collaborating with the Khomeini camp decided to remove Bakhtiar.[239] The situation came to a head on February 11. At a meeting of senior US officials, State Department officials, Warren Christopher and David Newsom argued that the US had to recognize a government led by Bazargan.[240]

Brzezinski, however, was still pressing for a coup. He warned that 'if the military made an accommodation with the Bazargan government, the armed forces would disintegrate, with major domestic and foreign implications'.[241] However, Carter had concluded that the US had no choice but to work with Bazargan and he wanted him to be asked to protect the lives of Americans in Iran.[242] When Huyser was contacted, he said that a coup 'was not feasible without a massive U.S. commitment'.[243] Huyser's assessment settled the debate. However, Brzezinski continued to argue that the US had to use its leverage.[244]

After the declaration of neutrality, General Khosrowdad and General Badre'i who sought to stage a military take-over were assassinated. The provisional government appointed Fardust as the chief of intelligence and Gharabaghi as Chief of Staff.[245] Generals Gharabaghi, Fardust, Moghaddam and Hatam were responsible for the Iranian military's declaration of neutrality, which was, in effect, capitulation to Khomeini's demands.[246]

The collapse of US strategy

As we have seen throughout this study, US officials had adequate intelligence to make better decisions. The fact that they did not was because of sharp disagreement over strategy. According to General Gharabaghi, the conflict between the two sharply divergent currents in US strategy was reflected in the Iranian government as well.[247] This was most notably the case in the Iranian military and security services. The result was further destabilization and the people's alienation. The Shah preferred to rely on US and British advice to get those countries to make decisions for him. Henry Kissinger's observation that the Shah was overthrown due to his lack of confidence in the Carter administration is very apt.[248]

Some observers of Iranian politics have suggested that the Shah could have avoided the tragedy that befell him by co-opting National Front politicians.[249] The author disagrees with this point of view. Firstly, National Front politicians were not the Shah's strongest opponents. Secondly, even had the Shah brought the National Front into government, it would not have guaranteed his survival. Politicians such as Bakhtiar and Bazargan were determined to oust the Shah. The Shah considered Bazargan to be one of Khomeini's staunchest allies and the man who introduced political Islam into Iranian universities.[250]

US political officer in Esfahan, McGaffey, later offered a trenchant analysis of the upheaval in Iran, arguing that 'venality at the top' and lack of ideological and personal integrity among political leaders and the intelligentsia had caused the chaos in the country.[251]

As Charles Naas later observed, the Iranian elite and the vast majority of educated Iranians firmly believed that foreign powers would somehow rectify the situation in their country.[252] Naas concluded that unlike most members of the Iranian intelligentsia, Khomeini had not relied on foreigners for assistance:[253]

Naas believed that Khomeini had exploited the Shia concept of martyrdom to turn the masses against the Pahlavi dynasty.[254] What Naas did not say was that Khomeini and his followers were just as anxious as the Shah to gain US support. State Department officials were wrong. Khomeini and his allies confirmed the worst fears of their opponents in Washington.

9

THE REGIONAL IMPACT OF THE IRANIAN REVOLUTION

The Iranian revolution had a huge regional and global impact. The fall of the Shah led to a massive increase in the price of oil and the revolutionary regime nationalized Iran's Consortium, thereby ending foreign control of Iran's oil industry. However, the dispute between National Security Adviser Zbigniew Brzezinski and Secretary of State Cyrus Vance hampered President Carter's efforts to formulate a coherent Middle East strategy. Vance sought to cultivate revolutionary Iran, while repairing the damage done to relations with Saudi Arabia and making efforts to broaden the framework of the Camp David Treaty. Brzezinski, on the other hand, increasingly viewed Iraq as the only regional power that was capable of replacing the Shah as the regional hegemon.

The Impact of the Iranian Revolution on the Middle East Peace Process

The Iranian revolution was a geopolitical setback for Israel. Israel had been increasingly isolated after the 1967 and 1973 Arab-Israeli wars and it greatly valued its de facto alliance with Iran. Khomeini and most of his followers considered the Jews as enemies of Islam and occupiers of holy Muslim lands and hated Israel for its support of the Shah.[1] Moreover, many Iranian revolutionaries had been trained at PLO camps. The PLO considered the Iranian revolution as a major victory for the Palestinian cause. Arafat and his colleagues saw Camp David as a major setback because it removed the largest Arab country, Egypt, as a front-line state. Arafat hoped that revolutionary Iran would replace Egypt. The PLO's involvement in the Iranian revolution had demonstrated its subversive capability.[2]

The PLO's main objective was to prevent other Arab leaders from emulating Egyptian President Anwar Sadat. It exploited its alliance with Khomeini to put pressure on Arab governments that wanted to make peace with Israel.[3] Initially it seemed that Arafat's optimism was warranted. Arafat was the first foreign leader to visit Iran. On 19 February, the former Israeli consulate in Iran was turned over to the PLO.[4]

The week following Arafat's visit, a PLO spokesman declared that during Arafat's discussions with Khomeini, the two men had discussed a common strategy against Israel and 'the liberation of Jerusalem'.[5] Iran stopped oil shipments to Israel and broke off diplomatic relations with Egypt. These actions cost Iran 700 million dollars in yearly revenues.[6] However, Israeli officials had already begun to diversify their sources of oil supply.[7]

The revolution was also an opportunity for Israel because it dramatically increased its strategic significance to the US and significantly reduced, at least for a while, the Carter administration's pressure on it to agree to a comprehensive solution to the Arab-Israeli conflict. Israeli Prime Minister Menachem Begin sought to manoeuvre the Carter administration into supporting Israel as the only reliable US ally in the Middle East.[8]

Brzezinski has best summed up the administration's approach to Camp David in the wake of the Iranian revolution, arguing that 'the strategic pivot of the American position in the Persian Gulf area, Iran, was literally crumbling before our eyes', therefore, 'to let the Camp David accords slip away would be to turn a triumph into disaster, with unforeseeable consequences for the Middle East as a whole'.[9] In early January 1979, the Carter administration re-assessed its policy towards the Arab-Israeli theatre. The administration sought to achieve two objectives. First, to conclude a bilateral Egyptian-Israeli treaty by offering Israel a memorandum of strategic co-operation. Secondly, to counter-act the adverse effects of the abandonment of a comprehensive settlement and the collapse of the Shah's regime on Saudi Arabia by emphasizing the gravity of the Soviet threat to the region.

The Carter administration concluded a memorandum on strategic co-operation with Israel even though Carter did not believe that Israel was a US strategic asset.[10] Moreover, the US agreed to extend the US guarantee of Israel's energy supplies.[11]

The impact of the Iranian Revolution on Saudi Arabia and the oil market

Khomeini had made it abundantly clear that he intended to export the revolution to neighbouring countries. Khomeini's vision of Islam was fundamentally different from that of the Saudi monarchy.[12] Moreover, the Syrian-Iraqi rapprochement strengthened radical opponents of Camp David in the Arab world. Saudi Arabia and other Arab sheikhdoms of the Persian Gulf saw the Iranian revolution as a major upheaval that had completely transformed their geopolitical environment. The Iranian revolution convinced the Saudis that instability in Iran could affect the whole region.[13]

These events exacerbated the power struggle and policy differences within the House of Saud and culminated in a serious split in the Saudi leadership. Crown Prince Fahd's strategy was discredited and Fahd was blamed for the precarious situation in which Saudi Arabia found itself.[14] King Khalid, Prince Abdullah, Foreign Minister Saud al-Faisal and their supporters sought to distance the kingdom from the US.[15] Saudi Arabia's defiance of Washington was made abundantly clear during Secretary of Defence Harold Brown's visit to the region between 9 and 19 February, 1979. The Saudis publicly revealed their disagreement with the Carter administration and cancelled Crown Prince Fahd's visit to Washington in March.[16]

Throughout 1979, the Arab states of the Persian Gulf feared that the Iranian regime's alliance with the PLO had the potential of being transformed into a Shi'a-Palestinian alliance covering the whole Persian Gulf region.[17] However, it would be wrong to argue that the Saudis turned against the US for fear of being attacked by the PLO. Saudi Arabia was far more powerful than the PLO and had been its main financier since 1977. In fact, despite its earlier threats, the PLO did its utmost to persuade Iran's neighbours that the new Iranian regime did not pose a threat to them.[18]

The Saudis concluded that changing Washington's policy towards revolutionary Iran was beyond their capability.[19] The main objectives of King Khalid and Prince Abdullah were to maintain ties with Iraq and to appease revolutionary Iran.[20] Thus both King Khalid and Prince Abdullah sent friendly messages to the Islamic Republic.[21] Saudi Arabia's pursuit of this regional strategy was combined with an effort to punish the US by changing the kingdom's oil policy.

The Iranian Revolution and the Second Energy Crisis

The Iranian revolution triggered the second oil crisis. Some observers even went so far as to declare that the era of cheap oil had come to an end.[22] Since 1969 US imports from the Middle East had almost doubled.[23] The Shah had posed a major threat to the oil companies' operations from the mid 1970s onwards when he indicated that he sought to substantially modify the Consortium agreement. However, the Consortium's policy of punishing the Shah by reducing its off-take of Iranian oil backfired because it dealt a severe blow to the Iranian economy and forced the Shah to cut back many of his programmes, thereby alienating the Iranian people. The Shah was replaced by a regime which pursued far more radical policies.

On 28 February, 1979, the National Iranian Oil Company (NIOC) unilaterally cancelled the Consortium agreement.[24] The National Iranian Oil Company monopolized the production and marketing of Iranian oil. According to the *Petroleum Intelligence Weekly*, Iran's policies seemed to 'spell 'finis'' for the consortium in its role as an oil-buying group and provider of technical services including oil field operations'.[25]

There was a difference of opinion on production policy among officials of the new regime. The so-called moderates and the oil company wanted to increase Iran's production to about 4 mb/d and exports to 3.1 mb/d. However, they were opposed by workers' councils which in effect, functioned as Tudeh party cells. These councils sought to expel foreign technicians. The leftist councils were also demanding thorough management changes.[26] Moreover, radicals in the Revolutionary Council, who were tacitly supported by religious leaders and other groups, wanted to keep daily oil production at much lower levels in order to prepare the ground for creating an 'oil-free' economy.[27]

The new Iranian government reduced the involvement of Consortium companies in the Iranian oil industry and Iran sold oil directly to a large number of customers.[28] British Petroleum and the Royal Dutch Shell companies were the largest customers, initially lifting over 350,000 and 200,000 barrels per day respectively.[29] In the wake of the Iranian revolution, a large number of customers were prepared to pay premium prices on the spot market for Iranian oil.[30]

However, arguments that the Iranian revolution caused the second oil crisis are wide of the mark. Oil-producing nations quickly compensated for the shortage caused by the stoppage of Iranian production. Saudi Arabia rapidly increased its production as Iranian exports decreased at the end of the year. Moreover, Iran itself began to export at 60% of its previous rate of production in March 1979.[31] However, it was Iran's non-aligned foreign policy which deeply concerned advocates of neo-containment in Washington.

The Neo-containment current and US strategy in the Persian Gulf

National Security Adviser Zbigniew Brzezinski, Secretary of Defence Harold Brown and Secretary of Energy James Schlesinger disagreed with the State Department's policy of reaching an accommodation with the new Iranian regime. They believed that the fall of the Shah had created a power vacuum, which the US had to fill in order to prevent Soviet expansion into the region. Schlesinger contended that the world was consuming its inventories at a rate of two million barrels a day greater than the seasonal average. US inventories alone were being depleted at a rate of 500,000 a day in excess of average. Schlesinger warned that the situation was more serious than the 1973 oil embargo.[32]

In the same month Schlesinger declared that the US had to resort to force if necessary to protect its interests in the Persian Gulf.[33] On 25 February 1979, Harold Brown declared that the US would resort to force, if necessary, to safeguard its oil interests in the Middle East.[34] On 28 February, Brzezinski sent a memorandum to Carter, arguing for constructing a new 'security framework' in the region. His proposal entailed the abandonment of the Carter administration's earlier plans such as neutralization of the Indian Ocean, a strategic objective that the State Department was still pursuing.[35]

Some Treasury Department officials believed that the Iranian regime was hostile to the US and was likely to withdraw Iran's assets from the US, thereby causing a banking crisis. In a 12 February legal memorandum requested by the Office of General Counsel, the possibility of an asset freeze was seriously contemplated.[36] Thus nine months before the hostage crisis, legal experts in the Department of Treasury contended that the necessary conditions for invoking the International Emergency Economic Powers Act existed.[37]

The emergency was allegedly caused by the vulnerability of the US financial and banking system to the threat of a withdrawal of Iranian assets. However, before the Treasury Department reached that conclusion, the Carter administration had repeatedly argued that even the withdrawal of all of OPEC's assets would not threaten the US financial system. Moreover, US had 'immediate access to several alternative sources of funds'.[38]

As late as April 1979, in a letter to the Government Accounting Office, Assistant Secretary Fred Bergsten stated that withdrawal of OPEC deposits would be problematic, but not 'catastrophic' for the US.[39] As a US Congressional investigation concluded: 'Such a case for a freeze made at that time on economic grounds was tenuous at best.'[40]

A significant cross-section of US business elite supported military intervention in the Persian Gulf.[41] On 5 March, the General Accounting office released a study seriously arguing that the oil shortage, allegedly caused by the Iranian revolution, was artificial.[42] However, a CIA report released on 21 March, 1979, expressed doubt as to whether the US economy was able to 'to recover from the loss of Iranian oil', and warned of 'major shortages, higher prices, and an economic slowdown'.[43] The report left little doubt that the US had to regain control over Iranian oil.[44] However, according to Assistant Secretary of State for Near Eastern and South Asian Affairs, Harold Saunders, Iran continued to supply the same amount of oil to the US as it had done before the revolution. Saunders explained that the administration had encouraged economic ties between the US and Iran to stabilize the situation in revolutionary Iran.[45]

In fact, the oil shortage was primarily caused by the oil companies determination to increase their profit margin and the US government's decision to improve the country's competitive position vis-à-vis its economic rivals, West Germany and Japan.[46] However, Carter was forced to change his policy by the summer because of the political consequences of high energy prices.

Saudi opposition to US regional strategies

The Saudi leadership decided to punish the US for its Middle East policy by cutting back supplies to Aramco and concluding bilateral agreements with several West European countries.[47] Carter's response to the Saudi backlash was to authorize Vance to seek to broaden the Camp David settlement by entering into secret talks with the PLO.[48] At the same time, Harold Brown told the Senate Foreign Relations Committee 'that the United States was not committed to defend Saudi Arabia against external or internal threats'.[49] On 15 April, the *Washington Post* reported that the CIA had warned that Saudi Arabia had become extremely unstable.[50]

Nevertheless, Saudi Arabia broke off diplomatic relations with Egypt and cut off economic and military assistance to it.[51] Vance later told the House Foreign Affairs Committee that 'American relations with Saudi Arabia had deteriorated because of 'clear and sharp differences' over the Egyptian-Israeli peace treaty.'[52]

The Saudis insisted that they were doing their utmost to prevent further oil price increases, but they also made it clear that the industrial countries had to cut back their imports.[53] The Carter administration remained divided on the issue. Schlesinger virtually encouraged the Saudis to increase their price when he said: 'OPEC's role is now less than it was earlier' since 'market forces have largely taken over'. A few days later, on 26 April, a senior Energy Department official made a similar point.[54] US threats to abandon Saudi Arabia led Saudi leaders to seek to improve relations with the US.[55] The US and Saudi Arabia agreed to prevent their serious dispute over Camp David from damaging their close relations in other areas.[56]

Oil prices increase despite the resolution of policy conflicts in Saudi Arabia

In 1979, the US was the only major industrial country to enjoy a significant improvement in its current account balance. Both West Germany and Japan, however, suffered current account deficits.[57] However, by the summer of 1979 the US, as well as Japan, West Germany, and other Western countries were imploring Saudi Arabia to prevent further price rises. A special presidential task force on energy met several times secretly and decided that the only short-term solution to the energy crisis before it destroyed the Carter presidency was to persuade Saudi Arabia to increase its production.[58] In June, Carter sent a letter to the Saudis asking them to increase their output. The US ambassador asked

Crown Prince Fahd to increase production and seek to prevent price increases.[59]

Despite the Carter administration's pleas, by mid June the Saudis could no longer postpone increasing their price.[60] The Saudis assured US officials that they would do their utmost to prevent further price increases. Despite the Saudi price increase, at the OPEC conference in June, Iran and African countries were still demanding higher prices.[61]

The failure of Western democracies to co-ordinate their energy policies

Differences between the US and its allies over the energy question and policy towards the Middle East resurfaced at the G-7 summit in Tokyo, on 28 and 29 June. Carter tried to persuade America's Western allies to accept reductions in their short-term petroleum imports and to make greater use of coal and nuclear energy in the long run. These measures would cause serious short-term problems for the allies.[62]

West German Chancellor Helmut Schmidt was irate and rejected Carter's proposals out of hand, adding that Carter's Middle East policy had caused the oil crisis.[63] Britain, France, Italy, and West Germany also opposed Carter's draconian measures.[64] Carter was in a quandary. In July, he fired Energy Secretary James Schlesinger. Before his departure Schlesinger warned of the consequences of ignoring the energy crisis: 'Today we face a world crisis of vaster dimensions than Churchill described half a century ago made more ominous by the problems of oil. There is little, if any, relief in prospect.'[65]

Not only did Saudi Arabia refuse to prevent oil price increases, but it also strongly opposed a US military build-up in the Persian Gulf.[66] Saudi Arabia and other Arab sheikhdoms were convinced that the US would check Soviet expansionism in the region, but it could not be relied upon to keep a ruling family in power.[67]

The Carter administration and the shift to neo-containment

During mid-June 1979, a series of very important meetings was held, in which US policy towards the Middle East was heatedly debated. Vance and his deputy Warren Christopher opposed greater US involvement in the Persian Gulf, while Schlesinger 'forcefully' called for balancing the Soviet Union. Not only did Brzezinski support Schlesinger, but he also argued that the US should be the preponderant power in the region.[68]

Despite the disagreement in the administration, it was reported that there was agreement on the need for a gradual US military build-up in the Persian Gulf and the Indian Ocean region in 1980.[69] In late June, Chairman of the Joint Chiefs of Staff, General Bernard Rogers, announced the formation of a 100,000-strong Rapid Deployment Force for intervention in the Persian Gulf.[70] The US, Great Britain and France deployed large naval forces in the Indian Ocean. Moreover, France and Germany indicated that they were prepared to intervene militarily, if necessary, in order to ensure their access to Middle Eastern oil.[71]

Saudi Oil Minister Zaki Yamani warned that oil-producing countries could sabotage their oil fields to dissuade Western powers from occupying them.[72]

Privately, however, the Saudis caved into Western diplomatic pressure and agreed to increase their oil production 'substantially' and for a 'significant' period.[73] Saudi Arabia increased its output from 8.5 to 9.5 million barrels a day in July, even though there was no longer any oil shortage and half this amount would have been sufficient to finance Saudi Arabia's development requirements.[74]

A few days later, the Carter administration presented its recommendation to Congress for the sale of 1.2 billion dollars worth of military equipment. State Department spokesman Hodding Carter denied that there had been a quid pro quo.[75] Despite the increase in Saudi output, oil prices continued to rise. It was reported that the spot market was tight because of 'fear of instability'. In reality, the oil companies were mainly responsible for pushing up the prices.[76]

Saudi Oil Minister Zaki Yamani pleaded with OPEC countries to curb the rise of oil prices. Yamani admitted: 'We're losing control over everything'.[77] Moreover, economic problems, particularly inflation, were damaging the US economy. Senator Ted Kennedy was sharply criticizing Carter and raised the issue of challenging him for the Democratic Party's nomination in the 1980 presidential elections. In mid July Carter made a speech saying that the nation was suffering from a 'crisis of spirit'.[78] In mid-September, Brzezinski sent a report to Carter on the administration's foreign policy. Marked 'Top Secret', the report sharply criticized Carter's policies towards Iran, the Soviet Union, Central America and Afghanistan. Brzezinski made it clear that Carter had to be a stronger leader.[79] It was against this background that the Carter administration began to discuss the question of whether to establish closer relations with Iraq.

The Carter administration changes US policy towards Iraq

Brzezinski had been arguing since January 1979 that Iraq could be weaned away from the Soviet Union and that it could fill the power vacuum in the Persian Gulf.[80] After the signing of the Algiers accord with Iran in March 1975, Saddam Hussein was searching for ways to clamp down on the Iraqi Communist Party (ICP).[81] However, Hussein wanted to proceed gradually because he feared that a sudden crackdown on the ICP would turn Moscow against the Ba'th or lead it to side with President Bakr.[82] By the spring of 1978, Hussein was in a position to move against the communist party and in May he announced that a number of communists had been executed, despite appeals for clemency from the Soviet and East European ambassadors.[83] The main reason for the executions was Hussein's determination to distance Iraq from the Soviet Union.[84]

Brzezinski was encouraged by Hussein's crackdown on the Communist Party and he believed that Iraq could be drawn into the US orbit.[85] However, the assumption in Washington was still that, despite the Iranian revolution, in the event of a US-Soviet war, Iran would be on the American side and Iraq would be on the Soviet side.[86] The Pentagon was also concerned about the Iraqi threat to the conservative Arab states of the Persian Gulf littoral.[87] However, Pentagon officials were primarily concerned about the Iraqi threat to Iran. The Iranian revolution and the collapse of the Iranian military had changed the force ratio in favour of Iraq and Iraq could play a critical role in any Soviet plans to invade Iran.[88]

Brzezinski favoured weaning Iraq from the Soviet Union in order to reduce the threat to Iran and the Persian Gulf, while balancing Iraqi power and meeting the threat in the Persian Gulf on its own terms.[89] A regional security system could not be established because of regional instability and Soviet power projection capability.[90] The US could not credibly issue a nuclear threat in response to an Iraqi-Soviet attack on Iran, and expanding a war in the Persian Gulf to other areas, such as NATO's northern flank, would frighten allies such as Norway.[91]

Meeting the threat on its own terms would require pre-positioning of equipment and a build-up of naval forces and tactical aircraft in the Indian Ocean and possibly the Persian Gulf. Moreover, the US had to ensure that its military build-up would not be politically destabilizing for Saudi Arabia.[92] The Brzezinski approach was accepted by the highest echelons of the CIA despite the fact that CIA experts advised against forming a de facto alliance with Iraq.[93]

US intelligence did not expect Iraq to go so far in its opposition to Soviet policy as to compel Moscow to halt the export of arms to Iraq or recall its advisers.[94] A National Intelligence Estimate on 'Iraq's Role in the Middle East' mistakenly concluded that Iraq would not change its policy towards the US unless a Palestinian state was created in the West Bank and Gaza and Syria retrieved the Golan.

The only factor which would lead Iraqi leaders to change their minds, US intelligence contended, was a major Soviet breakthrough such as the establishment of a leftist government in Iran.[95] The CIA was well aware of the Iraqi threat to Iran. Some analysts were bluntly told not to concentrate on Iraqi intentions, and only monitor the Iraqi military.[96] However, Iraq continued to pursue its policy of excluding great powers from the Persian Gulf.[97]

Policy currents in Iraq and Iraq's relations with revolutionary Iran

Iraq and Syria were so alarmed by Camp David that they even began to cooperate in the military arena. On 1 October 1978, Iraq announced that it was prepared to send troops to support Syria against Israel. Iraqi President Ahmad Hasan al-Bakr sought to unify his country with Syria in order to prevent Saddam Hussein from dominating Iraqi politics.[98]

The Syrian-Iraqi détente mainly affected the two countries' postures towards Israel.[99] However, the State Department's Bureau of Intelligence and Research (INR) had come to the conclusion that military co-operation did not 'mean a real boost in either country's military capabilities'.[100] Iraq's decision to form a union with Syria and the latter's strong support for Iran meant that any union would have to accommodate the Iranian regime. There were two currents of opinion in the Iraqi Revolutionary Command Council. Bakr and his allies wanted to maintain good ties with the new regime. Saddam Hussein and his supporters, however, called for a tough response to revolutionary Iran.[101]

The RCC adopted Bakr's approach. On 13 February, 1979, two days after Khomeini came to power, Iraq sent a memorandum to Prime Minister Bazargan in which it declared that it respected the principles of sovereignty, and non-interference in domestic affairs. Iraq also welcomed Khomeini's anti-Zionist attitude and declared its intention to 'deepen its friendly relations' with Iran and 'promote mutual interests'.[102]

The PLO and the attempt to form a new strategic axis

In the spring and summer of 1979, the PLO sought to construct a new alliance against Israel organized around the Baghdad-Damascus-Beirut axis. Iran would act as the 'strategic rear' of this alliance. Arafat hoped that the alliance would also be supported by the political, economic, and military power of Saudi Arabia.[103] PLO 'ambassador' to Iran, Hani al-Hasan, argued that the Iranian revolution had enabled the PLO to encircle Israel, and possibly defeat Israel, if there were 'a basic change in Turkey', which he thought was inevitable.[104]

In order to form a new regional alliance against Israel, the PLO sought to mediate between Iran and Iraq. PLO Chairman Yasir Arafat failed to persuade Saddam Hussein and other Iraqi officials to support his alliance with Iran.[105] On 15 April, however, Bakr sent a cable to Iran, congratulating Khomeini on the establishment of the Islamic Republic.[106]

Khomeini's opposition to rapprochement with Iraq and the escalation of the Iran-Iraq conflict

Khomeini was totally opposed to a rapprochement with Baghdad. The conflict between the two countries erupted as early as February 1979, when violations of airspace were reported.[107] Khomeini criticized Iraq's treatment of its Shi'a community and from April 1979 onwards, a propaganda war between Iran and Iraq began. Iraq accused Iran of fomenting Shi'a rebellion.[108]

Shi'a unrest in Iraq resulted in the arrest of Ayatollah Muhammad Baqer Sadr and other clerics. In response, several Iranian Ayatollahs, including Khomeini, Shari'atmadari and Najafi-Mar'ashi sent telegrams to the Iraqi regime, condemning Iraqi leaders as 'despotic', 'traitorous imperialist agents', and 'criminal' and warned them of 'the wrath of God and the anger of the Muslim people'.[109] Border clashes occurred in May.[110] Iranian propaganda attacks repeatedly accused the Iraqi regime of being hostile to Islam and called on the Iraqi people to overthrow the Ba'thist regime.[111]

Policy currents in Iraq, the failure of the Iraqi-Syrian détente, Saddam Hussein's coup d'etat

As the conflict with Iran escalated, the debate in Iraq over the choice of appropriate strategy intensified. Saddam Hussein sought to distance his country from the Soviet Union and move it closer to the West, while his opponents in the Ba'th Party sought to accelerate the union negotiations with Syria and negotiate a settlement with Iran. Saddam Hussein's opponents in the Ba'th party believed that Hafiz Asad would become the president of the union and would curb Hussein's power. Bakr himself had sent a message to Hafiz Asad asking him to accelerate the union negotiations.[112]

The KGB believed that Saddam Hussein's admiration of Stalin would enable it to cultivate him. Like Stalin, Hussein was a power-hungry and blood-thirsty paranoiac who was obsessed with 'traitors' in the ranks of the party (in his case the Iraqi Ba'th Party). However, Hussein was also deeply suspicious of the Soviet Union.[113] Some observers of Iraqi politics, such as Sa'id Aburish and Con Coughlin, have speculated that Saddam Hussein's connections with the CIA went back to the early 1960s when he lived in Cairo. According to Aburish and

Coughlin, Hussein was in contact with the CIA station in Cairo.[114] The CIA did support the 1963 Ba'thist coup which led to the removal and assassination of the increasingly pro-Soviet Abd al-Karim Qasim. The agency's most important purpose was to prevent a key Middle Eastern state from being dominated by the Soviet Union.[115] After the second Ba'thist coup in 1968, US and UK officials knew that Saddam Hussein represented a current of opinion in the Ba'thist leadership which sought to distance his country from the Soviet Union. For example, as early as 1969, Saddam Hussein had assured the British ambassador to his country that Iraq's relations with the Soviet bloc 'was forced upon it by the central problem of Palestine'. The British ambassador had reported that Saddam Hussein was 'a formidable, single-minded and hard-headed member of the Ba'thist hierarchy, but one with whom, if only one could see more of him, it would be possible to do business'.[116]

It is highly likely that Hussein's opponents enjoyed Soviet support.[117] The Iraqis even proposed to Asad that he become the new president of the union with Bakr and Saddam Hussein serving as vice-presidents. However, the Syrian president was not prepared to accept a limitation of his powers.[118] The US embassy in Damascus expected the Iraqi-Syrian union negotiations to fail.[119] US intelligence reported that Asad did not want to subordinate Syrian interests to those of Iraq.[120]

However, as Saddam Hussein began to prepare the ground for seizing the leadership of the party, opposition to his rule mounted in the ranks of the Iraqi Ba'th Party.[121] According to Saddam Hussein's biographer, Sa'id Aburish, during this period, Hussein sought Jordanian and Saudi, as well as CIA, backing for the coup against Bakr.[122] Aburish has argued that the CIA saw an Iraqi-Syrian alliance as a threat to Israel, Jordan and Saudi Arabia.[123] Hussein's opponents sought to persuade Bakr not to resign. However, on 28 July 1979, Hussein declared that he had uncovered a plot by 'a foreign side' soon named as Syria.[124]

According to some observers, there had indeed been a Syrian-backed coup attempt in Baghdad.[125] US officials in Baghdad believed that Hussein's opponents had discussed their fears with Syrians and sought ways of preventing him from staging a take-over.[126] In fact, three of the five 'plotters' were Shi'a and were suspected of supporting Hafiz Asad.[127]

The CIA saw Hussein's take-over not as a coup d'etat but as a political confrontation. The CIA's prediction that 'recent events in Iraq will have little or no effect on Iraq's inter-Arab policy', however, was wide of the mark.[128] At the end of July Hussein purged pro-Bakr and pro-Soviet officials and advocates of rapprochement with Syria.[129]

Saddam Hussein was deeply alarmed at the situation in Iran. He told French Premier Raymond Barre 'that Iran might descend totally into chaos and end up being effectively divided between US and Soviet spheres of influence'.[130]

Iraq's attempts at negotiating a modus vivendi with revolutionary Iran

Saddam Hussein had not yet lost hope of reaching a modus vivendi with Iran. As late as July-August 1979, Iraq invited Prime Minister Bazargan to visit Iraq to discuss ways of improving relations between the two countries. According to then Iraqi Foreign Minister Sa'dun Hammadi, Bazargan welcomed the idea.[131]

However, Iran's relations with Iraq were considerably strained during the summer of 1979 because of Khomeini's hostile propaganda against the Ba'thist regime, Iran's interference in Iraq's domestic affairs and Saddam Hussein's expansionist ambitions in the Persian Gulf. During this period, Iran also consolidated its ties with Syria.[132] Iran's emerging alliance with Syria was, in retrospect, the most serious threat to the Arab-Israeli peace process because Syria supported extremist Palestinian terrorist groups.[133]

The Iranian revolution also encouraged Islamist opponents of the Saudi regime, particularly those in the oil-rich Eastern province of Saudi Arabia where the Shi'as were in majority. In 1979 the Organization of the Islamic Revolution for the Liberation of the Arabian Peninsula began to operate in the Eastern Province.[134] Iran also began to destabilize Kuwait. In September Kuwait arrested and expelled a relative of Khomeini named Ahmad al-Mahri.[135]

The Iranian ambassador to Kuwait, Ali Shams-Ardakani, reiterated Iran's respect for the sovereignty of all the Persian Gulf states.[136] Iranian Foreign Minister Ebrahim Yazdi met Saddam Hussein in Havana during the non-aligned summit. He assured Hussein that Iran was not encouraging the Iraqi Shi'as to oppose the government, that Iran had no ambitions in Bahrain and that Iran was not seeking to export the revolution. The two men agreed to meet later in Tehran or Baghdad. In early September, Yazdi even invited Saddam Hussein to visit Iran.[137]

The Bazargan government was thinking about issuing a public statement that Iran had no intention of exporting its revolution and would not violate the territorial integrity of Iraq.[138] During this period Iran and Iraq ceased their propaganda campaigns for a while. However, in the same month, Hussein presented Yazdi with conditions for normalizing relations, among them the return of Shatt-al-Arab to Iraq.[139]

Yazdi condemned Saddam Hussein's actions. He described Arab nationalism and Ba'thism as 'bankrupt ideologies' and declared that only Islamic revolutions could help the Arab world.[140] The CIA knew that by the end of September Hussein had concluded that further negotiations with the Iranian regime would be futile because Iran's religious leaders were hostile to him.[141]

The Iran-Iraq conflict

Saddam Hussein took advantage of revolutionary Iran's threat to regional stability to make Iraq the protector of smaller Arab states of the Persian Gulf. On 22 September he sent the Iraqi defence minister to Bahrain and Kuwait to propose a security pact.[142] The CIA had a high-level agent in the PLO who regularly reported to it on Iran's domestic developments, and its relations with Arab countries and movements.[143] According to the source, Saddam Hussein had instructed Iraqi military officers to co-operate with Kurdish separatists.[144] Khomeini ordered the Iranian military to crush the Kurdish rebellion 'at any price'. Opposition forces, including leftist groups, the Tudeh Party, some members of the intelligentsia, and pro-Shari'atmadari forces organized demonstrations and co-ordinated their activities with the Kurds to weaken Khomeini.

Khomeini ordered the Revolutionary Guards to use brute force to suppress the demonstrations.[145] The PLO was also involved in mediating between the

Iranian regime and the Kurds. The situation was further complicated by the rivalry between different Palestinian groups, most notably, Arafat's Fatah and George Habbash's Popular Front for the Liberation of Palestine (PFLP). Iraq used the PFLP to channel arms and money to separatists in Iran's Khuzestan Province.[146]

Habbash was also supporting the Kurds, the radical leftist Cherikha-ye Fada'iye Khalq and elements in the Iranian Mojahedin-e Khalq. The PFLP had also infiltrated agents into Kurdistan, was organizing among the oil workers and training them in weapons and explosives. Habbash wanted to cut off Iran's oil supplies to the West, but he preferred to persuade the Iranian regime to do so. PFLP leader George Habbash wanted to strengthen his organization's position in Iran's power struggle in case his leftist allies increased their influence.[147]

The CIA informed the Bazargan government of Habbash's activities in Kurdistan. The agency also established contact with Kurdish leaders living in exile.[148] The CIA was particularly concerned about the Kurds' Soviet connection and Marxist groups' efforts to capitalize on the Kurds' demands for autonomy to form a broad coalition. Former Prime Minister Shapur Bakhtiar and the former head of Iranian military intelligence, General Palizban also worked with the Kurds and Iraq in an effort to overthrow the Iranian regime. The CIA believed that a co-ordinated uprising of Iran's ethnic and tribal groups might overthrow the regime.

The CIA reported that Bakhtiar had also formed an alliance with Ayatollah Shari'atmadari and Kurdish and other tribal leaders such as Khosrow Qashqa'i. Neither the CIA nor the State Department agreed with Bakhtiar's objectives, but they told him that they wished to use his group as a source of information. The CIA was also in contact with Sardar Jaaf who was closely collaborating with the Iraqi military intelligence.[149]

Jaaf was co-operating closely with Iraq to supply arms to the Jaaf Kurds who held an area east and West of Kermanshah.[150] Jaaf told the CIA that no other country except Iraq was helping the Kurds. Saddam Hussein's relations with the Soviets were strained, so the Kurds had to buy their weapons in Europe. Salar Jaaf thought that Hussein could later turn against the Kurds, but he believed that the Iraqi leader 'was the Kurds only friend at present'.[151]

Regional implications of the continuing crisis in Iran

The Iran-Iraq and Iraq-Syria conflicts, as well as fear of Soviet encirclement, led Saudi Arabia and Kuwait to move closer to Washington on the Arab-Israeli issue.[152] The US embassy in Riyadh concluded that for Saudi leaders security was of utmost importance and only the US was capable of protecting them. However, privately, even Crown Prince Fahd said that he thought the US had betrayed the Shah. Fahd said that he considered Khomeini as a tool of the Soviet Union and warned that it was a matter of time before Iran became 'another Ethiopia'.[153]

By September 1979, the Israelis had become acutely concerned about the Iraqi threat to Iran. The Begin government asked the Carter administration to support the Bazargan government. The Israelis believed that Brzezinski, who thought Bazargan was too weak to be a counterweight to leftists, preferred Iran to further decline into chaos until such time as a pro-US leader emerged.[154] The Israelis were also concerned about Brzezinski's support for Saddam Hussein.[155]

According to Israeli intelligence evaluations, Saddam Hussein sought to make Iraq a nuclear power and develop a nuclear arsenal. The prospect of an Iraqi occupation of Khuzestan and Iraqi control of the Persian Gulf frightened the Begin government.[156] However, before the Iraqi invasion of Iran the Iranian hostage crisis led to the total rupture of US-Iranian ties.

10

THE CARTER ADMINISTRATION'S MODUS VIVENDI WITH THE REVOLUTIONARY REGIME

Contrary to the popular academic belief, both of President Carter's principal foreign policy advisers; Zbigniew Brzezinski and Cyrus Vance, believed that militant Islam could be a de facto ally in the Cold War.[1] In recent years, analysts of US policy towards Islamism have tended to divide US policy-makers into two categories, the confrontationalists and the accommodationists.[2] However, in the Carter administration, Brzezinski and Vance represented the accommodationist current, albeit for entirely different reasons. Vance believed that the revolutionary regime would be primarily concerned about the Soviet threat and that it would seek to maintain its basic security ties with the US.

Brzezinski started thinking about Islamism before the establishment of the Islamic Republic of Iran. In a weekly NSC report to Carter written one day after Khomeini's arrival in Iran, Brzezinski noted that despite 'Ayatollah Khomeini's remarkable victory over the Shah', the emergence of Islamism as a force had 'mixed' consequences for US strategy. Brzezinski also sent Carter a report on differences between Shi'a and Sunni Muslims, arguing that 'Iranian Shiism is quite different from the Sunni rite of Islam found elsewhere in the Middle East. It is more populist and oppositionist for doctrinal and historical reasons.'[3]

Brzezinski concluded that Islamism in Iran and other countries would not be able to institutionalize itself. He contended that the clergy lacked experience of government and would be dependent on experts and bureaucrats to manage the affairs of state. Brzezinski concluded that the US had to work with individual Muslim countries and emphasize the importance of US 'support for a world of diversity, and our commitment to social justice'.[4]

David Farber has argued that 'Brzezinski had made an excellent start in rethinking American relations with the Islamic world.'[5] In fact, as we saw earlier, CIA analyst Ernest Oney and Ambassador Sullivan had already presented much more detailed analyses of Islamism. Oney had even warned of a de facto alliance between the Soviets and radical clerics as early as 1975. However, Oney and Sullivan had failed to define US policy towards Iran. Brzezinski turned out to be wrong on all the major points he dealt with; militant Sunni Islam emerged as a major global force in the 1980s and political Islam did establish strong institutions in Iran.

Other officials were just as wrong as Brzezinski. As we saw earlier, throughout the revolutionary crisis, Secretary Vance and his advisers on Iranian affairs had sought to reach an accommodation with Khomeini. On 2 February, just one day after Khomeini's return to Iran, a senior US embassy official, George Lambrakis, argued: 'Our best assessment to date is that the Shia Islamic movement is far better organized, enlightened, and able to resist communism than its detractors would lead us to believe.'

Lambrakis argued that Islamism supported 'a reformist/traditionalist view of Iran' which was more attractive to Iranians than Soviet or Chinese models of communism. Lambrakis believed that although an Islamic system was 'not guaranteed to operate in a parliamentary democratic fashion as we understand it in the West', Islamists would find it difficult not to accommodate 'Westernized ideas of government held by many in the opposition movement'.[6] After the Iranian revolution, the Carter administration made a government-wide effort to analyse the impact of Islamism on Saudi Arabia, Egypt and Jordan. According to the then Assistant Secretary of State for South Asian and Near Eastern Affairs, Harold Saunders, US officials realized that Islamism had become a more powerful force in Middle East politics. Saunders pressed US analysts to study the situation in Saudi Arabia in particular. However, US officials did not believe that the Saudi government would be overthrown by Islamists. They also believed that Egyptian President Anwar Sadat could deal with Islamist pressure on his regime.[7] CIA and State Department analysts concluded that Khomeini-style revolutions were unlikely to occur in other Middle Eastern countries. Therefore, most US officials were not concerned about the growing strength of Islamist groups.[8]

In the post-revolutionary period, the Bazargan government sought to maintain close ties with the US. Iran's withdrawal from the militarily insignificant Central Treaty Organization, CENTO, was not considered to be an important event. Far more significant was the new regime's reappraisal of Iran's military relationship with the US.[9] The Bazargan government, however, made clear its determination to resist Soviet expansionism.[10] However, it was suspicious of Secretary of Defence Harold Brown's statement that the US would defend its interests in the Persian Gulf by using force 'if appropriate'.[11]

Leftist groups becoming more powerful?

Meanwhile, leftist groups, including the Tudeh Party, were taking advantage of the revolutionary upheaval to increase their influence. More than 300,000 small arms had fallen into the hands of extremist religious groups and leftist guerrilla organizations such as Mojahedin-e Khalq and Fedayeen-e Khalq. These groups ignored Khomeini's decree calling for the return of looted weapons.[12]

Only three days after the collapse of the old regime, a group of leftist guerrillas had attacked the US embassy building, killing an Iranian employee and wounding a Marine guard. This operation was planned by Cherikha-ye Fada'iy-e Khalq. The assailants also took 109 hostages, including Ambassador Sullivan and most of his key entourage. The clergy immediately condemned this operation and after only two hours Ayatollah Beheshti, Deputy Prime Minister Ebrahim Yazdi and a group of Mojahedin-e Khalq guerrillas intervened and dispersed the hostage-takers.[13] Moreover, afterwards, Khomeini sent a cleric to apologise to Sullivan for the incident.[14] Subsequently a group of guerrillas were assigned to the embassy to protect American diplomats. However, Sullivan later discovered that the guards had previously been given the task of assassinating him.[15]

After the revolution, a number of American employees had also been taken hostage by airforce personnel who feared that they would not receive their salaries.[16] Sullivan managed to get the hostages released by arranging for payments to be made to the employees and the payments continued while he remained in Iran.[17] He persuaded Bazargan to maintain the security of the listening posts in northern Iran, which monitored the Soviet Union. Sullivan did not believe that American personnel could be deployed at the listening posts, but he persuaded Bazargan that the posts would provide valuable intelligence to Iran by tracking movements of Soviet forces.[18]

On 12 February, CIA Director Stansfield Turner had warned the Special Co-ordinating Committee that Khomeini and Bazargan could not control the situation in Iran.[19] Sullivan warned that the Bazargan government 'was buried somewhere in the middle of this chaos'.[20] He argued that the communists sought to take over the media and take advantage of the disintegration of the Iranian military.[21] Sullivan continued to argue that Washington needed to form a coalition between the military, Bazargan and Khomeini to counter the left.[22]

On 20 February 1979, the Tudeh Party Central Committee called for abandoning 'the internal class struggle' until the US was driven out of Iran.[23] In late February, the CIA again warned that Khomeini and Bazargan could not remain in power.[24] In March 1979 CIA Director Admiral Stansfield Turner argued that Marxists would be the main beneficiary of conflict between Bazargan and Khomeini.[25]

The State Department accepted Khomeini 'as a useful anti-Soviet force'.[26] Brzezinski, however, began to think of the global impact of Islamism. He instructed the NSC to draw up plans for using Islamism as a means of bringing about the disintegration of the Soviet Union.[27] After the Iranian revolution, Brzezinski began to explore the possibility of forming a de facto alliance with militant Islamists against the Soviet Union. Brzezinski believed that there was an 'arc of crisis' which stretched from Northeast Africa to Soviet Central Asia. According to Henry Precht, Brzezinski believed that 'there was an arc of crisis, and so an arc of Islam could be mobilized to contain the Soviets'.[28] In the case of Muslims under Soviet rule, the Polish-born Brzezinski was influenced by Alexander Bennigsen, the son of a Russian count. From the late 1950s onwards, Bennigsen had argued that Islam was emerging as an important force in the Soviet Union and that Islamism would pose a threat to the Soviet state. Brzezinski was also influenced by the ideas of former CIA official, Paul Henze, who served on the NSC staff under Brzezinski.

Brzezinski approved of the formation of an inter-agency task force called the Nationalities Working Group, which brought together officials from the CIA, the Pentagon and the State Department. Henze chaired the Nationalities Working Group. The officials on the Nationalities Working Group were influenced by Bennigsen's ideas.[29] Bennigsen called for encouraging the spread of Islamism in the Soviet Union, arguing that the most likely outcome of a Muslim uprising in the Soviet Union would be 'probably, a conservative Islamic radicalism comparable to that of the present-day "Islamic Revolution" in Iran'.[30]

However, as we shall see, as far as Iran and regional security issues were concerned, Brzezinski came to the conclusion that the US could not work with the Iranian regime. Worse still, some Soviet officials began to encourage the spread of radical anti-American Islamism in Iran in an effort to expel the US from Iran and the region.

The participation of so many American-educated Iranians in the revolution against the Shah led many to conclude that Khomeini had covert ties with the CIA.[31] After the revolution, General Hossein Fardust who was appointed as the head of the revolutionary regime's intelligence apparatus, SAVAMA, contacted former CIA Director Richard Helms. The Shah, Fardust and Helms had attended Le Rosey school in Switzerland. Fardust suggested that the two countries maintain their intelligence relations. Fardust visited the US in May 1979. However, what he did not say to Helms was that he was on a mission to prove his loyalty to the new regime by conveying fatwas to American Islamists. The fatwas called for the assassination of Iranian opposition leaders, such as Ali Akbar Tabataba'i, if they did not heed the warnings of the Iranian regime.[32] As we shall see in a later chapter, Tabataba'i would be assassinated in 1980.

The Carter administration, however, was anxious to establish intelligence contacts with revolutionary Iran. The CIA station and the US embassy in Tehran were instructed to establish a new and more effective network of agents. One of the CIA's most experienced Iran hands, George Cave, managed to establish close relations with Deputy Prime Minister Ebrahim Yazdi, Defence Minister Chamran, and another Deputy Prime Minister Abbas Amir-Entezam. He also supervised the recruitment of former SAVAK agents and military intelligence agents.[33] The embassy's political counsellor was also in contact with two of Khomeini's closest associates, Ayatollah Beheshti and Ayatollah Musavi Ardebili.[34]

The issue of the Shah's admission into the US

Some Iranian officials such as Deputy Prime Minister and later Acting Foreign Minister, Ebrahim Yazdi, knew full well that not all US officials and influential Americans were against the new regime. Yazdi later wrote that he believed that the oil companies and the arms manufacturers sought to crush the revolution, while the State Department, and American liberals, wanted the Shah out.[35]

The new regime did not want to sever Iran's economic ties with the US. However, given the Rockefeller family's and the Chase Manhattan Bank's longstanding association with the Shah, officials of the revolutionary regime feared that the Rockefellers might freeze Iran's assets in order to destabilize the Iranian economy and help the Shah regain his throne. Therefore, the new regime chose other US banks to handle the National Iranian Oil Company's accounts.[36]

It is imperative to note that it was only *after* the abolition of the Oil Consortium and the Iranian regime's decision to withdraw its assets from the Chase Manhattan Bank that David Rockefeller became interested in helping the Shah. Initially Rockefeller refused to help Henry Kissinger find a residence for the Shah because he thought that helping the monarch would 'jeopardize' the Chase Manhattan Bank's relations with the new regime.[37]

In mid-March the State Department asked Kissinger to advise the Shah not to seek admission to the US until the situation had stabilized in Iran.[38] The State Department's Director of the Bureau of Iranian affairs, Henry Precht, argued that the US had to ensure that the Shah would not go to the US, warning that this would damage the Western position in the region and perhaps even lead to the closure of the US embassy in Iran.[39]

Kissinger rejected the State Department's demand 'with some indignation.'[40] On 7 April, Kissinger called Brzezinski to argue for the Shah's admission into the US. He criticized Brzezinski 'in rather sharp terms' and complained about US policy towards the Shah.[41] Brzezinski advised Kissinger to call President Carter. The next day Kissinger called Carter and asked him to permit the Shah to enter the US.[42]

The following day, David Rockefeller met Carter and raised the question again. The President was annoyed with these attempts to get the Shah into the US. He also observed in his diary: 'Rockefeller, Kissinger, and Brzezinski seem to be adopting this as a joint project.'[43] Kissinger made a speech on 9 April, sharply criticizing the Carter administration for treating the Shah 'like a Flying Dutchman looking for a port of call.'[44] Brzezinski believed that the US had to demonstrate its credibility, and admit the Shah into the US for medical treatment.[45] As we will see in a later chapter, this issue would come to haunt the Carter administration and tear asunder the fabric of US-Iranian relations.

US Congressional opposition to the new regime

Khomeini's hostility to Jews and Israel was a major cause of the deterioration of relations between the US and Iran. After the revolution, Jews, Christians and Baha'is were increasingly criticized and their rights were violated. Some of them were even tried and executed, while others had their properties confiscated. However, Khomeini himself seemed to be obsessed with the activities of Jews whom he described as 'imperialist spies, agents and fifth columnists'. He charged that the Jews had distorted Islam and warned of a gigantic Jewish plot aimed at world domination.[46] By early spring, US Congress had begun to cooperate with opponents of State Department policy. Congress was primarily concerned about the fate of Iranian Jews and the new regime's maltreatment of Iranian Jews strengthened the opponents of accommodating the new regime. Congress sprang into action after the execution of the most prominent Jewish merchant in Iran, Habib Elghanian, who was charged with spying for and raising funds for Israel.[47] After Elghanian's execution, Israeli Prime Minister Menachem Begin declared that he had been 'a good Zionist and one who helped Israel'.[48]

Aryeh Dulzin, director of the Jewish Agency and World Zionist organization, warned the Khomeini regime not to harm the sixty-five thousand Jews remaining in that country, saying that Israel was prepared 'to take action' to defend them. One of Dulzin's assistants said that Israel might launch operations 'both orthodox and unorthodox' to facilitate the emigration of Iranian Jews.[49]

The Senate approved Walter Cutler's nomination as the new US ambassador to Iran, but it also unanimously passed a resolution, sponsored by one of Israel's most prominent supporters, Senator Jacob Javitz, condemning trials and executions in Iran. Iranian officials were furious that the Senate resolution was passed only three days after Secretary Vance assured the Iranian government that the US wanted to expand ties with Iran.[50] Deputy Iranian Information Minister Mehdi Momken declared: 'They have paid more attention and expressed more worry about this one than the sum of all other executions. The form and composition of the U.S. Senate is that they always support Israel and Zionists.'[51] However, the State Department's reaction to the execution of Elghanian was much milder.[52]

US assessment of the situation in Iran

The State Department sought to disassociate the Carter administration from the Shah and his entourage as much as possible to assure the Bazargan government that the US would not try to restore the Pahlavi dynasty.[53] However, the new regime still feared the Shah. On 13 May, Khalkhali, nicknamed 'Blood Judge', announced that the Revolutionary Court had given the Shah, his twin sister Ashraf and other members of the Royal Family, the death sentence. Later that same month, a member of the group code-named 'Muhammad Ali' was involved in a failed assassination attempt against the Shah in Bahamas. In June, Khalkhali pledged that the Shah would be assassinated by his group the Fada'iyan-e Eslam. On 27 June, it was announced that there had been a failed assassination attempt against the Shah in Mexico, but the Mexican authorities denied that there had been any assassination attempt.[54]

By the summer of 1979 US officials were convinced that the Bazargan government had failed to stabilize the situation in the country.[55] Moreover, Ebrahim Yazdi and Mostafa Chamran whom US officials characterized as 'holy Fascists' had become increasingly prominent.[56] Both Yazdi and Chamran were among Khomeini's closest advisers and were involved in carrying out purges. They had also established ties with revolutionary committees.[57]

The State Department was particularly alarmed at the negative reaction of Iranian officials to a Congressional resolution on human rights violations in Iran sponsored by Senator Jacob Javitz. It wanted to establish a relationship with the new regime and refuse the Shah permission to enter the US.[58] State Department officials' assessments of the situation in Iran were becoming increasingly pessimistic. For example, US political officer in Isfahan, McGaffey, predicted increasing violence and chaos, a theocracy ruling over 'a diminished Iran' or a leftist take-over.[59]

The State Department had concluded that 'Khomeini's views are almost totally dominated by a rejection of all things foreign, and especially American. He would probably welcome a complete break in diplomatic relations with US'.[60] The Bazargan government's failure to accept the appointment of the US ambassador designate Walter Cutler led some embassy officials to argue that Bazargan could not influence Khomeini. The media constantly attacked the US, and anti-American demonstrations were frequent. The Bazargan government had started to accuse the US of interfering in Iranian affairs. Even the embassy's guards were openly hostile.[61]

The embassy's political officer, John Stempel, argued that the US should adjust the size of its diplomatic posts in the country and await positive signals from the Iranian government.[62] He believed that the 'Islamic coalition' was breaking up. Ayatollah Shari'atmadari and 'more moderate ayatollahs' had openly expressed their opposition to Khomeini's plans. The embassy's counsellor Charles Naas believed that only some leftist groups, such as Cherikha-ye Fada'i-ye Khalq, had the capability to challenge Khomeini. Naas argued that Khomeini's Islamic movement would ultimately fail because of its own incompetence and obscurantism.[63]

Naas did not rule out the possibility that Iran would 'collapse into chaos and disintegration'.[64] He contended that the US should only agree to meet Khomeini if the Bazargan government requested such a meeting.[65] Naas advised Vance to avoid commenting on Iran and to limit US presence in the country. However, he recommended maintaining the US relationship with the Iranian military and supplying spare parts to it to the extent permitted by US Congress.[66]

Naas could see no 'visible' alternative to Khomeini if only because 'Revolutionary Guards and the armed mobs' were loyal to him.[67] Despite Khomeini's anti-Americanism and paranoia about the US, Naas argued that Khomeini's death would be a catastrophe because without him Iran would be anarchic.[68]

By mid-summer 1979, over 70 percent of the former regime's senior officer corps had been executed. Almost all ministers from previous governments who had stayed in Iran were also killed. Even junior army and SAVAK officers were being executed.[69] Up to 12,000 officers were arrested, cashiered or retired. More than 70 out of the 80 senior generals, as well as hundreds of junior officers, were tortured and executed. According to one estimate, by the end of the summer of 1979, almost 75 per cent of the senior officers were killed.[70] By July, the Islamic Revolutionary Guards Corps, which the regime had created to replace the regular army, had more than 7,000 members. The Guards Corps also co-operated with the revolutionary regime's secret service, SAVAMA.[71] In the 'reign of terror' started by Khomeini and his allies among the clergy thousands of Iranians were executed, killed or jailed. Most notably those executed included the last two directors of SAVAK Generals Ne'matollah Nasiri and Naser Moghaddam and former Prime Minister and Court Minister Amir Abbas Hoveyda.[72] Hoveyda and Moghaddam paid with their lives for their policies of destabilizing the country in furtherance of their objectives.

The main problem in Iran remained the absence of a democratic political culture. Khomeini made it clear that it was not sufficient to educate the Iranian people and that an Islamic government had to be imposed from above. Thus the regime established revolutionary tribunals to punish the 'enemies of the revolution' individuals. The public prosecutor of Islamic Revolutionary Tribunals Ayatollah Ahmad Azari-Qomi announced that the tribunals would also punish those guilty of 'counter-revolutionary' activity in industrial and commercial sectors.[73] By May, the Iranian economy was out of control. The currency had lost 50 per cent of its value and 35 per cent of the work force was unemployed. Moreover, laws governing private property were either ignored or suspended altogether and properties of 'counter-revolutionaries' were confiscated by revolutionary foundations. Not surprisingly, many industrialists and businessmen fled the country.[74]

Khomeini moves towards establishing the guardianship of the supreme jurisconsult

It is often argued that the debate over the Islamic constitution led to a fracture of the revolutionary coalition.[75] Moreover, some authors, such as Ofira Seliktar, have argued that in the spring and summer of 1979, US officials failed to understand that there was a duality of power in Iran.[76] However, it is important to note that the situation in Iran was far more complex and volatile. Prominent clerics, members of parliament and judges kept their own armed revolutionary guards. For example, such prominent revolutionary figures as Behzad Nabavi, Jalaleddin Farsi, Mostafa Chamran, Sadegh Ghotbzadeh, Akbar Hashemi-Rafsanjani and Asadollah Lajevardi each had their own revolutionary guards group.[77] Moreover, a number of foundations, such as the Martyr Foundation, the Foundation for the Dispossessed, the Imam Propaganda Office and the Housing Foundation, implemented the policies of the Revolutionary Council and completely ignored the Bazargan government.[78]

As of July 1979 the joint CIA/INR 'vulnerability' assessment of the situation in Iran indicated that no group had yet established effective authority:[79] US officials believed that the dual system of government was inherently unstable and would not last long.[80] The so-called referendum, which resulted in the creation of the Islamic republic, was a mere formality because Iranians were asked to choose between the monarchy and an Islamic republic.[81]

Indeed, Khomeini himself indicated that the referendum was 'superfluous'.[82] The most prominent cleric who opposed the guardianship of the supreme jurisconsult was Ayatollah Shari'atmadari.[83] Shari'atmadari did not boycott the referendum on the constitution, but he declared that people should be given more than two systems to choose from.[84] He declared that the guardianship of the supreme jurisconsult was contrary to the principles of sovereignty and democracy.[85]

Faced with strong opposition from Bazargan, Shari'atmadari and other groups, Khomeini and his allies among the clergy downplayed the principle of the guardianship of the supreme jurisconsult in the first and second drafts of the constitution.[86] However, the formation of the Islamic Republican Party, which was highly committed to establishing a theocratic state, indicated that the guardianship of the supreme jurisconsult would remain an important issue in Iranian politics. The constitution was symptomatic of Khomeini's and the Islamic Republican Party's (IRP) opposition to nationalism. It did not even require the jurisconsult to be an Iranian citizen.[87] Increasingly, the IRP resorted to violence to suppress the challenge to its rule.[88] However, despite their vehement opposition to nationalism, Khomeini's clerical allies cracked down on groups in Kurdistan, Azerbaijan and Khuzestan provinces which were trying to foment secessionist tendencies. A large number of people were killed or executed in the process of re-establishing the authority of the central government.[89] By mid-June it was apparent to US officials that Khomeini and the IRP would dominate Iranian politics.[90]

The Soviet Union and the Tudeh's strategy of forming an alliance with the clergy

National Front leaders and leftist groups, who had ignored Khomeini's writings and speeches during the revolutionary turmoil, began to call Khomeini a dictator. The Cherikha-ye Fada'i-ye Khalq accused the mullahs of being fascists.[91] The new regime had failed to disarm and disband the Mojahedin-e-Khalq and Cherikha-ye Fada'i-ye Khalq. These groups tried to create a 'people's army' controlled by elected officers and soldier committees.[92] Cherikha-ye Faday'i-ye Khalq were supported by a large number of youths and industrial workers.[93] This group was also involved in inciting ethnic opposition to the central government in Baluchestan Khuzestan, Kurdistan, and Torkaman-Sahra.[94]

Khomeini authorised the Hezbollah to attack the Cherikha-ye Fada'i-ye Khalq,[95] which subsequently split into two groups. The majority faction sided with the Tudeh Party and supported the IRP. The minority led by Ashraf Dehghani called for an armed uprising against the regime. Nevertheless, even the majority were involved in clashes with the Revolutionary Guards in Torkaman-Sahra. The Guards succeeded in defeating them and destroying their organization.[96]

The Tudeh Party lacked a popular base because of its association with the Soviet Union. Its ultimate objective was to sever Iran's links with the US and stage a take-over. Tudeh's general-secretary Nureddin Kianuri believed that Khomeini and his clerical supporters lacked a concrete and coherent programme and concluded that the Tudeh Party could manipulate Khomeini.[97]

At the time, most Soviet commentators contended that the Shah's harsh and repressive policies had prevented groups other than the clergy from leading the opposition to the Shah. Some Soviet observers described Islam as a 'catalyst of national attitudes' and some went so far as to argue that despite the clergy's leading role in the revolution, the Iranian revolution was 'in no way a religious movement'.[98] Moreover, Soviet theorists, such as Rostislav Ulyanovsky, distinguished between 'progressive' and 'reactionary' tendencies among the clergy.[99] During this period, the Soviets maintained contact with the Tudeh through the Soviet Communist Party's International Department. Tudeh General-Secretary Nureddin Kianuri regularly sent the International Department news and analyses and the replies bore Ulyanovsky's signature.[100]

Kianuri often exaggerated the Tudeh's role in developments.[101] As late as 1982, Ulyanovsky called for supporting the so-called 'progressive clergy'.[102] Ironically, when Iranian authorities arrested the leaders of the Tudeh in 1983, Ulyanovsky blamed the Tudeh for the failure of its policy.[103] Despite his conservatism, the Tudeh saw Khomeini as a catalyst that would facilitate the rise of the radicals.[104]

The Tudeh Party encouraged revolutionary bloodletting and called for more. The Tudeh had an extensive and highly committed covert network, including the Navid organization in the military, whose task was to operate within the system to prepare the ground for a take-over.[105] According to one estimate, the Navid organisation's military branch had approximately two hundred members.[106] Members included Admiral Bahram Afzali who later served as the commander of the Iranian Navy. Afzali had access to most sensitive intelligence and the leader of the Tudeh, Kianuri, was personally involved in protecting him.[107]

During the spring and summer of 1979, Soviet propaganda against the Iranian regime intensified. The Soviet Union was gradually concluding that Iran was responsible for the deterioration of its position in Afghanistan. On 20 August 1979, Iranian Islamic Revolutionary Guards Corps seized the headquarters of the Tudeh and the Fada'iyan and the authorities closed down the Tudeh Party's newspaper, *Mardom* [people].[108]

Khomeini himself directly criticized the leftists, describing them as 'sons of Satan', 'atheists' and the 'evil of the earth'. He also accused them of inciting ethnic minorities and trying to subvert the regime.[109] In August the Kremlin began to disapprove of Khomeini's actions because Islamic fundamentalists rigged the elections to exclude the left from the Majlis.[110] However, the Tudeh continued to call for unity among revolutionary forces and reiterated its support for Khomeini. Khomeini, in turn, toned down his criticism of the party.[111]

What particularly concerned US officials was Soviet exploitation of the revolutionary turmoil to stage a coup akin to the 1978 Afghan coup.[112] Some US officials argued that the only positive outcome of the Iranian revolution for the Soviets so far had been 'the loss of Western position in Iran and in the region'. However, this was 'counterbalanced' by the emerging threats to Soviet interests in Iraq and Afghanistan.[113] Some Soviet officials had commented that developments in Iran were a source of concern to both the East and the West.[114]

Beginning in February, Soviet ambassador to Iran, Vladimir Vinogradov, held meetings with Khomeini once every two months in the city of Qom. However, Khomeini lectured Vinogradov repeatedly during his meetings with him. Vinogradov told officials of other embassies that the Kremlin 'was a damned fool to keep sending me down to Qom for regular beatings'.[115]

One US report during this period concluded: 'This Soviet self-restraint is of a tactical nature and not a question of principle.'[116] The US embassy in Tehran observed that 'the Soviets have fared no better than any one else in doing business in post-revolutionary Iran'. The country's gas shipments to the Soviet Union had not even reached the pre-revolutionary levels. Iran had decided not only not to build another pipeline, it was also demanding an increase in the price of gas. US officials believed that the Soviet Union would turn against Khomeini if he threatened 'vital Soviet interests'. The Soviets were becoming increasingly alarmed at the impact of the Iranian revolution on their own economy.[117]

The Soviets jammed Iranian broadcasts and their propaganda in turn stressed the 'freedom' enjoyed by Soviet Muslims.[118] Soviet Muslims had told US officials that they followed religious broadcasts and Koran readings from Iran, Egypt, and the VOA and Soviet Muslims also closely followed events in Iran and Afghanistan. The British view, however, was that Iranians would not have a major influence on Soviet Muslims because they were Shi'a.[119]

US response to Khomeini's ascendance in Iran

Khomeini had steadily increased his control over the Bazargan government with the appointment of his closest advisers to the cabinet. Just before the constituent assembly elections, faced with the threatened resignations of 11 of his 17 cabinet ministers, Bazargan threatened to resign.[120] Key portfolios such as foreign affairs, defence, and deputy Prime Minister were given to Khomeini's closest confidants and advisers: Ebrahim Yazdi (acting foreign Minister); Sadegh Tabataba'i (deputy Prime Minister); and Mostafa Chamran (defence minister). These three and Sadegh Ghotbzadeh, who was appointed as the director of Radio and Television, were called 'The Syrian Group' because of their close relations with Syria and the PLO.[121]

Richard Cottam has described secularists and National Front politicians as these politicians' natural constituencies.[122] In fact, Yazdi, Ghotbzadeh and

Chamran were fully committed to combining religion and politics and they did not refrain from resorting to violence. Yazdi and Ghotbzadeh were among Khomeini's closest advisers and had taken far more uncompromising positions than the so-called radical clerics such as Beheshti and Rafsanjani before the triumph of the revolution.[123]

Abolhasan Bani-Sadr, who later became the first president of the Islamic Republic of Iran formed hundreds of alliances with revolutionary committees.[124] Bani-Sadr, Yazdi, and Ghotbzadeh also competed with one another for political power. Nevertheless, the cumulative effect of their activities was a weakening of the provisional government.

As Khomeini and his supporters gained strength, the consensus of opinion at the State Department was that the US should support Khomeini and his clerical allies. US officials were concerned that America's economic rivals, West Germany and Japan, had taken advantage of the revolutionary turmoil to supplant US influence in Iran.[125]

It is important to note that State Department officials were relying on the advice of 'experts' who had a rather superficial understanding of the Iranian political scene. For example, at a seminar held at the State Department, the participants reached the conclusion that, 'The U.S. State Department has never understood Iran, culturally, religiously, or economically. It had only meagre clues to the depth of the Iranian dissatisfaction. The few reports hinting at severe problems, were suppressed.'[126]

However, there was little doubt in the minds of US officials that Iran would be ruled by Khomeini and his allies and that the new constitution would have 'a distinctly religious cast'.[126] In late August Khomeini took several steps in order to consolidate his power-base. He combined the cabinet and the Revolutionary Council, assumed the post of supreme commander of the armed forces and issued orders for crushing the Kurdish insurgency.[128]

There is no doubt that the State Department was slow to acknowledge the emergence of Khomeini and his associates as the leading force in Iranian politics. For example, on 21 June 1979, deputy Prime Minister Abbas Amir-Entezam told US Charge D'Affaires Bruce Laingen that the Bazargan government had been 'constantly overshadowed' by radical Islamists and that Khomeini had rejected hundreds of requests to intervene in such disputes.[129] Despite such warnings from prominent Iranian officials, it was not until 20 August that Laingen reported that 'Khomeini and his entourage at Qom call all the shots', adding that the election to Iran's new leadership body, the Assembly of Experts 'symbolizes the essential rigidity of the Islamic forces in Qom'.[130] Gary Sick has held State Department officials, particularly the Director of the Iran desk, Henry Precht, responsible for the misguided policy of supporting 'moderates'.[131] According to Sick, Precht's colleagues failed to change US policy because Precht 'had the ear and the confidence of' Assistant Secretary of State for Near Eastern and South Asian Affairs, Harold Saunders.[132] Sick has gone so far as to claim that 'Henry Precht essentially ran a one-man show.'[133]

The CIA station in Iran, on the other hand, argued that Khomeini and his allies had failed to stabilize the country. The CIA believed that the US should form an alliance among groups that were becoming disaffected with Khomeini. The alliance would consist of Ayatollah Shari'atmadari's Muslim People's

Republican Party, and the National Front. However, US officials saw Khomeini as their best short-term hope of crushing leftist groups.

The CIA had concluded that the Iranian revolution had not established a 'moderate' pro-American regime in Iran. The US was facing persistent instability in Iran, increasing Soviet activity in Afghanistan and a global energy crisis. The CIA decided to galvanize support for forming a broad coalition against Khomeini, led by Ayatollah Shari'atmadari, in the event of the Carter administration's decision to change US policy towards Iran.[134]

Shari'atmadari's Muslim People's Republican Party only had a strong power-base in Azerbaijan. Nevertheless, Khomeini and his allies considered Ayatollah Shari'atmadari to be their strongest opponent.[135] The State Department and the CIA monitored the activities of Iranian generals and other opposition figures, but they quickly concluded that none of them could form a viable political force in Iran.[136]

At the same time, the CIA was trying to establish contact with officials of the revolutionary regime. One of the CIA's most productive informants was Cyrus Ramtin who was a former manager at Iranian Radio and Television. Ramtin's close relations with Ayatollah Taleghani's son, deputy Prime Minister Mostafa Chamran, and Iranian officials enabled him to supply valuable intelligence to the CIA.[137]

The CIA also attempted to put Abolhasan Bani-Sadr, who was a member of the Revolutionary Council and who later served as Iran's first president, on its pay roll. The fact that Bani-Sadr was close to Khomeini made him more valuable as a source of information. In early August 1979, one of the CIA's old Middle East hands, Vernon Cassin, posing as businessman Guy Rutherford, arrived in Tehran to establish contact with Bani-Sadr and develop him as a source of intelligence. He met Bani-Sadr three times (25, 29 August, 2 September).[138] By early September Cassin had concluded: 'An individual with the access he enjoys should be able to furnish info of value in the period ahead.'[139]

Four months after his contact with Cassin, Bani-Sadr was elected the first president of Iran. After the US embassy in Tehran was occupied, the hostage-takers published documents, saying that Bani-Sadr had been offered $1000 per month to act as an 'American company adviser'. There is no evidence that Bani-Sadr knew that Cassin was a senior CIA operative, but he later recalled that Cassin 'offered me $5,000 a month'. According to Bani-Sadr, he 'told him [Cassin] to go away'.[140]

During this period the CIA also had contacts with senior Iranian officials. In early August, John Stempel and George Cave met Deputy Prime Minister Abbas Amir-Entezam in Stockholm. Amir-Entezam was primarily concerned about internal threats to the Iranian regime, particularly those that had outside support. On 21 August, 1979, Robert Ames, one of the CIA's most experienced Middle East experts, briefed Prime Minister Mehdi Bazargan, Acting Foreign Minister Ebrahim Yazdi and Deputy Prime Minister Abbas Amir-Entezam on developments in Iraq, Afghanistan, the Arab-Israeli conflict, and Soviet policy. The participants concentrated on potential threats to the Iranian regime. US officials believed that this session had been 'well received' by the Iranians.[141]

The State Department accepts Khomeini as leader

Although US officials may have preferred to deal with the Bazargan government, they knew full well that Khomeini and the clergy would dominate Iranian politics.[142] In a long memorandum to Vance on 5 September 1979, Harold Saunders called for the establishment of a long-term relationship with a non-aligned Iran to gain access to oil and contain the Soviet Union.

Saunders argued that 'Iraq will not want to see a strong, secure Shia government in Iran'. He believed that the Soviets were cautious because they feared instability on their borders.[143] He advised Vance to recognize Khomeini as the leader of the revolution and arrange a meeting between a US representative and Khomeini despite the latter's hostility to the US. Saunders wanted to use the symbolic significance of a meeting with Khomeini to develop US contacts with other senior clerics such as Taleghani and Shari'atmadari and to assure them that the US had accepted the revolution.[144]

Saunders recommended maintaining close ties with the Iranian government because it 'might be [the] key to the future political orientation of the country'.[145] The Near Eastern Affairs Bureau (NEA) did not expect the clergy to rule Iran in the long run. NEA officials even expected Bazargan to be the first president of Iran. They also expected clerical influence to wane after Khomeini's death.[146]

The Saunders memorandum shows that the assistant secretary of state did not know who was a moderate and who was an extremist in Iran. Saunders describes Taleghani as a moderate. However, both Taleghani's sons were members of Mojahedin-e Khalq and he was very sympathetic to that organization himself. So radical was Taleghani that he was called the 'red mullah'.[147]

As early as September, Deputy Prime Minister Abbas Amir-Entezam told his CIA contact George Cave that people were being increasingly attracted to Marxism and that the Soviet Union would not tolerate the existence of an Islamic Republic. He asked Cave to provide intelligence on Soviet activities in Iran. Amir-Entezam was also concerned about the delay in exchanging ambassadors, and Cave assured him that the US had recognized the Islamic Republic. Amir-Entezam wanted to maintain contact with the US through the CIA.[148]

US officials also detected increased Soviet hostility to Khomeini. They concluded that the most effective means of containing Soviet influence was to support Khomeini.[149] On 21 September, the article of the new constitution which established the guardianship of the supreme jurisconsult was approved. However, embassy officials were still reluctant to believe that Khomeini and his clerical supporters would establish an Islamic government in the country.[150]

The US embassy in Tehran advised Washington to support the new regime and ignore Iranian émigrés, none of whom had the capability to overthrow it.[151] Vance did not believe that there were any alternatives to the new regime, and emphasized the necessity of refraining from supporting its opponents lest Iranian officials suspect the US of interfering in Iran's internal affairs.[152]

In the meantime, the CIA was trying to construct a broad anti-Khomeini coalition comprised of secular and religious 'moderates' through its collaboration with a prominent tribal leader, Khosrow Qashqai, to cultivate the National Front. Qashqai was also co-operating with the governor of the Khuzestan province, Admiral Ahmad Madani. The CIA also explored the possibility of establishing a pact between Qashqai and Ayatollah Shari'atmadari.[153]

Qashqa'i advised Madani to lead a coup d'etat against Khomeini, but he responded that the coup option was premature because the armed forces were too weak. However, the CIA made it clear to Qashqai that it would not support a coup d'etat against Khomeini.[154]

Until September, Ayatollah Beheshti and Ayatollah Lahuti were trying to persuade Khomeini to dismiss Bazargan and appoint Admiral Madani in his place, despite Beheshti's personal hostility to the admiral. Madani was alarmed at increasing Arab activities in Khuzestan.[155] Madani's problems were compounded by the fact that Defence Minister Chamran was hostile to him.[156] Khomeini, however, was satisfied with Madani's efforts to suppress the insurgency in Khuzestan. Khomeini had asked Qashqa'i to mobilize his tribe to assist Madani in defending Khuzestan.[157]

The Qashqa'is were well armed. The CIA station in Tehran reported that Qashqa'i was seeking to organize a coup d'etat against Khomeini.[158] It also reported that Shapur Bakhtiar had sent several messages to Qashqa'i, claiming that he enjoyed the support of elements in the military, Ayatollah Shari'atmadari and all of Iran's tribes, particularly the Arabs. He asked Qashqai to join his organization and offered him unlimited financial assistance. Qashqai, however, had informed the CIA that Shari'atmadari was too clever to make any commitment to Bakhtiar's programme. He believed that Bakhtiar was simply boasting.[159]

The Carter administration expands US co-operation with Iran

Secretary Vance tried to consolidate US ties with Iran. US officials held a series of meetings with Acting Iranian Foreign Minister Ebrahim Yazdi on October 3, 4, and 6, during the latter's visit to New York for the opening session of the United Nations General Assembly. Vance met Yazdi on 3 October, in what was the first meeting between senior officials of the two countries since the fall of the Shah. Vance said that the US supported 'Iran's independence and territorial integrity', and was not trying to destabilize the new regime. He suggested Iran and the United States should 'put the past behind them'.

When Yazdi enquired about US views on the future of the Shah and his assets, in a disarmingly revealing reply, Vance said that the Carter administration had told the Shah not to enter the US at this time, but he could not rule out the possibility of admitting him at some point in the future.[160] He wanted to test Yazdi's reaction to the Shah's admission into the US on medical grounds.[161] On the question of the Shah's assets, Vance advised Yazdi to pursue Iran's case against the Shah in American courts.[162]

Yazdi also met Harold Saunders, and sharply criticized the US for supporting the Shah, arguing that the US would not accept the Islamic revolution particularly because it had suffered economic losses. Yazdi declared that Iran had to be treated with 'equality and respect', adding that the way that the military issues had been dealt with suggested that there might have been a 'conspiracy against Iran'. US officials hoped that Yazdi's colleagues may have appreciated US 'sincerity'. However, even Saunders, who was keen on improving relations with revolutionary Iran, had to express concern about the violation of the rights of minorities and others in Iran.[163]

Senior State and Defence Department officials also met Yazdi and his assistants to discuss the issue of Iranian arms purchases and military cooperation.[164] Interestingly, during his stay in New York, Yazdi argued that the establishment of a theocracy 'would have 'no effect' on the representative character of the Islamic Republic'. He said that the president and the Majlis would exercise 'real political power'.[165] An American who had contacts with Iranian radicals observed that 'Yazdi aspires to the presidency.'[166] At a meeting with Khomeini in Qom to report to Khomeini on his meeting with Vance, Yazdi said that Vance had expressed support for the new regime. Khomeini, however, was already aware of the State Department's consideration of the possibility of admitting the Shah into the US. Khomeini jibed: 'Do you mean they didn't tell you about the Shah's going to America?'[167] Khomeini was informed of the State Department's policy by the clerics in the IRP who had access to documents provided by a highly-placed spy at the US embassy code-named Hafez.[168]

Soviet pressure on Iran

By October Iranian-Soviet relation had sharply deteriorated. In a conversation with East German leader, Erich Honecker, Soviet leader Leonid Brezhnev accused Iranian leaders of persecuting 'progressive forces' and trying to 'ruthlessly suppress the activities of national minorities'. According to Brezhnev, Iranian leaders were trying to 'blame us for the instigation of the activities'. The Soviet leader informed his East German counterpart that Soviet efforts to establish good relations with Iran were 'currently not gaining any practical results in Tehran'. However, Soviet policy was still aimed at improving relations with Iran because the Iranian revolution had 'undercut the military alliance between Iran and the USA' and also because Iran had been 'taking anti-imperialist positions'. According to Brezhnev, Soviet policy was also aimed at countering US efforts to 'regain its influence in the region'.[169]

Many Iranian officials suspected the Soviet Union of interfering in Kurdistan and fomenting secessionist tendencies among other minorities. For example Soviet ambassador Vinogradov told Charge d'affaires Laingen that Ayatollah Taleghani had complained to him that the Soviet Union was destabilizing Kurdistan. Vinogradov claimed that his country did not want to contribute to the dismemberment of Iran because this 'would leave a number of small and weak states on the Soviet southern border'. After Vinogradov's controversial meeting with Taleghani, the latter agreed 'to say something positive about Soviet interests in Iran. His death had prevented that'.[170]

Vinogradov had told Iranian officials, including Acting Foreign Minister Yazdi, that the Iranian government should emulate Lenin and offer Iran's minorities the right of secession. The Bazargan government, however, disagreed with him. Vinogradov later described Khomeini as 'a rigid personality with whom it was difficult to have a dialogue but nonetheless a very able man'. However, he opined that Khomeini's concept of an Islamic state 'was unrealistic for the long term'.[171] Iranian officials' failure to respond adequately to Vinogradov's threats reflected the weakness of the revolutionary regime.

The State Department's efforts to maintain relations with Iran

Although the State Department was considering the Shah's admission to the US, it continued to work for better relations with the Iranian regime. The chief of the Iran desk Henry Precht argued that because no group had the capability to overthrow the new regime, the US should seek to 'moderate the policies of the present regime'. Precht believed that a theocracy was not viable in the long run. He wanted to strengthen the military and 'moderate religious and secular groups'.

Precht wanted the administration to take measures to alleviate Iranians' suspicions. The State Department had already taken several measures to build a new relationship with Iran such as the releasing of military spare parts in the pipeline, Iranian purchase of spares, and contributing to the resolution of commercial disputes.[172]

The State Department had still not succeeded in appointing an ambassador to Iran mainly because clerics were reluctant to talk to US officials.[173] Precht argued that the French 'given their past assistance to Khomeini, would be in the best position' to approach Khomeini and 'to suggest very gently' to Khomeini that Bazargan needed help to contain communism.[174]

Precht believed that Iraq was probably destabilizing Iran by permitting Kurdish insurgents to use its territory. He recommended that the French and the Germans make separate approaches to Iraq to reduce the pressure on the Bazargan government.[175] Precht even claimed that the government was committed to promoting freedom of the press, free elections, and greater autonomy for provinces.[176]

US intelligence contacts with Iran

In mid-October one of the CIA's most experienced Iran experts George Cave, along with Charge d'affaires Bruce Laingen and energy specialist Ron Smith met representatives of the Bazargan government. The Iranians were represented by Acting Foreign Minister Ebrahim Yazdi and Iranian ambassador to Sweden Abbas Amir Entezam.[177]

The Iranians were unconvinced by Smith's presentation on the Soviet Union's energy problems and his argument that this posed a threat to the Persian Gulf.[178] Yazdi and Amir-Entezam were mainly concerned about the situation in Kurdistan. Yazdi believed that Iraq, Israel and possibly the US were co-operating in destabilizing Kurdistan. He was unconvinced by Laingen's argument that the US did not have an interest in destabilizing Kurdistan because it wanted to maintain the uninterrupted flow of oil. Yazdi argued that the CIA might have been involved in a covert operation in Kurdistan.[179]

In their reports US officials spoke of Yazdi's deep 'paranoia'. Yazdi thought the meeting was a fiasco. Amir-Entezam later met alone with Cave to say that what the Iranians really needed was intelligence on the Kurdish situation.[180]

Cave 'apparently successfully' convinced Amir-Entezam that Israel was not co-operating with Iraq. He told Amir-Entezam that there was 'some evidence' that Iraq was supporting the Kurds, but that Iraq would certainly not want an independent Iranian Kurdish state. Cave suggested that Iran should try to deal with the situation by co-operating with Turkey. He later reported that 'while it may seem incredible, what they really want is for us to devise solutions to their problems'.[181] A few days later, the occupation of the US embassy in Tehran abruptly brought intelligence contacts between the two countries to a halt.

11

US STRATEGIES AND THE IRANIAN HOSTAGE CRISIS

The Iranian hostage crisis dealt a severe blow to the Carter administration's attempt to re-establish ties with Iran. The crisis widened the division between the advocates of neo-containment and those of détente and new world order in the administration. National Security Adviser Zbigniew Brzezinski and Secretary of Defence Harold Brown tried to persuade President Carter to move against Ayatollah Khomeini and to increase US military presence in the Persian Gulf and Southwest Asia. Secretary Vance and his State Department colleagues, on the other hand, continued their efforts to maintain relations with the new regime, even though the evidence indicated that Khomeini was unwilling or unable to purge radical elements.

The Shah's admission into the US

Carter and the State Department had refused to permit the Shah to enter the US because they feared that his admission would have an adverse effect on relations with Iran. As early as 6 March, the State Department's head of Iran Desk, Henry Precht, had warned that the Shah's arrival in the US would be 'a disaster for US-Iranian relations', and pose a 'severe' security problem for US officials in Iran.[1]

Thus, when David Rockefeller's network informed the administration that the Shah was ill, Washington asked the US embassy in Tehran for an evaluation of the political situation. Embassy officials, including US Charge d'affaires Bruce Laingen, replied that US diplomats could be taken hostage.[2]

The Shah, who was living in Mexico, distrusted the Americans and was not keen on going back to the US. Kissinger and David Rockefeller persuaded him that Mexico did not possess the facilities to treat him.[3] The evidence suggests that Carter finally agreed to allow the Shah to go to the US despite his awareness that US diplomats might be taken hostage. What changed Carter's mind was undoubtedly the political pressure exerted on him by Kissinger and Rockefeller.[4] There is no evidence that US officials attempted to corroborate the Shah's condition independently and Carter decided to proceed before the safety of US diplomats could be guaranteed.[5] The head of the Iran desk at the State Department, Henry Precht, who was visiting Iran, was instructed to assure Iranian officials that the US had no intention of overthrowing the new regime.[6] On 21 October, Laingen and Precht met Prime Minister Bazargan and Acting

Foreign Minister Ebrahim Yazdi who did not believe that the Shah had cancer. The Iranian officials said that the Shah's admission into the US would cause serious problems[7] and they demanded that the Carter administration permit Iranian doctors to examine the Shah.

Bazargan and Yazdi preferred the Shah to be treated in Europe or Texas where they believed he would not be able to plan a coup.[8] Laingen and Precht agreed to give the names of two Iranian doctors identified by Yazdi to the Shah's doctors.[9] Laingen asked Bazargan and Yazdi to strengthen the embassy's security,[10] and Bazargan agreed to help.[11]

Iranian officials were still interested in intelligence co-operation with the US and saw such co-operation as a test of US sincerity. Yazdi suspected Israel and Iraq of destabilizing the country.[12] Precht and Laingen agreed to share intelligence with Iran, but said that the US had no intelligence that Israel was destabilizing Iran. Precht told Yazdi that 'we see no viable alternative to the present government'.[13]

On the same day, Carter decided to admit the Shah into the US. What finally convinced Carter was probably the Rockefeller network's report to the State Department, claiming that the Mexican President Lopez Portillo would grant the Shah political asylum.[14] However, Press Secretary Jody Powell later admitted someone in Rockefeller's office could have invented the story.[15] Moreover, the Carter administration rejected a suggestion by Bazargan and Yazdi that the Shah should be asked to go to Texas.[16]

On 24 October, the Shah's doctors operated on him to remove the gallstones that had caused his jaundice. They missed one stone and a doctor had to be flown in from Canada to carry out another complex operation, thereby exploding the myth that the Shah could have only been treated in the United States.[17]

Question of Iranian regime's stability

Iranian officials believed that there were plots against the regime. They were particularly perturbed by Senator Henry Jackson's prediction that the revolution would inevitably fail and that Iran was about to disintegrate. US diplomats in Tehran were 'horrified' by Jackson's comments. Iranian officials believed Jackson's statement meant that the US had a plan to dismember Iran.[18] Ayatollah Beheshti told Laingen and Precht that he was mainly concerned about monarchist 'counter-revolutionary activities'.[19]

One thing that nearly all State Department policy-makers agreed upon was avoiding contacts with Iranian exiles and removing the issue of human rights from the agenda.[20] Like most US officials, the CIA station chief in Iran, Thomas Ahern, was primarily concerned about leftist activities even though he observed that the left had not been particularly successful.[21] Ahern did not believe that Khomeini could contain communist influence in Iran, and proposed to form a coalition of westernized politicians, military officers and moderate clerics who could form a coalition around Ayatollah Shari'atmadari.[22] Ahern's proposal was too late.

Iranian reactions to the admission of the Shah into the US

Khomeini's initial reaction to the announcement of Carter's decision to permit the Shah to enter the US was rather subdued.[23] However, Khomeini saw the

Shah's arrival in the US as a plot to force him to abdicate in favour of his son.[24] In late October, he began to describe his opponents as 'traitors. . . dependent on the West'. He declared: 'Those American-loving rotten brains must be purged from the nation.'[25]

On 31 October, Khomeini called for a mass demonstration at the American embassy the following day. That same day, an Iranian Foreign Ministry official, Parsa Kia, urged a US embassy political officer to persuade Washington to ask the Shah to leave the US. Parsa Kia said that the Bazargan government feared a coup d'etat and that Khomeini and other clerics might do something rash and cause a major crisis, even possibly the severance of relations.[26]

Brzezinski-Bazargan meeting

Bazargan believed that Brzezinski was the main enemy of revolutionary Iran and he arranged to meet him in Algeria where both of them were due to attend Algeria's national day celebrations. Bazargan wanted to persuade Brzezinski to support close relations between the two countries.[27] Moreover, Laingen 'urged that Brzezinski or others in the U.S. delegation meet with the Iranians'.[28]

In order to demonstrate Iran's non-aligned status, Bazargan declared on 1 November that Iran would abrogate the 1959 Iran-US Mutual Assistance Agreement and 'certain offending clauses' in the 1921 Iranian-Soviet treaty. Moreover, the Iranian Foreign Ministry formally expressed its opposition to the Shah's presence in the US. However, Foreign Ministry officials privately informed the US embassy 'outside pressures' had led the ministry to make such a statement.[29]

On 1 November, Brzezinski met Bazargan, Acting Foreign Minister Ebrahim Yazdi, and Defence Minister Mostafa Chamran in Algiers. Vance has claimed that he was surprised to learn that Brzezinski had met Bazargan and Yazdi.[30] The documentary evidence, however, indicates that the State Department had actually organized the meeting! Brzezinski was conciliatory, declaring: 'The American government is prepared to expand security, economic, political, and intelligence relationships at your pace.'[31]

Bazargan and Yazdi raised the issue of the Shah and his assets. Yazdi 'mocked the idea that the Shah sought asylum for medical reasons'. Brzezinski was furious and responded that 'this discussion is humiliating and demeaning. I am not certain whether it is more humiliating for me to listen or for you to raise this'.[32]

Communists within the Algerian FLN informed the Tudeh Party of Bazargan's meeting with Brzezinski. The Tudeh Party, in turn, informed other radical Iranian groups of the meeting in Algiers. These groups later took part in occupying the US embassy.[33] After the meeting, the Iranian officials were filmed shaking hands and chatting with Brzezinski. The head of the Iranian Radio and Television Organization, Sadegh Ghotbzadeh, ordered the media to show the encounter. The hard-liners in Iran claimed that Khomeini had not been informed of the meeting.[34] According to Abolhasan Bani-Sadr, Khomeini believed that Bazargan wanted to open a separate channel of communications with the US.[35]

Preparations for attacking the US embassy

On 1 November, a crowd of some 3,500 people marched in front of the US embassy protesting at the Shah's presence in the US. During the rally, Khomeini's office released a statement, calling on students to 'expand their attacks against the United States and Israel, so that they may force the U.S. to return the deposed and criminal Shah'.[36] However, before the group could attack the embassy, leftist students and the government re-routed the demonstration to prevent supporters of right-wing clerics from taking over the embassy.[37] US diplomats, however, did not request additional protection for the embassy.

On 2 November, Khomeini referred to the Shah's presence in the US as a conspiracy, calling on the US to hand over Iran's 'enemy'.[38] The Students Following the Line of the Imam had decided to attack the US embassy on 4 November. When the Revolutionary Guards protecting the embassy were informed of the attack, they helped the assailants by withdrawing their forces[39] and the students later officially thanked them.[40] The Iranian hostage crisis was to become Jimmy Carter's nightmare.

The question of Khomeini's motive

Carter administration officials have argued that Khomeini either had foreknowledge of or approved of the hostage seizure.[41] Both groups have portrayed Khomeini as the central figure that directed events both before and after the hostage seizure. Cyrus Vance, Gary Sick and Harold Saunders have also explained the power struggle in terms of a clash between secular elements and the clerical establishment. Zbigniew Brzezinski has blamed Iranian extremists for holding US diplomats hostage. However, he held Khomeini responsible for what happened and he repeatedly advised Carter to take measures to overthrow him.[42]

In Iran, some observers argued that Khomeini capitalized on the hostage crisis to consolidate the Islamists' position by describing the seizure of the hostages as Iran's 'second revolution'. For example, a prominent cleric, Hadi Modaressi, who was close to Khomeini, observed that in order to radicalize the masses rapidly 'we wish and we welcome military aggression against us because it strengthens the revolution and rallies the masses around it'.[43] Analysts of the hostage crisis also tend to perceive Khomeini as the main actor on the Iranian side. One group of analysts such as Christos Ioannides, Richard Thornton, Stephen Walt and Sa'id Amir-Arjomand have argued that conservative clerics ordered the militants to take US diplomats hostage to prepare the ground for the removal of the Bazargan government.[44] Another group of analysts including Ruhollah Ramazani, Sepehr Zabih, James Bill, and Richard Cottam have argued that Khomeini took advantage of the militants' action to establish a theocracy.[45] More recently, Kenneth Pollack has argued that Khomeini supported the seizure of hostages because of his 'obsessive hatred for the United States' and also because he wanted to divert the Iranian people's attention from Iran's serious internal problems.[46] Other recent studies by David Farber, David Harris and Mark Bowden do not really add much to our knowledge of the hostage crisis or Khomeini's role.[47] Harris's study does not even contain the names of Mohammad Musari-Kho'iniha and Mohammad Hosseini-Beheshti in its index – an astonishing omission given the fact that both men played central roles in the hostage crisis.[48] Christos Inoannides's account of the crisis is the most valuable from a historical point of view if only because he managed to interview the militants. His study also influenced subsequent interpretations of the crisis.

A Critique of Ioannides's explanation of hostage crisis

According to Ioannides, senior clerics in the Islamic Republican Party (IRP), Ayatollah Beheshti, Hojjat ol-Eslam Mohammad Javad Bahonar, Hojjat ol-Eslam Ali Khamene'i and Hojjat ol-Eslam Akbar Hashemi-Rafsanjani knew that the Carter administration was considering the possibility of admitting the Shah into the United States. State Department documents were provided to the aforementioned clerics by a highly-placed spy in the US embassy, code-named Hafez. By mid-September they were in possession of several documents, including a memorandum written by Henry Precht, which predicted that US diplomats would be taken hostage if the Shah were admitted into the US.[49]

The IRP clerics informed Khomeini of the State Department's deliberations.[50] According to Ioannides, the Shah's early admission to the US frightened them and they decided to organize an attack against the embassy using a demonstration as a pretext to enable their agents to enter the embassy compound.[51] Again according to Ioannides, Beheshti tried desperately to pre-empt a leftist take-over of the embassy because of his own contacts with the US, which made him vulnerable to attacks by his opponents.[52]

The most serious error in Ioannides's argument is his assumption that the leader of the Students Following the Line of the Imam, Mohammad Musavi-Kho'iniha, was close to Beheshti and Rafsanjani and the Islamic Coalition Society.[53] Ioannides has even speculated that Kho'iniha discussed his plans with Beheshti and Bahonar.[54] Unfortunately, his account has also influenced the interpretations of others such as Ofira Seliktar who, despite her awareness of Kho'iniha's leftist connections, has speculated that Kho'iniha had access to the embassy's cable traffic because of his association with the aforementioned figures and that he might have provided intelligence to the hostage-takers.[55]

In fact, Kho'iniha was a leftist and fiercely anti-American cleric and the vast majority of the hostage-takers were radical Islamists whose views were diametrically opposite to those of Beheshti, Bahonar and Rafsanjani. Kho'iniha was one of Khomeini's radical students and he was close to Khomeini's son, Ahmad.[56] His association with the students ensured that they would not be labelled communists.[57] Dilip Hiro has argued that Ahmad Khomeini planned the occupation of the US embassy and that Kho'iniha was acting on his instructions.[58] However, the evidence suggests that Kho'iniha planned the attack. Ahmad Khomeini must have protected Kho'iniha. Khomeini changed his mind several times during the crisis, indicating that his motives were different from those of Kho'iniha.

An alternative explanation of the hostage crisis

Despite the fact that Khomeini described the occupation of the US embassy as Iran's second revolution, no Iranian official has claimed that Khomeini ordered or had foreknowledge of the embassy take-over. In fact, Kho'iniha has said that he did not inform Khomeini because he believed that Khomeini would not approve of their action.

Kho'iniha's account of Khomeini's opposition to such a take-over has been corroborated by none other than Ebrahim Yazdi, who was trying to maintain Iran's ties with the US under adverse conditions. According to Yazdi, Khomeini initially told him to get the students out of the embassy.[59] During the first three days of the hostage crisis, Khomeini was 'very angry' with the students and felt that their action was likely to provoke a confrontation with the US and endanger the revolution.[60]

According to an account by one of the hostage takers, 'It was the presence of Mr Kho'iniha that enabled us to resist.'[61] During the hostage crisis Khomeini made contradictory statements and changed his position on key issues.[62] By focusing on Khomeini's role analysts have lost sight of other forces that caused and perpetuated the hostage crisis.

There was simply no need for the Islamic Republic Party (IRP) to provoke a crisis with the US to institutionalize the Islamic Republic. There was no need to overthrow the Bazargan government either. Two weeks before the occupation of the embassy, the government had informed the Revolutionary Council that if Khomeini and the Revolutionary Council refused to support it, it would resign. The day before the embassy was occupied, the cabinet office approved the resignation of the Bazargan government.[63]

Radical organizations and the dynamics of the power struggle

All the accounts of the hostage crisis have ignored the far more significant conflict between Ayatollah Beheshti and radical clerics such as Kho'iniha.[64] This was symptomatic of the factional conflict within the IRP where the conservative Islamic Coalition Society and the Hojjatieh were pitted against the left-wing of the Mojahedin of the Islamic Revolution and radical clerics.

The Hojjatieh and the Islamic Coalition Society were primarily associated with bazaar merchants and businessmen.[65] Until the summer of 1981, the Hojjatieh group which included Beheshti and Mohammad Javad Bahonar, dominated the IRP.[66] Hojjatieh downplayed the importance of exporting the revolution and advocated strengthening the regime in Iran.[67]

The radicals had representatives among the militant students and younger clerics and Revolutionary Guards Corps. They wanted to align Iran with the Soviet Union at the global level and export the revolution at the regional level. However, in 1979, factionalism within the IRP had not become apparent to outsiders.[68]

The Islamic left charged that the Hojjatieh was representative of 'American Islam' and had taken no part in overthrowing the Shah.[69] The main factions involved in the hostage seizure were the Mojahedin of the Islamic Revolution and Habibollah Peyman's the Combatant Muslims Movement. There is some evidence that the Fada'iyan-e Eslam, a Islamist terrorist group involved in several assassinations in the 1940s and 1950s, was also represented among the militants.[70] Perhaps the reason that Khomeini vacillated during the hostage crisis was that he had close ties to both the IRP factions involved in the power struggle.

The Mojahedin of the Islamic Revolution

The leaders of the militants who stormed the embassy were Mohsen Mirdamadi, Abbas Abdi, Mohammad Ebrahim Asgharzadeh and Ma'sumeh Ebtekar.[71] They were close to the Mojahedin of the Islamic Revolution (MIR) and the leftist wing of the IRP, which later formed the Militant Clerics

Association in 1988. MIR members had broken away from the Mojahedin-e Khalq because they placed greater emphasis on the role of religion in politics. However, much of their programme was leftist.[72]

The MIR was a coalition of six small paramilitary organizations: *Fallah, Movaheddin, Falaq, Omat-e Vahedeh, Mansurun,* and *Tawhidi-Saf, Badr,* formed on 4 April, 1979. *Tawhidi Saf, Falaq* and *Mansurun* had been the most active urban guerrilla groups in Iran during the revolution.[73] MIR members claimed that they revered Khomeini and accepted his 'radical' political ideology.[74] However, their political platform opposed the involvement of all clerics, conservative and radical, in government.[75]

The left wing of the MIR was particularly opposed to conservative clerics such as Beheshti who supported free enterprise, relations with the West and export of revolution by example rather than by force.[76] However, the right-wing of the MIR was close to right-wing clerics, such as Beheshti and Rafsanjani, as well as bazaar merchants.

The most important reason for the formation of the MIR was the clerics' distrust of the armed forces. In fact, Beheshti and Rafsanjani encouraged the MIR to form a unified command.[77] The MIR formed the backbone of the Revolutionary Guards Corps (IRGC).[78] One of the founders of the MIR was Behzad Nabavi who was also a founder of the IRGC. Nabavi was an engineer who went to jail in 1971 as a Marxist and came out in 1978 as a follower of Khomeini.[79] He would later play a key role in negotiations with the US.

Several members of the MIR occupied key positions in the IRGC. For example, Mohsen Reza'i became its commander.[80] The MIR had several thousand armed members who would later play an important role in suppressing leftist guerrilla groups and purging the armed forces.[81] The MIR members had close ties with the PLO which informed them that the Shah's admission into the US was part of a plot to overthrow the new regime.[82]

The Combatant Muslims' Movement

Habibollah Peyman led the Combatant Muslims' Movement. Previously, Peyman had been a member of the guerrilla group, Jama, which was an offshoot of the Liberation Movement. Peyman had been sentenced to 20 years imprisonment for his involvement in attempts to overthrow the Shah. After the revolution, Peyman attached himself to the IRP and the Tudeh Party.[83] He also had ties with the PLO, and members of the Mojahedin-e Khalq Organization. Peyman's armed group had been involved in the embassy seizure on 14 February.[84] However, Peyman later denied that he was the leader of the hostage-takers.[85]

Peyman believed that Iran should pursue a Pan-Islamic foreign policy to prevent the US from defeating the revolution[86] and believed that the masses should establish relations with 'oppressed' masses such as the Palestinians, the Black Americans, Africans, etc.

Leftist groups and the question of Soviet influence

Interviews with the hostage-takers later revealed that many of them were leftists and some of them openly criticized Khomeini. They declared that Bazargan whom they saw as pro-American, was deceiving Khomeini.[87] One of the leaders of the students was a girl known as 'Mary', who declared: 'We don't accept the Cabinet, and if everyone listens to the Ayatollah, we won't have a revolutionary republic. Iran is not just for the mullahs.'[88] Mary was later identified as Ma'sumeh Ebtekar, who was a vice-president in the government of Mohammad Khatami.

The skill with which the hostage-takers interrogated the hostages and organized huge rallies led many observers to conclude that non-Iranians were involved in the operation. The most frequently mentioned outside group was George Habbash's Popular Movement for the Liberation of Palestine (PFLP). In fact, the hostage-takers later published documents on Habbash's involvement in destabilizing Khuzestan, indicating that they distrusted him.[89]

There have also been reports that Soviet intelligence agents played a role in planning the hostage seizure because some of the hostage-takers were graduates of Soviet training centres in Czechoslovakia and East Germany.[90] According to former CIA official Miles Copeland, an officer of Israel's foreign intelligence service, the Mossad, told him that the Mossad had identified half of the hostage-takers and that they were guided by ten or fifteen older persons who were KGB agents or mercenaries motivated by financial considerations.[91]

No evidence has surfaced as yet of the involvement of mercenaries. However, Bazargan and Bani-Sadr have both said that leftists and communists had infiltrated the ranks of the Student Following the Line of the Imam.[92] According to John Stempel, leftists, including Cherikha-ye Fada'iy-e Khalq, played an important role in the occupation of the US embassy.[93] After the seizure of the hostages, the Cherikha-ye Fada'i-ye Khalq resurfaced and strongly supported the hostage-takers to prevent a rapprochement between Iran and the US and facilitate a leftist take-over.[94]

The Tudeh Party also supported the hostage seizure. The party launched a massive propaganda campaign to persuade Iranian leaders to abrogate the 1959 Iranian-American security treaty, and to purge the armed forces of 'counter-revolutionary' elements.[95]

The premise behind the Tudeh's strategy was identifying and gaining control of the centre of gravity of the system.[96] In order to do so, they first had to help the IRP establish a theocracy in Iran.[97] Tudeh leader Nureddin Kianuri contended that Islamists would inevitably fail and the Tudeh would take power.[98]

However, the operation to occupy the US embassy in Tehran was planned and carried out by leftist Islamist organizations, which had their own ideologies. The hostage-takers were protected by their mentor Hojjatoleslam Mohammad Musavi-Kho'iniha.

Mohammad Musavi-Kho'iniha and the hostage seizure

The leader of the hostage captors, Kho'iniha, was close to the Soviet ambassador to Iran, Vinogradov, and he managed to establish contact between the radical students and the Soviet embassy. Some authors have described Kho'iniha as a KGB agent.[99] Others have argued that Kho'iniha had attended Patrice Lumumba University in Moscow and that he was sympathetic to the Tudeh Party.[100] Indeed, Egyptian journalist Mohammad Heikal met representatives of the hostage-takers at the Soviet embassy.[101] However, so far, no evidence has surfaced that Kho'iniha was a KGB agent.

Kho'iniha's pro-Soviet sympathies may well have prevented an attack on the Soviet embassy. According to Mohammad Ebrahim Asgharzadeh, one of the leaders of the Students following the Line of the Imam, five students attended the first planning meeting. Two of them wanted to attack the Soviet embassy because the Soviet Union was 'a Marxist and anti-God regime'. However, two other students Mohsen Mirdamadi and Habibollah Bitaraf supported Asgharzadeh's view that the US embassy must be temporarily occupied in protest at US policy towards Iran.[102] Subsequent events showed that the students were far more anti-American than anti-Soviet. Indeed, as we shall see, their selective use of US embassy documents to discredit politicians who favoured close relations with the US was rather like a Soviet-inspired active measures campaign.

Kho'iniha represented a populist current of opinion in Iran which found favour with the Soviet leadership. He has been remarkably frank about his role in the operation. He emerged as a leader of the reform movement in Iran in the 1990s. His newspaper *Salam*, which was shut down in 1999, frequently published articles and reports sharply criticizing injustice in the Islamic Republic.

Kho'iniha has argued that the hostage seizure must be understood in terms of the circumstances in 1979 and that the same people would definitely not take the same measures in 2000.[103] He has argued, however, that those involved in the seizure of the hostages feared a repetition of the CIA-backed 1953 coup d'etat which restored the Shah.[104]

At the time of the hostage seizure there were three CIA officials at the embassy. They were; the CIA station chief, Thomas Ahern, Bill Daugherty and Malcolm Kalp. None of these men had been in the country for more than four months and none of them could even speak Persian.[105] Ahern subsequently criticized the CIA for its failure to predict the fall of the Shah. He contended that the agency was so preoccupied with espionage that it failed to take note of the growing opposition to the monarch. He also lambasted the embassy and the administration for their failure to produce any reliable estimates on the future of Iran in 1979, adding that Washington merely wanted the embassy to be optimistic and support politicians such as Bazargan and Yazdi in the hopes of 'moderating or helping them moderate the regressive tendencies of the regime'.[106] In fact, as we saw in an earlier chapter, by the summer of 1979 senior State Department officials, such as Assistant Secretary of State for Near Eastern and South Asian Affairs, Harold Saunders, had come to the conclusion that the US had to work with Khomeini.

It is not clear from Kho'iniha's account how the hostage seizure would have helped Iran's case unless one assumes that the hostages were to serve as bargaining chips in complex negotiations. In fact, this is what happened later. Many years afterwards, the leaders of the militants claimed that their aim was to stage a brief sit-in, between three and seven days, to protest at the Shah's admission into the US.[107] The leader of the Students Following the Line of the Imam, Ebrahim Asgharzadeh, informed his associates that the attack on the embassy would not resemble the one in February. He likened that attack to a 'terrorist act or military action'. Asgharzadeh argued that this time around, they should plan for something like the civil disobedience campaign against the Shah.[108] According to David Harris, Asgharzadeh and his associates intended to occupy the embassy for 48 to 72 hours unless they were driven out of the building by the Bazargan government. They would try to capitalize on the publicity generated by the seizure of the embassy to 'articulate their grievances against the United States'.[109]

The Students Following the Line of the Imam did not expect to be supported enthusiastically by the regime or receive global media coverage.[110] Massoumeh Ebtekar has also said that they had only prepared for a three-day take-over. However, according to Ebtekar, the militants expected Khomeini to approve of their action.[111] According to Mark Bowden, who interviewed some of the militants long after the occupation of the embassy, Kho'iniha had his own agenda which was to establish an Islamic Republic by fomenting anti-Americanism in the country.[112] However, as we saw earlier, Khomeini and his closest advisers had already gone a long way towards establishing a theocracy. The key issue as far as Kho'iniha was concerned, was Iran's foreign policy orientation. Some clerics, such as Ayatollah Beheshti, wanted to maintain close relations with the US. Kho'iniha, however, saw the crisis as an opportunity to sever the ties between the two countries. This is the key issue as far as Kho'iniha's role is concerned.

Remaining true to Iran's conspiratorial tradition, former Iranian President Abolhasan Bani-Sadr, now living in exile in France, has argued that the hostage crisis was an American plot to re-establish US influence in Iran and Khomeini exploited the crisis to consolidate his position and defeat opponents of theocracy.[113] According to Bani-Sadr, the Students Following the Line of the Imam were controlled by a five-man committee whose members were Bani-Sadr, Hojjatoleslam Seyyed-Ali Khamene'i, Hojjatoleslam Mohammad Musavi-Kho'iniha, Hojjatoleslam Mojtahed-Shabastari and Ayatollah Musavi-Ardebili. Again according to Bani-Sadr, during the meetings of the Revolutionary Council, it became clear that only Kho'iniha had foreknowledge of the operation. Bani-Sadr says that Kho'iniha instructed the students to occupy the embassy and said that Khomeini would approve of their action afterwards.[114]

Khomeini's call on the students to attack US interests on the anniversary of the army's attack on Tehran university (1 November 1979) led the students to believe that Kho'iniha had discussed the matter with Khomeini. However, Kho'iniha had not informed Khomeini of the plan at all.[115] Bazargan has also said that Khomeini had no foreknowledge of what happened.[116]

Kho'iniha's own account essentially confirms Bani-Sadr's and Bazargan's accounts.[117] However, Kho'iniha promised the militants that he would discuss the matter with Khomeini.[118] It was not until after the take-over that the hostage-takers realized that Kho'iniha had not done so.[119]

The available evidence suggests that Kho'iniha saw the seizure of the hostages as a means of preventing the US from moving against the Iranian regime. He also used the documents seized in the US embassy to convince Khomeini to carry out a massive purge of advocates of maintaining relations with the US.

The Carter administration's response to the hostage seizure

President Carter and the State Department believed that the militants had no intention of staging a prolonged occupation of the embassy.[120] Vance later claimed that the militants took advantage of Brzezinski's meeting with Bazargan and Yazdi in Algiers to implement their own policies.[121] Vance's account, however, is misleading and self-serving. As we saw earlier, the State Department had actually organized the meeting.

Gary Sick warned Brzezinski that the hostage crisis was symptomatic of the conflict between secularists and the clergy, that Khomeini was quite prepared to get rid of the Bazargan government immediately and that he sought to politically exploit the issue of the Shah's presence in the US to unify the factions in Iran. He encouraged Brzezinski to consider the option of overthrowing Khomeini and the Iranian regime.[122] Nevertheless, Sick proposed that the US send a special emissary to Khomeini to persuade him to release the hostages.[123]

Brzezinski proposed sending 'a private emissary to Khomeini', but Carter was 'visibly reluctant' do so.[124] At a meeting of the Special Co-ordination Committee [SCC] on the Iranian hostage crisis on 5 November, all participants agreed that the rivalry between the 'moderates' and the 'extremists' had caused the crisis.[125]

The SCC decided to communicate with Khomeini and IRP mullahs directly, and former Attorney-General Ramsey Clarke, and William Miller, the staff director of the Senate Select Committee on Intelligence, were selected for this purpose.[126] Moreover, under Brzezinski's direction, the SCC began to consider contingency plans for military action in the event of the hostages being harmed or of Iran's disintegration. The planning concentrated on a rescue mission, punitive responses to hostile Iranian actions, and safeguarding the oil fields in south-western Iran.[127]

On 5 November, optimism about the success of the negotiations seemed warranted. Charge d'affaires Bruce Laingen spoke with Ayatollah Beheshti and asked him to urge the militants to release the hostages. Beheshti blamed the US for ignoring his warnings. He was reluctant to get involved but agreed that the hostages should be released immediately and unconditionally.[128]

That night, the State Department established contact with Beheshti who welcomed the idea of receiving an emissary. He promised to report the suggestion to the Revolutionary Council and inform the US of the outcome the following day. The State Department and Vance then briefed Clark and Miller on the situation and gave them their instructions.[129] Beheshti's behaviour indicates that at this stage he had no intention of using the crisis to purge his so-called 'secularist' rivals.

However, there was disagreement among State Department officials over the issue of sending emissaries to Iran.[130] Henry Precht believed that the Iranians had to resolve the crisis and argued that Carter should not get involved in the negotiations. Vance sought to define US policy. Precht was persuaded to draft a letter which 'was very forthcoming and tried to convey understanding of the revolution'. However, when the letter was sent to the White House, officials there changed the tone of the letter and made it 'more threatening'.[131]

On the same day, the PLO contacted the White House and the State Department through an intermediary and offered to mediate between Iran and the US. The PLO representatives were 'quietly encouraged'.[132] However, the Carter administration was well aware of the fact that the PLO sought to enhance its own reputation in the US.[133]

Laingen, who was not a hostage, had persuaded the Revolutionary Council to meet Clark and Miller.[134] By the time Carter and US officials met on the morning of 6 November to discuss the crisis, senior Iranian clerics had expressed their support for the hostage-takers. However, this did not necessarily mean, as Sick has claimed, 'that the original hopes of a quick solution to the crisis were no longer realistic'.[135]

In fact, Carter was informed that Clark and Miller were on their way and that the PLO had started to 'mediate' between Iran and the US. Despite these efforts, Brzezinski and Secretary of Defence Harold Brown contended that the US should threaten Khomeini.[136] This was a dramatic volte-face because the mediators had not even reached Tehran yet!

Brown said that if the Iranians murdered the hostages, the US should be prepared to occupy the Kharg island oil terminal and destroy Iran's oil production facilities.[137] By now it should have been clear to Carter that Brzezinski and Brown wanted to prolong the crisis to further their strategic objectives, namely, the build-up of US power in the Persian Gulf, overthrowing Khomeini and unifying the Western Alliance by threatening military action against Iran.

Carter disagreed with Brzezinski and Brown. He felt that any hostile US reaction could endanger the lives of the hostages. He instructed the State Department to persuade all Americans to leave Iran. He rejected Brown's recommendation, saying that 'it risked shutting down the world's oil supply from the Persian Gulf.[138] Carter argued that although it was possible to bomb the oilfields and Qom, that would not necessarily force the students to release the hostages. Brzezinski replied that the US only had to 'make the threat credible'. Vance disagreed with him. He recommended sending a message to the Iranians saying that they would be expected to guarantee the safety of Americans in Iran.[139]

Carter said that there should be no public statement except that the Iranians had guaranteed to protect the well-being of Americans. Carter thought that the presence of a few US officials would not prevent Iran from drifting into the Soviet camp. He felt that the Iranian regime 'could kill our people at any time'. He wanted to negotiate the release of hostages and sever US ties with Iran. He also wanted to cut off the supply of all military spares, examine the possibility of expelling all Iranian students, and expropriating Iranian assets in the United States.[140]

The President made it clear that under no circumstances would he agree to the Shah's extradition. However, much of the SCC meeting on 6 November was devoted to the discussion of the repercussions of an Iranian oil cut-off. Carter instructed his advisers to deal with the problem in small groups in the White House Situation Room. All the participants agreed that 'it was essential to avoid leaks'.[141]

On the same day, Bazargan's resignation was accepted and the Revolutionary Council took over the running of the country. However, by the time the afternoon session was convened, 'one of the few instances of a major breach of security during the crisis' had occurred. The media found out that Clark and Miller were going to Iran.[142] Judging from the available evidence, it is highly likely that the source of the leak was the NSC and/or the Pentagon because they wanted to polarize the situation. Carter could not prevent the media from reporting the story,[143] and the leak boxed in the Iranians.[144]

The Iranians were worried about a hostage rescue mission.[145] However, according to Bani-Sadr, Beheshti agreed to allow Clark to go to Tehran. Khomeini, who distrusted Beheshti, issued a declaration, saying that no one had the right to negotiate with the US.[146] Clark and Miller stayed in Turkey until 15 November, trying to negotiate the release of the hostages. Miller's contacts in Iran kept him informed of the developing power struggle. During the course of their stay it became increasingly clear to them that the crisis would not be resolved until a new constitution had been approved and a new government had been formed.[147]

Vance, Under Secretary of State David Newsom, and Harold Saunders have said that the leak sabotaged the mission.[148] The failure of the Clark-Miller mission, however, strengthened Brzezinski's position since it led Carter to centralize decision-making in the White House. Throughout the crisis, Brzezinski seemed to be co-operating with the Shah's friends; Henry Kissinger, David Rockefeller and John J. McCloy rather than with Carter and Vance. In his memoirs Brzezinski tries to convey the impression that PLO mediation began after Khomeini's refusal to allow the Revolutionary Council to negotiate with Clark and Miller.[149] In fact, PLO mediation began almost immediately after the hostages were seized.

Moreover, by now Admiral Turner had informed US officials that the CIA believed that the students holding the hostages 'had been infiltrated by the left', and that apparently Khomeini had approved of their action.[150] By the afternoon of 6 November, Carter was more willing to consider economic warfare and the military option. An Entebbe-style rescue mission was ruled out because Tehran was a crowded city. Most US officials argued that military intervention would lead to the collapse of the Iranian regime and the outbreak of civil war and the formation of an even more radical anti-American government. Moreover, US military intervention could provoke a US-Soviet confrontation and possibly lead to Soviet occupation of parts of Iran.[151]

US officials believed that a punitive strike would not resolve the issue. They also rejected Brzezinski and Brown's proposal to occupy part of Iranian territory such as an island. Others in the group believed that this would trigger off a long naval and air war in the Persian Gulf. Opponents of the use of force feared that attacking Iran might lead Iran to ask the Soviet Union for assistance.[152] Moreover, the Joint Chiefs of Staff argued that the US was not in a position to launch an immediate rescue mission since it lacked reliable intelligence.[153]

The option, which was given most serious consideration, was mining Iranian harbours or blockading Iran. However, even this was a risky option. The least serious fall-out of such a conflict would be a significant increase in tanker rates and a further increase in the price of oil. Moreover, Moscow could offer minesweepers to Iran, thereby increasing Soviet influence in that country. Opponents of the use of force did not believe that mining Iranian harbours would lead to the release of the hostages.[154] At the end of the 6 November meeting, US officials agreed that the US would use diplomatic means to increasingly make the holding of the hostages costly to Iran. Above all, Carter was determined to avoid a land war in Iran.[155]

The Shah's 'friends', however, were determined to prevent the State Department from negotiating with the Khomeini regime. Henry Kissinger called for a tough response.[156] On the fourth day of the crisis, John McCloy met Newsom and ambassador to the UN Donald McHenry and warned them that no talks must be held until the hostages were released.[157] The next day McCloy met the Shah and assured him that the Carter administration did not intend to ask him to leave the US.[158]

Embassy documents and the radicalization of Iranian politics

After the revelation of the Clark-Miller mission Khomeini decided to postpone the settlement of the hostage dispute until Iran's presidential 'election'. He put the Revolutionary Council in charge of dealing with the crisis and this decision enabled the militants to collect documentary evidence implicating senior Iranian officials in negotiations with the US during the revolutionary turmoil.

Habibollah Peyman's armed group had been involved in the embassy seizure on 14 February, and several members of his group had accurate information about the embassy's sensitive areas such as code rooms and the communication centre.[159]

The militants knew that Michael Holland was in US military intelligence, and they wanted the names of Iranian officers who were in contact with him. According to Holland, the militants had 'the telephone list'.[160] By the time the embassy was stormed, Laingen had moved some of the most sensitive documents back to the embassy compound. Thus, when the militants entered the embassy they found documents that compromised many senior Iranian officials and clerics including Beheshti, Shari'atmadari, Bazargan, Yazdi, Bani-Sadr and many others.

The evidence suggests that rather than use the embassy documents to discredit 'moderates' and 'secularists', as most authors have argued, the leaders of the militants actually used the documents to blackmail or remove some of Khomeini's closest advisers such as Beheshti, Yazdi and Bani-Sadr, and attack Ayatollah Shari'atmadari who was their most powerful opponent among the clergy. The documents on Beheshti and Yazdi's contacts with US officials were particularly damaging because they showed that Khomeini had approved of at least some of their contacts with American officials.[161]

After the revolution, Beheshti emerged as the regime's second most powerful figure after Khomeini. He had sought to maintain Iran's close ties with the US. In his case, the few documents that were published showed that he had been in contact with officials of the Shah's regime and the Bakhtiar government and that the Shah was thinking about giving him a seat on the Regency Council before leaving Iran. Contrary to the prevailing view, Khomeini did not fully approve of Beheshti's activities and distrusted him.[162]

According to Richard Cottam, because Beheshti had indirectly received 'state funds given for religious activities' during the reign of the Shah he was vulnerable to attacks by radicals and he had to adopt radical policies to 'restore' his 'lost credibility'.[163] In fact, Beheshti had been an employee of the Iranian Ministry of Education. All the documents on Beheshti's contacts with the US embassy were retrieved by Musavi-Kho'iniha.[164] However, the documents on Ayatollah Shari'atmadari's contacts with the embassy would later be published to label him a foreign agent. The evidence suggests that Kho'iniha used the documents to compel Beheshti to make significant political concessions.[165]

By early December it was clear to the Carter administration that many members of the Revolutionary Council wanted to end the crisis as soon as possible, but there was no guarantee that the hostage-takers or Khomeini would be willing to release the hostages.[166] The Carter administration continued to receive intelligence that Beheshti was emerging as the dominant figure in the Revolutionary Council, but the council itself seemed to have almost no authority.[167] The US received reports 'almost daily' that in a confrontation with the students, even 'Khomeini could not be certain he would prevail'.[168]

Indeed, it is likely that other radical clerics had begun to threaten Ayatollah Beheshti long before the hostage seizure. In February 1979 the revolutionaries had seized SAVAK documents, which documented SAVAK's ties with 1,200 clerics in Iran. The SAVAK documents were turned over to Ali Khamene'i (Iran's current supreme leader). According to Bani-Sadr, some of the SAVAK documents in Khamene'i's possession concerned SAVAK payments to Ayatollah Beheshti.[169]

The US had been in contact with Beheshti since January 1979, if not earlier.[170] Until the spring of 1979, he had maintained contact with Sullivan and other embassy officers. However, by the spring of 1979 these contacts had dried up.[171] After the occupation of the US embassy, Ayatollah Ostad Tehrani met the hostage-takers who showed him 'documents revealing that some of the most vocal anti-imperialists among the clerics had American contacts'. Tehrani prepared a report on these 'pro-American anti-imperialists' and sent it directly to Khomeini.[172] Beheshti and others who favoured the release of the hostages were so frightened that they even refused to speak to US officials directly on the telephone, preferring to communicate through an intermediary.[173]

The Revolutionary Council was the scene of a furious debate between Bani-Sadr and Ghotbzadeh, who wanted to resolve the issue immediately, and the militants who now had Beheshti's support if only because they could blackmail him. On many occasions, the Council was divided seven to six in favour of Beheshti.[174] Beheshti was worried that Peyman and his followers would try the hostages, although behind the scenes, he claimed that he too favoured the trial of the hostages to pressure the US into making concessions.[175]

Moreover, Beheshti appointed the leader of the hostage-takers, Musavi-Kho'iniha, as the liaison between the Revolutionary Council and the state radio and television. Thus the hostage-takers began to gain control of the media to broadcast anti-American propaganda and further radicalize the regime.[176]

By 20 November, another major escalation in the crisis had occurred. The release of thirteen of the hostages, including women and blacks who were not accused of espionage, led some to believe that the occupation of the embassy had been an 'accident'. After the occupation of the embassy, Khomeini had appointed his protégé Abolhasan Bani-Sadr as acting foreign minister. Bani-Sadr had proposed the formation of a UN Security Council commission or some other type of international forum 'to investigate the events of the Shah's rule' and to ensure the return of the Shah's assets to Iran.

Vance maintained close contact with UN Secretary-General Kurt Waldheim. However, the US opposed Bani-Sadr's proposal on the grounds that the hostages had to be released first. Moreover, in the negotiations held at the UN, the Iranian representatives had indicated that the rest of the hostages would be released in the near future.[177]

On 14 November, Bani-Sadr, who was worried that the US would freeze Iran's assets, threatened to withdraw those assets from US banks. According to Bani-Sadr, Iranian officials had found documents in the embassy, showing that the US was searching for a way to freeze Iran's assets. Bani-Sadr's threat backfired and the Carter administration went ahead and did just that. The asset freeze strengthened those officials who wanted to sever ties between Iran and the US. The Iranians repeatedly threatened to put the hostages on trial. On 20 November, Khomeini declared that 'if Carter does not send the shah, it is possible that the hostages may be tried, and if they are tried, Carter knows what will happen'. Khomeini added that Carter 'lacked the guts for military action'.[178]

The Soviet Union supported Iran on the same day. Soviet Foreign Minister Andre Gromyko expressed his country's support for the Iranian revolution and said that no country had the right to interfere in Iran's internal affairs. The attack on the US embassy in Pakistan and the seizure of the Grand Mosque in Saudi Arabia also demonstrated the kinds of regional crises the US had to confront. Paradoxically, Khomeini accused the US of being responsible for the occupation of the Grand Mosque.[179] However, on the same day, Soviet Foreign Minister Andre Gromyko expressed Soviet support for Iran.[180]

At an NSC meeting on 20 November, Carter approved of a slow military build-up in the region to increase the pressure on Iran.[181] By the middle of November the special committee chaired by Brzezinski had identified initial targets in Iran and was ready to activate the plan within two days if instructed by the president. Another crucial NSC meeting was held on 23 November. The participants ruled out the nuclear option from the beginning.[182] Carter wanted to expel Iranian diplomats from the US.

Carter declared that the US would take a series of steps to increase the pressure on the Khomeini regime – 'condemn, threaten, break relations, mine three harbors, bomb Abadan, total blockade'.[183] He also wanted to pursue the negotiating track, but Brzezinski, Powell, and Jordan persuaded him to warn Khomeini that trials of Americans could compel the US to take military action against Iran.[184] However, when Carter asked the Joint Chiefs of Staff for conventional military options to rescue the hostages and punish Iran, they responded that the US was virtually powerless to influence the situation.[185]

Vance said that the Iranian representatives were about to accept a four-point agreement to release the hostages and that Khomeini had approved of the plan.[186] He and Vice-President Mondale told Carter that threatening Iran would derail the negotiations. Vance convinced Carter to continue the negotiations. However, Carter wanted to launch a punitive attack on Iran even if the hostages were released. Vance strongly opposed the mining of harbours. Finally, the President decided to send a direct message to top Iranian officials expressing 'US preference for a peaceful solution', but warning that any harm done to any hostage, or a trial would compel the US to attack Iran.[187]

In retrospect, it appears that Soviet support for the occupation of the US embassy accelerated the administration's decision to build up US power in the area.[188] Although Iranian officials never acknowledged Carter's message, the Carter administration was assured by a government official acting as intermediary that senior Iranian officials had indeed received it.[189]

Carter's threat was not particularly effective. In an interview with *Le Monde*, Khomeini indicated that he had not approved of the students' decision to kill the hostages in the event of US military action. However, he said that he would be unable to control them under those circumstances.[190] The next day, the hostage-takers announced that the embassy compound had been mined.[191] Moreover, by now the Soviet Union had begun to take measures to prevent a US attack on Iran.

Soviet support for the militants

Undoubtedly, the most important international dimension of the crisis was Soviet infiltration of the Students Following the Line of the Imam. This enabled the Soviet Union to act as the protector of the revolution. Soviet semi-official commentary almost immediately repeated the students' charge that the embassy was a 'den of espionage'.[192] More importantly, on 9 November, *Pravda* reported that Brzezinski had met the Iranian delegation in Algiers to hatch 'a counterrevolutionary plot'.[193] Throughout November, the Soviet press was full of references to US' 'efforts to undermine the Iranian revolution'.[194] Moscow Radio's World Service in the Persian language supported the occupation of the US embassy because it was allegedly filled with 'agents of the CIA and US imperialists'.[195]

Despite Soviet propaganda, the Politburo privately disassociated the Soviet Union from the militants.[196] The available evidence suggests that the Carter administration was aware of Soviet influence over the hostage-takers. Indeed, the US asked the Soviets to tell the Czech ambassador to persuade the militants to free the hostages. The Soviets replied that they only supported the international agreements regarding the diplomatic corps.[197]

Moreover, Soviet Foreign Minister Andre Gromyko strongly discouraged PLO chairman Yasir Arafat from pursuing mediation efforts, saying that the Soviet Union did not 'wish to protect American interests, despite their request that we do so'.[198] Shortly afterwards, Arafat changed his position and supported the occupation of the US embassy.[199]

Soviet leaders also took advantage of the hostage crisis to revive their policy of forming a united front. Thus the Tudeh Party immediately declared its support for the hostage-takers and tried to infiltrate their ranks.[200] The party's purpose was to prepare the ground for a take-over.[201] The Tudeh also attacked nationalists, liberals, and Khomeini's clerical opponents, particularly Ayatollah Shari'atmadari.[202]

The attacks on Shari'atmadari were part of a KGB active measures campaign against the ayatollah. As we saw earlier, Shari'atmadari was Khomeini's rival and he disapproved of the guardianship of the supreme jurisconsult. He was also an ardent opponent of the Soviet Union. After the revolution, Shari'atmadari declared: 'The Iranian people's triumphant struggle constitutes a turning point in the history of world struggles and the best model to follow by the oppressed Muslim peoples of the world.' As an Azeri from Tabriz, Shari'atmadari was probably talking about Muslim Azeris under Soviet rule. The active measures campaign against Shari'atmadari probably contributed to his purge by the Iranian regime in 1982. Shari'atmadari was accused of being involved in a plot against the regime and, faced with the threat of his son's execution, he pled for Khomeini's forgiveness. He was defrocked and spent the last four years of his life under house arrest.[203] Khomeini also hated the Soviet Union. However, his extremism and his association with some of the most anti-American clerics in the country undoubtedly furthered Soviet foreign policy objectives.

After their arrest in 1983, Tudeh Party leaders 'confessed' that their long-term plan was to subvert the regime, while building up the Tudeh as the only alternative.[204] Like Khomeini, Tudeh's General-Secretary Nureddin Kianuri declared that the hostage crisis was the second Iranian revolution. He declared that 'a broad popular front' had to be formed to support Khomeini in 'the struggle against American domination'.[205]

The situation was brought to a head on 20 November when Khomeini threatened to put the hostages on trial. Soviet Foreign Minister Andre Gromyko declared his country's 'positive attitude toward the revolution' and warned that no country should interfere in Iran's internal affairs.[206] In late November, *Pravda* repeated Brezhnev's warning that the Soviet Union would not permit 'outside interference in Iran's internal affairs by anyone, in any form, and under any pretext'.[207]

At the same time, Soviet sources in Washington indicated that the Soviet Union retained the right under the 1921 treaty 'to intervene if it sees any U.S. military move in Iran as a threat to Soviet security'.[208] Some Soviet commentators warned of the dangers of US intervention.[209] Soviet commentary increasingly emphasized that US military action would be aimed at overthrowing Khomeini.[210]

Within a few weeks of the occupation of the US embassy in Tehran, the CIA discovered that the Soviet General Staff had drawn up contingency plans to occupy all of northern Iran in case the crisis jeopardized Soviet security or the US decided to attack Iran.[211] However, between November and mid-December Soviet commentary refrained from provoking the US.[212]

After the Soviets invaded Afghanistan, they tried to make political capital out of their support for Iran. On 28 December, Soviet Ambassador Vinogradov met Khomeini and told him 'in confidence' that US officials, including President Carter, had tried to persuade the Soviets to 'show understanding of the American position in the Iranian-American conflict'. However, according to Vinogradov, Soviet leaders had rebuffed US officials. Vinogradov also wanted Khomeini to understand the Soviet position in Afghanistan.[213] However, Khomeini said that 'there could be no mutual understanding between a Muslim nation and a non-Muslim government'.[214]

The Carter administration's response to Soviet support for Iran

Brzezinski and Brown sought to take advantage of the hostage crisis to construct a new security framework for the Persian Gulf. However, there was strong opposition within the State Department and the Pentagon to the development of a new security framework.[215]

Indeed, even Deputy National Security Adviser David Aaron was rather sceptical about military options. Within the Pentagon, the Joint Chiefs and individual services disagreed with Brown's views on regional security.[216] However, Brzezinski and Brown deliberately chose a step-by-step approach in order to overcome the State Department's and Pentagon's opposition to their strategy.[217] Moreover, planning for the rapid deployment force was carried out in secrecy.[218]

Nevertheless, the hostage crisis created an immediate requirement for some form of US military presence in the Persian Gulf. However, the leaders of Saudi Arabia, the United Arab Emirates, and Kuwait had informed the US that they would not support US military action against Iran.[219]

US neo-containment strategy and Iraq

Brzezinski and Brown believed that Iraq was the new regional power.[220] They pressed forward with their policy of strengthening Iraq even though they had received a detailed fifty-page report which strongly argued that Saddam Hussein threatened vital long-term US interests. That report was written by Howard Teicher of the Pentagon's International Security Assistance department.[221]

Teicher contended that Saddam Hussein's goal was to make his country the most powerful Middle Eastern oil-producing state. He warned that Hussein would invade Iran 'in nine months' to annex Iran's oil-rich province of Khuzestan. Teicher predicted that Iraq would find it difficult to defeat Iran. He argued that because of Iraq's close ties with Saudi Arabia, Iran might retaliate by attacking Saudi Arabia or other Persian Gulf littoral states and instil fear in world oil markets. Moreover, according to Teicher, Hussein would try to pressure Riyadh to reduce Saudi oil production so as to increase the price of oil. Teicher also warned that Hussein would inevitably renew Iraq's claim to Kuwait.

Teicher contended that Hussein might provoke a superpower confrontation over the Arab-Israeli issue and that even if Iraq could check the spread of Khomeinism in the Persian Gulf, one could not ignore the dangers that a revisionist Iraq posed US position in the region in the long run. Teicher was later informed that Harold Brown had disagreed with his report, saying that Iraq had 'moderated its behaviour'.[222] In fact, in early December, the Carter administration received intelligence through Western channels that Iraq was planning to occupy Khuzestan's oil fields.[223] The credibility of these reports was proved by the increasing guerrilla attacks on oil facilities and the escalation of border clashes between Iran and Iraq.[224]

Brzezinski's call for military action

The issue of taking military action against Iran also had to be assessed in the context of the increasing likelihood of Soviet military intervention in Afghanistan. However, most intelligence analysts did not believe that the Soviet Union would invade Afghanistan.[225] Meanwhile, Carter was thinking about imposing a total embargo on Iran.[226] The NSC meeting on 28 November was the most divisive of the entire crisis as far as the question of military action was concerned. At this meeting Brzezinski called for increasing the pressure on Iran 'in a measured way'. He contended that the longer the US waited, the more Iran would be capable of 'gradually undercutting existing world-wide support for the United States by focusing on the issue of U.S. intelligence activities'.[227]

Brzezinski argued that only a US attack on Iran's oil facilities, including mining them, would lead the allies to impose sanctions on Iran. While admitting that mining Iran's harbours 'would put the hostages under increased danger', Harold Brown argued that time was running out. Vance tried to eliminate the mining option by arguing that it could be implemented in the context of UN sanctions. Hamilton Jordan pointed out that the Soviets would certainly veto such a proposal and that would be 'the end of SALT II'.[228]

CIA Director Admiral Turner and Chairman of the Joint Chiefs of Staff General Jones both said that US position in the Middle East was deteriorating, but they did not believe that military action would resolve the hostage crisis.[229] Brzezinski 'was unable to demonstrate that military action would either free the hostages or significantly strengthen the U.S. position'.[230]

However, Brzezinski and Brown were determined to pursue the military option. On 1 December, Brown wrote 'a strongly worded memorandum' to Carter, arguing that military action would be inevitable after 10 to 15 days.[231] Continued deployment of military power in the region was aimed at dissuading the Soviet Union from attacking or occupying northern Iran.[232] Moreover, Brzezinski argued that the US had to maintain a large military force in the region on a permanent basis to contain the Soviet Union.[233]

Meanwhile, Vance had managed to persuade Carter that the Shah's departure for Mexico would contribute to the resolution of the issue.[234] However, on 29 November, the Mexican government announced that it had withdrawn its invitation to the Shah.[235] The Shah wanted to go to Egypt, but both Brzezinski and Vance feared that this would further destabilize the Middle East.[236] Carter was exasperated with Brzezinski whom he accused of 'conspiring with Kissinger and Rockefeller to get the Shah permanently into the country'.[237]

Indeed, the Shah's presence in the US undermined Vance's negotiating efforts and enabled Brzezinski to politically exploit the crisis. Before the NSC meeting on 4 December, Brzezinski warned Carter that 'the issue was becoming increasingly a matter of America versus Islam'. He advised Carter to enhance US military presence in the region and consider 'the possibility of assisting efforts to unseat Khomeini'.[238] Brzezinski argued:

> In effect, I felt that the question of the lives of the hostages should not be our only focus but that we should examine as well what needed to be done to protect our vital interests. I was painfully aware that at some point perhaps a choice between the two might even have to be made.[239]

Vance argued that US military build-up in the Persian Gulf might lead the Soviets to invade Afghanistan. The State Department saw the military option as merely a form of leverage in negotiations and a means of limiting the excesses of the Iranian regime.[240]

However, in order for the State Department strategy to succeed, the US had to behave like a weak power to enable Khomeini to consolidate his power base.[241] The 4 December NSC meeting was crucial in terms of long-term US policy. There was too much at stake for Carter to wait for the emergence of a stable government in Iran.[242]

The President finally accepted Brzezinski's proposal for the creation of a regional security framework and decided to authorize a major US military build-up in the region.[243] The decision to build up US power in the Persian Gulf and Southwest Asia was made *three weeks before* the Soviet invasion of

Afghanistan.[244] The Saudi government flatly refused to grant any facilities to the US. Other governments were more forthcoming, but they preferred to deal with the US on an informal basis.[245] As Brzezinski observed later, the Soviet invasion of Afghanistan 'permitted' politically a massive build-up of US power in the region.[246]

Oil and the Fracture in the Alliance

Brzezinski and Brown were the most vocal advocates of exerting pressure on America's allies to persuade them to impose economic sanctions on Iran. Vance took a much less hostile view of Japan and West Germany, although they disagreed sharply with the US over the issue of imposing sanctions on Iran. The Carter administration literally asked Japan to choose between its relations with the US and its ties with Iran, but Japan only agreed to reduce its purchase of Iranian oil to pre-hostage crisis levels.

The US embargo on Iranian oil also necessitated a redistribution of oil supplies around the world. The Iranians quoted fifty dollars a barrel for their oil to frantic Japanese trading companies.[247] Heavy stockpiling by Japan helped to keep spot market prices high. Japanese action put upward pressure on the price of oil and saddled the allies with higher energy costs.[248] Vance described Japan's action as 'insensitive', adding that the Japanese had, in effect, sided with Iran.

At the same time, Iran led a campaign to cut back production in OPEC. The US exerted diplomatic pressure on Saudi Arabia to increase its oil production. Not only could the Saudis not unify OPEC, but they also alienated radical Arab producers such as Libya. Higher energy costs began to fuel inflationary pressures in the US. Iran had vowed to destabilize the dollar and some oil producers indicated that they wanted to reduce the dollar's role in oil dealings.

The Carter administration took pre-emptive measures to ensure that the crisis would not increase the downward pressure on the dollar. A high-level mission led by Under-Secretary of State for Economic affairs Richard Cooper, and Under-Secretary of the Treasury Anthony Solomon visited European capitals on 6 December to convince America's West European allies to co-operate with the US in imposing financial sanctions on Iran.

West German officials were infuriated at the extra-territorial application of US law during the Iran asset freeze. Cooper and Solomon said that they were concerned that the crisis might drive a wedge between the US and Western Europe, if Iran continued to trade normally with the European Economic Community. Moreover, they argued, such trading could strengthen other radical OPEC states such as Libya.[249]

Cooper and Solomon failed to convince West German officials.[250] They also visited Switzerland to persuade Swiss authorities to use the money weapon against Iran. The Swiss strongly opposed the Carter administration's policy because they believed that it violated their sovereignty and jeopardized international monetary stability.[251]

The US also adopted measures to compel Western Europe and Japan to agree to energy conservation targets. At a press conference held on the same day that Cooper and Solomon visited European capitals, Secretary of Energy Charles Duncan announced that the US must prepare itself for oil supply interruptions. The new targets announced by Duncan represented more than a five percent reduction on 1978 petrol consumption.[252]

On the eve of the International Energy Agency meeting in Paris, well-placed sources expected that the meeting would end in a bitter dispute between the US and its Western allies. Even America's closest ally Britain refused to agree to substantial energy conservation targets.[253]

After the failure of Cooper and Solomon's mission, Carter was very disappointed and instructed Vance to force Chancellor Schmidt of West Germany 'to choose between Germany's broader relationship with the United States as opposed to Germany's temporary interest in Iran'. Vance was to warn European leaders that the alternative to peaceful sanctions was a unilateral US blockade of Iran, including the possibility of mining Iranian ports.[254]

These threats proved effective. On 15 December, Vance informed Carter that the allies would join the US in imposing sanctions on Iran even if the Soviet Union vetoed a UN Security Council resolution.[255] On 17 January, Western Europe and Japan made their decision public and announced their support for US policy.[256] However, Western European countries such as West Germany and France would soon decide to rely more heavily on the Soviet Union for their energy supplies. Needless to say, their decision had far-reaching implications for the cohesion of the Western alliance.

12

THE SOVIET INVASION OF AFGHANISTAN AND THE HOSTAGE CRISIS

The Soviet invasion of Afghanistan completely transformed the strategic landscape of Southwest Asia. However, most studies of US policy towards Iran during this period, including recent studies by Kenneth Pollack, David Farber, David Harris and David Patrick Houghton have virtually nothing to say about the inter-relationship of the two events.[1] Similarly, students of US and Soviet policy towards Afghanistan have said very little about US policy towards Iran. However, key decision-makers in both the US and the Soviet Union viewed the situation in Afghanistan through the Iranian prism.

US officials' perceptions of the Afghan situation prior to the Soviet invasion

The situation in Afghanistan had progressively deteriorated after the April 1978 coup d'etat. Afghans increasingly saw the Marxist regime as anti-Islamic.[2] The key question was whether Moscow would intervene to save the Afghan regime.[3] However, US intelligence officials did not believe that the Soviet Union would introduce a large number of ground forces into Afghanistan because this would 'seriously damage' Soviet relations with India and Pakistan.[4]

In the spring of 1979 the Carter administration learned that China, Pakistan and Saudi Arabia were willing to assist the Afghan Mujahedin.[5] On 3 July 1979, President Carter signed a finding to provide covert assistance to the Mujahedin.[6] Subsequently, President Zia ul-Haq of Pakistan began to put pressure on the US to provide military assistance as well.[7]

By June 1979, the US embassy in Afghanistan estimated that the Afghan regime controlled only half the country.[8] However, intelligence reports continued to downplay the possibility of Soviet military intervention because such intervention was viewed as highly detrimental to the SALT II Treaty and to Soviet relations with the Islamic world.[9]

Nevertheless, at a meeting with Carter on 23 July, National Security Adviser Zbigniew Brzezinski warned that the Soviets might try to overthrow the Afghan regime.[10] Then in January 1998, Brzezinski admitted that the first covert CIA aid to the Afghan Mujahedin was authorized six months before the Soviet invasion.[11] He also admitted that he warned Carter that 'this aid would result in military intervention by the Soviets'.[12]

Despite his defence of the operation, Brzezinski admitted that its deleterious consequences had not been taken into consideration at the time.[13] Former CIA Director Robert Gates and CIA official Charles Cogan have basically verified Brzezinski's account of the assistance provided to the Mujahedin.[14] However, it is important to note that at the time, Brzezinski was not sure about the success of the policy of entrapping the Soviets in Afghanistan. In fact, contemporaneous documents from the period immediately after the Soviet invasion demonstrate that Brzezinski was deeply worried about the Soviet invasion and its consequences.[15]

Soviet perceptions of the regional crises

Between late September and early December, Soviet leaders became deeply concerned about Afghan leader Hafizullah Amin's overtures to the US, as well as the possibility of an Islamic revolution in Afghanistan.[16] In a memo to Soviet leader, Leonid Brezhnev, KGB chief Yuri Andropov argued that the CIA had recruited Amin and that the agency was determined to create a 'New Great Ottoman Empire', including the Central Asian republics of the Soviet Union. He feared that the US would establish a military base in Afghanistan and deploy Pershing missiles there. He also feared that the US would provide assistance to Iran and Pakistan to acquire a nuclear capability and move into Central Asia. Andropov advised Soviet leaders to overthrow Amin and support Afghan communism.[17]

The decision to overthrow Amin was taken on 31 October 1979.[18] There were also several assassination attempts on Amin, one of which slightly wounded him.[19] However, it appears that both the timing and the nature of the Soviet intervention in Afghanistan were determined by Soviet fears of a US invasion of Iran. In early December, in an article with a pseudonym reserved for the Soviet leadership, *Pravda* charged that 'the United States was deliberately stirring up the most serious crisis since the Second World War'.[20]

Pravda condemned the US for 'sheltering a murderer and a plunderer'.[21] It reiterated Brezhnev's warning that the Soviet Union 'would not tolerate outside interference in Iran's internal affairs'.[22] By now Soviet leaders were convinced that détente was dead.[23] Moreover, the fall of the Shah provided a geopolitical opportunity to the Kremlin.[24] The internal Afghan situation was not so serious as to require an immediate Soviet invasion,[25] but the Soviets' fear of encirclement by the US strengthened the advocates of intervention.[26] The Soviet parliamentary commission of inquiry that investigated the Soviet decision also drew attention to the possibility of US intervention in Iran.[27]

Speaking at a conference of former American and Soviet officials involved in the Afghan crisis in Norway in September 1995, General Valentin Varennikov said that Soviet leaders feared and were militarily prepared for a US invasion of Iran to overthrow Khomeini.[28] However, according to KGB defector, Vasiliy Mitrokhin, the KGB was alarmed by the prospect of improvement of relations between Iran and Afghanistan or an Islamic revolution in Afghanistan.[29]

Brzezinski calls for pressure on Iran

US officials' perception of the situation in Iran was coloured by events in other parts of the Middle East and Southwest Asia. The seizure of the Grand Mosque in Mecca was one such event. Initially, there were reports that Saudi Shi'as, possibly backed by Iran, were responsible for the attack. US officials were concerned about the spread of Khomeini's influence beyond Iran.[30] However, there were also conspiracy theories about the seizure of the Grand Mosque, which were reflected in the factually incorrect reports that Israel had attacked the Grand Mosque with US support.[31] Within hours, a mob attacked the US embassy in Pakistan. Two Americans and four Pakistanis were killed and the embassy building was seriously damaged and badly burned.[32]

According to later CIA reports, President Zia ul-Haq of Pakistan had concluded that he was in no position to save the Americans inside the embassy and he might as well allow the riot to 'burn itself out'.[33] Secretary of State Cyrus Vance summoned ambassadors from 30 Islamic countries to discuss the crisis in Pakistan. Asked about the spread of Islamism, Vance responded: 'It's hard to say at this point whether a pattern is developing'.[34] However, there was 'a pattern'. There was an attack on US consul general in Lahore and on 22 and 23 November, there were 'rock-throwing demonstrations' at American diplomatic missions in Srinigar, India; Ismir, Turkey and Dacca, Bangladesh.[35] The most important effect of the spread of regional unrest was on US policy towards Iran. The spread of unrest and the gathering Soviet threat to Afghanistan strengthened the position of National Security Adviser Zbigniew Brzezinski who had been calling for the use of force against the Iranian regime.

At a Special Co-ordinating Committee meeting on 19 December, Brzezinski called for pressure on Iran.[36] At a smaller meeting, he warned that as long as Khomeini was in power the US could not resolve the crisis, adding that US covert operations should be related to military options.[37] Carter believed that the US must list punitive measures against Khomeini, without risking international condemnation.[38]

US intelligence reports continued to warn of 'a major' Soviet intervention by 25 December.[39] However, the US failed to deter the Soviet Union.[40] In a memorandum to Carter on 26 December, Brzezinski wrote that the US was facing a 'regional crisis' and warned of the Soviet threat to the Indian Ocean. He also warned that the 'collapse' of the Iranian pillar of US strategy would enable the Soviet Union to establish a presence in the Persian Gulf and the Gulf of Oman.[41] Brzezinski argued: 'With Iran destabilized, there will be no firm bulwark in Southwest Asia against the Soviet drive to the Indian Ocean'.[42]

He contended that while Afghanistan 'could become a Soviet Vietnam, the initial effects of the intervention are likely to be adverse for us'.[43] He argued that the US would be viewed as 'timid' and that Soviet action would lead to calls for US intervention in Iran.[44] Brzezinski called for co-operating with Islamic countries in conducting covert operations to assist the rebels. He also called for co-ordination with China and Pakistan.[45] Nevertheless, Brzezinski warned that the US 'should not be too sanguine about Afghanistan becoming a Soviet Vietnam' because the 'guerrillas are badly organized and poorly led'. They did not have an army or a sanctuary and unlike the US in Vietnam, Moscow did not have any doubts about its own military tactics.[46]

On the issue of Pakistan, Brzezinski's recommendation would come to haunt US strategy in the 1990s and early 21st century. He observed that the US would have to review its policy towards Pakistan and regretted that 'our security policy toward Pakistan cannot be dictated by our nonproliferation policy'.[47]

Unfortunately, the Reagan administration also ignored Pakistan's pursuit of a nuclear programme[48] – a decision that was probably as damaging to US national security in the long run as the Soviet invasion of Afghanistan because of the involvement of such figures as the father of Pakistan's atomic bomb, Abd al-Qadir Khan, and the army chief staff, Mirza Aslam Beg, in the illegal shipment of nuclear material to such radical states as Iran, Libya and North Korea.[49]

At an SCC meeting two days before the Soviet invasion, Brzezinski proposed sending a message to Brezhnev threatening to scuttle SALT and tilt towards China. Vance and Christopher disagreed with him.[50] After the Soviets invaded Afghanistan, Carter sent 'the sharpest message' of his presidency to Brezhnev, describing the Soviet invasion as 'a clear threat to the peace'. The Soviet leader's reply infuriated Carter because he claimed that the Soviets had been invited by the Afghan authorities.[51]

The Soviet invasion of Afghanistan and the Iran hostage crisis

The Soviet invasion led Carter to search for a negotiated solution to the Iranian hostage crisis. He pursued a proposal made by US ambassador to the UN Donald McHenry at an NSC meeting on 28 December. The UN would issue a resolution calling on the Secretary-General to seek a negotiated solution. If he did not succeed within a week, sanctions would be imposed on Iran.[52] UN Secretary-General Kurt Waldheim travelled to Iran on 31 December, but his visit was a disaster. Indeed, his life was threatened during the visit.[53] The Iranians, however, proposed that an international tribunal be established under the UN's auspices, and Waldheim agreed to report back to the Security Council.[54]

He told Carter and the UN Security Council that sanctions would be ineffective. However, the President refused to withdraw the resolution. On 13 January, the Security Council approved the resolution by a margin of 10–2. However, the Soviet veto ensured that the resolution could not be enforced.[55]. Moreover, European officials said that they would not impose sanctions on Iran because sanctions would only force Iran to rely on the Soviet Union.[56]

US officials' perception of the regional situation

What concerned Brzezinski most was that Carter would be prevailed upon to ignore what he saw as the broader geopolitical implications of the Soviet invasion.[57] Brzezinski himself saw the situation in terms of 'the objective consequences of a Soviet military presence so much closer to the Persian Gulf'.[58]

Vance saw the Soviet invasion as a setback for détente.[59] He believed that the Soviets' 'immediate aim was to protect Soviet political interests in Afghanistan which they saw endangered'.[60] Within the intelligence community, the Defence Intelligence Agency, [DIA], also saw the situation in terms of a Soviet drive for the warm waters of the Persian Gulf although it did not present any evidence in support of its case.[61]

Initially, Carter agreed with Brzezinski, describing the Soviet invasion as 'the greatest threat to peace since the Second World War'.[62] In an address to the nation on 4 January 1980, Carter declared that the Soviet invasion threatened Southwest Asia and world energy resources.[63]

Carter and Vance saw the Soviet invasion as a personal affront.[64] However, Brzezinski was primarily concerned about constructing a regional security framework.[65] Carter gave him the task of drafting the State of the Union address, and he patterned this on the Truman doctrine of 1947. Vance and White House Counsel Lloyd Cutler removed the section on the regional security framework, but Brzezinski and White House spokesman Jody Powell re-inserted it. James Schlesinger advised Brzezinski to resign to compel Carter to respond firmly to the Soviet invasion of Afghanistan. Indeed, Brzezinski has said that had Carter refused to accept his recommendations, he might well have resigned.[66]

In his speech, Carter said: 'Any attempt by any outside force to gain control of the Persian Gulf region will be regarded as assault on the vital interests of the United States of America, and such an assault will be repelled by any means necessary, including military force.'[67] The Carter Doctrine, as it became known, reflected Brzezinski's view on the interdependence of Western Europe, the Far East and the Middle East-Persian Gulf region. Brzezinski believed that Soviet control of Persian Gulf oil would enable the Kremlin to blackmail Western European and East Asian countries.[68]

The hallmark of the Carter Doctrine was Carter's willingness to commit resources to Southwest Asia. However, the President made this declaration without consulting any of his advisers except Brzezinski.[69] With regard to Iran, Carter announced a U-turn on policy, declaring that 'the United States was ready to cooperate with Iran in meeting the Soviet threat from Afghanistan and in establishing a new relationship once the hostages are released'.[70] Critics argued that the Soviet Union already shared a border with Iran that was closer to key targets than Iran's border with Afghanistan.[71] Moreover, the terrain from Afghanistan to Iran was extremely treacherous and was likely to impede any military movement.[72]

However, after a number of major US setbacks in the Third World, most recently the Iran hostage crisis, US policy-makers exaggerated the geostrategic significance of the Soviet invasion of Afghanistan.[73] They believed that military action against Iran would make it more difficult to mobilize Islamic resistance to the Soviet occupation of Afghanistan.[74] Brzezinski still saw Khomeini as a fervently anti-Communist figure.[75] However, he mistakenly believed that only Beheshti had the power to effect the release of the hostages.[76] In fact, as late as January 1980, most US officials shared Brzezinski's view.[77]

According to Brzezinski, the US could not establish contact with Beheshti.[78] However, a former Iranian diplomat, Mir-Ali Akbar Montazam, says that 'senior CIA officials and Carter's envoys' met Beheshti in West Germany on 12 January.[79] If such a meeting was ever held, not much seems to have been achieved.

US failure to construct a regional security framework

Most of the students of the Carter era, with the notable exception of Richard C. Thornton, have interpreted the Carter Doctrine as a major turning point in US strategy. As late as 2004, a prominent American historian, Andrew Bacevich, argued that the Carter Doctrine marked a major change in US global strategy in that it ushered the outbreak of World War IV, which he described as the war for global oil resources. According to Bacevich, the real import of the Carter doctrine was masked by the Cold War, which still served as the overarching framework for understanding international relations.[80] However, as we shall see in this chapter, Bacevich is wrong. Although Carter was temporarily swayed by Brzezinski's call for a tough response to the Soviet invasion of Afghanistan, he continued to explore the possibility of reviving US-Soviet détente. More importantly, as we shall see, he was prepared to make significant concessions to obtain the freedom of the hostages; concessions which could seriously undermine America's ability to maintain its primacy in the Persian Gulf.

One week before the enunciation of the Carter Doctrine, Brzezinski asserted that the US was willing to take military action to protect its 'vital interests' and that it sought to establish a 'co-operative security framework' with the states in the region, specifically mentioning Iraq and Libya as countries 'with whom we don't have irreconcilable differences'.[81] The tilt to Iraq was also a move against Iran.

However, Saudi Arabia publicly condemned the Carter Doctrine and preferred the US military presence to remain 'over the horizon'.[82] The Saudis were alarmed by Iran's support for the Shi'a minority in the Eastern Province which had become restive.[83] Moreover, Crown Prince Fahd signalled his country's desire to improve relations with the Soviet Union.[84] The Carter Doctrine fuelled regional countries' suspicions that the US might undertake military intervention in the region.[85]

In early February 1980, Brzezinski and Deputy Secretary of State Warren Christopher visited Pakistan and Saudi Arabia to discuss plans for security cooperation. President Zia of Pakistan mockingly described the administration's offer of 400 million dollars over two years as 'peanuts'.[86] However, Brzezinski and Zia ul-Haq did discuss an expanded covert action programme to assist the Afghan Mojahedin.[87]

The US officials' visit to Riyadh was more successful.[88] What changed the minds of Saudi leaders was a change of US policy on the Palestinian issue and a firm US commitment not to permit Iran to drift into the Soviet camp.[89] Brzezinski said that the US was willing to undertake military co-operation with Saudi Arabia and other states in the region.[90] The Saudis agreed to match US contribution to the Afghan Mojahedin.[91] However, they continued to argue that regional states were responsible for the security of the Persian Gulf.[92]

Saddam Hussein's concerns about Soviet strategy

As far as the Carter administration was concerned, the main breakthrough was in US relations with the Iraqi regime which was worried about a Soviet-backed coup along the line of the Afghan coup.[93] Despite the declaration of his intent to organize resistance to the Soviet invasion of Afghanistan[94], Saddam Hussein indicated that he would not abrogate the Iraqi-Soviet treaty.[95]

Hussein was not prepared to normalize diplomatic relations with the US, but he did favour contacts.[96] On 8 February, he promulgated the pan-Arab 'National Charter', designed to establish Iraq as the new hegemonic power in the Persian Gulf. It categorically ruled out any foreign military presence on Arab soil.[97]

The pan-Arab Charter exacerbated tensions between Iran and Iraq. Saudi Arabia, as well as most of the smaller Persian Gulf states, immediately supported the charter.[98] On 13 February, Hussein accused the Iranian regime of obliterating Khuzestan's 'Arab character'.[99] In response, Iran moved closer to radical Arab states, which also organized a major campaign to undercut efforts to organize Islamic opposition to the Soviet invasion of Afghanistan.[100] The Islamic Conference condemned the Soviet invasion of Afghanistan, but it also sharply criticized US attempts to gain base rights in Southwest Asia.[101]

The Iranian regime purges the armed forces

During this period, the Iranian regime accelerated the purge of the armed forces. It appears that at least one influential pro-Soviet official, the first commander of the Revolutionary Guards Corps, Abbas Zamani, played a key role in this purge. However, he resigned his post on 17 June, a day after Khomeini warned that traitors might have infiltrated the Revolutionary Guards Corps.[102]

After the defection of a KGB officer, Vladimir Kuzikchin, in 1982, it was revealed that Zamani had been one of the Soviets' contacts in Iran.[103] It is not known whether he was a Soviet agent in 1980, but his actions did assist the Soviet policy of encouraging a thorough purge of the armed forces. In 1983 when the CIA passed the names of Soviet agents in Iran to Iranian officials, Zamani, who was deputy intelligence director, was arrested.[104]

In a memorandum to President Carter and members of the NSC on 16 January, CIA Director Admiral Turner argued that the Soviet invasion of Afghanistan was unlikely to have been part of a grand design to dominate Southwest Asia.[105] However, Turner feared that the unrest in Iran might tempt the Kremlin to seek to increase its influence in that country to make up for its energy shortages.[106]

US support for a failed military coup in Iran

In late 1979, the State Department's Bureau of Intelligence and Research, INR, reported that 'the hostage crisis was a function of Iranian internal politics' and that the US could do nothing to influence Iranian domestic politics.[107] Moreover, in early 1980, 'a senior Islamic statesman' who knew Khomeini and other senior clerics informed Vance that the hostages would not be released until Khomeini had institutionalized the Islamic revolution.[108]

However, Vance refused to take heed of such reports.[109] His desperation provided a golden opportunity to shadowy Iranian operators, such as the Hashemi brothers, Cyrus and Jamshid Hashemi, to sell their services to Washington. Cyrus Hashemi advised Assistant Secretary of State Harold Saunders to contact former Defence Minister Admiral Madani and Khomeini's nephew Reza Pasandideh to discuss the release of the hostages and provide financial support to Madani in Iran's presidential election. Hashemi admitted that Madani was no longer one of Khomeini's favourite personalities, but he was a strong candidate.[110]

Despite the Iran Working Group's scepticism about Hashemi's reliability, Vance presented the proposal to Carter, saying that Hashemi had informed them that Khomeini had accepted a preliminary meeting between one or two US officials and three or four Iranians.[111] He advised Carter to explore the proposal. In late January 1980, Jamshid Hashemi, who used the alias

Mohammad Ali Balanian, tried to gain CIA and State Department support for a military coup led by Madani.[112] He was provided with funds to support Madani in the elections.[113]

At a meeting with Saunders on 2 January 1980, also attended by Cyrus Hashemi, Jamshid Hashemi offered to establish a channel of communication with Khomeini and Khomeini's brother, Ayatollah Pasandideh. After another meeting in London attended by Saunders, the CIA chief of the Near East Division, Charles Cogan and the Hashemi brothers, Cogan gave the Hashemis a portion of the 500,000 dollars in cash for Madani's presidential campaign and said that he wanted the hostages released unharmed.[114] The CIA would approach Khomeini through Pasandideh and ask him to intervene. Madani would be elected president. If the mediation effort failed and Madani were defeated in the elections, Madani would take military action to effect the hostages' release.[115]

According to US Congress: 'At the urging of the State Department a decision was made by the CIA to provide 500,000 dollars in cash to the Hashemi brothers for a sensitive covert operation in Iran.' Hashemi's mission for the CIA is still classified.[116]

The sensitive covert operation may have been aimed at instigating a coup d'etat since the issue had already been explored with regard to the so-called Madani-Pasandideh channel. On 16 January 1980, the Kuwaiti newspaper *Al-Ray al-Amm* reported that several army officers had been executed for planning to kidnap and assassinate Khomeini. On 18 January, another Kuwaiti newspaper A*l-Qabas* reported that Madani had masterminded the coup attempt. Still other Middle Eastern sources reported that 63 officers had been executed because of their involvement in the coup attempt.[117]

During this period, the CIA learned that Jamshid Hashemi was also using the name Mohammad Ali Balanian. The agency had previously issued warnings regarding Hashemi's reliability as a source and it terminated its relationship with Hashemi in February 1980 after he refused to take a polygraph test. Furthermore, in late February the CIA learned that Hashemi had been lying about his contacts with Madani.[118]

Also in late February, Charles Cogan discovered that Hashemi had only spent 90,000 or 100,000 dollars of the funds provided to him on the covert operation. Cyrus Hashemi returned 290,000 dollars to Cogan on 28 February.[119] Hashemi had also collaborated with other intelligence agencies.[120] It seems that Jamshid Hashemi was an agent provocateur who too was trying to entrap enemies of the Iranian regime, particularly in the armed forces. In February 1980, Defence Minister Mostafa Chamran announced that 7,500 military personnel, mostly senior officers, had been purged during the previous two months.[121] The State Department's decision to support Hashemi's activities had a calamitous impact on US foreign policy.

The Carter administration considers the Ghotbzadeh-Panama channel

According to Vance, after the 12 January UN vote, the State Department received messages through indirect channels that Iranian officials would welcome a sign from the US that would help them to persuade Khomeini to agree to the release of the hostages.[122] By early December, the US was in contact with more than 20 individuals and organizations.[123] On 11 December, Richard Cottam contacted Sadegh Ghotbzadeh who said that the Revolutionary Council was anxious to resolve the crisis.[124] Ghotbzadeh had been deeply concerned about the Soviet threat to Iran and had issued a strong condemnation of Soviet policies.[125]

Ghotbzadeh told *Le Figaro* that 'Iran may consider arming the 50,000 Afghan refugees in Iran to fight the Soviets.'[126] Moreover, Iran voted for a UN resolution condemning the Soviet invasion of Afghanistan.[127] However, Ghotbzadeh was a self-serving opportunist whom many Iranian intellectuals saw as an Iranian Mussolini.[128] He believed that the only way to resolve the crisis was to convince Khomeini that the seizure of the hostages had compelled the US to accept the Iranian revolution.[129]

He suggested that the Shah's extradition or trial or 'some other forum' would pave the way for the release of the hostages.[130] He also said that he knew that the US would not extradite the Shah, but he wanted the Americans to make some concessions.[131] However, the Shah had taken up residence in Panama and, as we will see, the Carter administration would find it enormously difficult to handle the issue of his extradition to Iran.

In fact, there had already been a confrontation between Ghotbzadeh and the hostage-takers regarding the status of US officials who were still at the Foreign Ministry, whom Ghotbzadeh said were free to leave, but whom the hostage-takers described as spies. Ghotbzadeh backed down and said that he could only ensure the safety of the officials at the Foreign Ministry.[132]

He did not even know the number of hostages in the embassy. Foreign Service Officers in Washington, however, telephoned the embassy almost every night and spoke to the militants.[133] In late December, Panamanian leader General Torrijos established contact between two French lawyers with high-level contacts in Iran, Hector Villalon and Christian Borguet, and Carter's adviser Hamilton Jordan. Villalon and Borguet wanted Jordan to act as an intermediary with Carter because they believed the State Department was 'controlled by Kissinger and Rockefeller'.[134]

Jordan was assured that Ghotbzadeh did not really want the Shah's extradition.[135] Carter, Brzezinski and Vance, however, suspected Torrijos of seeking to extradite the Shah to resolve the issue.[136] The Panamanians were informed that the US only wanted them to act as intermediaries.[137]

Ghotbzadeh had presidential ambitions, however, and he talked to Torrijos on the telephone every night, offering 'money, women, a share in Iran's oil exports and whatever else he could think of'.[138] Reportedly, on one occasion, Ghotbzadeh offered General Torrijos £800,000,000 to extradite the Shah to Iran.[139] Ghotbzadeh even hired PLO hit men to assassinate the Shah.[140]

Despite his misgivings, Carter decided to pursue the opening. On 12 January, Carter sent a message to Iranian leaders through UN Secretary General Kurt Waldheim, reiterating that the return of the hostages was 'essential to a resolution of other issues.' He agreed to the formation of a UN commission to investigate Iran's grievances without involving the hostages. The US would also facilitate any legal action by Iran in US courts to account for the Shah's assets. Once the hostages were released, the US would unfreeze Iranian assets and resume normal commercial relations with Iran if the latter settled US banks' claims and met its 'financial obligations'.[141]

The US would also agree to discuss with the Iranians the Soviet invasion of Afghanistan and the supply of military spare parts to Iran.[142] By now the US had persuaded Western Europe and Japan to support economic sanctions against Iran.[143] Shortly afterwards, Cuban leader Fidel Castro proposed a grand bargain, linking the release of the hostages to the restoration of détente.

The Castro channel and the proposal to resolve regional conflicts

By mid-January the multiplicity of the centres of decision-making in Iran had frustrated Vance.[144] However, his determination to revive détente with the Soviets provided the Kremlin with an opportunity to compel the US to change its regional strategy. Vance wanted an agreement with the Soviets that would prevent the introduction of troops or 'mutually threatening bases' in Iran or Pakistan. He sought to link the Soviet withdrawal from Afghanistan with a mutual restraint agreement covering Iran and Pakistan.[145]

Soon after the opening of the Panamanian channel, Cuban leader Fidel Castro informed President Carter that he wanted to discuss Iran and Afghanistan.[146] NSC's Latin America specialist, Robert Pastor, and Department of State executive secretary, Peter Tarnoff, held discussions with Castro in Cuba on 16 and 17 January. Castro expressed his desire to normalize relations with the US, but he said that he would not 'abandon' the Soviet Union.[147] He said that he would pull Cuban troops out of Ethiopia immediately, and Angola later. He also pledged not to send weapons to Latin American revolutionaries.[148]

In his memoirs, Carter merely says that Castro was embarrassed to be associated with the Soviets.[149] Castro apparently proposed a revival of US-Soviet détente, Soviet withdrawal from Afghanistan and the release of American hostages in Iran.[150] In return, Castro wanted the US to lift the sanctions placed on the Soviet Union, including the Olympic boycott, promise to ratify SALT II and extend economic assistance to Nicaragua. The Soviet Union would withdraw from Afghanistan after installing a 'neutral' government in Kabul and would also assist efforts to release the hostages in Iran.[151]

Only the Soviets themselves could have put forward such a wide-ranging proposal. As we saw earlier, the hostage-takers' mentor, Musavi-Kho'iniha, had pro-Soviet sympathies. Castro's proposal suggests that Kho'iniha would have persuaded the militants to release the hostages if the US had agreed to Moscow's terms.

However, on 20 January, Iranian Foreign Minister Sadegh Ghotbzadeh declared that the Soviets might not accept Iran's unilateral abrogation of the 1921 treaty. At the same time, he ruled out a US-Iran alliance against the Soviet Union. The Soviet embassy in Iran issued a statement saying that the Soviet Union would not attack Iranian oilfields.[152]

On 20 January, Carter declared that the US supported Iran's territorial integrity. He reiterated his concern for the 'release of the hostages without bloodshed', adding that 'the US would apply unilateral economic sanctions and would continue to seek support for sanctions among U.S. allies'.[153]

Iranian presidential elections and the stalemate in the negotiations

The next phase of the negotiations occurred against the background of the

Iranian presidential elections. Khomeini's distrust of Ayatollah Beheshti led him to declare that a cleric must not become president. The French-educated Abolhasan Bani-Sadr who had been Khomeini's close adviser in Paris emerged as his favourite candidate. On 16 January, Khomeini's son and grandson and several other religious leaders declared their support for Bani-Sadr.[154]

With Beheshti out of the presidential race, the Islamic Republican Party (IRP) had to nominate another candidate. However, the IRP's first choice, Jalaleddin Farsi, was rejected on the grounds of his Afghan background.[155] As a result, Bani-Sadr emerged as the strongest candidate. Ghotbzadeh who was worried about losing the election, insisted that the Panamanians should put the Shah under arrest.[156] However, Khomeini's description of Bani-Sadr as his 'devoted son' contributed substantially to Bani-Sadr's election victory.[157]

Meanwhile the issue of the Shah's extradition was being debated. Panamanian officials made contradictory statements about the Shah's status in Panama and possible extradition to Iran.[158] The Carter administration opposed his extradition.[159] Ghotbzadeh, who wanted to end the crisis, asked the Carter administration to postpone the UN vote on the imposition of sanctions on Iran. Carter immediately agreed to this request,[160] and on 24 January, Carter postponed the imposition of sanctions on the 'unanimous recommendation of his advisers'.[161]

Moreover, by now the Revolutionary Council was supporting Bani-Sadr and began to distance itself from the militants.[162] On Bani-Sadr's orders Kho'iniha was removed as the head of state media. However, Kho'iniha maintained his influence on internal security issues and, according to some reports, he invited Soviet advisers to Iran to reorganise Iran's intelligence services.[163]

Carter and Vance resume their efforts to restore détente

The Kremlin interpreted the Carter Doctrine as a cynical manoeuvre.[164] Protocol No. 181 of the Central Committee of the Soviet Communist Party sums up Soviet policy towards Iran during this period. The Soviets were to 'maintain a firm line in international affairs in opposition to the Carter administration's provocative steps' and to 'concentrate' their 'main efforts' on opposing 'the hostile activity of the USA and its allies on the Islamic countries of the Middle and Near East, particularly on Pakistan and Iran' and such 'influential' Asian countries as India. In the case of Iran, Soviet officials were instructed to 'Bring into life measures directed at the preservation of the anti-imperialist, primarily anti-American elements in the foreign policy of Iran, insofar as the continuation of the crisis in Iran-American relations limits the potential possibilities of the Khomeini regime to inspire anti-government uprisings on Moslem grounds in Afghanistan.'[165] In late January, Vance implored Carter to contact Brezhnev to say that the situation in Afghanistan jeopardised US-Soviet relations.[166] Carter refused to send another message to Brezhnev, but he instructed Vance to write a letter to Gromyko. They decided not to inform Brzezinski. Meanwhile, Carter allowed Brzezinski to build allied support for the containment of the Soviet Union.[167]

At the same time, Carter expressed a more relaxed attitude towards Cuban activities in the Western Hemisphere.[168] Despite the hostile tone of Soviet propaganda, a few days later Brezhnev responded to Carter's message. On 4

February, Brezhnev called for an end to regional conflicts, including in the Middle East.[169]

However, in Iran, the Carter administration's new interlocutor, Bani-Sadr, declared that the Soviets were 'trying to seize Iranian territory' and gain 'access to warm water ports'.[170] Despite Castro's offer of a grand bargain, Carter proceeded with the Bani-Sadr channel, which he described as 'the most encouraging development' since the beginning of the crisis. Bani-Sadr asked Carter not 'to identify him as a friend of the United States or as a moderate'. Carter believed that Bani-Sadr and Ghotbzadeh would seek to obtain the hostages' release.[171]

Khomeini increased Bani-Sadr's powers by appointing him as the Secretary of the Revolutionary Council, in place of Beheshti, and the commander-in-chief of the armed forces, a position which the Constitution had reserved for the leader (Khomeini).[172] However, Bani-Sadr also called for the export of the revolution,[173] to demonstrate that he too was a committed revolutionary.

Carter enunciates new positions on hostages and Afghanistan

Meanwhile secret negotiations between Ghotbzadeh and French lawyers Villalon and Bourget were under way.[174] In mid-February, Ghotbzadeh held a secret meeting with Hamilton Jordan in Paris.[175] He asked Jordan to instruct the CIA to kill the Shah to end the crisis.[176] Jordan was due to meet Beheshti's envoy Hasan Habibi when his mission was sabotaged by leaks to the European press.[177]

Carter, however, pressed forward with both the Ghotbzadeh and Castro channels, failing to realize that Ghotbzadeh's hostility to the Soviet Union could undermine his efforts. In a major volte face, Carter declared that he would be willing to accept a new UN commission of inquiry to be formed prior to the release of the hostages to study Iran's complaints.[178]

On Afghanistan, Carter proposed that the UN send a peacekeeping force, possibly including troops from Muslim countries, while 'a neutral and responsible government' was being formed.[179] However, Defence Secretary Harold Brown asserted that any Soviet attempt to gain control of Persian Gulf oil would be tantamount to a Soviet invasion of Western Europe or Japan.[180] Nevertheless, US officials said that the US might not even ask for a partial Soviet withdrawal from Afghanistan.[181]

On the issue of Afghanistan, Vance was undoubtedly influenced by his Soviet affairs adviser Marshall Shulman who argued that the Soviets 'probably genuinely believe that the scale of outside help to the Afghan insurgents justified and required the Soviet intervention'. Shulman contended that while détente 'in the 1972 sense of the word is not re-creatable', the US had to state 'at responsible levels' that it had a long-term interests 'in a more constructive relationship with the Soviet Union'. At the same time, Shulman argued that 'Soviet disclaimers of aggressive intent toward Iran, Pakistan and Yugoslavia cannot, of course be taken at face value'. However, he advised Vance that the US had to 'extract such commitments' from the Soviets when discussing the issue of Afghanistan.[182] The State Department strongly supported British Foreign Secretary Lord Carrington's proposal regarding the neutralization of Afghanistan and the withdrawal of Soviet troops.[183] In fact, the US and Britain closely co-ordinated their policies on this issue.[184] If the hostages were freed, Carter was prepared to press forward with the ratification of SALT II.[185] Between 14 and 21 February the Carter administration received intelligence indicating that Khomeini would support the release of the hostages before 21 March.[186]

However, on 22 February, an Iranian friend of Ghotbzadeh informed the Carter administration that 'something has developed underground against the release of the hostages and against Khomeini'. He said that there had been some fighting and that there was a 'real mess' inside the embassy.[187] As we will see below, after the incident Khomeini acceded to the militants' demands.[188]

Given the militants' possession of US documents on Bani-Sadr and Beheshti, had Khomeini agreed to a settlement, the entire state might have been destabilized because the militants might have publicized the documents.[189] Vance and his advisers, however, insisted on proceeding with the negotiations.

The Carter administration considers the Soviet channel

Carter's advisers were deeply divided over the issue of reviving détente. By 28 February, the Soviets had merely sent an indirect message through Brezhnev's son, indicating that they might consider withdrawal from Afghanistan in return for a change of US position on the Olympics.[190] Vance, however, was determined to proceed. He asked Carter to authorize him to meet Gromyko.[191] Brzezinski was 'appalled' that the US might be considering talks with the Soviets while calling for a united Western alliance.[192]

Vice-President Mondale agreed with Brzezinski, but Vance said that the Soviets had sent a message saying that they wanted 'a formal Gromyko-Vance meeting'. Carter himself believed that the Soviets wanted 'a puppet government' in Afghanistan.[193] Brzezinski insisted that a Vance-Gromyko meeting 'would confuse our allies and would be politically devastating at home'.[194]

Carter and his principal advisers could not come to a decision. On 3 March, Vance indicated that US sanctions would be lifted following a full Soviet withdrawal from Afghanistan.[195] He declared that the US did not want a resumption of the Cold War.[196]

Harold Brown, however, warned that US-Soviet conflict in the Middle East would trigger a global war.[197] It appears that Brzezinski and Brown's emphasis upon the importance of the Carter Doctrine led the Soviets to abandon their attempt to revive détente.[198] Brzezinski has claimed that Carter abandoned the idea of negotiating with the Soviets.[199] However, the President would try to make the Kremlin a better offer.

Bani-Sadr and Ghotbzadeh's failure to release the hostages

Iranian Foreign Minister Sadegh Ghotbzadeh continued to put pressure on the militants to release the hostages. Ghotbzadeh declared that they were using the embassy documents to threaten government ministers and called on them to stay out of politics and transfer all the documents to the government.[200] Many observers believed that Ghotbzadeh would be executed or jailed. However, Khomeini fully agreed with Ghotbzadeh's position.[201]

On 9 March, a spokesman for the militants declared that they were willing to transfer the hostages to the Revolutionary Council at any time, but they wanted to continue their work on the documents.[202] The issue was brought to a head on 10 March at a meeting between Khomeini and the Revolutionary Council. Bani-Sadr was not present at the meeting. The evidence suggests that during the meeting the hard-liners persuaded Khomeini to side with them.[203]

On 10 March Khomeini declared that the Majlis should decide the fate of the hostages. He tried to turn the UN commission into a propaganda vehicle by calling for the issuance of its report, even before it had met the hostages.[204] Khomeini also called on the students to return the documents to government, but the militants sought to turn them over to the UN commission of inquiry.[205] In effect, Khomeini said that he would allow the hostage-takers to dominate the Majlis, if they returned the documents.[206] The return of the documents could theoretically help Bani-Sadr, but the militants' behaviour made it clear that that Khomeini had little influence on them.

The new definition of the situation

After the failure of the UN commission of inquiry, Bani-Sadr declared that some of the 'students' were influenced by the Soviet Union, 'particularly through the Tudeh Party'.[207] In exile, Bani-Sadr charged that Khomeini deliberately delayed the release of the hostages because the IRP clerics had been colluding with the Republicans.[208] Bani-Sadr, however, has not provided any evidence to prove his claim regarding the collusion with the Republicans.

Hamilton Jordan concluded that Khomeini knew nothing of Ghotbzadeh's plan.[209] The NSC, on the other hand, concluded that Khomeini had deliberately sabotaged it.[210] Vance argued that Bani-Sadr was the emerging authority and that the US should deal with him.[211] Another reason that Vance wanted to proceed with the negotiations was reports of shootings, suicides, and attempted escapes.[212] Indeed, at this point, the administration was more concerned about the hostages' safety than their immediate release.[213]

The hostage-takers and conservative IRP clerics, led by Ayatollah Beheshti, called for the return of Iran's assets and US agreement to the trial of the Shah. Ghotbzadeh, however, publicly disagreed with Beheshti.[214] After the presidential elections, the leaders of the militants, Mohammad Musavi-Kho'iniha and Habibollah Peyman, concentrated their energies on the Majlis elections.[215]

Bani-Sadr indicated that Iran should pledge not to execute the Shah in the event of his extradition. He proposed a congressional investigation into US relations with the Shah, similar to that proposed by Congressman George Hansen, who had spoken with the hostage-takers in Iran. In November 1979, Bani-Sadr had supported Hansen.[216] Iran's Panamanian lawyer had already declared that the Iranian government would not execute the Shah, adding that 'the Shah would be arrested in the next few days and extradited to Iran by the end of April'.[217]

When Bani-Sadr's supporters failed to achieve a majority in the Majlis, he charged that there was a strong possibility of vote rigging. At the same time, he declared that Khomeini would increase his powers. However, Bani-Sadr now proposed that the US had to agree to the extradition and trial of the Shah and the return of his assets to Iran.[218]

Bani-Sadr's conditions were no different from those proposed by Beheshti and the radicals. As this point, US officials sought to reach out to the militants.

Assistant Secretary of State Harold Saunders met Egyptian journalist Mohammed Heikal on 16 March and persuaded him to make contact with Iranian clerics.[219] Heikal believed that US officials' decision to work with Bani-Sadr was symptomatic of their ignorance of Iranian realities.[220] He was also well aware of the militants' close relations with the Soviet embassy in Iran.[221] Heikal had a number of meetings with Saunders and Iranian officials but he failed to break the deadlock.[222]

The hostage crisis and schemes for the neutralization of Southwest Asia

In his desperation to obtain the freedom of the hostages, Carter revived the proposal for the neutralization of Iran, Afghanistan, and Pakistan. In effect, he had put the lives of the hostages before US geopolitical interests, something Brzezinski had warned against earlier. In order to indicate that there was no disunity on the issue within the administration, Brzezinski was chosen to convey Carter's proposal to the Soviets. That proposal was made at a time when Tudeh leader Nureddin Kianuri was boasting that his party could operate freely and that he supported the hostage-takers to prevent the normalization of US-Iranian relations.[223]

In March, a network of royalist military officers was arrested.[224] Iranian Defence Minister Mostafa Chamran stated that the Iranian army was at 75% of its pre-revolutionary strength and that Iran relied on the superpower stand-off to protect its security.[225] At the time, it was far more likely that the US would attack Iran. Other Iranian officials, however, were not so sanguine about the Soviet threat.[226]

The Shah's situation complicated US negotiating efforts. By now the Shah was convinced that Panamanian officials would either assassinate him or return him to Iran. On 15 March, he finally decided to leave Panama for Egypt,[227] but Carter believed that the Shah should return to the US. Vance and Harold Saunders both feared that in that case the militants might kill the hostages. Saunders feared that should this happen Carter would be forced to attack Iran, thereby destabilizing the entire Middle East.[228]

Hamilton Jordan was sent to Panama to dissuade the Shah from leaving. There he encountered French lawyer Christian Borguet who was about to present Iran's extradition papers to the Panamanians. Jordan informed Borguet that the administration wanted the Shah to stay in Panama or return to the US, but the lawyer said that the Shah's return to the US would lead the militants to kill the hostages.[229] In Jordan's presence, General Torrijos told Borguet that he was prepared to arrest the Shah, if the militants would transfer the hostages to the government by the following day. Jordan did not protest.[230]

It appears that Torrijos interpreted Jordan's silence as tacit approval.[231] The general said that the Shah must leave immediately because Borguet was going to present the extradition papers to the Panamanians.[232] Jordan contacted Carter and Vance to inform them of the Shah's decision to go to Egypt. Carter wanted the Shah to go back to the US, but Vance argued that the Shah should abdicate first in order to do so. As Jordan later said, Vance knew that the Shah would never agree to abdicate and would go to Egypt.[233]

A former senior State Department official later described Jordan's efforts as follows: 'They were trying to keep the Shah there and manipulated the signals

Panama gave the Shah to lull him into thinking he was safe there while at the same time they were hinting to the Iranians that he might be extradited'.[234]

On 18 March, Brzezinski met Soviet Ambassador Anatoly Dobrynin to discuss Carter's proposal for a grand bargain. Brzezinski said that the US would be prepared to accept 'a neutral Afghanistan, friendly to the Soviet Union like Finland, but not another vassal state like Mongolia'. Brzezinski even raised the question of Algerian or Syrian troops replacing Soviet troops as an interim measure.[235]

Dobrynin quickly concluded that Carter must have formulated the proposal. According to the ambassador, Brzezinski said that if Iran and Pakistan declared their neutrality, 'the United States was ready to respect it under a secret U.S.-Soviet agreement but not give official guarantees lest they create the impression that the Soviet Union's reach had extended to the Persian Gulf with American consent'.[236] Dobrynin did not respond to Brzezinski's proposal and the issue was not to come to a head until early April.

Meanwhile, Iranian official commentary held that the Soviet invasion of Afghanistan posed a threat to Iran.[237] Khomeini also expressed his opposition to the Soviet Union, declaring that 'the fight against Communism was the same as the fight against the United States and the West'. He also made it abundantly clear that he would not reconsider his policy of exporting the revolution[238]

On 21 March, Lloyd Cutler and Vance's adviser, Arnold Raphel, were dispatched to Panama to dissuade the Shah from going to Egypt.[239] Cutler had already been informed that Torrijos would arrest the monarch if the US gave him the green light.[240] Cutler and Raphel tried to persuade the Shah to abdicate and to refrain from travelling to Egypt.[241] The Shah's aide Robert Armao described their behaviour as 'manipulating a dying man'.[242] The Shah only agreed to abdicate if it was in favour of his son, and the Empress declared that the Pahlavi dynasty would never renounce its claim to the throne.[243]

Raphel said that the Shah and the Empress now had the opportunity to fulfil their pledge to sacrifice their lives for their country. The Empress was not sure what Raphel wanted the Shah to do: to surrender or to abdicate. Cutler and Raphel failed to persuade him to stay in Panama.[244] The Shah 'wanted to die with honour and not as a result of a medical error or a conspiracy financed by his enemies'.[245] He later wrote that trusting the Americans could have cost him his life.[246]

President Carter contacted President Sadat and tried, unsuccessfully, to persuade him to rescind his invitation to the Shah.[247] Sadat rebuffed Carter, saying that he had already sent a special presidential plane to Panama.[248] However, the American President did not give up. It seems that at this stage, US officials were trying to return the Shah to Iran in a desperate effort to resolve the hostage crisis. On 22 March, Cutler and Raphel were in Panama for yet another meeting with the Shah.[249]

There would be no need for Cutler and Jordan to go back to Panama unless there was something important to be discussed. Cutler asked the Shah not to travel to Egypt aboard Sadat's plane, adding that the US could provide a plane.[250] He then contacted a friend in the charter business.[251] The contract to fly the Shah and his entourage to Egypt was given to Evergreen International Airlines which had had ties with the CIA.[252]

Indeed, the available evidence suggests that the only purpose of Cutler's mission was to persuade the Shah to board the American plane.[253] The plane had to refuel at the Azores and it was revealed later that Hamilton Jordan had planned to delay its departure from the Azores to arrange for the return of the Shah to Panama and his extradition to Iran. Most accounts of the hostage crisis present Jordan's scheme as a spur of the moment decision.[254]

Torrijos wanted Iranian leaders to demonstrate that the hostages were about to be released to give him a pretext to arrest the Shah. The militants, however, refused to release them, indicating that the Shah's extradition was not their top priority. Iranian officials were divided. Ghotbzadeh wanted to use force to compel the militants to release the hostages, whereas Bani-Sadr opposed its use.[255] When the plane took off, Ghotbzadeh informed US officials through Borguet that he would deliver the hostages in one hour if the plane could be prevented from reaching Egypt. So when the plane arrived in the Azores, Jordan called Harold Brown and asked him to delay the plane there.[256]

Jordan also spoke with Cutler who said that the matter would be discussed upon his return to the US. According to one account, US officials could not agree to Borguet's suggestion.[257] Torrijos rejected Ghotbzadeh's plea to give him another twenty-four hours and the Shah's plane was cleared to leave the Azores.[258]

At a Special Co-ordinating Committee meeting on the same day, Brzezinski called for mining Iran's harbours and the occupation of Iran's main oil terminal at Kharg Island.[259] A rescue mission, however, was not yet a viable option. Vance argued that an 'elected' Majlis would enable Bani-Sadr to resolve the hostage crisis. He advised Carter to send a message to Bani-Sadr proposing the return of the UN commission and a transfer of the hostages to the government. However, Carter began to prepare for a military attack or a rescue mission, should the negotiations break down. He also authorized a reconnaissance flight to prepare for the rescue effort.[260]

Carter permitted Vance to continue the negotiations, but if by 31 March the hostages had not been released, the US would sever diplomatic relations, expel Iranian diplomats, impose economic sanctions and begin to adjudicate American companies' financial claims against Iran by using the assets frozen earlier.[261]

Vance met members of the UN commission and collaborated with French lawyers Borguet and Villalon in devising a 'revised scenario'.[262] However, the negotiations were undermined by numerous press reports alleging that Henry Kissinger and David Rockefeller had organized the Shah's flight to Egypt.[263] Ghotbzadeh suspected IRP clerics of maintaining contact with Kissinger and his associates through commercial channels.[264] Other Iranian officials believed that Kissinger had informed the Shah of Iran's decision to present extradition papers to Panama.[265]

Nevertheless, at a meeting of Carter's senior advisers on 31 March, Vance said that he had received a message from Bani-Sadr and Ghotbzadeh, saying that Iran would announce details of the hostage transfer the next day.[266] Moreover, Bruce Laingen informed the State Department that the Iranian Foreign Ministry was preparing to receive the hostages.[267] So Carter agreed to postpone the imposition of sanctions.[268] However, that night the White House received an advance copy of a statement attributed to Khomeini, rejecting the transfer of the hostages to the government.[269]

Despite Bani-Sadr's and Ghotbzadeh's lack of clout, US officials believed that the Bani-Sadr-Ghotbzadeh channel was their only viable option.[270] On 1 April,

Bani-Sadr declared that the Majlis would be the final arbiter, but he pledged that if the US eschewed hostile measures, the government would take control of the hostages. Carter immediately responded that this 'positive step' had led the US to postpone the imposition of sanctions.[271] However, the other component of Carter's policy, the revival of US-Soviet détente, would now collapse, leaving US regional strategy in a shambles.

Soviet leaders reject Carter's proposal for revival of détente

Anatoly Dobrynin was summoned to Moscow for consultations in April. The main issues on the agenda were the possibility of reviving détente, and the neutralization of Iran, Afghanistan, and Pakistan. Dobrynin argued that Carter and Brzezinski were acting in unison. He said that the anti-détente forces in the US had convinced the public that the Soviet Union had committed aggression in Afghanistan and was threatening vital US interests in the Middle East.

Dobrynin concluded that détente was finished and proposed that the Soviet Union seek closer ties with Western Europe. The Politburo was divided, but no one believed that Afghanistan in itself was so vital to the US as to cause such an aggravation of US-Soviet relations.[272] In addition, the Politburo did not trust either Carter or Brzezinski. It decided to press forward with détente in Europe, while seeking to reveal the Carter administration's reasons for 'undermining' détente.[273]

On 5 April, the Politburo instructed all Soviet ambassadors and KGB officials in the Persian Gulf and the Indian Ocean region to do their utmost to oppose or undermine the US military build-up in Southwest Asia.[274] Moreover, the Soviets strengthened military units in the Transcaucasian district contiguous to Iran, dispatched naval and amphibious forces to the Persian Gulf and offered 'emergency' economic assistance to Iran in the event of a US blockade.[275] However, the Soviets rejected Iranian demands to stop supplying arms to Iraq, arguing that this would lead Iraq to move into the Western camp.[276]

In late March Brzezinski had asked CIA Director Admiral Turner to present an assessment of whether the Soviet invasion of Afghanistan was 'an aberration' or a reflection of the Soviets' perception that the global balance of power favoured them. The response was that Afghanistan might well represent 'a qualitative turn' in Soviet policy towards the Third World.[277] It was against this background that Carter decided to launch a hostage rescue mission.

13

THE FAILURE OF THE HOSTAGE RESCUE MISSION AND THE CONTINUATION OF THE NEGOTIATIONS

By the spring of 1980, US officials had begun to see Iran as the greatest threat to US interests in the region. National Security Adviser Zbigniew Brzezinski took advantage of Iraqi leader Saddam Hussein's desire for an opening to Washington to put forward his case for the normalization of US-Iraq relations. Brzezinski saw the hostage crisis entirely in terms of US geopolitical and regional interests. Given this background, it is amazing that a number of students of the hostage crisis, such as Houghton, Moses, Farber and Harris have failed to take account of geopolitical considerations in US policy.[1]

The analogy, which seems to have guided Brzezinski during this period, was the Molotov-Ribbentrop pact, which gave the Soviets sufficient leeway to further their interests to the south of Batum and Baku. Brzezinski warned Carter that the Soviet Union was still pursuing the same objectives.[2] The failure of efforts to obtain the freedom of the hostages through negotiations led President Carter by April to contemplate military action. There was a 'clear danger' that the captors would still be holding the hostages during the Democratic National Convention in mid-August, perhaps even on Election Day.[3] Moreover, by April, if not much earlier, there was strong evidence that the hostage-takers were infiltrated by Soviet agents. Carter and Brzezinski feared a Soviet take-over of Iran.[4]

By early April, even the State Department had concluded that President Abolhasan President Bani-Sadr and Foreign Minister Sadegh Ghotbzadeh were losing in the power struggle in Iran.[5] When the Revolutionary Council voted in favour of accepting custody of the hostages, Khomeini vetoed the Revolutionary Council's decision.[6] At a formal NSC meeting on 7 April, Carter declared that 'it had been a mistake for him not to have acted more assertively sooner'.[7] He believed that the US was dealing not just with a group of hostage-takers, but with a 'a hostile government'. Vance opposed the use of force, but he was isolated. Brzezinski, Vice-President Walter Mondale and Secretary of Defence Harold Brown supported Carter's decision to increase the pressure on the Iranian regime.

The Carter administration improves US relations with Iraq

In keeping with Brzezinski's recommendations, the US increasingly relied on

Iraq, albeit indirectly, in order to maximize the pressure on Iran. If there were any doubts about Iraq's new foreign policy orientation, they were dispelled on 25 March when Iraq and Saudi Arabia signed a pact to strengthen North Yemen which was fighting the Soviet-backed South Yemen.[8] Saddam Hussein promised King Khalid that if the Soviet Union occupied any part of Saudi territory, Iraq would be the first country to join the Saudis in the war against the Soviet Union.[9]

After the signing of the Iraqi-Saudi pact, the Kremlin decided to organize its policy around Saddam Hussein's archenemy, Hafiz Asad.[10] In March Iraq openly turned against Syria and resumed its support for the Syrian Muslim Brotherhood.[11] In March the Brotherhood's violent actions provoked popular unrest in Aleppo, Hama, and Homs.[12] However, the disturbances and riots led Asad to consolidate his alliance with Iran. Iraqi and Syrian regimes destabilized each other by supporting insurgent groups.[13]

Iraq established contact with Iranian opposition leaders, Shapur Bakhtiar and General Gholamali Oveisi, in April.[14] By the spring of 1980, Saddam Hussein was publicly expressing his fear that Iraq might be broken up into Shi'a, Sunni, and Kurdish states.[15] According to one estimate, in April alone, at least 20 Iraqi officials were assassinated in bomb attacks by Shi'a underground organizations.[16] In early April the Iranian-backed Al-Da'wa al-Islamiya attempted to assassinate Foreign Minister Tariq Aziz.[17] It said that the attack was a response to the Ba'th's execution of nearly 40 of its members in March.[18] The Iraqis said that the attack had been carried out by an Iranian.[19]

Saddam Hussein made membership of al-D'awa punishable by death. Three days later Khomeini called on the Iraqi military to topple Saddam Hussein. Iraq responded by bombing Ghasr-e Shirin and executing the spiritual leader of al-D'awa, Ayatollah Mohammad Baqer Sadr, and his sister Bint Huda on 9 April.[20] The next day, 10 April, Under Secretary of State David Newsom announced that 'the United States is prepared . . . to resume diplomatic relation with Iraq at any time'.[21]

Carter decides to launch a rescue mission

According to Carter's diary entry of 10 April, 'The Iranian terrorists are making all kinds of crazy threats to kill the American hostages if they are invaded by Iraq-whom they identify as an American puppet.'[22] The threat to the captives, Carter has claimed, led him to launch a rescue mission.[23]

The evidence does not support Carter's claim. On 14 April – four days after the Carter administration had received a warning from the captors that they might kill the hostages – Brzezinski said on the MacNeil-Lehrer television news show:

> We see no fundamental incompatibility of interests between the United States and Iraq. We feel that Iraq desires to be independent, that Iraq wishes a secure Persian Gulf, and we do not feel that American-Iraqi relations need to be frozen in antagonism.[24]

Brzezinski's statement would, if anything, further strain US–Iran relations. Moreover, Carter's claim is not supported by US intelligence reports. A secret report in early April had concluded that the 'continuing turmoil in Iran posed no particular threat to the captives'. In fact, the rescue mission itself posed a greater threat to the hostages. One Pentagon estimate predicted twenty casualties among the hostages and fifty or more among the rescuers. Another report estimated that fifteen hostages and thirty rescuers would be killed.[25] There is very little evidence that Carter's decision to launch the rescue mission was influenced by domestic American politics.[26]

The most compelling reason for launching the rescue mission was the Soviet Union's influence over some of the hostage-takers, particularly their mentor, Kho'iniha. Vance, however, who had played the leading role in the negotiations with the Soviets, continued to call for restraint. As late as 1990, Vance argued that his opposition to the rescue mission was justified because the conflagration resulting from a rescue mission could have spread to the whole region.[27] He was pinning his hopes on Iranian Majlis elections.[28] However, planning for the mission continued when Vance was on vacation in Florida.[29]

On 8 April, NSC official Gary Sick sent Brzezinski a long memorandum arguing that the US had two options. First, it could either increase the pressure on Iran steadily and, if necessary, mine Iranian harbours. The second option was to launch a rescue operation because it would 'deprive' Khomeini 'of his bargaining leverage and would puncture his aura of invincibility'. Moreover, a hostage rescue mission would entail 'minimal loss of life' and would not lead to 'unpredictable escalation'.[30]

Brzezinski argued that a rescue mission was the only option to get the hostages back alive and that the US 'policy of restraint' was no longer effective.[31] He contended that the only other alternative was 'the direct application of force', which would 'drive Iran into the hands of the Soviets'.[32] On 11 April, in Vance's absence, Carter and his senior advisers decided that the rescue operation should be launched on 24 April.[33]

The failure of Israeli mediation and Vance's efforts to call off the rescue mission

The Israelis were anxious to strengthen Iran in order to prevent Iraq from becoming the dominant power in the region. On 13 April, Begin informed Carter that Israel had contacts in Iran that could be developed further if the US permitted Israel to sell arms to Iran. Carter rejected Begin's proposal and asked him for an assurance that his country would observe the US arms embargo. The Israelis promised that they would not sell arms to Iran, adding that if they decided to change their policy they would inform the US.[34]

Vance was angry that the decision to launch the rescue mission had been made in his absence.[35] At a private meeting with Carter on 15 April, he tried to get the mission cancelled by arguing that Khomeini would release the hostages once they were no longer useful to him politically.[36] Carter gave Vance the chance to defend his position at a NSC meeting, which was held later that same day. Vance argued that the rescue mission might result in the death of a number of hostages and a confrontation between the US and the Soviet Union.[37]

Vance argued forcefully for the continuation of the negotiations, but Carter rejected his recommendations. He said that he too was concerned about a confrontation with the Soviets, but that the rescue mission was the least risky military option.[38] Brzezinski had framed the issue in precisely the same fashion on 9 April. However, Vance apparently succeeded in persuading Carter to re-open the Ghotbzadeh channel. Despite Ghotbzadeh's failure to persuade the militants to release the hostages, Hamilton Jordan met the Iranian Foreign Minister in mid-April. He returned from Paris very optimistic.[39]

Miles Copeland and the rescue mission

Although planning for a rescue mission had been kept secret, supporters of the Republicans in the national security bureaucracy revealed some of the details, thereby endangering the lives of the hostages. On 20 April, the *Washington Star* published an article by former CIA official, Miles Copeland, who was working closely with the Republicans on an alternative rescue mission. The rescue plan described in Copeland's article was 'similar to the real one'.[40]

Only a handful of people had been aware of the hostage rescue plans and Vance. who opposed the use of force, had been circumvented. Initially, Brzezinski had even sought to keep the CIA out of the loop.[41] The publication of the Copeland article meant that Carter either had to call off the operation or a rescue mission had to be launched before the captors harmed the hostages.

Vance resigns, Carter approves the rescue mission

On 21 April, Vance tendered his resignation. However, he agreed not to make his decision public until after the rescue mission.[42] The publication of Copeland's article had an immediate effect. Persian language broadcasts indicated that the Iranians expected a blockade or a rescue operation. US intelligence had also received reports that Iranian forces had been placed on alert. US officials believed that Copeland's article had alerted the Iranians and the Soviets.[43]

Most worrying was a report from one of the CIA's agents in Tehran who reported that the guards were alert and that the safety of the operation could not be guaranteed.[44] However, another report from Iran indicated that the Tehran part of the operation would go smoothly. CIA Director Admiral Turner decided to disregard the report, which recommended postponing the operation.[45]

A military analysis of the rescue mission is beyond the scope of this study.[46] Suffice it to say that the reasons given for the failure of the mission are not convincing. Most importantly, the mission could have proceeded with five helicopters instead of the initial six.[47] Mission commander Charles Beckwith has claimed that if they had decided to proceed with only five helicopters, they would have been forced to leave behind eighteen to twenty men, thereby compromising the mission. Firstly, the damaged helicopter could have been repaired.[48] Secondly, there would have been casualties. Pentagon officials expected there to be between forty-five and seventy casualties among hostages and rescuers.[49] According to one account, the most optimistic CIA estimate held that no more than twenty hostages out of fifty-three would be taken out of Tehran alive.[50]

In fact, the operation endangered the lives of 300 other Americans in Iran.[51] After consultation with the mission commanders, it took Carter only twelve minutes to abort the mission.[52] Some critics, such as William Safire, argued that Carter had never intended to complete the mission.[53] Another possibility raised was that the Soviet Union threatened to attack the transport aircraft as they left Iran through Turkey. The Carter administration went to great lengths to demonstrate that the cover of the mission had not been blown. In a report on Defence Secretary Harold Brown's press conference, 'informed sources' were quoted as saying: 'There was no sign that the Russians either detected the mission or put forces on higher alert.'[54]

At a congressional inquiry and afterwards the Carter administration maintained that the failure of the mission had been due to a series of mishaps.[55] However, some intelligence sources claimed that the Soviets had sent their own fighters to intercept the American aircraft. According to these sources, the hotline between Washington and Moscow had been activated and Carter, fearing a confrontation, had agreed to abort the rescue mission. Moreover, there were hints that 'the conflagration' was caused by 'either gunfire or a small missile'.[56] Whatever the cause of the failure of the mission, the dispute over the choice of strategy only sharpened in the US.

US strategy after the rescue mission

Despite Secretary Vance's resignation, his successor Edmund Muskie was determined to pursue a negotiated solution to the crisis.[57] As a senator, Edmund Muskie had argued that the Carter administration had exaggerated the significance of the Soviet invasion of Afghanistan. After he became Secretary of State, Muskie made more ambiguous statements.[58] Like Vance, he realized that the US-Soviet relationship was highly competitive. However, he did not want to stop talking to the Soviets because they had invaded Afghanistan. Muskie believed that the invasion was primarily aimed at maintaining Soviet influence in a neighbouring country.[59] Thus the views of the NSC and the State Department of the situation in the Persian Gulf and Southwest Asia continued to diverge.[60]

After the failure of the rescue mission, Brzezinski immediately began to prepare for another rescue mission. However, this time the mission would entail even greater risks because the Iranians would be on a higher state of alert. Moreover, the captors moved the hostages to different locations around the country. As NSC official Gary Sick observed later, defeat seemed to have made Brzezinski even more determined to launch another rescue mission.[61] The second invasion was code-named Honey Badger. According to Brzezinski, the new plan would be 'less complicated and less dependent on high technology than the previous operation'.[62]

Some of the rescuers would enter Iran on commercial flights using fake passports. Others would enter the country by truck. The rescue forces would then launch several rescue missions in different parts of the country and the helicopters would arrive at those locations to fly the hostages and the rescuers out of the country.[63] The second rescue mission, required the participation of 20,000 troops. In the words of Martin and Walcott, it was 'more an invasion than a rescue mission'.[64] According to Brzezinski:

The second mission had some analogies with Entebbe while it was being planned because the second plan involved going into the airport at Tehran, taking the airport, landing an armoured mobile force, driving into the city, shooting up anything in the way, bombing anything that starts interfering, storming the embassy, taking out anybody who's alive after that process and then going back and taking off.[65]

When NSC official Gary Sick argued that the plan was not feasible, Brzezinski cut him out of the planning process.[66] The State Department continued to oppose the use of force against Iran.[67] Its policy towards Iran and its regional strategy were remarkably similar to the West Europeans' regional strategy. Brzezinski, however, attached equal importance to the Persian Gulf-Southwest Asia, Western Europe, and Japanese theatres.

The Carter administration's resumption of negotiations with Iran

After the rescue mission the Soviets once again attempted to negotiate an agreement on the demilitarization of the Persian Gulf and the Indian Ocean with the US.[68] America's West European allies, including Great Britain, also favoured a negotiated solution to regional conflicts, including the hostage crisis.[69]

On 22 May, West Europeans announced the imposition of sanctions on Iran. But this was only a token gesture. The only trade embargoed included the contracts signed after the hostage seizure.[70] After the failed rescue mission, the Special Co-ordinating Committee, SCC, discussed the possibility of expanding the CIA's covert activity in Iran. The agency had been in contact with pro-Shah figures and this concerned Brzezinski and Warren Christopher who thought association with 'reactionary' elements would damage US interests. Brzezinski and Christopher wanted the CIA to 'find new contacts'.[71]

CIA Director Admiral Turner 'was less interested in such long-term political concerns than in getting the hostages out'. Turner believed that none of the opposition groups that the CIA was supporting, or that Brzezinski wanted the agency to support, had a strong political base inside Iran.[72]

The SCC decided to wait for Iranian officials 'to negotiate on reasonable terms'.[73] The State Department still believed that President Bani-Sadr had the power to negotiate. Indeed Bani-Sadr had requested and received additional authority over the armed forces from Khomeini.[74] He believed that Iran had to release the hostages because Iraq was destabilizing Iran 'under the direction of the United States'.[75]

Shortly after the Tabas rescue mission, the State Department asked the Egyptian journalist, Mohamed Heikal, to open a channel of communication with Bani-Sadr. The directive Heikal was given clearly shows that the State Department pursued a defeatist strategy on the hostage issue to maintain Iran's non-aligned status. Heikal was told to emphasize that the failure of the rescue mission had shown 'the moral superiority of the Islamic Republic'. The State Department went so far as to suggest that the Iranians should make full use of the hostages' release to score a propaganda victory.[76] However, US intelligence indicated that the hostage issue had become less important to the Iranian regime.[77]

Power struggle in Iran: Beheshti splits the ranks of militants

Iranian politics were increasingly polarized between Islamic fundamentalist and left wing extremist groups.[78] After the failure of the rescue mission, Ayatollah Beheshti and his supporters once again called for trying the hostages. Beheshti's Islamic Republican Party (IRP) emerged as the leading party in the second round of parliamentary elections held on 9-10 May.[79]

At the same time, Beheshti split the ranks of the Students Following the Line of the Imam by reaching an agreement with the Mojahedin of the Islamic Revolution, which was the main group behind the hostage seizure.[80] The agreement excluded Habibollah Peyman's Combatant Muslims Movement.[81] Beheshti also ensured that the mentor of the Students Following the Line of the Imam, Hojjat ol-Eslam Mohammad Musavi-Kho'iniha, would be given a seat in the Majlis and 'elected' to the Deputy Speakership.[82]

At the same time, he also sought to take advantage of the banking dispute between Iran and the US to resolve the crisis. However, Beheshti was anxious to distance himself from the talks because he believed that his life and position would be endangered if radical factions in the regime discovered that he was negotiating with the Americans.[83]

The IRP's main objective was Bani-Sadr's gradual removal. Both Bani-Sadr and his opponents appeared to believe that Khomeini's illness meant that he would only provide spiritual guidance.[84] On 9 May, Bani-Sadr received an edict from Khomeini to form a cabinet, but the Revolutionary Council rejected his nominee for Prime Minister.[85] Moreover, the IRP-dominated Majlis repeatedly undermined Bani-Sadr. Khomeini was reluctant to intervene in this dispute.[86]

Bani-Sadr used his prerogative as commander-in-chief to bring the armed forces and the Revolutionary Guards Corps under his control.[87] In late April, after the dispersal of the hostages, the Revolutionary Guards were given the task of protecting the embassy compound as well as the military bases and hotels in provincial towns to which some of the hostages had been moved.[88]

However, the Guards saw Bani-Sadr as a threat to their existence and he failed to appoint a commander.[89] His opponents succeeded in appointing their ally, Mohsen Reza'i, as Guards commander in July 1980. Another ally of the IRP, Hojjatoleslam Fazlollah Mahallati, was appointed Guards' supervisor.[90] During the same period the regime also began to clamp down on the activities of the National Front and the Mojahedin-e Khalq.[91] Simultaneously, Khomeini launched a Cultural Revolution, which was designed to reduce the influence of secularists and secular leftists in Iran's universities.[92]

The crackdown on Mojahedin-e Khalq

The crackdown on the Mojahedin-e Khalq was considered to be so important that some members of the Islamic Republican Party, such as Hasan Ayat, were even prepared to form an alliance with the Tudeh Party in order to eliminate them. Ayat, a leading member of the IRP's central council and its chief ideologue, was also one of the leaders of the hostage-takers.[93] Much later, it was revealed that the Tudeh party had planned to stage a take-over by forming an alliance with the hostage-takers whom the Tudeh assumed would support the coup d'etat.[94]

In June Bani-Sadr revealed transcripts of a conversation in which Ayat called for Khomeini's replacement by Ayatollah Montazeri and using the hostage crisis to ensure Ayat's appointment as Prime Minister.[95] The IRP did not deny the authenticity of the tape, but claimed that it only reflected Ayat's view.[96]

Khomeini was reportedly upset. To counter the IRP's bid for power, Bani-Sadr formed a tacit alliance with the Mojahedin-e Khalq. Indeed it was they who had obtained transcripts of Ayat's conversation.[97] On 20 June, Ayat called Bani-Sadr an agent of the US who was 'acting like the Shah'.[98] The tug of war between Bani-Sadr and his opponents continued throughout the summer.

US Strategy and the Iran-Iraq Conflict

The escalating conflict between Iran and Iraq, which posed a threat to the security of the Persian Gulf, enabled Brzezinski, and Secretary of Defence Harold Brown to push through their policy of expanding the US military presence in Southwest Asia.[99] The main obstacle to the regional security framework was Saudi Arabia's opposition.[100]

Worse still, Saudi Arabia continued to indicate that it was prepared to reach an accommodation with the Soviet Union.[101] The Soviets recognized the significance of Riyadh's shift of strategy and continued to court Saudi Arabia.[102] However, the Iraqi regime's rhetoric became increasingly anti-Soviet.[103] Ever since the communist coup in Afghanistan in April 1978, the Ba'thist regime had feared that the Soviet Union would try to overthrow it.[104]

By May 1980 Saddam Hussein had concluded that he had no choice but to wage war against the Iranian regime.[105] Conservative Arab states such as Saudi Arabia, Jordan and Kuwait which feared the spread of the Iranian revolution, supported him.[106] The US also continued to signal that it desired to improve relations with Iraq. Deputy Assistant Secretary of State Morris Draper claimed that Iraq had softened its position on Israel, even though there was little evidence that this was the case.[107] He also noted that Iraq had reduced its dependence on the Soviet bloc.[108]

As Iraq stepped up its diplomatic efforts to isolate Iran, Iran moved closer to Syria. Syrian President Hafiz Asad considered Saddam Hussein as the main threat to his regime and saw his nascent alliance with Iran as a means of destabilizing Iraq and undermining the Camp David agreement.[109] On 27 April, Iran and Syria signed a joint communiqué in Damascus affirming their friendship and calling for opposition to the Camp David treaty.[110] Asad also believed that his alliance with Khomeini would enhance the religious legitimacy of his regime.[111]

Iran also stepped up his propaganda campaign against Saddam Hussein. Iranian officials and both Khomeini and Foreign Minister Ghotbzadeh called for the overthrow of the Iraqi regime.[112] Bani-Sadr and the Iranian defence minister made it clear that Iran would go to war with Iraq in the event of further deterioration of the border conflict.[113]

In June and July the Carter administration stepped up the supply of military equipment to Jordan and Saudi Arabia to prepare them for the conflict between Iran and Iraq.[114] In the summer of 1980, Saddam Hussein threatened to diversify the sources of Iraq's arms imports if the Soviet Union did not meet his country's needs.[115] In July, he demanded that Iran accept Iraqi control of the entire Shatt-al-Arab.[116] As Iraq continued to prepare for war, Saddam Hussein's chief ally, King Hussein of Jordan, redoubled his efforts to gain support for Baghdad in other Arab capitals.[117]

US contacts with Iraq

There have been a number of reports regarding US contacts with Saddam Hussein during this period. According to the *New York Times* and Iranian exiles, Brzezinski met Saddam Hussein in Amman during the first week of July 1980.[118] Reportedly, the purpose of Brzezinski's visit was to persuade Saddam Hussein 'to oppose Iran's reckless policies'. Brzezinski and NSC official Gary Sick, however, deny that such a meeting took place. But, Brzezinski did meet King Hussein, and he may have also met a senior Iraqi emissary to discuss the Iran-Iraq conflict.[119] Sick later said: 'Brzezinski was letting Saddam assume there was an U.S. green light for his invasion of Iran, because there was no explicit red light. But to say the U.S. planned and plotted it all out in advance is simply not true.'[120]

Naturally, Brzezinski did not need to create Hussein's motives for him. The question of whether he personally met Saddam Hussein is peripheral to the argument. After 1979 Brzezinski played a central role in directing US covert operations. According to Howard Teicher who was a Pentagon official at the time: 'In the months preceding his invasion of Iran, Saddam had received intelligence reports from King Hussein of Jordan and the Saudi leadership which summarized U.S. briefings on the steady decline in the military capabilities of the Iranians.' Teicher has said that US officials knew full well that US intelligence assessments would reach Saddam Hussein.[121]

According to Sa'id Aburish, Hussein did not meet Brzezinski, but he did meet three CIA officers, Rance Haig, Tom Twetten and Tom Alan.[122] Moreover, King Hussein also organized a meeting between Saddam Hussein and Iranian opposition leaders who assured the Iraqi president that Khomeini's popularity was declining and that he had to take advantage of the opportunity to attack Iran.[123]

The Nozheh Coup Attempt

Initially, Iraq concentrated its efforts on promoting a military coup in Iran. Former Iranian Prime Minister Shapur Bakhtiar and Tehran martial-law administrator under the Shah, General Gholamali Oveisi, had been collaborating on a plan with the Iraqis which recommended an Iraqi invasion of Iran, followed by Bakhtiar's take-over of Khuzestan Province.[124] It was reported that Egypt and Iraq were supporting Oveisi and that he had met US officials.[125] The two men visited Iraq several times throughout the summer and sent agents into Iranian provinces of Khuzestan and Kurdistan.[126]

The Nozheh coup d'etat was organized by Shapur Bakhtiar and General Oveisi from their exile in France and Iraq.[127] The Nozheh plot was revealed on 9 July, 1980. The Iranian regime declared that the Air Force had been planning to take over the Nozheh air base near Hamedan and to strike Khomeini's residence, the Tehran airport, the theological seminary in Qom, the Majlis, the headquarters of the Revolutionary Guards and selected military bases. Strike units were instructed to assassinate members of the Revolutionary Council and cabinet, as well as some clerics.[128] According to one Iranian account, the coup leaders initially wanted to eliminate Bani-Sadr, but they later decided to arrest him.[129] According to another account read out in the Majlis, had the coup succeeded there would have been mass public executions of Iranian leaders.[130]

Both the official account and Bani-Sadr's version of the Nozheh coup are self-serving and simplistic.[131] In fact an Israeli intelligence agent, Manuchehr Ghorbanifar, and the Soviet Union were chiefly responsible for informing the Khomeini regime of the Nozheh coup d'etat.[132] The US relied almost entirely on Israeli intelligence to keep abreast of developments in Iran,[133] because Israel had infiltrated the ranks of civilian and military coup leaders there.[134]

If Iraq had succeeded in occupying the oil-rich Iranian province of Khuzestan, it would have considerably increased its oil wealth and would have emerged as the leader of the Arab world. Israeli decision-makers believed that geopolitical realities would prevail and Iranian leaders would be tempted to resume their country's relationship with Israel. At the time of the Nozheh coup attempt Israeli leaders were deeply preoccupied with the Iraqi nuclear threat.[135]

Bakhtiar later said that some of his close colleagues had sold the coup plans to Bani-Sadr through the Iranian embassy in France.[136] Ghorbanifar blamed Bakhtiar, whom he accused of bragging to the Iraqis and blowing the cover of the mission.[137] Significantly, in July Israel resumed its arms shipment to Iran. According to Gary Sick, these shipments occurred as a result of an agreement William Casey negotiated with Cyrus Hashemi.[138] Ghorbanifar would play a major role in US and Israeli arms shipments to Iran in the 1980s.

The Soviet role in revealing the Nozheh coup

The Soviet Union also helped the Iranian regime to foil the Nozheh coup, despite the fact that Iran's increasing diplomatic isolation had not immediately resulted in its absorption into the Soviet orbit. On 2 July, Iran asked the Soviets to close their consulates in Rasht and Esfahan and reduce their staff at the embassy to nine.[139]

However, Soviet diplomats stationed in Tehran repeatedly warned the Iranians of threats and offered assistance to suppress opposition activities.[140] A Soviet diplomat passed information on the Nozheh coup to Bani-Sadr just before the officers involved were arrested.[141] Soviet foreknowledge of the coup was the result of Tudeh and, by extension KGB, infiltration of the armed forces. The Tudeh Party had succeeded in establishing secret cells in the armed forces and were waiting for an opportunity to stage a coup themselves.[142]

Until 1983 the party claimed that it had discovered the Nozheh plot and that it had co-operated with the Iranian regime in foiling it.[143] Indeed, even the official account of the Nozheh coup credits the Tudeh Party with passing intelligence to the Revolutionary Guards Corps. However, the official account downplays their role.[144]

The Soviet Union also influenced other leftist groups such as the Fada'iyan-e Khalq and elements of Mojahedin-e Khalq.[145] The Mojahedin-e Khalq, which had considerable support within the NCOs, also claimed credit for discovering the Nozheh coup attempt.[146] After the suppression of the left, the Revolutionary Guards claimed exclusive credit for uncovering the Nozheh coup attempt and purging the plotters.[147]

The impact of the Nozheh Coup on Iranian Politics

The Iranian regime's response to the Nozheh plot was brutal. Six hundred air force officers were arrested, and in July 1980, 81 of them were executed.[148] The regime also attempted to assassinate Shapur Bakhtiar in Paris, but failed.[149] However, the regime did succeed in assassinating another opposition leader, Ali Akbar Tabataba'i who was gunned down on 22 July 1980 by an American Islamist, David Belfield, aka Dawud Salahuddin. Tabataba'i had been a former press attaché at the Iranian embassy in Washington.[150] Salahuddin had been recruited and influenced by Sa'id Ramadan and an Iranian-born naturalized American rug merchant, Bahram Nahidian, who coordinated pro-Khomeini activities in Washington D.C.. Sa'id Ramadan had tasked Nahidian with recruiting young disillusioned African-American men. Salahuddin was one of Nahidian's recruits.[151] Salahuddin escaped to Iran and arrived there on 31 July 1980. Since then he has been living in Iran. He has also indicated that he is quite prepared to kill again or bomb buildings in pursuit of his political objectives. He also continued his association with Sa'id Ramadan and made contact with Libyan leader Mu'ammar Qadhafi and former Afghan President Borhanoddin Rabbani on Ramadan's behalf. Shortly after the first World Trade Center bombing, Salahuddin also established back-channel contacts with American officials and even talked about returning to the US to stand trial in the murder of Tabataba'i. US officials were trying to use the murder case as leverage to discover the motives of the World Trade Center bombers and Salahuddin informed them that the bombing was directly related to the US military presence in Saudi Arabia. Salahuddin was also disillusioned with the Iranian regime, particularly the clergy. He declared: 'The corruption here among the highest levels of the mullahs is incredible-it includes financial malfeasance, gross human rights violations, extrajudicial murder, and two systems of justice, one for the mullahs, and one for citizens.' Nevertheless, he worked as a journalist, writer, war correspondent and actor in Iran. In 1994, Salahuddin sent a letter to Attorney-General Janet Reno saying that he would agree to mediate between the US government and 'certain key figures in the worldwide Islamic movement' if all the charges against him in Bethesda were dropped.[152] As late as 2002 the CIA was interested in Salahuddin because it believed that he had access to the inner sanctum of the Iranian regime and had high-level contacts among Iranian 'moderates' who wanted to improve Iran's relations with the US.[153] In 1980, however, Salahuddin's action strengthened the most radical elements in the Iranian regime.

The Nozheh coup attempt actually strengthened the hostage-takers' position. Moreover, leftist and radical religious groups, such as the Organization of the Mojahedin of the Islamic Revolution, sought to intensify the purge of the armed forces.[154] The Revolutionary Guards took advantage of the coup to purge the armed forces and try to remove the president.[155] In a major U-turn, on 20 July Khomeini condemned Bani-Sadr's government as non-revolutionary and told him that he distrusted the military because it was pro-Shah.[156]

Bani-Sadr was also the victim of a Soviet active measures campaign aimed at portraying him as a US agent.[157] In 1980, the KGB conducted a joint operation code-named TAYFUN with the Bulgarian intelligence service. The operation made use of forgeries purporting to belong to a phantom underground Military Council for Salvation conspiring to overthrow Khomeini and restore the monarchy. The KGB claimed that the Iranian regime believed the forgeries and blamed the fictitious underground Military Council for the attacks on its supporters.[158] The KGB resident in Beirut, code-named KOLCHIN, supplied further disinformation to PLO leader Yasir Arafat on fictitious conspiracies against the Iranian regime, including an alleged plot to assassinate Khomeini by the CIA, Mossad, SIS, the French SDECE and the German BND. According to KGB reports, Arafat personally supplied the disinformation to Khomeini. The KGB also fabricated a report to the CIA from a fictitious Iranian agent providing further 'apparent evidence' of a CIA-sponsored attempt to assassinate Khomeini.[159]

The Formation of the Raja'i Government

Throughout August President Bani-Sadr was locked into a power struggle with the IRP over the selection of Prime Minister and the cabinet.[160] After much wrangling, the Majlis's choice, Muhammad Ali Raja'i was appointed Prime Minister on 11 August.[161]

The formation of the Raja'i government was, in effect, tantamount to a power grab by the leaders of the hostage takers. The Raja'i government was an alliance of the Mojahedin of the Islamic Revolution (MIR) and the *Hojjatieh* faction in the IRP, in which *Hojjatieh* played a subordinate role. Significantly, the Raja'i government included only one cleric, Hojjatoleslam Mahdavi-Kani, who was a member of Hojjatieh.[162]

Raja'i and his top aide, Minister for Executive Affairs, Behzad Nabavi, were co-founders of the MIR.[163] The MIR secured powerful cabinet posts in the Iranian government, including ministries of heavy industry and oil.[164] After the formation of the Raja'i government, Habibollah Peyman's followers either left the US embassy compound or were sent to guard the hostages outside Tehran.[165] The alliance between the conservative clerics and the MIR was an alliance of convenience, based on their opposition to Bani-Sadr. Moreover, Khomeini himself told Bani-Sadr that he would have no authority over either the interior or defence ministries.[166] Beheshti went much further, declaring 'that Bani-Sadr would have no more authority'.[167] Bani-Sadr also lost control of the Iranian broadcast media, particularly television.[168]

Purge of armed forces and debate about alliance with Tudeh

The Raja'i government saw the Iranian military as a bastion of pro-American and pro-Shah forces. Hence, during this period, it accelerated the purge of the armed forces to forestall another coup attempt. The planners sought to bring about the gradual disintegration of the military to replace it with the Revolutionary Guards,[169] who were given the task of defending the regime and exporting the revolution.[170] Contrary to Bani-Sadr's absurd claim, this plan did not serve the interests of the United States.[171] In fact, the Soviets considered the Iranian military as pro-American and preferred to see it replaced with the Revolutionary Guards Corps and militias armed by the Soviet Union.[172]

The Iranian regime established a new branch in the armed forces for political and religious indoctrination of the officer corps.[173] Ayatollah Beheshti and his supporters were still a powerful counterweight to leftists. Beheshti argued that the Tudeh was an arm of Soviet policy and described Marxists as traitors.[174]

However, his rhetoric reflected the ascendancy of the radicals.[175] So radical did Beheshti's rhetoric become that some accused him of being a Soviet agent.[176] It would be difficult to believe that Beheshti, a man who accumulated millions of dollars in Western banks believed in severing Iran's ties with the West.[177]

Increasingly, there emerged a rift in the IRP between advocates of forming an alliance with Communist and leftist parties and those who advocated a crackdown on all potential opponents of the regime.[178] However, until the summer of 1981, the anti-Communist Hojjatieh group led by Beheshti dominated the IRP. Hojjatieh was also more reluctant than the radicals to continue the conflict with Iraq.[179]

Escalation of Iran-Iraq conflict

The failure of the Nozheh coup may well have led Saddam Hussein to conclude that going to war with Iran would be necessary.[180] In August Bakhtiar and Oveisi assured him that the Iranian regime would collapse provided a foreign power gave it a push.[181] In July and August Saddam Hussein informed several Arab leaders that Iraq intended to invade Iran.[182]

On 4 August, the US declared that it would sell Iraq eight marine turbine engines licensed in February and that the Commerce Department was studying the sale of five Boeing jets to Iraq as well.[183] This was a vote of confidence in Saddam Hussein. On 5 August, he visited Riyadh where he met King Khalid, Crown Prince Fahd and other senior officials.[184] According to the then Saudi ambassador to the UK, Ghazi Al-Gosaibi, Saddam Hussein informed Crown Prince Fahd of his plan to attack Iran.[185]

A former aide to Saddam Hussein, Sa'ad Bazzaz, has confirmed this.[186] Hussein promised the Saudis that Iraq would only resort to military action after it had exhausted all peaceful alternatives and that it would 'limit military action while offering negotiations'.[187] However, it is unlikely that either Saudi Arabia or Iraq genuinely believed this was possible.[188] Crown Prince Fahd promised Iraq billions of dollars in aid and free use of the Saudi port of Jeddah.[189]

In a 1981 US government document, marked, 'top secret/sensitive', the then US Secretary of State Alexander Haig wrote: 'It was also interesting to confirm that President Carter gave the Iraqis a green light to launch the war against Iran through Fahd.'[190] The then CIA Director Admiral Stansfield Turner has said that he did not have any evidence that Saddam Hussein had cleared his invasion plan with the US, but he has admitted that the CIA had informed Carter of an imminent invasion.[191]

Egyptian President Anwar Sadat later told Brian Crozier that the Carter administration and the Saudis had approved of Saddam Hussein's decision to invade Iran.[192] Saddam Hussein told the Emir of Kuwait that General Oveisi 'could be in Tehran within days'.[193] Saddam Hussein's intelligence chief Barzan al-Takriti was so incompetent that he led the Iraqi leader to believe that the Iranians would surrender in the early hours of combat.[194]

According to former director of Iraq's Military Intelligence, General Wafiq Samarai, Saddam Hussein drew an analogy with Israel's victory in the 1967 six-day war.[195] Count Alexandre de Marenches, director of French intelligence, SDECE, at the time, held Hussein's intelligence chief Barzan al-Takriti responsible for Iraq's intelligence failure because he flattered the Iraqi leader, instead of telling him the truth.[196]

Iran-Iraq conflict and the deterioration of Iraqi-Syrian relations

What particularly complicated Saddam Hussein's calculation was that Iraq found itself in a three-front conflict situation with Iran, Israel and Syria. The most serious threat to the stability of the Asad regime was still the Muslim Brotherhood. According to various reports, the Brotherhood was supported by the US, Israel, Iraq, and Jordan during various stages of its development.[197] In 1980 both Iraq and Jordan supported it and Iraq's main ally, Jordan, had even permitted the Syrian Muslim Brotherhood to establish camps there.[198]

As soon as he secured Saudi Arabia's approval for his invasion plan, Hussein moved against Syria. On 18 August, Iraq declared that the Syrian embassy was planning to destabilize Iraq, and expelled the embassy's entire staff. The Syrians responded by expelling the Iraqi ambassador and 19 embassy officials.[199] Saddam Hussein also concluded a new agreement with Jordan, which secured a line of communication for Iraq in the event of the closure of Shatt-al-Arab and the Strait of Hormuz.[200]

Iran asked the PLO to inform Saddam Hussein that attacking Iran would be an act of folly, but he was impervious to these warnings. He assured Arafat that a lightning Iraqi victory would terrify the Israelis.[201] However, Hussein's greatest strategic mistake was that he alienated the Soviet Union.

The Soviet Union and the Iran-Iraq conflict

The Nozheh coup infuriated the Kremlin, and the Soviets declared that the US was involved in the coup. They feared that an Iraqi invasion of Iran would undermine their position there.[202] Meanwhile Moscow's relations with Baghdad had deteriorated to the point that it was prepared to risk its ties with Iraq in order to increase its influence in Iran. In July Soviet ambassador Vinogradov told Bani-Sadr that the Soviet Union had informed Iraq of its opposition to an invasion of Iran. He also noted that Iraqi-Soviet relations had deteriorated. According to Bani-Sadr, Vinogradov made it clear that as far as the Soviet Union was concerned, Saddam Hussein was behaving like Sadat and he would move into the US orbit.[203]

In August, Iran asked the Soviet Union to refrain from supplying arms to Iraq. The Soviets refused to comply with Iran's demand, but indicated that they were willing to supply arms to Iran.[204] Moreover, to show their 'good faith', the Soviets provided Iran with intelligence on Iraq's war plan. In fact, Iran was in possession of Iraq's war plans for nearly two months before the Iraqi invasion.[205] According to Bani-Sadr, the Iranian Foreign Minister Sadegh Ghotbzadeh purchased a copy of Iraq's invasion plan in August for 200,000 dollars from a Latin American security official in Paris.[206]

A few weeks later Bani-Sadr met with the Soviet ambassador, Vinogradov and asked him if he was behind supplying intelligence to Iran. According to Bani-Sadr, Vinogradov just 'chuckled'. 'It was his way of confirming it', said Bani-Sadr.[207] It was later reported that the plan had been formulated by a group of Iranian exiles, Israeli Generals, and Americans in Paris. The report also mentioned that Brzezinski had met Saddam Hussein in the first week of July in Jordan.[208] Bani-Sadr had also received other reports of a secret meeting between the two in which Brzezinski was said to have approved of an Iraqi attack on Iran.[209]

Shortly afterwards, Iran's ambassador to the Soviet Union, Mohammad Mokri, provided Bani-Sadr with the same information that Ghotbzadeh had supplied. In early August, Mokri returned to Iran for consultations. After his meeting with Bani-Sadr, he said that Iran had expressed its 'disapproval' of Soviet arms supplies to Iraq.[210] Mokri was later imprisoned for spying for the Soviet Union.[211]

Bani-Sadr has said that Iranian officials thought the Tudeh Party and the Soviets had invented the intelligence on Iraq's invasion plan to enhance their status in Iran.[212] Iran repeatedly asked the Soviet Union to cease its arms supplies to Iraq, and Ghotbzadeh was particularly active in this regard.[213]

As early as the spring of 1980 Ghotbzadeh had informed Moscow that if it failed to withdraw its troops from Afghanistan, Iran would provide military assistance to the Afghan Mojahedin. In July, he ordered the Soviet embassy in Tehran to reduce the number of its staff.[214] On 11 August, he sent a message to the Soviet Foreign Minister Andrei Gromyko, lambasting the Soviets as 'no less satanic than the United States'. Ghotbzadeh contended that the US and the Soviet Union had reached an informal agreement to divide Southwest Asia between them.[215]

He accused the Soviets of encouraging secessionist tendencies in Kurdistan, providing satellite intelligence to the Kurds, and espionage. He noted Moscow's refusal to accept Iran's abrogation of the 1921 treaty in order to commit 'aggression' against Iran.[216] However, in late August Soviet Foreign Minister Andre Gromyko claimed that the 1921 treaty guaranteed Iran's independence.[217]

The KGB conducted an active measures campaign against Ghotbzadeh to portray him as an American agent. The KGB's Service A forged a letter to Ghotbzadeh from Senator Harrison Williams whom Ghotbzadeh had met 20 years earlier when he was a student in the US. The letter advised the Iranian foreign minister 'not to release the American hostages in the immediate future'. It also contained material aimed at compromising Ghotbzadeh personally.[218] In July 1980, the Iranian ambassador to France received Soviet disinformation alleging that Ghotbzadeh was co-operating with the US to overthrow Khomeini. Ghotbzadeh was also accused of receiving 6 million dollars to help smuggle the six American diplomats who had taken refuge at the Canadian embassy out of Iran. It is not clear whether these active measures contributed to Ghotbzadeh's removal as foreign minister in August 1980.[219] The KGB, however, did not cease its campaign against Ghotbzadeh. Forgeries showing that Ghotbzadeh was a CIA agent probably contributed to his arrest in April 1982. He was charged with plotting to assassinate Khomeini. Even after Ghotbzadeh's arrest, the KGB's Service A continued to fabricate evidence against Ghotbzadeh. The KGB's Tehran residency believed that a fabricated CIA telegram provided in 'easily broken code' and an agent 'readily identifiable' as Ghotbzadeh was the 'final nail in his coffin'. Ghotbzadeh and about 70 military officers who were accused of colluding with him were shot in September 1982.[220]

Allegations of Republican efforts to delay the release of the hostages

President Carter's mismanagement of the hostage crisis led the Republicans and his opponents in the foreign-policy establishment to seek to capitalize on his predicament. The Republicans had hired a large number of former intelligence officials who had extensive contacts in various US intelligence agencies. Their co-operation ensured that there would be a steady flow of intelligence on the hostage situation to the Republican camp.[221] The fact that many officials held Carter responsible for the decline of US intelligence capabilities facilitated Republican efforts.[222]

According to former Israeli Military Intelligence official, Ari Ben-Menashe, in December 1979, Copeland gathered together a group of former CIA officials and associates who had been removed by Admiral Turner to formulate a hostage rescue plan. This group, which was closely associated with William Casey, was trying to persuade the Iranians to release the hostages and to ensure that if Iraq attacked Iran, it would not be able to annex the oil-rich Khuzestan Province.[223]

According to Ben-Menashe, Earl Brian and Robert McFarlane represented the Republicans in talks with Iranians in Tehran in January 1980. The Israelis agreed to the plan because Brian and McFarlane were both close to Israel.[224] Ben-Menashe has said that the meeting in Tehran, in January 1980, set in motion a series of other meetings between the Iranians, the Republicans and Israelis in Madrid and Paris.[225]

He is the only person who has said that meetings between representatives of the Republicans and the Iranians occurred as early as January 1980. It is extremely difficult to believe that McFarlane and Brian would have been able to attend a meeting in Tehran while the hostages were being held.

From April 1980 onwards, Reagan's campaign manager William Casey had been involved in a major effort to gather intelligence on Carter's policy towards Iran.[226] According to Copeland, it was not until 22 March 1980, that he formulated his alternative hostage rescue plan with the assistance of former CIA officials Kermit and Archibald Roosevelt, and Steven Meade. Copeland was also an adviser to the Joint Chief of Staff on the hostage situation.[227]

In the meantime, the State Department had reactivated the Hashemi channel.[228] On 2 July, Cyrus Hashemi and his lawyer met Khomeini's nephew, Reza Pasandideh. Pasandideh said that Khomeini's 'key people' wanted to end the crisis.[229] Pasandideh proposed that Muskie send a message directly to Bani-Sadr. The participants agreed that if Muskie agreed to send an envoy to Iran then Bani-Sadr would send a representative to the US. However, follow-up meetings never took place.[230]

According to a US congressional report, based on Harold Saunders' testimony, the meeting was not considered to be important because by then the Majlis was being formed and the US could communicate directly with the Iranian Prime Minister.[231] Saunders' testimony explodes the myth that US officials considered Khomeini as the main target of their negotiating efforts.

According to Bani-Sadr, Pasandideh told him that he had travelled to Madrid to meet 'Mr Reagan's envoys'.[232] Bani-Sadr told the US Congress that Pasandideh had threatened him, saying that he would be overthrown or eliminated if he did not agree to the proposal.[233]

Pasandideh's interlocutors certainly had Republican connections. Pottinger, who represented the State Department, was a former Justice department official in the Ford administration.[234] Hashemi also had Republican connections. Casey and Hashemi may have been brought together by their mutual association with an oil man, John Shaheen. Casey and Shaheen were close friends and had served in the OSS together during World War II. The US oil embargo on Iran had deprived Shaheen of millions of dollars of oil trade, and Cyrus Hashemi helped him prevent the collapse of his business empire.[235]

According to a report submitted to US Congress by Sergei Stepashin in 1993, who later served as Russia's Prime Minister, Soviet intelligence indicated that as early as July 1980 both the Carter administration and the Republicans were involved in arms for hostages negotiations.[236] According to the report, Pentagon representatives held a meeting with Iranian officials in July 1980 and agreed 'in principle' to deliver 'a significant quantity of spare parts for F-4 and F-5 aircraft and also M-60 tanks ... via Turkey'.[237] In return, the Iranians discussed a step by step normalization of relations and agreed to support Carter by releasing the hostages.[238]

Allegations of William Casey's contacts with Iranian officials

Cyrus Hashemi's brother, Jamshid, has said that he and his brother were involved in negotiations between William Casey and Hojjatoleslam Mehdi Karubi in July and August in Madrid. According to him, Karubi agreed to delay the release of the hostages in return for a pledge from Casey that Reagan would release Iran's frozen assets and assist Iran to purchase military spare parts. The deal was then finalized in Paris in October 1980. As part of that deal Israeli officials agreed to supply military equipment to Iran.[239] However, Hashemi told US Congressional investigators that Casey wanted the hostages to be freed 'as soon as possible'.[240]

Former Israeli intelligence official, Ari Ben-Menashe, and Arif Durrani, an arms dealer, have basically repeated Jamshid Hashemi's allegations, but said that Casey sought to delay the hostages' release.[241] Ben-Menashe has quoted Mehdi Kashani, the son of Ayatollah Kashani, and Israeli official Rafael Eitan as his sources.[242] He has also said that he read Israeli intelligence reports saying that there were four meetings in Madrid within the time frame of 25 July to 1 August or 26 July to 30 July.[243]

Arif Durani has said that Iranian Revolutionary Guards were his sources. Some of Jamshid Hashemi's associates, including a member of the opposition, Eslam Kazemieh, have said that he had participated in meetings with Iraqi officials in Madrid to persuade them to support Iranian opposition groups.[244] Kazemieh and other sources informed US Congressional investigators that Jamshid Hashemi 'had ties to the Iraqi government dating back to a period preceding the fall of the Shah'.[245]

According to Kazemieh, Jamshid Hashemi was using the names of Ali Amini and Admiral Ahmad Madani to 'extract money' from the Iraqis to overthrow the Iranian regime.[246] Admiral Hushang Aryanpour, who was a close associate of Admiral Madani, has said that Hashemi had asked Madani to go to Iraq to meet Saddam Hussein, who was 'prepared to give extensive assistance to Madani'.[247] Contemporaneous US intelligence reports indicate that Jamshid Hashemi had travelled to Madrid in early August to meet Iraqi officials.[248]

Aryanpour also told US Congressional investigators that Jamshid Hashemi told him in 1988 and 1991 that he had attended meetings in Spain in 1980 between William Casey and Mehdi Karubi. And other Iranian exiles had told Aryanpour of meetings between the Republicans and Iranian officials.[249] Admiral Madani also told US congressional investigators that Cyrus Hashemi had informed him of his contacts with William Casey and offered to arrange a meeting between Madani and Casey, but he had declined his offer.[250]

US Congressional investigators have used the testimonies of Islam Kazemieh and Admiral Aryanpour to refute Jamshid Hashemi's allegations. They were, however, unable to establish Casey's whereabouts.[251] Moreover, Congressional investigators dismissed contemporaneous evidence, including statements by the then Iranian Foreign Minister Sadeq Ghotbzadeh indicating that meetings may have been held between Republican representatives and representatives of the Iranian regime.[252]

However, the US congressional investigators concluded that Casey was 'fishing in troubled waters'. They decided that Hashemi had been a credible witness at the closed sessions and that he had endangered himself and his family by testifying. The investigators also concluded that there was no reason for Hashemi to lie about the Madrid meetings.[253] The US Congressional investigators argued:

> The totality of evidence does suggest that Casey was 'fishing in troubled waters'[254] and that he conducted informal, clandestine, and potentially dangerous efforts on behalf of the Reagan campaign to gather intelligence on the volatile and unpredictable course of the hostage negotiations between the Carter Administration and Iran.[255]

In 1993, Sergei Stepashin, who would later serve as Russia's Prime Minister, reported to the US Congress that Casey had met three times with representatives of Iranian leaders in Madrid and Paris to 'possibly' delay the release of the hostages.[256] A senior Russian diplomat later told investigative journalist Robert Parry that 'the Soviet Union had its own well-placed sources in key governments connected to the US-Iranian manoeuvring'.[257]

Analysis of the evidence

The fact that Jamshid Hashemi met with Iraqi officials in Madrid in early August 1980 does not mean that he and his brother Cyrus were not involved in arranging meetings between Casey and Karubi. Karubi represented the radical wing of the Iranian regime which had seized the hostages, and Casey represented the Republican elite.

During this period, right-wing elite groups associated with the Republicans were also trying to overthrow Khomeini. Brian Crozier, who headed a group known as 61, travelled to Egypt three times between July and November to explore the possibility of organizing a coup to remove Khomeini from power. He held discussions with Empress Farah Pahlavi and Reza Pahlavi, the Shah's eldest son. He was actively co-operating with the Republicans and their supporters in the CIA.[258]

Jamshid Hashemi's ties with the Iraqi regime are particularly significant since he was also in contact with the NSC on the hostage issue. In the weeks prior to the outbreak of the Iran-Iraq war, the Hashemi brothers concluded that Brzezinski did not want a negotiated settlement because he knew that Iraq would attack Iran.[259] Jamshid Hashemi's contact with Iraqi officials raises the question of his foreknowledge of Iraq's invasion plans.

The Republicans were also involved in revealing the plan for a second rescue mission. On 18 August, investigative journalist, Jack Anderson published the first in a series of columns alleging that the Carter administration was planning to invade Iran in mid-October to free the hostages. Anderson wrote that the attack would also be punitive and that US armed forces would hold parts of Iranian territory.[260]

White House spokesman Jody Powell described Anderson's allegations as 'absolutely false'. Jack Anderson and Dale Van Atta later said that they had received documents from a an NSC official and a member of the Joint Chiefs of Staff.[261] The commanders of the second rescue mission were concerned that Anderson's allegations would lead the hostage-takers to take action. Indeed, on 25 August, the hostage-takers did threaten to murder the hostages.[262]

Anderson said that he had learned of the plan from unidentified experts who believed that the alleged invasion was politically motivated and doomed to fail.[263] In a speech on 20 August, Reagan himself said that Carter might be 'tempted to take reckless actions'.[264] As we saw earlier, the available evidence does indicate that the second rescue mission would have been more like an invasion.

The Carter Administration's Policy

By the end of August the State Department was convinced that the IRP was the most powerful organization in Iran.[265] Thus, it sent its position paper on the hostage crisis to key religious figures such as Ayatollah Beheshti, Rafsanjani, and Prime Minister Raja'i.[266] Then on 1 September, the Carter administration was informed that Bani-Sadr and Ghotbzadeh were annoyed with Washington's attempt to approach Beheshti, Rafsanjani, and Raja'i.[267]

Bani-Sadr has said that he received information of continuing negotiations between the Republicans and the Beheshti-Rafsanjani group.[268] According to him, he strongly warned Beheshti against negotiating with the Republicans.[269] Bani-Sadr, however, has inflated his own importance by claiming that Beheshti and other conservative clerics negotiated with Reagan to overthrow him.[270]

14

IRAN-IRAQ WAR AND DEVELOPMENTS IN THE HOSTAGE CRISIS

The leadership crisis in Iran, caused partly by internecine warfare between President Bani-Sadr and Prime Minister Raja'i, had almost paralysed the decision-making process. Bani-Sadr had a very low opinion of Raja'i, but he failed to compel the prime minister to resign his post.[1] By early September, seven cabinet posts were still occupied by caretakers.[2] The president who had been increasingly undermined, turned to the military to strengthen his position.[3] However, Raja'i prevented him from weakening the Revolutionary Guards Corps.[4] As a result of US sanctions, Iran had no choice but to buy limited quantities of low technology weapons through countries such as North Korea, or pay exorbitant prices for high-technology items on the black market.[5] Moreover, by late August, the Soviet Union was also emerging as a threat.

Threat of Soviet intervention in the Iran-Iraq conflict

Tensions between Tehran and Moscow rose partly because of Iranian Foreign Minister Sadegh Ghotbzadeh's criticism of the Soviet policy and his statements about Soviet espionage. Soviet propaganda accused Ghotbzadeh of being pro-American and of opposing his country's 'independence'.[6] In the meantime, the Iran-Iraq conflict was escalating rapidly.[7] Both Khomeini and Ghotbzadeh criticized the superpowers for encouraging Iraq to attack Iran.[8]

On 5 September, the Carter administration received intelligence indicating that the Soviet troops on the Iranian border had been put on a higher state of alert.[9] Soviet military activity near Iran triggered off another major confrontation over the choice of strategy in the Carter administration. Secretary Muskie and Warren Christopher opposed US military action. Brzezinski, however, argued that the US should make it clear to the Soviets that military action would lead to superpower confrontation.[10]

US officials realized that short of resorting to nuclear war there was nothing they could do. Nevertheless, Carter sided with Brzezinski and Brown. The following day both Muskie and Christopher agreed to send a sharp message to the Soviets, reiterating that the Persian Gulf was in the US sphere of influence.[11]

Hostage negotiations: Sadegh Tabataba'i and the West German channel

By early September, Khomeini had become anxious to settle the hostage issue. He asked Sadegh Tabataba'i, the brother-in-law of his son Ahmad, to approach the Carter administration. According to Gary Sick, Bani-Sadr was not informed of Khomeini's decision.[12] However, according to Bani-Sadr himself, Khomeini decided to approach the Carter administration after Bani-Sadr threatened to reveal Iranian contacts with the Republicans.[13]

On 9 September, Tabataba'i told West German Ambassador Gerhard Ritzel that senior Iranian officials wanted to end the hostage crisis before the US presidential elections.[14] His message warned the US that Khomeini was ill and that his death might lead to a communist take-over. Above all, Tabataba'i offered an arms for hostages deal and omitted Khomeini's demand for an apology.

Undoubtedly, what had caused the turn-around in Iran was the Iraqi threat.[15] Nevertheless, in mid-September Khomeini declared that 'We are at war with America', adding that 'the hand of the US had appeared from the sleeve of Iraq'.[16]

US officials did not take seriously Tabataba'i's claim that Khomeini was dying. Nevertheless, Carter sided with the State Department and wanted to start negotiating with Iran immediately. Brzezinski contended that Iranian officials feared another hostage rescue mission and that the Iranian proposal 'could be a trap'.[17]

Carter, Muskie and Christopher hoped to confine the negotiations to the supply of non-lethal items, which, in effect, meant a tilt towards Iraq. Due to the destruction of Iranian records during the revolution, Iranian officials only had a vague notion of which weapons systems the Shah had ordered and the Carter administration wanted to keep them in the dark.[18]

Christopher-Tabataba'i negotiations

At an NSC meeting on 12 September, Carter approved instructions for Muskie, who was due to meet Soviet Foreign Minister Andre Gromyko, reaffirming America's 'strong interest in the stability of the region'. He also directed his advisers to develop military options for the defence of Iran and for horizontal escalation options, in the event of a Soviet invasion of Iran.[19] Carter instructed Muskie to read his talking points to Gromyko and give him 'a non-paper'.[20] The message must have been very firm since by mid-September Soviet forces had stood down.[21]

At his talks with Tabataba'i, on 16–18 September, mediated by West German Foreign Minister Hans Dietrisch Genscher, Christopher could not promise the Iranians that all US claims against Iran would be cancelled. Nor could he assure his interlocutor that Iran could retrieve the Shah's assets through American courts. Genscher generally supported Christopher's position.

Tabataba'i' basically wanted an arms for hostages deal as compensation for Iran's frozen assets, as well as a new military relationship with the US.[22] Christopher refused to trade arms for hostages and only mentioned the 50 million dollars order for non-lethal equipment already paid for by the Shah.[23] However, he said that the US would resume its arms supplies once the dispute was resolved.[24] Christopher and Tabataba'i agreed to meet later in September,[25] but that meeting never took place. Instead, the leaders of the hostage-takers, who were now in control of the Iranian government, chose Algeria, which did not have close relations with the US, as the intermediary.

The issue of Republican intervention

According to Reagan's adviser Peter Hannaford, in September, the Republicans discovered that the Carter administration was negotiating with Iran.[26] Various reports stated that the NSC was the source of the leak.[27] The Republicans' discovery of the Christopher-Tabataba'i negotiations led to a flurry of covert activity in the party.[28] In September, Iranian Foreign Minister Sadegh Ghotbzadeh said a number of times that the Republicans were trying to prevent the release of the hostages.[29] Ghotbzadeh indicated that the negotiations were part of high-level US-Soviet negotiations.[30] US congressional investigators have tried to portray Ghotbzadeh as a conspiracy theorist.[31] However, Sadegh Tabataba'i later said that he believed 'some of the radical mullahs had been paid to block a hostage settlement'.[32] An Iranian official, who wished to remain anonymous, told American investigative journalist Joseph Trento that the head of Saudi intelligence, Kamal Adham, had paid off 'several Iranian clerics' who had held meetings with the Republicans. According to this official: 'The amount of payments was between 16 million and 55 million dollars.'[33]

Other allegations of Iran's contacts with the Republicans

According to former Israeli intelligence official, Ari Ben-Menashe, Iranian and Israeli officials met in the second half of September in Amsterdam for two days.[34] The Iranians agreed to release the hostages in the first week of October, and, in return, Israel would funnel 52 million dollars to Iran. After the release of the hostages Israel would immediately start selling arms to Iran. Moreover, Israel would secure a pledge from the Republicans that if Reagan came to power, he would release all frozen Iranian assets in American banks.[35]

US Congressional investigators have argued that Ben-Menashe was not telling the truth. However, according to an official Israeli government report, Israel used its arms channel to Iran as a means of holding political discussions, including the release of US hostages.[36]

The implications of the Iran-Iraq War for US and Soviet Strategies

On 17 September 1980, Saddam Hussein unilaterally abrogated the Algiers agreement of 1975 and announced that the Shatt-al-Arab was returning to Arab sovereignty.[37] However, he failed to persuade Iraq's main arms supplier, the Soviet Union, to increase arms deliveries to Iraq.[38] KGB chief Yuri Andropov was irate because he thought an Iraqi invasion of Iran would destroy Soviet relations with radical Iranian clerics.[39] He persuaded Brezhnev to impose an arms embargo on Iraq.[40] However, soon after the outbreak of the Iran-Iraq war, Brezhnev called on both sides to end the conflict through negotiations.[41]

Saddam Hussein invaded Iran on 22 September. He expected to occupy Khorramshahr, Abadan, Ahvaz, Dezful, and Masjed Soleyman, the main centres of Iran's oil-rich province of Khuzestan.[42] The success of Carter and Brzezinski's policy depended on US ability to prevent Soviet intervention in the conflict and bring Iran to the negotiating table soon after the Iraqi invasion. Brzezinski, however, realized that the outbreak of the war might make Iranian leaders more intransigent.[43]

On the day war broke out Carter declared that the US was 'not taking a position' on the war.[44] Asked about the implications for the hostage situation, Carter responded that the Iranians 'need to get spare parts for their military weapons ... and therefore induce them to release the hostages'.[45]

By the time of the fall of the Shah, Iran had 12 billion dollars' worth of weapons orders in the pipeline. Moreover, the country had a positive balance of 400 million dollars in the Foreign Military Sales Account when President Carter froze Iran's assets.[46]

Contrary to Carter's expectations, the Iranian Foreign Ministry declared that they held the US responsible for all of Iran's problems.[47] The Majlis decided to postpone the discussion of the hostage issue until after the war with Iraq had ended.[48] On 25 September the US and the Soviet Union agreed to stay neutral in the war.[49] However, between 22 September and 10 October, the US was supporting Iraq and the Soviet Union was supporting Iran.

The threat to Saudi Arabia and the strategic debate in Washington

After the first week of fighting, the Iraqi offensive had ground to a halt.[50] Iranian retaliatory responses caused the suspension of Iraqi oil exports. Iran's strong response to Iraqi attacks alarmed Saudi Arabia.[51] Algeria, Pakistan and the PLO unsuccessfully sought to mediate between the two countries to bring the war to an end.[52] Iraqi forces failed to achieve a quick and decisive victory, and Saudi Arabia's problems were compounded by the fact that Iraq sought to portray that country as an ally.[53]

Iran considered Saudi Arabia to be a co-belligerent in the war. Saudi Arabia was also vulnerable to Iranian attempts to disrupt naval traffic through the Persian Gulf.[54] However, the threat to Saudi security also enabled the US to tighten its alliance with Saudi Arabia.[55] On 26 September, Brzezinski advised Carter:

> It is important to differentiate between the short-run danger to the oil supplies, which we are right in minimizing, and the longer-range threat to the region, which we should not underplay. The country must understand that the long-term effort in the area requires fortitude and sacrifice to accomplish there what Truman did in Europe.[56]

On the same day, Saudi Arabia urgently requested the deployment of American AWACs planes, and more intelligence-sharing arrangements to prepare for possible Iranian retaliatory attacks on Saudi oil fields.[57] Brzezinski and Defence Secretary Harold Brown called for a swift intervention to support Saudi Arabia, while Muskie and Christopher contended that US intervention would provoke Soviet intervention.[58] To Brzezinski's chagrin, Muskie and Christopher proposed to launch a joint US-Soviet plan to bring the war to an end. Brzezinski argued that the State Department policy 'would legitimate the Soviet position in the Gulf'. Muskie, however, believed that deploying the AWACs to Saudi

Arabia would lead to a war between the US and the Soviet Union.[59] Notwithstanding, Carter decided to deploy the AWACs to Saudi Arabia on 29 September.[60]

On 28 September, Muskie met Iraqi Foreign Minister Sa'dun Hammadi and emphasized US opposition to 'any escalation of the conflict'. Hammadi replied that Iraq was pursuing only 'limited objectives' and asked the US 'not to interfere in the conflict in any way'.[61] However, on the same day, Christopher declared that the US was 'strongly opposed to any dismemberment of Iran'.[62]

On 28 September, Saddam Hussein offered Iran a cease-fire and mediation or direct negotiations on condition that Iran recognized Iraq's 'legitimate rights'. Khomeini rejected Hussein's offer out of hand.[63] By now he was demanding Hussein's removal.[64] On 1 October, Iraq declared that it was willing to observe a cease-fire from 5 to 8 October on condition that Iran did the same. On the same day, Muskie sent a letter to Iranian Prime Minister Mohammad Ali Raja'i, asking him not to link the hostage crisis with the Iran-Iraq war.[65] However, also that day, Iran rejected the UN Security Council resolution of 28 September, and ignored Iraq's cease-fire proposal.[66]

The Iran-Israel channel and arms supplies to Iran

What made Iranian officials confident was Israeli arms supplies to Iran. On 28 September, Israeli Deputy Defence Minister Mordechai Zipori indicated that Israel was willing to supply arms to Iran.[67] By early October Ayatollah Beheshti had established a close intelligence and security relationship with Israel.[68] During the same period, Hushang Lavi, a Jewish-Iranian arms merchant, approached the CIA to negotiate an arms-for-hostages deal.[69] Lavi claimed that he represented Bani-Sadr. However, Bani-Sadr himself has said that Lavi was associated with his rivals Beheshti and Rafsanjani. Bani-Sadr also said that he complained to Khomeini about the negotiations with the Republicans.[70]

Lavi later retracted his claim and said that he had only spoken with Bani-Sadr once.[71] However, the diaries of Lavi's lawyer, Mitchell Rogovin, prove that Lavi had information on the activities of Bani-Sadr and the Beheshti-Rafsanjani faction. Lavi approached the CIA and proposed that the hostages be exchanged for an F-14 fighter jet. In a report to deputy National Security Adviser David Aaron, the CIA concluded that there was insufficient evidence to indicate that Lavi had ties with anyone to justify future contacts.[72] Lavi's approach to the CIA was apparently reported to the vice-presidential candidate, George Bush.[73]

October Surprise-The L'Enfant Plaza Hotel Meetings

Allegations of an 'October Surprise' collusion between the Republicans and Iranian officials were first made by American extremist politician Lyndon LaRouche.[74] The Iran-Contra scandal led to further investigations of October Surprise. A number of 'witnesses' such as Ari Ben-Menashe and Hushang Lavi had either worked for or were close to Israeli intelligence services. Indeed, Ben-Menashe's allegations finally led former NSC official Gary Sick to write a book on October Surprise. Sick's book led to media reports which, in turn, led to congressional investigations.[75]

The timing and the evolution of the allegations show that the allegations might have been part of a disinformation operation to tarnish Bush's image. Israeli hard-liners regarded Bush as their worst enemy in the US government. A January 1992 poll showed that 55 percent of Americans believed the allegations.[76]

Ari Ben-Menashe and Hushang Lavi who were both involved in Israeli arms sales to Iran told investigators that they met Allen, Silberman and McFarlane at L'Enfant Plaza Hotel.[77] Ben-Menashe has claimed that an agreement was reached to delay the release of the hostages, whereas Lavi has said that Silberman turned down his proposal to delay the release of the hostages.[78]

The Republicans have given two versions of the L'Enfant Plaza meeting. According to the first version published in 1987, Allen, Silberman and McFarlane met secretly in October 1980 with a North African man claiming to represent Iran. He offered to turn the hostages over to the Republicans to humiliate the Carter administration. Silberman terminated the meeting, saying, 'we have one president at a time.'[79]

Richard Allen has given yet another version of the L'Enfant Plaza meeting. According to Allen, the meeting took place on 2 September 1980 and the Republicans' interlocutor was a Malaysian, called Mr Muhammad. According to Allen, Mr Muhammad put forward a ludicrous scheme, saying that Khomeini would release the hostages to the Republicans when the Shah's son, Reza, was restored as a figurehead monarch. The Republicans rejected the proposal, adding that the Carter administration was responsible for negotiating with Iran.[80]

Apparently the Republicans chose not to inform the Carter administration because Mr Muhammad's proposal was ridiculous. All versions of the L'Enfant Plaza meeting agree that the Republicans turned down the Iranian emissary's proposal.[81]

On 3 October, Khomeini proposed three conditions for the resolution of the hostage crisis; an end to US intervention in Iran, a pledge against any future US interference and the return of the Shah's assets. The most notable omission was the absence of any reference to a formal apology.[82]

US and Soviet responses to the escalation of the Iran-Iraq war

On 3 October, Brzezinski told Carter that although the Iran-Iraq war had become a war of attrition which might spread to other Persian Gulf states, it also gave the US 'a unique opportunity' to improve its position. Brzezinski wanted to 'begin more subtle initiatives to help Iran enough to put pressure on Iraq in order to push it back from most if not all occupied territory', while preventing Soviet infiltration or the disintegration of Iran.[83]

Moreover, during this period the US seems to have linked the supply of AWACs to Saudi Arabia to an increase in Saudi oil production.[84] Despite Saudi denials, the magnitude of the increase and the fact that the oil companies accepted it with equanimity suggests that the increase was co-ordinated with the US.[85]

On 2 October, Tass reported that neither Iran nor Iraq nor any other state threatened Saudi Arabia, describing Brzezinski's warning to the Soviet Union to stay out of the conflict as 'a hypocritical and demagogic utterance'.[86] The Soviets also signalled via Jordan that they would look favourably upon Iraqi requests for materiel.[87] It seems that as a result of the Soviet offer, Iraq changed its position and announced that it would continue the war 'whatever its duration and the sacrifices required'.[88] Subsequently Jordan served as a logistical base for East European arms shipments to Iraq.[89]

It is highly probable that the Soviets were using Iraq's military pressure on the Iranian regime to increase their influence in Iran. On 4 October, the Soviet Ambassador to Iran, Vladimir Vinogradov, met Iranian Prime Minister Raja'i and offered military equipment to Iran. The Soviet ambassador declared that his country was against the Iran-Iraq war and would condemn whoever started the conflict.[90]

Despite Raja'i's claim that he had rejected the Soviet arms offer, by the end of the first week in October, Libya, North Korea, Syria, and Vietnam began to supply arms to Iran. Indeed, Moscow assisted those countries to do so.[91] Even before Raja'i's meeting with Vinogradov, Israeli television had reported that an Iranian delegation had secretly travelled to Moscow to purchase US weapons that had been captured by the Vietnamese and transferred to the Soviet Union.[92] Iran's revelation of the Soviet offer was undoubtedly meant to drive a wedge between Baghdad and Moscow.[93]

Nevertheless, Carter announced that Moscow wanted to prevent the escalation of the conflict to the entire Persian Gulf area.[94] Moreover, Muskie went so far as to state that there was no Soviet threat to the Persian Gulf.[95] Moscow sought to counter US regional strategy by drawing closer to Iran and Syria.[96] On 8 October, the Soviet Union signed a formal treaty of alliance with Syria.[97] This was similar to other Soviet treaties with Third World client states such as Iraq and South Yemen.[98] The Soviet side insisted on inserting a clause in the Soviet-Syrian treaty stressing the importance of the Iranian revolution.[99]

On 11 October, Iraq severed diplomatic relations with Syria, Libya, and North Korea because they were supplying weaponry to Iran.[100] Iraq's ally, Saudi Arabia threatened to cut off aid to Syria to compel Asad to change his strategy,[101] but the Syrian-Saudi confrontation was not to come to a head until December.

Israel's intervention and a change in Carter's strategy

By 10 October, if not earlier, it was clear to the Carter administration that the Iranian regime was no longer afraid of being defeated by Iraq and overthrown.[102] Faced with the failure of his strategy, if not his presidency, Carter informed Bani-Sadr that 'for geopolitical reasons' the US would not permit Iraq to defeat Iran.[103] According to Bani-Sadr, Carter assured him that AWACs 'would provide the Iraqis with no information' and that only the Soviets provided Iraq with intelligence on Iran. Carter went so far as to offer to supply spare parts to Iran if it agreed to settle the hostage issue quickly.[104]

In fact, the State Department had declared that the US would provide air defence information to America's Arab allies.[105] Moreover, Saudi Arabia and Kuwait were acting as co-belligerents in the war.[106] However, on 7 October, the US and the UK warned Jordan not to provide assistance to Iraq.[107] Perhaps to mollify King Hussein, senior US diplomats in Jordan said that Soviet weapons were not being shipped to Iraq through Aqaba.[108]

In the meantime, Hushang Lavi continued his efforts to draw the CIA or the Republicans into an arms-for-hostages deal.[109] Lavi's attorney, Mitchell Rogovin, apparently informed the Republicans of Lavi's contacts with the Carter administration.[110] On 9 October, Harold Saunders informed Christopher that Lavi had proposed that the US send F-14 spare parts to Iran as part of a hostage settlement and that the US would need to ask Bani-Sadr to confirm the proposal.[111] Saunders made it clear that he did not trust Lavi at all and advised Christopher to tell Rogovin that they had their own channels.[112] Rogovin, however, told Saunders that Bani-Sadr had instructed Lavi to make a deal,[113] but before such a deal could be made, Khomeini reactivated the Sadegh Tabataba'i channel.

Reactivation of Tabataba'i channel and arms-for-hostages negotiations

On 8 October Sadegh Tabataba'i informed Bani-Sadr of his meeting with Christopher.[114] The evidence strongly indicates that Khomeini instructed Tabataba'i to do so. On 12 October, Khomeini appointed Bani-Sadr chairman of the Supreme Defence Council, which had extensive powers to conduct the war.[115] Bani-Sadr was outraged by the Raja'i government's and the Islamic Republican Party's attempt to control the war effort.[116] On 10 October, Ambassador Ritzel informed the State Department that Tabataba'i had reiterated that the hostages would be released and had asked for a list of the military equipment ordered by the shah.[117] The NSC argued that discussing arms supplies with Iran might help accelerate the negotiations.[118] However, Gary Sick warned Brzezinski that it was unlikely that the hostages would be released before the election.[119]

Brzezinski later said that the Carter administration wanted an arms-for-hostages deal.[120] In fact, Bani-Sadr had declared that Iran never had any difficulty purchasing US weaponry through international arms dealers. He also held the US responsible for the Iran-Iraq war and threatened to close off the Strait of Hormuz.[121] Nevertheless, on 11 October, the US began to prepare a package of military equipment, omitting items that were highly lethal or sensitive.[122] The State Department, however, prepared a report arguing that it would be contrary to the president's declaration of neutrality not to supply the military spare parts.[123]

By 10 October, the front had stabilized and Iran was not planning to launch a major offensive until the spring. The equipment which the administration planned to supply to Iran would not enable Iran to defeat Iraq, but it was deemed sufficient to persuade the Iranians to release the hostages.

Reportedly, at a meeting between the head of the Iranian security service, SAVAMA, and CIA officials in the second week of October, the participants discussed a plan to release the hostages in return for US arms and spare parts. Shortly afterwards, Carter sent an official message to Iran, dated 11 October, offering 150 million dollars in weapons, including aircraft spare parts: 10 million dollars less than the CIA and the SAVAMA chief had reportedly discussed.[124]

US failure to close the Jordanian-Iraqi channel and the threat to US regional position

Despite the US demarche to Jordan, Jordanian arms shipments to Iraq continued.[125] As far as Iraqi oil exports were concerned, the blockading of the port of Basra made Iraq dependent on Syria's goodwill.[126]

As the battlefield situation deteriorated, Jordan and Iraq pressed Saudi Arabia to increase its assistance to Iraq.[127] After consultations with King Hussein of Jordan, the Saudis reportedly agreed to permit Iraqi imports, including arms and food, to arrive at the port of Jidda.[128] Jordanian and Saudi support for Iraq may well have led Iranian leaders to conclude that Carter was negotiating in bad faith.

Republican intervention

It appears that Iranian leaders were simultaneously negotiating with the Republicans. The Republicans feared two possibilities: a hostage rescue mission and an arms-for-hostages deal.[129] In fact, there is documentary evidence that Reagan's foreign policy adviser, Richard Allen, received classified information during the 1980 campaign. The Republicans obtained most of their information from Brzezinski's NSC. American investigative journalist Joseph Trento has argued that Brzezinski's relationship with the CIA pre-dated the advent of the Carter administration and that Carter's national security adviser was a protégé of Theodore Shackley, associate deputy director of the CIA's Directorate of Operations who left the agency during Stansfield Turner's tenure.[130] Shackley considered Turner to be an incompetent amateur. Turner held Shackley partially responsible for the activities of a rogue CIA agent Edwin Wilson who had established close relations with Qadhafi's Libya. Wilson was later found guilty of arms-smuggling and jailed for his illegal activities. Wilson claimed that between 1976 and 1979 he had 'regularly' provided Shackley with intelligence on Libya.[131]

According to Trento, Shackley used such connections to get his proteges onto the NSC to sabotage Carter's policies and ensure his defeat in the presidential elections. The best way this could be done in 1980, according to Trento, was to delay the release of US hostages held in Iran.[132] Trento has also suggested that Brzezinski hired Donald Gregg, who despite his official responsibilities for East Asian affairs was alleged to have been assisting the Republicans' efforts to delay the release of the hostages.[133]

Trento, has completely failed to prove his case. Firstly, there is hardly any evidence linking Brzezinski to Shackley's activities before, during or after the elections. Moreover, the KGB fabricated a story about Brzezinski's connection with the CIA to discredit the national security adviser. The material was supplied by the Bulgarian secret service. The KGB resorted to fabricating material about Brzezinski after it failed to cultivate him. The KGB officials who thought about cultivating about the Polish-born national security adviser must have been particularly obtuse because throughout his career Brzezinski had concentrated his efforts on defeating the Soviet Union.[134] There is some evidence that before the 1980 presidential elections, President Carter sought to reach out to Soviet leaders to help him get re-elected. In early October, industrialist billionaire Armand Hammer who had long-standing friendships with Soviet leaders approached Soviet ambassador to the US Anatoly Dobrynin and asked him to facilitate Soviet Jewish emigration in the hopes that this would encourage American Jews to vote for Carter. Allegedly, Hammer assured Dobrynin that 'Carter won't for get that service if he is reelected'.[135] Then two weeks before the election Brzezinski approached Dobrynin offering concessions on arms control, Afghanistan and Central America. Dobrynin later wrote: 'It was hard to say whether it was aimed at obtaining some positive gestures from Moscow on the eve of the poll.' However, Dobrynin believed that the gist of the message was: 'Moscow should not do anything to diminish Carter's chances in the election race and might even help a bit.'[136] It is highly unlikely that Brzezinski approved of the approach to the Soviets because the concessions to which Dobrynin refers in his memoirs were consistent with the Vance approach in the aftermath of the Soviet invasion of Afghanistan. Thus it is highly likely that Brzezinski was acting on Carter's instructions. Indeed, as we saw in an earlier chapter, Carter had approved of the approach to the Soviets after the Soviet invasion of Afghanistan.

There is enough evidence to prove that the policies Brzezinski recommended on such issues as Poland, the Soviet Union and Iran were closer to those of the Republicans than to those of the State Department. Indeed, Brzezinski has always prided himself on being bipartisan on foreign policy issues. After the elections, Brzezinski's endorsement of General Alexander Haig, Reagan's nominee for Secretary of State, angered the Democrats. Moreover, Brzezinski contended that the Democratic Party had moved 'excessively to the left' and accused it of becoming 'excessively preoccupied with what might be called the do-gooder agenda in international relations'.[137] He went on to serve as an adviser on his native Poland to the Reagan administration and was even involved in a CIA covert operation directed at Poland.[138] He was also a member of the President's Chemical Warfare Commission (1985); a member of the NSC-Defense Department Commission on Integrated Long-Term Strategy (1987–1988); and a member of the President's Foreign Intelligence Advisory Board (1987–1989). In 1988, he was co-chairman of the Bush National Security Advisory Task Force.[139]

Brzezinski's commitment to bipartisanship does not prove that he colluded with the Republicans in 1980. President Carter has certainly not held his national security adviser responsible for his predicament. However, the evidence clearly indicates that the Republicans had access to the Carter administration's secrets. According to former NSC official, Gary Sick, there were individuals in the White House who were determined to ensure President Carter's defeat in the presidential elections. Sick has written that Carter's opponents used 'code names and clandestine reporting channels' to supply intelligence on the hostages and other policy issues to the Republicans. The Republicans, according to Sick, had also agents in some of the most sensitive areas of the government such as the intelligence agencies, the Pentagon, and the State Department and these individuals 'were providing regular intelligence reports on the most highly classified policies and operations'.[140]

For example, on 10 October, Seymour Weiss, a former under secretary of state and US ambassador to the Bahamas, informed Richard Allen of plans for launching a second rescue mission.[141] On 10 October, Allen sent a memorandum to Fred Ikle, a prominent member of Reagan's inner circle dealing with the hostage crisis, warning of partial release of hostages for spare parts.[142]

By mid October, Carter had almost tripled his offer to the Iranian regime in a matter of weeks.[143] However, he chose not to send 'the additional' 150 million dollars 'of the most sensitive equipment' Iran needed.[144] Carter and his advisers assumed that the Iranians had no reliable way of knowing what the Shah had purchased from the US and that Iran could not obtain US spare parts from any other source.[145]

On the same day, Warren Christopher sent a cable to the West Germans, saying that Carter had approved a package consisting of military equipment, spare parts, and cash valued at approximately 230 million dollars that could be supplied following the release of the hostages.[146] However, Carter emphasized that only previously purchased non-lethal spare parts would be supplied to Iran upon the release of the hostages.[147] To make his proposal more attractive, on 12 October Carter sent a message to Bani-Sadr, saying that he would force Iraq to make peace if Iran would release the hostages.[148] The new element in US policy was Carter's opposition to the disintegration of Iran. On 13 October, Bonn reported that Tabataba'i had been informed of the cable and he had advised Bani-Sadr accordingly.[149]

Also on 13 October, Angelo Codevilla, a former intelligence officer who was on the staff of the Senate Select Committee on Intelligence, informed Richard Allen that the DIA knew that all the hostages had been brought back to the US embassy compound the week before and that the Carter administration had 'embargoed intelligence' on this subject.[150] Apart from commanders of the second rescue mission, no one but a few senior officials of the Carter administration had any knowledge of this. Yet the Republicans were informed of it only four days after it was reported to President Carter.[151]

Carter's offer of non-lethal items and 80 million dollars of cash was hardly enough to enable Iran to reverse Iraq's occupation of its territory. On 13 October, Hushang Lavi's lawyer, Mitchell Rogovin, noted in his diary that 'Lavi talked to Bani-Sadr, interested in who would win election'.[152] On 14 October, Lavi informed the Carter administration that Rafsanjani had proposed a partial release of the hostages for spare parts. Carter instructed Warren Christopher to protest strongly through German channels that such a deal would be unacceptable.[153]

Bani-Sadr, who had already publicly said that Iran was receiving arms from international dealers, may have asked Lavi to increase Iran's demands. Thus at a meeting with Harold Saunders on 15 October, Lavi added a new list of F-4 and F-5E jet fighter spare parts to the original list of F-14 parts he had claimed the Khomeini regime was prepared to exchange for the hostages.[154] Saunders, once again, emphasized that the Carter administration was awaiting Bani-Sadr's confirmation of Lavi's authority.[155] Lavi was disappointed with Saunders' reply and wanted to go to the Republicans.[156]

Carter sought to obtain the freedom of the hostages by publicly opposing the dismemberment of Iran, and enunciated the policy change on 15 October.[157] He called for a cessation of hostilities and for immediate negotiations to settle the border dispute. Brzezinski has written that the Carter administration was on the verge of reaching an agreement with Iranian leaders and contemporaneous accounts support his account.[158] Bani-Sadr has claimed that he responded 'affirmatively' to Carter's message, but he says that it had the opposite effect on Khomeini, who decided not to release the hostages.[159]

Bani-Sadr has said that his government had reached an agreement with the Carter administration.[160] However, Mitchell Rogovin's diary entries refute this. The diary also shows that Bani-Sadr was in contact with Lavi regarding the most sensitive and secret issues. The US Congress, however, simply ignored the evidence provided by Rogovin's diary entries,[161] although it indicated strongly that Lavi was in contact with Bani-Sadr and other senior Iranian officials.[162]

On 16 October, Lavi informed Rogovin that Raja'i would not deal with Carter under any circumstances.[163] Rogovin's diary entries for 16 and 17 October indicate that Lavi had spoken to Bani-Sadr and that the Iranians did not want to deal with Carter 'but did want to do a swap'.[164] The entries also show that Bani-Sadr was privy to Raja'i's decision to approach the Republicans. However, Bani-Sadr informed the Carter administration that Lavi did not represent him, and his claim has been taken at face value.[165]

Raja'i was due to arrive in New York on 17 October to address the UN Security Council. His visit to the UN was widely perceived as an attempt to repair Iran's image.[166] He was accompanied on this trip by Behzad Nabavi who was very close to the hostage-takers. The Carter administration failed to organize a meeting with Raja'i or even the Iranian ambassador to the UN. However, during this period, the US contacted Algerian officials, who, in turn, told Raja'i that releasing the hostages would serve Iran's interests.[167]

Nabavi held substantive discussions with representatives of Algeria, Syria, Pakistan, and Indonesia. The Algerian government offered to mediate between Iran and the US, and the four countries urged the Iranians to release the hostages before the US presidential elections, in case Reagan won the election.[168] At a meeting with Algerian officials in Algiers, Raja'i was advised to reach an agreement with Carter before the US elections to prevent a Reagan victory.[169]

By now Carter was so desperate to obtain the release of the hostages before the election that on 19 October, he declared that if this was done, 'I will unfreeze the assets in banks here and in Europe, drop the embargo against trade, and work toward resumption of normal commerce with Iran in the future.'[170] On 20 October, Muskie declared that 'the integrity of Iran is today threatened by the new Iraqi invasion'.[171] This was the first time that a senior US official had referred to an 'invasion' of Iran. At a meeting of the UN Security Council on 23 October, US ambassador to the UN, Donald McHenry, repeated Muskie's characterization of the war and called on Iraq to withdraw from Iranian territory.[172]

Undoubtedly, Muskie's and McHenry's statements were made in the hope of persuading Iranian leaders to release the hostages before the election.[173] The bankers, however, signalled that Carter was not in a position to return Iran's assets. David Rockefeller, Chairman of the Chase Manhattan Bank, declared: 'If the Iranians think they're going to get back all the assets they have here immediately, they're going to be very disappointed.'[174]

Robert Carswell, who as Deputy Secretary of the Treasury under Carter was involved in the hostage negotiations, later observed: 'the banks had substantial legal arguments for refusing to return the deposits until Iran settled its loans . . .' Moreover, Carter 'had no legal power to force loan settlements. A public dispute with the banks would be difficult to control and might well derail the Algerian intermediation that began in late 1980.'[175]

Rockefeller's declaration ensured that the issue would be dragged out. Some analysts have argued that the bankers warned the Iranians that unless they settled the issue before the election they would have to face an angry Reagan administration which would destroy Iran and accept the death of the hostages, if necessary, to teach Iran a lesson.[176] While this might have been true of some bankers, it is far more likely that Rockefeller was signalling the Iranians that they would have to deal with the Republicans.

According to Mitchell Rogovin's diaries, by 21 October Iranian leaders had decided to delay the release of the hostages in order to negotiate with George Bush after the election.[177] On 22 October, Raja'i reversed Iran's position and declared that Iran was not interested in an arms-for-hostages deal.[178] At the time, the Carter administration believed that Raja'i's statement was conciliatory in that it did not link the release of the hostages with shipment of spare parts to Iran. US officials thought that the Algerians had persuaded Iranian leaders to moderate their stance.[179] Indeed, Iranian radicals viewed the Reagan administration as a far greater threat to the Islamic Republic.[180] The hostage-takers' mentor, Musavi-Kho'iniha, said that the Majlis might make a decision by 26 October, adding that if the US accepted Iran's conditions, the hostages would be freed the following day.[181]

On the same day, an Iranian intermediary, Cyrus Hashemi, told the Carter administration that Khomeini had indicated that the hostages might still be released before the election. According to Gary Sick, Hashemi, who was also in contact with the Republicans, lied to the administration to lull it into a false sense of security.[182]

Paris Meetings-Allegations

What happened next has been the subject of debate ever since. Several arms dealers, former Iranian, US and Israeli officials have said that meetings were held between Iranians, Israelis, and Americans in Paris to decide the fate of the US hostages. Sergei Stepashin who served as first deputy minister of security of the Russian Federation in 1992-1993 and who would later serve as Russian prime minister, reported to US Congress in 1993 that Russian intelligence information indicated that George Bush, Ronald Reagan, William Casey and Robert Gates, then an NSC official, had been involved in secret contacts with Iran in 1980 and that Bush and Gates had taken part in the Paris meeting, which was aimed at 'possibly delaying' the release of the hostages.[183]

What makes the enquiry extremely difficult are the different accounts of the alleged Paris meetings. The most sensational account of the alleged Paris meetings has been provided by former Israeli Military Intelligence Official, Ari Ben-Menashe, who has claimed that he was a member of the Israeli delegation in Paris. According to him, the meetings took place in Paris in mid-October. The US delegation included George Bush and William Casey, Robert Gates, and former CIA official George Cave. The Israelis had also sent a high-powered delegation, including David Kimche, Yahoshua Saguy, Shmuel Morieh, Uri Simchoni, and Rafael Eitan. Ayatollah Mehdi Karubi led the Iranian delegation.[184] During these negotiations, according to Ben-Menashe, Karubi agreed to delay the release of American hostages in return for 52 million dollars, guarantees of arms sales for Iran, and unfreezing of Iranian assets in US banks.[185] If true, these were substantially better terms than those offered by Carter.

Ben-Menashe had a hard time establishing his bona fides as an Israeli official.[186] Indeed, his claims about having seen George Bush seriously damaged his credibility. The timing of Ben-Menashe's allegations suggests that he was trying to damage George Bush politically. At the time, the Bush administration was making efforts to pressure Israel into accepting a comprehensive Middle East settlement. Indeed, throughout his memoirs, Ben-Menashe is highly critical of the Reagan administration's support for Israel's enemy, Iraq.

The available evidence indicates that the Republicans had contacts with Israeli officials prior to the 1980 presidential election. The Israelis negotiated a pre-election arms deal with Iran, which delayed the release of the hostages until 31 October. The Republicans may have given the Begin government the go-ahead to supply US equipment to Iran. Nicholas Veliotes who served as Assistant Secretary of State for Middle Eastern Affairs in the Reagan administration, has said that he believes that the origins of Israel's shipments of American military equipment to Iran can be traced back to before the 1980 election.[187]

It is not clear whether the Republicans directly negotiated a delayed hostage release with the Iranians or whether Israeli and Soviet arms supplies to Iran prevented the release of the hostages before the 4 November presidential elections. Opponents of the 'October Surprise' theories have simply tried to disprove Bush and Casey's presence in Paris. It is difficult to believe that George Bush would have so recklessly jeopardized the Republicans' campaign. Iranian radicals could have simply publicized Bush's involvement to tarnish Reagan's image and negotiate a more favourable agreement with Carter.

On 22 October, the CIA reported that Israel had been in contact with Iran regarding a possible swap of 'hostages for spares'. The Israelis wanted to deliver F-4 aircraft tyres and possibly other materiel.[188] Carter was only informed of the plane's impending departure after it had actually landed in Israel.[189] According to Brzezinski:

> It was at this juncture that we learned, much to our dismay, that the Israelis had been secretly supplying American spare parts to the Iranians, without much concern for the negative impact this was having on our leverage with the Iranians on the hostage issue.[190]

After discussing the matter with Muskie, the US made 'a strong demarche' to Israel. Brzezinski has said, 'at least for a while the Israelis held back'.[191] However, the evidence shows that Carter failed to restrain Israel On 22 October, the State Department instructed US ambassador to Israel, Samuel Lewis, to inform the Israelis that the US recognized 'the long-term significance for Israel's position in the Middle East of the opportunity to begin to restore an Israeli relationship with Iran, especially at a time when Iran is engaging Iraqi forces . . .'[192]

On 23 October, Lewis met a high-level Israeli official and conveyed Carter's message that all Israeli arms shipments to Iran were to be stopped until the Iranians released the hostages. The Israeli official reiterated Israel's position that supplying military equipment to Iran could contribute to the settlement of the hostage issue.[193] According NSC official Gary Sick, Carter sent a message to Begin on 23 October, protesting at the shipment of aircraft parts to Iran. However, the evidence suggests that Begin continued to mislead him.[194]

The failure of Carter's regional strategy

It is important to note at this point that Carter was not oblivious to Republican attempts to establish contact with the Iranian regime. He also had an inkling that the CIA officials who were dismissed or alienated by CIA Director Stansfield Turner were collaborating with the Republicans. He said in the *Village Voice*: 'We knew that some of the people were loyal to Bush and not particularly loyal to me and Stan Turner. We were worried about revelations of what we were doing... I never did have an official report come to me and say that Bill Casey was meeting with Iranian officials in Paris or anything specific, just allegations and rumors... I didn't believe them.'[195]

Iranian leaders feared that their refusal to release the hostages before the election would lead Carter to attack Iran. On 22 October, some of the hostages were moved to the maximum security Evin prison.[196] However, so desperate was Carter to gain the support of the Jewish lobby for his re-election that he reversed his policy towards Saudi Arabia, in an attempt to placate Israeli leaders. He was particularly anxious to improve his position in New York State.[197] The evidence strongly indicates that Carter offered a quid pro quo to the Begin government. The US would refuse to sell sophisticated F-15 equipment to Saudi Arabia, if Israel refrained from shipping arms to Iran while the hostages were still in captivity.[198] Carter's refusal to sell F-15 related equipment to Saudi Arabia could not have occurred at a worse time for Saudi leaders. The kingdom had come under tremendous pressure from Iran and the radical Arab states for its close association with the US. After Carter announced his decision, Crown Prince Fahd threatened that his country would purchase the equipment elsewhere if necessary.[199] Carter's decision only strained US-Saudi relations further.

Iranian leaders refuse to release the hostages before the elections

President Carter's pressure on the Israelis to stop them from supplying arms to Iran led Iranian leaders to change their position yet again. On 23 October, Majlis Speaker Hashemi-Rafsanjani told French correspondent Eric Rouleau, 'Iranian opinion and the Iranian Majlis are so hostile to the United States... that there is a possibility that we would only ask for the money we paid for the weapons to be refunded.'[200] On 24 October, Khomeini declared that 'foreign media' had circulated rumours of an arms-for-hostages deal between Iran and the US.[201] On the same day, 24 October, arms dealer Hushang Lavi who was in contact with Iranian leaders informed his lawyer Mitchell Rogovin that the hostages would not be released before the election.[202] The hostage-takers mentor, Kho'iniha, who had previously indicated that the hostages would be released before the election, now said: 'We are not in a hurry to release the hostages. We have no intention of helping Jimmy Carter in his presidential campaign.' He pointed out that the Majlis debate might be 'long and tough'.[203] On 26 October, Rafsanjani said that if the US met Iran's conditions, the hostages would be freed soon, and pointed out that 'it makes no difference to us who comes to power in America'.[204]

The Israelis continued to press the Carter administration to approve Israeli arms shipments to Iran. On 27 October, Ambassador Lewis met Israeli officials to discuss the matter. The Israelis informed Lewis that upon the arrival of the

F-4 tyres on October 22, they had informed the Iranians that there would not be any further shipments due to Israel's pledge to the US. Lewis reported that the Iranians had approached Israel again for artillery pieces and ammunition. The Israelis had argued that even if the Iranians received Soviet equipment, they would not be able to use it. Once again Israeli officials said that should they supply arms to Iran, they would be able to persuade the Iranians to release the hostages.[205]

The Israelis were too clever by half. They had long considered Jimmy Carter as hostile to their interests. As early as February 1979, Brzezinski and other senior US officials had come to the conclusion that Begin wanted to ensure that Carter would lose the 1980 presidential election.[206] Begin must have known full well that the shipment of arms and spare parts to Iran would strengthen Iran's position in the hostage negotiations with the Carter administration. Not surprisingly the State Department rejected Israel's request. Warren Christopher instructed Ambassador Lewis to inform the Israelis that the negotiations had reached a 'delicate' stage and ask them not to do anything for a few days. 'Once our hostages are released, of course, the decision will be Israel's.'[207]

US officials expected the Majlis to make a decision and they knew that another Israeli shipment to Iran would strengthen Iran's position. Subsequently Warren Christopher and the Congressional committees investigating the 'October Surprise' theory failed to raise the most obvious questions about Prime Minister Begin's motives.[208] The State Department officials' concern was not unfounded. On 27 October, the Carter administration received reports that the best deal the Iranians were prepared to offer was a staggered release of the hostages.[209] Under the circumstances, such a deal would be a swap of military equipment for the hostages. Reports of an imminent arms-for-hostages deal had already led Saddam Hussein to distance his country from the US. On 26 October, Iraqi Foreign Minister Sa'doun Hammadi accused the US of abandoning 'neutrality' and supporting Iran. Iraq warned the US that it would retaliate if the US traded arms for hostages.[210] Iraq also asked the EEC countries to use their diplomatic influence to negotiate an end to the war, and not to resume arms supplies to Iran once US hostages had been released.[211]

Carter's pre-election concessions and the change in Iran's negotiating position

Despite President Carter's frantic efforts to persuade Iranian leaders to release the hostages, by late October the Iranians believed that Carter had little power to deliver on his promises. On 27 October, President Bani-Sadr wrote in his newspaper, *Enghelab-e Eslami*, that Carter was no longer in control of US foreign policy.[212] In late October, Carter decided to make a major concession to persuade Iranian leaders to release the hostages before the election. After discussing the hostage issue with Brzezinski, Muskie and Christopher, he decided to release a greater portion of the military equipment in the pipeline plus Iran's frozen assets in return for the release of the hostages.[213]

Carter put forward his proposal during his debate with Ronald Reagan the next day. The Republicans had succeeded in purloining President Carter's and Vice-President Mondale's foreign policy and defence briefing books.[214] During the 28 October debate, Reagan spoke of the humiliation suffered by the US and called for launching a congressional investigation after the hostages were released. Carter, however, pledged that the US would release the military equipment purchased by Iran which was in the pipeline and would also unfreeze Iran's assets.[215]

The equipment in the pipeline which Carter now proposed to release amounted to 240 million dollars in weapons, including spare tyres for Iran's American-made aircraft (F-4s, F-5s, and F-14s), several C-130 transports, over 8,600 anti-tank missiles, thousands of tank and artillery rounds, cluster bombs, land mines, and Hawk surface-to-air missiles.[216] Thus Carter proposed to send Iran nearly five times the amount of military equipment that the Republicans had allegedly promised. On the same day, 28 October, Iran received a very important message from Iraqi leader, Saddam Hussein, which was carried by the Cuban foreign minister. Hussein agreed to return his forces to the international border, followed by a cease-fire, and renunciation of Iraq's claim to the entire Shatt-al-Arab waterway.[217]

The Cuban Foreign Minister proposed a five-point plan. It called for withdrawal of Iraqi forces to the border, cease-fire, acceptance of the 1975 Algiers agreement, the deployment of a non-aligned peacekeeping force, and negotiations to settle all the other issues. According to Bani-Sadr, the Cuban proposal was exactly what Iran wanted.[218] The Iranian Supreme Defence Council had reservations about certain aspects of the Cuban proposal, but it accepted its essentials. The Iranians, however, amended parts of the proposal in order to prevent Iraq from renewing its aggression. The modified plan was sent to Baghdad.[219]

However, according to the diaries of Hushang Lavi's lawyer, Mitchell Rogovin, as late as 29 October, Iranian leaders still wanted to negotiate a hostage deal with the Republicans. According to Rogovin's diary entry: 'Lavi-Iran will send delegation to wrap up. Nov. 5–10.'[220] The power struggle in Iran continued to complicate efforts to negotiate the release of the hostages. On 29 October, President Bani-Sadr asked Khomeini to dismiss Prime Minister Raja'i and, basically, accept Carter's proposal of October 28.[221]

Carter makes further concessions to Iran

While Iranian leaders were weighing their options, the Carter administration made another major concession. On 31 October, the Pentagon declared that the US 'owed' Iran 500 million dollars worth of military equipment which could be 'delivered rapidly'. The materiel included cluster and laser-guided bombs, which had already been paid for by the Shah.[222] On 31 October, Beheshti, Nabavi, Raja'i and Rafsanjani met to discuss the hostage crisis, and decided to accelerate the parliamentary debate prior to the US elections on 4 November. Nabavi was given the task of neutralizing leftist opposition within the ranks of the hostage-takers and the secular political parties, as well as that from Bani-Sadr.[223]

Carter's proposal of 28 October apparently convinced Nabavi and Kho'iniha that they had achieved most of their objectives. However, the evidence suggests that Beheshti and Rafsanjani sought to delay the release of the hostages because they expected the Republicans to offer better terms.[224] In the meantime, Iran's battlefield position continued to deteriorate because the Iraqis were preparing for the long-term occupation of Khuzestan.[225]

Indeed, the Iraqi Foreign Minister declared in New York that an Iraqi withdrawal from Iran was 'unthinkable'.[226] Saddam Hussein merely sought to achieve his goals through a war of attrition.[227] He offered to withdraw completely from Iran in return for Iran's recognition of Iraq's 'national rights'. Not surprisingly, the Iranians rejected Hussein's proposals and demanded a complete withdrawal of Iraqi forces from their territory followed by a cease-fire.[228]

The Iranian radicals no longer needed the hostages because they had managed to gain control of the state apparatus. However, they feared that a Reagan administration would attack Iran and seek to overthrow the regime.[229] Thus the hostage-takers' mentor, Kho'iniha, made a U-turn and declared that the hostage seizure had served its purpose.[230] The decision to accelerate the Majlis 'debate' undoubtedly had Khomeini's support.[231]

Leaders of militants take control of negotiations, the opening of Algerian channel

By now the Iranian Majlis was considering Iran's proposal regarding the hostage issue. The proposal essentially repeated Khomeini's conditions as articulated on 2 October, namely the return of the Shah's assets to Iran, a non-interference pledge by the US, the abandonment of all American claims against Iran and the unfreezing of Iran's assets.[232] Moreover, during the Majlis debate, a number of deputies argued that the hostages could be used as bargaining chips to obtain the military equipment which the Shah had already paid for.[233]

According to Massoumeh Ebtekar, who was one of the leaders of the hostage-takers, the militants heard 'rumours' that 'a particular Majlis faction' wanted to influence the US presidential elections.[234] The militants believed that some deputies were quite prepared to ignore the official Majlis proposal.[235] On 2 November, the Majlis accepted the four conditions proposed by Khomeini in October. Following this decision, Iran appointed a committee in Prime Minister Raja'i's office headed by the Minister of State for Executive Affairs, Behzad Nabavi, to handle the Iranian side of the negotiations. Prime Minister Raja'i asked Algeria to serve as the sole intermediary in the negotiations between Iran and the US.[236] The timing of the Majlis decision was no coincidence. Indeed Iranian officials later indicated that the Majlis resolution would help Carter win the election.[237] However, when the release of the hostages was delayed, some observers speculated that the Majlis had sought to ensure a Republican victory.[238] Indeed, Massoumeh Ebtekar, has suggested, albeit rather elliptically, that the then Majlis Speaker Rafsanjani and his allies may well have made a deal with the Republicans.[239]

Nabavi's appointment as Iran's chief negotiator indicated that finally the US would be negotiating with one of the leaders of the hostage captors, though indirectly. The November 2 decision marked a significant policy shift on the part of the Iranian leadership. Until now West Germany had served as the intermediary between Iran and the US. On the Iranian side negotiations were handled by Beheshti and Sadegh Tabataba'i who had sought to maintain Iran's ties with the West. According to Algerian intermediaries, the radicals distrusted Tabataba'i because he was educated in the West and served in the Bazargan government.[240]

Nabavi, however, sought to sever Iran's ties with the US and favoured closer ties with the Soviet Union.[241] Indeed, Carter administration officials were aware of Nabavi's Marxist past.[242] The Majlis proposal on the hostage issue was conveyed to the Carter administration on 2 November. Carter's advisers were divided. They all agreed that Iranian leaders were using the hostages as a bargaining chip to gain additional concessions from Carter before the election.[243] Brzezinski was not sure if Iranian leaders were negotiating in good faith or were simply 'setting up' the administration.[244] Lloyd Cutler advised Carter to declare that the US would freeze the Shah's assets in the US to persuade the Iranians to release the hostages before the election.[245] Carter rejected Cutler's advice, but he also wanted to continue to negotiate with the Iranian leaders.

Islamic Republican Party's challenge to Bani-Sadr

It appears that it was at this point that Ayatollah Beheshti and his allies in the IRP decided to persuade some of the radical Majlis deputies to delay the release of the hostages until after the US presidential election. Moreover, on 3 November, IRP clerics persuaded Majlis members to sign a letter requesting Khomeini to dismiss Bani-Sadr as commander in chief of the armed forces.[246] There could be little doubt that the IRP's move was also a challenge to the authority of Khomeini who had himself chosen Bani-Sadr as Iran's commander-in-chief. The IRP's move exacerbated the leadership crisis in Iran, indicating that even Khomeini's position was not secure. That same day Bani-Sadr recorded in his journal that his opponents would delay the resolution of the hostage issue to enable the Republicans to win the presidential election.[247]

15

POST-ELECTION SHIFT OF US STRATEGY IN IRAN AND THE REGION

Proponents of the October Surprise theory, such as Gary Sick and Abolhasan Bani-Sadr, have argued that the Iranians continued to hold the hostages after the 1980 election to remind Reagan of the deal that he had made with Iranian officials. Moreover, according to the then Under-Secretary of State, Warren Christopher, and the then Assistant Secretary of State for Near Eastern and South Asian Affairs, Harold Saunders, the complex nature of the negotiations prevented the hostages' release before Reagan's inauguration.

The available evidence tells a different story. After Carter's defeat, the administration tilted to Iraq again and the Iranians sought to use the hostages as bargaining chips to exact concessions from the US. However, hardly any of the students of the Carter administration's foreign policy have focused on US policy during the transition period.

After the election, Carter decided to side with his National Security Adviser Zbigniew Brzezinski who recommended a tilt towards Iraq in the Iran-Iraq war. Brzezinski and Secretary of Defence Harold Brown also favoured closer security co-operation with Saudi Arabia. Brzezinski advised Carter to inform the Iranians that if they refused to release the hostages, the US would provide military assistance to Iraq.[1]

Secretary Muskie and his deputy Warren Christopher, on the other hand, de-emphasized the importance of military competition with the Soviet Union.[2] Muskie and Christopher wanted to continue to negotiate with Iranian leaders. They sought to reduce the pressure on Iran and the Soviet Union. Harold Brown and Robert Komer, who was in charge of planning for Persian Gulf security, prepared a long-term military plan aimed at constructing a regional security framework.[3] However, Muskie's opposition meant that the issue would remain unresolved.

Saudi Arabia turns to the Paris-Bonn axis to counterbalance the US

US relations with Saudi Arabia also continued to deteriorate during the transition period. Riyadh turned to the Franco-German axis for security cooperation and concluded major arms deals with both countries.[4] The Saudis indicated as well that they wanted a major oil for arms deal with West Germany.[5] Western Europe and Japan were hoping that their exports to Saudi Arabia would offset their huge oil import bills.[6]

Saudi Arabia's decision to broaden its security ties with France and West Germany had far-reaching implications for US regional and global strategy.[7] Paris and Bonn favoured the neutralization of Southwest Asia and sought to revive détente. Saudi Arabia refused to grant military base rights to the US, and its relations with the US went on deteriorating during the remainder of Carter's term in office. In February 1981 Crown Prince Fahd even raised the question of Saudi arms purchases from the Soviet Union.[8]

The Saudis may also have calculated that improving ties with Moscow would enable them to persuade the Kremlin to lift the arms embargo on Iraq. Indeed, this embargo was Iraq's main problem. Fortunately for Saddam Hussein, Iraq's second major arms supplier France, continued to sell arms to Baghdad.[9]

The Soviet Union still refused to sell arms to Iraq. Presumably, Hussein's opponents in the Soviet leadership calculated that the war would weaken him and force him to agree to the Iraqi communists' participation in government.[10]

Iraq's change of its war aims and the leadership crisis in Iran

On 11 November, Saddam Hussein reiterated Iraq's war aims. These included Iraq's 'national and sovereign rights' over Shatt-al-Arab and the disputed border area, and an Iranian pledge of non-interference in the internal affairs of Arab countries. Moreover, Hussein talked of overthrowing the Iranian regime.[11] As we saw in an earlier chapter, Hussein had been trying to negotiate a cease-fire. The only plausible explanation for Hussein's decision to change his war aims is that he must have received assurances from the US.

The Carter administration's change of position occurred at a particularly sensitive time for Iranian leaders. The crisis of authority in Iran continued unabated. By now two broad coalitions had formed: the Islamic Republican Party (IRP), the Mojahedin of the Islamic Revolution and the Tudeh Party on one side, and President Bani-Sadr, clerical opponents of the Islamic Republican Party and Mojahedin-e Khalq Organization (MKO) on the other. However, there were strains within each coalition, and Khomeini vacillated between the two.[12] The IRP placed inexperienced and incompetent political commissars in the military to supervise senior military officers, thereby hampering the war effort. So frightened were IRP clerics of the military's battlefield successes that they armed their supporters to prevent a coup against the regime.[13]

The IRP also used their shock troops, the Hezbollahis, to smash opposition groups and mobilize the masses to rally around Khomeini and impose censorship on the mass media.[14] The party's boldest move during this period was the arrest of former Foreign Minister Sadegh Ghotbzadeh on 7 November. According to Bani-Sadr, Ghotbzadeh was arrested because he had threatened to reveal the secret agreement between the Republicans and the IRP.[15]

Ghotbzadeh would shortly be released. On 15 November, there was a major demonstration outside the bazaar to celebrate his release. The demonstrators called for the dissolution of the IRP, describing IRP clerics as 'capitalists' who 'suck on the blood of the underprivileged'.[16] Several senior clerics, including Ayatollah Lahuti, Grand Ayatollah Abdollah Shirazi, and Ayatollah Hasan

Qomi, supported Bani-Sadr.[17] Bani-Sadr used his constitutional prerogative to reject six successive nominees for the post of foreign minister. He also prevented Prime Minister Raja'i from appointing ministers of finance and commerce.[18]

New US negotiating positions

It was against the background of increasing Iraqi battlefield successes that Warren Christopher presented the US negotiating position to Algerian intermediaries. The US pledged not to interfere politically or militarily in Iran. It would prevent the transfer of the Shah's assets out of the US, lift all economic sanctions on Iran and return 5.5 billion dollars of Iran's assets held in the US and by American banks abroad.[19] The Algerian mediators flew to Tehran on 12 November, where they spent the next ten days explaining the US proposal to a committee chaired by Iran's chief negotiator Behzad Nabavi.[20]

According to Christopher, the main obstacle to resolving the issue was the banks' refusal to unfreeze Iran's assets unless Iran brought its loan payments up to date.[21] However, the principal importance of the Carter administration's proposal lay in what it did not say. It made no mention of the 500 million dollars' worth of military equipment, which Carter had promised to Iran. Not surprisingly, Nabavi complained that 'the U.S. paper seemed to be a new proposal in its own right'.[22]

By now, Nabavi had emerged as the most vociferous advocate of delaying the release of the hostages until Reagan's inauguration.[23] He told Khomeini that the militants wanted to delay the release of the hostages until 20 January.[24] It has often been suggested that Khomeini delayed the release of the hostages in order to humiliate Carter. The record, however, suggests that there were far more important issues at stake than quenching Khomeini's thirst to belittle Carter. Indeed, the Ayatollah believed that Iran had already defeated the 'Great Satan'.[25]

Hostage negotiations come to a standstill

In November and December 1980, the State Department received intelligence from various sources saying that Iranian leaders had decided to release the hostages 'at noon on Inauguration Day'.[26] Nevertheless, a US Congressional task force later concluded that Iranian leaders wanted to settle the issue during the transition period.[27]

According to Lloyd Cutler, the Carter administration requested the Reagan transition team to honour any negotiated agreement, but the Republicans refused. However, the Carter administration used the Reagan threat to persuade Iranian officials to release the hostages.[28]

Iranian leaders were willing to make significant concessions to the US to end the crisis. After the US presidential election, they only demanded 200 million dollars' worth of military equipment instead of the 500 million dollars promised by Carter before the election. The evidence suggests that Iranian leaders had decided to ask Israel to supply the materiel to Iran in return for the hostages.

Israeli Prime Minister Menachem Begin passed Iran's request for American arms to Carter on 13 November during his visit to the US. The overall value of the deal was 200 million dollars and Begin declared that 'the arms deliveries might also be of assistance in the release of the hostages'.[29] Carter rejected Begin's request and reiterated his position that Israel must refrain from supplying arms to Iran.[30] However, the two men agreed that 'following the release of the hostages, there would be no reason to prevent arms deliveries from Israel to Iran'.[31]

Carter's refusal to release Iran's equipment and the turn-around in the negotiations

Given the change in Carter's position, it is not surprising that the Iranians changed their own position on banking issues. They informed Warren Christopher that the proposal known as Plan C which called on Iran to repay all its debts was unacceptable, and on 14 November said that they wanted an alternative plan.[32] They wanted to only repay some of Iran's loans, and asked for guarantees.[33] The bankers rejected this request and started to work on yet another plan known as Plan D.[34]

Plan D required Iran to repay all its loans that were due for repayment. The remaining loans would be brought up to date with overdue payments and interest being paid. The Iranian Central Bank would provide a guarantee that it would pay future claims. In return, Iran would receive a much greater proportion of its frozen deposits and the banks would pay interest on the remaining sums as guarantees. A large proportion of the cheap loans would also remain intact.[35]

On 20 November, Muskie indicated that the US had 'in principle' accepted all four conditions demanded by the Iranian Majlis.[36] On 21 November, Behzad Nabavi, presented Iran's reply to the US proposal to Algerian officials, who were mediating between the US and Iran, arguing that Iran could not 'deviate' from the Majlis' conditions and could not reply to the US' 'unrelated' proposals. The major unresolved points were the transfer of assets without exception to Iran, access to the Shah's assets, and the annulment of claims against Iran.[37]

The Algerians did not present Iran's proposal to the US until 26 November.[38] Given Algeria's support for Iran's positions on regional questions, it appears that the purpose of the delay was to enable Iran to improve its battlefield position in order to draw the US into an arms-for-hostages deal. Cyrus Hashemi, who had been acting as an intermediary in the negotiations with Iranian leaders, proposed the arms-for-hostages deal to the Carter administration.[39] By now Hashemi was openly boasting to his associates about his close relationship with William Casey.[40] However, there is no evidence that the Carter administration took Hashemi up on his offer.[41]

Iranian-Syrian alliance and the Syrian-Jordanian crisis

From late October onwards, Syria also began to supply small amounts of weapons, ammunition, and spares to Iran.[42] Syrian President Hafiz Asad called for supporting Iran and described the Iran-Iraq conflict as 'the wrong war'.[43] Moreover, Syria also indirectly supported Iraqi Kurds' demands for secession.[44]

Iraq was also involved in setting up a clandestine Syrian Islamist coalition with ties to the Muslim Brotherhood.[45] The groups involved carried out many acts of terrorism in Syria. According to former CIA official Robert Baer, Saudi

Arabia supported the Muslim Brotherhood and the CIA turned a blind eye to Saudi involvement.[46] It is difficult to measure the level of Iraqi support for the Brotherhood during this period.[47]

In November, seven Iraqi opposition groups united against the Ba'thist regime and sought to establish close relations with Iran and the Soviet Union.[48] Moreover, Iran and Syria co-operated closely in organizing the postponement of the Arab summit due to be held in Jordan.[49] Syria's move against Jordan was particularly important because Jordan served as Iraq's logistical base. The Soviet Union supported Syria's move against Jordan.[50]

At the same time, Iran persuaded Algeria and Libya to give it diplomatic support.[51] Iranian Majlis Speaker Akbar Hashemi-Rafsanjani also called for Iranian-Syria cooperation to overthrow Saddam Hussein.[52]

While the Arab summit was in progress, Syria increased the number of its troops on the Jordanian border[53], but the Arab summit was concentrating on providing support for Iraq in its war with Iran.[54] However, the resolution issued at the summit also called for a cease-fire and negotiations in the Iran-Iraq war.[55] Such a cease-fire, of course, would favour Iraq, which was occupying Iranian territory.

Iran-Iraq war enters a critical phase

Syria's move against Jordan coincided with a critical phase of the Iran-Iraq war. Iraq had just resumed its oil shipments through Turkey and was planning to export between 350,0000 and 400,000 barrels a day through Turkey.[56] The Iraqi armed forces had intensified their attacks on Ahvaz, Gilan-e Gharb, Susangerd, and Sumar. Iran rejected the mediation of the UN emissary, Olof Palme, who indicated that Saddam Hussein was prepared to end the war.[57] The Iranians claimed to be on the point of achieving victory.[58] Palme said that he would not return to the area until mid-December at the earliest.[59]

In the meantime, Iranian attacks on Iraqi oil terminals had reduced Iraq's oil export capacity from about three million barrels a day to about one million barrels a day. Iraq was having to rely on overland pipelines through Turkey and Syria.[60] Iraq's ally, Saudi Arabia, began to prepare the ground for an anti-Iranian security pact and also discussed internal security planning with Kuwait and Pakistan.[61] The Saudis almost certainly wanted to curb pro-Khomeini activities among the Shi'a population of the three countries.[62]

They also began to mediate between Syria and Jordan. Saudi support for Iraq and the Syrian Muslim Brotherhood enabled Saudi mediator, Prince Abdullah, to moderate Syrian opposition to Iraq.[63] Asad refused to withdraw his forces from the Jordanian border,[64] but he did, however, instruct Syrian oil industry officials to prepare for the resumption of the shipment of Iraqi oil. Iraq could export around 500,000 barrels a day and Syria could earn substantial transit fees.[65]

Soviet intervention

Syrian-Jordanian tensions escalated so sharply that US Under Secretary of State David Newsom asked Soviet Ambassador to the US Anatoly Dobrynin to get the Soviet Union to use its influence to prevent Syria from attacking Jordan.[66] First Deputy Chairman of the Supreme Soviet Presidium, Vassily Kuznetsov, told

Asad that the Soviet Union would not support a war against Jordan.[67] Less than a week later, Syria accepted Saudi mediation.[68]

On 2 December, the Iraqi high command declared that it was awaiting orders to launch a final offensive to occupy the rest of Khuzestan. However, Syria was still threatening Iraq's logistical base in Jordan,[69] and on 7 December, Saddam Hussein announced that Iraq was pursuing a defensive strategy.[70] By that day, Syria and Jordan had begun withdrawing their troops from the border region as a result of Saudi mediation.[71] However, tensions did not subside noticeably.[72]

The Carter administration considers Iran's proposal

It was against this background of increasing regional tension that the Algerian mediators presented Iran's reply to the US proposal. Brzezinski characterized Iran's response as 'insulting' and advised Carter to summarily reject it. Warren Christopher and his negotiating team, however, argued that the Iranian response was 'the opening gambit in a negotiating strategy'. Carter sided with Christopher.[73] Brzezinski and CIA Director Admiral Turner advised the president to make it clear to the Iranians that the US position was their 'final offer'.[74]

Carter discussed the issue with Muskie, and Christopher was instructed to inform the Iranians that the US had made its final offer. The US merely asked Iran to bring its loans current and pledge to meet its future payments. In return, the American banks would agree to release the frozen Iranian deposits.[75] The US informed Algerian intermediaries that if a settlement was not reached during the transition period, no one could predict what the incoming Reagan administration would do.[76]

The power struggle in Iran and the hostage crisis

Bani-Sadr's opposition to the hostage settlement and Khomeini's support for him made it difficult for the Raja'i government to resolve the hostage issue. The Central Bank's possession of damaging information on Beheshti's bank accounts strengthened Bani-Sadr's position considerably,[77] since the IRP saw his alliance with the Bank's Chairman Ali-Reza Nobari as a threat.[78]

On 3 December, in an effort to mediate between the president and the government, Khomeini summoned Bani-Sadr and Raja'i to end their infighting.[79] According to Bani-Sadr, at a meeting with Beheshti and Rafsanjani's clerical opponents on 6 December, he said that Beheshti and Rafsanjani had hatched a plot to overthrow him and that they had made a secret deal with the Republicans. Bani-Sadr warned them that his removal would bring down the regime. He asked his interlocutors to propose to Khomeini the formation of a committee to mediate between him and his opponents. Raja'i and Rafsanjani opposed the proposal, but Khomeini approved it.[80]

On 6 December, Khomeini asked Bani-Sadr, Raja'i and Rafsanjani to stop quarrelling and proposed the formation of a committee to mediate between them.[81] Bani-Sadr has written that the committee prevented his opponents from overthrowing him before 20 January.[82] Then, Beheshti, Rafsanjani and their supporters circulated rumours that Bani-Sadr was preparing to stage a military coup with US support to overthrow Khomeini and the revolution, but they failed to convince Khomeini. On 14 December, he once again asked Bani-Sadr and his opponents to settle their differences.[83]

However, on 16 December, sixty members of the Majlis signed a statement accusing Bani-Sadr of disclosing state secrets and of provoking conflict between the military and the nation.[84] Their move forced Khomeini to choose between them and Bani-Sadr. This leadership crisis in Iran coincided with a major Soviet initiative in Southwest Asia.

Brezhnev's proposal for a new regional security system and the hostage crisis

In December, Brezhnev revived his proposal for the neutralization of Southwest Asia. As we saw in an earlier chapter, Moscow had intelligence on contacts between the Republicans and Iranian officials. It seems that the election of Ronald Reagan, who had pledged to pursue a strongly anti-Soviet global strategy, and the prospect of an American attack against Iran led Soviet leaders to revive their proposal to prevent such an attack on Iran.

Brezhnev put forward his proposal during a speech to Indian parliamentarians on 10 December. He called for banning the use of force by great powers in the Persian Gulf, and a ban on foreign military bases 'such as Diego Garcia' and nuclear weapons in the area. Brezhnev went so far as to call for the return of Diego Garcia to Mauritius. He did not even mention Afghanistan, merely alluding to a 'negotiated political situation' for the region.[85]

In effect, Brezhnev's proposal sought to prevent the establishment of a US-led regional security framework and US naval deployments to the region, while leaving intact Soviet land-based military power in the vicinity of Southwest Asia.[86] The Carter administration rejected Brezhnev's proposal. Indeed, even France and West Germany opposed the proposal.[87]

What concerned the Soviets most was an American attack on Iran. Soviet broadcasts before and after the resolution of the crisis emphasized the importance of US non-interference in Iranian affairs.[88] It appears that the Carter administration's rejection of Brezhnev's proposal led Iran's chief negotiator, Behzad Nabavi, who was pro-Soviet, to suddenly reverse course to derail the negotiations with the US. Nabavi's demands and Brezhnev's proposal enabled the Soviet Union to use the hostages as a bargaining chip to compel Carter to agree to the neutralization of the Persian Gulf, or at least non-interference in Iranian affairs.

What made the situation more difficult for the US was that the Saudis made positive comments on Brezhnev's proposal in the last week of December.[89] The Saudi decision to support the neutralization of the Persian Gulf may well have been due to the shipment of Soviet arms to Iraq via Saudi Arabia.

Iran Reverses Course

On 19 December, in a message to the Carter administration, Behzad Nabavi made new demands. The new proposal stipulated:

(1) The US should deposit 9.6 billion dollars in Iranian assets, plus interest, and the gold on deposit with the Federal Reserve Bank, with the Central Bank of Algeria before the hostage release.

(2) The US should also deposit 4 billion dollars with Algeria as security for eventual repayment of Iranian frozen funds.
(3) The United States must accept liability for any claims against Iran for damages associated with the hostage seizure.
(4) The US should immediately report on the Shah's assets in the US and deposit 10 billion dollars as security against their eventual return to Iran.
(5) In return, Iran would agree to bring up to date all outstanding payments on its loans from US banks and would authorize the Central Bank of Algeria to hold 1 billion dollars as a guarantee of future Iranian payments against the loans.
(6) Iran accepted some form of claims settlement and would set aside another 1 billion dollars to cover payment of claims. This fund would be replenished to ensure that it did not drop below 500 million dollars until the settlement process was completed.[90]

These demands were called the '24 billion dollar misunderstanding.'[91] Carter later observed that only a total reversal of Iran's position would have resolved the issue.[92] Majlis Speaker Hashemi-Rafsanjani increased the pressure on the US by threatening to put the hostages on trial.[93] Behzad Nabavi declared that Iran could keep the hostages for 10 years if necessary.[94]

Bani-Sadr has claimed that Nabavi made these demands to delay the release of the hostages until the inauguration day.[95] There is no evidence for this contention. Moreover, this would only draw suspicion to the Republicans. Indeed this was one of the reasons that many Iranians and some Americans suspected collusion between the Republicans and Iranians.

The Algerians failed to dissuade Nabavi from making such demands.[96] The Carter administration began to prepare itself for hostage trials, although Carter was still hopeful that Iranian leaders would negotiate. However, he wanted to inform US allies of the US reaction both to the trials and to possible harm done to the hostages.[97] On 21 December, Iran published a summary of its demands. The administration responded by publishing the text of its own messages to Iran. Nevertheless, US officials believed that they could still make a deal with Iran.[98]

After holding consultations with Carter on 21 December, Christopher sent a message to the Algerians, describing the Iranian response as 'deeply disappointing'. The US proposed a draft Memorandum of Understanding (MOU) with Iran. The MOU would take into consideration the political problems facing the Nabavi commission and proposed the transfer of as many Iranian assets as possible to an escrow outside the US prior to the hostage release, with arrangements for their return to Iran as soon as the hostages were freed.[99] The US proposal 'expressly rejected' Iran's request for 24 billion dollars. However, 'it maximized the amount of Iranian assets that could realistically be collected, short of court action'.[100]

President-elect Reagan and his advisers considered Nabavi's demands to be tantamount to blackmail and Reagan made a strong statement to that effect.[101] However, US Congressional investigators have concluded that there were meetings between Iranians and the Republicans during the transition period to resolve the hostage crisis.[102]

The Iranian government takes control of the hostages

On 24 December, the US was informed that the three American diplomats who were at the Iranian Foreign Ministry, Bruce Laingen, Michael Howland and Victor Tomseth had been taken to the location where the other hostages were being held. According to the report, the Iranian government was holding all the hostages.[103] However, the Algerian intermediaries reported that the three diplomats were being held separately.[104]

On 28 December, the Algerian intermediaries informed the Carter administration that they had visited the hostages. They said that they would not be responsible for the failure of the negotiations or for refusal by Iran or the US to honour their commitments.[105] More importantly, they said that 49 of the hostages were now located in two separate places within ten to twenty minutes of the US embassy.[106]

Of course, the information provided by the Algerians could have led the US to launch a rescue mission.[107] The evidence suggests, rather strongly, that to prevent such a rescue mission, the Iranian government decided to take Laingen, Howland and Tomseth hostage. Carter was alarmed.[108] He was informed by various sources that there was a 'hot debate' between Iranian leaders. However, on 29 December, the Algerians informed the Carter administration that the Iranian government was preparing for the hostages' release.

After eight hours of negotiations, it was agreed that to overcome Iran's objection to signing an agreement with the US, the US proposal would be submitted in the form of a 'declaration' by the government of Algeria. The proposal called for: (1) the opening of an escrow account for Iran in which 7.3 billion dollars would be placed upon confirmation of the release of the hostages; (2) the establishment of a claims-settlement procedure; and (3) a US decision to freeze and provide information on the Shah's assets and facilitate Iran's access to US courts.[109]

Once again, it is extremely important to emphasize that the US proposal made no mention of the military equipment, which Iran had already paid for.[110] US officials feared hostage trials and they used the Reagan threat to compel the Iranians to release the hostages.[111] Rumours were circulating in Iran that if the hostages were not released by 20 January, Reagan would take military action.[112]

On 2 January, Carter instructed his advisers to prepare for the trial of the hostages. He decided to announce a state of belligerency or ask Congress to declare war on Iran. The US would freeze the Iranian assets permanently and ask the UN Security Council to impose comprehensive sanctions against Iran. The US would then proceed to blockade Iran or to mine its ports.[113] After consultations with the Algerian mediators, the Carter administration decided to continue the negotiations but it reiterated that the Iranians would have to deal with the Reagan administration if the hostage issue were not resolved before 16 January.

The Algerians conveyed the message to Behzad Nabavi on 3 January. Nabavi said that Iran would respond within the next two or three days. The Iranians responded by increasing the psychological pressure on the US. On 5 January, Washington was informed that Laingen, Howland and Tomseth had been taken away to join the other hostages at an unknown location.

The Algerians advised US officials to remain calm and relayed the Iranians' assurances that the government was holding all the hostages. On 6 January, the US ambassador to Algeria, Ulric Haynes, was informed that the hostages would be released soon. However, US officials were advised not to mention the 16 January deadline to avoid conveying the impression that Iran had been given an ultimatum.[114]

On 7 January, Warren Christopher and his aides flew to Algeria to accelerate the negotiations.[115] The banking and diplomatic channels merged on that same day, indicating that the Carter administration would not accept a settlement that was unacceptable to the banks.[116] Christopher made it clear to Algerian Foreign Minister Benyahya that Iran could either take the 7.3 billion dollars or wait until spring 1981 and deal with the Reagan administration. The Iranian negotiators promised to study the proposal.[117]

The Republicans' proposal and the threat to attack Iran

Reagan's appointees refused to be briefed by the Carter administration on the hostage situation, but Reagan nominated Fred Ikle to maintain contact with the Carter administration on the hostage issue.[118] In a memorandum on 29 December, 1980 to William Casey and Richard Allen, Ikle argued that the Iranian regime must not be permitted to humiliate Reagan the way they had humiliated Carter.[119]

Ikle realized that the hostage situation was complicated by the power struggle in Iran and proposed several alternatives, including launching another hostage rescue mission; declaring a state of belligerency; seizing Iranian territory and even seizing 'counterhostages'.[120]

He noted that covert action could result in the release of the hostages and bring to power a regime friendlier towards the US. However, it might also 'bring into power a group beholden to the Soviet Union'. Ikle cautioned that military action was also fraught with 'political costs and potential failure'.[121] For Fred Ikle, Iran's future geopolitical orientation was far more important than the hostage crisis.[122]

He proposed a series of options to bring the issue to a head within two weeks after Reagan's inauguration. He argued that the US could present the Carter administration's proposal as a final offer, which would expire after 30 days. Alternatively, it could reiterate Reagan's 13 September position that the safe return of the hostages was the pre-condition to any negotiations. Yet another alternative was to remain silent and keep the Iranians guessing.[123]

The Congressional committees investigating the October Surprise allegations argued that the Ikle memoranda indicated that the Republicans had not made a deal with Iran. However, these memoranda should be read in the context of Iran's new demands. Reagan and Bush were inclined to use force against Iran to obtain the hostages' freedom.[124]

Iran changes its negotiating position

The French lawyer, Christian Borguet, who was involved in the hostage negotiations, has said that IRP clerics pressured Behzad Nabavi to resolve the issue before 20 January. Nabavi reversed Iran's position on 15 January, i.e. the day before the US deadline, declaring that Iran would pay off all its loans.[125] In effect, Iran was proposing to implement Plan C which it had rejected on 14 November![126] Nabavi had, in effect, agreed to buy Iran out of the hostage crisis.[127] Bani-Sadr later argued that Nabavi's reversal of Iran's position was a charade.[128] Gary Sick subscribes to that view.[129]

A series of documents were signed in Washington on 18 January. The Iranians formally accepted the proposal on 19 January and Warren Christopher initialled the agreement in Algiers.[130] However, the release of the hostages was delayed because of a series of disagreements over technical details.[131] Moreover, Bani-Sadr wrote to Khomeini, urging him to prevent the signature of the agreement,[132] but Khomeini did not reply.[133]

The militants fear of US attack and the decision to release the hostages

Many years later, the Iranian negotiator, Behzad Nabavi, wrote that had Iran refused to reach a settlement, the US would have wreaked havoc on Iran as it did on Iraq during the war over Kuwait.[134] On the other hand, Bani-Sadr has contended that the Reagan administration would not have attacked Iran, and that Iranian leaders never feared such an attack.[135]

The Soviets were worried that after the resolution of the hostage crisis the US would move against Iran.[136] They rejected US claims that their reports were undermining the negotiations and reiterated their pledge to oppose 'foreign' (read US) intervention in Iran.[137] On 17 January, Secretary Muskie told Ambassador Dobrynin that Soviet broadcasts were 'unhelpful' to a diplomatic settlement of the hostage issue.[138]

In the final analysis, it appears that it was fear of US attack that compelled the militants to release the hostages in return for an arms-for-hostages deal. The resolution of the hostage crisis, however, neither ended the power struggle nor settled the debate over Iran's foreign policy orientation.

Impact of hostage crisis on Iranian foreign policy

The Reagan administration had a Soviet-centric view of the international system. Given the administration's perception of Iran's strategic importance, it sought to revive the strategy of containment.[139] Some US officials, particularly CIA Director William Casey and Secretary of State Alexander Haig, believed that the US could cultivate Iran as an ally against the Soviet Union despite their recent experience of the hostage crisis.

Reagan administration officials have claimed that they only acquiesced in Israeli arms supplies to Iran after Reagan took office. However, the available evidence shows that the Republicans had secretly approved of arms sales to Iran both before the election and during the transition period. There is no evidence indicating that Israeli and US shipments of arms to Iran were related to a secret agreement concluded between Iran and the Republicans prior to the 1980 presidential election.[140]

It is important to note that US Congressional investigators did not examine reports of direct US shipments to Iran. In December 1980, deputy Mossad director David Kimche secretly met on three occasions with McFarlane in Geneva, Washington, and Jerusalem to secure US authorization for Israeli arms sales to Iran. McFarlane later obtained Secretary of State Haig's approval for these Israeli deliveries to Iran. The Reagan administration began to sell arms to Iran in 1981. When asked about early Israeli arms shipments to Iran, McFarlane said that he was 'generally' aware of the 1981 Israeli arms deliveries, but claimed that he had not authorized them.[141]

The US began to sell arms to Iran immediately after the Reagan administration took office. Investigative journalist Seymour Hersh has concluded that several billion dollars of military equipment were sold to Iran,[142] which was a major reason why Iraq failed to defeat it.[143] However, by late 1981, as Iran threatened to defeat Iraq the Reagan administration tilted in Iraq's direction.[144]

Bani-Sadr has made public some of the invoices of the Israeli shipments to Iran. The earliest of these invoices is dated 8 March 1981. These shipments would have required a presidential finding to be legal. In fact, the day after the earliest of the invoices provided by Bani-Sadr, William Casey proposed a covert action programme to Reagan for supporting pro-US elements in Iran.[145]

US regional strategy and hostage crisis

The hostage crisis prevented the pursuit of a consistent presidential strategy in the Persian Gulf and Southwest Asia. The removal of Iran as a front-line state in the US confrontation with the Soviet Union resulted in a modified US global strategic posture, with increasing emphasis on vital US interests in Southwest Asia. The arrest of a large number of Soviet agents in Iran in 1983 showed that Soviet intelligence had succeeded in placing its agents in sensitive positions within the Iranian regime. So successful was the Soviet strategy that some members of the IRP even advocated forming an alliance with the Tudeh.[146]

The Carter and Reagan administrations both refrained from resorting to military action against Iran because of Iran's extremely sensitive geostrategic position. In the 1980s as evidence of Iran's involvement in international terrorism mounted, Washington refused to take direct military action for fear of driving the Iranian regime into the arms of the Soviets.[147] It was not until 1987, and the revival of US-Soviet détente, that the Reagan administration resorted to military action and intervened in the Iran-Iraq war to force Iran to change its policies. The Iran-Contra affair strengthened the advocates of détente, such as Secretary of State George Shultz, in the Reagan administration. Superpower détente ended US efforts to cultivate Iran as a strategic asset.

16

CONCLUSION

The rather sharp disagreement between National Security Adviser Zbigniew Brzezinski and Secretary of State Cyrus Vance over the choice of policy towards Iran was symptomatic of a massive dispute over global strategy in the Carter administration. It was this dispute, rather than any intelligence failures, which led to a major failure of US strategy in Iran. Vance advocated the implementation of the New World Order strategy, which was based on the premise that the world had become increasingly multipolar. He sought to reduce the military pressure on the Soviet periphery, take a more even-handed approach to Iran and Saudi Arabia and closely co-ordinate US Middle Eastern policies with those of Great Britain, West Germany and Japan.

From the very beginning, US strategy sought to achieve its goals by putting pressure on the Shah to change his oil-price policy, focusing his attention on Iran's internal development and strengthening the position of Saudi Arabia in the region. However, once the Shah had changed his oil policy, he decided to crack down on his opponents and he tried to persuade Carter to support him.

Brzezinski, who was an advocate of neo-containment, focused his attention on containing Soviet power and thus placed great emphasis upon the US's security relationship with Iran. Brzezinski did not believe that America could simply force the Shah to become a constitutional monarch. His and Vance's divergent strategic approaches towards Iran meant that when the crisis reached its denouement, the Carter administration could not speak with one voice. This led the Shah to suspect that Washington was plotting to overthrow him. Indeed, both Vance and Ambassador Sullivan did not believe that the Shah's ouster would be such a great catastrophe.

The ambassador's policy was based on the premise that the military and the conservative clerics would ally against the leftists and form a right-wing government to replace the Shah. Brzezinski did not agree with Sullivan's assessment and saw the military as the main institution keeping Iran in the US sphere of influence. However, by the time Brzezinski got involved in Iran policy, there was little he could do.

Ultimately, the Shah was overthrown as a result of the choices he had made during his rule. Like Carter, he was also trying to reconcile diametrically opposed policy options. His modernization programme alienated many clerics. However, his anti-communism enabled his clerical opponents to pursue their activities. The Shah saw his downfall as a plot hatched in London and Washington. He would never have believed that Iranians would dare to take to the streets to overthrow him.

For Carter, Brzezinski and Vance the fate of the Shah was far less important than Iran's foreign policy orientation. Brzezinski feared that a non-aligned Iran would pursue radical policies which would undermine the US position in the Middle East. Vance and his advisers, however, believed that even a non-aligned Iran would not necessarily harm US interests and that Iran would preserve its ties with the US because of the Soviet threat.

The Soviets sought to take advantage of the fall of the Shah and the hostage crisis to compel the US to agree to the neutralization of the Persian Gulf and the Indian Ocean. For a while, Brzezinski thought that Khomeini's anti-communism provided a basis for a de facto alliance with the US. However, the hostage crisis convinced him that the US had to remove Khomeini. Carter, on the other hand, was trying to save the lives of US hostages and revive détente even after the Soviet invasion of Afghanistan. However, the Soviets did not believe that Carter was strong enough to deliver on his promises.

Despite his pre-eminent position as the architect of the revolution, Khomeini was only one actor among many. Indeed, at first, he did not even approve of hostage taking. The situation was further complicated by the militants' extremely complex relationship with Ayatollah Beheshti who was one of the chief power brokers in Iran. They had found documents on Beheshti's contacts with US officials. However, despite their visceral anti-Americanism, they chose not to disgrace Beheshti and used the documents to persuade him to form an alliance with them.

In the 1980s, the leaders of the hostage-takers secured powerful cabinet posts in the Iranian government, including the ministries of heavy industry and oil.[1] Later on, several militants were given diplomatic posts. They were all deeply involved in the Iranian regime's terrorist operations, including the assassination of Iranian dissidents.[2] Khomeini realized that he had to accommodate different policy currents within the state apparatus in order to preserve the regime:[3]

The hostage crisis led to a major realignment in Iran's foreign policy in that it helped advocates of forming alliances with radical Third World states and the Soviet Union to gain the upper hand. After the seizure of hostages in Tehran, Brzezinski called for a tilt towards Iraq. Despite receiving warnings that Iraqi President Saddam Hussein had regional ambitions which conflicted with US interests, Brzezinski continued to see Iraq as a de facto ally in the effort to contain the Soviet Union and re-establish US influence in the Persian Gulf.

Brzezinski saw the Iran-Iraq war as an opportunity for regaining influence in Iran through an arms-for-hostage deal. However, Iraq's invasion of Iran had provided Iranian radicals with a justification for exporting their revolution to neighbouring countries.

Moreover, Iraq's invasion of Iran also enabled Israel to re-establish its security ties with Iran through arms sales. Israeli Prime Minister Menachem Begin saw Carter as a threat to Israeli strategy and used his country's relationship with Iran to undermine the US president. Carter's problems were compounded by his failure to fully understand his principal advisers' strategies.

The Iranian hostage crisis was a particularly complex event because of its implications for US regional and grand strategies. At the level of regional strategy, US failure to deal forcefully with the seizure of its hostages may well have encouraged other terrorist organizations to take US diplomats hostage. At the level of grand strategy, US failure to deal effectively with Khomeini's challenge led the Soviet Union to increase its support for Iranian radicals, who were determined to export the revolution in an effort to expel the US from the Persian Gulf. In the early 1980s, the CIA apparently passed on intelligence to the Iranian regime on the activities of the Tudeh Party. The intelligence had been collected by Soviet defector Vladimir Kuzikchin who reportedly provided British officials with 'a list of several hundred Soviet agents operating in Iran'. The Iranian authorities then arrested more than 1,000 Tudeh Party members. Iranian officials had already started monitoring the activities of many Tudeh Party members.[4] Former CIA official Melvin Goodman who was responsible for analysing Soviet policy towards the Third World has claimed that during the Kuzikchin affair, the CIA and SIS were working with former SAVAK officials who had joined the new regime.[5] However, such temporary successes in the field of intelligence activities did not lead to any breakthroughs in US relations with Iran. Moreover, despite the large number of Tudeh Party activists arrested, it is important to note that according to Kuzikchin himself the Soviet Union only had two agents in the Iranian government.[6] The key policy issue was the Iranian regime's expanding ties with the Soviet Union and its support for various terrorist organizations in the Middle East and elsewhere. Even after the disintegration of the Soviet Union, Iran continued to maintain a strategic relationship with Russia while continuing its support for some of the most anti-American terrorist organizations in the world such as the Lebanese Hezbollah.

At the same time, a massive US military response could well have led the Soviets to invade Iran. Neither the strategy of political containment of the Soviet Union, recommended by Vance, nor the strategy of military containment, propounded by Brzezinski, were likely to serve Carter's political interests in an election year.

In fact, so disenchanted were officials in the US national security bureaucracy that some of them started collaborating with the Republicans. By the time Carter left office, the US had lost a major ally, the Soviet Union had become more globally assertive and Saudi Arabia had lost faith in the US security guarantee. It is astonishing that despite his growing concern about Soviet support for radical movements, Brzezinski did not consider the Soviet Union to be responsible for the increase in international terrorism. Brzezinski's military assistant, William Odom, did not subscribe to the incoming Reagan administration's view that the Soviet Union was responsible for the increase in international terrorist incidents.

The policies which Brzezinski had initiated, however, such as the opening to Iraq and the alliance with Saudi Arabia and Pakistan, were implemented with greater vigour by the Reagan administration. The consequences of those policies in the long term turned out to be devastating for the US and the Middle East.

The rise of Sunni extremism and blowback thesis

Writers such as Chalmers Johnson, John Cooley, Stephen Kinzer, Gabriel Kolko and Peter Dale Scott have popularized the blowback thesis of US foreign policy.[7] The rise of Al-Qa'idah owed much to US covert operations in Southwest Asia. Brzezinski believed that Islamists would be able to destabilize the Soviet

Union and contribute to its disintegration. Speaking in an interview with *Le Nouvel Observateur* in 1998 (15–21 January 1998), i.e., after the Taleban had come to power in Afghanistan, Brzezinski still argued that the covert operation to assist the Mojahedin was a good idea.

During the Afghan war, the Reagan administration supported the activities of Usamah Bin-Ladin's mentor, Abdullah Azzam. Azzam himself toured the US in the early and mid 1980s to recruit fighters.[8] Azzam was also a founder of the Palestinian radical Islamist group, Hamas.[9] The fall-out from the covert operation in Afghanistan caused huge problems for the US, culminating in the horrific 11 September attacks.[10]

The reverberating impact of the hostage crisis

After the revolution, Brzezinski still argued that a coup would have been better than a revolution. He contended: 'I think given what transpired when Khomeini came to power, I think I was historically and politically vindicated.'[11] However, during the presidencies of Bill Clinton and George W. Bush, Brzezinski also called on US officials to improve their country's relations with Iran.[12] Significantly, in the 1990s, the hard-liners in the Iranian hostage crisis emerged as advocates of improving US-Iranian relations. In Iran, some leaders of the hostage-takers, such as Abbas Abdi and Ma'sumeh Ebtekar, emerged as key advisers to Iranian President Mohammad Khatami.[13] Abdi's metamorphosis was best exemplified by his decision to meet former hostage Barry Rosen and his being jailed in 2003 for allegedly fabricating an opinion poll indicating that the majority of Iranians favoured the normalization of relations with the US. Abdi's predicament amply demonstrated the kaleidoscopic nature of the Iranian polity. However, the hostage crisis continued to affect US relations with Iran. In July and August 2005 there were reports that Iran's new President Mahmud Ahmadinezhad had been one of the hostage-takers. The Iranian Foreign Ministry spokesman Hamid Reza Asefi described such reports as 'sheer lies, unfounded and baseless'.[14] Some of the hostage-takers denied the veracity of such reports.[15] However, the Bush administration took the reports seriously and began to conduct an investigation into the matter. It was even reported that the US would deny Ahmadinezhad a visa to prevent him from addressing the UN General Assembly. However, Ahmadinezhad was allowed to go to the UN.[16] Ahmadinezhad did address the UN, declaring that Iran had the right to pursue a nuclear programme.[17]

For the Bush administration Iran's nuclear programme was of paramount importance because US officials feared that the Iranian regime was trying to acquire a nuclear-weapons capability. By the summer of 2005 relations between the US and Iran had deteriorated to the point that former CIA official Philip Giraldi wrote that Vice-President Cheney's office had ordered the preparation of options for the use of tactical nuclear weapons against Iran in the event of another 9/11-style attack against the US.[18] The Carter administration must bear a heavy responsibility for the problems that beset US policy in the Islamic world after 1979. It is no exaggeration to say that the Carter administration's policy towards Iran was a major disaster for the US, the Middle East, and, indeed, the world.

NOTES

Chapter 1

1. Jimmy Carter, *Keeping Faith* (New York: Bantam Books, 1982), Zbigniew Brzezinski, *Power and Principle* (New York: Farrar, Strauss and Giroux, 1983), Cyrus Vance, *Hard Choices* (New York: Simon and Schuster, 1982), Gary Sick, *All Fall Down* (London, I.B. Tauris and Co Ltd, 1985), John Stempel, *Inside the Iranian Revolution* (Bloomington, Ind.:Indiana University Press, 1981), William Sullivan, *Mission to Iran* (New York, W.W. Norton, 1981)
2. See Brzezinski, *Power and Principle*.
3. See Michael Ledeen and William Lewis, *Debacle* (New York: Alfred A. Knopf, 1981), p. 142, Barry Rubin, *Paved with Good Intentions* (New York: Penguin Books, 1981)
4. See Ofira Seliktar, *Failing the Crystal Ball Test: The Carter Administration and the Fundamentalist Revolution in Iran* (Newport, CT, Praeger Publishers, 2000), p. xvi.
5. Ibid.
6. Nikki R. Keddie, *Iran and the Muslim World* (New York: New York University Press, 1995), p. 13.
7. See Martin Kramer, *Ivory Towers on Sand* (Washington D.C.: The Washington Institute for Near East Policy, 2001), p. 1.
8. See the chapter on the Iranian revolution for Cottam's report on his discussions with Khomeini's opponents.
9. See Richard Cottam's, *Iran and the United States* (Pittsburgh, University of Pittsburgh Press, 1988)
10. Seliktar, *Failing the Crystal Ball Test*, pp. 151–52.
11. Ibid.
12. James A. Bill, *The Eagle and the Lion* (New Haven and London, Yale University Press, 1988)
13. For the Iranian case see Joseph J. Trento, *Prelude to Terror* (New York: Carroll and Graf, 2005). For the Saudi case see Robert Baer, *Sleeping with the Devil* (New York: Crown Publishers, 2003). For the rest of the Middle East see Said Aburish, *A Brutal Friendship* (London: Victor Gollancz, 1997)
14. See chapter 2 and the chapters on the hostage crisis in this study.
15. See also Franz Schurmann: *The Foreign Politics of Richard Nixon* (Berkeley, California, Institute of International Studies, University of California, Berkeley, 1987), pp. 13–14.
16. See Walter Russell Mead, *Special Providence* (New York: Alfred A. Knopf, 2002), p. 39.
17. Ibid., p. 41.
18. John Lewis Gaddis, *Strategies of Containment: A Critical Appraisal of US National Security Policy* (New York, Oxford University Press, 1982).
19. See Seliktar, *Failing the Crystal Ball Test* and Richard E. Feinberg, *The Intemperate Zone: The Third World Challenge to U.S. Foreign Policy* (New York and London: W.W. Norton and Company, 1983).
20. Raymond Garthoff, *Détente and Confrontation: American-Soviet Relations from Nixon to Reagan*, revised edition, (Washington D.C.: Brookings Institution, 1994).
21. Seliktar, *Failing the Crystal Ball Test*, pp. 38–41.
22. Ibid, p. 125.
23. See for example, Ibid., pp. 146–160.
24. Richard Pipes, *Vixi: Memoirs of a Non-Belonger* (New Haven and London: Yale University Press, 2003), David Callahan, *Dangerous Capabilities: Paul Nitze and the Cold War* (New York: Harper Collins, 1990).

25 Richard C. Thornton, *The Carter Years* (New York: Paragon House, 1991), pp. 244–74.
26 Ibid., pp. 134–227.
27 Ibid., pp. 244–45.
28 Ibid., pp. xiii–xvi.
29 Ibid., pp. 8–9.
30 See Robert M. Gates, *From the Shadows* (New York: Simon and Schuster, 1996), p. 108.
31 Seliktar, Failing the Crystal Ball Test, p. 51.
32 See Steven L. Spiegel, *The Other Arab-Israeli Conflict* (Chicago, University of Chicago Press, paperback edition, 1986), p. 322.
33 See Brzezinski, *Power and Principle*, on Huntington's role and for Huntington's views see Samuel Huntington, *Political Order in Changing Societies* (New Haven and London: Yale University Press, 1968), p. 191.
34 Huntington, *Political Order in Changing Societies*, p. 179.
35 Seliktar, *Failing the Crystal Ball Test*, p. 55.
36 Ibid., pp. 49–50.
37 Ibid., p. 54.
38 Brzezinski, *Power and Principle*, p. 76.
39 Bill, *The Eagle and the Lion*, pp. 249–50.
40 Gates, *From the Shadows*, p. 72.
41 Sick, *All Fall Down*, pp. 119–20.
42 Ibid., pp. 303–304.
43 Ibid.
44 *Public Papers of the Presidents: Carter*, pp. 1–4, pp. 954–62.
45 Ibid., pp. 954–62.
46 Ibid., pp. 954–62, Carter, *Keeping Faith*, p. 143.
47 Anthony Lake and Roger Morris, 'The Human Reality of Realpolitik', *Foreign Policy* 4 (Fall 1971): 158.
48 Seliktar, *Failing the Crystal Ball Test*, pp. 37–57.
49 Ibid., p. 50.
50 See Mohammad Reza Pahlavi, *The Shah's Story* (London: Michael Joseph, 1980), p. 221, and Ibid., p. 54.
51 Ibid., p. 54, Ledeen and Lewis, *Debacle*, pp. 75, 145.
52 Jeane Kirkpatrick, 'Dictatorships and Double Standards', *Commentary*, November 1979, 34–45.
53 Rubin, *Paved with Good Intentions*, p. 176.
54 Samantha Power, *A Problem From Hell: America and the Age of Genocide* (London: Flamingo, an imprint of Harper Collins Publishers, 2003), p. 131.
55 Ibid., p. 147.
56 Maria Do Ceu Pinto, *Political Islam and the United States* (Durham, Ithaca Press, 1999), Fawaz A. Gerges, *America and Political Islam* (Cambridge, Cambridge University Press, 1999).

Chapter 2

1 See Babak Ganji, *From Regional Hegemony to Revolutionary Turmoil: An Examination of Policy Currents in US Relations with Iran* (Ph.D. Thesis, University of Newcastle-upon-Tyne, 2004).
2 Ibid.
3 Ibid.
4 See Bill, *The Eagle and the Lion* for a good discussion of the issue.
5 See Thornton, Richard C., *The Nixon-Kissinger Years: Reshaping America's Foreign Policy* (New York: Paragon House, revised paperback edition, 2001).
6 'Iran Reaches for Power: Implications fort U.S. Policy', Near Eastern Affairs, June 24 1974, in *Documents*, Vol 8, p. 108.
7 See Kissinger's account in Henry A. Kissinger, *Years of Renewal* (London: Weidenfeld and Nicolson, 1999), pp. 668–72.
8 See the chapter on the Kurdish conflict in Ibid.
9 Asadollah Alam, *The Shah and I: The Confidential Diary of Iran's Royal Court, 1969–1977*. Edited and translated by Alikhani, Alinaghi (London: I.B. Tauris, 1991), p. 437.
10 James A. Bill, *The Eagle and the Lion: The Tragedy of American-Iranian Relations* (New Haven Conn.: Yale University Press, 1988), p. 204 observes, 'When added to the unprecedented

NOTES 243

level of U.S. military sales to Iran, this highly publicized agreement seemed to weld the two countries in to one huge, commercial, binational conglomerate.' Bill does not discuss the policy conflicts in Washington, nor does he mention that the Shah decided to offer the agreement as a sop to his critics. Last but not least, he glosses over the fact that the agreement was not a success. As the record indicates, by 1977, the US was Iran's third largest trading partner.

11 See the Ernest Oney report in *Documents,* Vol 7 and Ganji, *From Regional Hegemony to Revolutionary Turmoil.*
12 Bill, *The Eagle and the Lion,* p. 417.
13 See the Ernest Oney report in *Documents,* Vol 7. On Oney's concern about the influence of religion in Iranian politics see Bill, *The Eagle and the Lion,* p. 417. For concerns about the Shah's independent policies see Ganji, *From Regional Hegemony to Revolutionary Turmoil.*
14 See Michael A. Palmer, *Guardians of the Gulf* (New York: Free Press, a division of Macmillan Inc, 1992), p. 91.
15 Zonis, *Majestic Failure,* p. 160.
16 The INR reports are 'Iranian Outlook,' Report no. 411, May 4, 1976, and 'The Future of Iran: Implications for the US,' Report no. 704, Jan 28, 1977, cited in Bill, *The Eagle and the Lion,* p. 423.
17 Zonis, *Majestic Failure,* p. 160.
18 See Robert Dreyfuss, *Devil's Game: How the United States Helped Unleash Fundamentalist Islam* (New York: Metropolitan Books, 2005), p. 232.
19 Ibid.
20 Ibid, pp. 232–33.
21 Bill, *The Eagle and the Lion,* p. 407.
22 Ibid., p. 408.
23 See From American Embassy, Tehran to Secretary of State, Washington, D.C. , July 10, 1975, Documents, Vol 7, p. 190.
24 See Asadollah Alam, *The Shah and I,* edited and translated by Alinaghi Alikhani, (London: I.B. Tauris, 1991).
25 See Stephen Gill, *American Hegemony and the Trilateral Commission* (Cambridge and New York: Cambridge University Press, paperback edition, 1991) and Holly Sklar (ed), *Trilateralism: Elite Planning for World Management* (Boston, Mass.: South End Press, 1980).
26 See Asadollah Alam, *The Shah and I,* pp. 441, 444, 448, 460.
27 See *The Washington Post,* 28 March 2005.
28 See Zdenek Cervenka and Barbara Rogers, *The Nuclear Axis* (Times Books, 1978).
29 Dreyfuss, *Devil's Game,* p. 231.
30 R.K. Ramazani, 'Iran's Foreign Policy: Contending Orientations', *Middle East Journal,* Vol 43, No. 2, Spring 1989, p. 203.
31 Ibid.
32 See Dreyfuss, *Devil's Game,* p. 233.
33 Mark Hulbert, *Interlock* (New York: Richardson and Snyder, 1982), pp. 99–100.
34 Ibid., p. 99.
35 Ibid., p. 100.
36 See Anoushiravan Ehteshami, *After Khomeini* (London and New York: Routledge, 1995), pp. 77–125.
37 Dankwart A., Rustow, *Oil and Turmoil* (New York: W.W. Norton, 1982), p. 157.
38 Hulbert, *Interlock,* p. 100.
39 Dankwart Rustow, 'U.S.-Saudi Relations and the Oil Crises of the 1980s', *Foreign Affairs,* p. 507.
40 Gold and Conant, *Access to Oil,* p. 61.
41 Ibid., p. 77.
42 Ibid., p. XI.
43 See Joseph Trento, *Prelude to Terror* (New York: Carroll and Graf, 2005), pp. 102–103.
44 Vance, *Hard Choices,* p. 315.
45 See Kai Bird, 'Co-Opting the Third Word Elites: Trilateralism and Saudi Arabia', in Sklar (ed), *Trilateralism,* p. 346.
46 *Documents, Vol 35,* p. 31.
47 Mordechai Abir, *Saudi Arabia in the Oil Era* (London: Croom Helm, 1988), p. 144.
48 See David E. Spiro, *The Hidden Hand of American Hegemony* (Ithaca and London, Cornell University Press, 1999)

49 Gold and Conant, *Access to Oil* p. XII.
50 Ibid., p. XII and pp. 60–61.
51 Charles Kupchan, *The Persian Gulf and the West* (London: Allen and Unwin, 1987), p. 59.
52 Marvin Zonis, *Majestic Failure: The Fall of the Shah* (Chicago and London: The University of Chicago Press, 1991), p. 231.
53 Amir Taheri, *The Unknown Life of the Shah* (London: Hutchinson, 1991), p. 238. Daniel Pipes, *The Hidden Hand: Middle East Fears of Conspiracy* (New York: St Martin's Griffin, paperback edition, 1998), p. 333.
54 R.K. Ramazani, *The United States and Iran* (Charlottesville: University of Virginia Press, 1980), pp. 92, 101, n. 40.
55 Seliktar, *Failing the Crystal Ball Test*, p. 64.
56 H.E. Chehabi, *Iranian Politics and Religious Modernism* (Ithaca: Cornell University Press, 1990), pp. 246–47.
57 Douglas Little, *American Orientalism* (London and New York, I.B. Tauris, 2002), p. 223.
58 Ibid., p. 223.
59 See Sohrab Sobhani, *The Pragmatic Entente: Israeli-Iranian Relations: 1948–1988* (New York: Praeger Publishers, 1989), p. 112.
60 See Vance, *Hard Choices*, p. 314.
61 Bill, *The Eagle and the Lion*, p. 423. Bill, however, ignores the change of policy and simply states that no change occurred.
62 Cottam, *Iran and the United States*, pp. 172–73, 284, n. 22.
63 Charles-Phillipe David, Nancy Ann Carrol and Zachary A. Selden, (henceforward referred to as David et al), *Foreign Policy Failure in the White House: Reappraising the Fall of the Shah and the Iran-Contra Affair* (Lanham, New York and London: University Press of America, 1993), pp. 61–62.
64 Seliktar, *Failing the Crystal Ball Test*, p. 55.
65 Brzezinski, *Power and Principle*, p. 177.
66 See David J. Rothkopf, *Running the World: The Inside Story of the National Security Council and the Architects of American Power* (New York: Public Affairs, 2005), p. 197.
67 Brzezinski, *Power and Principle*, p. 177.
68 Ibid.
69 See William J. Daugherty, *Executive Secrets: Covert Action and the Presidency*, foreword by Mark Bowden (Kentucky: The University Press of Kentucky, 2005), p. 186. Zbigniew Brzezinski has praised Daugherty's account, saying that readers 'may be surprised to learn' that President Carter made such a decision.
70 Henry Paolucci, *Iran, Israel and the United States* (New York: Griffon House Publications, 1991), pp. 133–67 for Sullivan's connections with Kissinger.
71 Ibid., 155.
72 See Dreyfuss, *Devil's Game*, p. 227.
73 See the argument in Brzezinski, *Power and Principle*
74 *Documents*, Vol 8, 1979, pp. 158–63.
75 Ibid., pp. 158–59.
76 Ibid., p. 158.
77 Ibid., pp. 159–160.
78 Ibid.
79 See Steven Emerson, *The American House of Saud*, (New York: Franklin Watts, 1985), p. 130 and Steven A. Schneider, *The Oil Price Revolution* (Baltimore: Johns Hopkins University Press, 1983), p. 400 on the rate of Saudi production.
80 John Loftus and Mark Aarons, *The Secret War against the Jews* (New York: St Martin's, 2000), pp. 335–36.
81 Thornton, *The Carter Years*, p. 422.
82 Ibid., p. 423.
83 Ibid., pp. 423–24.
84 Alam, *The Shah and I*, p. 535.
85 Ibid., p. 536.
86 Ibid., pp. 536–537.
87 Ibid., p. 537.
88 Sobhani, *The Pragmatic Entente*, p. 120.
89 Kimche, *The Last Option*, Ledeen and Lewis, *Debacle*.
90 See Nadav Safran, *Saudi Arabia: The Ceaseless Quest for Security* (Ithaca and London: Cornell University Press, paperback edition, 1988), p. 271.

91 Ibid., p. 271.
92 Gold and Conant, *Access to Oil*, p. 82.
93 Ibid., p. 84.
94 On this point see Gary Sick, *October Surprise* (London and New York: I.B. Tauris, 1991), p. 62.
95 Ibid.
96 Ibid., pp. 62–63.
97 Abir, *Saudi Arabia in the Oil Era*, pp. 142–43.
98 See Ibid., pp. 144, 162, n. 20, Schneider, *The Oil Price Revolution*, p. 400, 595 fn 295.
99 Ibid., p. 144.
100 Safran, *Saudi Arabia*, p. 429.
101 Ibid., p. 252.
102 Ian Seymour, *OPEC* (New York: St Martin's, 1981) p. 170.
103 Ibid.
104 Ibid.
105 Sullivan, *Mission to Iran*, p. 118.
106 Ibid.
107 Seliktar, *Failing the Crystal Ball Test*, p. 55.
108 David, et al, *Foreign Policy Failure in the White House*, pp. 65–66.
109 Seliktar, *Failing the Crystal Ball Test*, p. 55.
110 David, et al, *Foreign Policy Failure in the White House*, p. 62.
111 Parviz Radji, *In the Service of the Peacock Throne* (London: Hamish Hamilton, 1983), diary entry, July 6, 1977.
112 Vance, *Hard Choices*, p. 319.
113 Ibid., p. 318.
114 Raji, *In the Service of the Peacock Throne*, diary entry, July 6, 1977.
115 Bill, *The Eagle and the Lion*, p. 228. Bill, however, consistently tries to downplay the Carter administration role in encouraging the Shah's opponents.
116 Dreyfuss, *Devil's Game*, p. 227.
117 Seliktar, *Failing the Crystal Ball Test*, p. 56.
118 Sick, *All Fall Down*, p. 26.
119 Ramazani, *The United States and Iran*, p. 49.
120 Ibid.
121 Seliktar, *Failing the Crystal Ball Test*, p. 56.
122 Alam, *The Shah and I*, p. 542.
123 Carter, *Keeping Faith*, p. 435.
124 Sick, *All Fall Down*, p. 27.
125 Carter, *Keeping Faith*, p. 435.
126 For a good account see Seliktar, *Failing the Crystal Ball Test*, pp. 56–60.
127 Carter, *Keeping Faith*, p. 434.
128 Seliktar, *Failing the Crystal Ball Test*, pp. 64–65.
129 Carter, *Keeping Faith*, p. 435, Bill, *The Eagle and the Lion*, pp. 231–32.
130 Fereydoun Hoveyda, *The Fall of the Shah* (New York: Wyndham Books, 1979), p. 173.
131 SAVAK report in *Jostarhai'i Az Tarikh-e Moaser-e Iran* (Aspects of Contemporary Iranian History), p. 382, Taheri, *The Unknown Life of the Shah*, p. 238.
132 See Abbas Milani, *The Persian Sphinx: Amir Abbas Hoveyda and the Riddle of the Iranian Revolution*, (London: I.B. Tauris, 2000), p. 284.
133 Ramazani, *The United States and Iran*, pp. 93–94.
134 See Stempel, *Inside the Iranian Revolution*.
135 Jahangir Amuzegar, *The Dynamics of the Iranian Revolution* (New York: State University of New York Press, 1991), p. 227.
136 Pipes, *The Hidden Hand*, p. 244.
137 Ibid., pp. 75–86.
138 See for example, Bill, *The Eagle and the Lion*, p. 238, Stephen Walt, *Revolution and War*, (London: Cornell University Press, 1996), pp. 212–13, Said Amir-Arjomand, *The Turban for the Crown* (New York and Oxford: Oxford University Press, 1988) and Parviz Daneshvar, *Revolution in Iran* (London: Macmillan, 1996).
139 R.K. Ramazani, 'Iran's Revolution: Patterns, Problems and Prospects', *International Affairs*, No. 4, Autumn 1980, p. 446.
140 Mehran Kamrava, *Revolution in Iran* (London: Routledge, 1990), p. 86.
141 See Anthony Parsons, *The Pride and the Fall: Iran 1974–1979* (London, Jonathan Cape, 1984), p. 48, Zonis, *Majestic Failure*, p. 232–33.

142 See Ervand Abrahamian, *Iran Between Two Revolutions* (Princeton, NJ: Princeton University Press, 1982), p. 500, Chehabi, *Iranian Politics and Religious Modernism*, p. 227.
143 Chehabi, *Iranian Politics and Religious Modernism*, p. 228.
144 Ibid., pp. 228–29.
145 See, Abdolkarim Sanjabi, *Omidha Va Naomidiha* (Hopes and Hoplessness) (London, 1989).
146 See Gasiorowski, *US Foreign Policy and the Shah*, p. 214.
147 Chehabi, *Iranian Politics and Religious Modernism*, pp. 228–29.
148 Taheri, *The Unknown Life of the Shah*, p. 243.
149 Sick, *All Fall Down*, pp. 23–24.
150 Ramazani, *The United States and Iran*, pp. 92–93, 95, 101, n. 47.
151 Sullivan, *Mission to Iran*, p. 120.
152 Yergin, *The Prize*, p. 645.
153 Sullivan, *Mission to Iran*, p. 120.
154 Rubin, *Paved With Good Intentions*, p. 200.
155 Ibid., pp. 200–201.
156 Ibid., p. 258.
157 Ibid., p. 201.
158 Vance, *Hard Choices*, p. 322.
159 Ibid.
160 Ibid., pp. 321–22.
161 Ibid., p. 322.
162 Ibid., p. 322.
163 Rubin, *Paved with Good Intentions*, p. 200.
164 Seth Tillman, *The United States in the Middle East* (Bloomington: Indiana University Press, 1982), pp. 96–97.
165 See Little, *American Orientalism*, p. 223–24.
166 Sick, *All Fall Down*, p. 30.
167 Ibid., pp. 30–31.
168 David Kimche, *After Nasser, Arafat and Saddam Hussein, the Last Option: The Quest for Peace in the Middle East* (London: Weidenfeld and Nicolson, 1991), p. 198.
169 Ibid.
170 Sick, *All Fall Down*, p. 30.
171 Vance, *Hard Choices*, p. 323.
172 Menashri, *Iran: A Decade of War and Revolution*, p. 47.
173 Vance, *Hard Choices*, p. 323.
174 *Documents*, Vol 7(2), p. 205.
175 Ibid., pp. 204, 207–209.
176 Ibid., pp. 204–205.

Chapter 3

1   See Ervand Abrahamian, *Iran Between Two Revolutions* (Princeton, New Jersey, Princeton University Press, 1982), Shaul Bakhash, *The Reign of the Ayatollahs* (London: I.B. Tauris and Co Ltd, 1985), Vanessa Martin, *Creating an Islamic State* (London, I.B. Tauris, 2000), Baqer Mo'in, *Khomeini* (London: I.B. Tauris, 1999).
2   See John O Voll's foreword to Richard P. Mitchell, *The Society of the Muslim Brothers* (New York and Oxford, Oxford University Press, reprinted in 1993).
3   Daniel Pipes, *Militant Islam Reaches America* (New York and London, W.W. Norton and Company, 2002), p. 57.
4   Gilles Kepel, *The Prophet and the Pharaoh*, (Berkeley and Los Angeles, University of California Press, paperback edition, 1993).
5   On Khomeini's life see Moin, *Khomeini*. On his association with Kashani see Dreyfuss, *Devil's Game*, pp. 102–103, 110–19.
6   Ibid., p. 104.
7   Gasiorowski, *U.S. Foreign Policy and the Shah*.
8   Ibid., p. 180.
9   Ibid., pp. 169–170.
10 Ali Rahnema and Farhad Nomani, *The Secular Miracle* (London and New Jersey: Zed Books Ltd, 1990), p. 98.

11 See H.E. Chehabi, *Iranian Politics and Religious Modernism*.
12 Sick, *All Fall Down*, p. 199.
13 Esmail Shakeri, Ph.D. thesis, *Oil Nationalisation and the Hostage Crisis* (University of Toronto, 1992), p. 219.
14 Ibid.
15 Ali Rahnema and Farhad Nomani, *The Secular Miracle* (London: Zed Books, 1990), p. 100. On Bazargan's ties with Taleghani see also Joseph Alpher, 'The Khomeini International', *Washington Quarterly*, Vol. 61, Fall 1980, p. 65, and Shakeri, *Oil Nationalization and the Hostage Crisis*, p. 219.
16 See Ervand Abrahamian, *Radical Islam: The Iranian Mojahedin* (London: I.B. Tauris and Co Ltd, 1989).
17 See John Esposito, *The Islamic Threat: Myth or Reality?* (Oxford and New York: Oxford University Press, 1992), p. 108, Ali Rahnema, *An Islamic Utopian: A Political Biography of Ali Shari'ati* (London, I.B. Tauris and Co Ltd, 1998)
18 Esposito, *The Islamic Threat: Myth or Reality*, p. 107, Ian Buruma and Avishai Margalit, *Occidentalism* (New York: The Penguin Press, 2004), pp. 110–11.
19 See Hamid Algar, *The Islamic Revolution in Iran* (London: Open Press, 1980), p. 47, Rahnema and Nomani, *The Secular Miracle*, pp. 51–73, and Esposito, *The Islamic Threat: Myth or Reality?*, p. 106.
20 Rahnema and Nomani, *The Secular Miracle*, p. 67.
21 See Ervand Abrahamian, *Iran Between Two Revolutions* (Princeton, New Jersey, Princeton University Press, 1982), see also Gasiorowski, *US Foreign Policy and the Shah*, p. 191.
22 Abrahamian, *Radical Islam*, pp. 105–25, Rahnema, *An Islamic Utopian*, Sick, *All Fall Down*, p. 199.
23 Gasiorowski, *US Foreign Policy and the Shah*, pp. 194–95.
24 Ibid., p. 195.
25 Abrahamian, *Radical Islam*, pp. 145–69.
26 Gasiorowski, *US Foreign Policy and the Shah*, p. 196.
27 Ibid., p. 214.
28 Bill, *The Eagle and the Lion*, p. 266.
29 Ebrahim Yazdi, *Akharin Talashha Dar Akharin Ruzha* (Final efforts in the final days) (Tehran, Qalam Publications, 1984), pp. 12–14.
30 Abrahamian, *Iran Between Two Revolutions*, p. 479.
31 Daniel Brumberg, *Reinventing Khomeini* (Chicago, University of Chicago Press, 2001), pp. 75–79, see also Abrahamian, *Iran Between Two Revolutions*, p. 479.
32 David Menashri, *Revolution at a Crossroads* (The Washington Institute for Near East Policy, Washington D.C., 1997), p. 1.
33 Ibid., p. xiii.
34 Moin, *Khomeini*, chapters 1–7 and Vanessa Martin, *Creating an Islamic State*, chapters 1–5.
35 Amir Asadollah Alam, *Yaddashtha-ye Alam* (Alam's diaries), Vol. 1, (Tehran: Ketabsara, 1372 [1992–1993]), pp. 46–48.
36 See Moin, *Khomeini*, p. 69.
37 See also chapter 6.
38 See Moin, *Khomeini*, pp. 74–117.
39 See Vanessa Martin, *Creating an Islamic State*, pp. 69–70.
40 Moin, *Khomeini*.
41 Ibid., p. 161.
42 Ibid.
43 Ibid.
44 Ibid.
45 Rahnema and Nomani, *The Secular Miracle*, pp. 19–127.
46 Ibid., p. 169.
47 See Brumberg, *Reinventing Khomeini*, pp. 75–78, and Roy, *The Failure of Political Islam*, pp. 3–5, for good discussions of these issues.
48 Daniel Pipes, 'The Western mind of radical Islam', *First Things*, December 1995.
49 Brumberg, *Reinventing Khomeini*, pp. 80–97, Martin, *Creating an Islamic State*, pp. 112, 128.
50 Rahnema and Nomani, *The Secular Miracle*, pp. 167–70.
51 Stephen Walt, *Revolution and War* (London: Cornell University Press, 1996), p. 214.
52 Sick, *All Fall Down*, p. 198, Ervand Abrahamian, *Khomeinism* (London: I.B. Tauris, 1993).
53 See Rahnema and Nomani, *The Secular Miracle*, p. 169.

54 Ibid., p. 167, see also Brumberg, *Reinventing Khomeini*, pp. 76–78.
55 Pipes, *The Hidden Hand*, p. 143.
56 Hamid Algar, translator and editor, *Islam and Revolution: Writings and Declarations of Imam Khomeini* (Berkeley, California, 1981), p. 127.
57 Pipes, *The Hidden Hand*, p. 175.
58 See Gasiorowski, *US Foreign Policy and the Shah*, p. 214.
59 Stempel, *Inside the Iranian Revolution*, p. 44.
60 Bill, *The Eagle and the Lion*, p. 238.
61 Ibid., p. 238.
62 Amir Taheri, *The Spirit of Allah: Khomeini and the Islamic Revolution* (London: Hutchinson, 1985), p. 192.
63 Moin, *Khomeini*, pp. 178–79.
64 Ibid., p. 180.
65 Ibid., 180–81.
66 Ibid., p. 181.
67 Taheri, *The Spirit of Allah*, p. 192.
68 Ibid., pp. 193–94.
69 David Menashri, *Iran* (New York: Holmes and Meier, 1990), pp. 72–73.
70 See for example Bill, *The Eagle and the Lion*, p. 238.
71 Jahangir Amuzegar, *The Dynamics of the Iranian Revolution*, (New York: State University of New York Press, 1991), p. 167.
72 Ibid.
73 See Moin, *Khomeini*, p. 151.
74 Stempel, *Inside the Iranian Revolution*, pp. 27, 44. Stempel argues, unconvincingly, that SAVAK did not know much about the religious opposition.
75 Taheri, *The Unknown Life of the Shah*, p. 237. Taheri does not mention the policy differences within SAVAK.
76 See 'Reply to Enes Kasic' in Lewis Edwin Hahn, Randall E. Auxier, and Lucian W. Stone, Jr (eds), *The Philosophy of Seyyed Hossein Nasr* (Chicago and La Salle, Illinois,: Open Court, 2001), p. 793.
77 See Mark Sedgwick, *Against the Modern World* (New York: Oxford University Press, 2004), 157–58.
78 See Seyyed Hossein Nasr, 'An Intellectual Biography' in Hahn et al, *The Philosophy of Seyyed Hossein Nasr*, p. 72.
79 American Embassy Memo, October 22 1978, *Documents*, Vol 25, p. 80
80 Roy, *The Failure of Political Islam*, p. 187. However, Roy mistakenly observes that the Shah 'repressed the Shiite clergy within the country but supported their expansion abroad'.
81 Rahnema, *An Islamic Utopian*, p. 312.
82 Ibid.
83 Ibid., pp. 312–314.
84 Tolu'i, *Bazigaran-e Asr-e Pahlavi*, Vol 2.
85 See Milani, *The Persian Sphinx*, p. 199, Mostafa Alamuti, *Iran Dar Asr-e Pahlavi* (Iran in the Pahlavi era), Vol 12, (London, 1992), pp. 117–18.
86 Michael Rubin, *Into the Shadows: Radical Vigilantes in Khatami's Iran* (Washington: Washington Institute for Near East Policy, 2001), pp. 13–14.
87 Nikola B. Schahgaldian, *The Clerical Establishment in Iran*, (Santa Monica, Rand Corporation, 1989), pp. 62–63, fn. 80. Schahgaldian is less sure about Borujerdi's support for Hojjatieh.
88 Mir Ali Asghar Montazam, *The Life and Times of Ayatollah Khomeini* (London: Anglo-European Publishing Limited, 1994), pp. 257–58.
89 Taheri, *The Spirit of Allah*, p. 192, see also Schahgaldian, *The Clerical Establishment in Iran*, p. 62, fn. 73. According to Schahgaldian this was Hojjatieh's claim.
90 Roy, *The Failure of Political Islam*, pp. 173–74.
91 See Martin, *Creating an Islamic State*, pp. 64–74, Moin, *Khomeini*, pp. 178–81.
92 Moin, *Khomeini*, 179, Taheri, *The Spirit of Allah*, p. 192.
93 Schahgaldian, *The Clerical Establishment in Iran*, pp. 62–63.
94 Stempel, *Inside the Iranian Revolution*, p. 86.
95 Schahgaldian, *The Clerical Establishment in Iran*, p. 62.
96 Abrahamian, *Iran Between Two Revolutions*, pp. 442–46.
97 Akbar Hashemi-Rafsanjani, *Dowran-e Mobarezeh* (years of struggle), Vol 2, compiled and edited by Mohsen Hashemi, (Tehran, 1997), for SAVAK documents on Khomeini's activities.

98 Abrahamian, *Iran Between Two Revolutions*, p. 445.
99 Rahnema and Nomani, *The Secular Miracle*, pp. 100, 125, n. 185.
100 See Akbar Hashemi-Rafsanjani, *Dowran-e Mobarezeh* (years of struggle), Vol 1, compiled and edited by Mohsen Hashemi (Tehran, 1997).
101 Schahgaldian, *The Clerical Establishment in Iran*, pp. 63, 72–73, and Menashri, *Iran*.
102 Schahgaldian, *The Clerical Establishment in Iran*, p. 72.
103 Sick, *All Fall Down*, p. 199.
104 Rahnema, *An Islamic Utopian*, Rahnema and Nomani, *The Secular Miracle*, Abrahamian, *Radical Islam*.
105 Abrahamian, *Khomeinism*, see also Brumberg, *Reinventing Khomeini*, pp. 75–79.
106 Olivier Roy, in *Failure of Political Islam*, also refers to the influence of 'secular Islamists' in Iran. The term Secular-Islamist is meaningless.
107 Trento, *Prelude to Terror*, p. 186.
108 See Dreyfuss, *Devil's Game*, 72–79, 137–38.
109 Trento, *Prelude to Terror*, pp. 186–187.
110 Ibid.
111 Dreyfuss, *Devil's Game*, pp. 131–32. 136–46.
112 See Graham Fuller and Rend Rahim Francke, *The Arab Shi'a: The Forgotten Muslims* (New York: Palgrave/ St Martin's Press, 1999), pp. 47-48. See also Dreyfuss, *Devil's Game*, pp. 176–77.
113 See Trento, *Prelude to Terror*, p. 186.
114 Joseph Alpher, 'The Khomeini International', *Washington Quarterly*, Vol 61, Fall 1980, p. 59.
115 Moshe Maoz, *Syria and Israel* (Oxford: Clarendon Press, 1995), p. 187.
116 Ledeen and Lewis, *Debacle*, p. 110.
117 Ibid., pp. 109–110.
118 For a detailed account see Colonel Isa Pejman, *Asar-e Angosht-e SAVAK* (SAVAK's fingerprint), Vol 2 (Paris: Nima, 1995).
119 Ledeen and Lewis, *Debacle*, p. 110, Daniel Pipes, 'The Alawi capture of power in Syria', *Middle Eastern Studies*, 25 (1989).
120 Ledeen and Lewis, *Debacle*, p. 110, Alpher, 'The Khomeini International', p. 59.
121 Alpher, 'The Khomeini International', p. 59, does not consider Asad's regional strategy.
122 Daniel Pipes, 'Syria after Asad', and Eyal Zisser, 'Hafiz al-Asad discovers Islam'.
123 *London Keyhan*, 7 August, 1997, p. 4.
124 Stempel, *Inside the Iranian Revolution*, p. 53.
125 On unrest in Iraq see Ofra Bengio, 'Shi'is and Politics in Ba'thi Iraq', *Middle Eastern Studies*, No. 1, January 1985, p. 3–4.

Chapter 4

1 Thornton, *The Carter Years*, p. 194. Thornton, however, says nothing about the Iran-Iraq-Saudi Arabia talks, arguably, the most important component of the administration's regional strategy in terms of US-Soviet relations.
2 Ibid., pp. 134–71.
3 David Yallop, *To the Ends of the Earth: The Hunt for the Jackal* (London: Corgi Books, 1994), pp. 536–37. See also Christopher Andrew and Oleg Gordievsky, *KGB: The Inside Story* (London Hodder and Stoughton, 1991) p. 547. They say that KGB officials talked of assassinating Sadat. See Thornton, *The Carter Years* on South Yemen and the Horn of Africa.
4 Menashri, *Iran*, p. 47.
5 Ibid., pp. 46–47.
6 Nadav Safran, *Saudi Arabia: The Ceaseless Quest for Security* (Ithaca and London: Cornell University Press, paperback edition, 1988), pp. 272–73.
7 Ibid., p. 273, Oles M. and Bettie M. Smolansky, *The USSR and Iraq* (Durham and London, Duke University Press, 1991), p. 202.
8 Ibid.
9 See Christopher Andrew and Vasili Mitrokhin, *The Mitrokhin Archive II* (London: Penguin, Allen Lane, 2005), pp. 179–80.
10 Ibid., p. 178.
11 Ibid., pp. 178–79.
12 Ibid., pp. 178–79.

27 Ledeen and Lewis, *Debacle*, p. 209.
28 See Robert Dreyfuss, *Devil's Game*, p. 240.
29 Ibid, pp. 250–52.
30 Ibid, p. 253.
31 Draft, Metrinko: April 24, 1979, in *Documents*, Vol 14, p. 107, see also Sick, *All Fall Down*, p. 34.
32 See Trento, *Prelude to Terror*, pp. 190–91.
33 Taheri, *Nest of Spies*, p. 113.
34 Ibid., p. 115.
35 Yazdi, *Akharin Talashha Dar Akharin Ruzha*, pp. 10–11, 197–98.
36 Hulbert, *Interlock*, pp. 105–112.
37 Paolucci, *Iran, Israel, and the United States*, p. 268. Paolucci was not even aware of the nationalization of the Consortium.
38 Ibid., p. 270.
39 Ioannides, *America's Iran: Injury and Catharsis* (Lanham, Md.: University Press of America, 1984), p. 83.
40 Paolucci, *Iran, Israel, and the United States*, p. 270.
41 Brzezinski, *Power and Principle*, p. 473.
42 Carter, *Keeping Faith*, p. 452.
43 Ibid.
44 Sick, *All Fall Down*, 180.
45 Hamilton Jordan, *Crisis* (New York: G.P. Putnam's Sons, 1982), p. 29.
46 See for example, Seliktar, *Failing the Crystal Ball Test*, p. 138.
47 See John K. Cooley, *Pay Back: America's Long War in the Middle East*, (Washington D.C. Brassey's, 1991), p. 23.
48 Ibid.
49 Ibid., p. 24.
50 Paolucci, *Iran, Israel, and the United States*, p. 235.
51 Ibid., p. 234.
52 Cooley, *Pay Back*, p. 23.
53 Ioannides, *America's Iran*, pp. 106–107.
54 See Ibid., pp. 70–72–73, 111, Seliktar, *Failing the Crystal Ball Test*, p. 157.
55 From American Embassy Tehran, to Secretary of State, Washington D.C., June 14, 1979, in *Documents*, Vol 15, p. 86.
56 Ibid., pp. 132–33.
57 Cottam, *Iran and the United States*
58 Ibid., p. 143.
59 From Am Embassy, Tehran to Secretary of State, Washington D.C., June 14, 1979, *Documents*, Vol 15, p. 91.
60 Reporting cable by John Stempel, May 31, 1979, in *Documents*, Vol 15, p. 60.
61 Ibid.
62 Ibid., p. 65.
63 From American Embassy, Tehran to Secretary of State, Washington D.C., June 7, 1979, in *Documents*, Vol 15, p. 81.
64 Ibid., pp. 83–84.
65 *Documents*, Vol 34, pp. 89–90.
66 Ibid.
67 From Am Embassy Tehran, to Secretary of State, Washington D.C., June 8, 1979, *Documents*, Vol 34, pp. 91–92.
68 *Documents*, Vol 34, p. 94.
69 Stempel, *Inside the Iranian Revolution*, p. 207.
70 Seliktar, *Failing the Crystal Ball Test*, p. 128.
71 For a good account see Ibid., p. 135.
72 Ibid.
73 Ibid., p. 135 and 139–40 for a succinct account of the debate about economic policy in Iran.
74 Ibid., p. 139.
75 See for example Sick, *All Fall Down*, Amir Arjomand, *Turban for the Crown*.
76 See Seliktar, *Failing the Crystal Ball Test*, pp. 138, 141–42.
77 Nikola B. Schahgaldian, with the assistance of Gina Barkhordarian, *The Iranian Military Under the Islamic Republic* (Santa Monica: Rand Corporation, 1987), p. 66.

1988), p. 179, Thornton, *The Carter Years*, p. 189, Peter W. Rodman, *More Precious Than Peace*, (New York: Charles Scribner's Sons, 1994) p. 202.
61 Ghaus, *The Fall of Afghanistan*, p. 150.
62 Ibid., p. 151.
63 Sick, *All Fall Down*, p. 36.
64 Brzezinski, *Power and Principle*, p. 356.
65 Seliktar, *Politics, Paradigms and Intelligence Failures*, p. 77.
66 Ibid., p. 97.
67 Sick, *All Fall Down*, 36.
68 Thomas T. Hammond, *Red Flag Over Afghanistan* (Bowker, 1984), pp. 62–63.
69 See the evidence cited by Seliktar, *Failing the Crystal Ball Test*, p. 110.
70 Sick, *All Fall Down*, p. 36.
71 Vance, *Hard Choices*, p. 386.
72 See From American Embassy, Tehran to Secretary of State, Washington D.C., September 25, 1978, in *Documents*, Vol 29, pp. 68–69.
73 John K. Cooley, *Unholy Wars* (London: Pluto Press, third edition, 2002), p. 54. Cooley does not mention Nasiri's name.
74 Ibid., p. 54.
75 Thornton, *The Carter Years*, p. 193, Brzezinski, *Power and Principle*, p. 320, says the meeting occurred on 2 June.
76 Thornton, *The Carter Years*, p. 193.
77 Ibid., pp. 194–96 for a good analysis of Vance's moves.
78 Haim Shemesh, *Soviet Iraqi Relations, 1968–1988: In the Shadow of the Iran-Iraq Conflict* (London: Lynne Rienner, 1992), pp. 164–65.
79 Roger Hilsman, *George Bush vs Saddam Hussein: Military Success! Political Failure?* (Lyford Books, 1992), p. 15.
80 Shemesh, *Soviet-Iraqi Relations*, pp. 166–67, Andrew and Mitrokhin, *The Mitrokhin Archive II*, p. 177.
81 Smolansky and Smolansky, *The USSR and Iraq*, p. 202.
82 Safran, *Saudi Arabia*, p. 273.
83 Ibid.
84 Ibid., pp. 273–74.
85 Ibid., p. 274, mistakenly says 11 November 1979.
86 Amir Taheri, *The Unknown Life of the Shah* (London: Hutchinson, 1991), p. 268. Taheri does not mention the Bakr angle.

Chapter 5

1 Stempel, *Inside the Iranian Revolution*, p. 86. Stempel observes that their goal was to overthrow the regime. However, this is debatable.
2 Mansur Rafizadeh, *Witness* (New York: William Morrow, 1987), p. 248.
3 Taheri, *The Unknown Life of the Shah*, p. 242.
4 Alamuti, *Iran dar Asr-e Pahlavi* (Iran in the Pahlavi era, Vol 10, pp. 304–310.
5 Mahmoud Toloui, *Bazigaran-e Asr-e Pahlavi* (The King-Pins of the Pahlavi Era), Vol 2, (Tehran, Elm Publications, 1994).
6 Milani, *The Persian Sphinx*, pp. 222, 266.
7 Zonis, *Majestic Failure*, pp. 109, 302, n. 78.
8 Rafizadeh, *Witness*, pp. 250–51.
9 Toloui, *Bazigaran-e Asr-e Pahlavi*, Vol II.
10 Stempel, *Inside the Iranian Revolution*, pp. 36–37.
11 Ibid.
12 Joshua Muravchik, *The Uncertain Crusade* (Washington D.C.: American Enterprise Institute for Public Policy Research, 1988), p. 211.
13 Taheri, *The Spirit of Allah*, p. 214.
14 Ibid., pp. 172–73.
15 Ibid., p. 173.
16 Historical Documents Center, Ministry of Information, *The Islamic Revolution According to SAVAK Documents* (Tehran: Soroush Press, 1997), Vol 1, pp. 405–407.
17 Milani, *The Persian Sphinx*, p. 286.

18   Taheri, *The Spirit of Allah*, pp. 204, 207–209.
19   Ibid., p. 202. See also Toloui, *Bazigaran-e Asr-e Pahlavi*, Vol 1, p. 547.
20   Zonis, *Majestic Failure*, p. 91.
21   Milani, *The Persian Sphinx*, pp. 286–87.
22   Toloui, *Bazigaran-e Asr-e Pahlavi*, Vol 1, p. 547.
23   Alamuti, *Iran dar Asr-e Pahlavi (Iran in the Pahlavi Era)*,Vol 13, pp. 13–14.
24   Ibid., pp. 40–53, Taheri, *The Spirit of Allah*, pp. 202–203.
25   Taheri, *The Spirit of Allah*, p. 203.
26   Ibid.
27   Toloui, *Bazigaran-e Asr-e Pahlavi*, Vol 2.
28   Taheri, *The Spirit of Allah*, p. 204.
29   Taheri, *The Unknown Life of the Shah*, p. 250.
30   See SAVAK documents in *Farazhaii Az Tarikh-e Enghelab Be Ravayat-e Asnad-e SAVAK VA Amrika* (Turning-points in Iranian history according to SAVAK and American documents) (Tehran, 1996), p. 23.
31   Taheri, *The Spirit of Allah*, p. 204.
32   Taheri, *The Unknown Life of the Shah*, pp. 250–51.
33   Alamuti, *Iran Dar Asr-e Pahlavi*, Vol 10, pp. 296–97.
34   David Menashri, *Iran*, p. 34.
35   Chehabi, *Iranian Politics and Religious Modernism*, p. 232.
36   'Iran in 1977–78: The Internal Scene,' June 1, 1978, *Documents*, Vol 12, *no.2*, p. 121.
37   Milani, *The Persian Sphinx*, p. 291.
38   Ibid.
39   Alamuti, *Iran Dar Asr-e Pahlavi*, Vol 10, pp. 296–97. Alamuti says Sabeti wanted to arrest 3,500 people.
40   See Milani, *The Persian Sphinx*, pp. 222–23.
41   Taheri, *The Spirit of Allah*, pp. 200–201. Taheri does not mention the dispute over strategy.
42   Amuzegar, *The Dynamics of the Iranian Revolution*, pp. 248–49.
43   See Taheri, *The Spirit of Allah*, pp. 174, 194–95, 199–200 and Seliktar, *Failing the Crystal Ball Test*, p. 75.
44   Taheri, *The Spirit of Allah*, pp. 198–99, Seliktar, *Failing the Crystal Ball Test*, p. 79.
45   Toloui, *Bazigaran-e Asr-e Pahlavi*, Vol 2.
46   Zonis, *Majestic Failure*, p. 90. Zonis unconvincingly says, 'The magnitude of its [SAVAK's] failures was so great as to be inexplicable.'
47   See Walter Laqueur, *A World of Secrets* (New York: Basic Books, 1985), p. 97.
48   On the Church Committee see John Ranelagh, *The Agency: The Rise and Decline of the CIA* (London: Sceptre, 1988), pp. 592–622, Christopher Andrew, *For President's Eyes Only* (London: Harper Collins, paperback edition, 1996), pp. 414–22, and Seliktar, *Failing the Crystal Ball Test*, p. 52.
49   Seliktar, *Failing the Crystal Ball Test*, p. 52.
50   Ibid.
51   Ibid., pp. 46–47, 52, 68.
52   Ibid., p. 68.
53   William Blum, *The CIA: A Forgotten History* (London: Zed Books Ltd, 1986), p. 76.
54   See Trento, *Prelude to Terror*, p. 196.
55   Ibid., p. 187.
56   Sepehr Zabih, *Iran Since the Revolution* (London: Croom Helm, 1982), p. 9.
57   Stempel, *Inside the Iranian Revolution*, p. 288.
58   From American Embassy, Tehran to Secretary of State, Washington D.C., July 25, 1977, *Documents*, Vol 8, p. 179.
59   *Documents*, Vol 8, p. 179.
60   *Documents*, Vol 8, p. 181.
61   Stempel, *Inside the Iranian Revolution*, p. 86.
62   *Documents*, Vol. 12, part 2.
63   From Am Embassy, Tehran to The Department of State, Washington D.C., 11 January 1978, Documents, Vol 7(2), second series, pp. 204, 205, 207–209.
64   Zachary Karabell, "'Inside the US Espionage Den': The US Embassy and the Fall of the Shah." *Intelligence and National Security* 8, no. 1 (Jan. 1993): 44–59.
65   Sullivan, *Mission to Iran*, chapter 8, and pp. 100–102.
66   *Documents*, Vol. 2 part 1, see also, Karabel, 'Inside the US Espionage Den', p. 53.
67   Karabel, 'Inside the US Espionage Den', p.50.

68 Charles-Phillipe David, Nancy Ann Carrol and Zachary A. Selden, (henceforward referred to as David et al), *Foreign Policy Failure in the White House: Reappraising the Fall of the Shah and the Iran-Contra Affair* (Lanham, New York and London: University Press of America, 1993), p. 62.
69 Ibid., p. 89.
70 Amuzegar, *The Dynamics of the Iranian Revolution*, p. 250.
71 Confidential airgram Tabriz A-04, February 21, 1978, *Documents*, Vol 61.
72 David, et al, *Foreign Policy Failure in the White House*, p. 89, unconvincingly attempts to explain Vance's behaviour in terms of psychological factors.
73 Sick, *All Fall Down*, p. 35.
74 David et al, *Foreign Policy Failure in the White House*, p. 62.
75 Bill, *The Eagle and the Lion*, p. 245, see also Rubin, *Paved with Good Intentions*, p. 208.
76 Sick, *All Fall Down*, p. 36.
77 Confidential Tehran cable, April 25, 1978 in *Documents*, Vol 12, part 2.
78 Memorandum of Conversation, May 8, 1978, *Documents*, Vol 24, pp. 3–5.
79 See Memorandum of Conversation, Tehran, May 25, 1978, *Documents*, Vol 24, p. 7.
80 Ibid., pp. 6–8.
81 Memorandum of Conversation, *Documents*, Vol 24, p. 19.
82 Ibid.
83 From Charles Naas, Minister-Counsellor to Henry Precht, NEA/IRN, Department of State, Washington D.C., *Documents*, Vol 24, pp. 14–15.
84 Ashraf Pahlavi, *Faces in a Mirror* (Englewood Cliffs, N.J.: Prentice Hall, 1980).
85 See Stephen Dorril, *MI6: Fifty Years of Special Operations* (London: Fourth Estate, 2000), p. 654. See also For a detailed account of SAVAK and the Special Intelligence Bureau see Colonel Isa Pejman, *Asar-e Angosht-e SAVAK* (SAVAK's fingerprint), Volumes 1 and 2 (Paris: Nima, 1995). For Fardust's account which has been written under duress while he was in the custody of the Khomeini regime see: Hossein Fardust, *Khaterat-e Arteshbod-e Sabegh Hossein Fardust* (Memoirs of former Major-General Hossein Fardust) (Tehran: Ettela'at Publications, 1990).
86 Taheri, *The Spirit of Allah*, p. 200. Taheri does not present a shred of evidence in support of this conclusion.
87 See Fardust, *Khaterat*.
88 Cottam, *Iran and the United States*, p. 185.
89 See Rafizadeh, *Witness*, pp. 253–56.
90 Rubin, *Paved with Good Intentions*, p. 207.
91 Gholamreza Nejati, *Tarikh-e Siasi-ye Bisto Panj Sale-ye Iran* (Twenty-five years of Iranian political history), Vol 2 (Tehran: Rasa Publications, 1995), p. 75.
92 *Farazhaii Az Tarikh-e Enghelab*, p. 63.
93 See *Documents*, Vol 23, pp. 32–36 and Seliktar, *Failing the Crystal Ball Test*, p. 85.
94 Memorandum of Conversation between Eslaminia, George Lambrakis, and John Stempel, May 15, 1978, *Documents*, Vol 25, pp. 27–28, also May 23, 1978, See also Stempel, *Inside the Iranian Revolution*, p. 100. Stempel implies that the US embassy had been privy to these debates.
95 *Documents*, Vol 25, pp. 27–28.
96 Ibid.
97 Ibid., p. 29.
98 Rubin, *Paved with Good Intentions*.
99 Miles Copeland, *The Game Player* (London: Aurum Press, 1989), p. 249.
100 Ibid.
101 See the account by Ehsan Naraghi, *From Palace to Prison: Inside the Iranian Revolution*, translated by Nilou Mobasser (London: I.B. Tauris, 1994).
102 Copeland, *The Game Player*, 250.
103 Ibid., p. 251.
104 Ibid., 250.
105 Ibid., 251–52.
106 Ibid., p. 251.
107 Ibid., p. 254.
108 Sick, *All Fall Down*, pp. 36–37.
109 Brzezinski, *Power and Principle*, p. 355.
110 See the account by Robert Sherrill, *The Oil Follies of 1970–1980* (New York: Anchor Press, 1983).

111 Mohammad Reza Pahlavi, *Answer to History* (New York: Stein and Day, 1980), p. 22.
112 See for example, Pipes, *Hidden Hand*, p. 190.
113 See Staff Report, Subcommittee on Evaluation, Permanent Select Committee on Intelligence, U.S. House of Representatives, *Iran: Evaluation of U.S. Intelligence Performance Prior to November 1978*, U.S. Government Printing Office, Washington: 1979, p. 4fn.
114 Confidential Tehran Cable, May 21 1978, *Documents*, Vol 12, part 2.
115 Michael Donovan, 'National Intelligence and the Iranian Revolution', Intelligence and National Security, 12, no. 1 (Jan 1997), p. 145 and p. 161, n.8 for further references.
116 US Congress, *Evaluation of US Intelligence Performance*, p. 4.
117 See Stempel, *Inside the Iranian Revolution*, p. 55.
118 Seliktar, *Failing the Crystal Ball Test*, p. 83.
119 Sick, *All Fall Down*, p. 37.
120 Ledeen and Lewis, *Debacle*, p. 126, Seliktar, *Failing the Crystal Ball Test*, pp. 83–84.
121 Sick, *All Fall Down*, p. 37, Ledeen and Lewis, *Debacle*, p. 126.
122 Seliktar, *Failing the Crystal Ball Test*, p. 84.
123 Trento, *Prelude to Terror*, pp. 110–11.
124 Sick, *All Fall Down*, p. 37.
125 Ibid., pp. 37–41.
126 Vance, *Hard Choices*, p. 324, Seliktar, *Failing the Crystal Ball Test*, p. 83.

Chapter 6

1   On this point see William Engdahl, *A Century of War: Anglo-American Oil Politics and the New World Order* (London, Pluto Press, 2004), pp. 171–72.
2   Rodman, *More Precious Than Peace*, pp. 205–206.
3   See Andrew and Mitrokhin, *The Mitrokhin Archive II*, p. 181.
4   Ibid.
5   Ibid., pp. 181-82.
6   Ibid., p. 182.
7   Zonis, *Majestic Failure*.
8   See Jahangir Amuzegar, *Dynamics of the Iranian Revolution* (New York: State University of New York Press, 1991), p. 228.
9   Ibid., p. 244.
10 Robert M. Gates, *From the Shadows* (New York: Simon and Schuster, 1996), pp. 74–75. See also Seliktar, *Politics, Paradigms and Intelligence Failures*, pp. 77–78.
11 Seliktar, *Politics, Paradigms and Intelligence Failures*, p. 78.
12 See Seliktar, *Failing the Crystal Ball Test*, pp. 85–86 for an examination of all points of view on Precht's role.
13 See Ledeen and Lewis, *Debacle*, p. 170, Seliktar, *Failing the Crystal Ball Test*, p. 86.
14 Seliktar, *Failing the Crystal Ball Test*, p. 86.
15 See Sullivan, *Mission to Iran*, p. 177, see also Ibid.
16 Brzezinski, *Power and Principle*, p. 355.
17 Toloui, *Bazigaran-e Asr-e Pahlavi*, Vol 2, p. 999.
18 Rubin, *Paved with Good Intentions*, p. 207.
19 Toloui, *Bazigaran-e Asr-e Pahlavi*, Vol 2, p. 1000.
20 See Alamuti, *Iran dar Asr-e Pahlavi*, Vol 10, p. 294. See also chapter 5.
21 Seliktar, *Failing the Crystal Ball Test*, p. 86.
22 See Special Intelligence Bureau Document, 12 May 1978, From General Hossein Fardust, prepared by Colonel Amir Masoud Eftekhari, in *Farazhaii Az Tarikh-e Enghelab* (Tehran, 1996), pp. 60–62.
23 Stempel, *Inside the Iranian Revolution*, p. 99.
24 Rafizadeh, *Witness*, p. 259.
25 Alamuti, *Iran dar Asr-e Pahlavi*, Vol 10, pp. 283–303, Stempel, *Inside the Iranian Revolution*, pp. 100–101.
26 Chehabi, *Iranian Politics and Religious Modernism*, p. 238.
27 Cottam, *Iran and the United States*, p. 171.
28 Amuzegar, *The Dynamics of the Iranian Revolution*, p. 287. Amuzegar does not mention Sabeti's name. See also Toloui, *Bazigaran-e Asr-e Pahlavi*, Vol 2.
29 See Stempel, *Inside the Iranian Revolution*, for further discussion of this period.

30 Colonel Isa Pejman, *Arteshbod Hossein-e Fardust, Khedmat ya Khianat* (Major-General Hossein Fardust: Loyal servant or traitor?) (Paris, Mina Publications, 1994)
31 *Farazhaii Az Tarikh-e Enghelab*, pp. 71–73.
32 Alamuti, *Iran dar Asr-e Pahlavi*, Vol 10, p. 295.
33 Toloui, *Bazigaran-e Asr-e Pahlavi*, Vol 2, p. 1001.
34 Sobhani, *The Pragmatic Entente*, pp. 113–14.
35 Rafizadeh, *Witness*, p. 259.
36 See the account in Mohamed Heikal, *Iran: The Untold Story* (New York: Pantheon Books, 1982).
37 From American Embassy Tehran, to Department of State, Washington D.C., August 1, 1978, *Documents*, Vol 25, p. 51.
38 Alamuti, *Iran Dar Asr-e Pahlavi*, Vol 14 (Iran in the Pahlavi Era): (London: Book Press, Paka Print, 1992), p. 428.
39 Stempel, *Inside the Iranian Revolution*, p. 107.
40 Taheri, *The Unknown Life of the Shah*, pp. 263–64, 343, n. 5.
41 See Sullivan's account in Sullivan, *Mission to Iran*.
42 Bill, *The Eagle and the Lion*, pp. 445–46, Seliktar, *Failing the Crystal Ball Test*, p. xvi.
43 Brzezinski, *Power and Principle*, p. 397.
44 Vance, *Hard Choices*, pp. 325–26.
45 Rubin, *Paved with Good Intentions*, p. 209.
46 Carter, *Keeping Faith*, p. 438.
47 Ibid.
48 See Gary Sick's comments in America Abroad presents America and Iran: Cooperation and Conflict in the Post-Saddam Gulf?, (2003), Segment #3 'Eye Witness' with Marvin Kalb.
49 See Stansfield Turner's comments in Ibid.
50 Bill, *The Eagle and the Lion*, pp. 393–405 for institutional failures.
51 See Zbigniew Brzezinski's comments in America Abroad presents America and Iran: Cooperation and Conflict in the Post-Saddam Gulf?, (2003) Segment #3 'Eye Witness' with Marvin Kalb.
52 See Stansfield Turner's comments in America Abroad presents America and Iran: Cooperation and Conflict in the Post-Saddam Gulf?, (2003), Segment #3 'Eye Witness' with Marvin Kalb.
53 See Bill, *The Eagle and the Lion*, pp. 394–409.
54 Ibid., p. 392.
55 See Seliktar, *Failing the Crystal Ball Test*, p. 68.
56 This is one of the main themes of Sick's memoirs, *All Fall Down*.
57 Seliktar, *Failing the Crystal Ball Test*, pp. 175–180.
58 Stansfield Turner, *Secrecy and Democracy* (Boston: Houghton and Mifflin, 1985), pp. 116–17, Bill, *The Eagle and the Lion*, p. 445.
59 Seliktar, *Failing the Crystal Ball Test*, p. 110.
60 This indicates that the DIA was not aware of policy differences in SAVAK.
61 DIA Intelligence Appraisal, in *Documents*, Vol 63, pp. 2–11.
62 Michael Donovan, 'National Intelligence and the Iranian Revolution.' *Intelligence and National Security* 12, no. 1 (Jan. 1997), pp. 146, 161, n. 16.
63 Ibid., p. 146.
64 Sick, *All Fall Down*, p. 47, Rubin, *Paved with Good Intentions*, p. 210.
65 From American Embassy, Tehran, Action Secretary of State, Washington D.C., August 17, 1978, in *Documents*, Vol 12, pp. 9–10.
66 Ibid., pp. 12–13.
67 Ibid., p. 15.
68 Ibid., p. 18.
69 Ibid., pp. 15–16.
70 Ibid., pp. 12–13.
71 Ibid., pp. 16–17.
72 Ibid., p. 18.
73 Ibid., pp. 17–18.
74 Sick, *All Fall Down*, p. 48.
75 See Fardust's purported memoirs, *Khaterat-e Arteshbod-e Sabeq Hoseyn Fardust*, p. 577, which claim that Shari'atmadari also wanted the Shah to allow Khomeini to return to Iran.
76 See *Documents*, Vol 12, pp. 91–93, 97–98, 103–128, and *Documents*, Vol 25, pp. 39–42 and Seliktar, *Failing the Crystal Ball Test*, p. 84.

77 From American Embassy, Tehran, to Department of State, Washington D.C., August 1, 1978, *Documents*, Vol 25, pp. 50–51.
78 Ibid., pp. 51–52.
79 Ibid., p. 53.
80 Toloui, *Bazigaran-e Asr-e Pahlavi*, Vol 2, p. 1002, and From American Embassy, Tehran, Action Secretary of State, Washington D.C., August 17, 1978, *Documents*, Vol 12, p. 22.
81 From American Embassy, Tehran, to Secretary of State, Washington D.C., August 17, 1978, *Documents*, Vol 12, p. 22.
82 See Menashri, *Iran*, p. 34.
83 *Documents*, Vol 12, p. 23.
84 Menashri, *Iran*, p. 34.
85 *Documents*, Vol 12, p. 21.
86 Ibid., p. 22.
87 Sick, *All Fall Down*, p. 47.
88 Taheri, *The Unknown Life of the Shah*, p. 256.
89 Ibid., pp. 256–57.
90 Alamuti, *Iran dar Asr-e Pahlavi*, Vol 13, pp. 54–55, p. 111.
91 Ibid., pp. 54–87, Taheri, *The Unknown Life of the Shah*, p. 257.
92 Ibid., p. 82.
93 *Etteleat*, 3 June, 1990.
94 Ibid.
95 See Count De Marenches, interviewed by Christian Ockrent, *De Marenches: The Evil Empire*, (London: Sidgwick and Jackson, 1988), p. 123.
96 Ibid.
97 Sick, *All Fall Down*, p. 48.
98 Mohsen Milani, *The Making of Iran's Islamic Revolution* (Boulder: Westview Press, 1994), p. 116, Cottam, *Iran and the United States*, pp. 124–25, Milani, *The Persian Sphinx*, p. 289.
99 Taheri, *The Spirit of Allah*, p. 224.
100 Fardust, *Khaterat*, p. 579.
101 See Colonel Isa Pejman, *Asar-e Angosht-e SAVAK* (SAVAK's finger-print), Vol 1, (Paris, Zhen Publications, second edition, 1994), p. 414.
102 Alamuti, *Iran dar Asr-e Pahlavi*, Vol 13, p. 113.
103 Toloui, *Bazigaran-e-Asr-e-Pahlavi*, Vol 2, p. 1002.
104 *Documents*, Vol 12, pp. 87–89.
105 *Documents*, Vol 25, pp. 64–65.
106 Major-General Abbas Gharabaghi, *E'terafat-e Zheneral:Khaterat-e Arteshbod Abbas Gharabaghi (Mordad-Bahman 57)* (Confessions of a General: The Memoirs of Major-General Abbas Gharabaghi, July-August 1978-February 1979) (Tehran: Ney Publishers, 1366, [1987]) , pp. 16–17.
107 Sepehr Zabih, *The Iranian Military in Revolution and War* (London: Routledge, 1988), p. 21.
108 Taheri, *The Spirit of Allah*, p. 236.
109 Toloui, *Bazigaran-e Asr-e Pahlavi*, Vol 2, p. 555. See also *Documents*, Vol 12, p. 89.
110 Taheri, *The Spirit of Allah*, p. 225.
111 Nejati, *Tarikh-e Siasi-e Bisto Panj Sale-ie Iran (25 Years of Iranian Political History)*,Vol 2, p. 83, Taheri, *The Spirit of Allah*, p. 224
112 *Documents*, Vol 12, p. 89.
113 See Misagh Parsa, *States, Ideologies and Social Revolutions*, (Cambridge, Cambridge University Press, 2000) p. 143.
114 Donovan, 'National Intelligence and the Iranian Revolution', pp. 160, 163, n. 69.
115 Memorandum of Conversation, August 21, 1978, *Documents*, Vol 24, p. 21.
116 Chehabi, *Iranian Politics and Religious Modernism*, p. 239.
117 *Documents*, Vol 7, p. 236.
118 *Documents*, Vol 7, (2), p. 248.
119 Sick, *All Fall Down*, p. 49.
120 See Anthony H. Cordesman, *Iran and Iraq: The Threat from the Northern Gulf* (Boulder, Colo: Westview Press, 1994).
121 Donovan, 'National Intelligence and the Iranian Revolution', p. 161, n. 20.
122 David et al, *Foreign Policy Failure in the White House*, p. 63.
123 Bill, *The Eagle and the Lion*, pp. 408–409.

124 Ranelagh, *The Agency*, p. 649, fn.
125 Anthony Parsons, *The Pride and the Fall*, p. 67.
126 Alexander Moens, *Foreign Policy Under Carter: Testing Multiple Advocacy Decision Making* (Boulder, Westview Press, 1990), p. 142.
127 Brzezinski, *Power and Principle*, p. 360.
128 Carter, *Keeping Faith*, p. 441
129 On Zahedi, see the account in Bill, *The Eagle and the Lion*.
130 Taheri, *The Unknown Life of the Shah*, pp. 264–65.
131 Ibid., p. 264.
132 Sullivan, *Mission to Iran*, pp. 192–93.
133 Ibid.
134 Sick, *All Fall Down*, p. 49.
135 Brzezinski, *Power and Principle*, p. 357.
136 Sick, *All Fall Down*, p. 50.
137 Ibid.
138 Taheri, *The Unknown Life of the Shah*, p. 265.
139 Zabih, *The Iranian Military in Revolution and War*, pp. 21–22.
140 Sick, *All Fall Down*, pp. 51–52.
141 From American Embassy, Tehran to Secretary of State Washington D.C., September 10, 1978, in *Farazhaii Az Tarikh-e Enghelab*, pp. 108–111.
142 Sick, *All Fall Down*, pp. 51–52.
143 Pipes, *The Hidden Hand*, p. 173.
144 *Documents*, Vol 12 (3), pp. 59–60.
145 Ibid., p. 62.
146 Sick, *All Fall Down*, p. 55.
147 See Richard W. Cottam, *Nationalism in Iran*, (Pittsburgh, University of Pittsburgh Press, 1964), p. 239.
148 From American Embassy, Tehran, to Secretary of State, Washington D.C., Priority, September 21, 1978, *Documents*, Vol 12, pp. 67–68.
149 Ibid., p. 70.
150 *Documents*, Vol 12, pp. 70–71.
151 Secret Memorandum of Conversation September 15, 1978, *Documents*, Vol 63, p. 10–11.
152 Ibid.
153 See Memorandum from Secretary of State September 19, 1978, *in Documents*, Vol 12, p. 64.
154 From American Embassy, Tehran, Action Secretary of State, Washington D.C., August 17, 1978, *Documents*, Vol 12, pp. 17–18.
155 Country Team Meeting, September 27 1978, *Documents*, Vol 7, p. 235. The Soviet Union supported Ethiopia in its war with Somalia over Ogaden.
156 See Undated Special Bureau document, in *Farazhai Az Tarikh-e Enghelab*, pp. 164–67.
157 See SAVAK's report on Minachi's discussions, 28/6/2537, 19/9/1978, in Ibid.
158 Ibid., pp. 118–19, 121–22, 132–33.
159 Parsons, *Pride and the Fall*, p. 71. Parsons does not mention Shari'atmadari's name but the context is clear.
160 Ibid., p. 72.
161 Ibid., p. 72.
162 Stempel, *Inside the Iranian Revolution*, p. 127.
163 Parsons, *Pride and the Fall*, p. 74.
164 Ibid., pp. 74–75.
165 Stempel, *Inside the Iranian Revolution*, p. 127.
166 See *Documents*, Vol 24, pp. 25–31.
167 Stempel, *Inside the Iranian Revolution*, p. 129.
168 From American Embassy, Tehran to Secretary of State, Washington D.C., October 22 1978, Documents, Vol 25, p. 90.
169 Sick, *All Fall Down*, p. 57.
170 Toloui, *Bazigaran-e Asr-e Pahlavi*, Vol 2, p. 1001.
171 Taheri, *The Spirit of Allah*, pp. 221, Seliktar, *Failing the Crystal Ball Test*, p. 89.
172 Toloui, *Bazigaran-e Asr-e Pahlavi*, Vol 2, p. 574.
173 Ibid., see also Taheri, *The Unknown Life of the Shah*.
174 Taheri, *The Spirit of Allah*, p. 224.
175 From American Embassy, Tehran to Secretary of State, Washington, D.C., November 5, 1978, *Documents*, Vol 63 (12), pp. 12–13.

176 Alamuti, *Iran Dar Asr-e Pahlavi*, Vol 10, pp. pp. 307–308. For Sharif-Emami's account as narrated to Alamuti.
177 *Documents*, Vol 12, p. 64.
178 See the SAVAK document in Hamid Rowhani, *Shari'atmadari Dar Dadgah-e Tarikh* (Shari'atmadari before the Court of History) (Tehran: Qom Islamic Revolution Documentation Centre, 1982), pp. 151–53.
179 Sick, *All Fall Down*, p. 57.
180 Parsons, *Pride and the Fall*, p. 82.
181 Ibid., p. 83.
182 From American Embassy, Tehran, to Secretary of State, Washington, D.C., *Documents*, Vol 25, October 29, 1978, p. 99.
183 Parsons, *Pride and the Fall*, p. 81.
184 From American Embassy, Tehran, to Secretary of State, October 11, 1978, *Documents*, Vol 25, p. 67.
185 *Documents*, Vol 25, p. 70.
186 Parsons, *Pride and the Fall*, p. 87.
187 Menashri, *Iran*, pp. 55, 105, n. 3.
188 Parsons, *Pride and the Fall*, p. 85.
189 Steven A. Schneider, *The Oil Price Revolution* (Baltimore: Johns Hopkins University Press, 1983), p. 429.
190 Parsons, *Pride and the Fall*, pp. 83–84.
191 From American Embassy, Tehran, to Secretary of State, Washington D.C., October 16, 1978, in *Documents*, Vol 12, p. 96.
192 From American Embassy Tehran, to Secretary of State, *Documents*, Vol 25, October 24 1978, p. 95.
193 *Documents*, Vol 7, p. 237.
194 Taheri, *The Unknown Life of the Shah*, p. 288.
195 See Ibid. Contrary to Taheri's argument, Fardust was in daily contact with the Shah regarding the unrest in the country and the Shah sometimes even received him twice a day. See Pejman, *Arteshbod Hossein Fardust*, pp. 11–13, 17, 47–48.
196 Taheri, *The Spirit of Allah*, p. 236.
197 Ibid.
198 Parsons, *Pride and the Fall*, p. 84.
199 Brzezinski, *Power and Principle*, p. 362, says that Sullivan reported it afterwards.
200 Sick, *All Fall Down*, p. 68, Parsons, *Pride and the Fall*, p. 85.
201 Parsons, *Pride and the Fall*, p. 85.
202 Brzezinski, *Power and Principle*, p. 362.
203 Ibid.
204 Ibid.
205 Parsons, *The Pride and the Fall*.
206 Menashri, *Iran*, pp. 55, 105, n. 4.
207 Ibid.
208 Stempel, *Inside the Iranian Revolution*, p. 129.
209 Chehabi, *Iranian Politics and Religious Modernism*, pp. 242–43, says that Bazargan apparently did not know that Khomeini had always had a secret network in Iran. This is highly unlikely. All the clerics whom Bazargan chose were Khomeini's followers.
210 Ibid., pp. 242–43.
211 Sick, *All Fall Down*, p. 63, Sanjabi, *Omidha Va Naomidiha*, pp. 295–296.
212 Sanjabi, *Omidha Va Naomidiha*, p. 301.
213 See the accounts in Taheri, *The Unknown Life of the Shah*, Taheri, *The Spirit of Allah*.
214 Thornton, *The Carter Years*, p. 58.
215 Ibid., pp. 58–59.
216 Ibid.
217 *Petroleum Economist*, June 1978, p. 231.
218 Ibid., p. 230.
219 *Documents*, Vol 13 (4), pp. 69–71.
220 *Petroleum Economist*, July 1978, p. 301. The report does not mention the Shah's political concerns.
221 *Petroleum Economist*, August 1978, p. 327.
222 Ibid.
223 Zonis, *Majestic Failure*, p. 244.
224 *Petroleum Economist*, August 1978, p. 327.

225 See Thornton, *The Carter Years*, p. 59 for further details.
226 Ibid.
227 Carter, *Keeping Faith*, p. 439.
228 David, et al, *Foreign Policy Failure in the White House*, p. 63.
229 Sick, *All Fall Down*, p. 62.
230 From American Embassy Tehran to Secretary of State Washington D.C., October 31, *Documents*, Vol 12, p. 174.
231 Karabel, 'Inside the US Espionage Den', p.56.
232 Country Team meeting, November 1, 1978, *Documents*, Vol 7, p. 239.
233 Sick, *All Fall Down*, p. 72.
234 Ibid., p. 63.
235 Ibid., says unconvincingly that the Shah had threatened to abdicate. In fact, even after he left Iran, the Shah steadfastly refused to abdicate.
236 From Am Embassy, Tehran to Sec State, Washington, D. C. , November 2 1978, *Documents*, Vol 13 (4), pp. 12–14.
237 Hoveyda, *The Fall of the Shah*, p. 120.
238 Ibid., p. 137, observes that Brzezinski did not have much respect for Zahedi as a political operator either. However, this conclusion is rather dubious given the evidence.
239 From American Embassy, Tehran, to Secretary of State, Washington, D.C., November 5, 1978, *Documents*, Vol 63 (12), pp. 12–13.
240 *Documents*, Vol 63 (12), p. 13.
241 Ibid., p. 14.
242 From American Embassy, Tehran, to the Department of State, Washington D.C., November 2, 1978, *Documents*, Vol 13, pp. 21–22.
243 *Documents*, Vol 13, p. 22, and Sick, *All Fall Down*, p. 72.
244 *Documents*, Vol 13, pp. 17–20.
245 From INR-David E. Mark, Acting, to the Secretary, Department of State, Briefing memorandum, November 2 1978, *Documents*, Vol 13 (4), p. 10.
246 Ibid., p. 10.
247 Ibid., p. 11.
248 Ibid.
249 Thornton, *The Carter Years*, p. 251.
250 Sick, *All Fall Down*, pp. 67–68.
251 Vance, *Hard Choices*, p. 343, see also the analysis in Thornton, *The Carter Years*, p. 252.
252 Sick, *All Fall Down*, p. 68.
253 Brzezinski, *Power and Principle*, p. 364.
254 Moens, *Foreign Policy Under Carter*, pp. 150–51.
255 Sick, *All Fall Down*, p. 75.
256 Ibid., p. 72.
257 Parsons, *Pride and the Fall*, p. 85.
258 Pahlavi, *Answer to History*, pp. 169–70.
259 Stephen Kinzer, *All the Shah's Men* (New Jersey, John Wiley and Sons, Inc., 2003)
260 Gasiorowski, Mark J., 'The Qarani Affair and Iranian Politics', *International Journal of Middle Eastern Studies*, Vol 25, 1993.
261 Alam, Asadollah, *The Shah and I*, p. 444.
262 Rafizadeh, *Witness*, p. 278.
263 Ibid., pp. 279–80.
264 Parsons, *Pride and the Fall*, p. 90, says the meeting took place on 5 November. Sick, *All Fall Down*, p. 72, says the meeting was held on 4 November.
265 Ibid., pp. 90–91.
266 Ibid., pp. 90–91.
267 Ibid.
268 Sick, *All Fall Down*, p. 73.
269 Parsons, *Pride and the Fall*, pp. 91–92.
270 Ibid., p. 92.
271 Pahlavi, *Answer to History*, p. 165.
272 Sick, *All Fall Down*, p. 74.
273 Rubin, *Paved with Good Intentions*, pp. 227–28.
274 Ibid.
275 Rafizadeh, *Witness*, pp. 281–82. Taheri, *The Unknown Life of the Shah*, p. 279 says hard-line generals and SAVAK acted on their own to force the Shah to restore order.

276 See their accounts in Sullivan, *Mission to Iran*, Parsons, *Pride and the Fall*.
277 Rafizadeh, *Witness*, p. 282.
278 Donovan, 'National Intelligence and the Iranian Revolution', pp. 152, 162, n. 41.
279 William Shawcross, *The Shah's Last Ride* (London: Pan Books in association with Chatto and Windus, paperback edition, 1989), p. 12.
280 From Am Embassy, Tehran to Sec State, Washington D.C. November 9, 1978, *Documents*, Vol 13 (4), pp. 34–35.
281 Brzezinski, *Power and Principle*, p. 366.
282 Iranian government document reproduced in Yazdi, *Akharin Talashha Dar Akharin Ruzha*, p. 226.
283 Sick, *All Fall Down*, pp. 75–76.
284 Rubin, *Paved with Good Intentions*, p. 228.
285 *London Kayhan*, 4 December 1997, p. 8.
286 See *Documents*, Vol 13 (4), p. 34.
287 Ibid., pp. 29–32.
288 Sick, *All Fall Down*, p. 90.
289 Ibid., p. 91. See also Seliktar, *Failing the Crystal Ball Test*, p. 109 for a good account of the disputes over intelligence in Washington.
290 Ibid.
291 *Documents*, Vol 12 (3), p. 109.
292 Ibid., p. 117.
293 Ibid., p. 113.
294 Ibid., pp. 111, 117.

Chapter 7

1 *London Kayhan*, 8 January 98, p. 8.
2 Milani, *The Persian Sphinx*, p. 297.
3 Ibid.
4 Ibid., pp. 296–301.
5 Nikola B. Schahgaldian, with the assistance of Gina Barkhordarian, *The Iranian Military Under the Islamic Republic*, (Santa Monica: Rand Corporation, 1987), p. 18, fn. 27.
6 Thornton, *The Carter Years*, p. 255 and Sick, *All Fall Down*, p. 111.
7 Cottam, *Iran and the United States*, p. 178.
8 *Documents*, Vol 66, pp. 41, 45–46, Schneider, *The Oil Price Revolution*, p. 429.
9 *Documents*, Vol 12, p. 85.
10 See Brian Crozier, *Free Agent, the Unseen War, 1941–1991* (London: Harper Collins, 1993), p. 160.
11 Sick, *All Fall Down*, p. 124.
12 Parsons, *Pride and the Fall*, pp. 92–93.
13 See Stempel, *Inside the Iranian Revolution*
14 Carter, *Keeping Faith*, p. 440.
15 Ibid.
16 Sullivan, *Mission to Iran*, p. 203.
17 Ibid., pp. 202–203.
18 Brzezinski, *Power and Principle*, p. 368.
19 Ibid.
20 See Sullivan's argument in *Mission to Iran*.
21 Vladimir Kuzikchin, *Inside the KGB* (London: Andre Deutsche, 1990), p. 239.
22 Yodfat, *The Soviet Union and Revolutionary Iran*, p. 49.
23 Kuzikchin, *Inside the KGB*, p. 252.
24 Andrew and Mitrokhin, *The Mitrokhin Archive II*, p. 182. Despite these observations, Andrew and Mitrokhin seem to be unaware of Soviet support for the so-called 'progressive' and anti-American clerics and their account does not say much about Soviet support for the revolution.
25 Thornton, *The Carter Years*, p. 255.
26 Ibid., pp. 255, 281, n. 121.
27 Ibid., pp. 255, 281, n.122.
28 Sick, *All Fall Down*, p. 95.
29 Thornton, *The Carter Years*, pp. 256, 281, n. 126, Brzezinski, *Power and Principle*, p. 368.

NOTES

30 Cottam, *Iran and the US*, pp. 174–75, 285, n. 27, Sick, *All Fall Down*, p. 106.
31 Carter, *Keeping Faith*, p. 441.
32 Sick, *All Fall Down*, p. 95.
33 Pahlavi, *Answer to History*, p. 170.
34 Ibid.
35 Nureddin Kianuri, *Khaterat-e Nureddin-e Kianuri* (Nureddin Kianuri's memoirs), (Tehran, Etelaat Publishers, 1372 [1993]). pp. 488–89, 491.
36 Iraj Eskandari, *Khaterat-e Siasi-ye Iraj Eskandari*, (The political memoirs of Iraj Eskandari), compiled by Ali Dehbashi, (Tehran: Elmi Publishers, second edition, 1368, [1990]), p. 233.
37 Ibid., pp. 238–39.
38 From American Embassy Moscow to Secretary of State, Washington D.C., November 16, 1978, *Documents*, Vol 24, pp. 106–107.
39 From American Embassy, Tehran, to American Embassy, Moscow, Secretary of State, Washington D.C., November 20, 1978, *Documents*, Vol 24, p. 112.
40 Sick, *All Fall Down*, p. 93.
41 Ibid.
42 Ibid., p. 94.
43 Michael Donovan, 'National Intelligence and the Iranian Revolution', p. 152.
44 See *Documents*, Vol 13, pp. 9, 21–23, see also Seliktar, *Failing the Crystal Ball Test*, p. 105.
45 See William Shawcross, *The Shah's Last Ride* (London: Pan Books, 1989), p. 9.
46 Brzezinski, *Power and Principle*, p. 368, see also Seliktar, *Failing the Crystal Ball Test*, p. 102.
47 Carter, *Keeping Faith*, p. 441.
48 Vance, *Hard Choices*, p. 330.
49 Ibid.
50 Seliktar, *Failing the Crystal Ball Test*, p. 109.
51 Ibid., and Vance, *Hard Choices*, p. 330.
52 Ibid.
53 From American Embassy Tehran, Action: Secretary of State Washington D.C., November 30, 1978, *Documents*, Vol 13 (4), pp. 65–67.
54 Ibid.
55 Ibid.
56 Parsons, *Pride and the Fall*, p. 107.
57 From American Consul Isfahan to Department of State, Washington D.C., December 6, 1978, *Documents*, Vol 13 (4), p. 84.
58 See Gholamreza Nejati, *Tarikh-e Siasi-ye Bisto Panj Sale-ie Iran*, Vol 2.
59 Donovan, 'National Intelligence and the Iranian Revolution', p. 153.
60 Ibid., p. 154.
61 Ibid., pp. 154–55.
62 Ibid., p. 155.
63 Ibid.
64 From Secretary of State, Washington D.C. to All Near Eastern and South Asian Diplomatic Posts, November 24, 1978, *Documents*, Vol 48, Part 1 (2), p. 92.
65 From Secretary of State, Washington D.C., to All Diplomatic and Consular posts, November 29, 1978, in *Documents*, Vol 64, p. 65.
66 Thornton, *The Carter Years*, pp. 256, 281, n. 129.
67 Sick, *All Fall. Down*, p. 105.
68 See Michael A. Ledeen, *The War against the Terror Masters* (New York, St Martin's Press, 2002), p. 111.
69 Ibid.
70 Ibid.
71 From Secretary of State, Washington D.C., to American embassy, London, December 2, 1978, *Documents*, Vol 13 (4), pp. 73–74.
72 Ibid., p. 74.
73 Ibid., pp. 75–76.
74 Ibid., pp. 76–77.
75 Stempel, *Inside the Iranian Revolution*, pp. 148–49.
76 Ibid., Stempel does not mention Brzezinski's exact role in the Shah's decision.
77 Brzezinski, *Power and Principle*, p. 371.
78 Desmond Harney, *The Priest and the King* (London and New York: British Academic Press, 1998), pp. 103, 107–108.

79 Brzezinski, *Power and Principle*, p. 355.
80 See Moens, *Foreign Policy Under Carter*, p. 151.
81 Brzezinski, *Power and Principle*, p. 372.
82 Ledeen and Lewis, *Debacle*, pp. 171–73, Thornton, *The Carter Years*, pp. 257–58.
83 Sick, *All Fall Down*, pp. 102–103.
84 Ibid., pp. 103–104.
85 Vance, *Hard Choices*, p. 330.
86 Pahlavi, *Answer to History*, p. 170.
87 Vance, *Hard Choices*, p. 328, Brzezinski, *Power and Principle*, p. 372.
88 Sick, *All Fall Down*, pp. 125–27, Sullivan, *Mission to Iran*, 221.
89 Sick, *All Fall Down*, p. 108.
90 Ibid., pp. 108–109.
91 Thornton, *The Carter Years*, pp. 258–59.
92 Sick, *All Fall Down*, p. 110.
93 Ibid. Sick unconvincingly argues that US policy had not changed.
94 Naraghi, *From Palace to Prison*, p. 91.
95 Amir Arjomand, *The Turban for the Crown*, p. 120.
96 Naraghi, *From Palace to Prison*, p. 91.
97 Sick, *All Fall Down*, p. 105. Sick does not relate Carter's statement to the decision to lift the ban on demonstrations.
98 Gholam R. Afkhami, *The Iranian Revolution* (Washington D.C.: Middle East Institute, 1985), Chapter 4, Major-General Abbas Gharabaghi, *E'terafat-e Zheneral* (Confessions of a General) (Tehran, Ney Publishers, 1366 [1987]), and Bill, *The Eagle and the Lion*, p. 256.
99 See Major-General Abbas Gharabaghi, *Gofteguha-ye Arteshbod Gharabaghi*, (General Gharabaghi's interviews) (Santa Clara and St Jose, Zamaneh Publishers, 1995).
100 Zabih, *Iranian Military in Revolution and War*, p. 35.
101 Ibid., pp. 35–36.
102 Ibid., pp. 36, 55, n. 12.
103 Amir Arjomand, *The Turban for the Crown*, p. 121.
104 Fardust, *Khaterat*, pp. 593–94.
105 Zabih, *Iranian Military in Revolution and War*, p. 37.
106 Gharabaghi, *E'terafat-e Zheneral*, Amir Arjomand, *The Turban for the Crown*, p. 121, Schahgaldian, *Iranian Military*, p. 16.
107 Donovan, 'National Intelligence and the Iranian Revolution, p. 155.
108 Ledeen and Lewis, *Debacle*.
109 David, et al, *Foreign Policy Failure in the White House*, p. 63.
110 Sick, *All Fall Down*, p. 111.
111 Ibid.
112 Ibid.
113 Memorandum to the Files, From NEA/IRN-Henry Precht, December 12, 1978, *Documents*, Vol 18, pp. 115–19.
114 Brzezinski, *Power and Principle*, p. 373, Vance, *Hard Choices*, p. 331, and Sick, *All Fall Down*, p. 130. Brzezinski dates the Sullivan cable 12 December.
115 Sick, *All Fall Down*, pp. 130, 135, Vance, *Hard Choices*, p. 330.
116 Bill, *The Eagle and the Lion*, pp. 252–53.
117 Brzezinski, *Power and Principle*, p. 373, Sick, *All Fall Down*, p. 116.
118 Vance, *Hard Choices*, p. 331.
119 Sick, *All Fall Down*, p. 116.
120 Bill, *The Eagle and the Lion*, p. 253.
121 Ibid.
122 See Brzezinski, *Power and Principle*, 374. See also Sick, *All Fall Down*, pp. 115–17.
123 Pahlavi, *Answer to History*, p. 168, Menashri, *Iran*, p. 61, *Documents*, Vol 26, p. 40, See also Naraghi, *From Palace to Prison*, *Farazhaii Az Tarikh-e Enghelab*, pp. 310–11.
124 Vance, *Hard Choices*, p. 331.
125 Precht to Ambassador Sullivan and Assistant Secretary of State for Near Eastern and South Asian Affairs Harold Saunders, December 19, 1978, *Documents*, Vol 13, p.16.
126 *Documents*, Vol 13, p. 17.
127 Sullivan, *Mission to Iran*, pp. 211–12.
128 Sick, *All Fall Down*, pp. 119–120.
129 Brzezinski, *Power and Principle*, p. 374.
130 Vance, *Hard Choices*, p. 332.

131 David, *Foreign Policy Failure in the White House*, p. 64.
132 Pahlavi, *Answer to History*, p. 171.
133 Ibid.
134 Ibid.
135 Taheri, *The Unknown Life of the Shah*, p. 290.
136 See Memorandum to the Files, October 17, 1978, *Documents,* Vol 20 (1), p. 87.
137 See Memorandum of Conversation, October 22, 1978, *Documents,* Vol 20 (1), p. 88.
138 Ibid.
139 Ibid.
140 Nejati, *Tarikh-e Bisto Panj Sale-ye Iran*, Vol 2.
141 From American Embassy Tehran to Secretary of State, Washington D.C., January 2, 1979, *Documents,* Vol 24 (5), p. 44.
142 Ibid., p. 46.
143 Ibid., p. 45.
144 Ibid., pp. 44–45.
145 Amuzegar, *Dynamics of the Iranian Revolution*, p. 260.
146 Sick, *All Fall Down*, pp. 132–33, Sullivan, *Mission to Iran*, p. 207.
147 Sullivan, *Mission to Iran*.
148 Carter, *Keeping Faith*, p. 443.
149 Sick, *All Fall Down*, p. 135.
150 Ibid., Sullivan, *Mission to Iran*. However, neither Sullivan nor Sick give a detailed explanation of Ayatollah Beheshti's role.
151 Yazdi, *Akharin Talashha Dar Akharin Ruzha*, pp. 111–112.
152 Vance, *Hard Choices*, p. 334.
153 Sullivan, *Mission to Iran*, p. 213.
154 Ibid., p. 235.
155 Ibid.
156 Ibid., p. 222, Sick, *All Fall Down*, p. 136.
157 Ibid., and Sick, *All Fall Down*, p. 133.
158 Sick, *All Fall Down*, p. 133.
159 Vance, *Hard Choices*, p. 335.
160 Ibid., p. 335.
161 Carter, *Keeping Faith*, pp. 444–45.
162 Ibid., p. 445.
163 Sullivan, *Mission to Iran*, p. 223, Sick, *All Fall Down*, p. 133.
164 Brzezinski, *Power and Principle*, pp. 376–77, Sick, *All Fall Down*, p. 131, Vance, *Hard Choices*, p. 335.
165 Brzezinski, *Power and Principle*, p. 377, Sick, *All Fall Down*, p. 131.
166 Brzezinski, *Power and Principle*, p. 377.
167 Ibid., p. 378.
168 Vance, *Hard Choices*, p. 335.
169 Carter, *Keeping Faith*, p. 443.
170 Ibid., U.S. Congress, House of Representatives, Committee on Foreign Affairs, Subcommittee on Europe and the Middle East. *General Huyser's Mission to Iran, January 1979.* 97th Cong. 1st Sess, June 9, 1981.
171 Brzezinski, *Power and Principle*, pp. 378–79.
172 Ledeen and Lewis, *Debacle*, p. 178.
173 Sullivan, *Mission to Iran*, p. 235.
174 Carter, *Keeping Faith*, p. 443.
175 Brzezinski, *Power and Principle*, pp. 378–79.
176 Sullivan, *Mission to Iran*, p. 229.
177 Ibid., skirts the issue.
178 Parsons, *The Pride and the Fall*, p. 121.
179 Cottam, *Iran and the United States*, p. 185. Cottam mistakenly says that there is 'as yet no evidence' Huyser did not seriously explore the coup option.
180 Afkhami, *The Iranian Revolution*, pp. 131–32.
181 See Major-General Abbas Gharabaghi, *Asrar-e Ma'muriat-e Zheneral Huyser Dar Bohran-e Iran* (The Secrets of General Huyser's Mission during the Iranian Crisis), (Los Angeles, Maverick Publishers, 1989), p. 32–33.
182 Ibid., pp. 21–24.
183 Gharabaghi, *Goftoguhai-e Arteshbod Gharabaghii*, p. 377.
184 Gharabaghi, *Asrar-e M'amuriat-e Zheneral Huyser Dar Bohran-e Iran*, pp. 20–25.

185 Ibid., pp. 90–93.
186 Ibid., pp. 123–24.
187 See Ibid., 28–35, see also Huyser, *Mission to Tehran*, pp. 41, 49, 77.
188 Gholam R. Afkhami, *The Iranian Revolution*, pp. 131–32.
189 Gharabaghi, *E'terafat-e Zheneral*, p. 139.

Chapter 8

1 Cottam, *Iran and the United States*, p. 186.
2 Ibid., p. 177.
3 For a detailed account of Poniatowski's role see Nejati, *Tarikh-e Siasi-ye Bisto Panj Sale-ye Iran*, Vol 2 (Twenty-five Years of Iranian Political History), pp. 216–22.
4 Ibid., p. 221.
5 Rubin, *Paved with Good Intentions*, pp. 245–46.
6 Carter, *Keeping Faith*, p. 445.
7 Hoveyda, *The Fall of the Shah*, p. 143.
8 Valery Giscard D'Estaing, *Le Pouvoir Et La Vie*, p. 111, cited by Major-General Abbas Gharabaghi, *Asrar-e Ma'muriat-e Zheneral Huyser Dar Bohran-e Iran*, p. 34.
9 Carter, *Keeping Faith*, p. 445.
10 Sepehr Zabih, *The Iranian Military in Revolution and War*, (London: Routledge, 1988), p. 63.
11 Amuzegar, *The Dynamics of the Iranian Revolution*, p. 302.
12 Vance, *Hard Choices*, p. 336, Sullivan, *Mission to Iran*, p. 229.
13 Vance, *Hard Choices*, p. 335.
14 See Robert Huyser, *Mission to Tehran*, p. 23, Sick, *All Fall Down*, p. 132.
15 Brzezinski, *Power and Principle*, p. 380.
16 Carter, *Keeping Faith*, p. 445.
17 Brzezinski, *Power and Principle*, p. 380.
18 Thornton, *The Carter Years*, p. 265.
19 Carter, *Keeping Faith*, p. 445.
20 Brzezinski, *Power and Principle*, p. 380.
21 Carter, *Keeping Faith*, p. 445.
22 Brzezinski, *Power and Principle*, p. 380.
23 Huyser, *Mission to Tehran*, p. 52.
24 See the account in Ibid.
25 Ibid., p. 42. See Gharabaghi, *Asrar-e M'amuriat-e Zheneral Huyser Dar Bohran-e Iran*, pp. 40–44 for documentary evidence and refutation of Huyser's claims.
26 Cottam, *Iran and the United States*, p. 177.
27 See Ari Ben-Menashe, *Profits of War* (New York: Sheridan Square Press, 1992), pp. 40–41.
28 Sobhani, *The Pragmatic Entente*
29 See Segev, *The Iranian Triangle*, p. 108.
30 Ibid.
31 Ibid., pp. 108–109.
32 See Benjamin Beit-Hallahmi, *The Israeli Connection: Whom Israel Arms and Why* (London: I.B. Tauris and Co Ltd, 1988), p. 12.
33 Ibid.
34 Vance, *Hard Choices*, p. 336.
35 Carter, *Keeping Faith*, p. 445.
36 See Mohsen M. Milani, *The Making of Iran's Islamic Revolution*, (Boulder, Colo: Westview Press, second edition 1994), p. 131.
37 Said Amir Arjomand, *The Turban for the Crown* (New York and Oxford: Oxford University Press, 1988), pp. 123–24. Amir-Arjomand does not seem to have been aware of Israel's role.
38 Menashri, *Iran*, p. 69.
39 Ibid.
40 *Documents*, Vol 10. English version has no page numbers, Farsi translation, pp. 5–7.
41 Milani, *The Making of Iran's Islamic Revolution*, p. 131.
42 Afkhami, *The Iranian Revolution*, p. 132.
43 Gharabaghi, *E'terafat-e Zheneral*, pp. 138–39.
44 Huyser, *Mission to Tehran*, p. 68.
45 Ibid.
46 Sullivan, *Mission to Iran*, p. 235.

47 *Documents*, Vol 26, p. 112.
48 Huyser, *Mission to Tehran*, p. 49. See also Gharabaghi, *Asrar-e M'amouriat-e Zheneral Huyser Dar Bohran-e Iran*, pp. 62–63, says Huyser did not propose establishing contact between the Iranian High Command and religious leaders until 10 January.
49 *London Keyhan*, 27 November, 1997, p. 8.
50 Yazdi, *Akharin Talashha Dar Akharin Ruzha*, p. 143.
51 Ibid., p. 144.
52 *Documents*, Vol 10. English version has no page numbers, Farsi translation, pp. 5–7.
53 *London Keyhan*, 21 May, 1998, p. 8.
54 *Documents*, Vol 10. English version has no page numbers, Farsi translation, pp. 5–7.
55 Vance, *Hard Choices*, pp. 335–36.
56 Ibid., p. 336.
57 Brzezinski, *Power and Principle*, p. 380, Sick, *All Fall Down*, pp. 133, unconvincingly seeks to portray this as Sullivan's plan, but it leaves little doubt that the State Department approved of Sullivan's efforts.
58 Zabih, *Iranian Military in Revolution and War*, p. 45, Gharabaghi, *Asrar-e M'amuriat-e Zheneral Huyser Dar Bohran-e Iran*, p. 34.
59 Sullivan, *Mission to Iran*, pp. 224–26, see also arguments in Bill, *The Eagle and the Lion*, and Cottam, *Iran and the United States*.
60 *Private Papers of Ebrahim Yazdi*, in Nejati, *Tarikh-e Bisto Panj Sale-ie Iran*, Vol 2, p. 288, says the US 'proposed to directly maintain contact with the Imam [Khomeini].'
61 *Documents*, Vol 10, p. 114.
62 See Sullivan's account in, *Mission to Iran*.
63 *Documents*, Vol 10, pp. 114–15.
64 Sick, *All Fall Down*, p. 148.
65 Ibid., p. 149.
66 See the argument in Gharabaghi, *Asrar-e Ma'muriat-e Zheneral Huyser Dar Bohran-e Iran*.
67 Huyser, *Mission to Tehran*.
68 Brzezinski, *Power and Principle*, p. 383, see also Gharabaghi, *Asrar-e Ma'mouriat-e Zheneral Huyser Dar Bohran-e Iran*, p. 65.
69 Brzezinski, *Power and Principle*, p. 380.
70 Sick, *All Fall Down*, p. 137.
71 Brzezinski, *Power and Principle*, p. 381.
72 Kuross A. Samii, *Involvement by Invitation* (University Park and London: The Pennsylvania State University Press, 1987), p. 150. This message must have been sent to the Shah after the Guadeloupe summit.
73 Sick, *All Fall Down*, pp. 137–38.
74 Gharabaghi, *E'terafat-e Zheneral*, Zabih, *The Iranian Military in Revolution and War*, p. 44–45.
75 Gharabaghi, *Asrar-e M'amouriat-e Zheneral Huyser Dar Bohran-e Iran*, pp. 61–64.
76 Nejati, *Tarikh-e Bisto-Panj Sale-ie Iran*, Vol 2, p. 375.
77 Zabih, *Iranian Military in Revolution and War*, pp. 44–45 and other relevant sections.
78 Ibid.
79 Milani, *The Making of Iran's Islamic Revolution*, p. 127.
80 Mohammad Reza Pahlavi, *Answer to History*, (New York: Stein and Day, 1980).
81 Sullivan, *Mission to Iran*, p. 232.
82 Zabih, *Iranian Military in Revolution and War*, p. 49.
83 Sullivan, *Mission to Iran*, p. 233.
84 Ibid.
85 Ibid.
86 Sick, *All Fall Down*, pp. 138–39.
87 Brzezinski, *Power and Principle*, pp. 381–82, and pp. 563–64.
88 Ibid.
89 Gharabaghi, *E'terafat-e Zheneral*, pp. 152–53, Zabih, *Iranian Military in Revolution and War*, p. 49.
90 Yazdi, *Private Papers*, in Nejati, *Tarikh-e Bisto Panj Sale-ie Iran*, Vol 2, pp. 289–90.
91 Ibid.
92 Ibid., p. 293.
93 Ibid., p. 292.
94 Yazdi, *Akharin Talashha Dar Akharin Ruzha*, p. 145.
95 *Documents*, Vol 10, English version has no page numbers, Farsi translation, p. 16.
96 Ibid.
97 Huyser, *Mission to Tehran*, pp. 138–39.

98 *Daily Telegraph*, January 19, p. 4.
99 Gharabaghi, *E'terafat-e Zheneral*, pp. 201–203.
100 Ibid., pp. 227–28, 262.
101 Amuzegar, *The Dynamics of the Iranian Revolution*, p. 302.
102 Huyser, *Mission to Tehran*, p. 139.
103 Ibid., p. 141.
104 Ibid., p. 142.
105 Ibid.
106 Ibid., p. 141.
107 Menashri, *Iran*, p. 64.
108 Ibid., p. 72.
109 Ibid.
110 Ibid.
111 *Documents*, Vol 27(3), p. 46.
112 Ibid., pp. 43–44, pp. 47–48.
113 Huyser, *Mission to Tehran*, p. 141.
114 Parsons, *Pride and the Fall*, pp. 127–29.
115 Menashri, *Iran*, p. 66.
116 Ibid.
117 Rahnema and Nomani, *The Secular Miracle*, pp. 170–71.
118 Ibid.
119 Ibid., p. 171.
120 See Colonel Pejman, *Arteshbod Hossein Fardust* (Major-General Hossein Fardust) (Paris, Zhen Publications, second edition, 1992).
121 Fardust, *Khaterat*, pp. 620–21, 674.
122 Zabih, *Iranian Military in Revolution and War*, p. 112, n. 9.
123 Fardust, *Khaterat*.
124 Ibid., pp. 611–19, Alamuti, *Iran Dar Asr-e Pahlavi*, Vol. 14, pp. 56–58.
125 *Documents*, Vol 10, p. 13.
126 Ibid., pp. 19–24.
127 Ibid., pp. 11–14.
128 Huyser, *Mission to Tehran*, p. 143.
129 Ibid., p. 144.
130 *Daily Telegraph*, January 19, 1979, p. 4. Sick, *All Fall Down*, p. 171, mistakenly says Bakhtiar made this statement on 20 January.
131 *Daily Telegraph*, January 19, 1979, p. 4.
132 Ibid.
133 Ibid.
134 Huyser, *Mission to Tehran*, p. 146.
135 Ibid., p. 148.
136 Brzezinski, *Power and Principle*, p. 386.
137 Ibid., p. 386–88.
138 Ibid., p. 386.
139 Ibid., p. 387.
140 Ibid., pp. 386, 388. After the meeting Brown told Brzezinski, 'You got ninety percent of what you wanted. Your memo obviously had an impact on the President.'
141 Huyser, *Mission to Tehran*, pp. 159–60.
142 Ibid., pp. 155–157, 160.
143 Harney, *The Priest and the King*, 163.
144 *London Keyhan*, 13 November, 1997, p. 8.
145 Huyser, *Mission to Tehran*, p. 160.
146 Sick, *All Fall Down*, 171.
147 Sullivan, *Mission to Iran*.
148 Huyser, *Mission to Tehran*, pp. 277, 283, and 285.
149 From American Embassy Tehran to Secretary of State, Washington D.C., January 22, 1979, *Documents*, Vol 27 (3), p. 73.
150 Ibid.
151 *Documents*, Vol 27 (3), p. 102.
152 Ibid., p. 113.
153 From American Embassy, Tehran to Secretary of State, Washington. D.C., January 22, 1979, Documents, Vol 10, (pp. 30–32 Persian translation)

154 Yazdi, *Akharin Talashha Dar Akharin Ruzha*, 137.
155 Ibid., p. 138.
156 Ibid., pp. 138–39.
157 *Documents*, Vol 27 (3), p. 74.
158 Ibid., pp. 90–91.
159 Vance, *Hard Choices*, pp. 338–39.
160 Brzezinski, *Power and Principle*, p. 388.
161 Vance, *Hard Choices*, p. 339, see also Thornton, *The Carter Years*, pp. 270–71, 285.
162 Huyser, *Mission to Tehran*, pp. 176–77.
163 Ibid., p. 178.
164 Ibid., p. 184.
165 Vance, *Hard Choices*, p. 339.
166 Brzezinski, *Power and Principle*, p. 388.
167 Vance, *Hard Choices*, p. 339.
168 Brzezinski, *Power and Principle*, p. 388.
169 Ibid.
170 Yazdi, *Akharin Talashha Dar Akharin Ruzha*, pp. 146–48.
171 *Daily Telegraph*, January 25, 1979, p. 1.
172 Gharabaghi, *E'terafat-e Zheneral*, p. 228.
173 Sick, *All Fall Down*, p. 146, and Yazdi, *Private Papers*, in Nejati, *Tarikh-e Bisto Panj Sale-ie Iran*, Vol 2, p. 299–300.
174 Sick, *All Fall Down*, pp. 146–47, William Shawcross, *The Shah's Last Ride* (London: Pan Books in association with Chatto and Windus, paperback edition, 1989), p. 84.
175 Shawcross, *The Shah's Last Ride*, p. 84.
176 Ibid.
177 Ibid., p. 85.
178 See the documents in Yazdi, *Akharin Talashha Dar Akharin Ruzha*. Yazdi says that the documents were found in the Special Intelligence Bureau, pp. 249–99.
179 Sick, *All Fall Down*, p. 146, Taheri, *The Spirit of Allah*, p. 248.
180 See Alamuti, *Iran Dar Asr-e Pahlavi*, Vol 10, (London: Book Press, 1991), pp. 302–303.
181 See *Mesl-e Barf Ab Khahim Shod: Mozakerat-e Shora-ye Farmandehan-e Artesh, Dey-Bahman 1357* (We Will Melt like Snow, The Discussions of the commanders of the army, January-February 1979) (Tehran: Nashr-e Ney, Ney Publishers, 1365 [1986]), pp. 165–69. The book contains transcriptions of the recordings of the meetings of the Iranian military High Command.
182 See the account in Gharabaghi, *E'terafat-e Zheneral*.
183 Mansur Rafizadeh, *Witness*, p. 288. According to Rafizadeh, Moghaddam did not specify whether he had spoken to Khosrowdad or not.
184 Ibid.
185 Ibid., p. 289.
186 Yazdi, *Akharin Talashha Dar Akharin Ruzha*, p. 142.
187 Ibid.
188 Ibid., pp. 174–75.
189 Ibid., p. 175. Yazdi, nevertheless, attempts to downplay the significance of this extremely important intelligence warning presumably because it indicates a degree of co-operation between the French government and the Khomeini camp.
190 Ibid., pp. 175–76.
191 See Taheri, *The Spirit of Allah*, p. 248.
192 Huyser, *Mission to Tehran*, p. 191.
193 From American Embassy, Tehran to Secretary of State, Washington, D.C., January 25, 1979, *Documents*, Vol 27 (3), p. 97.
194 Alamuti, *Iran Dar Asr-e Pahlavi*, Vol 14, pp. 331–32.
195 Ibid., pp. 169–170.
196 Ibid., pp. 170–71.
197 Ibid., p. 168.
198 See Nejati, *Tarikh-e Siasi-ye Bisto Panj Sale-ie Iran*, Vol 2 (Twenty-five years of Iranian Political History), pp. 307–308.
199 From American Embassy, Tehran, to Secretary of State, Washington D.C., January 28, 1979, Documents, Vol 27(3) and other documents therein.
200 *London Keyhan*, 13 November, 1997, p. 8.
201 *London Keyhan*, 21 May, 1998, p. 8.
202 *Documents*, Vol 18, p. 120–21.

203 Yazdi, *Akharin Talashha Dar Akharin Ruzha*, pp. 233–48 for claims and counter-claims regarding Yazdi's and Beheshti's roles and Yazdi's replies to his critics.
204 Vance, *Hard Choices*, p. 340.
205 Ibid., p. 341.
206 Gharabaghi, *E'terafat-e Zheneral*, pp. 277–78.
207 Ibid., pp. 277–78.
208 *Mesl-e Barf Ab Khahim Shod*, pp. 203–230.
209 Ibid., pp. 245–47
210 Gharabaghi, *E'terafat-e Zheneral*, pp. 277–78.
211 Stempel, *Inside the Iranian Revolution*, p. 171.
212 Alamuti, *Iran Dar Asr-e Pahlavi*, Vol. 14, pp. 166–67, Gharabaghi, *'Eterafat-e Zheneral*, pp. 265, 410, n. 27.
213 Alamuti, *Iran Dar Asr-e Pahlavi*, Vol. 14, pp. 166–67.
214 Sick, *All Fall Down*, p. 150.
215 Najati, *Tarikh-e Siasi-ye Bisto-Panj Sale-ye Iran*, Vol 2, p. 354–55.
216 Ibid., p. 355.
217 Stempel, *Inside the Iranian Revolution*, p. 175, Sick, *All Fall Down*, p. 150.
218 Sick, *All Fall Down*, p. 150.
219 Ibid., pp. 150–51.
220 Brzezinski, *Power and Principle*, p. 389.
221 Huyser, *Mission to Tehran*, pp. 259–60.
222 Ibid.
223 Ibid. See also Sick, *All Fall Down*, p. 150.
224 Nejati, *Tarikh-e Siasi-ye Bisto-Panj Sale-ye Iran*, Vol 2, pp. 359–60.
225 Brzezinski, *Power and Principle*, p. 385.
226 Ibid., pp. 389–90.
227 Gharabaghi, *'E'terafat-e Zheneral*, pp. 265–68. See also Alamuti, *Iran Dar Asr-e Pahlavi*, Vol. 14, p. 167.
228 See the Special Intelligence Bureau document, dated 16/11/1357 (5 February 1979), in *Farazhaii Az Tarikh-e Enghelab*, pp. 366–67.
229 See Stansfield Turner, *Terrorism and Democracy* (Boston: Houghton Mifflin, 1991), pp. 77–78, 88, Ranelagh, *The Agency*, pp. 651–55 for the Brzezinski-Turner disagreement.
230 *Documents*, Vol 27, p. 130.
231 Ibid.
232 Ibid.
233 Huyser, *Mission to Tehran*.
234 Gharabaghi, *Asrar-e M'amuriat-e Zheneral Huyser Dar Bohran-e Iran*, pp. 155–56.
235 See the argument in Pejman, *Arteshbod Hossein Fardust*.
236 *Mesl-e Barf Ab Khahim Shod*, pp. 232–35, 240–43.
237 Gharabaghi, *E'terafat-e Zheneral*, pp. 321, and Gharabaghi, *Asara-e M'amuriat-e Zheneral Huyser Dar Bohran-e Iran*, p. 125.
238 Gharabaghi, *E'terafat-e Zheneral*, 323–26, Zabih, *The Iranian Military in Revolution and War*, pp. 71.
239 Fardust, *Khaterat*, p. 623–24.
240 Brzezinski, *Power and Principle*, pp. 390–91.
241 Ibid., p. 392.
242 Ibid., p. 392.
243 Ibid., pp. 392–93. See also Sick, *All Fall Down*, pp. 155–56.
244 Ibid., p. 393. See also Sick, *All Fall Down*, p. 156.
245 See the account in Fardust, *Khaterat*. See also Zabih, *The Iranian Military in Revolution and War*, p. 37.
246 See Alamuti, *Iran Dar Asr-e Pahlavi*, Vol 14, pp. 277–83.
247 See *Gofteguha-ye Arteshbod Gharabaghi*, p. 14.
248 Paolucci, *Iran, Israel, and the United States*, p. 254.
249 See Sepehr Zabih, *The Mossadegh Era* (Chicago: Lake View Press, 1982)
250 Ehsan Naraghi, *From Palace to Prison*, p. 39.
251 *Documents*, Vol 15, p. 91.
252 Ibid., pp. 80–81.
253 Ibid.
254 Ibid., p. 81.

Chapter 9

1. US Congress, *The Economic Consequences of the Iranian Revolution*, (Washington D.C. GPO, 1979), p. 186.
2. Ibid., p. 188.
3. Christos P. Ioannides, 'The PLO and the Iranian Revolution', *American-Arab Affairs*, 1980, no. 10, pp. 93–94.
4. Ibid., p. 89.
5. US Congress, *The Economic Consequences of the Iranian Revolution*, p. 188.
6. Ioannides, 'The PLO and the Iranian Revolution', p. 90.
7. Sobhani, *The Pragmatic Entente*.
8. Camille Mansour, *Beyond Alliance: Israel and U.S. Foreign Policy*, (New York: Columbia University Press, 1994), pp. 134–35.
9. Brzezinski, *Power and Principle*, William Quandt, *Camp David* (Washington D.C., The Brookings Institution, 1986), p. 290.
10. Quandt, *Camp David*, p. 306.
11. US Congress, *The Economic Consequences of the Iranian Revolution*, p. 187.
12. See Hanner Furtig, with a foreword by Anoushiravan Ehteshami, *Iran's Rivalry with Saudi Arabia Between the Gulf Wars* (Durham Middle East Monograph series, Ithaca Press, Garner Publishing Ltd, 2002), p. 26.
13. From American Embassy Jidda to Secretary of State, Washington D.C., January 3, 1979, *Documents*, Vol 35, pp. 19–20.
14. Abir, *Saudi Arabia in the Oil Era*, p. 146.
15. Ibid. and William B. Quandt, *Saudi Arabia in the 1980s* (Washington D.C. The Brookings Institution, 1981), p. 81.
16. Thornton, *The Carter Years*, p. 320.
17. Ioannides, 'The PLO and the Iranian Revolution', p. 94, see also John Cooley, 'Iran, the Palestinians, and the Gulf,', *Foreign Affairs*, Vol. 57, Summer 1979, pp. 1017–1034.
18. Ioannides, 'The PLO and the Iranian Revolution,', p. 95.
19. Safran, *Saudi Arabia*, p. 354.
20. Ibid., p. 308.
21. R.K. Ramazani, *Revolutionary Iran* (Baltimore: Johns Hopkins University Press, 1986), p. 88.
22. US Congress, *The Economic Consequences of the Iranian Revolution*, p. 120–21.
23. Ibid., p. 122.
24. Shaul Bakhash, *The Politics of Oil and Revolution in Iran*, (Washington D.C., Brookings Institution, 1982), pp, 6–7.
25. Mark Hulbert, *Interlock* (New York: Richardson and Snyder, 1982), p. 32.
26. Bakhash, *The Politics of Oil and Revolution in Iran*, p. 7.
27. Jahangir Amuzegar, *Iran's Economy Under the Islamic Republic* (London: I.B. Tauris, 1993), pp. 231–32.
28. Bakhash, *The Politics of Oil and Revolution in Iran*, p. 10.
29. Ibid.
30. Ibid., pp. 10–11.
31. Amuzegar, *Iran's Economy Under the Islamic Republic*, p. 233.
32. Hulbert, *Interlock*, p. 125.
33. Michael Klare, *Beyond the 'Vietnam Syndrome'* (Washington D.C.: Institute for Policy Studies, 1981), p. 24.
34. Ibid., pp. 70–71.
35. Brzezinski, *Power and Principle*, pp. 446–47.
36. US Congress, Committee on Banking, Finance and Urban Affairs House of Representatives, *Iran: The Financial Aspects of the Hostage Settlement Agreement*, 97th Congress, First Session, July 1981, p. 5.
37. Ibid., p. IV.
38. Ibid., p. 3.
39. Ibid., p. 4.
40. Ibid.
41. Klare, *Beyond the Vietnam Syndrome*, p. 24.
42. Hulbert, *Interlock*, p. 126.
43. Ibid., p. 127.
44. Bakhash, *The Politics of Oil and Revolution in Iran*, p. 7.
45. US Congress, Iran: *The Financial Aspects of the Hostage Settlement Agreement*, p. 8.

46 Thornton, *The Carter Years*, pp. 420–34.
47 Ibid., p. 432.
48 Brzezinski, *Power and Principle*, pp. 437–38.
49 Congressional Research Service, *Saudi Arabia and the United States*, Report, 97th Cong., 1st Sess, (1981), p. 55.
50 Ibid., Cordesman, *The Gulf and the Search for Strategic Stability*, pp. 186, 189, 192, n. 89.
51 Safran, *Saudi Arabia*, p. 311.
52 Thornton, *The Carter Years*, p. 432.
53 Pierre Terzian, *OPEC* (London: Zed Books, 1985), p. 267.
54 Ibid.
55 Safran, *Saudi Arabia*, p. 312.
56 Ibid., p. 313.
57 Thornton, *The Carter Years*.
58 Yergin, *The Prize*, p. 693.
59 Ibid.
60 Terzian, *OPEC*, pp. 267–68.
61 Ibid., p. 269.
62 Carter, *Keeping Faith*, pp. 111–12, see also Thornton, *The Carter Years*, p. 435.
63 Carter, *Keeping Faith*, pp. 111–12,
64 Ibid., Thornton, *The Carter Years*, p. 435.
65 Yergin, *The Prize*, p. 698.
66 US Congress, *US and Saudi Arabia*, p. 55.
67 Safran, *Saudi Arabia*, p. 355.
68 Brzezinski, *Power and Principle*, p. 447.
69 US Congress, *US and Saudi Arabia*, p. 55.
70 Ibid.
71 Terzian, *OPEC*, pp. 269–70.
72 Ibid., p. 270.
73 Ibid., p. 271.
74 Ibid., and Yergin, *The Prize*, p. 695. Yergin does not mention the threats to occupy Saudi oilfields.
75 US Congress, *US and Saudi Arabia*, p. 56.
76 Terzian, *OPEC*, p. 271.
77 Yergin, *The Prize*, p. 703.
78 David Farber, *Taken Hostage*, (Princeton and London: Princeton University Press, 2005), p. 116.
79 Ibid., p. 118.
80 Howard Teicher and Gayle Radley Teicher, *Twin Pillars to Desert Storm* (New York: William Morrow and Company, Inc., 1991).
81 See Haim Shemesh, *Soviet-Iraqi Relations, 1968–1988* (Lynne Rienner Publishers, 1992), pp. 164–65.
82 Ibid., pp. 165–166.
83 Ibid., p. 166.
84 Ibid., pp. 160, 166–67.
85 Teicher and Teicher, *Twin Pillars to Desert Storm*, pp. 61–62.
86 See Raymond Tanter, *Rogue Regimes*, (London, Macmillan, 1999), p. 303, n.32.
87 Ibid., pp. 104–105.
88 Ibid., p. 104, see also Teicher and Teicher, *Twin Pillars to Desert Storm*, pp. 60–61.
89 Ibid., pp. 105–106.
90 Ibid., p. 106.
91 Ibid.
92 Ibid.
93 Teicher and Teicher, *Twin Pillars to Desert Storm*, pp. 62–63.
94 Director of Central Intelligence, National Intelligence Estimate, 'Iraq's Role in the Middle East', June 21, 1979, in *Documents*, Vol 77, pp. 8–9, 19.
95 Ibid., pp. 8–9.
96 Teicher and Teicher, *Twin Pillars to Desert Storm*, p. 67.
97 Congressional Research Service, *Saudi Arabia and the United States*, p. 11.
98 Sa'id Aburish, *Saddam Hussein: The Politics of Revenge* (London: Bloomsbury, 2000), p. 162–63.

99 Director of Central Intelligence, National Intelligence Estimate, 'Iraq's Role in the Middle East', June 21, 1979, in *Documents*, Vol 77, p. 38.
100 Bureau of Intelligence and Research, Report No. 1211, July 6, 1979, in *Documents*, Vol 77, p. 156.
101 Majid Khadduri, *The Gulf War* (Oxford: Oxford University Press, 1988), p. 68.
102 Ibid., pp. 80–81.
103 Ioannides, 'The PLO and the Iranian Revolution', pp. 94–95.
104 Ibid., p. 94.
105 Ibid., p. 96.
106 Khadduri, *The Gulf War*, p. 81. Khadduri mistakenly says Abolhasan Bani-Sadr was Iran's president at the time.
107 Ibid., p. 83.
108 Shemesh, *Soviet-Iraqi Relations*, p. 161.
109 Menashri, *Iran*, p. 101.
110 McLachlan, 'Analyses of the Risks of War: Iran-Iraq Discord, 1979–1980, in Farhang Rajaee (ed)., *The Iran-Iraq War*, (Gainesville: University Press of Florida, 1993), pp. 25–26.
111 Menashri, *Iran*, p. 102.
112 Patrick Seale, *Asad* (London: I.B. Tauris, 1987), p. 355.
113 See Andrew and Mitrokhin, *The Mitrokhin Archive II*, pp. 176–77, 188.
114 See for example Con Coughlin, *Saddam Hussein: His Rise and Fall* (London: Harper Perennial, 2005), pp. 37–39, Aburish, *Saddam Hussein*, p. 54.
115 Ibid., pp. 38–39, Aburish, *Saddam Hussein*, pp. 55–56.
116 See British embassy, Baghdad to FCO, 15 November and 20 December 1969, FCO 17/871, The National Archives, Kew (copies available on National Security Archive web site). See also Andrew and Mitrokhin, *The Mitrokhin Archive II*, pp. 176, 533, n. 32.
117 See Kenneth R. Timmerman, *Ol Ins Feuer*, (Fanning the Flames: Guns, Greed and Geopolitics in the Gulf War), (Zurich: Orell Fusli, 1988), p. 26.
118 From American Embassy, Damascus to Secretary of State Washington D.C., June 22, 1979, *Documents*, Vol 77, pp. 145–46.
119 Ibid., p. 148.
120 Director of Central Intelligence, National Intelligence Estimate, 'Iraq's Role in the Middle East', June 21, 1979, in *Documents*, Vol 77, p. 39.
121 Malik Mufti, *Sovereign Creations*, (Ithaca: Cornell University Press, 1996), p. 213.
122 Aburish, *Saddam Hussein*, p. 168.
123 Ibid.
124 See From American Embassy, Damascus, to Secretary of State Washington D.C., *Documents*, Vol 77, pp. 161–62.
125 Mufti, *Sovereign Creations*, pp. 218–19. Mufti rejects the hypothesis of Syrian involvement.
126 See *Documents*, Vol 77, pp. 169–172.
127 Ibid., p. 171, see also Khadduri, *The Gulf War*, p. 77.
128 Cite Washington, to Tel Aviv Info Amman, Beirut, Cairo, Damascus, Jerusalem, Tehran, *Documents*, Vol 44, pp.
129 Shemesh, *Soviet-Iraqi Relations*, p. 149.
130 From American Embassy, Paris to Secretary of State, Washington D.C. Priority, July 17, 1979, in *Documents*, Vol 77, p. 204.
131 Ramazani, *Revolutionary Iran*, pp. 58–59. See also Khadduri, *The Gulf War*, p. 81.
132 David Jackson-Smith, *The Search for Strategic Stability in the Persian Gulf*, (Master's thesis, Washington D.C.: George Washington University, May 10, 1987), pp. 32–33.
133 Said K. Aburish, *A Brutal Friendship: The West and the Arab Elite* (London: Victor Gollancz, 1997), p. 177.
134 Abir, *Saudi Arabia in the Oil Era*, pp. 145–46.
135 Ramazani, *Revolutionary Iran*, p. 119, Menashri, *Iran*, p. 103.
136 Menashri, *Iran*, p. 103.
137 Ibid., p. 102.
138 Report entitled, 'Effect of Kurdish Fighting on Iranian Relations with Iraq', *Documents*, Vol 10, no page numbers.
139 Shemesh, *Soviet-Iraqi Relations*, p. 161.
140 Ioannides, 'The PLO and the Iranian Revolution,', p. 97, see also Menashri, *Iran*, p. 103.
141 Cite Director to: Stockholm Info Tehran, November 1, 1979, in *Documents*, Vol 10, pp. 3–4.

142 Safran, *Saudi Arabia*, p. 356.
143 *Documents*, Vol 44, for extensive documentation.
144 From Beirut to Director, September 6, 1979, *Documents*, Vol 44, p. 37. (Has no page numbers)
145 Cite Beirut to Director, Info Tehran, Documents, Vol 44, p. 35.
146 See DIA, *International Terrorism: A Compendium Volume II, Middle East (U)*, in *Documents*, Vol 43, pp. 57–58, Anthony H., Cordesman, and Abraham R. Wagner, *The Lessons of Modern War, Vol II: The Iran-Iraq War* (Boulder and San Francisco, Westview Press, 1990), p. 36, n. 1.
147 *Documents*, Vol 36, and Vol 42, pp. 92–94.
148 *Documents*, Vol 32, pp. 1–40.
149 From Bonn to Director, September 9, 1979, *Documents*, Vol 32, p. 44.
150 From Bonn to Director, October 1, 1979, *Documents*, Vol 32, p. 47.
151 Ibid., pp. 47–49.
152 From American Embassy Kuwait to Secretary of State, August 16, 1979, *Documents*, Vol 40, pp. 99–100.
153 From American Embassy Jidda to Secretary of State, October 10, 1979, *Documents*, Vol 35, p. 158.
154 Ari Ben-Menashe, *Profits of War* (New York: Sheridan Square Press, 1992), p. 49. See also Teicher and Teicher, *Twin Pillars to Desert Storm* on Brzezinski's support for Iraq, and Cottam, 'US and Soviet Responses to Islamic Political Militancy', in Nikki R. Keddie and Mark J. Gasiorowski (ed), *Neither East Nor West: Iran, the Soviet Union and the United States* (New Haven and London: Yale University Press, 1990), p. 277 on Brzezinski's opposition to Bazargan.
155 Ben-Menashe, *Profits of War*, p. 49.
156 Ibid., p. 53.

Chapter 10

1 Bill, *The Eagle and the Lion*, Amir Taheri, *Nest of Spies*, (London: Hutchinson, 1988)
2 Fawaz A. Gerges, *America and Political Islam* (Cambridge and New York: Cambridge University Press, 1999).
3 David Farber, *Taken Hostage* (Princeton and Oxford: Princeton University Press, 2005), pp. 105–106.
4 Ibid., pp. 106–107.
5 Ibid., p. 107.
6 Dreyfuss, *Devil's Game*, p. 219.
7 Ibid., pp. 271–72.
8 Ibid., p. 272.
9 See R.K. Ramazani, 'Iran's Foreign Policy: Contending Orientations', *Middle East Journal*, Vol. 43, No. 2, Spring 1989, p. 205.
10 *Middle East Journal*, Vol. 43, No. 2, Spring 1979, p. 206.
11 Ibid., p. 207.
12 Parviz Daneshvar, *Revolution in Iran*, (London: Macmillan, 1996), p. 131.
13 See Sullivan, *Mission to Iran*, pp. 248–68, David Patrick Houghton, *US Foreign Policy and the Iran Hostage Crisis*, (Cambridge, Cambridge University Press, 2001), pp. 76–77.
14 Sullivan, *Mission to Iran*, p. 265.
15 Ibid.
16 Ibid., p. 272.
17 Ibid.
18 Ibid.
19 See Robert M. Gates, *From the Shadows*, (New York: Simon and Schuster, 1996), p. 128.
20 Sullivan, *Mission to Iran*, p. 273.
21 Ibid.
22 Ibid., pp. 273–74.
23 Taheri, *Nest of Spies*, p. 111, Rahnema and Nomani, *The Secular Miracle*, p. 171.
24 Gates, *From the Shadows*, p. 128.
25 Rubin, *Paved with Good Intentions*, p. 286.
26 William Griffith, 'The Revival of Islamic Fundamentalism: The Case of Iran', Center for International Studies Massachusetts Institute of Technology Cambridge, Massachusetts, April 23, 1979, *Documents*, Vol 14, p. 95.

27 Ledeen and Lewis, *Debacle*, p. 209.
28 See Robert Dreyfuss, *Devil's Game*, p. 240.
29 Ibid, pp. 250–52.
30 Ibid., p. 253.
31 Draft, Metrinko: April 24, 1979, in *Documents*, Vol 14, p. 107, see also Sick, *All Fall Down*, p. 34.
32 See Trento, *Prelude to Terror*, pp. 190–91.
33 Taheri, *Nest of Spies*, p. 113.
34 Ibid., p. 115.
35 Yazdi, *Akharin Talashha Dar Akharin Ruzha*, pp. 10–11, 197–98.
36 Hulbert, *Interlock*, pp. 105–112.
37 Paolucci, *Iran, Israel, and the United States*, p. 268. Paolucci was not even aware of the nationalization of the Consortium.
38 Ibid., p. 270.
39 Ioannides, *America's Iran: Injury and Catharsis* (Lanham, Md.: University Press of America, 1984), p. 83.
40 Paolucci, *Iran, Israel, and the United States*, p. 270.
41 Brzezinski, *Power and Principle*, p. 473.
42 Carter, *Keeping Faith*, p. 452.
43 Ibid.
44 Sick, *All Fall Down*, 180.
45 Hamilton Jordan, *Crisis* (New York: G.P. Putnam's Sons, 1982), p. 29.
46 See for example, Seliktar, *Failing the Crystal Ball Test*, p. 138.
47 See John K. Cooley, *Pay Back: America's Long War in the Middle East*, (Washington D.C. Brassey's, 1991), p. 23.
48 Ibid.
49 Ibid., p. 24.
50 Paolucci, *Iran, Israel, and the United States*, p. 235.
51 Ibid., p. 234.
52 Cooley, *Pay Back*, p. 23.
53 Ioannides, *America's Iran*, pp. 106–107.
54 See Ibid., pp. 70–72–73, 111, Seliktar, *Failing the Crystal Ball Test*, p. 157.
55 From American Embassy Tehran, to Secretary of State, Washington D.C., June 14, 1979, in *Documents*, Vol 15, p. 86.
56 Ibid., pp. 132–33.
57 Cottam, *Iran and the United States*
58 Ibid., p. 143.
59 From Am Embassy, Tehran to Secretary of State, Washington D.C., June 14, 1979, *Documents*, Vol 15, p. 91.
60 Reporting cable by John Stempel, May 31, 1979, in *Documents*, Vol 15, p. 60.
51 Ibid.
62 Ibid., p. 65.
63 From American Embassy, Tehran to Secretary of State, Washington D.C., June 7, 1979, in *Documents*, Vol 15, p. 81.
64 Ibid., pp. 83–84.
65 *Documents*, Vol 34, pp. 89–90.
66 Ibid.
67 From Am Embassy Tehran, to Secretary of State, Washington D.C., June 8, 1979, *Documents*, Vol 34, pp. 91–92.
68 *Documents*, Vol 34, p. 94.
69 Stempel, *Inside the Iranian Revolution*, p. 207.
70 Seliktar, *Failing the Crystal Ball Test*, p. 128.
71 For a good account see Ibid., p. 135.
72 Ibid.
73 Ibid., p. 135 and 139–40 for a succinct account of the debate about economic policy in Iran.
74 Ibid., p. 139.
75 See for example Sick, *All Fall Down*, Amir Arjomand, *Turban for the Crown*.
76 See Seliktar, *Failing the Crystal Ball Test*, pp. 138, 141–42.
77 Nikola B. Schahgaldian, with the assistance of Gina Barkhordarian, *The Iranian Military Under the Islamic Republic* (Santa Monica: Rand Corporation, 1987), p. 66.

78 Seliktar, *Failing the Crystal Ball Test*, p. 137.
79 From Secretary of State to American Embassy, Tehran, July 11, 1979, in *Documents*, Vol 15, p. 123.
80 *Documents*, Vol 15, p. 133.
81 Sick, *All Fall Down*, p. 201.
82 Ramazani, 'Iran's Revolution: Patterns, Problems, and Prospects', *International Affairs*, p. 449.
83 Menashri, *Iran*, p. 72.
84 Ibid., p. 154.
85 Ramazani, 'Iran's Revolution', p. 451, Moaddel, *Class, Politics, and Ideology in the Iranian Revolution*, pp. 207–208, 300, n. 11.
86 Moaddel, *Class, Politics, and Ideology in the Iranian Revolution*, p. 208.
87 Menashri, *Iran*, p. 117.
88 Rahnema and Nomani, *The Secular Miracle*, p. 172.
89 Seliktar, *Failing the Crystal Ball Test*, p. 128.
90 Stempel, *Inside the Iranian Revolution*, p. 211.
91 Ibid., p. 213.
92 From American Embassy, Tehran to Secretary of State, July 22 1979, in *Documents*, Vol 15, p. 135, Daneshvar, *Revolution in Iran*, p. 140, Chubin, 'Leftist Forces in Iran', Sajjadpour, *Iranian-Soviet Relations in a Security Perspective*, p. 111.
93 Maziar Behrooz, *Rebels with a Cause* (London, I.B. Tauris, 1999), pp. 105–120
94 Sajjadpour, *Iranian-Soviet Relations in a Security Perspective*, p. 111, See also Moaddel, *Class, Politics, and Ideology in the Iranian Revolution*, p. 240.
95 Rahnema and Nomani, *The Secular Miracle*, pp. 171–72.
96 Daneshvar, *Revolution in Iran*, p. 140, see also Moaddel, *Class, Politics, and Ideology in the Iranian Revolution*, p. 241.
97 Cottam, *Iran and the United States*, p. 201.
98 On this point see Carol R. Saivetz, 'Superpower Competition in the Middle East and the Collapse of Détente', in Odd Arne Westad (ed), *The Fall of Détente: Soviet-American relations during the Carter years*, (Oslo, Scandinavian University Press, 1997), p. 87.
99 Shahrough Akhavi, 'Soviet Perception of the Iranian Revolution' in *Iranian Studies*, vol.xix, no. 1, winter 1986, p. 4, see also Behrooz, *Rebels with a Cause*, p. 127.
100 Kuzikchin, *Inside the KGB*, p. 288. Kianuri has denied most of Kuzikchin's allegations, see Nureddin Kianuri, *Khaterat-e Nureddin Kianuri* (Tehran, Ettela'at Publishers, 1372 [1993]), pp. 552–53.
101 Kuzikchin, *Inside the KGB*, pp. 290–93.
102 Behrooz, *Rebels with a Cause*, pp. 127, 212–13.
103 Ibid., p. 128.
104 M. Moaddel, *Class, Politics, and Ideology in the Iranian Revolution*, p. 217.
105 See Sajjadpour, *Iranian-Soviet Relations in a Security Perspective*, pp. 82–90. Milani 'Harvest of Shame'. See also Behrooz, *Rebels with a Cause*, p. 126–27.
106 Sajjadpour, *Iranian-Soviet Relations in a Security Perspective*, p. 88.
107 Ibid., pp. 88–89.
108 Menashri, *Iran*, p. 93.
109 Ibid.
110 Stempel, *Inside the Iranian Revolution*, p. 219.
111 Menashri, *Iran*, p. 94.
112 Stempel, *Inside the Iranian Revolution*, p. 219.
113 From US Mission USNAT to Secretary of State, Washington D.C. , July 27, 1979, *Documents*, Vol 49, p. 48.
114 Ibid.
115 Stempel, *Inside the Iranian Revolution*, p. 219.
116 From US Mission USNAT to Sec State, Washington D.C. , July 27, 1979, *Documents*, Vol 24, pp. 115–116 and *Documents*, Vol 49, p. 48.
117 *Documents*, Vol 49, p. 53.
118 Ibid., pp. 53–54.
119 From American Embassy Moscow, to Secretary of State Washington D.C., September 6 1979, *Documents*, Vol 49, p. 71.
120 Stempel, *Inside the Iranian Revolution*, p. 212.
121 Menashri, *Iran*, p. 113.
122 Cottam, *Iran and the United States*, p. 200.

NOTES

123 Ibid., p. 199.
124 Ibid., p. 200.
125 Iran Update, July 25–26, 1979, in *Documents*, Vol 1–6, pp. 322–23.
126 Ibid., p. 321.
127 From American Embassy, Tehran to Secretary of State, Washington D.C., August 30, 1979, in Documents, Vol 16, p. 57. See also From American Embassy, Tehran to Secretary of State, Washington D.C., 30 August, 1979, in *Documents*, Vol 16, p. 59, see also Stempel, *Inside the Iranian Revolution*, p. 213.
128 From American Embassy, Tehran, to Secretary of State, Washington D.C., August 30, 1979, in *Documents*, Vol 16, p. 58.
129 Rubin, *Paved with Good Intentions*, p. 291, Seliktar, *Failing the Crystal Ball Test*, p. 150.
130 Documents, Vol 16, pp. 42–52, and Seliktar, *Failing the Crystal Ball Test*, p. 150.
131 Sick, *All Fall Down*, pp. 187–88.
132 Ibid., p. 188.
133 Ibid., p. 187.
134 See From: The Director to Tehran, August 1 1979, *Documents*, Vol 56, p. 89.
135 Cottam, *Iran and the United States*, p. 206.
136 *Documents*, Vol 68, p. 106.
137 *Documents*, Vol 68, pp. 54–56.
138 Bill, *The Eagle and the Lion*, p. 287.
139 Ibid., p. 287.
140 Ibid., pp. 287–88.
141 Ibid., p. 291.
142 Embassy of the United States of America, Note for Mr. Limbert, in *Documents*, Vol 16, pp. 57–58.
143 From NEA-Harold H. Saunders through p-Mr. Newsom to: The Secretary, September 5 1979, in *Documents*, Vol 16, pp. 70–71.
144 Ibid., p. 72.
145 Ibid., p. 73.
146 Ibid., pp. 69–70.
147 Menashri, *Iran*, p. 73.
148 *Documents*, Vol 55, pp. 17–19.
149 From American Embassy, Moscow to Secretary of State, Washington D.C. Priority, September 10, 1979, in *Documents*, Vol 49, p.72 and From Am Embassy, Moscow, to Sec State, Washington D.C., Priority, September 17, 1979, in *Documents*, Vol 16, pp. 89–92.
150 From American Embassy Tehran to Secretary of State Washington D.C. Immediate, September 18, 1979, in *Documents*, Vol 16, pp. 93–94.
151 From American Embassy Tehran to Secretary of State Washington D.C., September 20, 1979, in *Documents*, Vol 16, pp. 99–100.
152 From Secretary of State, Washington D.C., to American Embassy Bern, September 22, 1979, in *Documents*, Vol 68, p. 129.
153 From Tehran to Director, May 1979, Documents, Vol 55, pp. 40–41.
154 See Report Class Secret, Country: Iran, (September 5 1979), *Documents*, Vol 56, p. 92. October 1979 cable undated, *Documents*, Vol 55, p. 96.
155 *Documents*, Vol 56, p. 92.
156 Ibid., p. 99.
157 Current Political Developments, late October, *Documents*, Vol 56, p. 99.
158 Ibid., p. 93.
159 Ibid., p. 94.
160 From US Del[egation] [with] Secretary [of State] in New York to Secretary of State, Washington D.C., October 4 1979, in *Documents*, Vol 34, pp. 170–74.
161 Vance, *Hard Choices*, p. 371.
162 *Documents*, Vol 34, pp. 170–74
163 Ibid., pp. 168–69.
164 From Secretary of State, Washington D.C., to American Embassy, Tehran, October 6, 1979, *Documents*, Vol 34, pp. 177–79.
165 From Secretary of State, Washington D.C., to American Embassy, Tehran, October 9, 1979, *Documents*, Vol 34, p. 182.
166 Ibid.
167 Heikal, *Iran*, p. 19.
168 See chapter 11.

169 See Brezhnev's conversation with Honecker on international affairs, October 4, 1979, Westad, *The Fall of Détente*, p. 314–15.
170 Memorandum of Conversation with Soviet Ambassador, October 10, 1979, in *Documents*, Vol 49, p. 98.
171 Ibid., p. 99.
172 Policy Initiatives-Talks with Permanent Representatives, October 13, 1979, *Documents*, Vol 16, p. 130.
173 Ibid., p. 131.
174 Ibid.
175 Ibid., p. 132.
176 Ibid., pp. 152–55.
177 From American Embassy Tehran to Secretary of State, Washington D.C., October 18, 1979, *in Documents*, Vol 10, has no page numbers.
178 Ibid. and Cite Tehran to Director, October 17, 1979, in *Documents*, Vol 10.
179 From American Embassy Tehran to Secretary of State, Washington D.C., October 18, 1979, *Documents*, Vol 10.
180 Cite Tehran to Director, October 18, 1979, in *Documents*, Vol 10, no page numbers.
181 Ibid.

Chapter 11

1 Ioannides, *America's Iran*, p. 83.
2 Ibid., p. 77, Hulbert, *Interlock*, pp. 140–41.
3 Hulbert, *Interlock*, pp. 147–48.
4 Ibid., p. 147, Shawcross, *The Shah's Last Ride*, p. 214, see also Carter, *Keeping Faith*, p. 454.
5 Ioannides, *America's Iran*, p. 87, Carter, *Keeping Faith*, p. 456.
6 Ledeen and Lewis, *Debacle*, p. 228.
7 Gary Sick, *All Fall Down*, p. 185.
8 Shawcross, *The Shah's Last Ride*, p. 214.
9 Sick, *All Fall Down*, p. 185.
10 Ioannides, *America's Iran*, p. 88.
11 Ibid., Shawcross, *The Shah's Last Ride*, p. 214.
12 From American Embassy, Tehran to Secretary of State, October 23 1979, in *Documents*, Vol 34, p. 198. See also, From American Embassy, Tehran, to Secretary of State, October 24, 1979, *Documents*, Vol 34, p. 201.
13 Ibid., p. 199.
14 Hulbert, *Interlock*, pp. 148–49.
15 Ibid., p. 151.
16 Ibid., p. 153, Sick, *All Fall Down*, p. 185.
17 Ibid., p. 152.
18 Bill, *The Eagle and the Lion*, p. 285.
19 From American Embassy, Tehran to Secretary of State, October 28 1979, *Documents*, Vol 7, p. 288, Ioannides, *America's Iran*, p. 116.
20 *Documents*, Vol 16, p. 159.
21 *Documents*, Vol 55 (5), p. 21.
22 Ibid., p. 22.
23 Sick, *All Fall Down*, p. 204.
24 *London Kayhan*, 12 February 1998, p. 8.
25 Sick, *All Fall Down*, p. 204.
26 From American Embassy, Tehran, to Secretary of State, October 31 1979, *Documents*, Vol 7, pp. 289–290.
27 *Documents*, Vols 1–6, p. 198.
28 Sick, *All Fall Down*, p. 189, Stempel, *Inside the Iranian Revolution*, p. 306, Bill, *The Eagle and the Lion*, pp. 295, 492, n. 59.
29 Sick, *All Fall Down*, p. 204.
30 Vance, *Hard Choices*, p. 373.
31 Brzezinski, *Power and Principle*, pp. 475–76.
32 Ibid., p. 476.
33 Chehabi, *Iranian Politics and Religious Modernism*, p. 272.
34 Rubin, *Paved with Good Intentions*, p. 298.

35 *London Kayhan*, 12 February 1998.
36 *Iran Hostage Chronology*, p. 35, see also, Thornton, *The Carter Years*, p. 448, and Sick, *All Fall Down*, p. 205.
37 Hulbert, *Interlock*, pp. 137–38, Ioannides, *America's Iran*, p. 102. Neither Hulbert nor Ioannides seemed to know the composition of different factions and groups in Iran.
38 Sick, *All Fall Down*, p. 205.
39 Ibid., Ioannides, *America's Iran*, p. 78, Katzman, *Warriors of Islam: Iran's Revolutionary Guard* (Boulder, Colo: Westview Press, 1992), pp. 35–36.
40 Katzman, *Warriors of Islam*, p. 36.
41 Sick, *All Fall Down*, pp. 197, 203–204. See also Thornton, *The Carter Years*, p. 447. The only author who sees the take-over as a move against Khomeini is Henry Paolucci. See Paolucci, *Iran, Israel and the United States*.
42 Brzezinski, *Power and Principle*, pp. 476–84, Sick, *All Fall Down*, pp. 197, 203–204, Vance, *Hard Choices*, pp. 375–76.
43 Rubin, *Paved With Good Intentions*, p. 303, Seliktar, *Failing the Crystal Ball Test*, p. 170.
44 Amir-Arjomand, *The Turban for the Crown*, Richard C. Thornton, *The Carter Years*, Stephen Walt, *Revolution and War* (London: Cornell University Press, 1996)
45 Bill, *The Eagle and the Lion*, Cottam, *Iran and the United States*, R.K. Ramazani, 'Iran's Foreign Policy: Contending Orientations', *Middle East Journal* (Spring 1989), 202–17, Zabih, *Iran Since the Revolution*.
46 On this point see Kenneth M. Pollack, *The Persian Puzzle: The Conflict between Iran and America* (New York: Random House, 2004), pp. 156–57.
47 See Farber, *Taken Hostage*, David Harris, *The Crisis* (New York and Boston, Little Brown and Company, 2004). Mark Bowden's study has not been published yet. See Terry Gross, 'Mark Bowden discusses the Iranian hostage crisis that began 25 years ago', National Public Radio, November 4 2004. See also Mark Bowden, 'Among the Hostage-Takers', *The Atlantic Monthly*, December 2004.
48 See Harris, *The Crisis*, p. 202. Harris refers to Kho'iniha as 'a mullah who was acting as their spiritual adviser'.
49 Ioannides, *America's Iran*, pp. 92–93.
50 Ibid., pp. 95–96.
51 Ibid., pp. 96–97, 115–17.
52 Ibid., pp. 100–102.
53 Ibid., p. 51.
54 Ibid., 113.
55 See Seliktar, *Failing the Crystal Ball Test*, pp. 140, 158.
56 Mo'in, *Khomeini*, p. 227.
57 Ibid.
58 See Dilip Hiro, *The Iranian Labyrinth* (New York: Nation Books, 2005), p. 246.
59 David Patrick Houghton, *US Foreign Policy and the Iran Hostage Crisis* (Cambridge, Cambridge University Press, 2001), pp. 55–56.
60 Ibid., p. 55.
61 Mo'in, *Khomeini*, p. 227, does not mention Kho'iniha's possession of documents on Beheshti.
62 Stempel, *Inside the Iranian Revolution*, p. 225.
63 Mehdi Bazargan, *Enghelab-e Iran Dar Do Harekat* (The Iranian Revolution in Two Moves), (Tehran, 1363 [1984]), p. 95, fn.1.
64 The only exception is Zabih, *Iran Since the Revolution*.
65 Yodfat, *The Soviet Union and Revolutionary Iran*, p. 141, Nikola B. Schahgaldian, *The Clerical Establishment in Iran* (Santa Monica, Rand Corporation, 1989), pp. 61–65.
66 Schahgaldian, *The Clerical Establishment in Iran*, pp. 62–63, Menashri, *Iran*, p. 221.
67 Yodfat, *The Soviet Union and Revolutionary Iran*, p. 141, completely misses the significance of the debate between the Hojjatieh and the radicals for Iran's foreign policy orientation.
68 On the issue of factionalism see Emadeddin Baqi, *Goftegu Ba Sa'id Hajjarian* (An interview with Sa'id Hajjarian), (Tehran, Ney Publications, 2000), p. 46–48.
69 See Menashri, *Iran*, pp. 268–70.
70 See Ioannides, *America's Iran*, pp. 52–57, 111–12.
71 See Christos Ioannides, 'The Hostages of Iran: A discussion with the militants', *Washington Quarterly* 3: 12–35, 1980, p. 14.
72 Katzman, *Warriors of Islam*, 32.

73 Rahnema and Nomani, *The Secular Miracle*, pp. 172–73. The authors mistakenly say that Khomeini's orders for a war against the Shah never came.
74 Katzman, *Warriors of Islam*, p. 34.
75 Ibid.
76 Ibid., p. 35. See also Schahgaldian, *The Clerical Establishment in Iran*, pp. 61–65, 74–77. Neither Katzman nor Schahgaldian appear to have known about the existence of a right-wing faction in the MIR.
77 Rahnema and Nomani, *The Secular Miracle*, p. 173.
78 Schahgaldian, *The Clerical Establishment in Iran*, p. 75, Katzman, *Warriors of Islam*, p. 33.
79 Abrahamian, *Radical Islam*, p. 211.
80 Katzman, *Warriors of Islam*, p. 33.
81 Shaul Bakhash, *The Reign of the Ayatollahs: Iran and the Islamic Revolution* (London: I.B.Tauris and Co Ltd, 1985), p. 67.
82 Stempel, *Inside the Iranian Revolution*, pp. 225–26, Katzman, *Warriors of Islam*, Schahgaldian, *The Clerical Establishment in Iran*.
83 Chehabi, *Iranian Politics and Religious Modernism*, pp. 272–73.
84 Zabih, *Iran Since the Revolution*, pp. 46–47.
85 Ibid., p. 50.
86 Ibid., p. 50.
87 Paolucci, *Iran, Israel, and the United States*, p. 285.
88 Ibid., pp. 285–86.
89 Zabih, *Iran Since the Revolution*, p. 48.
90 See Ray S. Cline and Yonah Alexander, *Terrorism: The Soviet Connection*, (New York: Crane Russak, 1984), p. 59.
91 Copeland, *The Game Player*, p. 256.
92 Bazargan, *Enghelab-e Iran Dar Do Harekat*, pp. 93–94, Cline and Alexander, *Terrorism: The Soviet Connection*, p. 59.
93 Stempel, *Inside the Iranian Revolution*, pp. 225–26.
94 Ibid., p. 227.
95 Sajjadpour, *Iranian-Soviet Relations in a Security Perspective*, pp. 90–96.
96 Mohsen M. Milani, *The Making of Iran's Islamic Revolution: From Monarchy to Islamic Republic* (Boulder, Colorado, Westview Press, 1994), p. 153.
97 Sajjadpour, *Iranian-Soviet Relations in a Security Perspective*, p. 82.
98 Daneshvar, *Revolution in Iran*, pp. 139–140.
99 Timmerman, *Ol Ins Feuer*, p. 117.
100 See for example, Ioannides, *America's Iran*, p. 110–11, Seliktar, *Failing the Crystal Ball Test*, p. 158 and the references therein.
101 Heikal, *Iran: The Untold Story*, p. 14.
102 Seliktar, *Failing the Crystal Ball Test*, pp. 158–59. See also Chubin, 'Leftist Forces in Iran', Khalilzad, 'Moscow Dual Track Policy', Sajjadpour, *Iranian-Soviet Relations in a Security Perspective*, pp. 91–95, 96–97.
103 See Seyyed Mousavi-Khoeiniha's preface to Massoumeh Ebtekar as told to Fred A. Reed, *Takeover in Tehran: The Inside Story of the 1979 U.S. Embassy Capture* (Vancouver: Talonbooks, 2000), p. 26.
104 Ibid., Milani, *The Making of Iran's Islamic Revolution*, pp. 165–66.
105 See Bowden, 'Among the Hostage Takers'. For Daugherty's account see, William J. Daugherty, *In the Shadow of the Ayatollah: A CIA Hostage in Iran* (Annapolis: United States Naval Institute Press, 2001)
106 See Dreyfuss, *Devil's Game*, pp. 222, 239.
107 Houghton, *US Foreign Policy and the Iran Hostage Crisis*, p. 54.
108 Harris, *The Crisis*, p. 200.
109 Ibid.
110 Zabih, *Iran Since the Revolution*, p. 52.
111 See Ebtekar, *Takeover in Tehran*, p. 54.
112 See Terry Gross, 'Mark Bowden discusses the Iranian hostage crisis that began 25 years ago', National Public Radio, November 4 2004.
113 *London Keyhan*, 19 February 1998, p. 8.
114 Ibid.
115 See Ebtekar, *Takeover in Tehran*, p. 54, see also Shakeri, *Oil Nationalization and Hostage Crisis*, p. 198.
116 Bazargan, *Enghelab-e Iran Dar Do Harekat*, p. 94.

117 Houghton, *US Foreign Policy and the Iran Hostage Crisis*, p. 54, Shakeri, *Oil Nationalization and the Hostage Crisis*, p. 198.
118 Ibid.
119 See Ebtekar, *Takeover in Tehran*, p. 58.
120 Doyle McManus, *Free at Last* (New York, 1981), p. 18.
121 Vance, *Hard Choices*, p. 373.
122 Sick, *All Fall Down*, p. 206.
123 Ibid.
124 Brzezinski, *Power and Principle*, p. 478.
125 Sick, *All Fall Down*, p. 207.
126 Ibid.
127 Ibid., see also Brzezinski, *Power and Principle*, p. 478.
128 Saunders, 'The Crisis Begins', in Warren Christopher et al, *American Hostages in Iran*, p. 44.
129 Sick, *All Fall Down*, p. 108.
130 Russel Leigh Moses, *Freeing the Hostages*, (PhD Thesis, University of Pittsburgh, later published by University of Pittsburgh Press, 1996), p. 100.
131 Ibid.
132 Sick, *All Fall Down*, pp. 208–209.
133 Ibid., p. 209.
134 Ibid., pp. 213–14, Vance, *Hard Choices*, p. 176.
135 Ibid.
136 Ibid., 209–210.
137 Ibid., p. 210.
138 Ibid., p. 210.
139 Sick, *All Fall Down*, pp. 209–210.
140 Ibid., p. 210.
141 Ibid.
142 Ibid., p. 214.
143 Ibid.
144 Moses, *Freeing the Hostages*, p. 103, fn. 98.
145 Ibid., p. 102.
146 *London Kayhan*, 12, 19 February 1998.
147 Saunders, 'Diplomacy and Pressure', in Warren Christopher et al, *American Hostages in Iran*, p. 77.
148 Ibid., p. 76, Vance, *Hard Choices*, p. 376–77.
149 Brzezinski, *Power and Principle*, p. 479.
150 Sick, *All Fall Down*, p. 214.
151 Assersohn, *The Biggest Deal*, p. 41.
152 Sick, 'Military Options and Constraints', in Warren Christopher et al, *American Hostages in Iran*, p. 145.
153 Ibid., p. 145.
154 Ibid., p. 146.
155 Ibid., pp. 146–47.
156 Bird, *The Chairman*, p. 652.
157 Ibid.
158 Ibid.
159 Zabih, *Iran Since the Revolution*, pp. 46–47.
160 Paolucci, *Iran, Israel, and the United States*, pp. 287–88.
161 Zabih, *Iran Since the Revolution*, p. 14.
162 For example, in January 1980, Khomeini was the source of press attacks on Ayatollah Beheshti. See *Iran Hostage Chronology*.
163 Cottam, *Iran and the United States*, p. 217.
164 Ioannides, *America's Iran*, pp. 102–103.
165 Ibid., p. 102, Zabih, *Iran Since the Revolution*, pp. 52–53. Both studies make similar, but implausible, arguments.
166 Sick, *All Fall Down*, p. 240.
167 Ibid., p. 245.
168 Ibid., pp. 245, 359–60, n.2.
169 See Bani-Sadr, *Khianat-e Be Omid*, p. 47.
170 *Joint Report*, p. 54, n. 60.

171 Bill, *The Eagle and the Lion*, p. 279. Bill was apparently unaware of the Hafez operation.
172 See Erfani, *Iran's Islamic Revolution*.
173 Saunders, 'Diplomacy and Pressure', p. 77.
174 Zabih, *Iran Since the Revolution*, p. 54.
175 Ibid., pp. 55–56.
176 Ibid., p. 47.
177 Sick, *All Fall Down*, 225–26.
178 Thornton, *The Carter Years*, p. 451.
179 *Joint Report*, 'A Chronology on Iran', p. 297, App. 0041.
180 Sick, 'Military Options and Constraints', p. 148.
181 Brzezinski, *Power and Principle*, p. 483. Brzezinski does not mention Gromyko's expression of support for the revolution on the same day that Khomeini threatened to put the hostages on trial.
182 Major Maxwell Orme Johnson, *The Military as an Instrument of U.S. Policy in Southwest Asia* (Boulder, Colo: Westview Press, 1983), p. 9.
183 Brzezinski, *Power and Principle*, p. 483.
184 Ibid.
185 See Johnson, *The Military as an Instrument of U.S. Policy in Southwest Asia*, p. 9. He says that the meeting was held on 24 November.
186 Sick, *All Fall Down*, p. 234.
187 Ibid.
188 Johnson, *The Military as an Instrument of U.S. Policy in Southwest Asia*, pp. 9–10.
189 Sick, *All Fall Down*, p. 235, says the message was sent by 'a friendly government'.
190 *Joint Report*, p. 297, App. 0041.
191 Ibid., p. 298, App. 0042.
192 Moses, *Freeing the Hostages*, p. 193.
193 Ibid., p. 194.
194 Ibid., pp. 193–94.
195 Roberta Goren, *The Soviet Union and Terrorism* (London: George Allen and Unwin, 1984), pp. 47–48.
196 Moses, *Freeing the Hostages*, p. 196.
197 Cline and Alexander, *Terrorism: The Soviet Connection*, p. 100.
198 Ibid., p. 100–101.
199 Ioannides, 'The PLO and the Iranian Revolution,', p. 98. It is not clear to what extent the Carter administration was aware of the Soviet's attempt to discourage the PLO.
200 Zabih, *The Left in Contemporary Iran*, p. 28.
201 Sajjadpour, *Iranian-Soviet Relations in a Security Perspective*, pp. 80–97.
202 Zabih, *Iran Since the Revolution*, pp. 233–34, Zabih, *The Left in Contemporary Iran*, pp. 27–28.
203 On the campaign against Shari'atmadari see Andrew and Mitrokhin, *The Mitrokhin Archive II*, pp. 185–86, 378. Andrew and Mitrokhin do not discuss the Tudeh Party's activities in the Shari'atmadari case.
204 See Dr Mostafa Alamuti, *Iran Dar Asr-e Pahlavi* (Iran in the Pahlavi Era), Vol 9, (Paka Print, London, 1991), p. 406.
205 Moses, *Freeing the Hostages*, p. 199.
206 Sick, 'Military Options and Constraints', p. 148.
207 Moses, *Freeing the Hostages*, p. 199.
208 Thornton, *The Carter Years*, pp. 453, 474, n. 151.
209 Moses, *Freeing the Hostages*, p. 200.
210 Herbert L. Sawyer, *Soviet Perceptions of the Oil Factor in US Policy* (Boulder, Colo: Westview Press, 1983), p. 120.
211 Gates, *From the Shadows*, p. 130.
212 See Aryeh Yodfat, *The Soviet Union and Revolutionary Iran*.
213 See Vasilyi Mitrokhin, *The KGB in Afghanistan*, Cold War International History Project, Working Paper No. 40, (Washington D.C.: February 2002), p. 110.
214 Ibid., p. 110.
215 See Charles Kupchan, *The Persian Gulf and the West* (London: Allen and Unwin, 1987), p. 86.
216 Ibid., p. 84.
217 Ibid., p. 86.
218 Ibid., p. 85.
219 See *Joint Report*, 'A Chronology on Iran', p. 298, App. 0042.
220 Teicher and Teicher, *Twin Pillars to Desert Storm*, p. 78.

221 Ibid., p. 69.
222 Ibid., pp. 68–70.
223 Sick, *All Fall Down*, p. 245–46. Sick's account does not mention Teicher's study.
224 Ibid., pp. 245–46.
225 Vance, *Hard Choices*, p. 387.
226 Sick, *All Fall Down*, p. 235.
227 Ibid., p. 236.
228 Ibid.
229 Ibid., p. 237.
230 Ibid.
231 Brzezinski, *Power and Principle*, p. 484.
232 Thornton, *The Carter Years*, pp. 455–56.
233 Sick, *All Fall Down*, p. 241.
234 Brzezinski, *Power and Principle*, 481.
235 Ibid.
236 Ibid., pp. 481–82.
237 Ibid., p. 482.
238 Ibid., p. 484.
239 Ibid.
240 Sick, 'Military Options and Constraints', p. 180, Vance, *Hard Choices*, p. 387, Thornton, *The Carter Years*, pp. 456–57.
241 Sick, 'Military Options and Constraints', p. 180, downplays the obvious conclusion that the State Department considered Khomeini to be a de facto ally against the Soviet Union.
242 Saunders, 'The Crisis Begins', p. 45.
243 Johnson, *The Military as an Instrument of U.S. Policy in Southwest Asia*, pp. 16–17. See also Kupchan, *The Persian Gulf and the West*, pp. 86–87.
244 Brzezinski, *Power and Principle*, p. 446, see also Garthoff, *Détente and Confrontation*, p. 731.
245 Johnson, *The Military as an Instrument of U.S. Policy in Southwest Asia*, pp. 17–18.
246 See the argument in Garthoff, *Détente and Confrontation*.
247 Yergin, *The Prize*, p. 702.
248 *The Times*, December 14, 1979, p. 17.
249 *The Times*, December 7, 1979, p. 17.
250 *The Times*, December 8, 1979, p. 1, Brendan Brown, *The Flight of International Capital* (New York: Routledge, 1987), p. 377.
251 *The Times*, December 8, 1979, p. 1.
252 *The Times*, December 7, 1979, p. 17.
253 Ibid.
254 Sick, *All Fall Down*, p. 241.
255 Ibid., p. 242.
256 *Iran Hostage Chronology*, p. 87.

Chapter 12

1 Farber, *Taken Hostage*, Harris, *The Crisis*, Pollack, *The Persian Puzzle*.
2 Douglas MacEachin, *Predicting the Soviet Invasion of Afghanistan* (Center for the Study of Intelligence, Central Intelligence Agency, 2003), p. 7.
3 Ibid.
4 Ibid., p. 8.
5 Gates, *From the Shadows*, p. 144.
6 Ibid., p. 146.
7 Ibid.
8 MacEachin, *Predicting the Soviet Invasion of Afghanistan*, p. 8.
9 Ibid.
10 Ibid., p. 9.
11 On this point see Cooley, *Unholy Wars*, p. 10.
12 Ibid.
13 Ibid., p. 11.
14 Ibid., p. 10, Gates. *From the Shadows*, p. 149.
15 See Steve Coll, *Ghost Wars* (New York: Penguin Books, paperback edition, 2005), p. 593, n. 17.

16 Garthoff, *Détente and Confrontation*, pp. 1011, 1031.
17 Coll, *Ghost Wars*, p. 49.
18 Garthoff, *Détente and Confrontation*, p. 1011..
19 Ibid. See also Coll, *Ghost Wars*, p. 49.
20 *The Times*, December 6, 1979, p. 8.
21 Ibid.
22 Ibid.
23 Garthoff, *Détente and Confrontation*, p. 1041, fn. 177, Diego Cordovez and Selig S. Harrison, *Out of Afghanistan* (New York and Oxford,: Oxford University Press, 1995), p. 47, Thornton, *The Carter Years*, p. 466.
24 Martin Sicker, *The Bear and the Lion: Soviet Imperialism and Iran* (New York, Praeger, 1988), p. 113.
25 Thornton, *The Carter Years*, p. 465.
26 See also the argument in Garthoff, *Détente and Confrontation*.
27 Rodman, *More Precious than Peace*, p. 209.
28 Cooley, *Unholy Wars*, p. 9.
29 See Mitrokhin, *The KGB in Afghanistan*, p. 89.
30 Thornton, *The Carter Years*, p. 452.
31 Ibid., p. 453.
32 Ibid., and Coll, *Ghost Wars*, pp. 21–37 for an account of the attack.
33 Coll, *Ghost Wars*, p. 32.
34 Ibid., p. 34.
35 Thornton, *The Carter Years*, p. 453.
36 Brzezinski, *Power and Principle*, p. 485.
37 Ibid.
38 Ibid., p. 566.
39 Thornton, *The Carter Years*, pp. 464, 478, n. 211, Gates, *From the Shadows*, p. 133.
40 Thornton, *The Carter Years*, p. 464.
41 See Memorandum for the President from Zbigniew Brzezinski, subject: Reflections on Soviet intervention in Afghanistan' in Westad (ed), *The Fall of Détente*, p. 329.
42 Ibid., p. 330.
43 Ibid., pp. 329–30.
44 Ibid., p. 330.
45 Ibid., p. 331.
46 Coll, *Ghost Wars*, p. 51.
47 Ibid.
48 Ibid., pp. 62–63.
49 On Aslam Beg see Ibid., pp. 220–21, and on Abd al-Qadir Khan see Graham Allison, *Nuclear Terrorism: The Ultimate Preventable Catastrophe* (New York: Times Books, 2004), pp. 20–23, 93, 160, 193–94. On Abd al-Qadir Khan's relations with Iran see Kenneth R. Timmerman, *Countdown to Crisis: The Coming Nuclear Showdown with Iran* (New York: Crown Forum, 2005), pp. 2, 39–41, 42, 78, 79–80, 118, 122, 149–51, 154–56, 262–66, 267 and other references therein.
50 Brzezinski, *Power and Principle*, pp. 428–29, Cyrus Vance, *Hard Choices*, p. 389 and Garthoff, *Détente and Confrontation*, p. 1055, fn. 218, ignores the intelligence dimension.
51 Brzezinski, *Power and Principle*, p. 429. Carter, *Keeping Faith*, p. 472, Garthoff, *Détente and Confrontation*, p. 1058–59.
52 Sick, *All Fall Down*, p. 247.
53 Ibid., p. 248.
54 Ibid.
55 Ibid.
56 Ibid.
57 Vance, *Hard Choices*, pp. 387–89 and Garthoff, *Détente and Confrontation*, p. 1056.
58 Brzezinski, *Power and Principle*, p. 430, Garthoff, *Détente and Confrontation*, pp. 1056–57.
59 Moses, *Freeing the Hostages*, pp. 210–11.
60 Vance, *Hard Choices*, pp. 387–88, Garthoff, *Détente and Confrontation*, p. 1056.
61 Garthoff, *Détente and Confrontation*, p. 1071, fn.273.
62 Ibid., p. 1067.
63 See Gerry Argyris Andrainopoulos, *Kissinger and Brzezinski*, (London: Macmillan, 1991), p. 199.
64 Garthoff, *Détente and Confrontation*, pp. 1060–61, 1067.

65 Ibid., p. 1064–65.
66 Ibid., p. 1064, Brzezinski, *Power and Principle*, pp. 444–45.
67 Ibid., p. 1063.
68 Brzezinski, *Power and Principle*, pp. 443–45, see also Andrianopoulos, *Kissinger and Brzezinski*, p. 22.
69 See the accounts in Brzezinski, *Power and Principle*, and Garthoff, *Détente and Confrontation*.
70 *Iran Hostage Chronology*, p. 90.
71 Robert H. Johnson, *Improbable Dangers* (London, Macmillan, 1997), p. 169.
72 Ibid.
73 See Garthoff, *Détente and Confrontation*, p. 1056.
74 Brzezinski, *Power and Principle*, p. 485, Sick, *All Fall Down*, p. 282.
75 See the account by Moses, *Freeing the Hostages*.
76 Brzezinski, *Power and Principle*, p. 486.
77 'Biography of Ayatollah Mohamed Beheshti,' App, 26–29, *Joint Report*, p. 54, n. 60.
78 Brzezinski, *Power and Principle*, p. 486.
79 See Mir Ali Asghar Montazam, *The Life and Times of Ayatollah Khomeini*, p. 252.
80 See Andrew Bacevich, *The New American Militarism: How Americans are Seduced by War* (Oxford and New York, Oxford University Press, 2005), pp. 177–83.
81 Thornton, *The Carter Years*, pp. 518–519.
82 Charles A. Kupchan, *The Persian Gulf and the West* (London: Allen and Unwin, 1987), p. 131.
83 Quandt, *Saudi Arabia in the 1980s*, p. 39.
84 Ibid., p. 41, Congressional Research Service, *Saudi Arabia and the United States*, p. 13, William Quandt, 'Riyadh between the Superpowers', *Foreign Policy*, No. 44, Fall 1981, p. 51.
85 Ramazani, *Revolutionary Iran*, p. 123.
86 Brzezinski, *Power and Principle*, pp. 449–50, Garthoff, *Détente and Confrontation*, p. 1063.
87 Gates, *From the Shadows*, p. 148.
88 Brzezinski, *Power and Principle*, pp. 449–50.
89 Ibid., p. 520, and Congressional Research Service, *Saudi Arabia and the United States*, p. 59
90 Congressional Research Service, *Saudi Arabia and the United States*, p. 59.
91 Gates, *From the Shadows*, p. 148.
92 Ramazani, *Revolutionary Iran*, pp. 120–21, 124.
93 Shemesh, *Soviet-Iraqi Relations*, p. 163.
94 Ibid., Thornton, *The Carter Years*, p. 518.
95 Ibid., pp. 165, 176, n. 83.
96 Thornton, *The Carter Years*, p. 519.
97 Safran, *Saudi Arabia*, p. 360.
98 Ibid., p. 361.
99 Jasim M, Abdulghani, *Iraq and Iran: The Years of Crisis* (Baltimore, Johns Hopkins University, 1984), p. 188.
100 Robert O. Freedman, *Moscow and the Middle East: Soviet Policy Since the Invasion of Afghanistan* (Cambridge and New York: Cambridge University Press, 1991), p. 74, Efraim Karsh, *The Soviet Union and Syria Since 1970* (London and New York: Macmillan and St Martin's Press, 1991), p. 51, for Syria's role.
101 Congressional Research Service, *Saudi Arabia and the United States*, p. 13.
102 See David Menashri, *Iran*, p. 131.
103 John K. Cooley, *Pay Back*, (New York: Brassey's, 1991), p. 119, Cooley, however, does not say anything about the role of the Guards in the purges and Zamani's role.
104 Ibid.
105 Gates, *From the Shadows*, p. 147.
106 Ibid., pp. 147–48.
107 Sick, *All Fall Down*, p. 249.
108 Ibid., p. 249.
109 Ibid.
110 U.S. Congress, *Joint Report of Task Force investigating 'October Surprise' Allegations* (Washington D.C.: U.S. Government Printing Office, 1992) (henceforward referred to as Joint Report), p. 37.
111 Ibid.
112 Ibid., p. 102.
113 Ibid.
114 Ibid., p. 38.
115 Ibid., p. 56, n. 131.

116 U.S. Congress, Committee On Foreign Relations, United States Senate: *Report of the Special Counsel to Senator Terry Sanford and Senator James M. Jeffords*, (henceforward referred to as Sanford-Jeffords Report), (Washington D.C.: U.S. Government Printing Office, 1992), p. 39.
117 *Iran Hostage Chronology*, pp. 86–87.
118 See *Joint Report*, p. 102.
119 *Sanford-Jeffords Report*, 39.
120 See *Joint Report*, sections on Jamshid Hashemi's background.
121 Dilip Hiro, *Iran under the Ayatollahs* (London, Routledge and Kegan Paul, 1985), p. 154.
122 Vance, *Hard Choices*, p. 400, Vance does not mention Bani-Sadr and Ghotbzadeh.
123 Sick, *All Fall Down*, p. 240.
124 Ibid., p. 239.
125 Alvin Rubinstein,'The Soviet Union and Iran Under Khomeini', *International Affairs*, pp. 606–607.
126 *Iran Hostage Chronology*, p. 88.
127 Freedman, *Moscow and the Middle East*, p. 74, Safran, *Saudi Arabia*, pp. 318–19.
128 Richard W. Cottam, *Iran and the United States*, p. 214.
129 Ibid.
130 Sick, *All Fall Down*, p. 239.
131 *Joint Report*, p. 39, 57, n. 176.
132 'A Chronology on Iran', pp. 299–300, App. 0043–44 in *Joint Report*.
133 Sick, *All Fall Down*, p. 246.
134 Hamilton Jordan, *Crisis* (New York: G.P. Putnam's Sons, 1982) pp. 104–105.
135 Ibid., p. 105.
136 William Shawcross, *The Shah's Last Ride*, pp. 292–93.
137 Ibid., p. 290.
138 Taheri, *The Unknown Life of the Shah*, pp. 317, 345, n. 31.
139 Ibid., p. 317.
140 Ibid.
141 Vance, *Hard Choices*, p. 401.
142 Ibid.
143 *Iran Hostage Chronology*, p. 87.
144 Ibid., p. 86.
145 Cordovez and Harrison, *Out of Afghanistan*, p. 54.
146 Carter, *Keeping Faith*, p. 479, Garthoff, *Détente and Confrontation*, p. 976, Thornton, *The Carter Years*, p. 483.
147 Carter, *Keeping Faith*, p. 480, see also Thornton, *The Carter Years*, p. 484.
148 Carter, *Keeping Faith*, p. 480
149 Ibid.
150 Thornton, *The Carter Years*, p. 484.
151 Ibid.
152 *Iran Hostage Chronology*, p. 89.
153 Ibid.
154 Ibid., p. 86.
155 See Kenneth R. Timmerman, *Ol Ins Feuer*, (Fanning the Flames: Guns, Greed and Geopolitics in the Gulf War), (Zurich: Orell Fusli, 1988), Zabih, *The Left in Contemporary Iran*.
156 Taheri, *The Unknown Life of the Shah*, pp. 317–18, 345, n. 32.
157 Cottam, *Iran and the United States*, p. 212, Moses, *Freeing the Hostages*, p. 358.
158 '*Iran Hostage Chronology*, p. 91.
159 Sick, *All Fall Down*, p. 244.
160 Jordan, *Crisis*, p. 107.
161 Vance, *Hard Choices*, p. 402.
162 *Iran, Hostage Chronology*, p. 88.
163 Timmerman, *Ol Ins Feuer*, p. 117–18.
164 See the account by Dobrynin, *In Confidence*.
165 See Top Secret to Comrades Brezhnev, Andropov, Gromyko, Suslov, Ustinov, Ponomarev, Rusakov, Report to Communist Party Politburo on Afghanistan, January 27, 1980, Protocol No. 181 of the CC CPSU Politburo session of January 28, 1980, in Westad (ed), *The Fall of Détente*, p. 323–25.
166 Vance, *Hard Choices*, p. 394, Thornton, *The Carter Years*, p. 485.
167 Thornton, *The Carter Years*, p. 486.
168 Ibid.

169 Ibid.
170 *Iran Hostage Chronology*, p. 87.
171 Carter, *Keeping Faith*, pp. 485–86.
172 Menashri, *Iran*, p. 134, does not mention Bani-Sadr's message to Carter.
173 Jasim M. Abdulghani, *Iran and Iraq: The Years of Crisis* (Baltimore: Johns Hopkins University, 1984), pp. 186, 220, n. 59.
174 Sick, *All Fall Down*, pp. 301–302, Vance, *Hard Choices*, pp. 400–401, see also Thornton, *The Carter Years*, p. 488.
175 Carter, *Keeping Faith*, p. 488, *Joint Report*, pp. 40, 57, n. 191.
176 Sick, *All Fall Down*, p. 254. Sick does not say that the official was Ghotbzadeh.
177 Taheri, *The Unknown Life of the Shah*, p. 317.
178 Thornton, *The Carter Years*, p. 488.
179 Ibid.
180 Congressional Research Service, *Saudi Arabia and the United States*, p. 60.
181 Thornton, *The Carter Years*, p. 489.
182 See Marshall Shulman's letter to Cyrus Vance on US-Soviet relations after Afghanistan, February 15,1980 in Westad, *The Fall of Détente*, pp. 351–355–56.
183 Grasselli, *British and American Responses to the Soviet Invasion of Afghanistan*, p. 90–93.
184 Ibid., p. 91.
185 Thornton, *The Carter Years*, p. 489.
186 Sick, *All Fall Down*, p. 263.
187 Ibid., p. 264.
188 Zabih, *Iran Since the Revolution*, p. 54, makes no mention of the Ghotbzadeh plan.
189 See Sick, *All Fall Down*, p. 265, for a different argument.
190 Brzezinski, *Power and Principle*, p. 435.
191 Ibid., Vance, *Hard Choices*, p. 395.
192 Ibid.
193 Ibid.
194 Ibid., p. 436.
195 Thornton, *The Carter Years*, p. 491.
196 Ibid.
197 Klare, *Beyond the Vietnam Syndrome*, p. 38.
198 Brzezinski, *Power and Principle*, pp. 436–37.
199 Ibid.
200 Pierre Salinger, *America Held Hostage: The Secret Negotiations* (garden City, NY: Doubleday, 1981), p. 199.
201 Ibid., p. 200.
202 For further details see *Iran Hostage Chronology*.
203 Sick, *All Fall Down*, pp. 268–69, Saunders, 'Diplomacy and Pressure', p. 132.
204 Sick, *All Fall Down*, pp. 268–69.
205 Ibid., p. 269, see also Salinger, *America Held Hostage*, pp. 199–200.
206 Moses, *Freeing the Hostages*, pp. 339–340, does not say who was affected by this decision.
207 *Iran Hostage Chronology*, p. 125.
208 Bani-Sadr, *My Turn to Speak*, pp. 26–28.
209 Jordan, *Crisis*, pp. 165–66.
210 Sick, *All Fall Down*, p. 312, see also Moses, *Freeing the Hostages*, pp. 316–19.
211 Moses, *Freeing the Hostages*, p. 319.
212 Ibid., pp. 320–21, Sick, *All Fall Down*, pp. 306–307, Salinger, *America Held Hostage*, pp. 180–81.
213 Ibid., p. 322.
214 *Iran Hostage Chronology*, pp. 124–25.
215 Zabih, *Iran Since the Revolution*, p. 54.
216 *Iran Hostage Chronology*, pp. 125–26, see also, Moses, *Freeing the Hostages*, p. 359.
217 *Iran Hostage Chronology*, p. 124.
218 Ibid., pp. 125–26, see also, Moses, *Freeing the Hostages*, p. 359–360.
219 Salinger, *America Held Hostage*, p. 206. For Heikal's account see Mohamed Heikal, *Iran: The Untold Story*, pp. 187–88.
220 Heikal, *Iran: The Untold Story*, p. 188, does not say whether he told Saunders that he had met the militants at the Soviet embassy.
221 Ibid., pp. 14, 22. Heikal's account does not raise the obvious question, which is why he should have met with the leaders of the militants in the Soviet embassy.
222 Ibid., p. 189.

223 Menashri, *Iran*, p. 144, Moses, *Freeing the Hostages*, p. 201.
224 Hiro, *Iran Under the Ayatollahs*, pp. 154–55.
225 *Iran Hostage Chronology*, p. 130.
226 Ibid., p. 131.
227 Salinger, *America Held Hostage*, p. 207.
228 Shawcross, *The Shah's Last Ride*, p. 334.
229 Ibid., p. 335–36.
230 Ibid., p. 336, see also Taheri, *The Unknown Life of the Shah*, p. 320.
231 Ibid., Taheri, *The Unknown Life of the Shah*, p. 320.
232 Assersohn, *The Biggest Deal*, p. 122.
233 Shawcross, *The Shah's Last Ride*, pp. 336–37.
234 Assersohn, *The Biggest Deal*, p. 123.
235 Dobrynin, *In Confidence*, pp. 450–51.
236 Ibid., p. 451.
237 *Iran Hostage Chronology*, pp. 130–31.
238 Rahnema and Nomani, *The Secular Miracle*, pp. 300–301.
239 Salinger, *America Held Hostage*, pp. 208–209.
240 Shawcross, *The Shah's Last Ride*, p. 334.
241 Taheri, *The Unknown Life of the Shah*, p. 320.
242 Salinger, *America Held Hostage*, pp. 209–210.
243 Shawcross, *The Shah's Last Ride*, p. 338.
244 Ibid., p. 338, Sick, *All Fall Down*, p. 271.
245 Taheri, *The Unknown Life of the Shah*, p. 321.
246 Pahlavi, *Answer to History*, pp. 32–33, Shawcross, *The Shah's Last Ride*, p. 338.
247 Shawcross, *The Shah's Last Ride*, p. 339.
248 Taheri, *The Unknown Life of the Shah*, p. 321.
249 Sick, *All Fall Down*, pp. 271, 285.
250 Shawcross, *The Shah's Last Ride*, p. 339, Assersohn, *The Biggest Deal*, p. 122.
251 Assersohn, *The Biggest Deal*, p. 122.
252 Shawcross, *The Shah's Last Ride*, p. 339.
253 Ibid.
254 Ibid., p. 342, Assersohn, *The Biggest Deal*, p. 122, Sick, *All Fall Down*, p. 271.
255 Ibid., p. 339–40.
256 Ibid., p. 341, see also Sick, *All Fall Down*, p. 271.
257 Assersohn, *The Biggest Deal*, pp. 122–23.
258 Shawcross, *The Shah's Last Ride*, p. 342.
259 Brzezinski, *Power and Principle*, p. 486.
260 Ibid., p. 487.
261 Ibid.
262 Vance, *Hard Choices*, pp. 405–407.
263 Carter, *Keeping Faith*, p. 501.
264 *Joint Report*, pp. 164–65, 179, n. 198.
265 Ibid., p. 163.
266 Carter, *Keeping Faith*, p. 502.
267 *Joint Report*, p. 57, n. 197.
268 Carter, *Keeping Faith*, p. 502.
269 *Joint Report*, p. 41.
270 Ibid., p. 57, n. 199.
271 Ibid., p. 41.
272 Dobrynin, *In Confidence*, p. 452.
273 Ibid.
274 Garthoff, *Détente and Confrontation*, p. 1104.
275 Thornton, *The Carter Years*, pp. 498–99.
276 Yodfat, *The Soviet Union and Revolutionary Iran*, pp. 81, 90, n. 49.
277 Gates, *From the Shadows*, p. 148.

Chapter 13

1 David Patrick Houghton, *US Foreign Policy and the Iran Hostage Crisis* (Cambridge: Cambridge University Press, 2001).

Notes

2   Brzezinski, *Power and Principle*, p. 427 and Garthoff, *Détente and Confrontation*, pp. 1050–51, for a refutation of Brzezinski's argument.
3   Thornton, *The Carter Years*, pp. 495–96.
4   Timmerman, *The Death Lobby*, p. 110.
5   *Joint Report*, pp. 41, 57, n. 203.
6   Thornton, *The Carter Years*, p. 493.
7   Brzezinski, *Power and Principle*, p. 491.
8   See Kenneth R. Timmerman, *Ol Ins Feuer*, (Fanning the Flames: Guns, Greed and Geopolitics in the Gulf War), (Zurich: Orell Fusli, 1988), p. 27.
9   Ibid.
10 Ibid.
11 Eberhard Kienle, *Ba'th v. Ba'th* (London: I.B. Tauris, 1990), p. 154.
12 Moshe Ma'oz, *Asad* (London: Weidenfeld and Nicolson, 1988), p. 154.
13 Anthony H. Cordesman and Abraham R. Wagner, *The Lessons of Modern War, Vol II: The Iran-Iraq War* (Boulder and San Francisco, Westview Press, 1990), p. 29.
14 Segev, *The Iranian Triangle*, p. 120.
15 Efraim Karsh and Inari Rautsi, *Saddam Hussein* (London: Futura, 1991) p. 148.
16 Ibid., p. 139.
17 Timmerman, *Ol Ins Feuer*, p. 29.
18 Cordesman and Wagner, *The Lessons of Modern War, Vol II*, pp. 29, 38, n. 23.
19 Marion Farouk Sluglett and Peter Sluglett, *Iraq Since 1958* (London and New York: I.B. Tauris and Co Ltd, 1990), p. 200.
20 Timmerman, *Ol Ins Feuer*, p. 29, Sluglett and Sluglett, *Iraq Since 1958*, p. 200, Cordesman and Wagner, *Lessons of Modern War, Vol II*, p. 29.
21 Thornton, *The Carter Years*, pp. 520–21.
22 Jimmy Carter, *Keeping Faith*, p. 506.
23 Ibid.
24 Thornton, *The Carter Years*, p. 521.
25 Ibid., pp. 497, 531, ns, 76 and 77, 532, n. 78.
26 Houghton, *US Foreign Policy and the Iran Hostage Crisis*, pp. 174–79.
27 Jeffrey D. Simon, *The Terrorist Trap* (Bloomington and Indianapolis, Indiana University Press, second edition, 2001), p. 148, p. 479, n. 73.
28 Ibid., pp. 148–149, 430, n. 78.
29 Sick *All Fall Down*, p. 290, and Vance, *Hard Choices*, p. 409.
30 Sick, *All Fall Down*, p. 290.
31 Ibid.
32 David Harris, *The Crisis* (New York, Little Brown, 2004), 341.
33 Sick, *All Fall Down*, pp. 290–92, Houghton, *US Foreign Policy and the Iran Hostage Crisis*, pp. 123–27.
34 *Joint Report*, p. 201.
35 Vance, *Hard Choices*, p. 409.
36 Ibid.
37 Houghton, *US Foreign Policy and the Iran Hostage Crisis*, pp. 127–29.
38 Stansfield Turner, *Terrorism and Democracy*, p. 109.
39 Ibid., p. 108, obfuscates the chronology.
40 Ibid., p. 116.
41 Ibid., p. 115, Houghton, *US Foreign Policy and the Iran Hostage Crisis*, pp. 119–121.
42 Vance, *Hard Choices*, p. 411.
43 Turner, *Terrorism and Democracy*, p. 116.
44 Ibid.
45 Ibid., p. 117.
46 James H. Kyle, *The Guts to Try* (New York: Orion Books, 1990), Thornton, *The Carter Years*, p. 532, n. 89.
47 Thornton, *The Carter Years*, p. 500.
48 Ibid., pp. 502–503.
49 Ibid., p. 504.
50 Assersohn, *The Biggest Deal*, p. 133.
51 Thornton, *The Carter Years*, pp. 499, 532, n. 90.
52 Carter, *Keeping Faith*, pp. 515–16.
53 Thornton, *The Carter Years*, pp. 505, 534, n. 116.
54 Ibid., p. 505.

55 Assersohn, *The Biggest Deal*, p. 133.
56 Ibid.
57 Saunders, 'Beginning of the End', p. 283.
58 Gabriella Grasselli, *British and American Responses to the Soviet Invasion of Afghanistan* (Aldershot: Dartmouth Publishing, 1996), p. 137.
59 Ibid.
60 Cottam, *Iran and the United States*, p. 222. Cottam seems oblivious to the different strategic mind-sets, which drove NSC and State Department policies respectively.
61 Sick, *All Fall Down*, pp. 303–304.
62 Ibid., p. 303.
63 Houghton, *US Foreign Policy and the Iran Hostage Crisis*, 137.
64 Ibid.
65 Ibid.
66 Ibid., p. 138.
67 Ibid., pp. 137–38, downplays Muskie's role. See Grasselli, *British and American Responses to the Soviet Invasion of Afghanistan*, p. 137, for Muskie's views.
68 Shahram Chubin, *Security in the Persian Gulf 4* (Montclair, NJ.:Allanheld, Osmun, 1982), p. 137.
69 Ibid., p. 105.
70 Turner, *Terrorism and Democracy*, p. 147.
71 Ibid., p. 148.
72 Ibid.
73 Ibid.
74 Katzman, *The Warriors of Islam*, p. 54.
75 See Congressional Research Service, Library of Congress, Report Prepared for Committee on Foreign Relations, US House of Representatives. *The Iran Hostage Crisis: A Chronology of Daily Developments*. 97th Congress., 1 Sess (Henceforward referred to as Iran Hostage Chronology), p. 131.
76 Heikal, *Iran: The Untold Story*, pp. 189–90.
77 Saunders, 'Beginning of the End', p. 288.
78 Stempel, *Inside the Iranian Revolution*, p. 249.
79 Ibid., p. 248.
80 Katzman, *Warriors of Islam*, pp. 34–35.
81 Zabih, *Iran Since the Revolution*, p. 55.
82 Ibid.
83 Assersohn, *The Biggest Deal*, pp. 167–68.
84 Menashri, *Iran*, pp. 134–35.
85 Ibid., p. 135.
86 See Daniel Brumberg, *Reinventing Khomeini* (Chicago and London: The University of Chicago Press, 2001), p. 114.
87 Menashri, *Iran*, p. 134. On Bani-Sadr's attempt to control the Guards see Katzman, *Warriors of Islam*.
88 Zabih, *Iran Since the Revolution*, p. 58.
89 See Katzman, *The Warriors of Islam*, p. 54, Bakhash, *The Reign of the Ayatollahs*, p. 109, *The Times*, June 18, 1980, and June 19, 1980.
90 See Katzman, *Warriors of Islam* for a detailed account of factionalism in the Guards.
91 Bakhash, *The Reign of the Ayatollahs*, pp. 121–24.
92 Paolucci, *Iran, Israel, and the United States*, pp. 317–18.
93 Zabih, *Iran Since the Revolution*, p. 122 and Sepehr Zabih, *The Left in Contemporary Iran* (Stanford: Hoover Institution Press, 1986).
94 Hunter, *Iran and the World*.
95 *The Times*, June 19, 1980.
96 Menashri, *Iran*, p. 135.
97 *The Times*, June 19, 1980.
98 Congressional Research Service, *Iran Hostage Chronology*, p. 213, *Joint Report*, pp. 41, 57, n. 207.
99 Grasselli, *British and American Responses to the Soviet Invasion of Afghanistan*, pp. 107–108.
100 Congressional Research Service, *Saudi Arabia and the United States*, Report, 97th Cong., 1st Sess, (1981), p. 35.
101 Shahram Chubin, 'Gains for Soviet Policy in the Middle East', *International Security*, Vol 6, Spring 1982, p. 135.

102 Ibid., pp. 134–35.
103 Chubin, *Security in the Persian Gulf*, p. 91.
104 Ibid.
105 Claudia Wright, 'Implications of the Iraq-Iran War,' *Foreign Affairs*, (Winter 1980–81), pp. 279–80.
106 Claudia Wright, 'Neutral or Neutralized?: Iraq, Iran and the Superpowers', in Shirin Tahir-Kheli, and Shaheen Ayubi (eds), *The Iran-Iraq War* (New York: Praeger, 1983), p. 176, Safran, *Saudi Arabia*, p. 361, Safran is less certain of the timing of the Saudis' decision.
107 Teicher and Teicher, *Twin Pillars to Desert Storm*, pp. 67–71.
108 House Committee on Foreign Affairs, *Export of Frigate Engines to Iraq*, 14 May 1980, 96th Congress, 1981, pp. 51–53.
109 Ephraim Karsh, *The Soviet Union and Syria*, (London, 1988), pp. 52, 113, n. 35.
110 Moshe Maoz, *Syria and Israel*, p. 187.
111 Maoz, *Asad*, p. 154.
112 Karsh and Rautsi, *Saddam Hussein*, p. 146.
113 Ibid.
114 Congressional Research Service, *Saudi Arabia and the United States*, p. 61.
115 Chubin, *Security in the Persian Gulf*, pp. 98–100.
116 Cordesman and Wagner, *Lessons of Modern War, Vol 2*.
117 See Jackson-Smith, *The Search for Strategic Stability in the Persian Gulf*, p. 93.
118 Timmerman, *The Death Lobby*, pp. 112–13.
119 Ibid., p. 112.
120 Ibid., pp. 112–13.
121 Teicher and Teicher, *Twin Pillars to Desert Storm*, p. 103. The Teichers try to downplay the importance of the US role.
122 See Aburish, *Saddam Hussein*, pp. 187–88.
123 Ibid., pp. 188.
124 Timmerman, *The Death Lobby*, p. 115, Cottam, *Iran and the United States*, 224.
125 Jackson-Smith, *The Search for Strategic Stability in the Persian Gulf*, p. 94.
126 Segev, *The Iranian Triangle*, p. 120.
127 Timmerman, *Ol Ins Feuer*, pp. 121–23, see also Nikola B. Schahgaldian, with the assistance of Gina Barkhordarian, *The Iranian Military Under the Islamic Republic* (Santa Monica: Rand Corporation, 1987), p. 23.
128 *The Times*, July 25, 1980, Zabih, *The Iranian Military in Revolution and War*, pp. 125–26, Hiro, *Iran under the Ayatollahs*, p. 156, and Edgar O'Ballance, *Islamic Fundamentalist Terrorism*, (London: Macmillan, 1997), pp. 54–55.
129 See Centre for Political Studies and Research, Kudeta-ye Nozheh (Nozheh Coup d'etat) (Tehran: Centre for Political Studies and Research, second edition, 1989), pp. 161–62.
130 O'Ballance, *Islamic Fundamentalist Terrorism*, p. 55.
131 Schahgaldian, *The Iranian Military Under the Islamic Republic*, p. 23, fn 42.
132 Timmerman, *Ol Ins Feuer*, p. 123, and 253–56. Despite presenting a detailed account of Ghorbanifar's connection with the Mossad, Timmerman does not draw the obvious conclusion.
133 Seale, *Asad*, p. 362.
134 Ibid.
135 Timmerman, *The Death Lobby*, pp. 104–105, Cordesman, *Iran and Iraq: The Threat from the Northern Gulf*, Adel Darwish and Gregory Alexander, *Unholy Babylon*: The Secret History of Saddam's War (London: Victor Gollancz Ltd, 1991).
136 Hiro, *Iran Under the Ayatollahs*, p. 156.
137 Taheri, *Nest of Spies*, p. 138.
138 *Sanford-Jeffords Report*, p. 184.
139 Stempel, *Inside the Iranian Revolution*, p. 248.
140 Chubin, 'Gains for Soviet Policy in the Middle East'., p. 141.
141 Timmerman, *The Death Lobby*, p. 116.
142 Chubin, 'Leftist Forces in Iran', *Problems of Communism*, (Washington, DC), July-August 1980, pp. 8–9, fn. 38, Chubin, 'The Soviet Union and Iran', p. 934, Zalmay Khalilzad, 'Moscow's Double-Track Policy, Islamic Iran: Soviet Dilemma', *Problems of Communism*, (Washington DC), January-February 1984, p. 9.
143 Taheri, *Nest of Spies*, p. 138.
144 Centre for Political Studies and Research, *Kudeta-ye Nozheh*, p. 193.

145 Chubin, 'Gains for Soviet Policy in the Middle East', p. 143.
146 See Zabih, *The Iranian Military in Revolution and War*, p. 125.
147 Ibid.
148 Behrouz Souresrafil, *Khomeini and Israel* (United Kingdom: C.C. Press Ltd, second edition, 1989), p. 51, Timmerman, *Ol Ins Feuer*, p. 121.
149 O'Ballance, *Islamic Fundamentalist Terrorism*, pp. 146–47. O'Ballance does not mention the connection between the coup and assassination attempts. See also, Sick, *October Surprise*, p. 93.
150 Ira Silverman, 'An American Terrorist', *New Yorker*, Issue 2002-08-05.
151 Trento, *Prelude to Terror*, pp. 186–87, 191–92. See also Ira Silverman, 'An American Terrorist'.
152 See Ira Silverman, 'An American Terrorist'.
153 Ibid.
154 Bakhash, *The Reign of the Ayatollahs*, pp. 119–120, Schahgaldian, *The Iranian Military Under the Islamic Republic*, pp. 23–24, fn. 44.
155 See Katzman, *The Warriors of Islam*, p. 55. The author mistakenly describes the Nozheh coup as 'a minor failed regular army coup'. See also Bakhash, *The Reign of the Ayatollahs*, p. 119.
156 Bakhash, *The Reign of the Ayatollahs*, p. 119.
157 See Andrew and Mitrokhin, *The Mitrokhin Archive II*, p. 184.
158 Ibid.
159 Ibid.
160 Sick, *All Fall Down*, p. 308.
161 Hiro, *Iran Under the Ayatollahs*, p. 161.
162 Ibid., p. 162. Hiro apparently did not know of Kani's membership of Hojjatieh. On Mahdavi-Kani's membership of Hojjatieh see Menashri, *Iran*.
163 Katzman, *Warriors of Islam*, p. 35.
164 Ibid., p. 37, does not mention the important ministries controlled by the MIR.
165 Zabih, *Iran Since the Revolution*, p. 56.
166 Assersohn, *The Biggest Deal*, p. 165.
167 *Joint Report*, pp. 41–42.
168 See Bakhash, *The Reign of the Ayatollahs*, p. 110.
169 Bani-Sadr, *My Turn to Speak*, pp. 15–16.
170 Katzman, *The Warriors of Islam*, p. 55.
171 Timmerman, *Ol Ins Feuer*, pp. 117–18, 295–96. Sicker, *The Bear and the Lion*, p. 118.
172 Shahram Chubin, 'Leftist Forces in Iran', p. 8, Shahram Chubin, 'The Soviet Union and Iran', *Foreign Affairs*, Spring 1983, p. 934, and Zalmay Khalilzad, 'Moscow's Double-Track Policy', p. 5.
173 Daneshvar, *Revolution in Iran*, pp. 152–53.
174 Zabih, *The Left in Contemporary Iran*, p. 47.
175 Yodfat, *The Soviet Union and Revolutionary Iran*, p. 114.
176 Ibid., p. 128, n. 84.
177 See Assersohn, *The Biggest Deal*, Timmerman, *Ol Ins Feuer*, and Cooley, *Pay Back!* For Beheshti's activities see also Yodfat, *The Soviet Union and Revolutionary Iran*, p. 128, n. 84 above.
178 Zabih, *The Left in Contemporary Iran*, p. 47, Yodfat, *The Soviet Union and Revolutionary Iran*, p. 123. Zabih only identifies two tendencies.
179 Yodfat, *The Soviet Union and Revolutionary Iran*, p. 141.
180 Anthony H. Cordesman and Abraham R. Wagner, *The Lessons of Modern War, Vol II*, p. 29.
181 Taheri, *Nest of Spies*, p. 139, Sick, *October Surprise*, p. 104.
182 Cordesman and Wagner, *The Lessons of Modern War, Vol II*, pp. 38–39, n. 25.
183 Thornton, *The Carter Years*, p. 521.
184 Jackson-Smith, *The Search for Strategic Stability*, p. 95.
185 Aburish, *Saddam Hussein*, p. 188.
186 Ibid.
187 Hiro, *The Longest War*, pp. 75–76.
188 Segev, *The Iranian Triangle*, p. 120, Karsh and Rautsi, *Saddam Hussein*, p. 158.
189 Aburish, *Saddam Hussein*, pp. 188–89.
190 See Robert Parry, October Surprise X-Files, 'Saddam Hussein's 'Green Light', www.consortiumnews.com.
191 See Christopher Hitchens, 'Realpolitik in the Gulf: A Game Gone Tilt', in Mikah Sifry (ed), *The Gulf War Reader* (New York: Random House Value Publishing, paperback edition, 1997), p. 111.

192 Crozier, *Free Agent*, pp. 162–163.
193 Seale, *Asad*, pp. 361–62.
194 Timmerman, *The Death Lobby*, pp. 120–21.
195 Aburish, *Saddam Hussein*, p. 195.
196 Timmerman, *The Death Lobby*, pp. 120–21.
197 Moshe Ma'oz, *Asad: The Sphinx of Damascus: A Political Biography* (London: Grove Pr, 1988), p. 152.
198 Ibid., pp. 152, 161, Ma'oz, *Syria and Israel*, p. 156, Seale, *Asad*, pp. 329, 335–36.
199 Jackson-Smith, *The Search for Strategic Stability in the Persian Gulf*, p. 96, Kienle, *Ba'th v. Ba'th*, pp. 155–56.
200 Jackson-Smith, *The Search for Strategic Stability in the Persian Gulf*, pp. 96–97.
201 Bani-Sadr, *My Turn to Speak*, pp. 69–70.
202 Robert O. Freedman, *Moscow and the Middle East: Soviet Policy since the Invasion of Afghanistan*, p. 85.
203 Bani-Sadr, *My Turn to Speak*, p. 70.
204 Chubin, *Security in the Persian Gulf*, pp. 96–97.
205 Bani-Sadr, *My Turn to Speak*, pp. 13–14, Bulloch and Morris, *The Gulf War*, p. 47.
206 Bani-Sadr, *My Turn to Speak*, p. 13.
207 Bulloch and Morris, *The Gulf War*, p. 47, Bani-Sadr, *My Turn to Speak*, p. 14, Timmerman, *Ol Ins Feuer*, p. 123.
208 Bani-Sadr, *My Turn to Speak*, p. 14,
209 Bulloch and Morris, *The Gulf War*, pp. 47–48.
210 Jackson-Smith, *The Search for Strategic Stability*, p. 100.
211 Bani-Sadr, *My Turn to Speak*, p. 14–15.
212 Terzian, *OPEC*, p. 281.
213 Yodfat, *The Soviet Union and Revolutionary Iran*, p. 81.
214 See Andrew and Mitrokhin, *The Mitrokhin Archive II*, p. 185.
215 Ibid., pp. 71–72, Sicker, *The Bear and the Lion*, p. 115.
216 Ibid., Sicker, *The Bear and the Lion*, p. 115.
217 Chubin, 'Gains for Soviet Policy in the Middle East', p. 137.
218 Andrew and Mitrokhin, *The Mitrokhin Archive II*, p. 185.
219 Ibid.
220 Ibid.
221 See *Sanford-Jeffords Report*, *Joint Report*, Sick, *October Surprise*, Honegger, *October Surprise*,.
222 Parry, *Trick or Treason*, pp. 49–50.
223 Ben-Menashe, *Profits of War*, pp. 52–53.
224 Ibid., pp. 53–54.
225 Ibid., p. 55.
226 Joseph E. Persico, *Casey* (New York: Penguin Books, 1990), p. 192, see also *Sanford-Jeffords Report*, pp. 25–26.
227 Parry, *Trick or Treason*, p. 51.
228 *Joint Report*, pp. 78–79, *Sanford-Jeffords Report*, pp. 21, 40.
229 *Joint Report*, pp. 38, 56, n. 154.
230 *Sanford-Jeffords Report*, p. 41.
231 *Joint Report*, pp. 38, 56, n. 155.
232 Ibid., p. 79, 131, n. 101.
233 See Robert Parry, 'Russia's prime minister and October Surprise', 15 May 1999, www.consortiumnews.com.
234 *Joint Report*, p. 78.
235 Parry, *Trick or Treason*, pp. 255–56.
236 See Robert Parry, 'Russia's prime minister and October Surprise', 15 May 1999, www.consortiumnews.com.
237 Ibid.
238 Ibid.
239 *Joint Report*, pp. 64–65, 71–72, *Sanford-Jeffords Report*, pp. 52–55.
240 *Sanford-Jeffords Report*, p. 54.
241 *Joint Report*, p. 65, *Sanford-Jeffords Report*, p. 56.
242 *Sanford-Jeffords Report*, p. 56.
243 Ibid., pp. 56, 188–89.
244 *Joint Report*, pp. 100, 137, n. 419.
245 Ibid., p. 137, n. 420.

246 Ibid., p. 137, n. 420.
247 Ibid., pp. 100, 137, nos. 421–24.
248 Ibid., p. 100.
249 Ibid., p. 77.
250 *Sanford-Jeffords Report*, pp. 49–50.
251 *Joint Report*, p. 103.
252 Ibid., p. 80, Appendix, pp. 771–80.
253 *Sanford-Jeffords Report*, p. 116.
254 Ibid., p. 116, fn. 837.
255 Ibid., pp.116–17.
256 Robert Parry, 'Russia's prime minister and October Surprise'.
257 Ibid.
258 Crozier, *Free Agent*, pp. 161–62, 164.
259 Seale, *Asad*, p. 363.
260 Sick, *October Surprise*, p. 25.
261 Ibid.
262 Ibid. 26.
263 Ibid., p. 25.
264 Ibid., p. 26.
265 Saunders, 'Beginning of the End', p. 289.
266 Ibid.
267 Ibid., p. 288. See also n. 99 above.
268 *Joint Report*, p. 79.
269 Ibid., pp. 78–79.
270 Ibid., pp. 78, 80.

Chapter 14

1 Bani-Sadr, *My Turn to Speak*, see also, Bakhash, *The Reign of the Ayatollahs*, 106–108, Daneshvar, Revolution in Iran, p. 149.
2 Sick, *October Surprise*, p. 94.
3 Bakhash, *The Reign of the Ayatollahs*, p. 119.
4 Discussions with former Iranian military officers.
5 Sick, *October Surprise*, p. 93.
6 Freedman, *Moscow and the Middle East*, p. 85.
7 Cordesman and Wagner, *Lessons of Modern War, Vol 2*, p. 30.
8 Yodfat, *The Soviet Union and Revolutionary Iran*, p. 82.
9 Brzezinski, *Power and Principle*, p. 451.
10 Ibid.
11 Ibid., pp. 451–52.
12 Parry, *Trick or Treason*, pp. 142–43.
13 See Robert Parry, 'October Surprise: Time for Truth?', Part 2, *The Consortium*, consortiumnews.com.
14 Sick, *October Surprise*, pp. 94–95.
15 Roy Assersohn, *The Biggest Deal*, p. 187.
16 Chubin, *Security in the Persian Gulf*, p. 31.
17 Brzezinski, *Power and Principle*, p. 504.
18 Sick, *All Fall Down*, p. 312.
19 Brzezinski, *Power and Principle*, p. 452.
20 Ibid.
21 Saivetz, *The Soviet Union and the Persian Gulf in the 1980s*, p. 34.
22 Sick, *October Surprise*, p. 99.
23 Ibid., p. 99, tries unsuccessfully to downplay the strategic aspect of the negotiations.
24 Sick, *All Fall Down*, p. 312.
25 Ibid., p. 313.
26 Honegger, *October Surprise*, p. 14.
27 Ibid.
28 Ibid., p. 12.
29 *Joint Report*, pp. 80, 81–82, 131, n. 108, n. 113.
30 Ibid., pp. 80, 131, n. 108.

31 Ibid., p. 82.
32 Parry, *Trick or Treason*, p. 171.
33 Trento, *Prelude to Terror*, p. 210.
34 Ben-Menashe, *Profits of War*, p. 70.
35 Ibid.
36 *Joint Report*, p. 201, 226, n. 20
37 Haim Shemesh, *Soviet-Iraqi Relations*, pp. 182, 235, fn. 7.
38 Ibid., p. 183, Timmerman, *Ol Ins Feuer*, p. 30.
39 Timmerman, *The Death Lobby*, pp. 122, 509, fn. 13.
40 Ibid., p. 122. See also Smolansky and Smolansky, *The USSR and Iraq*, p. 232.
41 Shemesh, *Soviet-Iraqi Relations*, p. 183.
42 Zabih, *Iranian Military in Revolution and War*, p. 156.
43 Jordan, *Crisis*.
44 Chubin, *Security in the Persian Gulf*, p. 25.
45 Thornton, *The Carter Years*, p. 522.
46 Kenneth Timmerman, 'October Surprise, part 6: Iran's hidden U.S. cash stash', *WorldNetDaily.Com*, 2000.
47 Text of Foreign Ministry statement, Tehran, 18 September 1980, in BBC Summary of World Broadcasts, ME/6528/A/3 20 September 1980.
48 Moses, *Freeing the Hostages*, p. 547.
49 Chubin, *Security in the Persian Gulf*, p. 25.
50 Thornton, *The Carter Years*, p. 523.
51 Ibid.
52 Bani-Sadr, *My Turn to Speak*, p. 76–77.
53 Safran, *Saudi Arabia*, p. 368.
54 Ibid., p. 410.
55 Ibid.
56 Brzezinski, *Power and Principle*, p. 568.
57 Ibid., p. 452.
58 Ibid., pp. 452–53.
59 Ibid., p. 453.
60 US Congress, *The US and Saudi Arabia*, p. 61.
61 *Keesing's Contemporary Archives*, August 7, 1981, p. 31011.
62 Bani-Sadr, *My Turn to Speak*, p. 94.
63 Thornton, *The Carter Years*, p. 523, see also Aburish, *Saddam Hussein*, p. 195.
64 Bani-Sadr, *My Turn to Speak*, p. 78.
65 Moses, *Freeing the Hostages*, pp. 547–48.
66 *Keesing's Contemporary Archives*, August 7, 1981, p. 31013.
67 *Joint Report*, pp. 201–202.
68 Sick, *October Surprise*, 45–49, see also *Joint Report*, p. 216. The Joint Report does not mention Ayatollah Beheshti's involvement. See also John Cooley, *Pay Back*, p. 42.
69 Honegger, *October Surprise*, p. 33, Parry, *Trick or Treason*, pp. 127–28.
70 Honegger, *October Surprise*, p. 34. See also Parry, *Trick or Treason*, p. 127 Parry argues that Lavi was close to Bani-Sadr.
71 Honegger, *October Surprise*, p. 34.
72 *Joint Report*, pp. 111, 140, n. 583.
73 Honegger, *October Surprise*, p. 34.
74 Pipes, *The Hidden Hand*, p. 319.
75 Ibid., p. 320.
76 Ibid.
77 Ben-Menashe, *The Profits of War*, p. 71. For Lavi's version see *Sanford-Jeffords Report)*, pp. 66–68.
78 *Sanford-Jeffords Report*, pp. 66–68.
79 Ibid., p. 65.
80 Ibid., p. 70.
81 Sick, *October Surprise*.
82 Moses, *Freeing the Hostages*, p. 548. Moses who appears to know very little about internal Iranian political dynamics, attributes Khomeini's decision to Ghotbzadeh's influence.
83 Brzezinski, *Power and Principle*, pp. 568–69.
84 US Congress, *US and Saudi Arabia*, p. 62, Safran, *Saudi Arabia*, p. 411.
85 Aburish, *Saddam Hussein*, pp. 194–95.

86 *Keesing's Contemporary Archives*, August 7, 1981, p. 31012.
87 Edgar O'Ballance, *The Gulf War* (London: Brassey's, 1988), p. 52. O'Ballance seems to think that East European countries were pursuing an independent policy. This is highly unlikely.
88 *Keesing's Contemporary Archives*, August 7, 1981, p. 31007.
89 Ibid., O'Ballance, *The Gulf War*, p. 52, Shemesh, *Soviet-Iraqi Relations*, p. 236, fn. 18.
90 'Iranian Prime Minister's Talks with the Soviet Ambassador', Tehran home service, BBC Summary of World Broadcasts, SWB ME/6542/A/3–4.
91 Thornton, *The Carter Years*, p. 523, and Dennis Ross, 'Soviet Views Toward the Gulf War', *Orbis*, Fall 1984, p. 438.
92 'Reported Iranian Approach to USSR for arms', BBC Summary of World Broadcasts, *Monitoring Report*, ME/6542/i.
93 *The Times*, October 6, 1980.
94 *The Times*, October 8, 1980.
95 Grasselli, *British and American Responses to the Soviet Invasion of Afghanistan*, p. 137.
96 Ross, 'Soviet Views Toward the Gulf War', p. 438.
97 Efraim Karsh, *The Soviet Union and Syria Since 1970*, (London and New York: Macmillan and St Martin's Press, 1991), p. 52.
98 *The Times*, October 9, 1980.
99 *Keesing's Contemporary Archives*, August 7, 1981, p. 31012, Jackson Smith, *The Search for Strategic Stability*, p. 149.
100 'Iraqi closure of Syrian, Libyan and N Korean embassies', BBC Summary of World Broadcasts/Monitoring Report, ME/6547/i, 13 October 1980, Jackson-Smith, *The Search for Strategic Stability*, pp. 157–58, *The Times*, October 29, 1980, Safran, *Saudi Arabia*, p. 323.
101 *The Economist*, November 1, 1980.
102 *Sanford-Jeffords Report*, p. 201.
103 Bani-Sadr, *My Turn to Speak*, p. 93.
104 Ibid.
105 *The Times*, October 10, 1980.
106 *The Times*, October 10, 1980.
107 *Keesing's Contemporary Archives*, August 7, 1981, p. 31009.
108 Ibid., *The Times*, October 9, 1980. Contemporaneous reports, of course, do not mention the arms-for-hostages angle.
109 *Joint Report*, pp. 111, 140, n. 584 and n. 586.
110 Honegger, *October Surprise*, p. 35.
111 Ibid.
112 *Joint Report*, pp. 112, 140, n. 589.
113 Honegger, *October Surprise*, p. 35.
114 Bani-Sadr, *My Turn to Speak*, pp. 30–31.
115 See, *Joint Report*, p. 42.
116 Ibid.
117 Ibid., p. 43, Sick, *All Fall Down*, p. 313.
118 Ibid.
119 Sick, *All Fall Down*, p. 313.
120 *Joint Report*, p. 43.
121 *The Times*, October 10, 1980.
122 *Joint Report*, p. 43.
123 Ibid.
124 Sick, *All Fall Down*, pp. 313–14, does not mention the SAVAMA chief's visit. on this point see Honegger, *October Surprise*, p. 55.
125 *The Times*, October 8, 1980.
126 Safran, *Saudi Arabia*, pp. 368–69.
127 Ibid., p. 369, Parrot, 'The Response of Saudi Arabia to the Iran-Iraq War', pp. 44–45.
128 Jackson-Smith, *The Search for Strategic Stability*, p. 158, Safran, *Saudi Arabia*, p. 369, Parrot, 'The Response of Saudi Arabia to the Iran-Iraq War', p. 45.
129 Sick, *October Surprise*, p. 137.
130 On Brzezinski and Shackley see Trento, *Prelude to Terror*, pp. 166.
131 Ibid., pp. 52, 58, 93, 113–15, 115, 127–28, 145–47, 155–56. On the tension between Turner and Shackley and Wilson's activities see also David Corn, *Blond Ghost: Ted Shackley and the CIA's Crusades* (New York: Simon and Schuster, 1994), pp. 341–53, 363–70.
132 Trento, *Prelude to Terror*, pp. 166, 195–211.

133 Ibid., p. 203.
134 See Christopher Andrew and Vasili Mitrokhin, *The Mitrokhin Archive: The KGB in Europe and the West* (London: Penguin Books, paperback edition, 2000)
135 Dobrynin, *In Confidence*, p. 460, see also Steven F. Hayward, *The Real Jimmy Carter* (Washington D.C.: Regnery Publishing, 2004), p. 181.
136 Dobrynin, *In Confidence*, p. 462, Hayward, *The Real Jimmy Carter*, pp. 181-82.
137 See Seliktar, *Politics, Paradigms and Intelligence Failures*, p. 80.
138 See Gates, *From the Shadows*, p. 238.
139 See Zbigniew Brzezinski's biography on the Center for Strategic and International Studies' web site.
140 Sick, *October Surprise*, pp. 27–28.
141 Ibid., pp. 26,137. See also Honegger, *October Surprise*.
142 Sick, *October Surprise*, p. 138.
143 Sick, *October Surprise*, p. 132, notes that Carter 'substantially increased the offer of arms to Iran'.
144 Ibid.
145 Ibid.
146 *Joint Report*, pp. 43, 58, n. 246, does not mention the vast discrepancies between the two proposals.
147 Ibid., p. 43.
148 Bani-Sadr, *My Turn to Speak*, p. 94.
149 *Joint Report*, p. 43.
150 Sick, *October Surprise*, p. 137.
151 Ibid., p. 138.
152 Honegger, *October Surprise*, p. 36.
153 Sick, *October Surprise*, pp. 138–39.
154 Honegger, *October Surprise*, p. 36.
155 Ibid.
156 *Joint Report*, pp. 112, 141, n. 590.
157 *Keesing's Contemporary Archives*, August 7, 1981, p. 31011.
158 Brzezinski, *Power and Principle*, p. 504, see also See Honegger, *October Surprise*, p. 55.
159 Bani-Sadr, *My Turn to Speak*, p. 94.
160 See Honegger, *October Surprise*, p. 55.
161 *Joint Report*, p. 111.
162 Parry, *Trick or Treason*, p. 129.
163 *Sanford-Jeffords Report*, p. 90.
164 Parry, *Trick or Treason*, p. 129.
165 *Joint Report*, pp. 112, 141, n. 593.
166 Sick, *October Surprise*, p. p. 158.
167 Sick, *All Fall Down*, p. 315.
168 Zabih, *Iran Since the Revolution*, p. 58.
169 Ibid.
170 Sick, *October Surprise*, p. 159.
171 Ibid., p. 160.
172 Ibid.
173 Ibid. Sick evades the issue.
174 Hulbert, *Interlock*, p. 189.
175 Robert Carswell, 'Economic Sanctions and the Iran Experience', *Foreign Affairs*, Winter 1981/1982.
176 Hulbert, *Interlock*, p. 192.
177 Parry, *Trick or Treason*, p. 129.
178 *Iran Hostage Chronology*, p. 348, Sick, *All Fall Down*, p. 315. See also, *Sanford-Jeffords Report*, p. 27. None of these sources mention the significance of Lavi's message.
179 Sick, *All Fall Down*, p. 315.
180 See *Joint Report*.
181 Congressional Research Service, *Iran Hostage Chronology*, p. 350. See also Sick, *October Surprise*, p. 164.
182 Sick, *October Surprise*, pp. 164–65.
183 See Robert Parry, 'Russia's prime minister and October Surprise', 15 May 1999, consortiumnews.com.
184 Ben-Menashe, *Profits of War*, p. 73–74.

185 Ibid., p. 75.
186 Ibid.
187 Parry, *Trick or Treason*, p. 161.
188 Sick, *October Surprise*, p. 165.
189 Ibid., pp. 165–66.
190 Brzezinski, *Power and Principle*, p. 504.
191 Ibid.
192 *Joint Report*, pp. 202–203.
193 Ibid., p. 203.
194 Sick, *October Surprise*, p. 166.
195 Trento, *Prelude to Terror*, p. 209.
196 Sick, *October Surprise*, p. 163.
197 Chubin, *Security in the Persian Gulf*, p. 52.
198 Ibid., US Congress, *US and Saudi Arabia*, p. 62.
199 Safran, *Saudi Arabia*, p. 414.
200 Sick, *All Fall Down*, p. 314.
201 Sick, *October Surprise*, p. 169.
202 Parry, *Trick or Treason*, pp. 129–30.
203 Sick, *October Surprise*, p. 169.
204 Christopher dep, *Sanford-Jeffords Report*, p. 22.
205 *Joint Report*, p. 203.
206 Brzezinski, *Power and Principle*, p. 279 and Thornton, *The Carter Years*, p. 524.
207 Ibid. The Joint Report does not raise any questions about Begin's motives.
208 *Joint Report*, p. 204.
209 Brzezinski, *Power and Principle*, p. 505.
210 *The Times*, October 27, 1980.
211 *The Times*, October 27, 1980.
212 Bani-Sadr, *My Turn to Speak*, p. 39.
213 Brzezinski, *Power and Principle*, p. 505, indicates Carter may not have properly consulted his advisers.
214 Sick, *October Surprise*, pp. 170–71.
215 Ibid., p. 171.
216 Thornton, *The Carter Years*, p. 522.
217 Bani-Sadr, *My Turn to Speak*, p. 96.
218 Ibid., p. 37.
219 Ibid., p. 96.
220 Parry, *Trick or Treason*, p. 130.
221 Bani-Sadr, *My Turn to Speak*, p. 37. See David Menashri, *Iran*, pp. 170–71 on the power struggle during this period.
222 O'Ballance, *The Gulf War*, p. 53.
223 Zabih, *Iran Since the Revolution*, pp. 58–59.
224 See Bani-Sadr, *Seir-e Siasat-e Amrika dar Iran* (The Course of American Policy in Iran) (Place of Publication not specified: Entesharat-e Enqelab-e Eslami [Islamic Republic Publications] 1991), p. 266, see also Bani-Sadr, *My Turn to Speak*, p. 98. See also Ebtekar, *Takeover in Tehran*, p. 229.
225 *The Economist*, November 1, 1980, pp. 32–33.
226 Ibid.
227 Ibid.
228 *The Economist*, November 8, 1980, pp. 34, 36.
229 Hulbert, *Interlock*, p. 192–194.
230 Bakhash, *The Reign of the Ayatollahs*, p. 150.
231 See Bani-Sadr, *Seir-e Siasat-e Amrika dar Iran*, p. 266, see also Bani-Sadr, *My Turn to Speak*, p. 98.
232 Ebtekar, *Takeover in Tehran*, p. 228.
233 Ibid., p. 229.
234 Ibid.
235 Ibid.
236 Christopher deposition, *Sanford and Jeffords Report*, p. 22, Saunders, 'Beginning of the End', p. 292.
237 Hulbert, *Interlock*, pp. 193, 254, n. 9.
238 Ebtekar, *Takeover in Tehran*, p. 228.

239 Ibid., pp. 229–30.
240 See *Joint Report*, p. 49.
241 Sick, October Surprise, p. 177. Sick skirts the issue.
242 See for example, Sick, *All Fall Down*, pp. 359–360, refers to Bakhash's study, *Iran Under the Ayatollahs* to describe Nabavi's role.
243 Ibid.
244 Brzezinski, *Power and Principle*.
245 Sick, *All Fall Down*.
246 See Bani-Sadr, *Seir-e Siasat-e Amrika Dar Iran* (The Course of American Policy in Iran), p. 266.
247 Ibid., p. 567.

Chapter 15

1 Brzezinski, *Power and Principle*, p. 506.
2 Ibid.
3 Ibid., p. 469.
4 Chubin, *Security in the Persian Gulf*, p. 65–66.
5 Ibid., p. 66.
6 William B. Quandt, *Saudi Arabia in the 1980s*, p. 73.
7 Ibid., p. 72.
8 Ibid., pp. 142–43.
9 Jackson-Smith, *The Search for Strategic Stability in the Persian Gulf*, pp. 170–71.
10 Shemesh, *Soviet-Iraqi Relations*, p. 222.
11 Jackson-Smith, *The Search for Strategic Stability in the Persian Gulf*, p. 174.
12 Menashri, *Iran*, p. 172.
13 Daneshvar, *Revolution in Iran*, p. 157.
14 Chubin and Tripp, *Iran and Iraq at War*
15 See Abolhasan Bani-Sadr, *Seir-e Siasat-e Amrika dar Iran* (The Course of American Policy in Iran) (Place of publication not specified: Entesharat-e Enqelab-e Eslami, 1370, 1991), p. 267.
16 Menashri, *Iran*, p. 171.
17 Ibid.
18 Ibid.
19 Sick, *All Fall Down*, pp. 321–22, US Congress, *Iran: The Financial Aspects of the Hostage Settlement Agreement*, p. 24.
20 House of Representatives, *Iran: The Financial Aspects of the Hostage Settlement Agreement*, p. 24.
21 *Sanford-Jeffords Report*, p. 28.
22 Sick, *All Fall Down*, p. 324, skirts the issue and makes no mention of the vast difference between Carter's proposals of 28 October and 10 November.
23 Taheri, *Nest of Spies*, p. 135.
24 Zabih, *Iran Since the Revolution*, pp. 59–60.
25 Ibid., p. 59.
26 *Sanford-Jeffords Report*, p. 30.
27 Ibid., p. 31.
28 Ibid., p. 29.
29 *Joint Report*, p. 204–205.
30 Ibid.
31 Ibid., p. 205.
32 Hulbert, *Interlock*, p. 198.
33 Assersohn, *The Biggest Deal*, p. 200.
34 Ibid., pp. 200–201.
35 Ibid., p. 201.
36 *The Times*, November 21, 1980.
37 Sick, *All Fall Down*, p. 324.
38 Ibid. Sick does not explain the reason for the delay.
39 *Sanford-Jeffords Report*, p. 97.
40 Ibid., p. 49.
41 Ibid., p. 97.
42 See Edgar O'Ballance, *The Gulf War*, (London: Brassey's, 1988), p. 53.

43 Ibid., Maoz, *Syria and Israel*, p. 187.
44 Ibid., p. 169.
45 Kienle, *Ba'th u Ba'th*, pp. 159, 209, fns. 59,60.
46 *The Economist*, December 6, 1980. On Saudi Arabia's support for the Muslim Brotherhood see Robert Baer, *Sleeping with the Devil* (New York: Crown Publishers, 2003), pp. 91–105.
47 Kienle, *Ba'th u Ba'th*, pp. 159–60.
48 Chubin, *Security in the Persian Gulf 4*, p. 91.
49 Jackson-Smith, *The Search for Strategic Stability in the Persian Gulf*, p. 175.
50 Ibid., pp. 169–70, *The Times*, November 19, 1980, November 22, 1980.
51 Jackson-Smith, *The Search for Strategic Stability in the Persian Gulf*, p. 175.
52 Ibid., p. 178.
53 Ibid.
54 *The Times*, November 26 , 1980.
55 See Safran, *Saudi Arabia*, p. 324.
56 *The Times*, November 25, 1980.
57 Ibid., *The Times*, November 24, 1980.
58 *The Times*, November 26, 1980.
59 Ibid.
60 Anthony Cordesman, *The Gulf and the Search for Strategic Stability* (Boulder, Colo.: Westview Press, 1984), p. 667.
61 Ibid., p. 627.
62 *The Times*, November 22, 1980.
63 Safran, *Saudi Arabia*, p. 369, *The Economist*, December 6, and December 13, 1980, pp. 32–33, *The Times*, December 2, 1980, Jackson-Smith, *The Search For Strategic Stability in the Persian Gulf*, pp. 184–85.
64 *The Times*, December 2, 1980.
65 *The Times*, December 1, 1980.
66 *The Times*, December 3, 1980.
67 Ibid., Ramet, *The Soviet-Syrian Relationship Since 1955*, pp. 145–46, Efraim Karsh, *The Soviet Union and Syria Since 1970*, (London and New York: Macmillan and St Martin's Press, 1991), p. 56, *The Economist*, December 6, 1980, p. 35.
68 Ramet, *The Soviet-Syrian Relationship Since 1955*, pp. 146, Jackson-Smith, *The Search for Strategic Stability in the Persian Gulf*, pp. 183–84.
69 Jackson Smith, *The Search for Strategic Stability in the Persian Gulf*, p. 185.
70 Efraim Karsh, *The Iran-Iraq War*, (London: International Institute for Strategic Studies, Adelphi Paper 220, 1987), p. 21.
71 *The Times*, December 8, 1980.
72 Ibid., and *The Times*, December 9, 1980.
73 Sick, *All Fall Down*, p. 324.
74 Ibid., p. 325.
75 Hulbert, *Interlock*, p. 200.
76 *Sanford-Jeffords Report*, p. 29.
77 Assersohn, *The Biggest Deal*, p. 206.
78 Shaul Bakhash, *The Reign of the Ayatollahs* (London: I.B. Tauris and Co Ltd, 1985), p. 152.
79 Menashri, *Iran*, pp. 172–73.
80 Bani-Sadr, *Seir-Siasat-e Amrika dar Iran*, pp. 281–82.
81 Menashri, *Iran*, pp. 172–73.
82 Bani-Sadr, *Seir-Siasat-e Amrika dar Iran*, pp. 281–82.
83 Menashri, *Iran*, pp. 172–73.
84 Ibid.
85 Robert O. Freedman, *Moscow and the Middle East: Soviet Policy Since the Invasion of Afghanistan* (Cambridge and New York: Cambridge University Press, 1991), pp. 95, *The Times*, December 11, 1980, Garthoff, *Détente and Confrontation*, p. 1108, and fn. 84. Garthoff completely misses the connection between Brezhnev's proposals and the hostage negotiations.
86 Chubin, *Security in the Persian Gulf*, p. 138.
87 *The Times*, December 12, 1980.
88 Moses, *Freeing the Hostages*, p. 637.
89 Safran, *Saudi Arabia*, p. 414.
90 Sick, *October Surprise*, pp. 182–183, Salinger, *America Held Hostage*, p. 288, *Sanford-Jeffords Report*, p. 23, *The Times*, December 21, 1980.

91 Sick, *October Surprise*, p. 183.
92 Carter, *Keeping Faith*, p. 590.
93 Congressional Research Service, *Iran Hostage Chronology*, pp. 411–12.
94 *The Times*, December 22, 1980.
95 Bani-Sadr, *My Turn to Speak*, p. 47.
96 Assersohn, *The Biggest Deal*, p. 205.
97 Brzezinski, *Power and Principle*, pp. 506–507.
98 Sick, *All Fall Down*, p. 329, see also Assersohn, *The Biggest Deal*, p. 207.
99 Sick, *All Fall Down*, p. 330.
100 Ibid., pp. 330–31.
101 Sick, *October Surprise*, p. 185.
102 See *Sanford-Jeffords Report* and *Joint Report*.
103 Sick, *All Fall Down*, p. 331.
104 Ibid., pp. 331–32.
105 Carter, *Keeping Faith*, p. 590.
106 Ibid.
107 Ibid. Carter does not mention the significance of the intelligence provided by the Algerians.
108 Ibid., p. 592.
109 Sick, *All Fall Down*, p. 332.
110 Ibid.
111 Ibid. Sick does not mention this important fact. See also *Sanford-Jeffords Report*, p. 29.
112 Assersohn, *The Biggest Deal*, p. 207.
113 Carter, *Keeping Faith*, p. 591.
114 Sick, *All Fall Down*, pp. 332–33.
115 Ibid., p. 333.
116 Hulbert, *Interlock*, p. 200.
117 Sick, *All Fall Down*, p. 334.
118 Carter, *Keeping Faith*, p. 591.
119 *Sanford-Jeffords Report*, p. 94.
120 Ibid., p. 94–95.
121 Ibid., p. 95.
122 Ibid., pp. 95, 230.
123 Ibid., p. 95.
124 Ibid., pp. 93–95.
125 Sick, *October Surprise*, p. 187–188, Bani-Sadr, *My Turn to Speak*, p. 47.
126 See for example Hulbert, *Interlock*.
127 Sick, *October Surprise*, p. 187–188, Sick, *All Fall Down*, pp. 335–36, Bani-Sadr, *My Turn to Speak*, p. 47.
128 Bani-Sadr, *My Turn to Speak*, p. 47, Sick, *October Surprise*, p. 187.
129 Sick, *October Surprise*, p. 187.
130 Sick, *All Fall Down*, p. 336.
131 Ibid., pp. 336–38.
132 Bani-Sadr, *My Turn to Speak*, p. 48.
133 Sick, *October Surprise*, p. 189.
134 Bani-Sadr, *Seir-e Siasat-e Amrika Dar Iran*, p. 505.
135 Ibid., pp. 505–508.
136 Freedman, *Moscow and the Middle East*, p. 97.
137 Moses, *Freeing the Hostages*, pp. 635–36.
138 Ibid., p. 636.
139 Sick, *October Surprise*, p. 195.
140 *Sanford-Jeffords Report*, p. 119.
141 Sick, *October Surprise*, pp. 198–99.
142 Bruce W. Jentleson, *With Friends Like These: Reagan, Bush and Saddam: 1982–1990* (New York and London: W.W. Norton and Company. 1994), pp. 56–57.
143 Ibid., p. 57.
144 Teicher and Teicher, *Twin Pillars to Desert Storm*.
145 Honegger, *October Surprise*, p. 161.
146 Zabih, *The Left in Contemporary Iran*, p. 26–27.
147 Gates, *From the Shadows*.

Chapter 16

1. Katzman, *Warriors of Islam*, p. 37, Menashri, *Iran*.
2. Ibid., pp. 37, 100.
3. Saeed Rahnema and Sohrab Behdad (eds), *Iran after the Revolution*, p. 89.
4. Bill, *The Eagle and the Lion*, p. 273, Dreyfuss, *Devil's Game*, p. 296.
5. See Dreyfuss, *Devil's Game*, p. 296.
6. Kuzikchin, *Inside the KGB*, pp. 104–105, Dreyfuss, *Devil's Game*, p. 295, Andrew and Mitrokhin, *The Mitrokhin Archive II*, p. 173, 178–79, 180, 183, 186, 191–92.
7. See Chalmers Johnson, *Blowback* (London, Time Warner Paperbacks, 2002), John Cooley, *Unholy War* (London: Pluto Press, Third edition, 2002), Gabriel Kolko, *Another Century of War?* (New York, The New Press, 2002), Peter Dale Scott, *Drugs, Oil and War* (Rowman and Littlefield, 2003)
8. On Azzam see Rohan Gunaratna, *Inside Al Qaeda Global Network of Terror* (London: Hurst and Company, 2002), pp. 19–25, Gilles Kepel, *Jihad* (London, I.B. Tauris, 2002), pp. 144–51.
9. Cooley, *Unholy War*, p. 69, see also the references in Kepel, *Jihad*.
10. The best account is Coll, *Ghost Wars*. But see also Norman Friedman, *Terrorism, Afghanistan and America's New Way of War* (Annapolis, Maryland: Naval Institute Press, 2003), 37–38.
11. See America Abroad presents America and Iran: Cooperation or Conflict in the Post-Saddam Gulf? (2003) Segment #3 'Eye Witness' with Marvin Kalb.
12. See Zbigniew Brzezinski, Brent Scowcroft and Richard Murphy, *Differentiated Containment: U.S. Policy toward Iran and Iraq – Report of an Independent Task Force* (New York: Council on Foreign Relations, 1997), Zbigniew Brzezinski and Robert M. Gates, *Iran: Time For a New Approach* (New York: Council on Foreign Relations, 2004)
13. Daniel Brumberg, *Reinventing Khomeini* (Chicago, The University of Chicago Press, 2001), 236–37.
14. Islamic Republic of Iran News Agency (IRNA), 5 August 2005.
15. IRNA, 1 July 2005.
16. *Washington Post*, August 12, 2005 and *Washington Times*, August 12, 2005.
17. For a good account see: Radio Free Europe/Radio Liberty, 'Iran report', 20 September 2005, Volume 8, Number 37.
18. See Michael Schwartz, 'The Bush Administration's Iranian Nightmare', Tom Dispatch.com, 11 August 2005.

BIBLIOGRAPHY

Primary sources in English

Documents

US embassy Documents, Volumes 1–80, 80 Volumes. (Tehran, Entesharat-e Daneshjuyan-e Peyro-ye Khatt-e Emam, 1980–1987)
Foreign Relations of the United States, FRUS series
FRUS 1955–1957, XII: The Near East
FRUS 1958–1960, Vol XII: The Near East
Foreign Relations of the United States, 1964–68, Iran, Volume XXII, Internet version
Foreign Relations of the United States, 1964–68, Volume XXXIV: Energy, Diplomacy and Global Issues (Internet version)

US Congress

Gold, Fern Racine, and Conant, Melvin A., US Congress, Committee on Energy and Natural Resources, United States Senate, *Access to Oil: The United States Relationships with Saudi Arabia and Iran*, December 1977 (US Government Printing Office, Washington D.C.: 1977)
Congressional Research Service, *Saudi Arabia and the United States*, Report, 97th Cong., 1st Sess, (1981)
Congressional Research Service, Library of Congress, Report Prepared for Committee on Foreign Relations, U.S. House of Representatives. *The Iran Hostage Crisis: A Chronology of Daily Developments*. 97th Congress., 1st Sess
US Congress, *Economic Consequences of the Iranian Revolution (Washington D.C.* GPO, 1979)
U.S. Congress, House of Representatives, Committee on Foreign Affairs, Subcommittee on Europe and the Middle East. *General Huyser's Mission to Iran, January 1979*. 97th Cong. 1st Sess, June 9, 1981
U.S. Congress, House of Representatives, Committee on International Relations, Subcommittee on International Organizations. *Human Rights in Iran*. 94th Cong., 2d Sess., Aug. 3, Sept. 8, 1976.
U.S. Congress, House of Representatives, Staff Report, Subcommittee on Evaluation, Permanent Select Committee on Intelligence. *Iran: Evaluation of U.S. Intelligence Performance Prior to November 1978*
U.S. Congress, House of Representatives, Committee on Banking, Finance and Urban Affairs. *Iran: The Financial Aspects of the Hostage Settlement Agreement*. 97th Cong., 1st Sess, July 1981.
U.S. Congress, House of Representatives, Report of the Subcommittee on Europe and the Middle East of the Committee on Foreign Affairs. *Saudi Arabia and the United States, The New Context in an Evolving "Special Relationship"* (Washington D.C., GPO, August 1981)
U.S. Congress, Senate, Committee on Foreign Relations Subcommittee on Foreign Assistance, *Sale of AWACs to Iran*. 95th Cong., 1st Sess, July 18, 22, 25, 27, Sept. 19, 1977.
U.S. Congress, Committee On Foreign Relations, United States Senate: *Report of the Special Counsel to Senator Terry Sanford and Senator James M. Jeffords*, (Washington D.C.: U.S. Government Printing Office, 1992)
U.S. Congress, *Joint Report of Task Force investigating "October Surprise" Allegations* (Washington D.C.: U.S. Government Printing Office, 1992)
U.S. Congress, Senate, Committee on Foreign Relations, *U.S. military Sales to Iran* (1976)
Arms Control and Disarmament Agency
World Military Expenditures and Arms Transfers, 1970–1979 (Washington D.C.: U.S. Government printing Office, 1982)

Central Intelligence Agency
Heuer Jr., Richards, *Psychology of Intelligence Analysis* (History Staff, Center for the Study of Intelligence, Central Intelligence Agency, 1999)
MacEachin, Douglas, *Predicting the Soviet Invasion of Afghanistan: The Intelligence Community's Record* (Center for the Study of Intelligence, Central Intelligence Agency, 2003)

Published Memoirs, Diaries, speeches, declarations

Alam, Asadollah, *The Shah and I: The Confidential Diary of Iran's Royal Court, 1969–1977*. Edited and translated by Alikhani, Alinaghi (London: I.B. Tauris, 1991)
Algar, Hamid, translator and editor, *Islam and Revolution: Writings and Declarations of Imam Khomeini* (Berkeley, California, 1981)
Ball, George, *The Past Has Another Pattern: Memoirs* (New York: Norton, 1982)
Baer, Robert, *See No Evil: The True Story of a Ground Soldier in the CIA's War On Terrorism* (New York: Crown Publishers, 2002)
Baer, Robert, *Sleeping with the Devil: How Washington Sold Our Soul for Saudi Crude* (New York: Crown Publishers, 2003)
Beckwith, Charles A., and Knox, Donald, *Delta Force* (New York: Harcourt Brace Jovanovich, 1983)
Ben-Menashe, Ari, *Profits of War: Inside the Secret U.S.-Israeli Arms Network* (New York: Sheridan Square Press, 1992)
Brzezinski, Zbigniew, *Power and Principle: Memoirs of the National Security Adviser, 1977–1981* (New York: Farrar, Straus and Giroux, 1983)
Carter, Jimmy, *Keeping Faith: Memoirs of a President* (New York: Bantam Books, 1982)
Crozier, Brian, *Free Agent: The Unseen War, 1941–1991* (London: Harper Collins Publishers, 1993)
Daugherty, William J., *In the Shadow of the Ayatollah: A CIA Hostage in Iran* (Annapolis: United States Naval Institute Press, 2001)
Ebtekar, Massoumeh, as told to Fred A. Reed, *Takeover in Tehran: The Inside Story of the 1979 U.S. Embassy Capture* (British Columbia, Canada: Talon Books, 2000)
Gates, Robert M. From the Shadows: The Ultimate Insider's Story of Five Presidents and How they Won the Cold War (New York, Simon and Schuster, 1996)
Harney, Desmond, *The Priest and the King: An Eyewitness Account of the Iranian Revolution*, (London and New York, British Academic Press, an imprint of I.B. Tauris and Co Ltd, 1998)
Hoveyda, Fereydoun, *The Fall of the Shah* (New York: Wyndham Books, 1979)
Huyser, Robert, *Mission to Tehran* (New York: Harper and Row, 1986)
Jordan, Hamilton, *Crisis: The Last Year of the Carter Presidency* (New York: G.P. Putnam's Sons, 1982)
Kimche, David, *After Nasser, Arafat and Saddam Hussein, the Last Option: The Quest for Peace in the Middle East* (London: Weidenfeld and Nicolson, 1991)
Kissinger, Henry A., *White House Years*, (Boston: Little Brown, 1979)
Kissinger, Henry, *Years of Upheaval* (Boston: Little Brown, 1982)
Kissinger, Henry A., *Years of Renewal: The Concluding Volume of His Memoirs* (London: Weidenfeld and Nicolson, 1999)
Kuzikchin, Vladimir, *Inside the KGB: My Life in Soviet Espionage*, translated by Thomas B. Beattie (New York: Pantheon Books, 1990)
Naraghi, Ehsan, *From Palace to Prison: Inside the Iranian Revolution* translated by Nilou Mobasser, (London: I.B. Tauris, 1994)
Pahlavi, Ashraf, *Faces in a Mirror: Memoirs from Exile* (Englewood Cliffs, N.J.: Prentice-Hall, 1980)
Pahlavi, Mohammad Reza, *Answer to History* (New York: Stein and Day, 1980)
Parsons, Anthony, *The Pride and the Fall: Iran 1974–1979* (London, Jonathan Cape, 1984)
Rafizadeh, Mansur, *Witness: From the Shah to the Secret Arms Deal*, (New York: William Morrow, 1987)
Secord, Richard with Wurts, Jay, *Honoured and Betrayed: Irangate, Covert Affairs, and the Secret War in Laos* (New York: John Wiley & Sons, Inc., 1992)
Shirley, Edward, *Know Thine Enemy: A Spy's Journey into Revolutionary Iran* (New York: Farrar, Straus and Giroux, 1997)
Sick, Gary, *All Fall Down: America's Fateful Encounter with Iran* (London, I.B. Tauris and Co Ltd, 1985)

Stempel, John, *Inside the Iranian Revolution* (Bloomington, Ind.:Indiana University Press, 1981)
Sullivan, William, *Mission to Iran* (New York, W.W. Norton, 1981)
Teicher, Howard and Teicher, Gayle Radley, *Twin Pillars to Desert Storm: America's Flawed Vision in the Middle East from Nixon to Bush* (New York: William Morrow and Company, Inc., 1991)
Vance, Cyrus, *Hard Choices: Critical Years in America's Foreign Policy (New York: Simon and Schuster, 1982)*

Secondary Sources in English

Books

Abir, Mordechai, *Saudi Arabia in the Oil Era: Regime and Elites; Conflict and Collaboration* (London: Croom Helm, 1988)
Abdulghani, Jasim M., *Iraq and Iran: The Years of Crisis* (Baltimore, Johns Hopkins University, 1984)
Abrahamian, Ervand, *Iran Between Two Revolutions* (Princeton, NJ: Princeton University Press, 1982)
Abrahamian, Ervand, *Radical Islam: The Iranian Mojahedin* (London: I.B. Tauris and Co Ltd, 1989)
Abrahamian, Ervand, *Khomeinism* (London: I.B. Tauris, 1993)
Aburish, Said K., *A Brutal Friendship, The West and the Arab Elite* (London: Victor Gollancz, 1997)
Aburish, Said K., *Saddam Hussein: The Politics of Revenge* (London: Bloomsbury, 2000)
Aburish, Said K., *The Rise, Corruption and Coming Fall of the House of Saud* (London: Bloomsbury, paperback edition, 1995)
Afkhami, Gholam R., *The Iranian Revolution: Thanatos on a National Scale* (Washington D.C.: Middle East Institute, 1985)
Akhavi, Shahrough, *Religion and Politics in Contemporary Iran* (Albany, N.Y.: State University of New York Press, 1980)
Alexander, Yonah, and Nanes, Allan (eds), The United States and Iran (Frederick, Md.: Aletheia Books, 1980)
Algar, Hamid, *The Islamic Revolution in Iran* (London: Open Press, 1980)
Amir-Arjomand, Said, *The Turban for the Crown: The Islamic Revolution in Iran* (New York and Oxford: Oxford University Press, 1988)
Amjad, Mohammed, *Iran: From Royal Dictatorship to Theocracy*, (Westport, Conn: Greenwood Press, 1989),
Amuzegar, Jahangir, *Dynamics of the Iranian Revolution: The Pahlavis' Triumph and Tragedy* (New York: State University of New York Press, 1991)
Amuzegar, Jahangir, *Iran's Economy Under the Islamic Republic*, (London: I.B. Tauris, 1993)
Andrainopoulos, Gerry Argyris, *Kissinger and Brzezinski: The NSC and the Struggle for Control of US National Security Policy* (London: Macmillan, 1991)
Anderson, Jack with Boyd, James, *Fiasco* (New York: Times Books, 1983)
Andrew, Christopher, *For the President's Eyes Only: Secret Intelligence and the American Presidency from Washington to Bush* (London: Harper Collins Publishers, paperback edition, 1996)
Andrew, Christopher and Gordievsky, Oleg, *KGB: The Inside Story* (London Hodder and Stoughton, 1991)
Andrew, Christopher and Mitrokhin, Vasili, *The Mitrokhin Archive: The KGB in Europe and the West* (London: Penguin Books, paperback edition, 2000)
Andrew, Christopher and Mitrokhin, Vasili, *The Mitrokhin Archive II* (London: Penguin, Allen Lane, 2005)
Ansari, Ali M., *Modern Iran Since 1921: The Pahlavis and After* (London: Longman, Pearson Education Limited, 2003)
Ashton, Nigel John, *Eisenhower, Macmillan and the Problem of Nasser: Anglo-American Relations and Arab Nationalism, 1955–59* (New York: St Martin's Press, 1996)
Assersohn, Roy, *The Biggest Deal* (London, Methuen, 1982)
Bacevich, Andrew J., *American Empire: The Realities and Consequences of U.S. Diplomacy* (Cambridge, Mass and London: Harvard University Press, 2002)
Bakhash, Shaul, *The Reign of the Ayatollahs: Iran and the Islamic Revolution* (London: I.B. Tauris and Co Ltd, 1985)
Bakhash, Shaul, *The Politics of Oil and Revolution in Iran*, staff paper, (Washington D.C., Brookings Institution, 1982)
Ball, George W., and Ball, Douglas B., *The Passionate Attachment: America's Involvement With Israel, 1947 to the Present* (New York and London: W.W. Norton and Company, 1992)

Bashiriyeh, Hossein, *The State and Revolution in Iran* (New York, St Martin's Press, 1984)
Behrooz, Maziar, *Rebels With A Cause: The Failure of the Left in Iran* (London and New York: I.B. Tauris, 1999)
Beit-Hallahmi, Benjamin, *The Israeli Connection: Whom Israel Arms and Why* (London: I.B. Tauris and Co Ltd, 1988)
Bell, J. Bowyer, *Murders on the Nile: The World Trade Center and Global Terror* (San Francisco, Encounter Books, 2003)
Benard, Cheryl and Khalilzad, Zalmay, *"The Government of God": Iran's Islamic Republic* (New York: Columbia University Press, 1984)
Bill, James A., *The Eagle and the Lion: The Tragedy of American-Iranian Relations* (New Haven Conn.: Yale University Press, 1988)
Blum, William, *The CIA: A Forgotten History: US Global Interventions Since World War 2* (London: Zed Books Ltd, 1986)
Bobbitt, Philip, *The Shield of Achilles: War, Peace and the Course of History* (London: Penguin Books, 2003)
Brisard, Jean-Charles and Dasquie, Guillaume, *Forbidden Truth: U.S.-Taliban Secret Oil Diplomacy and the Failed Hunt for Bin Laden*, translated by Lucy Rounds with Peter Fifield and Nicholas Greenslade, (New York, Thunder's Mouth Press/Nation Books, 2002)
Brown, L. Carl, *International Politics and the Middle East: Old Rules, Dangerous Game* (London: I.B. Tauris and Co Ltd, 1984)
Brown, L Carl, *Religion and State: The Muslim Approach to Politics* (New York: Columbia University Press, 2000)
Bromley, Simon, *American Hegemony and World Oil: The Industry, the State System and the World Economy* (London: Cambridge and Oxford, Polity Press in association with Basil Blackwell Ltd, 1991)
Brumberg, Daniel, *Reinventing Khomeini: The Struggle for Reform in Iran* (Chicago and London: The University of Chicago Press, 2001)
Bundy, William, *A Tangled Web: The Making of Foreign Policy in the Nixon Presidency* (London: I.B. Tauris, 1998)
Burrows, William E. and Windrem, Robert, *Critical Mass: The Dangerous Race for Superweapons in a Fragmented World* (New York: Simon and Schuster, 1994)
Calvert, Peter, *Revolution and International Politics* (London: Pinter, second edition, 1996)
Chase, Robert S., Hill, Emily B., and Kennedy Paul, (eds.), *The Pivotal States: A New Framework for US Policy in the Developing World* (New York: W.W. Norton and Co., 1998)
Chehabi, H.E., *Iranian Politics and Religious Modernism: The Liberation Movement of Iran Under the Shah and Khomeini* (Ithaca: Cornell University Press, 1990)
Chomsky, Noam, *Deterring Democracy* (London and New York: Verso, 1991)
Chomsky, Noam, *Hegemony or Survival: America's Quest for Global Dominance* (New York: Metropolitan Books, Henry Holt and Company, 2003)
Chubin, Shahram, *Security in the Persian Gulf 4: The Role of Outside Powers*, (London: International Institute for Strategic Studies, 1981)
Chubin, Shahram and Tripp, Charles, *Iran and Iraq at War* (London: I.B. Tauris, 1988)
Citino, Nathan J., *From Arab Nationalism to OPEC: Eisenhower, King Saud, and the Making of U.S.-Saudi Relations* (Bloomington and Indianapolis: Indiana University Press, 2002)
Claes, Dag Harald, *The Politics of Oil-Producer Cooperation: The Political Economy of Global Interdependence* (Boulder, Colorado, Westview Press, 2001)
Cleva, Gregory D., *Henry Kissinger and the American Approach to Foreign Policy* (London and Toronto, Associated University Presses, 1989)
Cline, Ray S., and Alexander, Yonah, *Terrorism: The Soviet Connection*, (New York: Crane Russak, 1984)
Coll, Steve *Ghost Wars* (New York: Penguin Books, paperback edition, 2005)
Cook, Fred J. *The Great Energy Scam: Private Billions vs Public Good* (New York: Macmillan Publishing Company, 1982)
Cooley, John K., *An Alliance Against Babylon: The U.S., Israel and Iraq*, foreword by William R. Polk (London: Pluto Press, 2005)
Cooley, John K. *Libyan Sandstorm* (Boston: Holt, Rinehart and Winston, 1982)
Cooley, John K., *Unholy Wars: Afghanistan, America and International Terrorism* (London: Pluto Press, third edition, 2002)
Cordesman, Anthony H., *Iran and Iraq: The Threat from the Northern Gulf* (Boulder, Colo: Westview Press, 1994).
Cordesman, Anthony H., *The Gulf and the Search for Strategic Stability: Saudi Arabia, the Military*

Balance in the Gulf, and Trends in the Arab-Israeli Military Balance (Boulder, Colo.: Westview Press, 1984)

Cordesman, Anthony H., and Wagner, Abraham R., *The Lessons of Modern War, Vol II: The Iran-Iraq War* (Boulder and San Francisco, Westview Press, 1990)

Cordovez, Diego, and Harrison, Selig S., *Out of Afghanistan: The Inside Story of the Soviet Withdrawal* (New York and Oxford,: Oxford University Press, 1995)

Cottam, Richard W., *Iran and the United States: A Cold War Case Study* (Pittsburgh, University of Pittsburgh Press, 1988)

Cottam, Richard W., *Nationalism in Iran* (Pittsburgh, University of Pittsburgh Press, 1964)

Coughlin, Con, *Saddam Hussein: His Rise and Fall* (London: Harper Perennial, 2005)

Daalder, Ivo H. and Lindsay, James M., *America Unbound: The Bush Revolution in Foreign Policy* (Washington D.C.: Brookings Institution Press, 2003)

Daneshvar, Parviz, *Revolution in Iran* (London: Macmillan, 1996)

Darwish, Adel and Alexander, Gregory, *Unholy Babylon: The Secret History of Saddam's War* (London: Victor Gollancz Ltd, 1991)

Daugherty, William J., *Executive Secrets: Covert Action and the Presidency*, foreword by Mark Bowden (Kentucky: The University Press of Kentucky, 2005)

David, Charle-Phillipe, Carrol, Nancy Ann and Selden, Zachary A., Foreign Policy Failure in the White House: *Reappraising the Fall of the Shah and the Iran-Contra Affair* (Lanham, New York and London: University Press of America, 1993)

Dorril, Stephen, *MI6: Fifty Years of Special Operations* (London: Fourth Estate, 2000)

Dreyfuss, Robert with LeMarc, Thierry, *Hostage to Khomeini* (New York: New Benjamin Franklin House Publishing Company, Inc, 1980)

Dreyfuss, Robert, *Devil's Game: How the United States Helped Unleash Fundamentalist Islam* (New York: Metropolitan Books, 2005)

Dumbrell, John, *The Carter Presidency: A Re-Evaluation* (Manchester and New York: Manchester University Press, second edition, 1995)

Ehteshami, Anoushiravan, *After Khomeini: The Iranian Second Republic* (London and New York: Routledge, 1995)

Elman, Colin, and Elman, Miriam Fendius, *Bridges and Boundaries: Historians, Political Scientists, and the Study of International Relations* (MIT Press, Cambridge, Mass, 2001)

Emerson, Steven, *The American House of Saud* (New York: Franklin Watts, 1985)

Eshed, Haggai, *Reuven Shiloah, The Man Behind the Mossad: Secret Diplomacy in the Creation of Israel*, Forewords by Shimon Peres and Haim Herzog, translated from Hebrew by David and Leah Zinder (London: Frank Cass and Co Ltd, 1997)

Esposito, John L., *The Islamic Threat: Myth or Reality?* (New York and Oxford: Oxford University Press, 1992)

Esposito, John L., *Unholy War: Terror in the Name of Islam* (Oxford: Oxford University Press, 2002)

Farber, David, *Taken Hostage* (Princeton and Oxford: Princeton University Press, 2005)

Feinberg, Richard E., *The Intemperate Zone: The Third World Challenge to U.S. Foreign Policy* (New York and London: W.W. Norton and Company, 1983)

Forbis, William H., *The Fall of the Peacock Throne* (New York: McGraw Hill, 1981)

Freedman, Robert O., *Moscow and the Middle East: Soviet Policy Since the Invasion of Afghanistan* (Cambridge and New York: Cambridge University Press, 1991)

Friedman, Norman *Terrorism, Afghanistan and America's New Way of War* (Annapolis, Maryland: Naval Institute Press, 2003)

Friedman, Norman, *The Fifty-Year War: Conflict and Strategy in the Cold War* (London: Chatham Publishing, 2000)

Fuller, Graham E. *The Center of the Universe: The Geopolitics of Iran*, A RAND Corporation Research Study (Boulder, Colorado: Westview Press, 1991)

Fuller, Graham E., *The Future of Political Islam* (New York and Houndmills, Basingstoke: Palgrave Macmillan, 2003)

Furtig, Henner, with a foreword by Anoushiravan Ehteshami, *Iran's Rivalry with Saudi Arabia between the Gulf Wars*, (Durham Middle East Monograph Series, Ithaca Press, Garner Publishing Ltd, 2002)

Gaddis, John Lewis, *Strategies of Containment: A Critical Appraisal of Postwar American National Security Policy* (New York: Oxford University Press, 1982)

Gaddis, John Lewis, *We Now Know: Rethinking Cold War History* (Oxford: Clarendon Press, 1997)

Garthoff, Raymond, *Détente and Confrontation: American-Soviet Relations from Nixon to Reagan*, revised edition, (Washington D.C.: Brookings Institution, 1994)

Gasiorowski, Mark J., *U.S. Foreign Policy and the Shah: Building a Client State in Iran* (Ithaca, Cornell University Press, 1991)
Gerges, Fawaz A., *America and Political Islam: Clash of Cultures or Clash of Interests?* (Cambridge and New York: Cambridge University Press, 1999)
Gerges, Fawaz A., *The Superpowers and the Middle East: Regional and International Politics, 1955–1967*, with a foreword by William Quandt, (Boulder: Westview Press, 1994)
Gill, Stephen, *American Hegemony and the Trilateral Commission* (Cambridge and New York: Cambridge University Press, paperback edition, 1991)
Gold, Dore, *Hatred's Kingdom: How Saudi Arabia Supports the New Global Terrorism* (Washington D.C.: Regnery Publishing, Inc., 2003)
Goode, James F., *The United States and Iran: In the Shadow of Musaddiq* (London: Macmillan Press Ltd, 1997)
Goodwin, Jeff, *No Other Way Out: States and Revolutionary Movements, 1945–1991* (New York and Cambridge: Cambridge University Press, 2001)
Graham, Robert, *Iran: The Illusion of Power* (New York: St Martin's Press, 1980)
Gray, Colin S., *The Geopolitics of Superpower* (Lexington: The University Press of Kentucky, 1988)
Green, Jerrold, *Revolution in Iran: The Politics of Countermobilization* (New York, Praeger, 1982)
Grummon, Stephen, *The Iran-Iraq War* (Washington D.C.: Council on Foreign Relations, 1982)
Gunaratna, Rohan, *Inside Al Qaeda Global Network of Terror* (London: Hurst and Company, 2002)
Guzzini, Stefano, *Realism in International Relations and International Political Economy: The Continuing Story of a Death Foretold* (London and New York, Routledge, 1998)
Halliday, Fred, *Arabia Without Sultans* (Harmsworth: Penguin, 1974)
Halliday, Fred, *Cold War, Third World: An Essay on Soviet-US Relations* (London: Hutchinson, 1989)
Halliday, Fred, *Iran: Dictatorship and Development* (New York: Penguin Books, 1979)
Halliday, Fred, *Revolution and World Politics: The Rise and Fall of the Sixth Great Power* (London: Macmillan, 1999)
Halliday, Fred, *The Making of the Second Cold War* (London and New York: Verso, second edition, 1989)
Hammond, Thomas, *Red Flag Over Afghanistan: The Communist Coup, the Soviet Invasion, and the Consequences* (Boulder, Colorado: Westview, 1984)
Harris, David, *The Crisis: The President, the Prophet, and the Shah: 1979 and the Coming of Militant Islam* (New York and Boston, Little Brown and Company, 2004)
Heikal, Mohamed *Iran the Untold Story: An Insider's Account of America's Iranian Adventure and Its Consequences for the Future* (New York: Pantheon Books, 1982)
Hersh, Seymour, *The Samson Option: Israel's Nuclear Arsenal and American Foreign Policy* (New York: Random House, 1991)
Hiro, Dilip, *Iran under the Ayatollahs* (London, Routledge and Kegan Paul, 1985)
Hiro, Dilip, *The Iranian Labyrinth: Journeys through Theocratic Iran and its Furies* (New York: Nation Books, 2005)
Hiro, Dilip, *The Longest War: The Iran-Iraq Military Conflict* (London: Routledge, 1991)
Hiro, Dilip, *War Without End: The Rise of Islamist Terrorism and Global Response* (Revised edition, London and New York, Routledge, 2002)
Hirsh, Michael, *At War with Ourselves: Why America is Squandering its Chance to Build a Better World* (Oxford and New York: Oxford University Press, 2003)
Hogan, Michael J. and Paterson, Thomas G. (eds), *Explaining the History of American Foreign Relations* (Cambridge, Cambridge University Press, 1991)
Houghton, David Patrick, *US Foreign Policy and the Iran Hostage Crisis* (Cambridge, Cambridge University Press, 2001)
Hoveyda, Fereydoun, *The Fall of the Shah* (New York: Wyndham Books, 1979)
Hulbert, Mark, *Interlock* (New York: Richardson and Snyder, 1982)
Hunt, Michael H., *Crises in U.S. Foreign Policy: An International History Reader* (New Haven: Yale University Press, 1996)
Huntington, Samuel, *Political Order in Changing Societies* (New Haven and London: Yale University Press, 1968)
Ioannides, Christos P. *America's Iran: Injury and Catharsis* (Lanham, Md.: University Press of America, 1984)
Irfani, Suroosh, *Revolutionary Islam in Iran: Popular Liberation or Religious Dictatorship* (London: Zed, 1985)

Jain, Rajendra K. *Germany, the Soviet Union and Eastern Europe: 1949–1991* (London: Sangam Books, 1993)
Jawad, Haifaa A., *Euro-Arab Relations: A Study in Collective Diplomacy* (Reading: Ithaca Press, 1992)
Jentleson, Bruce W., *With Friends Like These: Reagan, Bush and Saddam: 1982–1990* (New York and London: W.W. Norton and Company, 1994)
Jervis, Robert, *Perception and Misperception in International Politics* (Princeton, New Jersey, Princeton University Press, 1976)
Jervis, Robert, *System Effects: Complexity in Political and Social Life* (Princeton, New Jersey, Princeton University Press, paper back edition, 1999)
Johnson, Chalmers, *Blowback: The Costs and Consequences of American Empire* (London: Time Warner Paperbacks, 2002)
Johnson, Major Maxwell Orme, *The Military as an Instrument of U.S. Policy in Southwest Asia: The Rapid Deployment Joint Task Force, 1979–1982*, (Boulder, Colo: Westview Press, 1983),
Johnson, Robert H., *Improbable Dangers: U.S. Conceptions of Threat in the Cold War and After* (London, Macmillan Press Ltd, paperback edition, 1997)
Kamrava, Mehran, *Revolution in Iran: The Roots of Turmoil* (London: Routledge, 1990)
Karsh, Efraim and Inari Rautsi, *Saddam Hussein: A Political Biography* (New York and London: The Free Press and Brassey's, 1991)
Karsh, Efraim, *The Iran-Iraq War: A Military Analysis*, Adelphi Papers no. 220, (London: International Institute for Strategic Studies, 1987)
Karsh, Efraim *The Soviet Union and Syria Since 1970*, (London and New York: Macmillan and St Martin's Press, 1991)
Katouzian, Homa, *The Political Economy of Modern Iran: Despotism and Pseudo-Modernism, 1926–1979* (New York, New York University Press, 1979)
Katzman, Kenneth, *The Warriors of Islam: Iran's Revolutionary Guard* (Boulder, Colo: Westview Press, 1992)
Kaufman, Burton I., *The Presidency of James Earl Carter, Jr.* (Kansas, The University Press of Kansas 1993)
Keddie, Nikki R., *Iran and the Muslim World: Resistance and Revolution* (New York: New York University Press, 1995)
Keddie, Nikki, and Gasiorowski, Mark (eds), *Neither East Nor West: Iran, the Soviet Union and the United States* (New Haven and London: Yale University Press, 1990)
Kelly, J.B., *Arabia, the Gulf and the West* (London: Basic Books, 1980)
Kennan, George F., *The Nuclear Delusion: Soviet-American Relations in the Atomic Age* (New York: Pantheon, 1982)
Kennedy, Paul (ed), *Grand Strategies in War and Peace* (New Haven and London: Yale University Press, 1991)
Kepel, Gilles, *Jihad: The Trail of Political Islam*, translated by Anthony F. Roberts (London and New York: I.B. Tauris Publishers, 2002)
Kepel, Gilles *The Prophet and the Pharaoh: Muslim Extremism in Egypt*, translated from the French by Jon Rothschild (Berkeley and Los Angeles, University of California Press, paperback edition, 1993)
Khadduri, Majid, *The Gulf War: Origins and Implications of the Iraq-Iran Conflict*, (Oxford: Oxford University Press, 1988)
Kienle, Eberhard, *Ba'th v. Ba'th: The Conflict Between Syria and Iraq, 1968–1989* (London: I.B. Tauris, 1990)
Kinzer, Stephen *All the Shah's Men: An American Coup and the Roots of Middle East Terror* (New Jersey, John Wiley and Sons, Inc., 2003)
Klare, Michael, *Beyond the "Vietnam Syndrome"* (Washington D.C.: Institute for Policy Studies, 1981)
Kolko, Gabriel, *Another Century of War?* (New York, The New Press, 2002)
Krasner, Stephen, *Defending the National Interest: Raw Materials Investments and U.S. Foreign Policy* (Princeton, N.J.: Princeton University Press, 1978)
Kupchan, Charles, *The Persian Gulf and the West: The Dilemmas of Security* (London: Allen and Unwin, 1987)
Laing, Margaret, *The Shah* (London, Sidgwick and Jackson, 1977)
Lake, Anthony, *Third World Radical Regimes: US Policy Under Carter and Reagan* (New York: Foreign Policy Association, 1985)
Ledeen, Michael and Lewis, William, *Debacle: American Failure in Iran* (New York: Alfred A. Knopf, 1981)
Ledeen, Michael A., *The War Against the Terror Masters: Why It Happened. Where We Are Now. How We'll Win* (New York: Truman Tally Books, St Martin's Press, 2002)

Leebaert, Derek, *The Fifty-Year Wound: How America's Cold War Victory Shapes Our World* (Boston, New York and London: Back Bay Books, Little Brown and Company, paperback edition, 2002)
Lenczowski, George (ed), *Iran Under the Pahlavis* (Stanford, Hoover Institution Press, 1978)
Lesch, David W., *1979: The Year that Shaped the Modern Middle East* (Boulder, Colorado, Westview Press, 2001)
Levy, Walter J. *Oil Strategy and Politics: 1941–1981* (Boulder Colo: Westview Press, 1982)
Lewis, Bernard, *The Crisis of Islam: Holy War and Unholy Terror* (New York, The Modern Library, 2003)
Little, Douglas, *American Orientalism: The United States and the Middle East Since 1945* (London and New York, I.B. Tauris, 2002)
Litwak, Robert, *Détente and the Nixon Doctrine: American Foreign Policy and the Pursuit of Stability, 1969–1976* (New York, Cambridge University Press, 1984)
Litwak, Robert S., *Rogue States and U.S. Foreign Policy: Containment After the Cold War* (Washington D.C. The Woodrow Wilson Center Press, 2000)
Loftus, John and Aarons, Mark, *The Secret War against the Jews: How Western Espionage Betrayed the Jewish People* (New York: St Martin's, 2000)
Long, David E., The United States and Saudi Arabia: Ambivalent Allies (Boulder, Westview, 1985)
Louis, William Roger and Bill, James A. (eds), *Mussadiq, Iranian Nationalism and Oil* (London, I.B. Tauris and Co., 1988)
Luttwak, Edward N., *Strategy: The Logic of War and Peace* (Cambridge, Mass, and London: Belknap Press of Harvard University Press, 1987)
Lytle, Mark Hamilton, *The Origins of the Iranian-American Alliance, 1941–1953* (New York, Holmes and Meier, 1987)
McLellan, David S., *Cyrus Vance* (New Jersey, Rowman and Allanheld, 1985)
Mann, Michael, *Incoherent Empire* (London and New York: Verso, 2003)
Mansour, Camille, *Beyond Alliance: Israel and U.S. Foreign Policy*, translated from the French by James A. Cohen, (New York: Columbia University Press, 1994)
Ma'oz, Moshe, *Syria and Israel: From War to Peace-making* (Oxford: Clarendon Press, 1995)
Marr, Phebe, *The Modern History of Iraq* (Boulder, Co: Westview Press, 1985)
Marshall, Jonathan, Scott, Peter Dale and Hunter, Jane, *The Iran-Contra Connection: Secret Teams and Covert Operations in the Reagan Era* (Boston: South End Press, 1987)
Martin, David C. and Walcott, John, *Best Laid Plans: The Inside Story of America's War against Terrorism* (New York: Harper and Row, 1988)
Mead, Walter Russell, *Special Providence: American Foreign Policy and How it Changed the World* (New York: Alfred A. Knopf, 2002)
Melanson, Richard A., *Reconstructing Consensus: American Foreign Policy Since the Vietnam War* (New York, St Martin's Press, 1991)
Menashri, David, *Iran: A Decade of War and Revolution* (New York: Holmes and Meier, 1990)
Menashri, David, *Revolution at a Crossroads: Iran's Domestic Politics and Regional Ambitions* (The Washington Institute for Near East Policy, Washington D.C., 1997)
Milani, Abbas, *The Persian Sphinx: Amir Abbas Hoveyda and the Riddle of the Iranian Revolution* (London and New York: I.B. Tauris Publishers, 2000)
Milani, Mohsen M., *The Making of Iran's Islamic Revolution* (Boulder, Colo: Westview Pess, second edition 1994)
Miniter, Richard, *Losing Bin-Laden: How Bill Clinton's Failures Unleashed Global Terror* (Washington D.C. Regnery Publishing Inc, 2003)
Mitchell, Richard P. *The Society of the Muslim Brothers* (New York and Oxford, Oxford University Press, reprinted in 1993)
Mitrokhin, Vasilyi, *The KGB in Afghanistan*, Cold War International History Project, Working Paper No 40, Introduced and Edited by Christian F. Ostermann and Odd Arne Westad (Washington D.C.: Woodrow Wilson Center for Scholars, February 2002)
Moaddel, Mansoor, *Class, Politics, and Ideology in the Iranian Revolution*, (New York: Columbia University Press, 1993),
Moin, Baqer, *Khomeini: Life of the Ayatollah* (London and New York: I.B. Tauris and Co Ltd, 1999)
Motyl, Alexander J., *Revolutions, Nations, Empires: Conceptual Limits and Theoretical Possibilities* (New York: Columbia University Press, 1999)
Mufti, Malik, *Sovereign Creations: Pan-Arabism and Political Order in Syria and Iraq* (Ithaca: Cornell University Press, 1996)

Muravchik, Joshua, *The Uncertain Crusade: Jimmy Carter and the Dilemmas of Human Rights Policy*, Foreword by Jeane Kirkpatrick (Washington D.C.: American Enterprise Institute for Public Policy Research, 1988)

Mylroie, Laurie, *The War Against America: Saddam Hussein and the World Trade Center Attacks*, Foreword by former CIA Director R. James Woolsey (Washington D.C. Regan Books, an imprint of Harper Collins, Publishers, revised edition, 2001)

Naftali, Timothy *Blind Spot: The Secret History of American Counterterrorism* (New York: Basic Books, 2005)

Napoleoni, Loretta, *Modern Jihad: Tracing the Dollars Behind the Terror Networks* (London: Pluto Press, 2003)

Nonneman, Gerd, *Iraq, the Gulf States and the War: A Changing Relationship* (London: Ithaca Press, 1986)

Noyes, James H., *The Clouded Lens*, (Stanford, Calif: Hoover Institution Press, 1982)

O'Ballance, Edgar *The Gulf War*, (London: Brassey's, 1988)

Odell, Peter, *Oil and World Power* (Middle sex, Penguin Books, 1986)

Oye, Kenneth, Rothschild, Donald, and Lieber, Robert J. (eds), *Eagle Entangled: U.S. Foreign Policy in a Complex World* (New York: Longman Publishers, 1979)

Palmer, Michael A., *Guardians of the Gulf: A History of America's Expanding Role in the Persian Gulf, 1833–1992*, (New York: Free Press, a division of Macmillan Inc, 1992)

Paolucci, Henry, *Iran, Israel and the United States: An American Foreign Policy Background Study* (New York: Griffon House Publications, 1991)

Parsa, Misagh, *States, Ideologies and Social Revolutions: A Comparative Analysis of Iran, Nicaragua and the Philippines* (Cambridge, Cambridge University Press, 2000)

Pastor, Robert A., *Condemned to Repetition: The United States and Nicaragua* (Princeton, New Jersey, Princeton University Press, 1987)

Payne, Richard J., *The West European Allies, The Third World and U.S. Foreign Policy: Post Cold War Challenges* (New York, Westport, Connecticut, London: Praeger, 1991)

Persico, Joseph E., *Casey: The Lives and Secrets of William J. Casey: From the OSS to the CIA* (New York: Penguin Books, 1990)

Pinto, Maria Do Ceu, *Political Islam and the United States: A Study of U.S. Policy towards Islamist Movements in the Middle East* (Durham, Ithaca Press, 1999)

Pipes, Daniel, *Conspiracy: How the Paranoid Style Flourishes and Where it Comes From* (New York: The Free Press, paperback edition, 1999)

Pipes, Daniel and Garfinkle, Adam (eds), *Friendly Tyrants: An American Dilemma* (London: Macmillan, 1991)

Pipes, Daniel, *Greater Syria: The History of an Ambition* (New York and Oxford: Oxford University Press, 1990)

Pipes, Daniel, *In the Path of God: Islam and Political Power* (New Delhi: Voice of India, reprint 2001)

Pipes, Daniel, *Militant Islam Reaches America* (New York and London, W.W. Norton and Company, 2002)

Pipes, Daniel, *The Hidden Hand: Middle East Fears of Conspiracy* (New York: St Martin's Griffin, paperback edition, 1998)

Pollack, Kenneth M., *The Persian Puzzle: The Conflict between Iran and America* (New York: Random House, 2004)

Prados, John, *Keepers of the Keys: A History of the National Security Council from Truman to Bush* (New York: William Morrow and Company, Inc., 1991)

Prados, John, *Lost Crusader: The Secret Wars of CIA Director William Colby* (Oxford and New York: Oxford University Press, 2003)

Prados, John, *President's Secret Wars: CIA and Pentagon Covert Operations Since World War II* (New York: William Morrow, 1986)

Pryce-Jones, David, *The Closed Circle: An Interpretation of the Arabs* (London: Phoenix Press, paperback edition, 2002)

Putnam, Robert D., and Bayne, Nicholas, *Hanging Together, The Seven Power Summits* (Cambridge: Harvard University Press, 1984),

Quandt, William B., *Camp David: Peace-making and Politics* (Washington D.C., The Brookings Institution, 1986)

Quandt, William B., *Saudi Arabia in the 1980s: Foreign Policy, Security, and Oil*, (Washington D.C. The Brookings Institution, 1981)

Rahnema, Ali, *An Islamic Utopian: A Political Biography of Ali Shari'ati* (London and New York: I.B. Tauris Publishers, 1998)

Rahnema, Ali and Nomani, Farhad, *The Secular Miracle: Religion, Politics and Economic Policy in Iran* (London and New Jersey: Zed Books Ltd, 1990)
Rajaee, Farhang (ed), *The Iran-Iraq War: The Politics of Aggression*, (Gainesville: University Press of Florida, 1993)
Ramazani, R.K., *Iran's Foreign Policy, 1941–1973: A study of Foreign Policy in Modernizing Nations* (Charlottesville, Va.: University of Virginia Press, 1975)
Ramazani, R.K., *Revolutionary Iran: Challenge and Response in the Middle East* (Baltimore: Johns Hopkins University Press, 1986)
Ramazani, R.K., *The United States and Iran: Patterns of Influence* (Charlottesville, Va.: University of Virginia Press, 1980)
Ramet, Pedro, *The Soviet-Syrian Relationship Since 1955: A Troubled Alliance*, (Boulder, Colo.: Westview Press, 1990)
Ranelagh, John, *The Agency: The Rise and Decline of the CIA* (London: Sceptre, a division of Hodder and Stoughton paperbacks, 1988)
Razavi, Hossein, and Vakil, Firouz, *The Political Environment of Economic Planning in Iran, 1971–1983*, (Boulder, Colo: Westview Press, 1984),
Reeve, Simon, *The New Jackals: Ramzi Yousef, Osama bin Laden and the Future of Terrorism* (London: Andre Deutsch, 1999)
Rodman, Peter W., *More Precious Than Peace: The Cold War and the Struggle for the Third World* (New York: Charles Scribner's Sons, 1994)
Rosati, Jerel A., *The Carter Administration's Quest for Global Community: Beliefs and their Impact on Behaviour* (South Carolina, University of South Carolina Press, 1987)
Roy, Olivier, *The Failure of Political Islam* (London and New York: I.B. Tauris, reprinted 1999)
Rubin, Barry, *Paved with Good Intentions: The American Experience and Iran* (New York: Penguin Books, 1981)
Rubin, Barry, *The Tragedy of the Middle East* (Cambridge, Cambridge University Press, 2002)
Rubin, Michael, *Into the Shadows: Radical Vigilantes in Khatami's Iran* (Washington D.C., The Washington Institute for Near East Policy, Policy Papers, No. 56, 2001)
Rubinstein, Alvin, *Soviet Policy Towards Turkey, Iran and Afghanistan: The Dynamics of Influence* (New York: Praeger Publishers, 1982)
Rustow, Dankwart A., *Oil and Turmoil: America Faces OPEC and the Middle East* (New York: W.W. Norton, 1982)
Ryan, Paul B., *The Iranian Rescue Mission: Why It Failed* (Annapolis, Maryland: Naval Institute Press, 1985)
Ryn, Claes J., *America the Virtuous: The Crisis of Democracy and the Quest for Empire* (New Brunswick and London: Transaction Publishers, 2003)
Safran, Nadav, *Saudi Arabia: The Ceaseless Quest for Security* (Ithaca and London: Cornell University Press, 1988, paperback edition)
Saivetz, Carol, *The Soviet Union and the Gulf in the 1980s* (Boulder, Westview Press, 1986)
Salinger, Pierre, *America Held Hostage: The Secret Negotiations* (Garden City, NY.: Doubleday, 1981)
Samii, Kuross A. *Involvement by Invitation: American Strategies of Containment in Iran* (University Park and London: The Pennsylvania State University Press, 1987)
Sampson, Anthony, *Seven Sisters: The Great Oil Companies and the World They Made* (Great Britain: Coronet Books, Hodder and Stoughton, updated edition, 1988)
Sampson, Anthony, *The Money Lenders: Bankers in a Dangerous World* (Great Britain: Coronet Books, Hodder and Stoughton, fifth impression, 1985)
Sawyer, Herbert L., *Soviet Perceptions of the Oil Factor in US Policy: The Middle East-Gulf Region*, (Boulder, Colo: Westview Press, 1983)
Schahgaldian, Nikola B., *The Clerical Establishment in Iran* (Santa Monica, Rand Corporation, 1989)
Schahgaldian, Nikola B., with the assistance of Barkhordarian, Gina, *The Iranian Military under the Islamic Republic* (Santa Monica, Rand Corporation, 1987)
Schneider, Steven A., *The Oil Price Revolution* (Baltimore: Johns Hopkins University Press, 1983)
Schurmann, Franz, *The Foreign Politics of Richard Nixon: The Grand Design*, (Berkeley, California, Institute of International Studies, University of California, Berkeley, 1987)
Schurmann, Franz, *The Logic of World Power* (New York: Random House, 1974)
Scott, Peter Dale, *Drugs, Oil and War: The United States in Afghanistan, Colombia and Indochina* (Lanham, Maryland, Rowman and Littlefield Publishers, Inc, 2003)
Segev, Samuel, *The Iranian Triangle: The Untold Story of Israel's Role in the Iran-Contra Affair*, translated by Haim Watzman (New York: The Free Press, A Division of Macmillan, Inc., 1988)

Sela, Avraham, *The Decline of the Arab-Israeli Conflict: Middle East Politics and the Quest for Regional Order* (Albany: State University of New York Press, 1998)
Seliktar, Ofira, *Failing the Crystal Ball Test: The Carter Administration and the Fundamentalist Revolution in Iran* (Newport, CT, Praeger Publishers, 2000)
Seliktar, Ofira, *Politics, Paradigms and Intelligence Failures: Why So Few Predicted the Collapse of the Soviet Union* (New York and London: M.E. Sharpe, 2004)
Servan-Schreiber, Jean Jacques, *The World Challenge*, (New York: Simon and Schuster, 1981)
Seymour, Ian, *OPEC, Instrument of Change* (New York: St Martin's Press, 1981)
Shalom, Stephen Rosskamm, *Imperial Alibis: Rationalizing U.S. Intervention after the Cold War* (Boston, MA: South End Press, 1993)
Shawcross, William, *The Shah's Last Ride: The Story of the Exile, Misadventures and Death of the Emperor* (London: Pan Books in association with Chatto and Windus, paperback edition, 1989)
Shemesh, Haim, *Soviet-Iraqi Relations, 1968–1988: In the Shadow of the Iraq-Iran Conflict*, (Lynne Rienner Publishers, 1992)
Sherrill, Robert, *The Oil Follies of 1970–1980, How the Petroleum Industry Stole the Show* (and Much More Besides) (New York: Anchor Press, 1983)
Shulsky, Abram N, and Schmitt, Gary J., *Silent Warfare: Understanding the World of Intelligence* (Brassey's, Washington D.C, third edition, 2002)
Shultz, Anne Tibbits, *Buying Security: Iran Under the Monarchy* (Boulder, Colo: Westview Press, 1989)
Sick, Gary, *All Fall Down* (London, I.B. Tauris and Co Ltd, 1985)
Sick, Gary, *October Surprise: America's Hostages in Iran and the Election of Ronald Reagan* (London and New York, I.B. Tauris and Co Ltd, 1991)
Simon, Jeffrey D., *The Terrorist Trap* (Bloomington and Indianapolis, Indiana University Press, second edition, 2001)
Sivan, Emmanuel, *Radical Islam: Medieval Theology and Modern Politics* (New Haven and London, Yale University Press, enlarged edition, 1990)
Skidmore, David, *Reversing Course: Carter's Foreign Policy, Domestic Politics and the Failure of Reform* (Nashville and London: Vanderbilt University Press, 1996)
Sklar, Holly (ed), *Trilateralism: Elite Planning for World Management* (Boston, Mass.: South End Press, 1980)
Sloan, G.R., *Geopolitics in United States Strategic Policy, 1890–1987* (Brighton: Wheatsheaf Books, 1988)
Sluglett, Marion Farouk and Sluglett, Peter, *Iraq Since 1958: From Revolution to Dictatorship* (London and New York: I.B. Tauris and Co Ltd, 1990)
Smolansky, Oles M and Smolansky, Bettie M., *The USSR and Iraq: The Soviet Quest for Influence* (Durham and London, Duke University Press, 1991)
Sobhani, Sohrab, *The Pragmatic Entente: Israeli-Iranian Relations: 1948–1988* (New York: Praeger Publishers, 1989)
Solingen, Etel, *Regional Orders at Century's Dawn: Global and Domestic Influences on Grand Strategy* (Princeton, NJ: Princeton University Press, 1998)
Souresrafil, Behrouz, *Khomeini and Israel* (United Kingdom: C.C. Press Ltd, second edition 1989)
Spiro, David E., *The Hidden Hand of American Hegemony: Petrodollar Recycling and International Markets* (Ithaca and London, Cornell University Press, 1999)
Taheri, Amir, *Nest of Spies: America's Journey to Disaster in Iran* (London: Hutchinson, 1988)
Taheri, Amir, *The Spirit of Allah: Khomeini and the Islamic Revolution* (London: Hutchinson, 1985)
Taheri, Amir, *The Unknown Life of the Shah* (London: Hutchinson, 1991)
Tahir-Kheli, Shirin, and Ayubi, Shaeen (eds), *The Iran-Iraq War: New Weapons, Old Conflicts*, (New York: Praeger, 1983)
Tanter, Raymond, *Rogue Regimes: Terrorism and Proliferation* (London, Macmillan, paperback edition, 1999)
Terzian, Pierre, *OPEC: The Inside Story*, (London: Zed Books, 1985)
Thornton, Richard C., *The Nixon-Kissinger Years: Reshaping America's Foreign Policy* (New York: Paragon House, 1989)
Thornton, Richard C., *The Nixon-Kissinger Years: Reshaping America's Foreign Policy* (New York: Paragon House, revised paperback edition, 2001)
Thornton, Richard C., *The Carter Years: Towards a New Global Order* (New York: Paragon House, 1991)
Tibi, Bassam, *The Challenge of Fundamentalism: Political Islam and the New World Disorder* (Berkeley, Los Angeles and London, University of California Press, updated edition, 2002)

Tillman, Seth, *The United States in the Middle East*, (Bloomington: Indiana University Press, 1982)
Timmerman, Kenneth R., *The Death Lobby: How the West Armed Iraq* (London, New York, etc, Bantam Books, 1992)
Trento, Joseph, *Prelude to Terror* (New York: Carroll and Graf, 2005)
Villiers, Gerard de, *The Imperial Shah: An Informal Biography*, translated by June P. Wilson and Walter B. Michaels (Boston: Little, Brown, 1976)
Walt, Stephen, *Revolution and War* (London: Cornell University Press, 1996)
Wohlforth, William Curti, *The Elusive Balance: Power and Perceptions during the Cold War* (Ithaca and London: Cornell University Press, 1993)
Wurmser, David, *Tyranny's Ally: America's Failure to Defeat Saddam Hussein*, with a foreword by Richard Perle (Washington D.C. The American Enterprise Institute Press, 1999)
Yallop, David, *To the Ends of the Earth: The Hunt for the Jackal* (London: Corgi Books, 1994)
Yergin, Daniel, *The Prize: The Epic Quest for Oil, Money and Power* (New York: Simon and Schuster, 1991)
Zabih, Sepehr, *Iran Since the Revolution* (London: Croom Helm, 1982)
Zabih, Sepehr, *The Iranian Military in Revolution and War* (London: Routledge, 1988)
Zabih, Sepehr, *The Left in Contemporary Iran* (Stanford: Hoover Institution Press, 1986)
Zabih, Sepehr, *The Mossadegh Era: Roots of the Iranian Revolution* (Chicago: Lake View Press, 1982)
Zonis, Marvin, *Majestic Failure: The Fall of the Shah* (Chicago and London: The University of Chicago Press, 1991)

Book in German

Timmerman, Kenneth R., *Ol Ins Feuer*, (Fanning the Flames: Guns, Greed and Geopolitics in the Gulf War), (Zurich: Orell Fusli, 1988)

Journal articles in English

Akhavi, Shahrough "Soviet Perception of the Iranian Revolution", *Iranian Studies*, vol.xix, no. 1, winter 1986
Alpher, Joseph, "The Khomeini International", *Washington Quarterly*, Fall 1980, Vol. 61
Bengio, Ofra, "Shi'is and Politics in Ba'thi Iraq", *Middle Eastern Studies*, No. 1, January 1985
Bowden, Mark, 'Among the Hostage-Takers', *The Atlantic Monthly*, December 2004.
Carswell, Robert, 'Economic Sanctions and the Iran Experience', *Foreign Affairs*, Winter 1981/ 1982
Chubin, Shahram, "Gains for Soviet Policy in the Middle East", *International Security*, Vol 6, Spring 1982
Chubin, Shahram, "Leftist Forces in Iran", *Problems of Communism*, (Washington, DC), July-August 1980
Chubin, Shahram, "The Soviet Union and Iran", *Foreign Affairs*, Spring 1983
Cooley, John, "Iran, the Palestinians, and the Gulf", *Foreign Affairs*, Vol 57, Summer 1979,
Donovan, Michael. "National Intelligence and the Iranian Revolution." *Intelligence and National Security*, 12, no. 1 (Jan. 1997): 143–163.
Gasiorowski, Mark J., "The Qarani Affair and Iranian Politics", *International Journal of Middle Eastern Studies*, Vol 25, 1993
Glazov, Jamie Symposium: Pakistan: Friend or Foe?, *Frontpage Magazine*, October 17, 2003, www.frontpagemag.com
Ioannides, Christos P., "The PLO and the Iranian Revolution", *American-Arab Affairs*, 1980, no. 10
Karabell, Zachary, "'Inside the US Espionage Den': The US Embassy and the Fall of the Shah." *Intelligence and National Security* 8, no. 1 (Jan. 1993): 44-59.
Kennedy, Edward, "The Persian Gulf: Arms Race or Arms Control?" *Foreign Affairs*, October 1975
Khalilzad, Zalmay "Moscow's Double-Track Policy, Islamic Iran: Soviet Dilemma", *Problems of Communism*, (Washington DC), January-February 1984
Kirkpatrick, J. "Dictatorships and double standards", *Commentary*, 68, 5, November 1979
Komer, Robert, "Maritime Strategy vs. Coalition Defense", *Foreign Affairs*, Summer 1982
Legvold, Robert, "The Superpowers: Conflict in the Third World," *Foreign Affairs*, Spring 1979
Lenczowski, George, "The Arc of Crisis: Its Central Sector", *Foreign Affairs*, Spring 1979

Levy, Walter J., "Oil and the Decline of the West", *Foreign Affairs*, Summer 1980
Levy, Walter J. "World Oil Cooperation or International Chaos", *Foreign Affairs*, 52, 4, 1974
Parry, Robert "Russia's Prime Minister and October Surprise", 15 May 1999, at *www.consortiumnews.com*.
Pipes, Daniel, "Syria after Asad", *World and I*, February 1987
Pipes, Daniel, "The Alawi capture of power in Syria", *Middle Eastern Studies*, 25 (1989)
Pipes, Daniel, "The Western mind of radical Islam", *First Things*, December 1995
Podhoretz, Norman, "How to Win World War IV", *Commentary Magazine*, February 2002
Pryor, Leslie M., "Arms and the Shah", *Foreign Policy*, Summer 1978.
Ramazani, R.K., "Iran's Foreign Policy: Contending Orientations", *Middle East Journal*, Vol. 43, No. 2, Spring 1989, p. 205.
Ramazani, R.K., "Iran's Revolution: Patterns, Problems and Prospects", *International Affairs*, No. 4, Autumn 1980
Ross, Dennis, "Soviet Views Toward the Gulf War", *Orbis*, Fall 1984
Silverman, Ira, 'An American Terrorist', *New Yorker*, Issue 2002-08-05.
Turner, Louis, "Oil and the North-South dialogue", *The World Today*, February 1977
Zisser, Eyal "Hafiz al-Asad discovers Islam", *Middle East Quarterly*, March 1995

Thesis and dissertations in English

Jackson-Smith, David, *The Search for Strategic Stability in the Persian Gulf: The United States and the Start of the Iran-Iraq War*, (Master's thesis, Washington D.C.: George Washington University, May 10, 1987)
Moses, Russel Leigh, *Freeing the Hostages: US-Iranian Negotiations and Soviet Policy, 1979–1981*, (PhD Thesis, University of Pittsburgh, later published by University of Pittsburgh Press, 1996)
Samii, Abbas William, *The Role of SAVAK in the 1978–79 Iranian Revolution* (PhD thesis, Cambridge University, 1994)
Shakeri, Esmail, *Oil Nationalisation and the Hostage Crisis: A Comparative Analysis of Iran's Foreign Conflict Behaviour under the Charismatic Leaderships of Mossadegh and Khomeini*, (PhD thesis, University of Toronto, 1992)

Documentaries

America Abroad presents America and Iran: Cooperation or Conflict in the Post-Saddam Gulf (2003)
Terry Gross, 'Mark Bowden discusses the Iranian hostage crisis that began 25 years ago', National Public Radio, November 4 2004.

Persian language sources

Primary sources

Documents,
Historical Documents Center, Ministry of Information (intelligence), *The Islamic Revolution According to SAVAK Documents*, Two volumes (Tehran, Soroush Press, 1998)
Mesl-e Barf Ab Khahim Shod: Mozakerat-e Shora-ye Farmandehan-e Artesh, Dey-Bahman 1357 (We Will Melt like Snow: The talks held by the army's command council, January-February 1979) (Tehran: Nasr-e Ney, Ney Publishers, 1365 [1986])
Memoirs, autobiographies and oral history collections
Bani-Sadr, Abolhasan *Khianat-e Be Omid* (Betrayal of Hope), (Paris: np, 1983)
Bani-Sadr, Abolhasan, *Seir-e Siasat-e Amrika dar Iran* (The Course of American Policy in Iran) (Place of publication not specified: Entesharat-e Enqelab-e Eslami, 1370, 1991)
Bozorgmehr, Esfandiar, *Karvan-e Omr (Vicissitudes of Life): Political Memoirs*, (London: Satrap Publishing, first edition, 1993)
Gharabaghi, Major-General Abbas, *Asrar-e Ma'muriat-e Zheneral Huyser Dar Bohran-e Iran* (The Secrets of General Huyser's Mission during the Iranian Crisis), (Los Angeles, Maverick Publishers, 1989)

Gharabaghi, Major-General Abbas, *E'terafat-e Zheneral: Khaterat-e Arteshbod Abbas Gharabaghi (Mordad-Bahman 57)* (Confessions of a General: The memoirs of Major-General Abbas Gharabaghi, July-August1978-February 1979) (Tehran, Ney Publishers, 1366 [1987])

Gharabaghi, Major-General Abbas, *Gofteguha-ye Arteshbod Gharabaghi*, (Santa Clara and St Jose, Zamaneh Publishers, 1995)

Fardust, Hossein, *Khaterat-e Arteshbod-e Sabegh Hossein Fardust: Zohur va Soghut-e Saltanat-e Pahlavi* (The memoirs of former Major-General Hossein Fardust: The Rise and Fall of the Pahlavi Dynasty), (Tehran: Etela'at Publications, 1990)

Kianuri, Nureddin, *Khaterat-e Nureddin Kianuri (Tehran, Etela'at Publishers, 1372 [1993]*

Rafsanjani, Akbar Hashemi, *Dowran-e Mobarezeh (Years of struggle)*, Two volumes, compiled and edited by Mohsen Hashemi, (Tehran, Daftar-e Nashr-e Ma'aref-e Enghelab [The office for the publication of the principles of the revolution], 1376 [1997])

Sanjabi, Abdolkarim, *Omidha Va Naomidiha* (Hopes and Hopelessness) (London, 1989)

Yazdi, Ebrahim, *Akharin Talashha Dar Akharin Ruzha*, (Final efforts in the final days), (Tehran, Qalam Publishers, 1363 [1984])

Yazdi, Ebrahim, Private Papers in Nejati, Gholamreza *Tarikh-e Siasi-ye Bisto Panj Sale-ie Iran*, (Twenty-five years of Iranian Political History), Volume II (Tehran: Rasa publications, 1995)

Secondary sources

Alamuti, Mostafa, Iran Dar Asr-e Pahlavi, *Vols 3–16 (London: Book Press, Paka Print, 1989–1994)*

Nejati, Gholamreza *Tarikh-e Siasi-ye Bisto Panj Sale-ie Iran*, (Twenty-five years of Iranian Political History), Volumes I and II (Tehran: Rasa publications, 1995)

Pejman, Colonel Isa, *Arteshbod Hossein Fardust, Ra'is Sabegh-e Daftar-e Vizhe-ye Ettela'at va Bazsrasi-ye Shahanshahi: Khedmat ya Khianat?"* (Major-General Hossein Fardust, former head of the Special Intelligence Bureau and the Imperial Inspectorate: Honourable Service or Treachery?" (Paris, Zhen Publications, second edition, 1992)

Toloui, Mahmoud, *Bazigaran-e Asr-e Pahlavi (The King-Pins of the Pahlavi Era), Vol II*, (Tehran, Elm Publications, 1994)

INDEX

Aaron, David 7–8, 54, 164, 210
Abdalaziz, Crown Prince Fahd ben 10, 17, 22, 48, 119, 123, 129, 174, 199, 220, 226
Abdi, Abbas 152, 240
Abdullah, Prince 10, 17, 119–20, 229
Abrahamian, Ervand 29, 33
Aburish, Sa'id 126–7, 195
Adham, Kamal 208
Afghan Mojahedin 169–70, 174, 201, 240
Afzali, Bahram 139
Ahern, Thomas 148, 155
Ahmadinezhad, Mahmud 240
Al-Qa'idah 239
al-Takriti, Barzan 48, 199
Ala, Hossein 29
Alam, Asadollah 13, 20–1, 24, 32, 81
Alan, Tom 195
Aliev, Heidar 88
Allen, Richard 211, 214–16, 234
Ames, Robert 142
Amin, Hafizullah 170
Amini, Ali 11, 30, 50, 74, 78, 89, 94, 103, 203
Amir-Arjomand, Sa'id 150
Amir-Entezam, Abbas 104, 134, 141–3, 146
Amuzegar, Jahangir 34
Amuzegar, Jamshid 24, 49–51, 58, 64, 69–70
Anderson, Jack 205
Andropov, Yuri 45, 63, 170, 208
Ansari, Hushang 13, 58, 77, 79
Arafat, Yasir 43, 45–6, 118, 126, 129, 163, 198, 200
Ardakani, Ali Shams 128
Ardebili, Musavi 104, 134, 156
Armao, Robert 184
Aryanpour, Hushang 203–4
Asad, Hafiz 38–9, 42–3, 126–7, 188, 194, 212, 228–30
Asefi, Hamid Reza 240
Asgharzadeh, Mohammad Ebrahim 152, 155
Ashraf, Princess 31, 56, 58, 136, 139
Askariyun 36
Association of the Combatant Clergy 37
Atherton, Alfred 22
Atta, Dale Van 205
Ayadi, Abdolkarim 33, 37
Ayat, Hasan 193–4
Azari-Qomi, Ahmad 137
Azerbaijan KGB 88
Azhari, Gholamreza 84, 86, 88
Aziz, Tariq 188
Azmun, Manuchehr 71, 76
Azzam, Abdullah 240

Bacevich, Andrew 173–4
Badre'i, General 102, 116

Baer, Robert 228
Baheri, Mohammad 71
Bahonar, Mohammad-Javad 34, 151
Bakhash, Shaul 29
Bakhtiar, Shapur 25, 54, 93, 95–9, 101–17, 129, 144, 160, 188, 195–7, 199
Bakhtiar, Teimur 82
Bakr, Ahmad Hasan 39–40, 42, 47–8, 124–7
Balanian, Mohammad Ali (alias of Jamshid Hashemi) 176
Ball, George 67, 91–2, 94
Bani-Sadr, Abolhasan 109, 113, 141–2, 149, 154, 156, 159–62, 179–83, 185–7, 192–8, 200–2, 205–7, 210, 212–13, 216–17, 221–2, 224–7, 230–2, 235–6
Banna, Hasan al- 29, 37
Bar-On, Hanan 27
Barre, Raymond 127
Barry, Rosen, 240
Bazargan, Mehdi 25, 30–1, 37, 52, 54, 56, 71, 77–8, 87, 96, 104–5, 107–8, 110, 112–17, 125, 127–9, 132–3, 136–8, 140–50, 152–8, 160, 223
Bazzaz, Sa'ad 199
Beaupuy, Alain de 74
Beckwith, Charles 190
Beg, Mirza Aslam 172
Begin, Menachem 43, 46, 60, 102, 119, 129–30, 135, 189, 219–21, 227–8, 238
Beheshti, Mohammad Hosseini 33–4, 36–7, 49, 51, 53–4, 78, 86, 96, 103–6, 110, 112–14, 132, 134, 141, 144, 148, 150–3, 156–7, 159–61, 173, 179–82, 193, 198–9, 205, 210, 222–4, 230, 238
Belfield, David (aka Dawid Salahuddin) 197
Ben-Menashe, Ari 102, 202–3, 208, 210–11, 218–19
Bennigsen, Alexandre 133
Benyahia, Muhammad Seddik 234
Bergsten, Fred 121
Bill, James 2, 29, 55, 66–7, 103, 150
Bitaraf, Habibollah 155
'Blood Judge' see Khalkhali, Sadegh
Blumenthal, Michael 26, 79, 89, 91
BND 198
Bojnurdi, Kazem 33
Borguet, Christian 177, 183, 185, 234
Borujerdi, grand ayatollah 32, 36
Bourget 180
Bowden, Mark 150, 156
Bowie, Robert 91–2
Bowling, John 12
BP (British Petroleum) 56, 62, 78, 95, 120
Brezhnev, Leonid Ilyich 42, 88, 145, 164, 170, 172, 179–80, 208, 231

Brian, Earl 202
British Petroleum (BP) 56, 62, 78, 95, 120
British Secret Intelligence Service 56
Brown, George (Lord George-Brown) 95
Brown, Harold 82, 86, 91, 94, 98, 104, 107–11, 119, 121–2, 132, 147, 158–9, 164–7, 180–1, 185, 187, 191, 194, 206, 209, 225
Brzezinski, Zbigniew 1–10, 18–19, 44–7, 53, 55, 58–9, 64, 66–8, 72, 78–9, 81–93, 95, 97–8, 100–1, 103–6, 108–9, 111, 114–16, 118–19, 121, 123–5, 129–35, 147, 149–50, 157–9, 162–7, 169–74, 177, 179, 181, 183–92, 194–5, 201, 205–9, 211, 213–16, 219, 221, 224–5, 230
Bureau of Intelligence and Research (INR) 14, 17–18, 22–3, 55, 71–2, 79, 81, 89, 93, 95, 125, 138, 175
Bureau of Political and Military Affairs 4, 27, 64
Burroughs, Frank 115
Bush, George 210, 218–19, 234
Butler, William 8
Byrd, Robert 26, 109

Caffery, Jefferson 38
Callaghan, James 100
Callahan, Arthur 93
Carrington, Lord 180
Carswell, Robert 217
Carter, Hodding 124
Carter, Jimmy 1, 8–10, 17–20, 22, 24, 26–7, 44, 46–7, 51, 53–4, 56, 58–9, 61, 63–4, 66–8, 70, 73, 79, 87–9, 91–2, 94, 96–8, 100–1, 103–6, 108–11, 114–16, 118–19, 122–4, 131, 135, 147–8, 150, 156–9, 162, 164–6, 168–9, 171–5, 177–81, 183–91, 199, 202, 206–7, 209–17, 219–22, 224–5, 228, 230, 232–3, 238
Casey, William 196, 202–4, 218–20, 228, 234–6
Cassin, Vernon 142
Castro, Fidel 178, 180
Cave, George 134, 142–3, 146, 218
Ceausescu, Nicolae 45
CENTO (Central Treaty Organization) 132
Central Intelligence Agency see CIA
Central Treaty Organization (CENTO) 132
Chamran, Mostafa 31, 65, 134, 136, 138, 140–2, 144, 149, 176, 183
Chase Manhattan Bank 134, 217
Cherikha-ye Fada'i-ye Khalq 38, 90, 129, 132, 137–9, 154
Christopher, Warren 98, 116, 123, 172, 174, 192, 206–10, 213, 216, 221, 225, 227–8, 230, 232, 234–5
Church Committee 53
CIA (Central Intelligence Agency) 8, 13–14, 16, 20, 27, 29–30, 53–4, 56, 58–60, 63, 65–6, 72–3, 82, 84–5, 89–91, 93, 98, 102, 112, 115, 121–2, 125, 127–9, 132–4, 139, 141–4, 155, 159, 164, 169–71, 173, 175–6, 180, 184, 190, 192, 195, 197–9, 202, 210, 213–15, 219–20, 229, 239
Clarke, Ramsey 157
Codevilla, Angelo 216
Cogan, Charles 14, 19, 170, 176
Cohen, Stephen 7
Combatant Muslims Movement 152–3, 193
Committee on the Present Danger 4–5

Consortium 11, 14, 47, 56, 59, 62, 78, 118, 120, 134
Cooley, John 239
Cooper, Richard 167–8
Copeland, Miles 58–9, 154, 190, 202
Cottam, Richard 2, 6, 29, 50, 56, 74, 96, 102–3, 140, 150, 160, 177
Coughlin, Con 126–7
Crozier, Brian 86, 199, 204
Cutler, Lloyd 173, 184–5, 224, 227
Cutler, Walter 135–6

Daugherty, Bill 155
De Beaupuy, Alain 74
de Marenches, Alexandre, Count 25, 70, 199
Defence Intelligence Agency (DIA) 68, 90, 172
Delta Force 44
Department Three 35, 37, 44, 49, 52, 65, 76
Derian, Patricia 3–4, 7, 24
DIA (Defence Intelligence Agency) 68, 90, 172
Dispossessed, Foundation for the 138
Dobrynin, Anatoly 184, 186, 214–15, 229, 235
Draper, Morris 194
Duncan, Charles 98, 167
Durrani, Arif 203
D'awa al-Islamiya (Islamic Call) 35
d'Estaing, Valery Giscard 100–1

Ebtekar, Ma'sumeh 152, 154, 156, 223, 240
Eitan, Rafael (Rafi) 102, 203, 218
Elghanian, Habib 135–6
Eliot, Theodore L., Jr. 97, 103
Energy Research and Development Agency (ERDA) 20
Engdahl, William 62
Eqbal, Manuchehr 11, 33
ERDA (Energy Research and Development Agency) 20
Eskandari, Iraj 88–9
Eslaminia, Hedayatollah 36, 50–1, 53, 57–8, 66, 69, 107
Evergreen International Airlines 184
Ezri, Meir 21

Fada'iyan-e Eslam 29–30, 136, 152
Fada'iyan-e Khalq 31, 196
Fadeykin, Ivan Anisimovich 63
Fahd ben Abdalaziz, Crown Prince 10, 17, 22, 48, 119, 123, 129, 174, 199, 220, 226
Faisal, Saud al- 119
Falaq 153
Fallah 153
Falsafi, Mohammad Taghi 36
Farah Pahlavi, Empress 35, 48, 64–6, 70, 184, 204
Farber, David 131, 150, 169, 187
Fardust, Hossein 15, 35–6, 52–3, 56–7, 62, 64–6, 69–70, 74, 77, 93, 100, 107–8, 112, 115–16, 134
Farsi, Jalaleddin 138, 179
Fatah 45, 129
Fedayeen-e Khalq 132
Ford, Gerald 15, 109
Foreign Policy (journal) 3
Foundation for the Dispossessed 138

G-2 93

Index

Gates, Robert 6, 63, 170, 218
Gazit, Shlomo 60
Gelb, Leslie 3–4, 24, 27, 64, 68
Gemayel, Bashir 65
Genscher, Hans Dietrisch 207
Gerges, Fawaz 9
Ghadhafi, Muammar 65, 197
Ghaffari, Hadi 51
Gharabaghi, Abbas 93, 99–100, 102, 104–6, 109, 111, 113–14, 116–17
Ghorbanifar, Manuchehr 196
Giraldi, Philip 240
Giscard d'Estaing, Valery 100–1
Golpayegani, Ayatollah 36, 77
Goodman, Melvin 239
Gosaibi, Ghazi Al- 199
Gregg, Donald 214
Gromyko, Andrei 162–4, 179, 181, 201, 207
GRU 46

Habbash, George 45, 129, 154
Habibollahi, Admiral 83–4
Haddad, Wadi 45
Hafez (spy in US embassy) 145, 151
Haig, Alexander 199, 215, 235
Haig, Rance 195
Haj Seyyed Javadi, Ali-Asghar 23
Hakim, Muhsin al- 38
Halperin, Morton 3
Hammadi, Sa'dun 127, 210, 221
Hammer, Armand 214
Hannaford, Peter 208
Hansen, George 182
Harris, David 150, 155, 169, 187
Hasan, Hani al- 126
Hasemi, Jamshid 203
Hashemi, Cyrus 175–6, 196, 202–4, 218, 228
Hashemi, Jamshid 175–6, 203–5
Hashemi-Rafsanjani, Ali Akbar 78, 86, 113, 138, 141, 151, 153, 205, 210, 216, 220, 222–3, 229–30, 232
Hatam, General 116
Haynes, Ulric 234
Heikal, Mohammed 154, 183, 192
Helms, Richard 17, 19, 22, 54, 134
Henze, Paul 133
Hersh, Seymour 236
Hezbollah 51, 107, 139, 239
Hiro, Dilip 151
Hirschman, Robert 93
Hojjatieh 36–7, 152, 198–9
Holland, Michael 160
Homayun, Dariush 51
Home, Lord 14
Honecker, Erich 145
Houghton, David Patrick 169, 187
Hoveyda, Amir Abbas 14, 21, 23–4, 36–7, 41, 49–52, 58, 64, 72, 80, 84, 86, 91, 137
Howland, Michael 233
Huda, Bint 188
Human Rights Bureau 22, 58–9
Hunter, Robert 7
Huntington, Samuel 7, 18
Hussein, King of Jordan 194–5, 212, 214
Hussein, Saddam 39, 42, 47–8, 54, 70, 124–30, 165, 174–5, 187–8, 194–5, 199–201, 203, 208, 210, 221–3, 226, 229–30, 238
Huyser, Robert 97–101, 103–11, 114–16

ICP (Iraqi Communist Party) 47, 124
Ikle, Fred 215, 234
Imam Propaganda Office 138
INR (Bureau of Intelligence and Research) 14, 17–18, 22–3, 55, 71–2, 79, 81, 89, 93, 95, 125, 138, 175
Ioannides, Christos 150–1
Iran Committee for the Defence of Human Rights 52
Iran Liberation Movement 6, 31
Iran Working Group 175
Iraqi Communist Party (ICP) 47, 124
Iraqi Da'wah (Call) Party 38
Iraqi Revolutionary Command Council 125
IRGC (Revolutionary Guards Corps) 137, 139, 152–3, 175, 193, 196, 198, 206
IRP 138–9, 145, 151–4, 157, 179, 182, 185, 193–4, 198–9, 205, 224, 226, 230, 234, 236
Islamic Centre of Geneva 38
Islamic Coalition Society 32–4, 36–7, 151–2
Islamic Group 38
Islamic Nations Party 33
Islamic Republican Party 138, 151, 179, 193, 213, 224, 226

Jaaf, Salar 81
Jaaf, Sardar 129
Jackson, Henry 'Scoop' 26, 91
Jama 153
Javadi, Ali-Asghar Haj Seyyed 23
Javits, Jacob 45, 135–6
Johnson, Chalmers 239
Jones, General 114, 166
Jordan, Hamilton 162, 166, 177, 180, 182–5, 190

Kalp, Malcolm 155
Karubi, Mehdi 203–4, 218
Kashani, Abolqasem 29
Kashani, Mehdi 203
Kazakov, Viktor 63
Kazemieh, Eslam 203–4
Keddie, Nikkie 1
Kennedy, Ted 124
KGB 40–6, 63, 66, 88, 126, 154, 163, 170, 186, 196–8, 201, 214
Khalid, King of Saudi Arabia 17, 21, 119–20, 188, 199
Khalkhali, Sadegh 51, 136
Khamene'i, Seyyed-Ali 37, 151, 156, 161
Khan, Abd al-Qadir 172
Khan, Daoud 46–7
Khatami, General 14, 82
Khatami, Mohammad 240
Khomeini 2, 5–6, 9–10, 19, 25, 29–40, 42–3, 47–59, 64–5, 68–71, 73–81, 83–4, 87–119, 125–6, 128–9, 131–53, 155–64, 166, 170, 173, 175–6, 179–82, 184–5, 187–9, 192–8, 202, 204, 206–7, 210–11, 213, 216, 218, 220, 222–4, 226–7, 230–1, 235, 238–40
Khomeini, Ahmad 151
Khomeini, Mossadeq 29
Khosrowdad, Manucher 91, 102, 112, 116
Kho'i, Grand Ayatollah 36, 90
Kho'iniha, Mohammad Musavi 150–2, 154–6, 160–1, 178–9, 182, 189, 193, 218, 220, 222–3
Khruschev, Nikita 44

Kia, Parsa 149
Kianuri, Nureddin 88–9, 139, 154, 164, 183
Kimche, David 27, 218, 235
Kinzer, Stephen 239
Kirkpatrick, Jeane 9
Kissinger, Henry 1, 5–7, 12–16, 19, 62–3, 67, 109, 117, 134–5, 147, 159, 166, 177, 185
Kolko, Gabriel 239
Komer, Robert 225
Kramer, Martin 29
Kuzikchin, Vladimir 41, 44, 175, 239
Kuznetsov, Vassily 229

Lahuti, Ayatollah 144, 226
Laingen, Bruce 141, 145–9, 157–8, 160, 185, 233
Lajevardi, Asadollah 138
Lake, Anthony 3–4, 7–8, 24
Lambrakis, George 57, 69, 95, 132
Laqueur, Walter 53
LaRouche, Lyndon 210
Lavi, Hushang 210–12, 220, 222
Ledeen, Michael 91
Lewis, Bernard 30
Lewis, Samuel 219–21
Liberation Movement 25, 30–1, 52, 56, 64–5, 71, 74–5, 77–8, 88, 104, 106, 113–14, 153
Long, David 14
Lubrani, Uri 15, 60, 102
Lyalin, Oleg 44

McCloy, John J. 159–60
McFarlane, Robert 202, 211, 235–6
McGaffey (US political officer) 117, 136
McGovern, George 3, 7
McHenry, Donald 160, 172, 217
McKelvey, Vincent 20
Madani, Ahmad 143–4, 175–6, 203–4
Mahallati, Fazlollah 193
Mahdavi-Kani, Mohammad Raza 36–7, 49, 78, 198
Mahdiyun 36
Mahri, Ahmad al- 128
MAN (KGB code name) *see* Mogharebi, Ahmad
Mansur, Hasan Ali 33–4
Mansurun 153
Marbod, Eric Von 104
Marenches, Alexander de, Count 25, 70, 199
Martin, Vanessa 29, 191
Martyr Foundation 138
Marxist Mojahedin 31
Mar'ashi, Grand Ayatollah 36, 77
Matin-Daftari, Hedayatollah 57
Mawdudi, Abul-Ala 29, 38
Mead, Walter Russel 3
Meade, Steven 202
Metrinko, Mike 55
MI6 56
Miklos, Jack 22
Militant Clergy Society 34
Militant Clerics Association 152
Miller, Judith 91
Miller, William 157
Minachi, Naser 77, 104, 110
MIR (Mojahedin of the Islamic Revolution) 193, 197–8, 226
Mirdamadi, Mohsen 152, 155
Mitrokhin, Vasiliy 170

MKO (Mojahedin-e Khalq Organization) 31, 37–8, 90, 107, 129, 132, 138, 143, 153, 193–4, 196, 226
Modaressi, Hadi 150
Mofatteh, Mohammad 34
Moghaddam, Naser 35, 52–3, 57–9, 62, 64–6, 69–70, 73–7, 83, 92–3, 95, 107–8, 110, 112–16, 137
Mogharebi, Ahmad 41
Mohagheghi, General 113
Mojahedin *see* Afghan Mojahedin; Marxist Mojahedin; Mojahedin-e Khalq Organization; Mojahedin of the Islamic Revolution; Mojahedin Organization
Mojahedin-e Khalq Organization (MKO) 31, 37–8, 90, 107, 129, 132, 138, 143, 153, 193–4, 196, 226
Mojahedin of the Islamic Revolution (MIR) 193, 197–8, 226
Mojahedin Organization 31–2
see also Mojahedin-e Khalq Organization
Mojtahed-Shabastari, Hojjatoleslam 156
Momken, Mehdi 136
Mondale, Walter 3, 7, 53, 98, 109, 162, 181, 187, 221
Montazam, Mir Ali Akbar 36, 173
Montazeri, Mohammad 37, 65, 193
Moses, Russel Leigh 187
Moss, Robert 87
Mossad 15, 30, 44, 47, 59–60, 91, 154, 198, 235
Mossadeq, Mohammad 11, 29–30, 56, 72, 96
Mottahari, Morteza 31, 33–7, 51, 53, 78, 86, 113
Movement of Combatant Muslims 37
Mo'in, Baqer 29
Mo'inian, Nosratollah 65
Mo'tazed, General 64
Mr Muhammad 211
'Muhammad Ali' 136
Mullah Ernie *see* Oney, Ernest R.
Muravchik, Joshua 9
Muskie, Edmund 191, 202, 206–7, 209–10, 212, 217, 219, 221, 225, 228, 230, 235
Muslim Brotherhood 29–30, 37–9, 44, 188, 200, 228–9
Muslim Mojahedin 31
Muslim People's Republican Party 142
Muslim World League 38

Naas, Charles 23, 64, 68, 117, 137
Nabavi, Behzad 138, 153, 198, 217, 222–4, 227–8, 231–5
Nada, Youssef 38
Nahavandi, Hushang 71
Nahidian, Bahram 197
Najafi-Mar'ashi, Ayatollah 126
Nasiri, Ne'matollah 33, 35, 37, 49, 52–3, 57–9, 64, 76, 86, 137
Nasr, Seyyed Hoseyn 35
Nasser, Gamal Abd al- 12, 30
Nathanson, George 115
National Front 6, 23, 25–6, 30–1, 52–3, 55, 57, 64–5, 70, 75, 77–8, 83–4, 89–91, 93, 95–6, 106, 117, 138, 140, 142–3, 193
National Iranian Oil Company (NIOC) 79, 120
National Security Council *see* NSC
National Voice of Iran (NVOI) 41, 86

INDEX

Nationalities Working Group 133
Navid organization 86, 139
Navvab-Safavi, Mostafa 29
NEA (Near Eastern Affairs Bureau) 143
Near Eastern Affairs Bureau (NEA) 143
Newsom, David 8, 116, 159–60, 188, 229
Ngo, Din Diem 18–19
NIOC (National Iranian Oil Company) 79, 120
Nitze, Paul 4
Nixon, Richard 1, 12
Nobari, Ali-Reza 230
NSC (National Security Council) 6–8, 18, 27, 45–6, 61, 73, 98, 106, 131, 133, 158, 162, 165–6, 172, 175, 182, 187, 189, 191, 204–5, 207–8, 210, 213–14, 218–19
NVOI (National Voice of Iran) 41, 86

Odom, William 18, 44–5, 239
Oil Consortium 11, 14, 47, 56, 59, 62, 78, 118, 120, 134
Oney, Ernest R. 2, 13, 54, 67, 131
Oveisi, Gholamali 73, 77, 80, 82–4, 91–2, 102, 188, 195, 199

Pahlavi, Ashraf, Princess 31, 56, 58, 136, 139
Pahlavi, Empress Farah 35, 48, 64–6, 70, 184, 204
Pahlavi, Reza 63, 204
Pakravan, Hasan 32
Palme, Olof 229
Paolucci, Henry 19
Park, Chun Hee 9
Parry, Robert 204
Parsons, Anthony 25, 72, 74–5, 77–8, 80–1, 83–4, 87, 98, 103, 107, 113
Pasandideh, Reza 175–6, 202
Pastor, Robert 178
Pejman, Isa 116
Perez, Carlos Andres 21
Peyman, Habibollah 37, 152–3, 160–1, 182, 193, 198
PFLP (Popular Front for the Liberation of Palestine) 42, 45, 129, 154
Pinto, Maria Do Ceu 9
Pipes, Daniel 29
Pipes, Richard 4
PLO 38, 40, 42–5, 65, 106, 118–20, 122, 126, 128, 140, 153, 157–9, 163, 177, 198, 200, 209
Political and Military Affairs, Bureau of 4, 27, 64
Pollack, Kenneth 150, 169
Poniatowski, Michel 100
Ponomarev, Boris 88
Popular Front for the Liberation of Palestine (PFLP) 42, 45, 129, 154
Portillo, Lopez 148
Powell, Jody 148, 173, 205
Pravda 163–4, 170
Precht, Henry 6, 9, 15, 64, 82, 91–5, 133, 135, 141, 146–8, 151, 157
Puzanov, Alexander 46

Qadhafi, Mu'ammar 65, 197
Qarani, Valiollah 11, 30, 57, 82
Qashqa'i, Khosrow 129, 144
Qasim, Abd al-Karim 127
Qoddumi, Faruq 43

Qomi, Hasan 226
Qomi, Hossein 37
Qutb, Muhammad Sayyid 29

Rabbani, Borhanoddin 197
Rabi'i, Amir-Hossein 83, 102, 105
Rafizadeh, Mansur 49, 57, 82–4, 112
Rafsanjani, Ali Akbar Hashemi 78, 86, 113, 138, 141, 151, 153, 205, 210, 216, 220, 222–3, 229–30, 232
Rahimi, General 113
Raja'i, Muhammad Ali 198, 205–6, 210, 212–13, 217–18, 222–3, 227, 230
Ramadan, Sa'id 37–8, 197
Ramazani, Ruhollah 150
Raphel, Arnold 184
Rapid Deployment Force 47, 123
Rastakhiz Party 50
Razmara, Haji Ali 29, 82
RCC 125
Reagan, Ronald 5, 10, 45, 79, 172, 202–5, 208, 214–15, 217–19, 221, 223, 225, 227, 230–6, 239–40
Reno, Janet 197
Reporter, Shapoor 13
Resistance Corps 76
Resurgence Party 37
Revolutionary Guards Corps (IRGC) 137, 139, 152–3, 175, 193, 196, 198, 206
Revolutionary Organization of the Tudeh 31 *see also* Tudeh Party
Reza'i, Mohsen 153, 193
Ribicoff, Abraham 45
Ritzel, Gerhard 207, 213
Rockefeller, David 134–5, 147, 159, 166, 177, 185, 217–18
Rockefeller, Nelson 81
Rogovin, Mitchell 210, 212–13, 216–18, 220, 222
Roosevelt, Archibald 202
Roosevelt, Kermit 58–9, 202
Rosenfeld, Stephen 91
Rostow, Walt 12
Royal Dutch Shell 120
Rudolph, Charles C. 54
Rutherford, Guy (alias of Vernon Cassin) 142

Sabeti, Parviz 37, 44, 49–52, 65, 75–6
Sadat, Anwar 39–40, 42, 118, 132, 184, 199–200
Sadegh Ghotbzadeh 38, 65, 95, 138, 140–1, 149, 161, 176–82, 185, 187, 190, 194, 200–1, 204–6, 208, 226
Sadighi, Gholam Hossein 93–4
Sadr, Muhammad Baqer al- 38, 188
Sadr, Musa 35, 43
Safavi, Navvab 29
Safire, William 191
Saguy, Yahoshua 218
Sahabi, Ezatollah 56, 114
Salahuddin, Dawud 197
Samarai, Wafiq 199
Sanjabi, Karim 52, 78, 93–5
Saunders, Harold 6, 68, 92, 122, 132, 141, 143–4, 150, 155, 159, 175–6, 183, 202, 213, 216, 225
SAVAK 24, 26, 30, 32–8, 41, 43–4, 47, 49–53, 56–9, 62–5, 70–1, 74–6, 82–4, 86, 92–3, 102, 108–9, 112, 116, 134, 161, 239
SAVAMA 116, 134, 137, 213

SCC 192
Schlesinger, James 53, 86, 98, 121, 123, 173
Schmidt, Helmut 100, 123, 168
Schurmann, Franz 3
Scott, Peter Dale 239
SDECE 60, 198–9
Second National Front 30
Seliktar, Ofira 1, 3, 8, 66–7, 137, 151
Shackley, Theodore 214
Shah 1–2, 4–44, 46–109, 111–12, 116–21, 129, 131, 134–6, 139, 144–5, 147–53, 155, 157–61, 166, 177, 179–80, 182–5, 195, 203, 207, 228, 233, 237
Shaheen, John 203
Shaker, Sa'dun 70
Sharif-Emami, Ja'far 65–6, 69–73, 75–8, 80, 82
Shari'ati, Ali 31–2, 35, 37, 96
Shari'atmadari, Ayatollah 34, 51, 53, 55–8, 64, 68–70, 74–8, 80–1, 88, 90, 107, 109–10, 126, 128–9, 136, 138, 141–4, 148, 160, 163
Sharon, Ariel 102
Shell, Royal Dutch 120
Shirazi, Abdollah 226
Shmuel Morieh 218
Shulman, Marshall 7, 180
Shultz, George 236
Sick, Gary 1, 8, 25, 27, 33, 46–7, 55, 60, 67, 70, 72–4, 78, 85, 87, 95–6, 103, 141, 150, 157–8, 189, 191–2, 195–6, 207, 210, 213, 215, 218–19, 225, 235
Simchoni, Uri 218
Simon, William 13
Solarz, Stephen 95
Solomon, Anthony 26, 167–8
Somoza, Anastazio 3, 9
Sorenson, Theodore C. 53
Special Forces Operational Detachment-DELTA 44
Special Intelligence Bureau 15, 35, 56–7, 62, 70, 74
Special Operations Group (PFLP breakaway group) 45
State Department 1–4, 6, 8, 12, 14–17, 19, 22–4, 27, 46–7, 50, 55, 59–61, 63–4, 66, 68, 71–3, 78, 81–2, 85, 87, 89–93, 95–7, 109–10, 115–17, 121, 124, 129, 132–6, 141–2, 145–9, 151, 155–7, 159, 164, 166, 175–7, 180, 183, 185, 187, 191–2, 202–3, 205, 207, 209, 212–13, 215, 219, 221, 227
Stempel, John 1, 33, 53–7, 66, 71, 75, 77, 87, 104, 108, 114, 136, 142, 154
Stepashin, Sergei 203–4, 218
Students Following the Line of the Imam 150–1, 154–6, 163, 193
Sullivan, William 1, 6, 9, 19, 22–7, 54–5, 59–61, 64, 66, 68–70, 73–4, 76–85, 87, 89, 92–8, 101–10, 113–15, 131–3, 161, 237
Sultan, Prince 41

Tabataba'i, Ali Akbar 134, 197
Tabataba'i, Sadegh 140, 207–8, 213, 216, 223
Taheri, Amir 29, 56
Taleban 240
Taleghani, Ayatollah 31, 37, 142–3, 145
Tarnoff, Peter 178
Tavakkoli, Mohammad 56, 71

Tawhidi-Saf 153
Tehrani, Ostad 161
Tehrani, Seyyed Jalaleddin 108–9
Teicher, Howard 165, 195
Thornton, Richard C. 5, 150, 173
Tibi, Bassam 29
Tomseth, Victor 233
Torrijos, General 177, 183–5
Trento, Joseph 54, 208, 214
Trilateral Commission 14, 17
Tuchman, Jessica 7
Tudeh Party 11, 30–1, 34, 41, 65, 68–9, 71, 74–6, 86, 88, 90, 106, 111, 128, 132–3, 138–40, 149, 153–4, 163–4, 182, 193, 196, 198, 201, 226, 236, 239
Tufanian, Hasan 21, 83, 102
Turner, Stansfield 47, 53–4, 58, 60, 67–8, 72, 82, 86, 90, 98, 115, 133, 159, 166, 175, 186, 190, 192, 199, 202, 214, 220, 230
Twetten, Tom 195

Ulyanovsky, Rostislav 139
Underground Committee for Vengeance 76

Vadi'i, Kazem 71
Vahedeh, Omat-e 153
Van Atta, Dale 205
Vance, Cyrus 1, 3–10, 16–17, 19, 22–4, 40–1, 44, 46–7, 55, 61–4, 66, 68, 74, 81–2, 86–92, 94–5, 97–8, 101, 103–5, 109–11, 113–15, 118, 122–3, 131–2, 135, 137, 143–5, 147, 149–50, 156–9, 161–2, 166–8, 171–3, 175–85, 187, 189–91, 215, 237–9
Varennikov, Valentin 170
Veliotes, Nicholas 219
Villalon, Hector 177, 180, 185
Vinogradov, Vladimir 41, 140, 145, 154, 164, 200, 212
von Marbod, Eric 104

Walcott 191
Waldheim, Kurt 161, 172, 177
Walt, Stephen 150
Washburn, John 73–4
Weiss, Seymour 215
Williams, Harrison 201
Wilson, Edwin 43, 214
Wilson, Harold 12
World Bank 27

Yamani, Zaki 16, 123–4
Yazdi, Ebrahim 31–2, 50, 65, 78, 93–6, 103, 106, 110–13, 128, 132, 134, 136, 140–2, 144–6, 148–9, 151, 155, 157, 160

Zabih, Sepehr 150
Zahedi, Ardeshir 58–9, 72, 78, 80–2, 84, 86, 89, 91–2, 95, 111
Zamani, Abbas 175
Zanjani, Ayatollah 78, 113
ZHAMAN 41
Zia-ul-Haq, Mohammad see Zia-ul-Haq, Mohammad
Zimmerman, Warren 104, 106, 111
Zipori, Mordechai 210
Zonis, Marvin 93

www.ingramcontent.com/pod-product-compliance
Lightning Source LLC
Chambersburg PA
CBHW061427300426
44114CB00014B/1579